THE CANTER

broadview editions

series editor: L.W. Conolly

GEOFFREY CHAUCER

THE CANTERBURY TALES

A SELECTION

EDITED BY ROBERT BOENIG

& ANDREW TAYLOR

SECOND EDITION

broadview editions

Library and Archives Canada Cataloguing in Publication

Chaucer, Geoffrey, -1400, author
   The Canterbury tales : a selection / Geoffrey Chaucer ; edited by Robert Boenig & Andrew Taylor. – Second edition.

(Broadview editions)
Includes bibliographical references.
ISBN 978-1-55481-136-6 (pbk.)

   I. Boenig, Robert, 1948-, editor   II. Taylor, Andrew, 1958-, editor   III. Title.
IV. Series: Broadview editions

PR1866.B64 2013   821'.1   C2013-902279-1

Broadview Press is an independent, international publishing house, incorporated in 1985.

We welcome comments and suggestions regarding any aspect of our publications—please feel free to contact us at the addresses below or at broadview@broadviewpress.com.

North America:
PO Box 1243, Peterborough, Ontario, Canada K9J 7H5
2215 Kenmore Ave., Buffalo, NY, USA 14207
Tel: (705) 743-8990; Fax: (705) 743-8353
E-mail: customerservice@broadviewpress.com

UK, Europe, Central Asia, Middle East, Africa, India, and Southeast Asia:
Eurospan Group, 3 Henrietta St., London, UK WC2E 8LU
Tel: 44 (0) 1767 604972; Fax: 44 (0) 1767 601640
Email: eurospan@turpin-distribution.com

Australia and New Zealand:
NewSouth Books, c/o TL Distribution
15-23 Helles Ave., Moorebank NSW, Australia 2170
Tel: (02) 8778 9999; Fax: (02) 8778 9944
Email: orders@tldistribution.com.au

This book is printed on paper containing 50% post-consumer fibre.

Broadview Press acknowledges the financial support of the Government of Canada through the Book Publishing Industry Development Program (BPIDP) for our publishing activities.

www.broadviewpress.com

Book design and composition by George Kirkpatrick
PRINTED IN CANADA

CONTENTS

ACKNOWLEDGEMENTS

We would like to thank Carolyn P. Collette, Richard Gyug, and Jocelyn Wogan-Browne for their generous response to inquiries, the editors of the *Broadview Anthology of British Literature* for many valuable suggestions, Stuart Rutten for carefully checking our transcriptions, Mary Hamel for her meticulous corrections to the first printing, and A.G. Rigg for providing the core of the glossary.

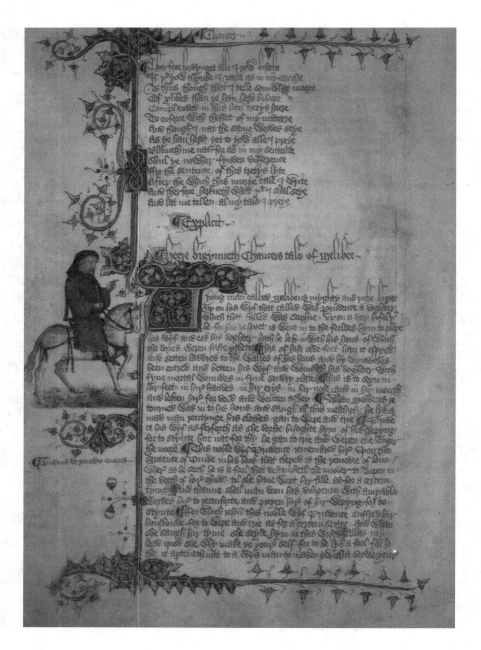

The first page of Chaucer's *Tale of Melibee,* from *The Canterbury Tales.* The figure on horseback is generally taken to be a representation of Chaucer. The actual size of pages in the Ellesmere manuscript is approximately 15¾ x 11⅛″. Ellesmere Manuscript EL 26 C9 f. 153v. Reprinted by permission of The Huntington Library.

INTRODUCTION

Chaucer's Life and Times

Chaucer's biographers reckon the approximate date of his birth by testimony Chaucer himself gave in October 1386 during a legal proceeding to determine which of two families, the Scropes or the Grosvenors, had the right to bear a certain coat of arms. Chaucer then claimed to be "forty years old and more." He adds that he had been "armed for twenty-seven years," a reference to his participation in a campaign of the Hundred Years' War in 1359, when King Edward III besieged the French city of Rheims. If we assume that when Chaucer was first armed in 1359 he was nineteen (which, as far as we can tell from the dates given by his fellow witness in the Scrope-Grosvenor inquiry, was the average age at which men of his class entered military service), 1340 is a good year to nominate as that of Chaucer's birth, though a year or two later is possible.

Chaucer was born to a family that eventually rose from the peasantry to the nobility. His great-grandfather Andrew de Dynyngton (d. 1288), also known as Andrew de Ipswich or Andrew le Taverner, was by evidence of his various names an itinerant tavern-keeper who migrated from a small village to the larger town of Ipswich in East Anglia, on the east coast of England. Andrew's son Robert (c. 1288–1314) moved to London and was apprenticed to a man named John le Chaucer. "Chaucer," like "Taverner," was a name drawn from an occupation. In French a "chaucier" was a maker of shoes and boots. When John le Chaucer was killed in a brawl, Robert, who was a beneficiary in his will, adopted his name as a mark of respect. Robert's son John (1312–66) took a further step up the social ladder, making his mark as a vintner, one who imported wine from abroad; in 1347 he became deputy in the important port of Southampton to John de Wesenham, who was in charge of the king's wine cellar. This position meant that John was in the royal service, just as his son Geoffrey would be in due course. In Southampton, John, his second wife Agnes, and the young Geoffrey weathered the Great Plague of 1348–49, the epidemic that killed somewhere between a quarter and a half of England's population. John survived and found himself heir to the estates of many relatives who were the plague's victims. Now quite a wealthy man, he moved back to London with his family, where he continued to procure wine for the royal court. Chaucer was probably between seven and nine years old when he found himself back in London. His family's home was on Thames Street close to St. Paul's Cathedral, where there was a celebrated school run by the almoner (the official responsible for distributing the cathedral's charity). Chaucer may have begun his education at this school, although there is no hard evidence of this. He certainly would have attended some kind of grammar school, however, where he would have learned to read and write Latin, using as textbooks works such as Aesop's

Fables and the *Distich*, a collection of moral sayings attributed in the Middle Ages to the Roman senator Cato.

John Chaucer's connections at the court allowed him to place his son in one of the royal households, probably as a page. By 1357, the teenage Geoffrey had become a member of the household of Elizabeth, Countess of Ulster, who was married to the king's second surviving son, Lionel. It was normal for married couples in the upper nobility to maintain separate households. As a page, Chaucer would have run errands, helped at meals, performed a fair number of menial tasks, and made himself generally useful. In exchange, he would have had an opportunity to familiarize himself with the ways of the court, to make influential connections, and also to acquire a considerable education. Over the years, Chaucer was to work for several of these households. He moved from Elizabeth's service to that of her husband when the two households were merged in 1359, the same year that he was armed, and it was probably at this point he was promoted to "valettus," one step below a squire. By 1367 he had been transferred into the household of Edward III and granted an annuity of 20 marks for life. Chaucer remained in the royal service until the king's death ten years later, and by 1372 the king had made him a squire. By 1374, however, Chaucer was no longer a member of the royal household but was instead living in his own quarters in London and working for the king in the custom's house in the port of London, a job he continued to perform for Richard II.

From the perspective of later decades, the late 1350s seemed the heyday of English chivalry. Edward III, born in 1312, was still vigorous, and his queen, Philippa of Hainault, was a generous patron, whose court included the poet and chronicler Jean Froissart. The Hundred Years' War, begun in the late 1330s, was at its most successful stage from the English point-of-view. The king's stirring victory at Crécy in 1346, when he had been greatly outnumbered, had improbably been surpassed by the victory of his eldest son, Edward the Black Prince, in 1356 at the battle of Poitiers. Outnumbered but supported by the formidable English longbow, the prince captured the French king, John the Good, bringing him home to England to await what was both literally and figuratively a king's ransom, three million golden crowns. King John's "prison" was the great Palace of Savoy in London, and there he was allowed to bring all the courtiers, servants, and entertainers he might need. The musicians, poets, and composers attending him helped set English artistic taste, and French music and literature became all the rage. In particular, the French courtiers shared with their captors their admiration for the work of Guillaume de Machaut, not only one of the greatest musical composers of his day but also the author of elaborate poems on courtly love that were to provide Chaucer with some of his early models. At the end of his life, in his Retractions, Chaucer claimed to have written "many a song and many a lecherous lay," that is, many a love poem. If he did so, which seems likely, he would probably have written them in French, the court language of the day. Some of them may even survive. A collection of medieval French court lyrics from this period in a manuscript that is now in Philadelphia contains a number of pieces by an author identified only as "Ch."[1] There is no evidence of who this "Ch" might be, but Chaucer is certainly a possible candidate.

In 1359 Chaucer followed Edward III over to France on the military expedition he mentioned in his testimony at the Scrope-Grosvenor inquiry. Edward III's objective was to besiege Rheims, where the French traditionally held their coronations, and have himself crowned King of France. English military luck, though, was beginning to run out. It rained heavily, and the countryside around Rheims had been stripped bare, making it hard to feed the besieging army. During the campaign, Chaucer was captured by the French and quickly ransomed by the king for £16—as much as Chaucer's salary for a year when he was a royal bureaucrat. Chaucer tells us nothing about his experiences as a prisoner of war. Although Rheims eventually surrendered, Edward had already pressed on to Paris, which he besieged unsuccessfully for several weeks, and then to Chartres. Here a hail storm so violent that it killed some of their troops persuaded the English to accept a compromise treaty, bringing Chaucer's brief military career to an end.

Events in Chaucer's life are deduced from a series of documents, usually referred to as the Chaucer Life Records, that have survived over the years; they mostly involve monetary or legal transactions and contain not a single reference to Chaucer's activities as a poet. For the six or seven years after Chaucer's military experience, the records fall silent. According to Thomas Speght, who wrote a life of Chaucer for his edition of 1598, a certain "Master Buckley" claimed to have seen a document in the Inner Temple that recorded Chaucer being fined two shillings for beating a Franciscan friar in Fleet Street. The Inner Temple was one of the four so-called Inns of Court, which provided housing for law students, and Speght's claim has led to much speculation that Chaucer returned from the army to be educated as a lawyer. There was indeed a William Buckley in the Inner Temple in the sixteenth century, and he was in charge of its records. Unfortunately neither he nor Speght is an entirely reliable witness: Speght, a staunch Protestant, was keen to show that Chaucer was a harsh opponent of the friars, while Buckley might have wanted to claim a distinguished alumnus for his institution. There is no evidence that Chaucer attended either Oxford or Cambridge Universities, although both possibilities have sometimes been suggested. Chaucer was extremely well read, but he could easily have picked up his education while serving in the royal households.[2]

---

1   The poems have been edited by James I. Wimsatt in *Chaucer and the Poems of "Ch" in University of Pennsylvania MS French 15* (Cambridge: D.S. Brewer, 1982).

2   The view that Chaucer would have needed to go to university or the Inns of Court to acquire his education is sharply criticized by T.F. Tout, "Literature and Learning in the English Civil Service in the Fourteenth Century," *Speculum* 4 (1929): 365–89. The kind of literary education

By 1366 Chaucer had married. His wife was the daughter of Gilles de Roet (also known as Paon de Roet), a nobleman from the Duchy of Hainault, about one hundred miles north of Paris, the homeland of Edward III's wife Philippa. Chaucer's new wife was named Philippa after the Queen. Philippa Chaucer's sister Katherine is better known by her married name, Katherine Swynford. In 1368 she married a minor knight, Sir Hugh Swynford, who died fighting in the south of France four years later. At some point, possibly even before Hugh's death, Katherine became the mistress of John of Gaunt, third son of the King, and three years before his death in 1399, John of Gaunt—to much scandal—married her. These loose connections to the royal family, his administrative abilities, or even his growing reputation as a poet may explain Chaucer's numerous political and administrative appointments. Philippa Chaucer was a lady-in-waiting to the royal family, including John of Gaunt's second wife, Costanza of Castile, and Chaucer had increasing duties outside the court, so they were often separated. Philippa died in 1387. We know they had had two sons, Thomas, born in 1367, and Lewis, born in 1380, and there is some ambiguous evidence of a daughter as well. Chaucer composed his *Treatise on the Astrolabe* (an astronomical instrument) for Lewis, who seems to have died young. Thomas, however, survived to become a powerful courtier for the Lancastrian kings Henry IV and Henry V in the early fifteenth century. Thomas's daughter Alice married the Duke of Suffolk, completing both the family's return to East Anglia and its rapid rise up the ladder of social, political, and economic success.

In the late 1360s, Chaucer began his career as a diplomat. In the spring of 1366 he was in the Spanish kingdom of Navarre on a diplomatic mission evidently related to English intervention in the disputed succession of the Kingdom of Castile. In the summer of 1368 he again was out of the country on the King's business, probably in France. In both 1369 and 1370 he was part of John of Gaunt's military entourage in France; no major action occurred, however, in either year. At this stage Chaucer seems to have been working largely for Gaunt rather than for the king. This great prince was the richest man in England, and as his father grew older and his elder brother, the Black Prince, devoted himself to wars in France, Gaunt became the center of English court culture. He was also for a time a strong supporter of the reformer John Wycliffe. Gaunt granted Chaucer an annuity of £10 in 1374, and Chaucer wrote his first major poem, *The Book of the Duchess*, as an elegy for Blanche, Gaunt's first wife, who had died in 1368. This provides one of the very few reasonably firm dates for one of Chaucer's poems (and even in this case there is some debate about how long after Blanche's death the poem was composed). It is possible to work out a rough chronology of Chaucer's

---

that would have been available to Chaucer in one of the royal households is described by Richard Firth Green, *Poets and Princepleasers: Literature and the English Court in the Late Middle Ages* (Toronto: U of Toronto P, 1980), chap. 3.

works, however, and we know that at about this time he also translated into English some portions of the enormously popular French allegorical dream vision, *The Romance of the Rose.*

Chaucer soon shifted from military to more generally diplomatic matters, undertaking a mission to Genoa from December 1372 to the following May, as part of a delegation to discuss trade. Most of his biographers speak of this mission as the first of two journeys to Italy (the second coming in 1378) and date his exposure to the Italian literature that was soon to influence him heavily. Though this is likely the case, there remains the possibility that he had traveled to Milan back in 1367 when Prince Lionel (who had been widowed in 1363), married his second wife, Violante Visconti, daughter of the Duke of Milan. The wedding had been lavish, and the guests included the great poet Petrarch, to whom Chaucer pays tribute in the Clerk's Tale. It is tempting to place the young English poet in his proximity there and then, but there is no evidence that he had made the trip, though he had been in service to Lionel's first wife.

In June 1374, Chaucer was appointed to an administrative position that would occupy him for approximately the next dozen years. He became Controller of Customs for wool (and related commodities like hides and skins) for the port of London, and also (although he seems only to have held the position briefly) for the Petty Custom, which controlled wine and cloth. Chaucer's appointment is a good example of the way in which England was beginning to develop a professional bureaucracy staffed by men who were not necessarily clerics. As Derek Pearsall observes in his biography of Chaucer, "the royal household was becoming the civil service and the armed retainer was giving way to the bureaucratic official."[1]

As Controller, Chaucer received an annual salary of nearly £17. He was not the Customs Collector, a position which was usually given to a wealthy London merchant. Chaucer's task was instead to audit the accounts, making sure that the collector did not profit too outrageously and that the king received his due. The sums at stake were enormous: in the 1370s, the annual revenue generated for the king was normally about £70,000.[2] Chaucer was instructed to keep the accounts in his own hand, but this instruction was not taken literally. Chaucer had the assistance of various clerks and scribes to do much of the actual writing, including Adam Pinkhurst, the scribe who copied the Ellesmere manuscript. Chaucer did, however, have to go to work in the customs' house most days. To make this attendance easier, Chaucer was given the lease of a "house" (we would now call it a "flat" or "apartment") above one of the seven gates in the wall to the old city—Aldgate, about ten minutes' walk north of the Tower of London. It was during his time audit-

---

1   *The Life of Geoffrey Chaucer* (Oxford: Blackwell, 1995), 146.
2   W.M. Ormrod, *The Reign of Edward III: Crown and Political Society in England, 1327–1377* (New Haven: Yale UP, 1990), 207.

ing the accounts and living over Aldgate that Chaucer found firm footing as a writer. Apparently he was good at his job, for in 1382 he was re-appointed Controller of the Petty Custom.[1] Customs Controller Chaucer must have been markedly different from the genial and naïve narrator we see in the General Prologue. As George Lyman Kittredge observed, Chaucer was a professional tax collector and "a naïf Collector of Customs would be a paradoxical monster."[2]

The House of Fame, The Parliament of Fowls, and Troilus and Criseyde were all written when Chaucer lived over Aldgate. The first two of these were, like his earlier Book of the Duchess, dream visions in the French style, in which the poem's speaker falls asleep and dreams the events recounted in the poem. The House of Fame describes how the poet, buried in his books, is borne aloft by an eagle to hear news about love; it turns into a reflection on fame (including literary fame) and rumor. The basic framework of the journey owes a debt to Dante's Divine Comedy: the timorous narrator and pedantic eagle are comic counterparts of Dante and his guide to Hell, Purgatory, and Heaven, Virgil. The Parliament of Fowls recounts the efforts of birds to find mates at a meeting held on St. Valentine's Day. It was likely written in about 1380 as an allegory of the efforts to find a wife for the young King Richard II, for the details of the marriage negotiations match well with the events of the poem, and there is evidence that Chaucer himself took part in the negotiations. In a moment that anticipates some of those in The Canterbury Tales, the debate over which of the three aristocratic male eagles should marry the beautiful female eagle degenerates into a squabble when the lower-class birds burst in impatiently. Troilus and Criseyde, Chaucer's longest finished poem, is based on Giovanni Boccaccio's Filostrato, the story of a tragic love affair between the Trojan Prince Troilus and the court lady Criseyde, who eventually abandons him. Their affair, which follows many of the elaborate conventions of courtly love also seen in the Knight's Tale, becomes an occasion for more general reflections on human existence, for which Chaucer draws heavily from the famous Consolation of Philosophy of the late Roman statesman Boethius, which he had translated not long before.

In 1380 according to a document in the court of Chancery, Chaucer was released from legal action relating to the raptus of Cecily Champain or Chaumpaigne, the daughter of a London baker. Since it was first discovered by F.J. Furnivall in 1871, this document has provoked unease and disagreement among Chaucerians.[3] The Latin term raptus could mean either

---

1   Exactly when Chaucer first held the position of Controller of the Petty Custom is somewhat difficult to determine. See Samuel Moore, "New Life-Records of Chaucer," Modern Philology 16 (1918): 49–52 and John Manly, "Chaucer as Controller," Modern Philology 25 (1927): 123.

2   G.L. Kittredge, Chaucer and His Poetry (Cambridge, MA: Harvard UP, 1915), 45. Kittredge gets Chaucer's title wrong.

3   Furnivall, Parallel-Text Edition of Chaucer's Minor Poems (London, 1871), 136–44.

"rape" or "abduction." Chaucer's own father, John, had been abducted by an aunt when a child for the purpose of forcibly marrying him off to her daughter and thus procuring his inheritance, and the legal document says that she and her helpers "rapuerunt et abduxerunt" (raped and abducted) him. Christopher Cannon has argued that when the term *raptus* is used alone in fourteenth-century English legal documents, it usually means rape in the modern sense of forced coitus, but has also acknowledged that medieval English law was "hopelessly confused" about the distinction between rape and abduction.[1] Of course, Chaucer was only *accused* of *raptus* and the action was dropped, but there is some evidence that Chaucer made at least one payment of £10 to Cecily through intermediaries, a sum equal to over half his yearly salary as Controller (although he had other sources of income). Pearsall, for one, argues "[that] Chaucer was guilty of *something* is clear from the care he took to secure immunity from prosecution, but it need not have been rape."[2] They could, for example, have been having an affair.[3] It is hard to tell what light (if any) the affair sheds on Chaucer's character, but one thing it does make clear is how well connected he was. The five men he called as witnesses to the document of release were, in addition to Richard Morel (a prosperous grocer), Sir William Beauchamp, who was king Richard's chamberlain (the officer responsible for the day-to-day management of his personal household), Sir John Clanvowe and Sir William Neville, who were both chamber knights (that is, members of the king's inner circle who served him personally), and John Philpot, a wealthy London merchant who was Collector of Customs while Chaucer was Controller and later became Lord Mayor of London.

In June 1381 the famous Peasants' Revolt took place, during which farmers and tradespeople in Kent and East Anglia marched on London. Their demands were no less than a revision of the economic and social order in which everything would be held in common and all men would be equal—a form of what we would now call communism, although still under the head of the king. The rebels entered London on 14 June, many of them through Chaucer's own Aldgate, and together with poorer Londoners, burned the

---

1   Compare "*Raptus* in the Chaumpaigne Release and a Newly Discovered Document Concerning the Life of Geoffrey Chaucer," *Speculum* 68 (1993): 74–94, esp. 92, to the more complex position Cannon takes in "Chaucer and Rape: Uncertainty's Certainties," *Studies in the Age of Chaucer* 22 (2000): 67–92. Cannon notes in the later article that because medieval English law was concerned to protect male property rights, it considered the woman's consent irrelevant, so that the term *raptus* might also cover what we would now consider elopement (76).

2   *Life of Geoffrey Chaucer*, 137.

3   A further complication is the possibility suggested by Haldeen Braddy, in "Chaucer, Alice Perrers, and Cecily Chaumpaigne," *Speculum* 5 (1977): 906–11, that Cecily Champain can be identified as the step-daughter of Alice Perrers, the king's mistress. This view has gained some currency but is convincingly refuted by Marta Powell Harley, "Geoffrey Chaucer, Cecilia Chaumpaigne, and Alice Perrers: A Closer Look," *Chaucer Review* 28 (1993): 78–82.

Palace of Savoy (then owned by John of Gaunt), and hunted down and killed a number of wealthy citizens, lawyers, and Flemish weavers (who were resented by English weavers). The fourteen-year-old king met with the rebels the following day and promised them some concessions, but in a moment of anger or fear the mayor of London struck down their leader, Wat Tyler. The crowds were dispersed and many members of the rising subsequently executed. Chaucer mentions the turmoil in the Nun's Priest's Tale, when he says the noise made by the rebels when they were chasing down Flemings to kill them was not half as loud as the noise made chasing the fox who has stolen Chauntecleer.

About this time, Chaucer was working on another retelling of a work by Boccaccio—this time the Italian poet's epic poem about Duke Theseus of Athens, the *Teseida*, which recounts the rivalry of two captured Theban knights for the hand of the Duke's sister-in-law. Though there is no evidence that Chaucer had yet conceived of *The Canterbury Tales*, this work later became incorporated into it as the first tale, the Knight's Tale. At this time also, Chaucer was translating a theological treatise by the early thirteenth-century Pope Innocent III, which is usually known as *The Miserable Condition of Mankind*. This work does not survive—except in some versified excerpts that Chaucer incorporated into the Man of Law's Tale.

Beginning in 1386, some major changes happened in Chaucer's circumstances. He gave up his controllership and his house over Aldgate and became one of the Justices of Peace for the county of Kent (of which Canterbury was the main city) and served as Member of Parliament for Kent in the autumn of that year. Paul Strohm suggests that Chaucer's move from the court and the city to the country, together with his giving up his annuities in 1388, was a deliberate effort on his part to keep a lower profile.[1] If so, Chaucer was very wise. There was mounting hostility among the great lords to the alleged abuses of the king's favorites, and in 1388 a group of five great lords, led by Thomas Woodstock, Duke of Gloucester (Edward III's youngest son and Richard's uncle), launched a coup d'état. The Lords Appellant, so-called because they had "appealed" against the king's counselors in Parliament, defeated the royal army near Oxford and effectively took over control of the country. They forced the king, who had holed up in the tower of London, to agree to the execution of many of his closest advisors, including Simon Burley, his former tutor who had become one of his chamber knights, and to the exile of many others. The young Richard, still only 22, would reassert himself the following year, throwing off the counsel that had been set up to watch over him. Nearly ten years later, in 1397, he finally secured his revenge, arresting Gloucester—who then mysteriously died in prison—and two of the other leading Appellants, Richard, Earl of Arundel, who was

---

1   *Social Chaucer* (Cambridge, MA: Harvard UP, 1989), 36–41.

executed, and Thomas Beauchamp, Earl of Warwick, who was sentenced to life imprisonment after begging for his life. Chaucer must have been canny to keep out of trouble during these shifts in power and to maintain ties to both sides (for he managed to develop a connection to the Lancastrians even before the future Henry IV seized power from Richard in 1399). A number of Chaucerians have suggested possible parallels between these professional skills and Chaucer's literary attitudes, some condemning, most praising his prudence, moderation, and openness to conflicting views.

In 1387 Chaucer's wife Philippa died. At this time he was working on *The Legend of Good Women*, a collection of stories about good women that was allegedly written to make amends to Queen Anne for his depiction of Criseyde's betrayal of Troilus. The prologue to the *Legend* begins like a traditional French dream vision, but its structure signaled greater things to come, for, like *The Canterbury Tales*, it is a framework collection of what we would now call "short stories"—but one that does not yet show the marvelous variety of the later collection. Its theme is that of good women betrayed in various ways by bad men. As far as we know, Chaucer did not finish the collection, but it may have suggested the framework of *The Canterbury Tales* to him, although Boccaccio's great prose masterpiece *The Decameron* might have done so as well. About this time (1387), Chaucer began work on the great poem that would occupy the rest of his life. He incorporated some earlier works, like the reworking of Boccaccio's *Teseida*, which became the Knight's Tale, and also his translation into verse of the Life of St. Cecilia, which became the Second Nun's Tale. But most of the stories that became *The Canterbury Tales* were new works showing an independence from the French and Italian genres that had so enthralled him in the past. Over the next thirteen years he occasionally put *The Canterbury Tales* project aside to work on other things—short poems and, in 1391, the scientific *Treatise on the Astrolabe*. Another scientific work that may be his—though many scholars dispute this—is *The Equatorie of the Planets*, written in 1392. After the death of Richard's beloved queen, Anne of Bohemia, in 1394, Chaucer revised the Prologue of *The Legend of Good Women*, although he seems not to have finished the work as a whole.

In 1389 Chaucer had taken up another administrative post in Richard II's government, becoming Clerk of the King's Works. This was an influential position full of responsibility, and it represents the pinnacle of Chaucer's career as a civil servant. His duties included hiring and paying workers on the many building projects undertaken by the government and overseeing the procurement of materials. He worked with the king's master mason, Henry Yevele (whose role was rather like that of a modern architect) on projects including work on the Tower of London and the construction of lists for a court tournament—this last a kind of fourteenth-century sports stadium. Chaucer also planned renovations to St. George's Chapel in Wind-

sor Castle, though these were never begun. His tenure in this position, how-
ever, only lasted two years, till June 1391. The previous September he was
robbed and beaten twice in one week while carrying his payroll, and this
violence may have contributed in some way to his resignation.

Then Chaucer seems to have been retired for a while, living off some
pensions and annuities he had gathered during his career as a civil servant.
Perhaps the lion's share of *The Canterbury Tales* was written during this
period of relative freedom from the hustle and bustle of administrative life.
There is evidence that he took up residence in Greenwich at this time. In
the mid-1390s, though, he took on one last job—that of Deputy Forester for
the forest of North Petherton in Somerset, a hunting preserve belonging to
the Mortimers, cousins to the King. Roger Mortimer was heir presumptive
to the throne, since Richard II had no children. This was an administrative
post of lesser importance than his customs controllership and his clerkship of
the King's works.

By the late 1390s Chaucer was back in London, and late in 1399 he took
out a lease on a house within the precincts of Westminster Abbey. This was
an even more turbulent year politically than 1386. Though still young, King
Richard had been declining mentally—falling into episodes of paranoia and
megalomania, devising violent revenge on those he considered his enemies.
He had exiled John of Gaunt's eldest son Henry, his first cousin, and on
Gaunt's death in 1399—while Richard was away on an expedition to Ire-
land—Henry came back to claim his inheritance as Duke of Lancaster. Tired
of Richard's excesses, the nobility welcomed Henry, and Henry realized he
could claim more than just his heritage. He deposed his cousin, imprisoning
him, and proclaimed himself king. Richard soon died in prison. Thus began
the dynasty of the Lancastrians. One of Chaucer's last poems was an ironi-
cally humorous "Complaint to his Purse," praising Henry as the rightful
king and requesting the continuation of Chaucer's pensions and annuities—
a request the new king granted to the man who had always known how
to make himself useful and whose literary works were already becoming a
source of national pride.

Chaucer spent what was to be the last year of his life at Westminster
Abbey, in a small house looking over the garden of the Lady Chapel. Medi-
eval monasteries often functioned as what we would now term "rest homes"
for retired civil servants, so there is nothing particularly surprising in this
arrangement. In October 1400, aged somewhere in the vicinity of sixty,
Chaucer died. He was buried inside the abbey, which, from the time of
Edward the Confessor (d. 1066), had been the burial place of kings and dig-
nitaries. Originally his grave was at the entrance to St. Benedict's chapel,
where the monks would have crossed it on their way from the dormitory to
prayer. In 1556 his remains were reinterred in a sarcophagus against the east
wall of the Abbey's south transept, where it remains until this day.

The Construction of *The Canterbury Tales*

Chaucer was a poet rich in inventive genius, but he did not invent the genre of *The Canterbury Tales*. His great work is a framework-collection of stories in which there is a main story (the framework) whose characters themselves narrate other, smaller stories. There are a number of earlier classical and medieval works that—with greater or lesser flexibility—can also be considered works of this type. Ovid's *Metamorphoses*, a massive collection of stories of mythological transformations, is one example, as is, surprisingly, Dante's *Divine Comedy* (because various souls in the afterlife recount to the character Dante how they got there). John Gower, Chaucer's friend, was at work on a framework-collection, his *Confessio Amantis*, at the time Chaucer was producing *The Canterbury Tales*. A small number of the same stories appear in both Chaucer's and Gower's collections.

The closest analogue is Giovanni Boccaccio's prose collection, *The Decameron*, which begins with a group of Florentine nobles gathering in a villa outside the city to escape the plague and deciding to spend their days telling stories. It has never been absolutely proven that Chaucer knew this work, since he never refers to it, but Boccaccio was otherwise arguably the greatest influence on Chaucer, who reworked both his *Il Filostrato* (*Troilus and Criseyde*) and his *Il Teseida* (the Knight's Tale) and drew on his *De Casibus Virorum Illustrium* (*About the Fall of Famous Men*) for the Monk's Tale. Several of the *Canterbury Tales*, moreover, are versions of stories found in *The Decameron*, so it is highly likely that Chaucer knew the work and quite possible that it suggested its structure to him as a model for his own work. In Boccaccio's book, ten young nobles, seven women and three men, escape from their city of Florence during the outbreak of the Plague there in 1347–48, retire to a country estate for ten days (hence the work's title, which is Italianate Greek for "The Ten Days"), and pass the time telling each other stories and otherwise generally enjoying life.

As has often been noticed, the characters of *The Decameron* are not (with the exception of the cynical Dioneo, who tells the last tale each day) highly differentiated from each other, and the framework is rather static, with the only thing distinguishing each of the ten days being the general topic the stories must follow. If Chaucer did indeed take his cue from *The Decameron*, he saw possibilities for the framework that Boccaccio did not. His characters are highly differentiated, and the framework provides dramatic conflict out of which the stories develop. At the same time, we know that Chaucer recycled at least two poems he had written before into tales for his new collection. The Prologue to *The Legend of Good Women* provides a list of works he had written, including a *Palamon and Arcite* and a *Life of St. Cecilia*, which became the Knight's Tale and the Second Nun's Tale. Most scholars also assume that *The Tale of Melibee* and the Parson's Tale had independent lives before the conception of *The Canterbury Tales*, as well: they are inordinately long for a "wayside" tale, and are in prose, unlike the rest of *The Canterbury Tales*. Both also circulated in some manuscripts independently of the larger work, as did the Monk's Tale, which was likely also originally an independent work.

Boccaccio's *Decameron* is neat and satisfying mathematically. Ten people each tell one tale a day for ten days, giving us a number of tales exemplary in its completeness—one hundred. Boccaccio, energetic craftsman that he was, fails to disappoint us, for he finished each tale, providing us with the contracted number. (The final tale, included in part in the appendix, is the earliest recorded version of Chaucer's Clerk's Tale.)

Chaucer's numbers are more chaotic than Boccaccio's. There are, he tells us, twenty-nine pilgrims in the company that sets out towards Canterbury. This number itself is rather confusing, for if you count the number of pilgrims, things do not seem to add up, unless the "preestes thre" who accompany the Prioress are her own chaplain (the Nun's Priest) plus the Monk and Friar, whose portraits follow (not the Nun's Priest and two otherwise unremarked companions). Twenty-nine is a messy number, even if we can make it accord with the pilgrims Chaucer includes on his list in the General Prologue. It does not divide easily—by two's, three's, four's, five's, or anything. It stands alone. It seems to have been a favorite number of Chaucer's, though, for he uses it again towards the very end of *The Canterbury Tales*, where, in the Prologue to the Parson's Tale, we are told that it is getting late, for the afternoon sun stands in the sky at just 29 degrees. The tale-telling game that the Host outlines in the General Prologue demands four tales from each pilgrim—two told on the way to visit the shrine of St. Thomas Becket in Canterbury Cathedral and two on the way back. That would give us a total of 116 tales—a number divisible by four and twenty-nine, among others, but still rather awkward compared to Boccaccio's neat 100.

Perhaps Chaucer's 29/116 is, however, a ruse. Near the end of *The Canterbury Tales*, the Canon's Yeoman joins the pilgrimage, raising the number of pilgrims to thirty. If his intrusion had been planned from early on, that would give us a total number of tales that is far more numerologically satisfying—120. Its factors are a Boccaccian ten and also twelve, the latter venerable in association (the twelve apostles, the twelve patriarchs, the twelve months of the year, etc.). The significance of this number is perhaps less in its possible allegorical associations than in its magnitude: according to the structure announced in the General Prologue and augmented by the arrival of the Canon's Yeoman, *The Canterbury Tales* would have topped the already lengthy *Decameron* by a whopping twenty tales. Chaucer must have realized early on that such a plan was entirely unrealistic, however, given the length of his longer tales. Perhaps he allowed the Host's reference to two tales out and two tales back to remain in the General Prologue, which he probably revised on several occasions, to indicate that *The Canterbury Tales* was a work that could never be finished.

If Chaucer did intend to outdo Boccaccio and envisaged a work of 120 tales, he came nowhere near completing it. He has left us only twenty-four, including three (possibly four) fragments. Moreover, the two-there-two-back framework is challenged by a competing structure, announced most fully in the Prologue to the Parson's Tale, while the sun is hovering 29 degrees above the horizon. There the Host calls out to the Parson, claiming that everyone but he has told a tale, and it is time for him to complete the game. (In fact, a number of the pilgrims beside the Parson have not told a tale—the Plowman, the Yeoman, and the five Guildsmen.) As the Parson's Prologue makes clear, the pilgrims have not quite made it to Canterbury. The Parson complies by refusing to recite a fiction in verse and offers instead a long treatise on moral theology. This alternative structure implies only one tale per pilgrim (though Chaucer himself has already told two, his first interrupted and fragmentary). This structure also implies no return journey.

Which of these two competing structures is the "correct" or "intended" one? Two fifteenth-century writers, one of them the prolific poet John Lydgate and the other anonymous, seem to have felt that Chaucer should have taken his pilgrims at least as far as Canterbury and written tales for the return journey. Since then, critics have often debated this question, with a large number seeking artistic "unity" in the one-tale structure, which more closely approaches completion than the one outlined in the General Prologue. There has been debate about which of the structures was the first: was the Parson-structure a scaled-down version that the aging poet developed after realizing the impossibility of his task, or was the General Prologue-structure a whimsical afterthought? Probably the most common view is that *The Canterbury Tales*, as an unfinished work, has some inner contradictions that Chaucer never resolved. Its mathematics and its structure remain chaotic and messy. Others, however, have wondered if the work he envisaged could ever have been finished or whether it was, as Donald R. Howard argues, "unfinished but complete," that is, that Chaucer had created "a literary form and structure, a literary idea, whose possibilities were inexhaustible."[1]

What is clear is that the framing device of the pilgrimage served Chaucer well. It allowed him to explore the social tensions and moral debates of his day more freely than would otherwise be possible, transposing all conflict into an apparently innocent tale-telling competition. The question of who will tell the tale that offers the "best sentence and moost solaas" (line 798), i.e., the best moral meaning and the most enjoyment, is a standing invitation to probe beneath the surface and ask what each tale's meaning really is. The pilgrimage frame also allowed Chaucer to experiment with almost every major literary genre of his day. The variety is astonishing. The Knight's Tale, the Squire's Tale, and the *Tale of Sir Thopas* are courtly romances deal-

---

1   *The Idea of the Canterbury Tales* (Berkeley: U of California P, 1976), 1, 385.

ing with chivalry and courtly love. The first of these began life as an epic (in Boccaccio's *Il Teseida*) and is serious in its intent. The other two satirize the genre. The Wife of Bath's Tale and the Franklin's Tale are "Breton lays"— short courtly romances originally performed musically and dealing with love and the supernatural. The Miller's Tale, the Reeve's Tale, the fragmentary Cook's Tale, the Summoner's Tale, the Merchant's Tale, and the Shipman's Tale are all fabliaux: short, often funny stories usually set in a bourgeois or peasant environment, which involve trickery, most often sexual trickery. The Canon's Yeoman's Tale is mostly given over to descriptions of alchemical work, but it too has a kind of fabliau at its core: the story of how a canon tricks a priest into buying a phony alchemical recipe. The Man of Law's Tale, originally taken from an historical chronicle, has similarities to a Saint's Life, while the Prioress's Tale and the Second Nun's Tale are Saints' Lives proper. The Physician's Tale, lifted from another historical work, is an exemplum, as are the Friar's Tale, the Clerk's Tale, and the Pardoner's Tale. Exempla were stories that served as examples of moral values; they were often incorporated into medieval sermons. *The Tale of Melibee* is a moral treatise, and the Parson's Tale is a penitential manual, a work of instruction to help a priest hear confession or a parishioner prepare for confession. The Monk's Tale is a collection of tragedies, while the Nun's Priest's Tale and the Manciple's Tale are beasts' fables—a genre familiar to readers today from the famous fables of Aesop—though the Manciple's Tale began life in Ovid's *Metamorphoses* as a myth of the gods and goddesses and could easily be reclassified as a myth.

In the late seventeenth century the poet John Dryden, the first to translate some of *The Canterbury Tales* into modern English, used the phrase "God's plenty" to describe the work's astounding variety of characters. The phrase is still wholly appropriate and applicable to its genres as well. Chaucer seems to have constructed it with the intention of giving his readers the experience of as many genres as possible. At the same time, he assembles an encyclopedic compilation of ancient wisdom, history, and moral lessons, the kind of collection many of his early readers found immensely useful. The learned aspect of this compilation is reinforced in the Ellesmere manuscript by the large number of marginal glosses, which identify the source for quotations and draw attention to particularly sententious passages. In both its range of genres and its love of old learning, *The Canterbury Tales* sums up the literary world of the late Middle Ages.

Chaucer's English

Historians of the English language divide it into three broad periods—Old English, Middle English, and Modern English. The terms are of course simplifications, for the language is always changing, but they are convenient. Old English extends from the beginnings, when the Germanic peoples—including the Angles and the Saxons—invaded England in the fifth century, to approximately 1100, when the Normans with their French dialect began to alter the language after they conquered England in 1066. The Middle English period extends to about the year 1500, when, for reasons that are still not entirely clear, there was a sweeping transformation in the language, particularly in its pronunciation and inflections (the way grammatical information is conveyed by changing the form of a word). Chaucer wrote in a form of Middle English that was beginning to develop in London, with some influence from other parts of the country, including Oxford and Cambridge, and was becoming accepted as the appropriate kind of English for government business. This is the ancestor of what is still often called "standard" English. Chaucer's English as a consequence is easier to read, pronounce, and translate than that of contemporary works such as *Sir Gawain and the Green Knight*, which is written in the dialect of the West Midlands.

Chaucer wrote before the age (the eighteenth century) when people expected languages to employ standard spelling, so the modern reader is sometimes amused or irritated to see the same word spelled in different ways. Usually the alternate spellings were pronounced roughly the same. The second reaction a modern reader of Chaucer's language typically has when first encountering it is dismay in the face of unfamiliar words. This is a real obstacle for the reading of Chaucer's poetry, but it is a much smaller one than appears at first. A statistical analysis of Chaucer's language would reveal that the vast majority of his words survives somehow into Modern English with roughly the same meaning. It is the small minority that gains our attention.

Chaucer's pronunciation was different from that of Modern English. In fact it is in some ways more difficult to understand Chaucer when he is read aloud in Middle English than when he is read silently. It is not necessary to understand how he was pronounced to understand the meaning of what he wrote, but the lover of the audible aspects of poetry will doubtless want to know about this, so we have included a rough guide to Chaucer's pronunciation below.

The major change that ushered in early Modern English about the year 1500 is called the "Great Vowel Shift," which affected most long vowels in English. European languages today pronounce long vowels differently than does English. Thus Spanish *vino* and French *dire* are pronounced more or less as if they were written *veeno* and *deer* in English. In Chaucer's Middle English, long vowels were pronounced much the way they are pronounced in Spanish, Italian, French, and German today. The first thing someone who wants to read Chaucer aloud must learn is to use these so-called "Continental" long vowels. (Helge Kökeritz provides some basic rules for recognizing when a vowel is long or short in *A Guide to Chaucer's Pronunciation*, but many people will find it easier to follow John Gardner's advice, "Make them long or short exactly as you would in modern English.")[1] There were, more-

---

1   *A Guide to Chaucer's Pronunciation* (1961. Rpt. Toronto: U of Toronto P, 1978) and *The Life and Times of Chaucer* (New York: Knopf, 1977), 316.

over, almost no "silent" letters—either consonants or vowels—in Chaucer's Middle English. *Knight*, for instance, was pronounced with the sound of the *k* before that of the *n*, and the *gh* digraph (a digraph being a two-letter symbol representing only one sound like modern *th* or *sh*) was pronounced, not silent. The sound of this *gh* digraph has largely disappeared from Modern English: it approximated the sound of German *ch* in the word *ich*, Spanish *x* in the Spanish pronunciation of *Mexico*, or, for that matter, roughly the sound of a cat hissing. This "pronunciation of all letters" rule necessitates pronouncing some words with two syllables that we pronounce today with one—like *name*, pronounced in Chaucer's day *nah-meh*, with the long *a* given a pre-vowel shift value, and the short *e* at the end pronounced. The exception to the "pronounce all letters" rule, though, is the final *e*. Chaucer lived at the exact time of transition, when the final *e*'s were ceasing to be pronounced. People of his day sometimes did and sometimes did not pronounce them. An earlier English writer like the mystic Richard Rolle, who died a few years after Chaucer was born, likely would have pronounced them all, while a later English writer like Thomas Malory, who was born somewhat more than a decade after Chaucer died, likely pronounced none of them—our practice today. For Chaucer, a good approximation is to pronounce the final *e*'s followed by consonants only, for the elision of the final *e* into a vowel beginning the next word was a major cause of this change.

These suggestions are by no means complete, and they give only a rough approximation of Chaucer's pronunciation. Kökeritz offers a fuller treatment in her useful manual. For most people, however, the easiest way to learn to pronounce Middle English is by listening to others read it. The Chaucer Studio has made a wide range of recordings and good samples can also be found on various Chaucer websites, such as that of Larry Benson.[1]

Chaucer's Versification

All of *The Canterbury Tales* except for the *Tale of Melibee* and the Parson's Tale are in verse. The vast majority of tales with their attendant links are written in rhyming iambic pentameter couplets. That is, each line rhymes with a "partner," and it has five metrical feet. A metrical foot is a unit that—in English at least—has a set number of syllables, usually two but sometimes three. Most of Chaucer's metrical feet are iambic, meaning they comprise two syllables, the first unaccented, the second accented, although he introduces other metrical patterns for variety.

Chaucer seems to have been the first poet to use the rhyming iambic pentameter couplet extensively. The old traditions of English versification were different. Stretching back centuries to the Old English period and beyond,

---

1   See http://www.courses.fas.harvard.edu/~chaucer/. Many other sites are listed by the New Chaucer Society at http://artsci.wustl.edu/~chaucer/.

alliteration was the major way to structure lines. In Old and Middle English, alliterative lines, ones based on similar *initial* sounds of words, normally did not rhyme and had no set number of syllables. The best known examples of alliterative poetry from Chaucer's day are the poems in the Cotton Nero manuscript, including *Pearl* and *Sir Gawain and the Green Knight,* and William Langland's *Piers Plowman,* which begins: "In a somer seson whan soft was the sonne,/I shope me in shroudes as I a shepe were" ("In a summer season, when the sun was soft,/I dressed myself in garments as if I were a sheep.") Near the end of *The Canterbury Tales,* the Parson refuses to provide a poetical tale when he rejects both alliteration and rhyme emphatically: "I kan nat geeste 'rum, ram, ruf,' by lettre,/Ne, God woot, rym holde I but litel bettre ..." ("I cannot versify in 'rum, ram, ruf,' by letter/And, God knows, I hold rhyme but little better.")

There was no shortage of rhyming English poetry before Chaucer, including the powerful lyrics of Rolle, but often rhyme was used for popular romances of the kind Chaucer mocks in the *Tale of Sir Thopas,* or for works of basic religious instruction, where rhyming helped memorization. In France, on the other hand, rhyming was the norm for fashionable court poetry, and it is likely Chaucer chose to rhyme in English because he admired French poetry. The dominant rhyming scheme in France was the octosyllabic couplet—rhyming lines of four feet (usually eight syllables). Chaucer employs it in early poems like *The Book of the Duchess* and *The House of Fame.* English seems at times to demand more syllables than does French—possibly because rhymes in English are hard to find. As Chaucer himself remarked in his short poem "The Complaint of Venus," there is a great scarcity of rhyme in English. This may be one reason why Chaucer eventually preferred the longer line.

Not all the poetry of *The Canterbury Tales* is in iambic pentameter couplets. Several of the tales are in more elaborate stanza forms. The Man of Law's Tale, the Clerk's Tale, the Prioress's Tale, and the Second Nun's Tale are all in the so-called rhyme royal stanza, which consists of seven lines of iambic pentameter with a rhyme scheme of ababbcc (each letter here representing a different rhyme). This stanza got its name because the Scottish king James I, who was also a poet, in the early fifteenth century used it, imitating Chaucer. Chaucer first used (or invented) it in his dream vision *The Parliament of Fowls.* In *The Canterbury Tales* he seems to have associated this "royal stanza" not with royalty but with women. All of the tales employing it are about vulnerable women, except the Prioress's Tale, which is told by a woman and is about a vulnerable little boy.

The Monk's Tale employs an eight-line stanza, similar to rhyme royal, rhyming ababbcbc. Like rhyme royal, it is in iambic pentameter, though in the Prologue to that tale the Monk announces that he will tell his tale in lines "Of six feet, which men clepen [call] *exametron.*" A hexameter line, as the Monk explains, is of six feet rather than five. Several lines of this tale, including the first, are indeed hexameters; Chaucer seems to have been caught between the rock of the Monk's intentions and the hard place of what he had already written. Perhaps a further revision would have expanded the lines throughout to hexameters.

Chaucer's own *Tale of Sir Thopas* is also in stanzas rather than iambic pentameter couplets. It is, however, more difficult to describe than the Monk's Tale's stanza and the rhyme royal used in the other tales employing stanzas. This is because the format changes as the tale progresses. It starts out straightforwardly enough in six-line stanzas of octosyllabic lines, rhyming aabccb. Somewhere near the middle it gains a two-syllable "bob" line with a new rhyme scheme of aabcddc. For the next stanza immediately following it, the original format returns as the first six lines, but it is followed by the "bob" line and a further three long lines. After three stanzas like this, the new form disappears and the original returns, but the nine-line form shows up again for a final appearance near the end. Chaucer, of course, is having fun with this, casting the "pilgrim" version of himself as an inept poet who is never quite clear about what stanzaic form he is using.

The Reception of Chaucer's Poetry

In her massive compilation of references to Chaucer, Caroline Spurgeon divides the reception of Chaucer into six stages. The first stage, which covers nearly a century, is marked by the "enthusiastic and reverential praise" of the poets of his day and his immediate successors. The second stage (falling in the same period but in a different country) sees Scottish poets such as Robert Henryson imitating his style. Henryson (c. 1475) was so affected by reading Chaucer's *Troilus and Criseyde* that he took it upon himself to write a sequel recounting the heroine's demise. The third stage, beginning in the Elizabethan period, sees a range of attitudes. While many poets continue to praise Chaucer, a sense begins to develop that he "was obsolete, that his language was very difficult to understand, his style rough and unpolished and his versification imperfect."[1] Spurgeon also notes the way in which Chaucer was enlisted in the religious controversies of the day, something recent critics have stressed more strongly. In the fourth stage, which covers most of the seventeenth century, Chaucer's reputation is at a low ebb and no edition of his works is published. The fifth stage is one of "modernization," in which Chaucer's works are rewritten for eighteenth-century taste, just as some of Shakespeare's plays were (most notoriously *King Lear*), and starts with Dryden's *Fables* in 1700. Finally, beginning with Thomas Tyrwhitt's learned edition of the *Canterbury Tales* in 1775, we move into a stage when Chaucer

---

1   Caroline F.E. Spurgeon, *Five Hundred Years of Chaucer Criticism and Allusion, 1357–1900*, 3 vols. (Cambridge: Cambridge UP, 1925), 1: x. Many of the key texts are also available in Derek Brewer's edition, *Chaucer: The Critical Heritage*, 2 vols. (London: Routledge, 1978). We have modernized the spellings.

is celebrated, but by scholars rather than poets. Spurgeon began her project, which took her nearly twenty-three years, in 1900. If she were writing today, she would need to add at least one more stage. Sometime in about the mid-twentieth century, scholarly study of Chaucer, which tended to concentrate on questions such as Chaucer's sources and historical references, gave way to close critical reading and interpretation of his work.

As Spurgeon notes, we are all "inclined to feel that the way we regard an author, a classic, for instance like Chaucer, is the truest and only way he can be regarded," but the record of criticism shows the force of "the prevailing bias of the age, the standards, ideals and fashions, change in which constitutes change in taste."[1] Contemporary Chaucer scholars might well resist the suggestion that their work is no more than a reflection of the biases of their day. Are not the great scholarly editions such as the *Riverside Chaucer*, the wisely skeptical biography of Chaucer by Derek Pearsall, or the revised edition of the *Sources and Analogues* rather the reflection of progress, as scholarly standards become ever more rigorous, old myths are debunked, and true knowledge gradually accumulates? There is room for endless debate about Chaucer and his attitudes to religion, for example, but this debate now involves evidence that is very different from that used in the sixteenth century, when it was believed that the so-called Plowman's Tale, a Wycliffite or Lollard satire on the established church, had been written by Chaucer. We now know it was not. And, although the question would be a harder one to address, is there not progress in the critical appreciation of Chaucer's works? Our understanding of Chaucer's use of his literary sources, while filled with debate and uncertainty, has become more sophisticated. The Victorian critics who looked to historical records to find the identities of the real people whom they assumed lay behind Chaucer's characters now seem simply naïve. At the same time, some recent Chaucer critics have taken Spurgeon's interest in radical new directions. Chaucer's status as the father of English literature and the first great English canonical poet is often now seen as a reflection not just of the excellence of his writing but also of the needs of the various people who first copied and later edited him.

Spurgeon's work is limited to direct references to Chaucer, and during his life itself these are rare. For his younger contemporary, Eustache Deschampes, writing in about 1385, Chaucer is a Socrates in wisdom, a second Ovid in his poetry, and the "grant translateur" ("great translator") who has made *The Romance of the Rose* available in English. In his *Testament of Love*, which he wrote while in prison before being executed, the unfortunate London official Thomas Usk praises Chaucer as a "noble philosophical poet." Chaucer's friend John Gower has the God of love in his *Confessio Amantis* (c. 1390) praise Chaucer as his poet and his disciple of Venus—doubtless because love is a frequent subject of his poetry. But such references do not tell us

---

1 *Chaucer Criticism and Allusion*, 1: cxxxv–cxxvi.

much about who was reading Chaucer, or how. For that, we must turn else-where.

It was long assumed that Chaucer wrote and even performed his poetry for the royal court. In the opening lines of *Troilus and Criseyde*, Chaucer calls himself a servant of the servants of the God of Love, that is, of young aristo-cratic lovers, and works such as the *Book of the Duchess*, *Troilus and Criseyde*, and the Knight's Tale do indeed seem to meet these lovers' needs, in part by posing—directly or by implication—questions about the code of love for them to debate. *The Legend of Good Women* implies that the account of Cri-seyde's betrayal of Troilus was regarded by the court as a slander on women, and in one of the two prologues, the God of Love tells Chaucer that when he had written stories of good women to make amends he was to bring them to Queen Anne in her palace at Sheen. Furthermore, with its vivid dia-logue and narrators who sound like characters, Chaucer's poems are clearly made to be read aloud. As J.A. Burrow argues, in a lively introduction to the working conditions of medieval writers, in the Middle Ages people "treated books rather as musical scores are treated today," making reading "a kind of performance."[1] The kind of delivery this conjures can actually be seen in what must be the most widely reproduced image of Chaucer, the frontis-piece of an early fifteenth-century manuscript of Chaucer's *Troilus and Cri-seyde* that once belonged to King Henry V, which shows Chaucer reading or reciting his poetry in a garden to an audience of nobles.[2] But an analysis of the friends whom Chaucer mentions in his poetry provides us a rather differ-ent picture. According to this, Chaucer's first circle of readers was composed not of great aristocrats (both men and women), but of men, and men rather like himself—professional civil servants who were members of King Rich-ard's "affinity," the king's personal followers. These readers would include men like the Lollard knights Lewis Clifford and John Clanvowe, "who sprang from the lesser gentry and made their way ... by their wits" as well as lawyers and intellectuals like "philosophical" Ralph Strode (who appears to have been first an Oxford logician and then a London lawyer) and "moral" John Gower, to whom Chaucer dedicates *Troilus and Criseyde*.[3] What these men made of Chaucer's poetry we can only surmise, but they were a book-ish and sophisticated group. Clanvowe wrote both a courtly love poem, *The Book of Cupid*, and a religious treatise, *The Two Ways*. These men formed

---

1 *Medieval Writers and Their Work: Middle English Literature and Its Background, 1100–1500* (Oxford: Oxford UP, 1982), 47.

2 Chaucer is shown in a pulpit as if reading but no book is actually visible. The reasons why this picture (which was painted at least a decade after Chaucer died) cannot be regarded as a reliable witness to how Chaucer actually delivered his poetry were first advanced by Derek Pearsall in "The Troilus Frontispiece and Chaucer's Audience," *Yearbook of English Studies* 7 (1977): 68–74.

3 K.B. McFarlane, *Lancastrian Kings and Lollard Knights* (Oxford: Oxford UP, 1972), 162. The evidence for this readership and its social makeup is analyzed by Paul Strohm in *Social Chaucer*, 41–46.

something of a coterie, a small group who knew each other well enough to share insider jokes. In the fifteenth century, a rather similar class of educated and prosperous Londoners formed part of the market for elegant copies of Chaucer's works.

In approximately the first 120 years of the reception of Chaucer's poetry— a crucial period encompassing the last fifteen years of his life and including the first editions of *The Canterbury Tales* produced on the printing press— Chaucer's reputation is closely tied to the status of English as a literary language. He is generally depicted as a philosophical poet who illumined the English language with ornate rhetoric. To most English poets who mention him during this period he is a "master"—a teacher whom the present writer is striving to imitate through decorous language. The poet Thomas Hoccleve, for example, who was, like Chaucer, a civil servant although a more junior one, praises him as his "maistir deere and fadir reverent/Mi maistir Chaucer, flour of eloquence," making Hoccleve the first on record to describe Chaucer as his literary "father."

This fulsome praise must not always be taken at face value, however: for fifteenth-century poets Chaucer was an inspiring model but also an overwhelming presence, and an element of rivalry, and sometimes moral criticism, appears in their tributes.[1] In the early fifteenth century the Benedictine monk John Lydgate depicts Chaucer as his master, one who was the first to rain "the gold dew-drops" of rhetoric on the "rude" (that is, rough or unsophisticated) English language. In his *Siege of Thebes*, a prequel to the Knight's Tale, Lydgate actually inserts himself into *The Canterbury Tales*, describing how he joined the pilgrims at an inn in Canterbury and accompanied them back to London, telling his long story of bad Theban kings (including Oedipus), and ending, where Chaucer begins, with Creon's defeat at the hands of Theseus.

Lydgate was not the only one fascinated by the pilgrims' journey. An anonymous author, possibly a monk at Canterbury, added the tale of the young merchant Beryn, which he had the Merchant tell on the return journey. The introduction to the tale of Beryn includes a lengthy account of the pilgrims' arrival in Canterbury and how they passed the day there, visiting the Cathedral and town (see Background Documents, p. 428).

These continuations are some indication of how popular *The Canterbury Tales* had become. Not surprisingly, William Caxton, the entrepreneur who in 1476 first brought the printing press to England, soon printed them.[2] In his edition of 1484 he praises Chaucer as a "noble and great philosopher"

---

1   Robert R. Edwards discusses Lydgate's ambivalent attitude to his master Chaucer in his edition of *The Siege of Thebes* (Kalamazoo, MI: TEAMS, 2001), 5–6.
2   The best general introduction to the editing of Chaucer through the ages is the collection of essays edited by Paul G. Ruggiers, *Editing Chaucer: The Great Tradition* (Norman, OK: Pilgrim, 1984).

who "for his ornate writing in our tongue may well have the name of laure-
ate poet" since he has "by his labor embellished, ornated [decorated], made
fair our English" which was previously "rude" and "incongruous." Caxton
also printed Chaucer's translation of Boethius and his *House of Fame*, but the
first complete edition of Chaucer's works did not appear for another fifty
years. In 1532 William Thynne, who served King Henry VIII as the clerk
in the royal kitchen, brought out his edition. Thynne owned no fewer than
twenty-two manuscripts of various Chaucer works and made some effort to
compare them to determine the best readings. Thynne included a number of
works in his edition, notably the *Testament of Love* (which we now know to
have been written by Thomas Usk), and *The Plowman's Tale*, a satire on the
evils of the church in which a reforming pelican debates with a greedy and
bullying griffin. Thynne apparently realized these works were not by Chau-
cer, but he did not make this very clear, and the business of pruning Chau-
cer's canon of these spurious works was not completed until Walter Skeat
published his edition of Chaucer at the very end of the nineteenth century.
Like his royal master, Thynne shifted religious allegiance, and it is telling
to watch how the positioning of *The Plowman's Tale* reflects these shifts. It
first appears as a supplementary tale or appendix to Thynne's revised edi-
tion of 1542, suggesting that it is not really one of Chaucer's tales, but in the
third edition of 1550, it is incorporated into the tales themselves, appearing
between the tales of the Manciple and the Parson.

As James Simpson points out, the effect of these editorial changes was
to render Chaucer a Protestant.[1] That was not an inevitable development.
For the Lancastrian kings, who saw Lollardy as a major threat to political
stability, *The Canterbury Tales* seemed thoroughly respectable because it was
about a pilgrimage, something the religious reformers condemned. Chau-
cer's apparent religious orthodoxy may even have encouraged Lancastrian
civil servants to promote the copying of his manuscripts in the early fif-
teenth century.[2] A century later, however, John Foxe, who wrote the lives of
the Protestant martyrs who died under the Catholic Queen Mary, claimed
Chaucer as a faithful witness to the true faith that had emerged during the
late fourteenth century through the writings of John Wycliffe. For Foxe,
Chaucer was a "right Wicklevian." The anti-clericalism of *The Canterbury
Tales*, where monks and friars are implicitly and explicitly criticized, saved
Chaucer, it seems, from summary dismissal among some Protestants. Many,
however, would have agreed with the Protestant martyr and Bible transla-

---

1   The Oxford English Literary History, vol. 2. 1350–1547, *Reform and Cultural Revolution* (Oxford:
    Oxford UP, 2002), 41–42.
2   According to what is sometimes called the "Lancastrian thesis," Henry IV (who usurped the
    throne) and his son Henry V actively promoted the use of English and of Chaucer as the pre-
    eminent English poet; this was part of a propaganda effort designed to legitimize their regime.
    The view was first advanced by John H. Fisher in "A Language Policy for Lancastrian England,"
    PMLA 107 (1992): 1168–80.

tor William Tyndale, writing just eleven years (1528) after Martin Luther initiated the Protestant Reformation: Tynedale complained that though the Bible was illegal, at least in the vernacular, corrupting books like Chaucer's *Troilus and Criseyde*, filthy and full of wantonness, were not.

The biggest concern by the mid-sixteenth century, however, as Spurgeon notes, was that Chaucer's language was too old-fashioned to be easily understood. In 1546, Peter Ashton, a Cambridge scholar, wrote that he himself tried to use a plain style in his translations, and not words like Chaucer's, which had fallen out of use. Even among those who praise Chaucer, there is a growing sense that he belongs to a distant age. Queen Elizabeth's tutor, Roger Ascham, in 1552 compared Chaucer to Homer, Sophocles, and Euripides. This is, of course, high praise from the pen of a humanist scholar, but it likewise signals a shift in the reception of Chaucer's poetry: earlier he had elevated "our" language to new heights of golden rhetoric, but now he is distanced, likened to classic poets of another time and language. In 1575, the poet George Gascoigne called Chaucer "our father" as well as "my master." "Master," of course, means "teacher," and that had been the dominant metaphor among fifteenth-century commentators on Chaucer. But "father," a metaphor that will soon become dominant, is something different. A father has a closer, more affectionate, relationship to one than does a teacher, but one is free—or compelled—to be different. Edmund Spenser was heavily influenced by Chaucer, and drew upon the Squire's Tale for the story of Cambel (Chaucer's Cambalo) in Book IV of *The Faerie Queene*. Here he calls Chaucer a "well of English undefiled" and as the "pure wellhead of poesie," but he also laments that the "famous moniment" (monument) of Chaucer's account has been defaced by "wicked Time." With Sir Philip Sidney's monumental *Apology for Poetry* (1581), the distancing from the father figure becomes even more marked. Neoclassic in taste, Sidney lamented Chaucer's lack of regularity and his inconsistency in tone, where the comic and the tragic could freely mingle.

Spurgeon's third phase ends with the appearance in 1598 of a new edition of Chaucer's works edited by Thomas Speght. Drawing on the works of the great antiquarian John Stow, best known for his history of London, Speght included a life of Chaucer that took account of many of the medieval documents that were eventually grouped together in the Life Records. Speght also provided a glossary. Four years later, he brought out a revised edition, in which he had done a rather better job of determining Chaucer's text. Then follows nearly a century, Spurgeon's fourth phase, when Chaucer was neither edited nor translated, and the sense that he was old-fashioned prevailed. As late as 1694, the famous essayist Joseph Addison found Chaucer a "merry Bard," whose language is "rusted" and "worn out"; Chaucer, for Addison, jests in vain, for he is incapable any more of making his readers laugh.

By the time Addison made this remark, however, things were beginning to change. There was a growing demand for access to Chaucer, either through translations or through a proper edition. He was widely regarded as the first great English poet, but he was only available in the editions of the sixteenth and seventeenth century, which were inaccurate, expensive, and hard to read in their early black-letter typeface, and provided no help with the Middle English. Despite all these disadvantages, Speght's edition of 1602 was reissued in 1687, one sign of a renewed interest. But what really marks the turn is the publication of John Dryden's *Fables Ancient and Modern* (1700), in which he offered verse paraphrases of tales by Ovid, Boccaccio, and Chaucer. Dryden, an influential literary critic as well as a poet and playwright, remarks that the purity of English as a literary language had begun with Chaucer, who came at the "Dawning of our Language." He wrote with simplicity (not golden rhetoric) and followed nature closely. He is "the Father of English poetry," as Homer was to the Greeks and Virgil to the Romans. His meter is "not Harmonius to us" but it has a "rude Sweetness"—this because of his inability to provide ten syllables per line regularly. (Here Dryden fails to understand the history of English pronunciation, a matter that was finally corrected by Thomas Tyrwhitt in his edition of 1775.) Yet we find, maintains Dryden, "God's Plenty" in his poetry. "Mankind is ever the same," Dryden declares, implying that *The Canterbury Tales* may serve as a mirror to any age. Alexander Pope followed Dryden's example when he retold Chaucer's *House of Fame* as his *Temple of Fame* and in 1711 noted the difficulties in reading Father Chaucer's language—but with an historical sense rare among early commentators: "Our Sons their Father's *failing Language* see,/And such as Chaucer is, shall *Dryden* be."

By the start of the eighteenth century, the time was ripe for a proper edition, one that would satisfy the scientific standards of the age, which saw huge developments in scholarly editing, and the needs of a wider reading public that now looked to the major poets of the past—Chaucer, Milton, and Shakespeare—not as models of how to write poetry nor even as sources of philosophical wisdom, but as material for genteel relaxation. Editing Chaucer proved no easy matter, however. The first major attempt was undertaken—reluctantly—by John Urry, a junior fellow (rather like a modern graduate student) at Christ Church College, Oxford, whose Master thought that his fellows were too idle and was looking for projects to keep them busy. The edition finally appeared, after the death of both Urry and his no less reluctant successor Thomas Ainsworth, in 1721. Urry's text, however, proved little better than those of the black letter editions and was a large and expensive folio volume. There were a few other unsuccessful efforts before Thomas Tyrwhitt, a distinguished classical scholar who had been deeply influenced by the new developments in classical editing, produced his edition in 1775.

Tyrwhitt's edition of *The Canterbury Tales* represented a huge step forward for the editing of Chaucer and vernacular texts in general and was also very popular. It provided the educated reader with an elegant text in an affordable and portable octavo format that was based on a systematic consultation of the original manuscripts and a sound understanding of Middle English. Copiously annotated, it drew upon the deep knowledge of medieval vernacular literature that Tyrwhitt had acquired by fifteen years' reading in the British and Bodleian libraries. Tyrwhitt was the first to raise the question of the order of the tales, and he provided a solution that is still widely accepted (basically that of the Ellesmere manuscript, although this was still in private hands and not yet known to Chaucerians). Tyrwhitt was also the first to establish clearly the principles of Chaucer's versification and to recognize that making sense of these required a proper understanding of his particular form of Middle English, above all, the frequent sounding of the final *e*. He pruned Chaucer's canon of several spurious works and in his notes provided a wealth of information about Chaucer's sources and the meaning of obscure words or references. In all these ways, he laid the groundwork for the later edition of Walter Skeat, which in turn laid the groundwork for modern editions, notably those of F.N. Robinson and Larry Benson.

The next great edition of Chaucer, that of Skeat, came 120 years later and drew upon the massive and wide-ranging Victorian efforts to catalogue and study medieval historical records and recover the history of the language and the texts of its early writers. This was the period that saw the establishment of the Rolls Series for the publication of medieval English historical texts, the establishment of the British Museum, and the appearance of the first volumes of *A New English Dictionary Edited on Historical Principles* (better known as the *Oxford English Dictionary*), to name but a few of the major projects. A number of factors combined in the nineteenth century to bring things medieval into prominence. Walter Scott's Waverley novels—historical tales about heroic knightly deeds—excited a nation, and slightly later Alfred, Lord Tennyson's *Idylls of the King* made the Arthurian story all the rage. The interest in the Middle Ages also extended to architecture and the visual arts. In the middle years of the nineteenth century, a group of young painters who called themselves the Pre-Raphaelite Brotherhood began to revive what they thought were medieval painterly techniques and subjects, and found some support in the writings of John Ruskin. The *animus* of this group was the painter-poet Dante Gabriel Rossetti, who soon guided two younger friends into the Pre-Raphaelite mode—the painter Edward Burne-Jones and the polymath William Morris. A poet, designer of decorative arts, reviver of lost craft techniques (including stained glass), political agitator, and much else, Morris set off on a crusade to reform English society through medievalistic art and later through a leftist political activism that he traced back to the Peasants' Revolt of 1381.

The study of Chaucer and the esteem in which Chaucer was held both gained immensely from all this nostalgic and sometimes uninformed consumption of the medieval. Second only to King Arthur, Chaucer inspired Victorian England with his medieval Englishness. Burne-Jones presented his friend Morris with a cabinet painted over with scenes from the Prioress's Tale as a wedding gift. (The violent anti-Semitism of the tale does not seem to have troubled him, any more than it did Mathew Arnold, who praised its "delicate and evanescent" charm.) Decades later, in the 1890s, Burne-Jones and Morris collaborated on the *Kelmscott Chaucer*—a compete edition of Chaucer's works done for Morris's Kelmscott Press. It has often been called the most beautiful book ever printed. Burne-Jones designed the many illustrations for it, while Morris designed both lavish borders and a neo-black letter typeface. Morris also carefully chose the paper and the ink, and the works of Chaucer thus shimmer across the page with a startling beauty. For Morris and Burne-Jones, Chaucer is above everything else the iconic figure of the Poet whose work is unadulterated by the modern world.

This artistic appropriation of Chaucer was matched by one more scholarly. The late Victorian era was the great time for English philologists, that is, historians of the language, to explore the riches of their medieval past. There were numerous publishing ventures, most notably the Early English Text Society, founded in 1864 by Frederick James Furnivall, who was a brilliant linguist, an indefatigable enthusiast, and a bit of a rogue. The EETS provided cheap and accurate editions of early texts, partly for the use of the editors of the monumental *Oxford English Dictionary*, which endeavored to provide the full range of uses of a word back to the Old English period. Chaucer was, of course, one of the medieval writers these scholars pursued. A six-volume edition of his works had appeared in 1845 in a series called the Pickering Aldine Poets, and it included a more critically informed life of the poet than had appeared before. In 1868 Furnivall founded the Chaucer Society, which published transcriptions of many of the Chaucer manuscripts, including the two most influential manuscripts, the Ellesmere and Hengwrt (discussed below), which only came to light at this time. Today these publications, which can usually be found in the Chaucer section of most university libraries, tend to gather dust, but they remain useful tools, especially the *Six-Text Print of the Canterbury Tales* (which allows easy comparison of the readings in Ellesmere, Hengwrt, and four other of the best manuscripts of *The Canterbury Tales*). But the towering achievement of nineteenth-century Chaucerian scholarship, which drew on much of this work, was the six-volume edition of Chaucer's works done for the Clarendon Press in 1894 by W.W. Skeat (with a seventh volume presenting Chaucerian verse by other medieval poets). Although he did not actually consult the full range of manuscripts any more extensively than Tyrwhitt did, Skeat had the advantage of being able to draw on both Ellesmere and Hengwrt. Above all, Skeat's notes are a huge advance, drawing on the powerful philological and historical knowledge that had been accumulated since Tyrwhitt worked on his edition.

Close Reading and Interpretation

The Chaucer criticism of the twentieth century might be divided very roughly into three phases. For the first few decades, the prevailing tendency was to see criticism as a lighter business, essentially one of popularization, as opposed to the hard work of real scholarship. John Manly, for example, established his reputation by his massive collation (that is, systematic, line-by-line comparison) of the manuscripts of *The Canterbury Tales* which he did with Edith Rickert to produce their eight-volume edition. In comparison, Manly's major critical study, *Some New Light on Chaucer* (1926), was based on a series of public lectures and in his introduction he warned that it was "merely a collection of suggestions of a more or less speculative character" and not "a formal treatise for experts" (ix). The second phase might be characterized as "professional" criticism and was largely devoted to close reading, drawing heavily on the methods of the so-called New Criticism, which saw poems as complex artistic structures, filled with tension and irony. Derek Brewer points to Rosamund Tuve's study of Chaucer's imagery in *Seasons and Months*, published in 1933, as the turning point between amateur and professional criticism, but the real expansion of professional criticism did not begin until after World War II. In part this change reflected the massive increase in size of the post-war universities, in which English Literature was a popular subject. The New Criticism, with its close attention to the text in front of one and nothing else, flourished under these conditions because it was an approach well suited to the needs of students. It was, however, by no means the only form of Chaucer criticism during this period. In particular, one school of critics turned to medieval interpretation of the Bible, exegesis, as a model. Finally, there is a third phase when, some time in the 1980s, Chaucer criticism begins to be first affected and then dominated by the complex theories of psychoanalysis, feminism, Marxism, deconstruction, and, moving into the late 1990s, queer theory and postcolonialism.

After about three quarters of a century of professional criticism, the distinctions between differing interpretations in Chaucer criticism have become progressively finer and the language more complex. Above all, the sheer quantity of criticism on Chaucer (or indeed on most other major English poets) has become overwhelming. Anyone writing on Chaucer today runs the risk of reinventing the wheel and, for those who have arrived on the scene more recently, it is not always easy to get a sense of the broader patterns. A number of guidebooks are available. The notes to major scholarly editions, such as those of Larry Benson or more recently Jill Mann, or the volumes in the *Variorum Chaucer* (which now covers the General Prologue and seven of the tales) provide references to the most important commentary on particular passages or issues. The Chaucer bibliographies published by the University of Toronto Press (which now cover about a third of the tales) offer a comprehensive bibliography of almost everything that has been written since 1900 (no matter how foolish) and include useful précis of each argument. If one wants to know when critics started to see the Miller's Tale as a comic masterpiece rather than an embarrassing bit of vulgarity, for example, this is the place to go. There are also numerous general critical surveys. Perhaps the best is Helen Cooper's volume in the *Oxford Guides to Chaucer* (1996), which provides a judicious review of especially influential commentary tale by tale.

As Cooper notes, "there are as many interpretations of Chaucer as there are readers."[1] But this does not mean that Chaucer criticism is a formless mass of individual opinions. Rather, as a study like Cooper's makes very clear, Chaucer criticism consists of a series of recurring debates which coalesce around particular difficulties: what are we to make of the impossibly patient Griselda in the Clerk's Tale? Why does the Pardoner try to sell his relics to the pilgrims after he has told them he is a con man? Why is the genteel Prioress so violent in her tale? Is the long and earnest *Tale of Melibee* to be taken at face value or is it a joke? How do the Parson's Tale or the Retractions affect our reading of *The Canterbury Tales* as a whole? Often the answers reflect differences between the moral values of the critics at least as much as differences of analysis: the question of whether the Wife of Bath subverts or confirms medieval stereotypes about women is a particularly forceful example. Since critics often avoid announcing their moral values or critical allegiances directly, it can be helpful to have some sense of the differing camps they belong to.

The criticism of the first phase is amateur in the best sense of the word: filled with a deep enjoyment of Chaucer's works and anxious to share this, genial, and approachable. The pre-eminent practitioner is George Lyman Kittredge, a Harvard professor whose work included editions of Shakespeare and of traditional ballads, but who was also a popular lecturer. Kittredge endowed Chaucer studies with two of its most enduring (but also repeatedly criticized) concepts: the "marriage group," which sees the tales of Wife, Clerk, Merchant, and Franklin as thematically linked around the question of marriage; and the "roadside drama," in which the central interest of *The Canterbury Tales* is the way in which the pilgrims, psychologically realistic characters, interact, using their tales to score off each other. The concept of the "roadside drama" continues to generate debate to this day. It has been extended by R.M. Lumiansky in *Of Sundry Folk: The Dramatic Principle in the Canterbury Tales* (1955) and by Bertrand Bronson in *In Search of Chaucer* (1960)—who goes so far as to imagine which of the pilgrims might have been riding beside each other—and has also been attacked by any number of critics, perhaps most directly by Robert Jordan and C. David Benson. In *Chaucer and the Shape of Creation: The Aesthetic Possibilities of Inorganic Structure* (1967), Jordan turned to the medieval cathedral for a model of artistic unity

---

1   *Oxford Guides to Chaucer: The Canterbury Tales.* 2nd ed. (Oxford: Oxford UP, 1996), 2.

that would include diverse elements (depictions of both heaven and hell, for example), without seeking to merge them into a single unified vision or organic whole. Benson is one of many critics who pursue this line, arguing that dramatic approach distracts attention from the relation between the tales and the diversity of their styles. For Benson, "*The Canterbury Tales* is a collection of absolutely different kinds of poetry; each contributes a special artistic vision, and thus a special view of the world, to the collection as a whole."[1] Others, however, have defended modified notions of character. A notable example is H. Marshall Leicester, Jr., who advances the concept of "impersonated artistry" according to which *The Canterbury Tales* is a collection of "individually voiced texts"; the Miller's Tale, for example, while not a direct reflection of his character, does reflect the Miller's concerns (including the assumption that he or men like him were too boorish to tell a sophisticated story).[2]

By the 1950s Chaucer criticism had been transformed, and while the issues that Kittredge raised continued to be pursued, his approach was largely abandoned. Instead it was replaced by a new sense that criticism was a serious professional practice, even a science, in its own right and by a new set of critical values. As Larry Benson notes, in a useful summary of Chaucer criticism up to 1974, "A generation that admired Joyce's fiction, Yeats's poetry, and the critical doctrines in I.A. Richards's *Practical Criticism* and T.S. Eliot's *Tradition and the Individual Poetic Talent* could not regard 'realism' as the highest literary value, was inclined to respect rather than scorn 'tradition,' and found the touchstone of poetic merit in 'complexity.'"[3]

If one wanted to take a single work to represent the advent of the new "professional" Chaucer criticism, and demonstrate the connection between close reading and the so-called "New Criticism" that developed in the 1930s, one might well choose Charles Muscatine's *Chaucer and the French Tradition* (1957). Muscatine's title might at first suggest that he was a historicist critic of a quite traditional kind, dealing with one particular set of Chaucer's sources. A reader selecting a passage more or less at random—say his description of the opening scene of the Nun's Priest's Tale, contrasting Chauntecleer's colorful splendor to the restrained and humble setting of the poor widow's yard—might well be puzzled to understand why Muscatine can be classified as a New Critic in particular, or why he needs to be located as a member of any school at all, since this kind of close reading now seems so familiar and mainstream. But Muscatine makes his debt to the New Critical principles clear when he announces his study "seeks to determine Chaucer's 'meaning'

---

1   "The Canterbury Tales: Personal Drama or Experiments in Poetic Variety" in Piero Boitani and Jill Mann, eds., *The Cambridge Chaucer Companion* (Cambridge: Cambridge UP, 1986), 93–108 (107).

2   *The Disenchanted Self: Representing the Subject in the Canterbury Tales* (1990), 9–11.

3   "A Reader's Guide to Writings on Chaucer" in Derek Brewer, ed. *Geoffrey Chaucer: The Writer and His Background* (Woodbridge, Suffolk: Boydell and Brewer, 1974), 321–51.

as a complex whole; by giving form and style their due attention as essential, inseparable concomitants of meaning, it will try to balance the traditional preoccupation with 'content' alone. It sees realism as a technique and a convention, not as an end in itself, and it sees convention as a powerful tool, not as something to be avoided or rebelled against, or even necessarily to be remoulded" (1).

Muscatine's understanding of how form and style give a poem its meaning can be seen in his analysis of symmetry in the Knight's Tale. For Muscatine, it is entirely appropriate that the two knights, Palamon and Arcite, are almost indistinguishable (something that had previously often been regarded as a weakness), for the Knight's Tale celebrates order and this is reflected in the poem's structure, specifically in its use of symmetrical patterns:

> When we look at the poem's structure, we find symmetry to be its most prominent feature. The character-grouping is symmetrical. There are two knights, Palamon and Arcite, in love with the same woman, Emilye. Above the three and in a position to sit in judgment, is Duke Theseus, who throughout the poem is the centre of authority and the balance between the opposing interests of the knights.... In the tournament each knight is accompanied by one hundred followers, headed by a particularly notable king, on one side Lygurge, on the other Emetrius. (178)

Muscatine supports his reading by drawing attention to numerous details in the text that might not otherwise appear significant. He points out that at the tournament the two parties of knights are arranged symmetrically "in two renges" (files) and that this echoes the appearance of the mourning ladies who appeal to Theseus at the very beginning of the poem and enter "twye and tweye,/Ech after oother," and that even Palamon and Arcite, cousins, "of sustren two yborn," are found in the heap of bodies "liggynge by and by,/Booth in oon armes" (179). Through analysis of this kind, Muscatine shows again and again how the fine details of the text have a significance that goes beyond mere verisimilitude and contributes to the overall meaning.

In the 1950s a new movement emerged to challenge the prevailing New Critical norms, exegetical or patristic criticism, becoming a major force with the publication in 1962 of the influential *A Preface to Chaucer* by the movement's leading light, D.W. Robertson, Jr. This approach argued that medieval poetry had to be read in accordance with the moral values of the Middle Ages, that is, the values of medieval Christianity, and with medieval symbolic codes. The exegetical critics turned to the interpretation of the Bible by the Church fathers, such as Saint Augustine, and by medieval theologians for their basic model. For Robertson, medieval literature reflected a world view in which human emotion and human goals were always meant to be judged against higher religious truths, and the literature was therefore

"rigorously non-psychological" (34). Good medieval literature, when prop-
erly understood, was always morally serious and taught a single powerful
lesson—to place the love of God (charity) above the love of earthly things
(cupidity). To see this lesson, however, one needed to read allegorically, sep-
arating the wheat of true doctrine from the chaff of the story, just as the
Nun's Priest says we must do with his tale.

Robertson saw his own work as an effort to read medieval poetry on its
own medieval terms, and when his works first appeared Robertson was often
called a historicist. His criticism was certainly based on an immense knowl-
edge of medieval culture (not just the writings of the Church fathers but
also art history, especially iconography, and, surprisingly, social history—
he showed as much interest in the details of the English cloth trade as any
Marxist critic). He believed that humanist critics were imposing sentimental
and anachronistic readings on medieval texts. Of course, there are as many
kinds of history as there are historians, but Robertson's vision of the Middle
Ages as one of "quiet hierarchies" (51) is certainly at odds with that of recent
historicist critics, who tend to deride his work for its politically conservative
nostalgia, arguing that the Middle Ages was filled with religious, political,
and social conflict. For humanist critics confronting Robertson in the 50s
and 60s, however, the problem was not that Robertson was wrong about
medieval culture but that he used his knowledge to impose a single pre-
determined interpretation on every poem he found. In opposition, E. Tal-
bot Donaldson, one of the liveliest of Robertson's opponents, insists on "the
right of a poem to say what it means and mean what it says, and not what
anyone, before or after its composition, thinks it ought to say or mean."[1]

Donaldson, following the older pattern of Kittredge or Manly, made his
scholarly reputation as an editor and delivered his criticism as lectures, giv-
ing them an engagingly approachable style, as reflected in the title of his
collected essays, *Speaking of Chaucer*. Donaldson is anxious to share his own
pleasures in reading Chaucer (and to show that reading poetry is a manly
thing to do), as when he describes May in the Knight's Tale as "not only
the embodiment of all pretty young girls in the Spring, but a proof that the
Spring of pretty young girls is a permanent thing" (49). But under the breezy
manner, Donaldson makes two important points. The first is that if May
is a flat character it is because Chaucer has worked very hard, for his own
artistic purposes, to make her that way. The second is that human nature
remains constant. Again and again, Donaldson evokes his sense of kinship
with Chaucer and his characters across half a millennium. Above all, Don-
aldson believed in the enduring value of great poetry, rejecting the sugges-
tion that it was merely "chaff" concealing the "fruit" of moral doctrine. In
response to Robertson's remark that medieval art, if properly understood,
could provide "the food of wisdom as well as more transient aesthetic satis-

---

1 *Speaking of Chaucer* (New York: Norton, 1970), 135.

factions," Donaldson countered that "great poetic art offers something very close to the ultimate reality" (152) and that the wisdom it offers, which is not specifically doctrinal, is part of "a humane tradition that is as old as western civilization" (153).

The opposition between the two camps did Chaucer studies no harm. There had been a long-standing tendency for English Chaucerians to claim Chaucer as a representative Englishman; now he was being claimed (although by implication, not explicitly) as a representative American. Robertson and Donaldson spoke in part for two strong forces in American society, a Bible-centered Christianity that could unite Protestant and Catholic interests (*A Preface to Chaucer* appeared the year after the United States inaugurated, for the first time, a Catholic president) and a democratic secular humanism.[1] In Chaucer studies these forces were brought into productive debate. Whether one saw him as the first great democratic writer, the medieval Walt Whitman, or the first English Christian writer, the medieval English Dante, Chaucer was important. Publication flourished. In part to handle the increase in Chaucer criticism, a new journal was established in 1966, *The Chaucer Review.*

With a sense of mission and two well-developed professional approaches, Chaucer criticism was ready for the next major step, a consideration of the aesthetics of *The Canterbury Tales* as a whole. In 1963 Robert Payne commented that there was almost no discussion of *The Canterbury Tales* in their entirety, perhaps in his view—only "about a third (or less) seem really superior poetry."[2] The next twenty years would see a spate of books that did address *The Canterbury Tales* as a whole, in the process showing the crucial role played by tales that Payne so readily dismissed. These included Robert Jordan's *Chaucer and the Shape of Creation* (1967), mentioned above for its attack on Kittredge's notion of the roadside drama, Donald Howard's *The Idea of the Canterbury Tales* (1976), Helen Cooper's *The Structure of the Canterbury Tales* (1984), and V.A. Kolve's *Chaucer and the Imagery of Narrative*, Volume I (1984). The collection of excerpts edited by Corinne Saunders for the *Blackwell Guides to Criticism* (2001) provides a useful introduction to some of these efforts.

In each case, the author turned to one specific branch of medieval culture to find an underlying principle to unify the tales. For Jordan, the roots of Chaucer's "inorganic structure," with its tolerance of diverging perspectives, is best illustrated by the Gothic cathedral. Howard also turned to Gothic architecture (including the labyrinths traced on the floors of some medieval cathedrals) but he also stressed the importance of the art of memory, suggesting *The Canterbury Tales* was akin to one of the "memory palaces," collections of memorable images carefully placed in a mental grid by classical orators and

---

1   Robertson, however, according to several accounts, was not himself a Christian.
2   *The Key of Remembrance: A Study of Chaucer's Poetics* (New Haven, CT: Yale UP, 1963), 150.

medieval preachers and scholars who needed to store information in their head. For Cooper, the tales resemble the great medieval encyclopedias or summas of Thomas Aquinas and Vincent de Beauvais, which were intended not just to allow one to locate information on a particular topic but also "to show the wholeness, the unity, of all creation and all abstract or intellectual thought in all their diversity."[1] Kolve turned to medieval iconography and explored the ways in which the tales are organized around certain recurring images, such as that of Fortune and her wheel, or the enclosed garden, the unbridled horse (a symbol of uncontrolled desire), or death as a tapster, opening a spigot so the barrel would run dry. Kolve only managed to deal with the First Fragment (Knight to Cook), but showed, with an attention to the details of the text worthy of Muscatine, how the tales respond to each other, so that the Reeve's Tale, for example, reverses the images and values of the Miller's "green world." Taken together, these works offer a powerful case that the tales form a purposeful sequence, in which each plays a vital role.

In 1979 *The Chaucer Review* was joined by a second journal, *Studies in the Age of Chaucer*, whose inaugural volume begins with an essay by Florence Ridley, "The State of Chaucer Studies: A Brief Survey." Ridley provides a pugnacious account of what was going on in the field, expressing particular disapprobation for "a whole rash" of clinical studies which draw on Freudian psychoanalysis to explain Chaucer's characters (11) and arguing that major book-length readings of *The Canterbury Tales* such as those of David, Howard, and Spearing "are more the result of creative collaboration between poet and critic than interpretation of the work of one by the other" (16). Ridley's essay serves as a useful reminder of how long some Chaucerians have been making explicit appeals to theory while others charge them with anachronistic over-reading.

The professional criticism of Chaucer from the 50s to the 80s (what we have dubbed "phase two"), was, then, dominated by two schools: one at least vaguely New Critical and the other exegetical. In comparison, no single term can easily summarize the diversity of approaches of the Chaucer criticism of the last thirty-five years which make up the third phase. Since the 1980s, Marxism, poststructuralism and deconstruction, New Historicism, various forms of feminism, psychoanalysis, gender criticism, and queer theory have all been powerfully influential. These approaches might all be loosely characterized as "theorized," since they frequently appeal to political, social, or interpretive theorists—Michel Foucault, Jacques Derrida, Karl Marx, Sigmund Freud, and Jacques Lacan being among the most prominent. For their opponents, these recent critical approaches might be termed "ideological," since they can be overtly partisan and frequently use their analysis of medieval culture to offer a political critique of contempo-

---

1   *The Structure of the Canterbury Tales* (Athens, GA: U of Georgia P, 1984), 72.

rary society. For their supporters, however, the notion that any criticism can
be ideologically neutral or that the opinions of, say, Kittredge or Donaldson
represent simple common sense, is naïve. Moreover, we saw earlier how crit-
ics such as Muscatine, Donaldson, and Robertson do have their theoretical
positions, although they are not always as prominently announced as they
might be today. Borrowing a phrase from the Romantic essayist and opium
addict Thomas de Quincey, we might call the new readers "dark interpret-
ers": although they do not all reveal "the worlds of pain and agony and woe
possible to man"—as Quincey's night-time visions did—they are certainly
less inclined to celebrate either Chaucer or his poetry as uniformly benign.
In addition they have much to say about political and sexual repression and
their readings push far beyond what Chaucer might have recognized or
admitted to himself.[1]

Why literary criticism should have gone through such a massive method-
ological transformation during the last thirty years is a question far beyond
the scope of this brief survey. Terrence Hawkes begins his general introduc-
tion to the handy *New Accents* series of guides to new critical approaches as
follows: "It is easy to see we are living in a time of rapid and radical social
change" and adds that this will "inevitably affect the nature of those dis-
ciplines that both reflect our society and help to shape it." Perhaps that is
as good a starting point as any for an explanation of the rapid and radi-
cal change in literary criticism during this period. Such criticism does not
make for easy reading. It demands a considerable familiarity with various
philosophical or theoretical works—works that were in many cases writ-
ten for other philosophers, and that, in their effort to challenge our familiar
mental habits, often break with comfortable stylistic conventions.[2] For those
who have some familiarity with psychoanalysis, or Marxism, or poststruc-
turalism, however, it may be of interest to see how these approaches can be
applied to medieval texts.

★ ★ ★

One way of following the shifts in Chaucer criticism is to consider the re-
sponse to one of Chaucer's most dynamic and controversial pilgrims, the
Wife of Bath. For this, a useful guide is Peter G. Beidler's 1996 volume in the
series *Case Studies in Contemporary Criticism*, which provides introductions to
the major avant-garde critical movements and some of their key terms and

---

1   The term is employed by Tillotoma Rajan in her deconstructionist account of Romantic poetry
    Dark Interpreter: The Discourse of Romanticism (Ithaca: Cornell UP, 1980).

2   In response to this difficulty, there has developed a significant group of manuals and introduc-
    tory textbooks, including Jonathan Culler's *Structuralist Poetics: Structuralism, Linguistics and the
    Study of Literature* (London: Routledge, 1975) and *On Deconstruction: Theory and Criticism after
    Structuralism* (Ithaca: Cornell UP, 1982), and the volumes in the New Critical Accents series,
    several of them mentioned below.

then sample essays applying each of these "methods" to the Wife of Bath. Of course few contemporary critics fit neatly and exclusively into a single one of these boxes, and the notion that Marxism or feminism is no more than a "method" to be picked up for the sake of writing a critical article and then dropped is one that can and should be questioned; but this simplified approach is extremely helpful for those confronting such a bewildering and diverse field.

One of the first major contributions to our understanding of the Wife of Bath comes very early indeed, when Thomas Tyrwhitt, in his edition of 1755, noted that she is in part based on the character *La Vielle* in the *Romance of the Rose*, the old woman who helps the lover win his beloved, symbolized by the rose. Victorian critics, however, remained convinced that Chaucer drew his most vivid details from real people he had encountered. As late as 1926, Manly—while acknowledging that Chaucer borrowed "some traits" from the *Roman de la Rose*—could still write "There are many indications that Chaucer had a particular person in mind. Not only is her name given—Alisoun—and her striking costume described in much detail, her personality included two characteristics by no means borrowed or typical; she is deaf and 'gat-toothed.' Moreover, Chaucer writes as if he had seen her native place."[1] Later critics would argue that all these details are symbolically coded, but for Manly they are clues to the identity of real people.

The Wife of Bath has had numerous supporters. Kittredge, who thought she told her tale in part to goad the Clerk, clearly admired her zest and her independent mind and called her "too jovial to be ill-natured."[2] For Donaldson, she is "a high and gallant symbol of humanity."[3] Not surprisingly, D.W. Robertson dismisses such views as sentimental and anachronistic. For Robertson, the Wife of Bath is "not a 'character' in the modern sense at all, but an elaborate iconographic figure," a "literary personification of rampant 'femininity' or carnality."[4] This means, first of all, that she personifies certain vices that the patristic writers such as Saint Jerome often associated with women, being lecherous, talkative, and quarrelsome. But Robertson's interpretation goes deeper. His understanding of carnality is rooted in Saint Paul's comment that the letter, or literal meaning, of the Bible kills, whereas the spirit, or deeper meaning, gives life (2 Cor 3:6). For medieval theologians, the literal level was closely associated with the body; blinded by sin, people could not penetrate beyond a superficial reading. Hence, the Wife's insistence that the Old Testament patriarch Solomon's multiple marriages

---

1   *Some New Light on Chaucer*, 231.
2   "Chaucer's Discussion of Marriage," *Modern Philology* 9 (1911–12): 435–67 (xx), rept. Schoeck and Taylor, 136.
3   E.T. Donaldson, ed., *Chaucer's Poetry: An Anthology for the Modern Reader* (New York: Wiley, 1975), 1076.
4   *Preface to Chaucer*, 330, 321.

license hers, and her other willful misinterpretations of the Bible are not just examples of her duplicity and willfully sinful nature (her spiritual deafness), but a vivid illustration of "the abuses of false scriptural interpretation" (334). In Robertson's view, Chaucer intended the Wife to be a model of how not to read.

For exegetical critics the Wife is a negative example, but for feminist critics she is a conundrum, since she both defies and reinforces patriarchal stereotypes. What is clear is that what is sometimes called the Wife's performance (the combination of her prologue and tale) raises many of the issues of power and representation that have been central to feminist criticism. Her opening appeal to her own experience against "auctoritee," the writings of male clerics, sets out the terms of a recurring struggle; and in fact *The Authority of Experience* is the title of one of the earliest collections of feminist essays to deal with medieval texts (the Wife of Bath's performance among them).[1]

Feminist critics have offered different understandings of what exactly the Wife means by "experience," but all agree that her experience is fundamentally linked to her being a woman. For Mary Carruthers, who published "The Wife of Bath and the Painting of Lions" in the influential journal *PMLA* in 1979, the Wife's experience is that of a "wealthy west-country clothier endowed with the property of her deceased spouses" (209). Carruthers makes extensive use of economic history, dealing with such matters as cloth production in the area around Bath and the Wife's legal rights to her property, stressing that she is "not a weaver but a capitalist clothier, one of those persons who oversaw the whole process of cloth manufacture—buying the wool, contracting the labor of the various artisans involved in the manufacture, and sending bales of finished broadcloths off to Bristol and London for export" (210). Even her red tights (which for Robertson would carry obvious associations with sin) are defined in terms of the medieval cloth trade, for which scarlet cloth was the "choicest material" (213). It is from this experience, "her practical concord with her world and time" (218), that she can challenge the male authorities represented in her fifth husband's book and their presentation of what women are like, just as Aesop's lion challenges the depiction of lions by human artists.

Carruthers's article provoked indignant letters from Robert Jordan (always an opponent of any "dramatic" reading of *The Canterbury Tales*), who accused Carruthers of mistaking Alisoun for a real person and not knowing enough about the theory of poetry (including the work of Derrida). Another response came from James Wimsatt, who claimed that Carruthers was looking at the wrong kind of historical material—economics rather than spiritual writings, since (echoing Robertson) the Wife was "an emblem of human

---

1   See Ruth Evans and Lesley Johnson, *Feminist Readings in Middle English Literature: The Wife of Bath and All Her Sect* (London: Routledge, 1994).

carnality." In an "Afterword" to her essay, when it was republished by Ruth Evans and Lesley Johnson as the first essay in their collection *Feminist Readings in Middle English* (1994), Carruthers argues that what really offended Chaucerians about her essay was "the insistence that Chaucer had created in [the Wife] a fiction whose power was a quality that I enjoyed" (39). She also explored at some length the question of what kind of existence a fictional character can have (suggesting that her critics should read Sir Philip Sidney's *Defence of Poetry* before they accused her of not understanding poetics), and chastised a broad range of critics, including a fair number of feminists, for their efforts "to shut the Wife up" (44).

Carruthers's celebration of the Wife provoked the—predominantly male—Chaucer establishment of her day, but there was nothing particularly radical about her method, which drew upon her personal response to the character whom she admired and a mass of information about the late medieval English cloth industry around Bath, the milieu where this character would have lived had she been a real woman. Carruthers offers a wealth of economic information, but makes no use of economic or sociological theory and celebrates the Wife's resistance to male authority without referring to feminist theory. As Evans and Johnson point out in their introduction, initially Carruthers did not even see her article as a feminist one, although it has become one in retrospect, by the readings it generates: "Despite Carruthers's lack of theoretical framework within which to articulate her response, her awareness that textual representations offer *resistance* is invaluable in the production of feminist readings" (8, italics in original). By the 1990s, an explicit theoretical framework was a requirement, but even by 1979, as Jordan's evocation of Derrida suggests, it was something of a liability not to have one.

In this regard, an influential harbinger of the new approaches was Jill Mann's *Chaucer and Medieval Estates Satire* of 1973. Initially, this might seem a relatively traditional historical study. The three estates—those who pray (the clergy), those who fight (the chivalric aristocracy), and those who work (the peasantry)—were the three basic divisions of medieval society, even though, by Chaucer's day, a great number of people belonged to a middling group of merchants and upper artisans who no longer fitted into this scheme. As Mann shows, there was a huge body of satire, in Latin and the various vernacular languages, devoted to the vices that were considered to be typical of each estate or group, showing proud knights and court ladies, gluttonous monks, avaricious merchants, duplicitous and hypocritical friars, and so forth. Comparing Langland's *Piers Plowman* to Chaucer's General Prologue, Mann shows how by the late fourteenth century this satirical tradition had altered in response to the complex new cash economy that was penetrating the older feudal economy of exchange. In passages such as the one where his hero Piers enlists the various members of society to help him plough his half acre (see Background Documents), Langland shows "the practical bases for, and effects of, specific moral injunctions" (192). Chaucer responded to this changing socio-economic situation by showing a world in which moral judgment was impossible. He has "no systematic platform for moral values" (192). Instead, he depicts his pilgrims as if he thought they were just amiable rogues, stressing how good they are at their jobs and omitting any reference to consequences of their behavior or the sufferings of their victims. In this way, Mann argues, Chaucer shows that we live "in 'a world of experts,' where the moral views of the layman become irrelevant.... A world of means rather than ends" (194).

So far Mann's work seems relatively traditional, although it does show more fully than ever before how much Chaucer was drawing on a literary tradition when he wrote the General Prologue, as opposed to drawing on his observations of the people he met in inns. It is in one of her endnotes to this discussion, however, that Mann takes a new methodological approach in Chaucer criticism, when she appeals to an elaborate sociological theory, that of Max Weber (as opposed to her own lay understanding), to explain where Chaucer's attitude comes from: "The concentration on means rather than ends has been held by sociologists to be characteristic of the social ethic of societies dominated by economic markets, and particularly of capitalism" (291 n22).

Mann's criticism thus links a specifically literary tradition with the social and economic world, but it is the world of the author, not that of the characters. Rather than accepting the information about people's jobs that is given so freely in the General Prologue as a mirror of society, for example, she asks why we are given so much information, all of which is presented by the narrator to assure us that each pilgrim is an expert at his or her trade (12). When she turns to the Wife, Mann explores the debt to the figure of La Vielle in the *Romance of the Rose*, first noted by Tyrwhitt, and to other satirical figures like her, showing how a number of details, such as the Wife's cloth-making, her insistence on making her offering in church before anyone else, her love of pilgrimages, and her "outrageous head-dresses" are all typical of the genre. The great difference between these depictions of women and Chaucer's, Mann notes, is that in them "the beautiful young woman who is able to carry on love-affairs and the ugly old woman who knows all theory of love but cannot practice it" (103) are always two different figures, whereas Chaucer fuses them.

Mann's argument is not specifically Marxist, but it does follow general Marxist lines in suggesting that the prevailing economic situation will determine to a very significant degree the kind of art that is produced in any particular period. Two explicitly Marxist studies appeared in 1986, one by Stephen Knight entitled *Geoffrey Chaucer* and the other by David Aers entitled even more simply *Chaucer*. In his general introduction to Knight's book, Terry Eagleton, perhaps Britain's leading Marxist critic, has harsh words for those who see Chaucer as a "sane, middling sort of chap, ... refreshingly free of grim-lipped hectoring or false heroics, eschewing extremes in the name of that well-nigh biological common humanity which undercuts whatever superficial ideological differences may divide us." For Eagleton, this "sentimental humanism" (which is, more or less, that of Kittredge, Donaldson, or any number of other Chaucerians) is deeply conservative, lulling us into the illusion that nothing has ever really changed and thus nothing ever will. But if we must avoid sentimentalizing the poet we can still celebrate the works. For both Knight and Aers, Chaucer's poems function as a predominantly positive force because they question outmoded chivalric and aristocratic forms and point towards new kinds of identity. As Aers puts it, "The dominant ideology [of the period] did not have as total a hold as we are often led to believe, and at least some surviving works were produced in an actively critical relation with it. [Chaucer's poetry] is largely of this kind. It works over ruling ideas, conventional pieties and the unexamined norms of official culture in a way that subjects them to processes of criticism, processes which can include estrangement, distancing and even subversion" (3). In this respect, an illuminating contrast is offered by David Carlson's analysis in *Chaucer's Jobs* (2004), which condemns Chaucer as "an official of the repressive apparatus of the state" and opens with the blunt statement "Chaucer was the police."

In the case of the Wife of Bath, Knight rejects "the usual literary critical approach" which "merely validates its own bourgeois individualism, seeing her as a bold free spirit and ignoring her historical and social context" (98). He praises her, but always in terms of economic forces. Thus, when she speaks of her fourth husband, ending by saying that now that the flour is gone she must sell the bran, for Knight a "courageous, self-conscious, domestic and mercantile person has emerged" (100). When the Wife calls into question the definition of gentility, claiming that it is what one does (not one's birth) that makes one gentle, her comments are "potentially revolutionary," although Knight acknowledges that there are also elements of political conservatism in the story, as when the Wife praises the joys of poverty, where the tale seeks to contain the energies it is releasing. Aers's reading is no less grounded in the details of medieval social and economic practice, but it is grimmer. The Wife "exhibits the fate of woman as a commodity ... in a society where 'al is for to selle'" (69), and she rebels "within the framework of market relations" (70).

These early Marxist critics, with their insistence on local detail and the hard facts of property ownership, tend to write about the characters as if they were real people and to credit them with agency, pointing to the ways in which they resist the dominant forces of their day, much as Carruthers does. In comparison, more recent critics, often more influenced by post-structuralism, find themselves echoing Robertson, for whom the Wife is a textual construction, not a realistic character. The crucial recognition here, drawing on the work of the linguist Ferdinand de Saussure, is that basic notions such as that of character and self "are not *given* but *produced* in a specific society by the ways in which that society talks and thinks about itself and its experience."[1] Lee Patterson provides an early example in *Chaucer and the Subject of History* (1991), a study of Chaucer's explorations of subjectivity, or what Patterson calls "an inward sense of selfhood" and "the claims of the historical world," that is, the various ways in which identity is socially shaped at a particular period (11). Patterson begins his work with a critique of the prevailing notion of the individual as a totally free agent and of literary characters as stable representations of these agents. In keeping with this view, his interest in the Wife is not with her character but with her ways of speaking and story-telling, the "rhetoric of [her] discourse" (296). The result, oddly, is that in places Patterson sounds a lot like Robertson, as when he refers to "the carnality that characterizes [the Wife] as a woman" (287) and sees a sustained analogy between her "joly body" and the body of her text (315). Patterson specifically rejects Robertson, however, in favor of a humanist celebration of literary freedom (although a more nuanced one than, say, had been provided by Donaldson thirty years earlier), claiming that although in some ways the Wife is "confined within the prison house of masculine language" (313), she manages to turn exegesis upside down, thus opening up "a space in which what we have come to call literature can find its home" (316).

Ironically, the debt to Robertson is even stronger in Carolyn Dinshaw's *Chaucer's Sexual Poetics* (1989), a work that repudiates Robertson's conservative social vision as emphatically as possible but nonetheless draws heavily on his understanding of *The Canterbury Tales* as an allegory of how we should read. Of course, Robertson does not provide Dinshaw's predominant theoretical framework. Her work is in part a continuation of Sandra Gilbert and Susan Gubar's massive study, *The Madwoman in the Attic* (1979), which explores the ways in which women are defined as blanks or ciphers within the tradition of male writing, but her understanding of the operations of patriarchal discourse also makes extensive use of the work of poststructuralist psychoanalyst Jacques Lacan and the poststructuralist French feminist Luce Irigaray.[2] Whereas for Donaldson, the critic should respect "the right of a poem to say what it means and mean what it says," for Dinshaw, the poem is filled with conflicts and silences. Thus, the Man of Law's tale of Constance, who is given by her father, the emperor of Rome, in marriage to the Sultan of Syria, is structured around that which it cannot say: that, as in many of the folk tales that are analogues to the story, what drives the heroine into exile is flight from the incestuous desires of her father. In order to tell his tale, the Man of Law cannot recognize these undertones. He must also be

---

1   Catherine Belsey, *Critical Practice* (London: Routledge, 1980), 3. Belsey provides a useful guide to such fundamental concepts in poststructuralist cultural criticism as "the interpellation of the subject in ideology."

2   A useful introduction to the ways in which poststructuralism and psychoanalysis expanded the feminist critique is Toril Moi, *Sexual/Textual Politics: Feminist Literary Theory* (London: Routledge, 1985).

able to deny all independent female desire, excluding women who actively pursue their desires (the wicked mothers-in-law) as monstrous non-women, utterly unlike passive and virtuous Constance. She, with her pale face, is a blank on which the Man of Law can write his tale.

The question of who does the writing is more ambiguous in the Wife of Bath's Tale. With her "independent feminine will" (114), she might be said to embody "everything that the Man of Law cannot say" (115). Here, however, Dinshaw moves into tricky ground, as she herself acknowledges, for in many ways the Wife seems to do just the reverse, "enacting precisely what patriarchal discourse *does* say, and says endlessly"(118). But for Dinshaw she does this as an act of mimicry, a mode in which, according to Irigaray, women can "convert a form of subordination into an affirmation" (115).

The figure who performs this subversive mimicry, according to Dinshaw, is not a rounded character but part of "an allegorical representation of the act of reading" (120). Here Dinshaw borrows Robertson's premise that the Wife represents the literal text, but she adds another dimension, noting (which Robertson had not observed) that the Wife's fifth husband—a student at Oxford who hits her when she rips a page from his collection of misogynistic writings—is also a glossator. As the Wife observes, he could "gloss" her when he wanted sex, and while "gloss" here means in the first instance "flatter," it was connected to another meaning, to interpret or write commentary on a text. For Dinshaw, the Wife "speaks as the literal text, insisting on the positive, significant value of the carnal letter as opposed to the spiritual gloss" (120), although she makes her points by borrowing the techniques of the glossators and mimicking them. Overall, Dinshaw insists, Chaucer recognizes the violence that masculine glossing can do to the feminine; he "has imagined patriarchy from the Other's point of view and has duly reckoned the costs of clerical discourse in terms of the feminine body" (130).

The debate on Chaucer and the politics of gender continues as we move into what, starting in the 1990s, begins to be called "queer theory."[1] A good example is *Chaucer's Queer Nation* (2003), in which Glenn Burger explores the "weird centrality of bourgeois marriage" in *The Canterbury Tales* (44), asking a question that Kittredge never asked directly: why this should be such a major concern? For Burger, the point of queer theory for Chaucer studies is not to identify with particular characters, like the Wife or the Pardoner, who might be considered "queer," but rather to consider more broadly "the constructedness of modern regimes of sex/gender/sexuality and the identities founded on them" (x); in other words, to consider how these ways of classifying humans, and the ways societies have shaped identity through these systems of classification, have shifted over time. "Fluidity" is for Burger a key value, while "stability" is suspect; the term "queer" is not only broader than any set of categories of sexuality (lesbian, gay, straight,

---

1   See Annamarie Jagose, *Queer Theory: An Introduction* (New York: New York UP, 1996).

bisexual, transgendered, etc.) but also more mobile; it is not so much an abstract category, a box in which to put someone, as something one does, a verb. "Performativity" is a crucial term for Burger, one he borrows from the theorist Judith Butler, and applies to the Wife, who in his view has no stable gender identity. To characterize the Wife's performance and her subversive claims to authority, Burger turns to another theorist, Judith Halberstam, and her term "female masculinity," which she uses to designate various kinds of "heroic" behavior "which have been produced by and across both male and female bodies."[1] As Halberstam notes, "far from being an imitation of maleness, female masculinity actually affords us a glimpse of how masculinity is constructed as masculinity" (1), a principle Burger extends to the Wife. The Wife presents herself as "quintessentially female and feminine" (85), but there are good reasons not to trust her. She has no stable identity. She is queer.

Kittredge's "marriage group" ended with the Franklin's Tale, and as Kittredge remarked, "The Franklin's Tale is a gentleman's story and he tells it like a gentleman."[2] Burger, however, argues that "gentle" and even "man" were contested terms in the late Middle Ages. He sees the period as one of hybrid identities, as the divisions between lay and cleric became less clear and the number of people who were part of the ill-defined "middle" class increased. In regards to the Wife, Burger argues that in concentrating on the feminist/antifeminist conflict, we forget "the room for maneuver made possible by the conflicting legal and social definitions of 'wife' and 'middle' class during this period" (90). For confirmation, Burger turns back to Carruthers's article on the painting of lions, and elsewhere he draws heavily on the evidence of social historians and historicist critics to describe a Middle Ages that is not so much one of brutal conflict (as it might be in a Marxist account) but of continual instability.

Burger's efforts to read in the Wife of Bath's performance a challenge to contemporary constructions of gender and sexuality take us back to the argument presented so forcefully by D.W. Robertson that contemporary Chaucer critics are distorting Chaucer by attempting to read into him the tensions of their own day, or, as Paul Olson put it in 1986, making the poet into "the Narcissus image of our own historical or semiological fantasies."[3] Although Olson's remarks are directed against Marxist and feminist as much as against psychoanalytic readings of Chaucer, it is the latter that have most often provoked objections of this kind. Burger's version of queer theory is actually more often historicist than psychoanalytic, but it does share with psychoanalysis the conviction that sexual desire is the most fundamental of human drives and that identity is largely a matter of sexual identity. It is a

1   Judith Halberstam, *Female Masculinity* (Durham: Duke UP, 1998), 2.
2   Kittredge, "Chaucer's Discussion of Marriage," 60.
3   Paul Olson, *The Canterbury Tales and the Good Society* (Princeton: Princeton UP, 1986), 18.

view that has provoked strong opposition, as in Florence Ridley's comment in 1979 that what psychoanalysis offers is "merely a new, *if rather unpleasant*, way of approaching Chaucer's old familiar characters" and her advice to Chaucerians is to "leave clinical psychology alone" (11–12, italics added).

Psychoanalytic criticism of Chaucer first appeared in the 1960s. Most of the early efforts, however, were clinical studies of characters, dealing with topics such as the infantile narcissism of January or the Prioress's anal eroticism, and they often provoked the objection that you cannot psychoanalyze a fictional character. Of course traditional critics since the days of Kittredge had engaged in elaborate accounts of characters' psychology; but the highly technical idiom of psychoanalysis, and its willingness to probe into remote corners of the characters' psyches, and even events in their early lives—none of which may have actually been mentioned in the text—struck most Chaucerians as unpersuasive. Judith Ferster remarks, in a generally sympathetic account of psychoanalysis, that one 1962 article "reads more like the work of a clinician than that of a literary critic."[1]

A more sophisticated approach emerged in the 1980s with a series of articles by Louise (now Aranye) O. Fradenburg. In the first of these she explored the Wife's view of the past, specifically her nostalgia for romance, the "olde dayes of Kyng Arthour" when the land was still filled with fairies and had not yet been disenchanted.[2] The mourning for a lost past, both in medieval texts and on the part of the modern medievalist, has been an ongoing concern of Fradenburg's. Reworking her essay on the Wife of Bath for the *Case Studies in Contemporary Criticism*, for example, she turns to the Wife's evocation of the joys of her fourth marriage and her lost youth and notes, "The haunting, recognized by psychoanalysis, of our moments of greatest happiness by the memory of something lost is one way of accounting for the frequently elegiac tone of the Wife's exuberant defense of embodied pleasures" (214). This interest is one Fradenburg pursues in *Sacrifice Your Love: Psychoanalysis, Historicism, Chaucer* (2002).

For Fradenburg, psychoanalytic theories of mourning may help to account for the insistence of historicists that the Middle Ages is, on the one hand, absolutely and consistently different from modernity (often referred to as the "alterity" of the Middle Ages) and, on the other hand, that the particular historicist somehow has a privileged understanding of the period. In an article published in 1990, Fradenburg turns her attention to D.W. Robertson's psychological investment in his vision of the Middle Ages. In keeping with the psychoanalytic principle that the patient's contradictions suggest suppressed anxieties, she points to a contradiction in his rigorous historicism in his response to the Wife. Although for Robertson the Wife is an icono-

---

1   "'Your Praise is Performed by Men and Children': Language and Gender in the Prioress's Prologue and Tale," *Exemplaria* 2.1 (1990): 149–68 (151).
2   "The Wife of Bath's Passing Fancy," *Studies in the Age of Chaucer* 8 (1986): 31–58.

graphic figure of carnality constructed from medieval symbolic codes and not a plausible character, he writes "That she still seems feminine to us is a tribute to the justness of the ideas which produced her."[1] Here, momentarily, Robertson appeals to an eternal, transhistorical feminine. Having caught Robertson in an apparent contradiction, Fradenburg goes on to argue that Robertson projects his own anxieties upon the Wife: "When Robertson looks into the mirror of Narcissus, he sees, not an image of his own face, but that of the aging queen in Snow White, an aging woman whose fear of losing her youth and beauty leads her (as in Robertson's interpretation of the Wife) not to true renewal but to desperation, fantasy, and violence" (176). This language is more violent than Robertson's, who would surely have wondered how he could be accused of attributing such passions to an emblem merely by saying that the Wife's sermon is "designed to resist ... rejuvenation" (330). But Fradenburg's references to the mirrors of Narcissus and of the wicked queen in the story of Snow White are not her imposition. It is Olson, drawing upon Robertson, who first refers to the former; while Robertson makes the allusion to the mirror in Snow White when he warns that in anachronistic readings, "history, although it may seem to flatter us with the consoling message, 'Thou art the fairest of all,' becomes merely an instrument for the cultivation of our own prejudices" (3). In Fradenburg's reading, classical mythology and folklore, two of Freud's great sources, and the actual words or expression that one uses (that is, the things that "slip out," as opposed to the more general sense of what one meant to say)—which were one of the basic materials for his clinical analysis (the other being dreams)—suggest a range of unconscious desires and fears that psychoanalytic criticism seeks to bring to the surface.

Psychoanalysis remains a problematic method for literary critics. Freud's work is highly readable and provides clear answers to questions, but many of these answers now appear to be wrong.[2] The writings of Jacques Lacan, on the other hand, are frequently inscrutable. Feminists in particular have criticized the theory of the "castration complex" (developed by Freud and modified by Lacan) and its portrayal of female identity as one defined by a sense of lack. In general, the relation between clinical theory and literary criticism is not clear. The psychoanalytic critics of the 60s wrote with confidence that Freudian analysis provided a scientific account of the psyche, with precise and objective terms. This has given way to a more tentative sense that even if the accounts of Freud or Lacan are incomplete, unverifiable, or partially

---

1   Louise O. Fradenburg, "'Voice Memorial': Loss and Reparation in Chaucer's Poetry," *Exemplaria* 2.1 (1990): 169–202 (176 quoting *Preface to Chaucer*, 331).

2   The case against using psychoanalysis on Middle English literature is set out by Lee Patterson in "Psyche and Clio in Medieval Literary Studies: Chaucer's Pardoner on the Couch," *Speculum* 76 (2001): 638–80. Fradenburg responds in *Sacrifice Your Love: Psychoanalysis, Historicism, Chaucer* (Minneapolis: U of Minnesota P, 2002).

misguided, they nevertheless provide some explanation of psychological patterns that are otherwise completely inexplicable. Thus Carolyn Dinshaw, discussing the character of the Pardoner, refers to the castration complex as a "myth" and a "story" (something which need not be literally true to have explanatory power): "In the psychoanalytic story—a reworking of the myth of original loss and the desire for restitution, a myth that informs the Christian analysis of human history as well—the loss of an ideal, a loss of fullness, plenitude, is always associated with castration: the original fullness of continuity with the mother is lost as the child, first perceiving physical differentiation from the mother, fears for the integrity of its own body" (165).

Where Chaucer studies will go next is hard to tell. One major development is the way in which Middle English studies is shifting its attention from Chaucer, and other canonical literary authors such as the author of *Sir Gawain and the Green Knight* and *Pearl*, and turning to a much broader range of writings, often not of a particularly literary kind, such as theological and devotional treatises, penitential manuals, works of practical instruction, or bureaucratic and legal documents. These works, which might once have been considered merely background to the great canonical poems, are now increasingly seen as vital parts in a broad field of discourse. The centrifugal tendency is very much in evidence in the latest versions of the Oxford and Cambridge histories of medieval English literature. David Wallace, the editor of *The Cambridge History of Medieval English Literature* (1999), takes one approach by assembling a team of over thirty writers to cover everything from the afterlife of Old English to the writings of the sixteenth-century Protestant reformers. Chaucer is now but one of thirty-one chapters. James Simpson, the single author of the Oxford volume of 2002, takes another approach, covering the entire field himself but making a highly personal selection that often gives the major canonical works relatively brief treatment. It is characteristic of this volume that it begins almost at the end of the period it covers and begins not with a famous poet but with John Leland, who wrote an account of English geography for King Henry VIII.

An elegant example of the centrifugal tendency, which owes a good deal to the New Historicism developed by such Renaissance critics as Stephen Greenblatt, is Paul Strohm's *Hochon's Arrow: The Social Imagination of Fourteenth-Century Texts* (1992). Among the many stories that Strohm explores are two reports of women who allegedly murdered their husbands with the help of a priest. Strohm's account has something to say about the Wife of Bath, but only tangentially, for it suggests the kind of anxieties about women's status that were in circulation in this period. Strohm argues, surprisingly, that women's economic *expectations* had improved (even though their legal rights had not) and that husbands were beginning to feel threatened, hence the stories of murderous wives. Following the path taken by most Chaucerians, Strohm sees Chaucer's work as fundamentally positive or emancipatory, in this case because it links sexual and economic drives explicitly, thus revealing the social forces that other male commentators tried to contain through mockery.

It might at first seem that the most recent new theoretical approach, postcolonialism, would have little to say about medieval texts, since the term appears to refer to the period after the dissolution of the colonial empires. Indeed, a number of prominent postcolonial theorists, including Edward Said, Benedict Anderson, and Homi Bhabha, have begun their histories of colonial trauma in the Early Modern period or later, casting the Middle Ages as an age of relative stability unmarked by modern tensions, "a field of undifferentiated alterity against which modern regimes of power have arisen" as Jeffrey Cohen puts it in his introduction to *The Postcolonial Middle Ages* (3). This collection of essays offers two very different readings of how postcolonial theory can be applied to Chaucer. For John Bowers, Chaucer is a postcolonial writer with a "decolonizing project" (54) and the colonial power whose cultural hegemony he must resist is that of France. Chaucer approaches this task as a member of the French-speaking elite, whose "primary literary authorities belonged to the nonindigenous tradition," and in this uneasy situation he makes much use of "buffoonery" (55). In his efforts to shape a distinctive English culture, he uses "selective recall," omitting any reference to the Norman Conquest in his accounts of English history. "Heavy-handed promotion of London would have worked against any sense of English unity" (60), so Chaucer avoids direct references to London, although his pilgrims all speak London English. A traditional view of Chaucer links his decision to write in English with the rise of the Middle Class (who could increasingly read, but in English, not French) and thus with democratic tendencies, the development of national identity, and even with the eventual triumph of English as a world language. Bowers retells this story, but not as one of splendid progress, ending with Chaucer serving as "an agent of Lancastrian *cultural* imperialism" (63).

Sylvia Tomasch also considers the role that Chaucer played in the formation of English identity, but does so by exploring his representation of the Jews. Since Edward I expelled all Jews from England in 1290, it has sometimes been suggested that Chaucer and his readers cared little about them, so that in the Prioress's Tale they are no more than remote bogeymen. Tomasch argues that, on the contrary, the absence of the Jews was vital to the English sense of identity. She quotes James Shapiro, who claims that between 1290 and 1656, when Jews in limited numbers were allowed once more to settle in England, "the English came to see their country defined in part by the fact that Jews had been banished from it."[1] Thus in the Prioress's Tale, "a polluted Asia—polluted through Jewish presence and actions—is implicitly contrasted with a purified England, whose sanitized state is founded on the displacement of the Jews" (248). In the Pardoner's Tale, on the other

---

1   James Shapiro, *Shakespeare and the Jews* (New York: Columbia UP, 1996), 42.

hand, Flanders, where the three rioters meet Death, "stands for England as a corrupted place" (248). The old man who tells the rioters where to meet Death has often been associated with the legend of the Wandering Jew. For Tomasch, the old man "performs a perfect displacement" of the Jews, personifying them through his associations with gold and death (as Tomasch notes, Jews were accused of poisoning wells and murdering Christian children, and were also associated with usury) without ever being explicitly identified as a Jew. Borrowing from the study of cyberculture, Tomasch employs the term "virtual Jew" to stress "the integral connections between imaginary constructions and actual people" (252). Chaucer participated in this construction, "the ongoing, postcolonial, allosemitic production of the virtual Jew" (255).[1]

Postcolonial Chaucerians read his tales to see how they could have contributed to (or possibly resisted) the colonialising forces in his own day, and they do so with a strong sense that more traditional approaches have assumed the centrality of Europeans and Christians in the history of the Middle Ages. In an essay for the collection *Chaucer and the Jews* (2002), Sheila Delany offers one final challenge to such traditional assumptions. She approaches the depiction of Jews in the Prioress's Tale in terms of medieval Christian European attitudes to Judaism and Islam. The Prioress's Tale is set in "Asye" or Asia, which for Chaucer could have covered Turkey, Asia Minor, Asia, and large parts of the Arab world; although these regions were virtually all under Islamic control, there is no reference to Islam in the tale. It is "conspicuous by its absence" (48). Yet medieval Christians often associated Jews with Muslims, regarding them as dangerous allies. Chaucer's Prioress may have little knowledge of the world outside England, but Chaucer was a well-traveled diplomat, and we must not assume that his knowledge of Jews was completely circumscribed by their absence from England. In particular, his travels in Spain would have exposed him to cities in which there were large Jewish communities, and to examples of both tolerance and violent repression. On this basis, Delany suggests two possible readings of the tale: one as a veiled critique of what we now call religious tolerance, of the kind John of Gaunt practiced when he allied himself with pro-Jewish Muslims in Spain (52), and the other as a veiled critique of the Prioress's bigotry. Delany is unsure as to which reading Chaucer favored, but she is sure that for Chaucer, "the Islamic east was no merely figurative realm, but was pressing its intellectual and political claims as literally as it does today" (53).

For the various critical approaches we have reviewed, "today" is a crucial word. The differing assessments of what forces are at work on us today— whether the most important are political, economic, cultural, religious, or

---

1   Zygmunt Bauman defines allosemitism as an intense anxiety surrounding Jews as the embodiment of "incongruence, artificiality, sham and frailty of the social order and the most earnestly drawn boundaries" in "Allosemitism: Premodern, Modern, Postmodern," *Modernity, Culture, and "the Jew*," ed. Bryan Cheyette and Laura Marcus (Stanford: Stanford UP, 1998), 143–56 (150).

sexual, how much freedom these forces leave us, whether they should be celebrated or resisted, and how much they may have changed in the last six hundred years—continue to shape the approaches taken by Chaucerians.

Editorial Principles

This volume presents an edition of one of the two earliest manuscripts of *The Canterbury Tales*, the Ellesmere Manuscript, which is now housed in the Huntington Library in San Marino, California. This edition does not try to be a critical edition; that is, one which attempts to arrive at the author's original version by comparing readings from a large number of manuscripts. This kind of liberal editing requires a sense of the author's style that is precise enough to allow one to recognize where the scribes are likely to have gone wrong. It also normally requires that the editor group the manuscripts into a family tree, known as a stemma. One would normally expect editors to favor the readings in earlier manuscripts, as well as those readings that are found in the largest number of manuscripts. Manuscripts survive in haphazard ways, however, and they can be copied down from a version that is quite recent, or from one that has been sitting around for years. It is possible, then, to have several relatively early manuscripts that are all descended from a single (and bad) copy, all preserving a reading that is wrong; while at the same time, a single, later manuscript that is copied from a very early (and good) copy, whose reading is correct, may also survive. Establishing a stemma provides some sense of how much authority to give to any particular manuscript or group of manuscripts. Unfortunately, it has proven very difficult to do this in the case of Chaucer. The last systematic attempt was that of Manly and Rickert in their eight-volume edition, and powerful as their contribution was, the stemma they produced is generally considered to be mistaken. Manly and Rickert are the only ones who have attempted to produce a full critical edition of *The Canterbury Tales*. Most editions are eclectic editions, that is, they are based on a single manuscript, and turn to others only when this manuscript proves deficient. Skeat, F.N. Robinson and then Larry Benson, John Fisher, and Jill Mann have all produced eclectic editions based on the Ellesmere and N.F. Blake an eclectic edition based on Hengwrt. What separates these editions from our more modest effort is the degree to which their editors are prepared to emend lines that are merely weak (as opposed to completely nonsensical), especially lines that appear to them metrically unsatisfactory, and how systematically they have consulted a range of alternative readings.

An edition like this one pursues the more modest goal of making sense of a specific manuscript. Our edition reproduces the text of the Ellesmere manuscript, preserving its spellings and modifying only its word division and punctuation, and expanding the abbreviations. Where the Ellesmere Manuscript is clearly defective, we have consulted the second of the earliest

manuscripts, the Hengwrt Manuscript, now housed in the National Library
of Wales in Aberystwyth. In all cases, however, we have noted the original
reading in the Ellesmere either in the margin (for minor variations) or in
the notes at the foot of the page (for slightly longer ones). The manuscript
often provides large capitals, decorates the initial letter, or inserts the symbol
¶, all to act as paragraph markers. As an equivalent, we have set the whole
initial word in capitals, but we have not attempted to distinguish between
the sizes of capitals found in the manuscript. The exceptions to this practice
are Chaucer's two long prose tales, *The Tale of Melibee* and the Parson's Tale.
There we have omitted the large capitals, for the manuscript intersperses its
capitals and paragraph marks liberally throughout; to reproduce them would
run counter to modern practices and would therefore be more of an impedi-
ment than an aid to understanding. We have also, as far as possible, noted the
glosses (brief comments or explanations) that were copied in the margins by
the original scribe. Our edition may not always capture Chaucer's intention,
but it does present a version of a text as it was experienced by early readers.

   This text is one about which we are (by the standards of medieval manu-
scripts) very well informed. We know that both Ellesmere and Hengwrt
were copied by the same professional scribe, Adam Pinkhurst, in the first few
years after Chaucer's death in 1400, or just possibly in the last year or two
of Chaucer's life. Pinkhurst was doubtless the "Adam" to whom Chaucer
addresses his short poem, "Chaucers Wordes unto Adam, His Owne Scriv-
eyn," a humorous appeal to him to be careful at his work. Linne Mooney
has demonstrated that an oath Pinkhurst wrote and signed upon joining the
Scriveners' Company of London is in the same hand as that of both Heng-
wrt and Ellesmere.[1] This means that both manuscripts were copied by a man
whom Chaucer had already employed to copy out his translation of Boethi-
us's *Consolation of Philosophy* and his *Troilus and Criseyde*.

   The connection further augments the authority of these two manuscripts,
but it also makes the differences between the two even more puzzling,
bringing us back to one of the great questions in Chaucerian scholarship:
how close did Chaucer come to finishing *The Canterbury Tales*? Ellesmere,
generally agreed to be slightly later, presents the tales in an order that many
modern readers have found to make strong artistic sense and contains mate-
rial—in particular the Canon's Yeoman's Tale, an account of a fraudulent
alchemical workshop—that is missing from Hengwrt. It also ascribes the
interruption of the Squire's Tale to the Franklin, whereas Hengwrt (less
plausibly) ascribes it to the Merchant. On the other hand, many individual
lines in Ellesmere contain small errors or are missing words and need to be
corrected, as the reader will notice.[2] Why Pinkhurst, having managed to

---

1   Linne R. Mooney, "Chaucer's Scribe," *Speculum* 81 (2006): 97–138.
2   It must be remembered, however, that Hengwrt also contains a fair number of errors that can
    be corrected from Ellesmere. See Jill Mann, "Chaucer's Meter and the Myth of the Ellesmere
    Editor of *The Canterbury Tales*," *Studies in the Age of Chaucer* 23 (2001): 71–107.

get an accurate (although incomplete) text to copy when he was writing the
Hengwrt manuscript, should then have failed to do so when writing Elles-
mere remains unclear.

The Ellesmere manuscript is large—its pages measuring roughly 15 by
11 inches—and elegantly decorated. With its fine miniatures and elaborate
border decorations, it is the kind of luxury volume that might have been
commissioned by an aristocrat, a prosperous London merchant, or a senior
civil servant of the early fifteenth century. Various personal inscriptions in
the manuscript indicate that it once belonged to John de Vere, who became
the twelfth earl of Oxford in 1417, and whose guardians (possibly the book's
first owners) were Thomas Beaufort, Duke of Exeter (one of the sons of John
of Gaunt) and Henry IV's third son, John, Duke of Bedford—a great book
collector.

CHAUCER TIMELINE

(Note: Times are often approximate for both modern historians of the fourteenth century and fourteenth-century people themselves. The imprecision is by necessity reflected here.)

c.1288   Death of Chaucer's great-grandfather Andrew de Dynyngton. He was a villager who moved to the large town of Ipswich and set up a tavern there.

Probably the birth year of Chaucer's grandfather Robert le Chaucer. Robert eventually migrated to London, which remained for years the family's home. He gained his last name by inheriting the estate of John le Chaucer, with *chaucier* referring to the making of shoes and boots.

1312   Birth of Chaucer's father John le Chaucer. He becomes a wealthy vintner, an importer of wines from the English territory of Gascony, the old duchy of Aquitaine.

Birth of the future king Edward III.

1314   Death of Robert le Chaucer.

1337   The intermittent Hundred Years' War begins; it lasts 116 years, until 1453.

1340–43   Birth of Geoffrey Chaucer, probably near the start of this time span.

1346, 23 August   The outnumbered English win the Battle of Crécy under the generalship of King Edward III.

1347   John le Chaucer moves, presumably with his family (wife Agnes, son Geoffrey, and possibly a daughter named Katherine) to Southampton, where he becomes deputy to John de Wesenham, who is in charge of procuring wines for the royal household.

1348–49   The Great Plague, also known as the Black Plague or Black Death after the dark-colored tumors the disease caused, enters England in October of 1348, eventually killing somewhere between one quarter and one half of its population. John le Chaucer and his immediate family somehow survive. He inherits property in London from an uncle, and, with considerable financial stability, moves back to that city.

1350 (?)   Geoffrey Chaucer possibly begins his course of study at the school based at St. Paul's Cathedral, situated not far from Thames Street, where the Chaucer family set up their home so they could be near the docks of the Thames.

1356, 19 September   The outnumbered English win the Battle of Poitiers under the generalship of Edward, Prince of Wales, otherwise known as the Black Prince after the color of his armor. John the Good, King of France, is captured at this battle. Later he is brought to England and held for over three years in luxurious conditions until the down payment of his large ransom arrives with important hostages as security. While in England, John's musicians and poets help set musical and literary fashion there, establishing a French style that the young Chaucer admires and imitates in his early work.

1357   By this year, the teenaged Chaucer has become a page in the household of Elizabeth de Burgh, Countess of Ulster and wife of Prince Lionel, Edward III's second son.

1359   Chaucer is granted arms and serves as a soldier during a failed campaign to capture the city of Rheims, where the kings of France were traditionally crowned. The purpose is to crown Edward III, whose mother Isabella was the daughter of King Philip IV of France, thus making Edward a plausible heir to the French throne. Chaucer is captured during this campaign and ransomed for £16, a considerable sum for one so young.

Chaucer moves from the household of the Countess of Ulster to that of her husband, Prince Lionel.

early 1360s (?)   There is a dubious report that Chaucer is learning law at the Inner Temple and is fined for attacking a Franciscan Friar on nearby Fleet Street.

1366   By this year Chaucer has married Philippa de Roet,
        sister of Katherine Swynford, who will shortly become
        the mistress of John of Gaunt, the third son of Edward
        III, a man destined to dominate English politics and
        foreign affairs during the late 1370s and the 1380s.

        Chaucer serves as a diplomat in Spain, where John of
        Gaunt is getting involved in power politics.

        Death of John le Chaucer.

1367   Birth of Chaucer's son Thomas. He later becomes an
        important figure in the courts of Henry V and Henry
        VI, wielding much power.

        Thomas's daughter Alice, through marriage into the
        powerful de la Pole family, becomes Duchess of Suffolk
        in East Anglia.

1368   Marriage of Prince Lionel to his second wife, Violante
        Visconti. Petrarch attends the ceremony, and possibly
        so too does Chaucer, who at this time is in Prince
        Lionel's service. Lionel dies in Italy before he can return
        to England, and Chaucer enters the service of King
        Edward III.

        Death of Blanche, Duchess of Lancaster, first wife of
        John of Gaunt. She dies, probably of complications aris-
        ing from childbirth. Chaucer's first long poem, *The Book
        of the Duchess*, is written as an elegy for her death—but it
        is possible that it is written a few years thereafter.

        Approximate date of Chaucer's fragmented translation of
        the French poem *The Romance of the Rose*.

1368-70 Chaucer serves in various diplomatic missions in France.

1372   By this year, and possibly some time before, King
        Edward III has made Chaucer a squire.

        Chaucer is a member of an important trade delegation to
        Genoa, one of the Italian city-states.

1374   John of Gaunt grants Chaucer an annuity of £10, and
       Edward III grants him a daily pitcher of wine.

       Chaucer is appointed Controller (auditor) of Customs for
       wool and related commodities, a lucrative position, and
       granted a "house" (apartment or flat) above Aldgate, one
       of the seven gates to the old city of London, to occupy
       while in this position. He will hold this position and live
       here for twelve years. It is here that he writes a num-
       ber of his important poems—*The House of Fame, The
       Parliament of Fowls*, and *Troilus and Criseyde* among them.

       Adam Pinkhurst becomes Chaucer's scribe during
       this period; it is he who copies out the Ellesmere
       Manuscript.

1376   Death of Edward, Prince of Wales, leaving his young
       son as heir to the throne.

1377   Death of King Edward III; his grandson becomes King
       Richard II.

1378   Chaucer again travels to Italy as a member of a trade
       delegation.

1380   Chaucer is granted a quit-claim in a judicial proceeding
       against him accusing him of *raptus* (either rape or abduc-
       tion) of Cecily de Champaigne.

       Birth of Chaucer's son Lewis. Lewis dies, possibly in
       a military campaign in Wales, in the early fifteenth
       century.

       The Parliament of Fowls is possibly written in this year
       as an allegory of the protracted negotiations, of which
       Chaucer is a part, to arrange a marriage with Anne of
       Bohemia.

1381, June   The Peasants' Revolt. Enraged by an oppressive poll
             tax and frustrated by laws that kept wages low, peasants
             and village leaders across Kent and East Anglia revolt,
             killing a number of powerful people and burning John
             of Gaunt's palace in London. Soon brutally suppressed,

the Revolt leaves an impression on Chaucer, who refers to it in the Nun's Priest's Tale.

1381–82   Chaucer possibly begins work on his adaptation of Boccaccio's *Il Teseida*, a poem that will later be incorporated into *The Canterbury Tales* as the Knight's Tale.

1382   Chaucer is briefly appointed Controller of Petty Custom (the custom for wines and cloth) for the port of London.

King Richard marries Anne of Bohemia.

1386, October   Chaucer is a witness in the civil lawsuit involving Sir Richard Scrope and Sir Robert Grosvenor over the right to bear a certain coat of arms. It is during this legal proceeding that Chaucer gives evidence useful to determine an approximate year for his birth.

1386   Chaucer gives up his Customs Controllership and becomes Justice of the Peace and Member of Parliament for the County of Kent.

1387   Death of Philippa Chaucer. Chaucer is working on *The Legend of Good Women* and begins work on *The Canterbury Tales*.

1388   A number of courtiers, including King Richard's cousin, the future Henry IV, effect a *coup d'état* to purge the court of many of Richard's advisors. The Lords Appellant, as these courtiers were called, execute the most powerful of those advisors, occasioning King Richard's lasting enmity.

1389   Chaucer is appointed Clerk of the King's Works, a position in which he supervises building projects of the royal household. He also serves as paymaster in this position.

1390, September   Chaucer is robbed of his payroll money while effecting duties as Clerk of the King's Works.

1391, June   Chaucer is robbed a second time of his payroll money, leading either to his resignation or dismissal from this important administrative position.

1391   Chaucer finishes *A Treatise on the Astrolabe*, the first piece of scientific writing in English since Anglo-Saxon days, dedicating it to his son Lewis.

1392   Chaucer possibly finishes a second scientific treatise, *The Equatorie of the Planets*, though many scholars now argue against its ascription to Chaucer.

1394   Death of Richard II's queen, Anne of Bohemia. Chaucer revises his Prologue to *The Legend of Good Women*, originally dedicated to her.

mid-1390s   Chaucer takes up a position as Deputy Forester for the forest of North Petherton, in Somersetshire, his last administrative post. This was a hunting preserve owned by Roger Mortimer, Earl of March and Ulster, at that time presumptive heir to the throne of the childless Richard II.

1397   Richard II starts a series of maneuvers to take revenge on the Lords Appellant, his old enemies. He becomes increasingly irrational, tending toward megalomania and thus engendering political unrest.

1398   Richard exiles his cousin Henry Bolingbroke, one of the Lords Appellant, for a term of ten years.

1399   Death of John of Gaunt, Henry's father; Richard subsequently increases Henry's term of exile to life. Henry responds by returning to England, gathering supporters, reclaiming his inheritance, and, when he perceives it as possible, deposing his cousin Richard from the throne.

In the midst of all the political turmoil, Chaucer leases a house on the grounds of Westminster Abbey, possibly because he is ailing and seeking caretaking by the Abbey's monks.

He writes a poem dedicated to the new king acknowledging his right to be king and requesting continuation of his pensions and annuities. This is granted.

1400   The former King Richard dies under suspicious circumstances.

Death of Chaucer, aged approximately 60, with his great masterpiece *The Canterbury Tales* unfinished. It nevertheless circulates widely in manuscripts. Chaucer is buried in Westminster Abbey, near the entrance to St. Benedict's Chapel.

1398–1415 (?)   At some point in the early fifteenth century, or possibly even in the last year or two of the fourteenth, the Ellesmere Manuscript and its sister Hengwrt Manuscript are copied by Adam Pinkhurst.

1450?   In approximately this year, the printing press is invented in Germany and first used by Johannes Gutenberg.

1476   William Caxton brings to England its first printing press and sets it up in Westminster. Its first issue while in England is Caxton's first edition of *The Canterbury Tales*.

1483   Caxton prints his second edition of *The Canterbury Tales*.

1556   Chaucer's remains are moved from before the entrance to St. Benedict's Chapel in Westminster Abbey to a stone sarcophagus in the Abbey's South Transept, which today is known as Poets' Corner because of Chaucer's presence there and because of subsequent burials of, and memorials to, other famous writers.

THE GENERAL PROLOGUE

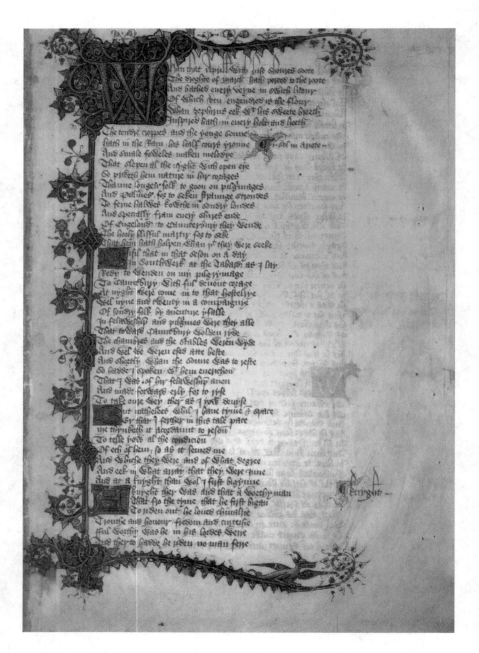

Opening page of *The General Prologue*. Ellesmere Manuscript EL 26 C9 f. 1r. Reprinted by permission of The Huntington Library.

THE GENERAL PROLOGUE

WHAN that Aprill with hise shoures° soote°   *showers, sweet*
The droghte° of March hath perced° to the roote   *drought, pierced*
And bathed every veyne° in swich° licour°   *vein, such, liquid*
Of which vertu° engendred is the flour,°   *power, flower*
5 Whan Zephirus[1] eek° with his sweete breeth   *also*
Inspired hath in every holt° and heeth°   *woods, heath*
The tendre croppes and the yonge sonne
Hath in the Ram[2] his half cours yronne°   *run*
And smale foweles° maken melodye   *birds*
10 That slepen al the nyght with open eye,
So priketh° hem nature in hir corages,°   *excites, their hearts*
Thanne longen folk to goon° on pilgrimages   *go*
And palmeres° for to seken straunge strondes°   *pilgrims, shores*
To ferne halwes° kowthe° in sondry londes.   *far-off shrines, known*
15 And specially, fram° every shires° ende   *from, shire's*
Of Engelond to Caunterbury they wende,°   *travel*
The hooly blisful martir[3] for to seke
That hem° hath holpen° whan that they were seeke.°   *them, helped, sick*
BIFIL° that in that seson° on a day   *It happened, season*
20 In Southwerk[4] at the Tabard[5] as I lay
Redy to wenden° on my pilgrymage   *travel*
To Caunterbury with ful devout corage,
At nyght were come into that hostelrye°   *inn*
Wel nyne and twenty in a compaignye
25 Of sondry° folk by aventure yfalle°   *various, encountered by chance*
In felaweshipe, and pilgrimes were they alle
That toward Caunterbury wolden ryde.
The chambres and the stables weren wyde,°   *wide*
And wel we weren esed° atte beste.   *made comfortable*
30 And shortly, whan the sonne was to reste,

[handwritten annotations: "where 'I' is?", "are In Southwerk at the Tabard", "'fall'"]

---

1 Zephyrus was the name given to the personified west wind. A marginal Latin gloss notes "Sun in Ares."

2 This is a reference to the sign of the Zodiac for the early spring.

3 St. Thomas Becket, Archbishop of Canterbury, was murdered on 29 December 1170 during a dispute with King Henry II, by four knights who thought the king wished his death. Becket was canonized in 1173, and blood from his wounds, mixed with the water used to wash the steps in Canterbury Cathedral where he was killed, was prized for its powers of healing.

4 Southwark is the region on the southern bank of the Thames (now officially part of London but not so during Chaucer's time), directly across from the old city of London. Approximately two hundred years after Chaucer, it became home to Shakespeare's Globe Theatre.

5 This is the name of Harry Bailly's Inn. A "tabard" was a type of tunic often worn over chain-mail armor.

So hadde I spoken with hem° everichon° — *them, everyone*
That I was of hir° felaweshipe anon° — *their, at once*
And made forward° erly° for to ryse — *made a pact, early*
To take oure wey ther as I yow devyse.° — *as I will tell you*
35 BUT nathelees,° whil I have tyme and space — *nevertheless*
Er that I ferther° in this tale pace,° — *further, go*
Me thynketh it° acordaunt° to resoun — *It seems to me, according*
To telle yow al the condicioun
Of ech of hem,° so as it semed me, — *each of them*
40 And whiche they were and of what degree° — *rank*
And eek° in what array° that they were inne, — *also, clothing*
And at a knyght than wol I first bigynne.
A KNYGHT ther was and that a worthy man,[1]
That fro the tyme that he first bigan
45 To riden out, he loved chivalrie,
Trouthe and honour, fredom and curteisie.[2]
Ful worthy was he in his lordes werre° — *war*
And therto hadde he riden, no man ferre,° — *further*
As wel in Cristendom as in hethenesse° — *pagan lands*
50 And evere honoured for his worthynesse.
At Alisaundre[3] he was whan it was wonne.
Ful ofte tyme he hadde the bord bigonne[4]
Aboven alle nacions in Pruce.
In Lettow hadde he reysed° and in Ruce, — *raided*
55 No Cristen man so ofte of his degree.
In Gernade at the seege eek° hadde he be — *also*
Of Algezir, and riden in Belmarye.
At Lyeys was he and at Satalye
Whan they were wonne and in the grete see.

---

1   Knighthood is both a rank and an occupation. Knights did not inherit their title but had to earn it, often by military service, unlike earls, barons, dukes, or titled aristocrats (known as peers), who were higher on the social scale. In Chaucer's day, of a total population in England of perhaps five million, there were about a thousand knights and perhaps as many squires.

2   Keeping one's word, preserving one's reputation or honor, generosity, and courtesy or courtly manners are central values in the code of chivalry.

3   The locations of the Knight's battles are as follows: Alexandria in Egypt (1365); Prussia; Lithuania; Russia (the scenes of much fighting against hold-out pagans in the last decades of the fourteenth century); Grenada (in Spain), whose city Algezir was captured in 1344; Banu Merin (in North Africa); Ayash ("Lyeys," in Syria, captured in 1367); Antalya ("Satalye," in modern Turkey, captured in 1361); Tlemcen (in modern Algeria); Balat ("Palatye," in modern Turkey, involved in campaigning in both the 1340s and 1365); and Turkey. The places not identified with a specific date of battle saw protracted hostilities between Christian and non-Christian during the period in question. The "great sea" is the Mediterranean. It would, of course, have been impossible for a real knight to have taken part in all these campaigns.

4   "Had the board begun" means "sat at the first table"—an honor in victory banquets.

60 At many a noble armee° hadde he be.   *expedition*
   At mortal batailles hadde he been fiftene
   And foughten for oure feith° at Tramyssene   *faith*
   In lystes° thries—and ay slayn his foo.   *jousting stations*
   This ilke° worthy knyght hadde been also   *same*
65 Somtyme with the lord of Palatye
   Agayn another hethen° in Turkye,   *heathen*
   And everemoore he hadde a sovereyn prys.°   *reputation*
   And though that he were worthy,° he was wys,°   *brave, prudent*
   And of his port° as meeke as is a mayde.   *behavior*
70 He nevere yet no vileynye ne sayde
   In al his lyf unto no maner wight.°¹   *kind of person*
   He was a verray,° parfit,° gentil° knyght.   *true, perfect, noble*
   BUT for to tellen yow of his array,°   *appearance*
   His hors° weren goode, but he was nat gay.°   *horses, finely dressed*
75 Of fustian° he wered a gypon°   *rough cloth, tunic*
   Al bismotered° with his habergeon,°   *soiled, mail coat*
   For he was late ycome° from his viage°   *arrived, voyage*
   And wente for to doon° his pilgrymage.   *do*
   WITH hym ther was his sone, a yong SQUIER,²
80 A lovyere° and a lusty bacheler   *lover*
   With lokkes crulle° as they were leyd° in presse.°   *curled, laid, press*
   Of twenty yeer of age he was, I gesse.°   *guess*
   Of his stature he was of evene lengthe°   *moderate height*
   And wonderly delyvere° and of greet strengthe.   *quick*
85 And he hadde been somtyme in chyvachie°   *cavalry expedition*
   In Flaundres, in Artoys, and Pycardie³
   And born hym weel as of so litel space°   *in so short a time*
   In hope to stonden in his lady grace.°   *lady's favor*
   Embrouded° was he as it were a meede,°   *embroidered, meadow*
90 Al ful of fresshe floures whyte and reede.°   *white and red*
   Syngynge he was or floytynge° al the day.   *playing the flute*
   He was as fressh as is the monthe of May.
   Short was his gowne with sleves longe and wyde.
   Wel koude he sitte on hors and faire ryde.

---

1 "He was never rude to anyone." Middle English often uses double or even triple negatives to
  intensify each other rather than to cancel each other out.
2 A squire would serve a knight, especially by helping to arm him, and would fight with him in
  battle. In some cases, as here, squires were young men training to be knights, but squires could
  also be older men, such as Chaucer.
3 These places in Flanders and northwestern France saw military action in 1383, as the English
  troops fought for Pope Urban VI against his rival, Anti-Pope Clement VII. The campaign, led
  by the war-loving Bishop of Norwich, was a great disaster for the English.

95 He koude songes make and wel endite.°	*compose (songs)*
Juste° and eek° daunce and weel putreye° and write.	*joust, also, draw*
So hoote he lovede, that by nyghtertale°	*nighttime*
He slepte namoore° than dooth a nyghtyngale.	*no more*
Curteis° he was, lowely,° and servysable°	*courteous, humble, helpful*
100 And carf° biforn his fader at the table.	*carved (meat)*
A YEMAN°[1] hadde he and servantz namo°	*yeoman, no more*
At that tyme for hym liste° ride so,	*desired*
And he was clad in cote° and hood of grene	*coat*
A sheef° of pecok arwes° bright and kene°	*sheaf, peacock arrows, sharp*
105 Under his belt he bar ful° thriftily.°	*very, carefully*
Wel koude he dresse his takel° yemanly.°	*equipment, yeomanly*
His arwes drouped° noght with fetheres° lowe,	*drooped, feather*
And in his hand he baar° a myghty bowe.	*bore*
A not heed° hadde he, with a broun visage.°	*close-cropped head, face*
110 Of wodecraft° wel koude° he al the usage.°	*woodcraft, knew, customs*
Upon his arm he baar° a gay bracer,°	*bore, leather arm guard*
And by his syde° a swerd° and a bokeler°	*side, sword, small shield*
And on that oother syde a gay° daggere	*bright*
Harneised wel° and sharpe as point of spere.°	*well-sheathed, spear*
115 A cristophere° on his brest of silver sheene.°	*St. Christopher medal, bright*
An horn he bar;° the bawdryk° was of grene.	*bore, shoulder-belt*
A forster° was he, soothly° as I gesse.°	*forester, truly, guess*
THER was also a Nonne,° a Prioresse,°[2]	*Nun, Prioress*
That of hir smylyng was ful° symple and coy°	*very, modest*
120 Hire gretteste ooth was but "By Seint Loy!"[3]	
And she was cleped° Madame Eglentyne.[4]	*called*
Ful weel she soong° the service dyuyne,°[5]	*sang, divine service*
Entuned° in hir nose ful seemely.°	*intoned, MS semeely, seemly*
And Frenssh she spak ful faire and fetisly°	*elegantly*
125 After the scole° of Stratford atte Bowe:[6]	*school*

---

1   A yeoman is a small landholder or tenant farmer, often prosperous enough to serve as an infantryman or archer in a knight's retinue.

2   A prioress is either the second-in-command of an abbey, a large nunnery governed by an abbess, or is in charge of a priory, a smaller nunnery.

3   St. Loy is St. Eligius, a seventh-century Bishop of Noyon in France. Like St. Dunstan, the tenth-century Archbishop of Canterbury, he was a goldsmith. He is patron saint of both goldsmiths and blacksmiths.

4   Eglantine, also known as sweet briar, is an early species of rose. It is known for its sweet, applelike scent (which even the leaves emit if crushed) and five-petaled coral flowers, which appear once a year, in spring. Eglantine was not a common name in the Middle Ages.

5   The phrase "service divine" refers to the Office (or Canonical Hours)—the round of services dominated by psalm-singing that monks and nuns sing on a daily basis. The names of the individual services were Matins, Lauds, Prime, Terce, Sext, None, Vespers, and Compline.

6   Stratford-at-Bow is in Middlesex, just to the east of London. Chaucer's point, elaborated in the

For Frenssh of Parys was to hire unknowe.° *unknown*
At mete° wel ytaught° was she withalle. *dinner, taught*
She leet° no morsel from hir lippes falle, *let*
Ne wette hir fyngres in hir sauce depe.
130 Wel koude she carie a morsel and wel kepe,° *take care*
That no drope ne fille upon hire brist.° *breast*
In curteisie° was set ful muchel° hir list.° *courtesy, much, pleasure*
Hir over-lippe° wyped° she so clene,° *upper lip, wiped, clean*
That in hir coppe° ther was no ferthyng° sene *cup, coin-sized spot*
135 Of grece° whan she dronken hadde hir draughte.° *grease, draft*
Ful semely after hir mete° she raughte.° *food, reached*
And sikerly° she was of greet desport° *surely, geniality*
And ful plesaunt and amyable° of port° *amiable, bearing*
And peyned° hire to contrefete cheere° *took pains, manners*
140 Of court and to been estatlich° of manere *stately*
And to ben holden° digne° of reverence. *held, worthy*
—But for to speken° of hire conscience,° *speak, tenderness of conscience*
She was so charitable and so pitous,° *compassionate*
She wolde wepe° if that she saugh° a mous° *weep, saw, mouse*
145 Kaught in a trappe if it were deed° or bledde.° *dead, bleeding*
Of smale houndes hadde she that she fedde
With rosted flessh or milk and wastel breed.°¹ *white bread*
But soore wepte she if any of hem were deed° *dead*
Or if men smoot it with a yerde° smerte.° *yardstick, smartly*
150 And al was conscience and tendre herte.° *tender heart*
Ful semyly hir wympul² pynched was,
Hir nose tretys,° hir eyen° greye as glas. *shapely, eyes*
Hir mouth ful smal, and therto softe and reed.° *red*
But sikerly,° she hadde a fair forheed. *surely*
155 It was almoost a spanne brood,° I trowe,° *a [hand's] span, believe*
For hardily° she was nat undergrowe.° *certainly, not undergrown*
Full fetys° was hir cloke, as I was war.° *elegant, aware*
Of smal coral aboute hire arm she bar
A peire° of bedes, gauded° al with grene,³ *pair, divided*
160 And theron heng a brooch of gold ful sheene,° *very shiny*

---

next line, is that the Prioress does not speak French properly but rather with a provincial accent.
The Benedictine Priory of St. Leonard's was at Stratford-at-Bow; in Chaucer's day it had nine
nuns, one of them named Argentine. The similarity of the names is suggestive, but Argentine
was not the prioress there.

1 White bread in the Middle Ages was a delicacy reserved for the nobility.
2 A wimple was a cloth that was folded to cover the neck and sides of the head, leaving only the
   face exposed. It was worn by both nuns and lay women.
3 She carries a set of coral rosary beads, a chain of prayer beads divided at intervals by green beads
   as indication of a shift in the prayer to be uttered.

On which ther was first write° a crowned "A"   *written*
And after, "Amor vincit omnia."[1]
ANOTHER Nonne with hire hadde she
That was hir chapeleyne,° and Preestes° thre.   *chaplain, priests*
165   A MONK ther was, a fair for the maistrie,°   *i.e., better than all*
An outridere°[2] that lovede venerie,°   *outrider, hunting*
A manly man, to been an abbot able.
Ful many a deyntee° hors hadde he in stable.   *fine*
And whan he rood, men myghte his brydel heere°   *hear*
170   Gynglen° in a whistlynge wynd als cleere°   *jingling, as clear*
And eek as loude as dooth the chapel belle.[3]
Theras° this lord was kepere of the celle,[4]   *where*
The Reule° of Seint Maure or of Seint Beneit,[5]   *rule*
Bycause that it was old and somdel streit,°   *somewhat restrictive*
175   This ilke° monk leet olde thynges pace°   *same, pass*
And heeld after the newe world the space.°   *course*
He yaf nat° of that text a pulled° hen   *gave not, plucked*
That seith that hunters beth nat hooly° men,   *not holy*
Ne° that a monk whan° he is recchelees°   *nor, when, negligent*
180   Is likned til° a fissh that is waterlees.   *likened to*
This is to seyn,° a monk out of his cloystre.°   *say, cloister*
But thilke° text heeld he nat worth an oystre.°   *that same, MS oystr*
And I seyde his opinioun was good.
What° sholde he studie and make hymselven wood°   *why, crazy*
185   Upon a book in cloystre° alwey to poure°   *cloister, pore*
Or swynken° with his handes and laboure°   *work, labor*
As Austyn[6] bit.° How shal the world be served?   *commands*
Lat Austyn have his owene[7] swynk to hym reserved!
Therfore he was a prikasour aright.°   *hard rider*
190   Grehoundes° he hadde as swift as fowel° in flight.   *grayhounds, bird*

---

1   The Latin phrase means "Love conquers all."
2   An outrider was a monk designated to leave the cloister (which, as Chaucer makes clear below, was not the ideal thing for a normal monk to do) to take care of his monastery's business in the world at large. One of the common accusations made against monks was that they loved hunting and kept expensive horses and hounds.
3   The scribe originally forgot the word "the," and it has been squeezed in later above the line.
4   A cell is a priory or outlying house that is governed by the central monastery.
5   St. Benedict, a sixth-century Italian monk and abbot, compiled the famous Rule that goes by his name. It became normative for most of Western monasticism. St. Maurus, by legend one of his monks, was credited with bringing his Rule to France.
6   "Austin" is the typical Middle English abbreviation for "Augustine," the great Doctor of the Church and Bishop of Hippo in Northern Africa (354–430 AD). He was famous for his theological writings, particularly *The City of God* and *The Confessions*, the latter his spiritual autobiography. He is also credited with writing the Rule (followed by Augustinian canons and monks) to which this passage alludes.
7   Hengwrt omits "owene," thus producing a more regular metrical line.

Of prikyng° and of huntyng for the hare ———————— *riding*
Was al his lust.° For no cost wolde he spare. ———————— *pleasure*
I seigh his sleves° ypurfiled° at the hond° ———————— *sleeves, lined, hand*
With grys°—and that the fyneste of a lond. ———————— *expensive gray fur*
195　And for to festne° his hood under his chyn° ———————— *fasten, chin*
He hadde of gold ywroght° a ful° curious pyn:° ———————— *made, very, pin*
A love knotte in the gretter° ende ther was. ———————— *bigger*
His heed was balled,°¹ that shoon as any glas, ———————— *bald*
And eek° his face as it hadde been enoynt.° ———————— *also, annointed*
200　He was a lord ful fat and in good poynt.²
Hise eyen° stepe° and rollynge in his heed,° ———————— *eyes, bright, head*
That stemed as a forneys° of a leed.° ———————— *furnace, lead*
His bootes souple,° his hors in greet estaat.° ———————— *supple, in best shape*
Now certeinly he was a fair prelaat.° ———————— *prelate*
205　He nas nat° pale as a forpyned goost.° ———————— *was not, distressed ghost*
A fat swan loved he best of any roost.° ———————— *roast*
His palfrey°³ was as broun° as is a berye.° ———————— *horse, brown, berry*
A FRERE° ther was, a wantowne° and a merye,° ———————— *friar, pleasure-seeking, merry*
A lymytour,°⁴ a ful solempne° man. ———————— *limiter, very imposing*
210　In alle the ordres foure°⁵ is noon° that kan° ———————— *four orders, no one, knows*
So muchel° of daliaunce° and fair langage. ———————— *much, flirtation*
He hadde maad° ful° many a mariage ———————— *made, very*
Of yonge wommen at his owene cost.
Unto his ordre he was a noble post!° ———————— *pillar*
215　And wel biloved and famulier was he
With frankeleyns° ever al in his contree ———————— *franklins (gentry)*
And with worthy wommen of the toun,
For he hadde power of confessioun,
As seyde hymself moore than a curat.° ———————— *curate (local priest)*
220　For of his ordre he was licenciat.° ———————— *licensed*
Ful swetely° herde he confessioun, ———————— *sweetly*
And plesaunt was his absolucioun.
He was an esy° man to yeve° penaunce, ———————— *easy, give*
Theras° he wiste° to have a good pitaunce.° ———————— *where, thought, donation*
225　For unto a povre° ordre for to yive° ———————— *poor, give*

1　Monks shaved the crowns of their heads in a haircut known as a "tonsure."
2　"In good point" is an idiom meaning, roughly, "in good condition."
3　A palfrey was an everyday horse, as opposed to a destrier (warhorse) or a plowhorse.
4　A limiter was a friar licensed to preach, minister, and hear confessions in a specified, limited area.
5　There were four main orders of friars in the later Middle Ages—the Franciscans, the Dominicans, the Carmelites, and the Augustinians. Like monks, the friars took vows of poverty, chastity, and obedience, but they were supposed to go out in the world and preach to the laity, whereas monks were supposed to live apart from the world and devote themselves to prayer.

Is signe that a man is wel yshryve.° confessed
For if he yaf° he dorste° make avaunt.° gave, dared, assert
He wiste that a man was repentaunt.[1]
For many a man so hard is of his herte,
230 He may nat wepe° althogh hym soore smerte.° weep, sorely hurts
Therfore instede of wepynge and preyeres,° weeping and prayers
Men moote yeve° silver to the povre freres. should give
His typet[2] was ay farsed° ful of knyves stuffed
And pynnes° for to yeven yonge wyves.° pins, give to young women
235 And, certeinly, he hadde a murye note.° merry singing voice
Wel koude he synge and pleyen on a rote.° play on a lyre
Of yeddynges° he baar outrely° the pris.° songs, completely, prize
His nekke° whit° was as the flour-de-lys.° neck, white, lily
Therto he strong was as a champion.
240 He knew the tavernes wel° in al the toun well
And everich hostiler and tappestere° each innkeeper and barmaid
Bet° than a lazar° or a beggestere.° better, leper, female beggar
For unto swich° a worthy man as he such
Acorded nat as by his facultee[3]
245 To have with sike lazars aqueyntaunce.° sick lepers acquaintance
It is nat honeste.° It may nat avaunce.° respectable, advance (one)
For to deelen° with no swich poraille° deal, poor folk
But al with riche° and selleres of vitaille.° rich, sellers of food
And overal theras profit sholde arise,
250 Curteis he was and lowely° of servyse. humble
Ther nas no° man nowher so vertuous. was not
He was the beste beggere in his hous.°[4] convent
For thogh a wydwe° hadde noght a sho,° widow, not a shoe
So plesaunt was his "In principio,"[5]
255 Yet wolde he have a ferthyng° er° he wente. farthing (coin), before
His purchas° was wel bettre than his rente.°[6] income, expenses
And rage° he koude as it were right a whelp.° cavort, dog

---

1 "For if a man gave money then he [the Friar] knew that man was repentant." The Friar is impos-
   ing a light penance in exchange for a donation to his order.
2 A tippet is a long ornamental piece of cloth worn either as a kind of scarf, as part of a hood, or as
   sleeves. It provided a convenient place to put small objects.
3 "It was not appropriate according to his profession."
4 Hengwrt adds at this point the following two lines, usually numbered in editions 252b and 252c:
   "And yaf a certeyn ferme for the graunt/Noon of his bretheren cam ther in his haunt" (And he
   paid a certain annual amount for the rights [to beg]/so that none of his brother friars came into
   his territory).
5 The opening line of the Gospel of John is "In the beginning was the word." The first fourteen
   lines were often used in devotions or to drive off evil spirits.
6 The exact meaning of the line is disputed, but the implication is clearly that the Friar is cheating
   in his accounts.

In love-dayes ther koude he muchel° help,   *could he (offer) much*
For ther he was nat lyk a cloystrer°   *not like a monk*
260 With a thredbare cope° as is a povre scoler.°   *cloak, poor student*
But he was lyk a maister or a pope.
Of double worstede° was his semycope°   *thick cloth, short cloak*
That rounded as a belle out of the presse.°   *mold*
Somwhat he lipsed° for his wantownesse°   *lisped, affectation*
265 To make his Englissh sweete upon his tonge.
And in his harpyng, whan that he hadde songe,
Hise eyen° twynkled in his heed aryght°   *eyes, aright*
As doon° the sterres° in the frosty nyght.   *do, stars*
This worthy lymytour° was cleped° Huberd.   *limiter, named*
270 A MARCHANT was ther with a forked berd.°   *beard*
In motlee° and hye° on horse he sat,   *multi-colored cloth, high*
Upon his heed a Flaundryssh° bevere° hat.   *Flemish, beaver*
His bootes clasped faire and fetisly.°   *elegantly*
Hise resons° he spak ful solempnely,°   *opinions, very solemnly*
275 Sownynge° alwey th'encrees° of his wynnyng.°   *concerning, increase, profit*
He wolde° the see° were kept for anythyng   *wished, sea*
Bitwixe° Middelburgh and Orewelle.¹   *Between*
Wel koude he in eschaunge° sheeldes selle.²   *exchange*
This worthy man ful wel his wit bisette.°   *employed*
280 Ther wiste no wight that he was in dette,³
So estatly° was he of his governaunce,°   *dignified, management*
With his bargaynes and with his chevyssaunce.°   *commerce for interest*
Forsothe,° he was a worthy man withalle.°   *truly, for all that*
But sooth to seyn, I noot how men hym calle.⁴
285 A CLERK ther was of Oxenford° also⁵   *Oxford*
That unto logyk hadde longe ygo,°   *Who had [committed himself] to*

---

1   These two ports were respectively in the Netherlands and in England. There was much trade in
    the late Middle Ages between the two countries, particularly in textiles.
2   A "shield" or *écu* was a French coin. This kind of trade between national currencies was re-
    garded with suspicion. It was often illegal and could be used as a way of surreptitiously charging
    interest on a loan (which the Church condemned as usury).
3   The syntax is ambiguous. Either "No one knew that he was in debt" (implying he was) or "No
    one knew him to be in debt" (implying he was not) or, since merchants were normally in debt,
    "No one knew how much he was in debt."
4   "To tell the truth, I don't know what he was called."
5   The term "clerk" can mean student or professor, priest or priest's assistant, or learned man or
    philosopher, depending on the context. University students were supposed to be preparing for
    the priesthood. Some became priests, which required a vow of celibacy, and could then win
    promotion in the ranks of the Church. Others only took minor orders (which meant they could
    marry), and either remained at university or, in many cases, became members of the growing
    royal, baronial, and civic administration. Chaucer's Clerk, who is studying advanced logic, is
    roughly the equivalent of a graduate student or junior professor.

And leene° was his hors as is a rake.   *lean*
And he nas nat right° fat, I undertake,°   *was not very, declare*
But looked holwe° and therto sobrely.°   *hollow, soberly*
290 Ful thredbare was his overeste courtepy,°   *overcoat*
For he hadde geten hym yet no benefice[1]
Ne was° so worldly for to have office.   *nor was (he)*
For hym was levere° have at his beddes heed°   *would rather, bed's head*
Twenty bookes clad in blak or reed°   *bound in black and red*
295 Of Aristotle and his philosophie°   *MS philophie*
Than robes riche or fithele° or gay sautrie.°   *fiddle, psaltery*
But al be that he was a philosophre,
Yet hadde he but litel gold in cofre.°[2]   *little gold in a chest*
But al that he myghte of his freendes° hente.°   *friends, obtain*
300 On bookes and on lernynge° he it spente   *learning*
And bisily° gan for the soules preye°   *busily, prayed*
Of hem° that yaf° hym wherwith to scoleye.°   *them, gave the means to study*
Of studie took he moost cure and moost heede.°   *care and attention*
Noght o° word spak he moore than was neede,   *one*
305 And that was seyd in forme and reverence°   *formally and respectfully*
And short and quyk and ful of hy sentence.°   *meaning*
Sownynge in° moral vertu was his speche.   *tending towards*
And gladly wolde he lerne and gladly teche.
A SERGEANT of the Lawe[3] war° and wys°   *shrewd, wise*
310 That often hadde been at the Parvys[4]
Ther was also, ful riche of excellence.
Discreet he was and of greet reverence.
He semed swich, his wordes weren so wise.
Justice° he was ful often in assise°   *judge, court*
315 By patente and by pleyn commissioun,[5]
For his science° and for his heigh renoun.°   *knowledge, renown*

---

1 A "benefice" was a position as a priest or clergyman. In the Middle Ages there had developed
   a much-criticized custom of granting the income from some benefices to people who would
   apportion a small amount of the income to a poorer clergyman to do the work and then live off
   the rest. This practice made some bishops with multiple benefices very wealthy, and it became
   a means of supporting a well-connected scholar at one of the universities.
2 Chaucer is punning on the word "philosopher," which can also mean alchemist.
3 In late fourteenth-century England, a Sergeant of Law was not simply a lawyer; he was one of
   about twenty or so lawyers who functioned as legal advisors to the king and served as judges.
4 "Parvys" is a shortened form of "Paradise," a name given to the porch in front of large church-
   es. Here the reference is to the porch of Saint Paul's Cathedral in London, where lawyers
   would meet with their clients, the "lawyer's office" being unknown to late fourteenth-century
   England.
5 Letter patents were royal letters of appointment that were "open," i.e., public documents that
   anyone was allowed to read. The full commission gives the Sergeant the right to hear all legal
   cases in the court of Assizes, circuit courts that would move from county to county.

Of fees and robes hadde he many oon;°   *many a one*
So greet a purchasour was nowher noon.[1]
Al was fee symple[2] to hym in effect.
320 His purchasyng myghte nat been infect.°   *invalidated*
Nowher so bisy° a man as he ther nas,°   *busy, was not*
And yet he semed bisier° than he was.   *seemed busier*
In termes° hadde he caas° and doomes alle°   *files, cases, judgments*
That from the tyme° of Kyng William[3] were yfalle.°   *time, given*
325 Therto he koude endite° and make a thyng.°   *write, brief*
Ther koude no wight° pynchen° at his writyng.   *nobody, quibble*
And every statut koude he pleyn by rote.°   *recite by heart*
He rood but hoomly° in a medlee° cote.   *simply, multi-colored*
Girt with a ceint° of silk with barres° smale   *belt, ornaments*
330 Of his arraye tell I no lenger tale.
A FRANKELEYN was in his compaignye.[4]
Whit° was his heed° as is a dayesye.°   *white, head, daisy*
Of his complexioun he was sangwyn.[5]
Wel loved he by the morwe a sope in wyn.[6]
335 To lyven° in delit° was evere his wone,°   *live, delight, custom*
For he was Epicurus[7] owene sone.°   *son*
That heeld opinioun that pleyn delit°   *full delight*
Was verray° felicitee parfit.°   *true, perfect happiness*
An housholdere and that a greet was he.
340 Seint Julian[8] was he in his contree.
His breed,° his ale was alweys after oon[9]   *bread*
A bettre envyned man° was nevere noon.   *man stocked with wine*
Withoute bake mete° was nevere his hous   *baked food*

---

1 A "purchaser" was someone who acquired feudal property by money rather than feudal service. "Nowhere none" simply means nowhere at all, another example of the Middle English use of multiple negatives to intensify negation rather than cancel each other out.

2 "Fee simple" means ownership without feudal obligations.

3 This King William is William the Conqueror, who ruled England from 1066 to 1087. His reign, of course, marked a turning point in English governance.

4 The Franklin (from the word franc or free) is a wealthy independent landowner and a member of the minor gentry.

5 The Franklin is dominated by blood, one of the four humors, which makes him red-faced and cheerful.

6 "He greatly loved in the morning bread soaked in wine." Such was the preferred breakfast for those wealthy enough to afford wine, which had to be imported from Gascony, the sole remaining territory England retained in what we now call France.

7 Epicurus (341–270 BC) was the Greek philosopher who maintained that the pursuit of pleasure was the natural state of humankind.

8 St. Julian, a legendary character like St. Christopher, was in the Middle Ages the patron saint of hospitality. This was because, in penance for unwittingly killing his parents (who had unknowingly lodged in his house while journeying), Julian set up a way-station for travelers.

9 The idiom "after one" means "consistent," i.e., consistently good.

	Of fissh and flessh and that so plentevous,°	*plentiful*
345	It snewed° in his hous of mete and drynke,	*snowed*
	Of alle deyntees° that men koude thynke.	*delicacies*
	After the sondry° sesons° of the yeer	*various, seasons*
	So chaunged he his mete° and his soper.°	*dinner, supper*
	Ful° many a fat partrich° hadde he in muwe°	*very, partridge, coop*
350	And many a breem° and many a luce° in stuwe.°	*bream, pike, pond*
	Wo° was his cook but if° his sauce were	*woe, unless*
	Poynaunt° and sharpe and redy° al his geere.°	*Spicy, ready, utensils*
	His table dormant¹ in his halle alway	
	Stood redy° covered al the longe day.	*ready*
355	At sessiouns° ther was he lord and sire.	*court sessions*
	Ful° ofte tyme he was Knyght of the Shire.²	*very*
	An anlaas° and a gipser° al° of silk	*dagger, pouch, all*
	Heeng° at his girdel whit° as morne° milk.	*hung, white, morning*
	A shirreve° hadde he been and countour.°	*sheriff, tax-collector*
360	Was nowher swich a worthy vavasour.°	*feudal land holder*
	AN Haberdasshere³ and a Carpenter,	
	A Webbe,° a Dyere, and a Tapycer,°	*weaver, tapestry-maker*
	And they were clothed alle in o° lyveree°⁴	*one, livery*
	Of a solempne and a greet fraternitee.⁵	
365	Ful fressh and newe hir geere° apiked° was.	*equipment, polished*
	Hir knyves were chaped° noght° with bras°	*mounted, not, brass*
	But al with silver, wroght ful clene and weel°	*made very elegantly and well*
	Hire girdles° and hir pouches everydeel.°	*belts, every bit*
	Wel semed° ech of hem a fair burgeys°	*seemed, citizen*

---

1   The Franklin's table is "dormant," meaning that it is always standing. Most medieval tables on which meals were set were trestle tables, i.e., a long board placed on top of what we would call saw-horses. After the meal was over, the table would normally be taken down—but not so the Franklin's.

2   "Knight of the Shire" was an official designation for people chosen to represent their region in Parliament. Chaucer himself, while he was never knighted and only held the rank of squire, served as Knight of the Shire for Kent in 1386, the year before the fictitious pilgrimage to Canterbury takes place. The Franklin has also presided at the sessions of the Justices of the Peace (line 355) and served as Sherif, the chief royal officer in a county who was responsible for collecting its taxes, and as the county auditor, who assisted the Sherif.

3   A haberdasher sells ribbons, buttons, hats, gloves, and small articles of clothing.

4   "Livery" is roughly equivalent to our "uniform." Members of craft or religious guilds as well as retainers of various lords wore liveries. At this time the wearing of liveries encouraged faction-alism and attendant violence, and there were some legal attempts to curb abuses.

5   Fraternities or brotherhoods were either trade guilds or religious guilds. The trade guilds regulated who was allowed to follow a given trade in a given town, and the religious guilds functioned as mutual aid societies, burying their dead and helping members who were sick or had fallen into poverty. These guildsmen, though identified by their trades, are members of a religious guild, since trade guilds admitted only members of a single trade.

370 To sitten in a yeldehalle° on a deys.°	*guildhall, raised platform*
Everich° for the wisdom that he kan°	*everyone, knew*
Was shaply° for to been an alderman.¹	*suitable*
For catel° hadde they ynogh° and rente,°	*belongings, enough, rent*
And eek° hir wyves° wolde it wel assente°	*also, wives, agree*
375 And elles° certeyn were they to blame.	*otherwise*
It is ful fair to been ycleped° "Madame"	*called*
And goon to vigilies°² al bifore	*vigils*
And have a mantel roialliche ybore.°	*cloak royally carried*
A COOK° they hadde with hem° for the nones°	*cook, them, for the occasion*
380 To boille° the chiknes° with the marybones°	*boil, chickens, marrowbones*
And poudre-marchant tart and galyngale.³	
Wel koude he knowe a draughte of Londoun ale.	
He koude rooste and sethe° and boille° and frye,°	*simmer, boil, fry*
Maken mortreux° and wel bake a pye.	*stews*
385 But greet harm° was it as it thoughte me°	*pity, seemed to me*
That on his shyne° a mormal° hadde he.	*shin, ulcer*
For blankmanger⁴ that made he with the beste.	
A SHIPMAN was ther wonynge° fer by weste.°	*living, far in the west*
For aught I woot,° he was of Dertemouthe.⁵	*all I know*
390 He rood° upon a rouncy° as he kouthe°	*rode, nag, could*
In a gowne of faldyng° to the knee.	*woolen cloth*
A daggere hangynge on a laas° hadde he	*lace*
About his nekke under his arm adoun.°	*downwards*
The hoote° somer hadde maad° his hewe° al broun.°	*hot, made, color, brown*
395 And certeinly he was a good felawe.	
Ful many a draughte° of wyn° had he drawe	*draft, wine*
Fro Burdeuxward whil that the chapman° sleepe.⁶	*merchant*
Of nyce° conscience took he no keepe.°	*scrupulous, notice*
If that he faught° and hadde the hyer hond,°	*If he fought, upper hand*
400 By water he sente hem hoom° to every lond.⁷	*home*

---

1 In late medieval England, as in some cities today, the board of "aldermen" governs under the mayor. The five guildsmen have prospered, rising from apprentices to masters. They are successful businessmen who run their own shop or shops, participate in civic government, and aspire, with their wives, to the status of the lesser gentry.

2 In the Middle Ages, vigils were church services held the night before an important holy day. The aldermen and their wives would lead the procession, with their cloaks carried by a servant.

3 "And tart ground spice and aromatic roots (such as ginger)."

4 Blancmanger is a stew of milk, rice, almonds, and chicken or fish.

5 Dartmouth is a port on the English Channel in the southwest of England, near Plymouth.

6 Sailing home from Bordeaux with a cargo of wine, the Merchant would secretly steal some while the [wine] merchant ("chapman") was asleep.

7 That is, he threw his prisoners overboard.

But of his craft° to rekene° wel his tydes,°   *ability, reckon, tides*
His stremes° and his daungers° hym bisides,°   *currents, dangers, all around him*
His herberwe° and his moone,° his lodemenage,°   *harborage, moon, piloting*
Ther nas noon swich° from Hull to Cartage.[1]   *was not anyone such*
405 Hardy he was and wys to undertake.°   *wise in his endeavors*
With many a tempest hadde his berd° been shake.°   *beard, shaken*
He knew alle the havenes° as they were   *havens*
Fro Gootlond to the Cape of Fynystere[2]
And every cryke° in Britaigne° and in Spayne.°   *inlet, Brittany, Spain*
410 His barge ycleped was the Maudelayne.
WITH us ther was a Doctour of Physik.[3]
In al this world ne was ther noon hym lik°   *there was no one like him*
To speke of phisik° **and of surgerye,**   *medicine*
For he was grounded in astronomye.[4]
415 He kepte° his pacient a ful greet deel   *watched over*
In houres by his magyk natureel.[5]
Wel koude he fortunen the ascendent°   *calculate a planet's position*
Of hise ymages[6] for his pacient.
He knew the cause of everich° maladye,°   *every, malady*
420 Were it of hoot or coold or moyste or drye,[7]
And where they engendred and of what humour.
He was a verray, parfit praktisour:°   *practitioner*
The cause yknowe° and of his harm the roote,°   *known, root*
Anon he yaf° the sike man his boote.°   *gave, remedy*
425 Ful redy hadde he hise apothecaries°   *pharmacists*
To sende hym drogges° and his letuaries.°   *drugs, syrups*
For ech° of hem° made oother for to wynne.°   *each, them, profit*
Hir° frendshipe nas nat newe to bigynne.°   *their, was not recently begun*

---

1 Hull is a port in northern England, "Cartage," either Carthage on the Mediterranean coast of North Africa or Cartagena in Spain.

2 Gotland is an island in the Baltic Sea off the coast of southern Sweden; Cape Fisterra is the point of land that juts out into the Atlantic Ocean in northwest Spain.

3 "Doctor of Physic" meant "physician." The term "doctor" means "teacher," as everyone in the Middle Ages knew, so the type of doctor who taught medicine and sometimes practiced it needed to be distinguished from other types of doctors, who taught academic subjects in the universities.

4 In the Middle Ages, physicians often based their schedules of treatment on astrological tables.

5 "Hours" refers here to the times in the day when the various planetary influences were pronounced, when the Physician watched over ("kepte") his patient. "Natural magic" is opposed to "black magic," which involves supernatural contact with malicious spirits.

6 The practice of astrologically based medicine involved the use of images of the planets as talismans.

7 Medieval medicine was also based on a theory, traceable back to Greek physicians like the ones Chaucer mentions below, of the balance of the four bodily humors (blood, phlegm, black bile, and yellow bile) and their qualities of hot, cold, moist, and dry mentioned in this line.

Wel knew he the olde Esculapius[1]
430 And Deyscorides and eek Rufus,°   *MS Risus*
Olde Ypocras, Haly, and Galyen,
Serapion, Razis, and Avycen,
Averrois, Damascien, and Constantyn,
Bernard, and Gatesden, and Gilbertyn.
435 Of his diete° mesurable° was he,   *diet, moderate*
For it was of no superfluitee°   *excess*
But of greet norissyng° and digestible.   *nourishment*
His studie was but litel on the Bible.[2]
In sangwyn° and in pers° he clad was al,   *red, blue*
440 Lyned with taffata and with sendal.[3]
And yet he was but esy of dispence.°   *moderate in spending*
He kepte that he wan° in pestilence.°[4]   *what he earned, plague*
For gold in phisik° is a cordial.°   *medicine, heart medicine*
Therfore he lovede gold in special.°   *especially*
445 A GOOD Wif was ther of biside Bathe,[5]
But she was somdel deef,° and that was scathe.°   *somewhat deaf, a shame*
Of clooth makyng she hadde swich an haunt,°   *skill*
She passed hem of Ypres and of Gaunt.[6]
In al the parisshe° wif° ne was ther noon°   *parish, wife, none*

---

1 A list of famous physicians begins in this line. Aesculapius was a mythological demi-god, son to
   Apollo (and subject of Chaucer's Manciple's Tale). Dioscorides, Rufus of Ephesus, Hippocrates
   (associated with the Hippocratic Oath physicians still swear), and Galen were famous Greek
   physicians. Galen (129–199 AD) was particularly influential, since he set out the theory of four
   humors which was the basis of medieval medicine. "Haly" is probably the Persian physician
   Ali Ben el-Abbas (d. 994 AD). Rhazes (d. c. 930 AD) was an Arab astronomer and physician.
   Avicenna or Ibn Sina (980–1037 AD) and Averroes (1126–98 AD) were Islamic philosophers
   and physicians. John of Damascus was a Syrian physician of the ninth century. Constantine
   the African came from Carthage, converted to Christianity, became a Benedictine monk, and
   taught at Salerno in Italy in the eleventh century. His work on aphrodisiacs earns him the title
   the "cursed monk" in the Merchant's Tale, line 1810. Islamic science was widely influential in
   the Middle Ages; it first brought Greek thought to the Latin West. The last three authorities are
   British. Bernard Gordon was a Scottish physician who taught at Montpellier in the fourteenth
   century. John Gaddesden (d. c. 1349) taught at Oxford and served as court doctor to Edward II.
   Gilbert was an English physician in the thirteenth century and the author of a major medical
   treatise.
2 In the Middle Ages physicians were often thought to be religious skeptics, partly because of
   their knowledge of classical astronomy.
3 Taffeta and sendal are types of silk cloth; silk, imported from Asia, was a mark of status and
   wealth.
4 Possibly a reference to the Black Death, which killed from a quarter to a half of the population
   of England between 1348 and 1349, although there were later outbreaks of plague in 1362, 1369,
   and 1376.
5 Bath is a town in southwest England near Bristol. It is famous for its hot springs (hence its name)
   and Roman ruins. The parish of St. Michael's, just north of Bath, was famous for its weavers.
6 Ypres and Ghent are cities in Flanders (now northwestern Belgium) known for cloth trading.
   There were also skilled weavers from these cities working in England.

450 That to the offrynge°¹ bifore hire sholde goon.   *offering*
And if ther dide, certeyn so wrooth° was she,   *angry*
That she was out of alle charitee.
Hir coverchiefs° ful fyne were of ground°—   *kerchiefs, of a fine texture*
I dorste swere° they weyeden° ten pound—   *dared swear, weighed*
455 That on a Sonday weren upon hir heed.
Hir hosen weren of fyn° scarlet reed,°   *fine, red*
Ful streite yteyd° and shoes ful moyste° and newe.   *tightly laced, supple*
Boold° was hir face and fair and reed° of hewe.°   *bold, red, color*
She was a worthy womman al hir lyve.
460 Housbondes at chirche dore° she hadde fyve,°²   *church door, five*
Withouten° oother compaignye in youthe.   *apart from*
But therof nedeth nat to speke as nowthe.°   *for now*
And thries° hadde she been at Jerusalem.³   *three times*
She hadde passed many a straunge strem.°   *foreign waters*
465 At Rome she hadde been and at Boloigne,
In Galice at Seint Jame and at Coloigne.
She koude muchel of wandrynge by the weye.⁴
Gat-tothed⁵ was she, soothly for to seye.
Upon an amblere° esily° she sat.   *saddle horse, easily*
470 Ywympled°⁶ wel and on hir heed° an hat   *wimpled, head*
As brood° as is a bokeler or a targe,°   *broad, shield (two types)*
A foot mantel° aboute hir hipes large   *outer skirt*
And on hir feet a paire of spores° sharpe.   *spurs*
In felaweshipe wel koude she laughe and carpe.°   *joke*
475 Of remedies of love she knew perchaunce,°   *as it happened*
For she koude° of that art the olde daunce.°   *knew, dance*
A GOOD man was ther of religioun
And was a povre Persoun° of a toun,   *Parson (parish priest)*
But riche he was of hooly thoght° and werk.°   *holy thought, work*
480 He was also a lerned man, a clerk,   *learned, scholar*
That Cristes° gospel trewely wolde preche.°   *Christ's, preach*

---

1   In medieval eucharistic services, the Offering was the time the people brought their gifts to the altar.
2   Marriage vows were exchanged on the church steps and were followed by a mass inside the church.
3   Jerusalem was the greatest of all pilgrimages. From England, a trip there and back could take a couple of years. The other pilgrimages mentioned below are Rome, where the apostles Peter and Paul were buried, Boulogne-sur-mer in France, famous for its miraculous image of the Blessed Virgin, Compostella in Galicia, where the relics of St. James were venerated, and Cologne, where the relics of the Three Kings (or Three Magi) were kept.
4   "She knew much about wandering along the road."
5   According to medieval physiognomy, a gap between the teeth was a sign that a woman was bold, lecherous, faithless, and suspicious.
6   Wimpled means wearing a wimple.

Hise parisshens° devoutly wolde he teche. — *parishioners*
Benygne° he was and wonder diligent — *benign*
And in adversitee° ful pacient,° — *adversity, patient*
485 And swich° he was preved° ofte sithes.° — *such, proven, many times*
Ful looth° were hym to cursen° for hise tithes,[1] — *reluctant, excommunicate*
But rather wolde he yeven° out of doute° — *give, without doubt*
Unto his povre° parisshens aboute — *poor*
Of his offryng and eek of his substaunce.
490 He koude in litel thyng have suffisaunce.[2]
Wyd° was his parisshe and houses fer asonder,° — *wide, far apart*
But he ne lefte° nat for reyn° ne° thonder — *did not neglect, rain, or*
In siknesse nor in meschief° to visite — *trouble*
The ferreste° in his parisshe muche and lite.° — *farthest, of greater or lesser rank*
495 Upon his feet and in his hand a staf° — *staff*
This noble ensample° to his sheepe he yaf,° — *example, gave*
That firste he wroghte° and afterward that he taughte.[3] — *acted*
Out of the gospel he tho° wordes caughte,° — *those, took*
And this figure° he added eek therto,° — *figure of speech, to it*
500 "That if gold ruste, what shal iren° do?" — *iron*
For if a preest be foul on whom we truste,
No wonder is a lewed man° to ruste, — *layman*
And shame it is if a preest take keepe°— — *heed*
A shiten° shepherde and a clene° sheepe. — *soiled with excrement, clean*
505 Wel oghte° a preest ensample for to yeve° — *ought, give*
By his clennesse how that his sheepe sholde° lyve.° — *should, live*
He sette nat° his benefice to hyre — *did not offer*
And leet° his sheepe encombred° in the myre° — *left, stuck, mud*
And ran to Londoun unto Seint Poules[4]
510 To seken hym° a chauntrie° for soules — *seek for himself, chantry*
Or with a bretherhed°[5] to been withholde,° — *brotherhood, hired*
But dwelleth at hoom and kepeth wel his folde° — *sheepfold (i.e., flock)*
So that the wolf ne made° it nat myscarie.° — *would not make, come to grief*
He was a shepherde and noght° a mercenarie,° — *not, mercenary*
515 And though he hooly were and vertuous,

---

1 Tithes were periodic assessments of one tenth a person's goods, harvest, and animals, claimed by the Church. Parish priests could excommunicate parishioners who would not pay them.
2 "He was able to have enough in little things."
3 Hengwrt omits "that," making for a more metrically regular line.
4 St. Paul's is the cathedral in London. The custom Chaucer refers to is related to the issue of benefices, outlined on p. 12, note 1. A "chantry" is an endowed position, usually at large churches and cathedrals, in which a priest sings masses for the soul of the person who left money for the endowment. The position involved very little work, unlike the Parson's toil described in his section of the General Prologue.
5 The "brotherhood" here is a guild. Guilds hired priests to serve as their chaplains.

He was nat to synful men despitous,°   *scornful*
Ne° of his speche daungerous° ne digne,°   *nor, proud, haughty*
But in his techyng discreet and benygne,°   *kind*
To drawen folk to hevene by fairnesse,
520 By good ensample. This was his bisynesse.
But it were any persone obstinat,[1]
Whatso° he were of heigh or lough estat,°   *whether, high or low class*
Hym wolde he snybben° sharply for the nonys.°   *rebuke, occasion*
A bettre preest, I trowe,° that nowher noon ys.   *believe*
525 He waiteth after° no pompe and reverence,   *expected*
Ne maked° hym a spiced° conscience.   *did not make, fastidious*
But Cristes loore° and hise apostles twelve   *teaching*
He taughte. But first he folwed it hymselve.
WITH hym ther was a Plowman, was° his brother,   *[who] was*
530 That hadde ylad° of dong ful many a fother.°   *hauled, cartload*
A trewe swynkere° and a good was he,   *true worker*
Lyvynge in pees and parfit° charitee.   *perfect*
God loved he best with al his hoole herte
At alle tymes, thogh he gamed or smerte.[2]
535 And thanne° his neighebore right° as hymselve.   *then, just*
He wolde thresshe° and therto dyke° and delve°   *thresh, dig, shovel*
For Cristes sake for every povre wight°   *poor person*
Withouten hire° if it lay in his myght.   *without pay*
Hise tithes[3] payde he ful faire and wel,
540 Bothe of his propre swynk° and his catel.°   *own work, possessions*
In a tabard° he rood upon a mere.°   *over-shirt, mare*
THER was also a Reve° and a Millere,   *Reeve*
A Somnour° and a Pardoner also,   *Summoner,*
A Maunciple° and myself. Ther were namo.°   *Manciple, no more*
545 The Millere was a stout carl° for the nones.°[4]   *sturdy fellow, occasion*
Ful byg he was of brawn and eek of bones.
That proved wel,° for overal ther° he cam°   *was clear, where, came*
At wrastlynge° he wolde have alwey the ram.[5]   *wrestling*
He was short-sholdred,° brood,° a thikke knarre.°   *stocky, broad, thick fellow*
550 Ther was no dore that he ne wolde heve of harre[6]
Or breke it at a rennyng° with his heed.   *by running at it*

Big/dumb

---

1 "But if anyone were obstinate."
2 "At all times, whether he rejoiced or suffered."
3 See p. 19, note 1.
4 "For the nonés" or "for the occasion" is a largely meaningless phrase that Chaucer occasionally
   uses to fill out a line.
5 A ram was a typical prize for victors at trade fairs.
6 "There was not a door that he would not heave off its hinges."

His berd° as any sowe° or fox was reed,°	beard, sow, red
And therto brood° as though it were a spade.	broad
Upon the cope° right of his nose he hade	ridge
555 A werte° and theron stood a toft of herys.°	wart, tuft of hairs
Reed° as the brustles° of a sowes erys.°	red, bristles, sow's ears
Hise nosethirles° blake° were and wyde.°	nostrils, black, wide
A swerd and a bokeler° bar° he by his syde.	shield, bore
His mouth as greet° was as a greet forneys.°	large, furnace
560 He was a janglere° and a goliardeys,[1]	joker
And that was moost of synne° and harlotries.°	sin, obscenities
Wel koude he stelen° corn° and tollen thries.°	steal, grain, count thrice
And yet he hadde a thombe[2] of gold, pardee.°	to be sure
A whit cote° and a blew° hood wered° he.	white coat, blue, wore
565 A baggepipe wel koude he blowe and sowne,°	sound
And therwithal he broghte us out of towne.	
A GENTIL° Maunciple was ther of a temple[3]	gracious
Of which achatours° myghte take exemple	buyers
For to be wise in byynge° of vitaille.°	buying, food
570 For wheither that he payde or took by taille,°	credit
Algate he wayted so in his achaat	
That he was ay biforn and in good staat.[4]	
Now is nat that of God a ful faire grace	
That swich a lewed° mannes wit shal pace°	unlearned, surpass
575 The wisdom of an heepe° of lerned men?	heap
Of maistres hadde he mo° than thries ten°	more, three times ten
That weren° of lawe° expert and curious,°	were, law, skilled
Of whiche ther weren a duszeyne° in that hous	dozen
Worthy to been stywardes° of rente and lond	be stewards
580 Of any lord that is in Engelond,	
To maken hym lyve° by his propre good°	live, own means
In honour dettelees°—but if he were wood°—	without debt, crazy
Or lyve as scarsly° as hym list desire°	frugally, as he wanted
And able for to helpen al a shire°	an entire county
585 In any caas° that myghte falle or happe.°	situation, happen
And yet this Manciple sette hir aller cappe.°	cheated them all

---

1 "Goliard" is the term for wandering scholars in the eleventh and twelfth centuries, who were known for their rowdy life. By Chaucer's time the term "goliard" had become less specific, and it referred to people who told dirty stories.

2 According to Skeat, the reference is either to the proverb "An honest miller has a golden thumb," which implied that there was no such thing as an honest miller, or to the distinctive shape millers' thumbs acquired by continually feeling the grain while it was being ground, so that the "golden thumb" was a sign of a prosperous miller.

3 A manciple was a manager at one of the Inns of Court, the legal brotherhoods in London. The inns of court were also called temples.

4 "He always sought an occasion for his purchasing ('achaat')/So that he always ('ay') came out ahead ('biforn') and did well."

THE Reve was a sclendre,° colerik° man.[1]   *slender, choleric*
His berd° was shave° as ny° as ever he kan.°   *beard, shaven, closely, can*
His heer° was by his erys° ful° round yshorn.°   *hair, ears, very, cut*
590 His tope was dokked° lyk a preest biforn.[2]   *clipped*
Ful longe were his legges and ful lene.°   *lean*
Ylyk° a staf° ther was no calf ysene.°   *like, staff, seen*
Wel koude he kepe° a gerner° and a bynne.°   *keep, granary, bin*
Ther was noon auditour koude of hym wynne.°   *get the better of*
595 Wel wiste° he by the droghte° and by the reyn°   *knew, drought, rain*
The yeldynge° of his seed and of his greyn.°   *yield, grain*
His lordes sheepe, his neet,° his dayerye,°   *cattle, dairy cows*
His swyn,° his hors, his stoor,° and his pultrye°   *swine, livestock, poultry*
Was hoolly° in this Reves governyng,   *wholly*
600 And by his covenant° yaf° the rekenyng°   *contract, gave, reckoning*
Syn° that his lord was twenty yeer of age.   *since*
Ther koude° no man brynge hym in arrerage.°   *could, arrears*
Ther nas baillif ne hierde nor oother hyne,
That he [ne] knew his sleighte and his covyne.[3]
605 They were adrad° of hym as of the deeth.°[4]   *afraid, death*
His wonyng° was ful faire upon an heeth.°   *dwelling, heath*
With grene trees shadwed was his place.
He koude° bettre than his lord purchace.°   *could, buy land*
Full riche he was, astored pryvely.°   *had a secret store [of goods]*
610 His lord wel koude he plesen subtilly,°   *please subtly*
To yeve° and lene° hym of his owene good°   *give, loan, goods*
And have a thank and yet a gowne and hood.[5]
In youthe he hadde lerned° a good myster.°   *learned, craft*
He was a wel good wrighte,° a carpenter.   *craftsman*
615 This Reve sat upon a ful good stot°   *farm horse*
That was al pomely° grey and highte° Scot.   *dappled, was named*
A long surcote° of pers° upon he hade,   *overcoat, blue*
And by his syde he baar° a rusty blade.   *carried*

---

1 A reeve was someone, often originally a peasant, who served as a supervisor on a lord's estate.
   Among other things, reeves collected the portion of the harvest due the lords and made sure
   peasants performed their customary labor for the lords. They were much resented. Chaucer's
   Reeve is dominated by choler or yellow bile, which makes him suspicious and irritable.
2 "The top of his head was cut short in the front like a priest's haircut." This would have been an
   unfashionable cut for a layman and suitable for a man who was either poor or miserly or austere.
3 "There was not a bailiff (foreman), herdsman, or other worker/whose tricks and deception he
   did not know."
4 Death in general or possibly the plague.
5 This reeve cheats his lord by storing away the lord's goods as his own and then providing from
   them loans to the lord, receiving payment and thanks. Payment in the Middle Ages was most
   often in tangible goods, like the clothing mentioned here, rather than in money.

Of Northfolk° was this Reve of which I telle,   *Norfolk*
620 Biside a toun men clepen Baldeswelle.¹
Tukked° he was as is a frere° aboute,²   *tucked, friar*
And ever he rood the hyndreste of oure route.°   *last of our company*
A SOMONOUR³ was ther with us in that place
That hadde a fyr reed,° cherubynnes° face,⁴   *fire red, cherub-like*
625 For saucefleem° he was with eyen narwe.°   *blotchy, narrow eyes*
As hoot° he was and lecherous as a sparwe,°⁵   *hot, sparrow*
With scaled browes blake and piled berd.⁶
Of his visage° children were aferd.°   *face, afraid*
Ther nas quyksilver, lytarge, ne brymstoon,
630 Boras, cerice, ne° oille of Tartre noon,⁷   *nor*
Ne oynement° that wolde clense° and byte°   *ointment, cleanse, bite*
That hym myghte helpen of the whelkes° white _   *blemishes*
Nor of the knobbes sittynge° on his chekes.°   *sitting, cheeks*
Wel loved he garleek, oynons, and eek lekes°   *also leeks*
635 And for to drynken strong wyn reed as blood.
Thanne wolde he speke and crie° as he were wood.°   *yell, as if crazy*
And whan that he wel dronken hadde the wyn
Thanne wolde he speke no word but Latyn.°   *Latin*
A fewe termes hadde he, two or thre,
640 That he had lerned° out of som decree.°   *learned, legal document*
No wonder is, he herde it al the day,
And eek ye knowen wel how that a jay°   *chattering bird*
Kan clepen "Watte"° as wel as kan° the Pope.   *call out Walter, can*
But whoso koude in oother thyng him grope,°   *examine*
645 Thanne hadde he spent al his philosophie.
Ay "Questio quid iuris!"⁸ wold he crie.
He was a gentil harlot and a kynde,°   *noble and kindly scoundrel*

---

1 Bawdeswell is a town in the northern part of Norfolk, the northernmost county in East Anglia on the east coast of England.

2 Franciscan friars wore habits tied about the waist with ropes.

3 A summoner delivered legal summonses to appear before either a secular or an ecclesiastical court, although more often the latter. The ecclesiastical courts were run by the Church and had jurisdiction over all clerics, but also over any lay person charged with a moral offense such as adultery or fornication.

4 Cherubim, the second highest order of angels, were bright red. See Ezekiel 1:13.

5 Since sparrows travel in flocks, they had a reputation in the Middle Ages for being lecherous, similar to the more modern reputation of rabbits.

6 The Summoner's eyebrows have a disease called the scall, and his beard has been losing tufts of hair.

7 The unsuccessful remedies are mercury (sometimes known as quicksilver), lead monoxide ("lytarge"), sulfur (sometimes known as brimstone), borax, white lead ("cerice"), and cream of tartar.

8 "Question: what point of the law?" The expression was often used in the ecclesiastical courts.

A bettre felawe° sholde men noght° fynde.   *fellow, not*
He wolde suffre for a quart of wyn
650 A good felawe to have his concubyn°   *mistress*
A twelf monthe° and excuse hym atte fulle.°   *a year, fully*
Ful prively° a fynch° eek° koude° he pulle.[1]   *secretly, finch, also, could*
And if he foond° owher° a good felawe,   *found, anywhere*
He wolde techen° hym to have noon awe°   *teach, no respect*
655 In swich caas of the Ercedekenes curs—[2]
But if° a mannes° soule were in his purs.°   *unless, man's, purse*
For in his purs he sholde ypunysshed be.°   *should be punished*
Purs is the Ercedekenes Helle, seyde he.
But wel I woot° he lyed° right in dede.°   *know, lied, indeed*
660 Of cursyng° oghte ech gilty man him drede.   *excommunication*
For curs wol slee° right as° assoillyng° savith.   *kill, just as, absolution*
And also war° him of a "Significavit"![3]   *beware*
In daunger° hadde he at his owene gise°   *power, pleasure*
The yonge girles[4] of the diocise°   *diocese*
665 And knew hir conseil° and was al hir reed.°[5]   *their counsel, advisor*
A gerland° hadde he set upon his heed   *garland*
As greet° as it were for an ale stake.°[6]   *large, ale-sign*
A bokeleer° hadde he, maad° hym of a cake.°   *shield, made, loaf of bread*
WITH hym ther was a gentil Pardoner[7]   *noble*
670 Of Rouncivale,[8] his freend and his compeer,°   *companion*
That streight° was comen fro the court of Rome.   *straight*
Ful loude° he soong° "Com Hider, Love to Me."[9]   *loudly, sang*
This Somonour bar to hym a stif burdoun.[10]

---

1   "To pull a finch" was an expression that meant, "pluck a bird" literally; figuratively it meant "cheat a person," although it also had sexual connotations.

2   "In such a case of the excommunication (curse) of the archdeacon." An archdeacon was the ecclesiastical official in charge of a diocese's ecclesiastical court.

3   This Latin word means "It signified," and it is the first word in a writ authorizing the civil court to imprison someone who had been excommunicated.

4   In Middle English "girls" can mean young people of both sexes, but here may just mean young women.

5   "Was all their advice" is an idiom meaning that the Summoner was in their confidence.

6   A long pole hung with a garland that stuck out into the street and showed that ale was being sold on the premises.

7   A pardoner sold indulgences, which were writs authorized by the Church to raise money for charitable causes. Indulgences usually promised reduction of time in penance and, after death, in Purgatory.

8   The Pardoner belongs to the Hospital of the Blessed Mary of Roncesvalles in London, a dependent house of the larger one at Roncesvalles, the mountain pass between Spain and France which many pilgrims used when they traveled to St. James of Compostella. Hospitals in the Middle Ages were not purely medical facilities; they also served as inns and poor houses.

9   This song, "Come Here Love to Me," does not survive.

10   "The Summoner accompanied him with a strong bass." In medieval carols, each sung verse was

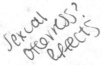
Sexual overtones? effects?

Was nevere trompe° of half so greet° a soun!°	trumpet, loud, sound
675 This Pardoner hadde heer° as yelow as wex,°	hair, wax
But smothe it heeng° as dooth a strike° of flex.°	hung, bunch, flax
By ounces° henge° hise lokkes° that he hadde,	strands, hung, locks
And therwith he hise shuldres° overspradde.°	shoulders, spread over
But thynne° it lay by colpons° oon° and oon.	thin, strands, one
680 But hood for jolitee° wered° he noon,	fun, wore
For it was trussed° up in his walet.°	packed, bag
Hym thoughte° he rood al of the newe jet.°	seemed to him, fashion
Dischevelee° save° his cappe° he rood° al bare.	disheveled, except, cap, rode
Swiche° glarynge° eyen° hadde he as an hare.¹	such, bulging, eyes
685 A vernycle² hadde he sowed° upon his cappe.	sewn
His walet° biforn° hym in his lappe,°	wallet, before, lap
Bretful° of pardoun, comen from Rome al hoot.°	brimful, hot
A voys° he hadde as smal° as hath a goot.°	voice, high-pitched, goat
No berd hadde he, ne never sholde° have:	nor ever would
690 As smothe° it was as° it were late [y]shave.°³	smooth, as if, shaven
I trowe° he were a geldyng° or a mare.⁴	believe, gelding
But of his craft fro° Berwyk into Ware⁵	from
Ne was ther swich° another pardoner.	there was not such
For in his male° he hadde a pilwe beer,°	bag, pillowcase
695 Which that he seyde was oure Lady veyl.°⁶	Virgin Mary's veil
He seyde he hadde a gobet° of the seyl°	piece, sail
That Seint Peter hadde when that he wente	
Upon the see° til Jhesu Crist hym hente.°⁷	sea, grabbed him
He hadde a croys° of latoun° ful of stones,	cross, brass
700 And in a glas° he hadde pigges bones.	glass
But with thise relikes whan that he fond	
A povre° person° dwellynge upon lond,	poor, parson
Upon a day he gat hym° moore moneye	got himself
Than that the person gat in monthes tweye.	
705 And thus with feyned° flaterye° and japes°	pretended, flattery, jokes

Fabulous hair
Woman? Gay?
Authority? devient. what does it say about church
relics (fraud)
selling "relics" to poor people
desire

---

separated by a "burden," a kind of refrain. Carols originally had many subjects, not just the joys of Christmas.

1 According to medieval lore, hares were hermaphroditic, becoming both male and female in order to reproduce. Bulging eyes were thought to be a sign of lust and folly.

2 A vernicle was a badge depicting Veronica's veil, a relic at Rome. St. Veronica pressed her veil against Jesus' face as he carried the cross, and by miracle his image was imprinted upon it. Pilgrims to Rome often came back with such badges.

3 The emendation is from Hengwrt.

4 "I believe he was either a gelding (a castrated horse) or a mare."

5 Berwick is in the extreme north of England near the border with Scotland; Ware is near London.

6 Chaucer's point is that the Pardoner carries fraudulent relics (sacred objects associated with Jesus or the saints) to help him in his money-making activities.

7 The reference is to Peter's unsuccessful attempt to imitate Christ by walking on the water. Christ had to rescue him. See Matthew 14:22–33.

He made the person and the peple his apes.°   *dupes*
But trewely, to tellen atte laste,
He was in chirche a noble ecclesiaste.°   *churchman*
Wel koude he rede a lessoun° or a storie.°   *lesson, story (from the Bible)*
710 But alderbest° he song° an offertorie,[1]   *best of all, sang*
For wel he wiste° whan that song was songe,   *knew*
He moste preche° and wel affile° his tonge°   *must preach, file, tongue*
To wynne° silver as he ful wel koude.   *acquire*
Therfore he song° the murierly° and loude.   *sang, more merrily*
715 Now have I toold yow shortly° in a clause   *briefly*
Th'estaat,° th'array,° the nombre, and eek the cause *social position, appearance*
Why that assembled was this compaignye
In Southwerk at° this gentil hostelry°   *MS as, noble inn*
That highte° the Tabard, faste by the Belle.[2]   *was named*
720 But now is tyme° to yow° for to telle   *time, you*
How that we baren° us that ilke° nyght   *behaved, same*
Whan we were in that hostelrie alyght.°   *arrived*
And after wol I tell of oure viage°   *journey*
And al the remenaunt of oure pilgrimage.
725 But first I pray yow of youre curteisye°   *courtesy*
That ye n'arette it nat my vileynye,[3]
Thogh that I pleynly° speke in this mateere   *plainly*
To telle yow hir wordes and hir cheere,°   *comportment*
Ne thogh I speke hir wordes proprely.°   *exactly*
730 For this ye knowen also wel as I:
Whoso shal telle a tale after a man,
He moot° reherce as ny° as ever he kan   *should, closely*
Everich a word° if it be in his charge,°   *every word, power*
Al° speke he never so rudeliche° or large,°   *although, crudely, freely*
735 Or ellis° he moot° telle his tale untrewe°   *else, must, falsely*
Or feyne° thyng or fynde wordes newe.   *falsify*
He may nat spare althogh he were his brother;
He moot as wel seye o word as another.
Crist spak hymself ful brode° in Hooly Writ,°   *freely, Holy Scripture*
740 And wel ye woot° no vileynye is it.   *know*
Eek Plato seith, whoso° kan hym rede,   *whoever*

---

1 The Offertory was chanted when the congregation was bringing gifts to the altar.
2 Previous editors have capitalized this word, guessing that it was the name of another inn—there
   were several called the Bell in that area—or perhaps a house of prostitution. Perhaps the word
   should not be capitalized, as it may imply a notable bell in the neighborhood.
3 "That you not attribute it to my lack of manners." "Vileynye" does not mean "villainy" in the
   modern sense. A "villein" was originally an inhabitant of a rural village; thus the word signifies
   the state of being rustic rather than civilized.

[handwritten: appologizing & defending his word → "degree"]

The wordes moote be cosyn° to the dede.°[1]   cousin, deed
Also I prey yow to foryeve° it me   forgive
Al° have I nat° set folk in hir degree°   although, not, rank
745 Heere in this tale as that they sholde stonde.
My wit° is short, ye may wel understonde.   intelligence

[handwritten: Is he making fun of rank/degree]

GREET chiere° made oure Hoost us everichon,°   cheer, everyone
And to the soper sette he us anon.
He served us with vitaille° at the beste.   food
750 Strong was the wyn, and wel to drynke us leste.°   it pleased us
A semely° man oure Hoost was withalle   suitable
For to been a marchal° in an halle.°[2]   marshal, hall
A large man he was, with eyen° stepe.°   eyes, bright
A fairer burgeys° was ther noon in Chepe,°[3]   citizen
755 Boold of his speche and wys and wel ytaught,°   learned
And of manhod hym lakked° right naught.°   lacked, nothing
Eek therto he was right a myrie man,

[handwritten: happy/marry Host]

And after soper pleyen° he bigan°   play, began
And spak of myrthe amonges othere thynges
760 Whan that we hadde maad oure rekenynges[4]
And seyde thus, "Now lordynges trewely,
Ye been° to me right welcome hertely.°   are, heartily
For by my trouthe, if that I shal nat lye,
I saugh nat this yeer so myrie a compaignye
765 Atones° in this herberwe° as is now.   at once, inn
Fayn° wolde I doon yow myrthe, wiste° I how.   gladly, knew
And of a myrthe I am right now bythoght°   in mind
To doon yow ese.° And it shal coste noght.°   do you ease, nothing
YE goon to Caunterbury. God yow speede!°   God bring you success!
770 The blissful martir° quite yow youre neede!°   martyr, reward
And wel I woot° as ye goon° by the weye,   know, go
Ye shapen yow° to talen° and to pleye.°   intend, tell tales, play

[handwritten: Host speaking]

For trewely,° confort° ne myrthe is noon   truly, comfort
To ride by the weye doumb as the stoon.°[5]
775 And therfore wol I maken yow disport,°   entertainment
As I seyde erst,° and doon yow som confort.°   first, bring you some comfort

---

1 The reference is to Plato's *Timaeus*, the only one of his dialogues available in translation to the Latin West in the Middle Ages. The quotation is found in section 29. The passage is also discussed by Boethius in his *Consolation of Philosophy* (3, prose 12), a work that Chaucer had translated and drew upon frequently.
2 A marshal is a steward or chief butler; a hall is a manor house or town house of a lord.
3 Cheapside was the merchants' district in London.
4 "When we had paid our bills."
5 "For truly there is neither comfort nor mirth/in riding along as silent as a stone."

And if yow liketh° alle by oon assent°   *pleases you, unanimously*
For to stonden at° my juggement°   *abide by, judgment*
And for to werken° as I shal yow seye,   *proceed*
780 Tomorwe, whan ye riden by the weye,
Now by my fader soule° that is deed,°   *father's soul, dead*
But if ye be myrie, I wol yeve° yow myn heed!°   *give, my head*
HOOLD up youre hondes° withouten moore speche."   *MS honde*
Oure conseil° was nat° longe for to seche.°   *counsel, not, seek*
785 Us thoughte° it was noght worth to make it wys°[1] *seemed to us, wise*
And graunted hym withouten° moore avys°   *MS witouten, more debate*
And bad° hym seye his voirdit° as hym leste.°   *asked, verdict, as he wanted*
"LORDYNGES," quod he, "now herkneth for the beste,
But taak it nought, I prey° yow, in desdeyn.°   *beg, disdain*
790 This is the poynt, to speken short and pleyn,
That ech of yow to shorte° with oure weye   *shorten*
In this viage° shal telle tales tweye°.   *journey, two*
To Caunterburyward,° I mene° it so,   *towards Canterbury, mean*
And homward he shal tellen othere two
795 Of aventures that whilom° han bifalle°   *once, have happened*
And which of yow that bereth hym° best of alle,   *conducts himself*
That is to seyn, that telleth in this caas°   *occasion*
Tales of best sentence° and moost solaas,°   *meaning, enjoyment*
Shal have a soper° at oure aller° cost°   *supper, of us all, cost*
800 Heere in this place, sittynge by this post,
Whan that we come agayn fro° Caunterbury.—   *from*
As for to make yow the moore mury,°   *merry*
I wol myself goodly° with yow ryde,   *gladly*
Right at myn owene cost, and be youre gyde.
805 And whoso wole my juggement withseye°   *resist*
Shal paye al that we spenden by the weye.°   *along the way*
And if ye vouchesauf° that it be so,   *grant*
Tel me anon withouten wordes mo,
And I wol erly° shape me° therfore."°   *early, get ready, for it*
810 THIS thyng was graunted and oure othes° swore° *oaths, sworn*
With ful glad herte and preyden° hym also   *asked*
That he wolde vouchesauf° for to do so   *would agree*
And that he wolde been oure governour
And of oure tales juge° and reportour°   *judge, referee*
815 And sette a soper at a certeyn pris°   *certain price*
And we wol reuled been at his devys°   *at his wish*
IN heigh and lough.° And thus by oon° assent   *all matters, one*

Handwritten margin notes: "Who Judges Stories? Host"; "contest held by host"; "What wins? best meaning and entertaining"

---

1   This idiom means approximately "make a big deal of it."

We been acorded° to his juggement.   *agreed*
And therupon the wyn was fet° anon.°   *fetched, immediately*
820 We dronken and to reste wente echon°   *each one*
Withouten any lenger taryynge.°   *longer delaying*
Amorwe,° whan that day gan° for to sprynge,°   *the next day, began, dawn*
Up roos° oure Hoost and was oure aller cok°   *rose, rooster for us all*
And gadrede° us togidre° all in a flok.°   *gathered, together, flock*
825 And forth we ridden,° a° litel moore than paas,°   *rode, at a, a horse's walking pace*
Unto the Wateryng of Seint Thomas.[1]
And there oure Hoost bigan his hors areste°   *rein in*
And seyde, "Lordynges, herkneth if yow leste!°   *please*
YE woot youre foreward° and it yow recorde,°   *contract, recall*
830 If evensong and morwesong accorde,[2]
Lat se° now who shal telle the firste tale.   *Let us see*
As evere mote° I drynke wyn or ale,   *might*
Whoso be rebel to my juggement
Shal paye for al that by the wey° is spent.   *along the way*
835 Now draweth cut er that we ferrer twynne.[3]
He which that hath the shorteste shal bigynne.
Sire Knyght," quod he, "my mayster and my lord,
Now draweth cut,° for that is myn accord.°   *draw a straw, my decision*
Cometh neer,"° quod he, "my lady Prioresse   *near*
840 And ye, sire Clerk, lat be youre shamefastnesse.°   *shyness*
Ne studieth noght.° Ley° hond° to every man."   *stop studying, lay, hand*
Anon to drawen every wight° bigan,   *person*
And shortly for to tellen as it was,
Were it by aventure or sort or cas,[4]
845 The sothe° is this: the cut° fil° to the Knyght,   *truth, straw, fell*
Of which ful blithe° and glad was every wyght.   *very happy*
And° telle he moste his tale as was resoun,°   *MS A, reasonable*
By foreward° and by composicioun,°   *contract, agreement*
As ye han herd. What nedeth wordes mo?
850 And° whan this goode man saugh° that it was so,   *MS An, saw*
As he that wys was and obedient
To kepe his foreward° by his free assent,   *contract*
He seyde, "Syn° I shal bigynne the game,   *since*

---

1 The Watering of St. Thomas was the name given to a brook just outside London on the way to
   Canterbury.
2 That is, "if you will fulfill now what you agreed to do last night." Evensong and Matins (morn-
   ing prayer) are two services in the monastic Daily Office, held respectively, of course, in the
   evening and in the morning.
3 "Now draw a straw before we depart further."
4 "Adventure," "sort," and "case" mean roughly the same: "chance."

What, welcome be the cut, a Goddes° name!   *in God's*
855 Now lat us ryde and herkneth what I seye."
And with that word we ryden forth oure weye.
And he bigan with right a myrie cheere°   *cheerful expression*
His tale anon and seyde in this manere:[1]

---

1   Hengwrt and some other manuscripts read "and seyde as ye may heere," not "and seyde in this manere," a suggestion that *The Canterbury Tales* were to be read aloud as well as silently.

THE KNIGHT'S TALE

Opening page of *The Knight's Tale*. Ellesmere Manuscript EL 26 C9 f. 10r. Reprinted by permission of The Huntington Library.

THE KNIGHT'S TALE

Iamque domos patrias, Scithice post aspera gentis Prelia, laurigero[1]

HEERE BIGYNNETH THE KNYGHTES TALE

WHILOM,° as olde stories tellen us,	*once*
860 Ther was a duc° that highte° Theseus.	*duke, was named*
Of Atthenes° he was lord and governour,	*Athens*
And in his tyme swich° a conquerour	*such*
That gretter° was ther noon under the sonne.	*greater*
Ful many a riche contree hadde he wonne,°	*won*
865 What with his wysdom and his chivalrie.°	*knightly prowess*
He conquered al the regne of Femenye°	*land of the Amazons*
That whilom was ycleped° Scithia[2]	*called*
And wedded the queene Ypolita°	*Hippolita*
And broghte hire hoom° with hym in his contree	*home*
870 With muchel° glorie and greet solempnytee°	*much, great ceremony*
And eek° hir faire suster Emelye.°	*also, Emily*
And thus with victorie and with melodye	
Lete° I this noble duc to Atthenes ryde	*let*
And al his hoost° in armes hym bisyde.°	*host, beside him*
875 AND certes,° if it nere to long to heere,°	*certainly, were not too long to hear*
I wolde° yow have toold fully the manere°	*would, manner*
How wonnen° was the regne of Femenye	*won*
By Theseus and by his chivalrye°	*knights*
And of the grete bataille° for the nones°	*great battle, for that occasion*
880 Bitwixen° Atthenes and Amazones	*between*
And how asseged° was Ypolita,	*besieged*
The faire, hardy queene of Scithia	
And of the feste° that was at hir weddynge	*feast*
And of the tempest at hir hoomcomynge.°	*homecoming*
885 But al that thyng I moot° as now forbere.°	*must, for the moment resist [telling]*
I have, God woot,° a large feeld to ere,°	*God knows, plow*
And wayke° been° the oxen in my plough.	*weak, are*

endorsed by chaucer.

---

1   The Latin poet Statius (40–c. 96 AD) wrote an epic poem about the Theban war, the *Thebaid*, which was one of Chaucer's sources for the Knight's Tale. This passage describes the triumphant return of Theseus at the very end of the poem: "And now Theseus, [drawing near] his native land in a chariot covered with laurels, after fierce battle with the Scythians [is heralded by glad applause and the shouts of the people to the heavens and the merry trumpet celebrating the end of the war.]"

2   Scythia was an ancient country in the Caucasus region, inhabited by nomads, and was believed to be the homeland of the Amazons (i.e., women warriors).

The remenant of the tale is long ynough:°   *enough*
I wol nat letten° eek noon° of this route.°   *hinder, none, company*
890 Lat° every felawe° telle his tale aboute!°   *let, fellow, in turn*
And lat se° now, who shal the soper wynne.   *let us see*
And ther° I lefte I wol ayeyn° bigynne.[1]   *where, again*
THIS duc of whom I make mencioun,
Whan he was come almoost unto the toun
895 In al his wele° and in his mooste pride,°   *prosperity, great pride*
He was war° as he caste his eye aside   *aware*
Where that ther° kneled° in the weye°   *there, kneeled, road*
A compaignye of ladyes tweye and tweye,°   *two by two*
Ech after oother clad in clothes blake.
900 But swich a cry and swich a wo° they make,   *woe*
That in this world nys° creature lyvynge   *is no*
That herde° swich another waymentynge.°   *heard, sorrowing*
And of this cry they nolde° nevere stenten°   *would not, cease*
Til they the reynes of his brydel henten.°   *grasped*
905 "WHAT folk been° ye,° that at myn° homcomynge   *are, you, my*
Perturben° so my feste° with criynge,"   *disturb, feast*
Quod° Theseus. "Have ye so greet envye°   *said, envy*
Of myn honour that thus compleyne and crye?
Or who hath yow mysboden° or offended?   *harmed*
910 And telleth me if it may been amended
And why that ye been clothed thus in blak."
THE eldeste lady of hem° alle spak°   *them, spoke*
Whan she hadde swowned° with a deedly° cheere°   *fainted, deathly, face*
That it was routhe° for to seen° and heere,°   *pity, see, hear*
915 And seyde, "Lord to whom fortune hath yeven°   *given*
Victorie and as a conquerour to lyven,°   *live*
Nat greveth us° youre glorie and youre honour,   *We are not grieved by*
But we biseken° mercy and socour.°   *ask, help*
Have mercy on oure wo° and oure distresse!   *woe*
920 Som drope of pitee thurgh° thy gentillesse°   *through, nobility*
Upon us wrecched wommen lat thou falle.
For certes,° lord, ther is noon of us alle   *certainly*
That she ne hath been a duchesse or a queene.
Now be we caytyves,° as it is wel seene,   *miserable people*
925 Thanked be Fortune and hire false wheel,[2]

---

1   There is a Latin gloss in the margin "Narrat" ("he tells"), indicating the Knight has resumed his story.
2   The Wheel of Fortune first made its appearance in Boethius's *Consolation of Philosophy*, a work Chaucer translated into English. The goddess Fortune turns her Wheel, and those on the top in prosperity fall miserable to the bottom.

That noon estaat assureth to be weel!°   assures no estate prospers
And certes, lord, to abyden° youre presence,   await
Heere in the temple of the goddesse Clemence°   Clemency (mercy)
We han° been waitynge al this fourtenyght.°   have, two-week period
930 Now help us, lord, sith° it is in thy myght.   since
I, WRECCHE° which that wepe° and crie thus,   wretched one, weep
Was whilom° wyf to Kyng Cappaneus[1]   once
That starf° at Thebes, cursed be that day!   died
And alle we that been° in this array°   who are, condition
935 And maken al this lamentacioun,
We losten alle oure housbondes at that toun
Whil° that the seege° theraboute lay.   while, siege
And yet now the olde Creon,[2] weylaway,°   alas
That lord is now of Thebes the citee,
940 Fulfild of ire° and of iniquitee,°   filled with anger, wickedness
He for despit° and for his tirannye   spite
To do the dede bodyes vileynye°   villainy or disgrace
Of alle oure lordes whiche that been slawe,°   killed
He hath alle the bodyes on an heepe° ydrawe°   heap, gathered together
945 And wol nat suffren hem by noon assent°   permit them on any terms
Neither to been yburyed° nor ybrent,°   buried, burned (cremated)
But maketh houndes° ete° hem° in despit!"°   dogs, eat, them, spite
And with that word, withouten moore respit,°   delay
They fillen gruf° and criden° pitously,   fell groveling, cried
950 "Have on us wrecched wommen som mercy,
And lat oure sorwe synken° in thyn herte!"   sink
THIS gentil° duc doun from his courser° sterte°   noble, horse, jumped
With herte pitous° whan he herde hem speke.   pitying
Hym thoughte° that his herte wolde° breke.   He thought, would
955 Whan he saugh° hem so pitous° and so maat,°   saw, pitiful, downcast
That whilom° weren° of so greet estaat.   once, were
And in his armes he hem alle up hente°   took
And hem conforteth in ful good entente°   with good will
And swoor his ooth as he was trewe knyght
960 He wolde doon° so ferforthly° his myght   would do, completely
Upon the tiraunt° Creon hem° to wreke°   tyrant, them, avenge
That al the peple of Grece sholde speke
How Creon was of Theseus yserved°   dealt with
As he that hadde his deeth ful wel deserved.
965 And right anoon° withouten moore abood,°   immediately, delay

---

1 King Cappaneus was one of seven leaders who attacked and besieged Thebes.
2 Creon was the king of Thebes and brother of Jocasta, mother of Oedipus.

His baner° he desplayeth and forth rood°   *banner, rode*
To Thebesward° and al his hoost° biside.   *towards Thebes, army*
No neer° Atthenes° wolde he go ne° ride   *No nearer, Athens, nor*
Ne° take his ese° fully half a day,   *nor, rest*
970 But onward on his wey° that nyght he lay   *way*
And sente anon° Ypolita the queene   *immediately*
And Emelye hir yonge° suster° sheene°   *young, sister, bright*
Unto the toun of Atthenes to dwelle.
And forth he rit;° ther is namoore to telle.   *rides*
975 THE rede° statue of Mars with spere° and targe°   *red, spear, shield*
So shyneth in his white baner large
That alle the feeldes glyteren° up and doun.   *glitter*
And by his baner born is his penoun°   *is carried his pennant (a narrow flag)*
Of gold ful° riche, in which ther was ybete°   *very, embroidered*
980 The Mynotaur[1] which that he slough° in Crete.   *killed*
THUS rit° this duc.° Thus rit this conquerour,   *rides, duke*
And in his hoost° of chivalrie the flour,°   *army, flower of chivalry*
Til that he cam to Thebes and alighte°   *dismounted*
Faire in a feeld theras° he thoughte fighte.   *where*
985 But shortly for to speken of this thyng,
With Creon, which° that was of Thebes kyng,   *who*
He faught and slough hym° manly as a knyght°   *killed him, in a manly way*
In pleyn bataille° and putte the folk to flyght.   *open battle*
And by assaut° he wan° the citee° after   *assault, captured, city*
990 And rente adoun° bothe wall and sparre° and rafter.   *pulled down, beam*
And to the ladyes he restored agayn
The bones of hir° housbondes that weren slayn   *their*
To doon obsequies° as was tho the gyse.°   *funeral rites, then the custom*
But it were al to° longe for to devyse°   *too, narrate*
995 The grete° clamour° and the waymentynge°   *great, noise, lamentation*
That the ladyes made at the brennynge°   *cremation*
Of the bodies and the grete° honour   *great*
That Theseus the noble conquerour
Dooth° to the ladyes whan they from hym wente,   *does*
1000 But shortly for to telle is myn entente.°   *intent*
WHAN that this worthy duc, this Theseus
Hath Creon slayn and wonne Thebes thus,
Stille° in that feeld he took al nyght his reste   *quietly*

---

1 An earlier adventure of Theseus's is his killing of the Minotaur, a half-bull, half-human mon-
ster, who was kept in the labyrinth on the island of Crete and there given Athenian youths to
devour for food. The Cretan King Minos's daughter Ariadne helped Theseus in this feat by
giving him a ball of thread to roll out behind him so he could find his way out of the labyrinth
once his deed was accomplished.

And dide with al the contree as hym leste.° | *as he desired*
1005 To ransake° in the taas° of the bodyes dede | *search, pile*
Hem for to strepe° of harneys° and of wede° | *strip, armor, clothes*
The pilours° diden bisynesse and cure[1] | *scavengers*
After the bataille and disconfiture.° | *defeat*
And so bifel° that in the taas they founde | *befell*
1010 Thrugh girt° with many a grevous,° blody° wounde | *pierced, grievous, bloody*
Two yonge knyghtes liggynge° by and by,° | *lying, side by side*
Bothe in oon armes wroght ful richely,[2]
Of whiche two Arcita highte° that oon | *was named*
And that oother knyght highte Palamon.
1015 Nat° fully quyke° ne° fully dede° they were, | *not, alive, nor, dead*
But by hir cote-armures° and by hir gere° | *coat of arms, equipment*
The heraudes° knewe hem best in special° | *heralds, particularly*
As they that weren° of the blood roial° | *were, royal*
Of Thebes and of sustren° two yborn.° | *sisters, born*
1020 Out of the taas the pilours han hem torn° | *had pulled them*
And han° hem caried softe° unto the tente | *had, softly*
Of Theseus. And ful° soone he hem sente | *very*
To Atthenes to dwellen in prisoun
Perpetuelly. He nolde no° raunsoun.[3] | *would not take any*
1025 And whan this worthy duc hath thus ydon,° | *done*
He took his hoost° and hoom he rood anon° | *army, immediately*
With laurer° crowned as a conquerour. | *laurel*
And ther he lyveth in joye and in honour
Terme of [his] lyve.° What nedeth wordes mo? | *for the rest of his life*
1030 And in a tour° in angwissh° and in wo | *tower, anguish*
This Palamon and his felawe° Arcite | *companion*
For everemoore ther° may no gold hem quite.° | *where, buy them back*
THIS passeth yeer by yeer and day by day,
Til it fil° ones° in a morwe° of May | *fell, once, morning*
1035 That Emelye, that fairer was to sene° | *see*
Than is the lylie° upon his stalke grene | *lily*
And fressher than the May with floures newe,
For with the rose colour stroof° hire hewe. | *competed*
I noot° which was the fyner° of hem two! | *do not know, finer*
1040 Er° it were day, as was hir° wone° to do, | *before, her, custom*

---

1   "Did business and care" is an expression that roughly means they worked hard.
2   "Both in one [coat of arms] fashioned very richly." As members of the same family, Palamon and Arcite have the same heraldic markings on a light cloth jacket worn over their armor.
3   In the fourteenth century, the custom was to try to capture enemy soldiers in battle rather than kill them, for ransoming was profitable. Although the tale is ostensibly set in classical antiquity, the descriptions of warfare and the social customs are based on those of Chaucer's own day.

She was arisen and al redy dight.°   *dressed up*
For May wol have no slogardrie° anyght.°   *laziness, at night*
The sesoun° priketh° every gentil° herte°   *season, incites, noble, heart*
And maketh hym° out of his slep to sterte°   *him, jump*
1045 And seith,° "Arys and do thyn observaunce!"°   *says, pay your respects*
This maked Emelye have remembraunce
To doon honour to May and for to ryse.
Yclothed was she fressh for to devyse.°   *describe*
Hir yelow heer° was broyded° in a tresse°   *hair, braided, plait*
1050 Bihynde hir bak, a yerde° long, I gesse.°   *yard, guess*
And in the gardyn at the sonne upriste°   *at sunrise*
She walketh up and doun, and as hire liste°   *as she desired*
She gadereth° floures,° party° white and rede,   *gathers, flowers, partly*
To make a subtil° gerland for hire hede.   *intricate*
1055 And as an aungel hevenysshly° she soong.   *heavenly*
The grete tour that was so thikke and stroong
Which of the castel was the chief dongeoun,[1]
Theras° the knyghtes weren in prisoun,   *where*
Of whiche I tolde yow and tellen shal,
1060 Was evene joynaunt° to the gardyn wal   *next to*
Theras° this Emelye hadde hir pleyynge.°   *where, enjoyment*
Bright was the sonne and cleer that morwenynge.
And this Palamoun, this woful prisoner,
As was his wone° by leve° of his gayler°   *custom, leave, jailor*
1065 Was risen and romed° in a chambre° an heigh°   *roamed, room, on high*
In which he al the noble citee seigh°   *saw*
And eek the gardyn ful of braunches grene,
Theras this fresshe Emelye the shene°   *bright*
Was in hir walk and romed up and doun.
1070 This sorweful prisoner, this Palamoun,
Goth in the chambre romynge° to and fro,   *roaming*
And to hymself compleynynge of his wo,
That he was born. Ful ofte° he seyde, "Allas!"   *very often*
And so bifel by aventure or cas°   *it happened by chance or accident*
1075 That thurgh a wyndow thikke of many a barre°   *thickly set with bars*
Of iren° greet° and square as any sparre,°   *iron, great, beam*
He caste his eye upon Emelya.
And therwithal° he bleynte° and cride, "A!"   *with that, went pale*
As though he stongen° were unto the herte.   *stung*

---

1 In the Middle Ages the term "dungeon" primarily meant a tower, often part of a castle. Dungeons were sometimes indeed used as prisons, as is the case here, but they had other functions as well, both domestic and military. The word here does not imply a dark or subterranean cell.

1080 And with that cry Arcite anon° up sterte°   *immediately, rose*
     And seyde, "Cosyn° myn, what eyleth° thee   *cousin, ails*
     That art so pale and deedly° on to see?   *deathly*
     Why cridestow?° Who hath thee doon° offence?   *did you cry, done*
     For Goddes love, taak° al° in pacience   *take, all*
1085 Oure prisoun, for it may noon oother be.°   *may not be otherwise*
     Fortune hath yeven° us this adversitee.   *given*
     Som wikke° aspect or disposicioun   *wicked*
     Of Saturne by som constellacioun
     Hath yeven us this, although we hadde it sworn.
1090 So stood the hevene whan that we were born.[1]
     We moste endure. This is the short and playn."°   *simple truth*
     THIS Palamon answerde and seyde° agayn,°   *said, in reply*
     "Cosyn,° forsothe° of this opinioun   *cousin, in truth*
     Thow hast a veyn° ymaginacioun.°   *foolish, misconception*
1095 THIS prison caused me nat° for to crye.   *not*
     But I was hurt right now thurghout myn eye
     Into myn herte. That wol my bane° be.   *death blow*
     The fairnesse of that lady that I see
     Yond° in the gardyn romen° to and fro   *yonder, roaming*
1100 Is cause of al my cryng and my wo.
     I noot where° she be woman or goddesse,   *do not know whether*
     But Venus[2] is it, soothly° as I gesse!"°   *truly, guess*
     And therwithal on knees doun° he fil   *down*
     And seyde, "Venus, if it be thy wil,
1105 Yow in this gardyn thus to transfigure°   *change shape or take human form*
     Bifore me, sorweful wrecche° creature,   *wretched*
     Out of this prisoun helpe that we may scapen.°   *escape*
     And if so be my destynee be shapen°   *predetermined*
     By eterne° word to dyen° in prisoun,   *eternal, die*
1110 Of oure lynage° have som° compassioun   *lineage, some*
     That is so lowe ybroght° by tirannye."   *brought low*
     And with that word Arcite gan espye°   *began to see*
     Wheras° this lady romed to and fro.   *where*
     And with that sighte hir beautee hurte hym so,
1115 That if that Palamon was° wounded soore,   *MS omits was*
     Arcite is hurt as muche as he or moore.
     And with a sigh he seyde pitously,

---

1 "Some evil aspect or alignment/of Saturn with some other constellation/has given us this fate,
   [which we must endure] although we had sworn [to do otherwise]./The stars were arranged
   that way when we were born." In Roman mythology, Saturn was the god of time and old age.
   Saturn describes his destructive influence in detail at lines 2454–69.
2 In Roman mythology, Venus was the goddess of love, reproduction, and peace.

"The fresshe beautee sleeth° me sodeynly°   *kills, suddenly*
Of hire° that rometh in the yonder place,   *her*
1120 And but° I have hir mercy and hir grace,   *unless*
That I may seen hire atte leeste° weye,   *at least*
I nam but deed!° Ther is namoore° to seye."   *I am as good as dead, no more*
THIS Palamon, whan he tho° wordes herde,   *those*
Dispitously° he looked and answerde,   *angrily*
1125 "Wheither seistow° this in ernest° or in pley?"°   *do you say, seriously, jest*
"NAY," quod° Arcite, "in ernest, by my fey!°   *said, faith*
God helpe me so, me list ful yvele pleye!"[1]
THIS Palamon gan° knytte° his browes tweye.°   *began, knit, two*
"It nere,"° quod he, "to thee no greet honour   *were not*
1130 For to be fals ne° for to be traitour   *nor*
To me that am thy cosyn and thy brother
Ysworn° ful depe° and ech of° us til oother   *sworn, very deep, each to*
That nevere for to dyen in the peyne[2]
Til that deeth departe shal us tweyne,°   *two*
1135 Neither of us in love to hyndre° oother   *hinder*
Ne° in noon oother cas,° my leeve° brother,   *Nor, chance, beloved*
But that thou sholdest trewely° forthren° me   *truly, help*
In every cas as I shal forthren thee.
This was thyn ooth and myn also, certeyn,
1140 I woot° right wel, thou darst° it nat° withseyn.°   *know, dare, not, deny*
Thus artow° of my conseil° out of doute,°   *are you, counsel, doubtless*
And now thow woldest° falsly been aboute°   *would, set about*
To love my lady, whom I love and serve
And evere shal, til that myn herte° sterve.°   *heart, dies*
1145 Nay, certes,° false Arcite, thow shalt nat so.   *certainly*
I loved hire first and tolde thee my wo
As to my conseil° and to my brother sworn   *my counselor*
To forthre° me as I have toold biforn,°   *help, before*
For which thou art ybounden° as a knyght   *obligated*
1150 To helpen me if it lay in thy might,
Or elles artow fals,° I dar° wel seyn."°   *you are false, dare, say*
THIS Arcite ful proudly spak ageyn.
"Thow shalt," quod° he, "be rather fals than I.   *said*
And thou art fals, I telle thee outrely,°   *completely*
1155 For paramour° I loved hire first er thow.°   *as a lover, before you*
What wiltow seyn,° thou wistest nat° yet now   *will you say, know not*
Wheither she be a womman or goddesse.
Thyn is affeccioun of hoolynesse,°   *feeling of religious devotion*

---

1   "I desire to play very little."
2   "Even if we were to die by torture."

And myn is love, as to a creature,°   *human being*
1160 For which I tolde thee myn aventure°   *experience*
And as to my cosyn and my brother sworn.
I pose° that thow lovedest hire biforn.   *suppose*
Wostow nat wel the olde clerkes sawe[1]
That 'Who shal yeve° a lovere any lawe?'°[2]   *give, law*
1165 Love is a gretter° lawe, by my pan,°   *greater, skull*
Than may be yeve° of any erthely man.   *given*
And therfore positif lawe°[3] and swich° decree   *positive law, such*
Is broken alday,° for love in ech degree.°   *daily, each social rank*
A man moot nedes° love, maugree his heed.°   *must needs, despite his intentions*
1170 He may nat flee it thogh he sholde be deed,°   *dead*
Al be she° mayde or wydwe° or elles° wyf.   *even if she is, widow, else*
And eek, it is nat likly al thy lyf
To stonden in hir grace.° Namoore° shal I.   *have her favor, no more*
For wel thou woost° thyselven° verraily,°   *know, yourself, truly*
1175 That thou and I be dampned° to prisoun   *condemned*
Perpetuelly. Us gayneth no raunsoun.°   *no ransom will free us*
We stryven° as dide the houndes for the boon.°   *quarrel, bone*
They foughte al day, and yet hir° part was noon.   *their*
Ther cam a kyte° whil they weren so wrothe°   *kite (bird), angry*
1180 And baar awey° the boon bitwixe hem° bothe.   *carried away, them*
And therfore at the kynges court, my brother,
Ech man for hymself. Ther is noon oother.
Love if thee list,° for I love and ay shal!°   *if you like, always shall*
And soothly,° leeve° brother, this is al.°   *truly, dear, all*
1185 Heere in this prisoun moote we endure°   *must remain*
And everich of us° take his aventure."   *each of us*
GREET was the strif and long bitwix hem tweye,°   *between the two of them*
If that I hadde leyser° for to seye.   *leisure*
But to th'effect:° It happed° on a day   *result, happened*
1190 To telle it yow as shortly as I may,
A worthy duc° that highte Perotheus,   *duke*
That felawe° was to Duc Theseus   *companion*
Syn° thilke° day that they were children lite.°   *since, the same, little*
Was come to Atthenes his felawe to visite
1195 And for to pley,° as he was won° to do.   *amuse himself, accustomed*
For in this world he loved no man so.
And he loved hym als° tendrely agayn.   *as*

---

1 "Do you not know well the old scholar's saying."
2 There is a Latin gloss in the margin, "Who might give a law to lovers."
3 "Positive law" is that written into the statute books, as opposed to "natural law," which is self-
   evident from God's creation.

So wel they lovede, as olde bookes sayn,
That whan that oon° was deed,° soothly° to telle,   *one, dead, truly*
1200 His felawe wente and soughte hym doun° in Helle!¹   *down*
But of that storie, list me nat° to write.   *I do not desire*
Duc Perotheus loved wel Arcite
And hadde hym knowe at Thebes yeer by yere.°   *year by year*
And finally at requeste and preyere
1205 Of Perotheus withouten any raunsoun,
Duc Thesuus hym leet out° of prisoun   *let him out*
Frely° to goon wher that hym liste° overal   *freely, to go where he wanted*
In swich a gyse° as I you tellen shal.   *such a manner*
THIS was the forward° pleynly for t'endite,°   *agreement, to write it plainly*
1210 Bitwixen Theseus and hym Arcite:
That if so were that Arcite were yfounde°   *found*
Evere in his lif by day or nyght or stounde°   *hour*
In any contree of this Theseus
And he were caught, it was acorded° thus: *agreed*
1215 That with a swerd he sholde lese° his heed.°   *lose, head*
Ther nas noon oother° remedie ne reed,°   *was no other, counsel*
But taketh his leve° and homward he him spedde.   *leave*
Lat hym bewar!° His nekke° lith to wedde!°   *beware, neck, lies as a pledge*
HOW greet a sorwe suffreth now Arcite.
1220 The deeth he feeleth thurgh his herte smyte.°   *strike*
He wepeth, wayleth, crieth pitously.
To sleen° hymself he waiteth prively.°   *kill, waits for an opportunity secretly*
He seyde, "Allas that day" that he "was born!²
Now is my prisoun worse than biforn!
1225 Now is me shape° eternally to dwelle   *it is ordained for me*
Nat in my Purgatorie but in Helle.
Allas, that evere knew I Perotheus,
For elles hadde I dwelled with Theseus
Yfetered° in his prisoun everemo!°   *chained, evermore*
1230 Thanne hadde I been in blisse and nat in wo.
Oonly the sighte of hire whom that I serve,
Though that I nevere hir grace may deserve,

---

1   The classical legend is that Theseus accompanied Pirithous (Chaucer's "Perotheus") to the Underworld in his unsuccessful attempt to rescue Proserpina, who had been abducted by Pluto, king of that region. Both men eventually returned alive, although Theseus was imprisoned and rescued by Hercules. The suggestion that Theseus went down to rescue Pirithous because he had died probably comes from the long thirteenth-century medieval allegory *The Romance of the Rose* (lines 8186 ff.), which Chaucer translated from French.

2   Many editions prefer the reading, found in several other manuscripts, "Allas the day that I was born." The Ellesmere variant (which we have preserved, although it may indeed be an error) would originally have been less awkward, since the quotation marks are a modern addition.

Wolde han° suffised right ynough° for me.   *would have, enough*
O deere cosyn Palamon," quod he,
1235 "Thyn is the victorie of this aventure.
Ful blissfully in prisoun maistow dure.°   *may you remain*
In prisoun certes,° nay° but in Paradys!   *certainly, no*
Wel° hath Fortune yturned° thee the dys°   *well, turned, dice*
That hast the sighte of hire and I th'absence.
1240 For possible is syn° thou hast hire presence   *since*
And art a knyght, a worthy and an able,
That som cas,° syn Fortune is chaungeable,   *event*
Thow maist to thy desir somtyme atteyne.°   *attain*
But I that am exiled and bareyne°   *lacking*
1245 Of alle grace and in so greet dispeir
That ther nys° erthe, water, fir, ne eir,°   *is not, nor air*
Ne° creature that of hem° maked° is   *nor, them, made*
That may me heele° or doon confort° in this.   *heal, bring comfort*
Wel oughte I sterve° in wanhope° and distresse.   *die, despair*
1250 Farwel my lif,° my lust,° and my gladnesse!   *life, desire*
ALLAS, why pleynen° folk so in commune°   *complain, commonly*
On° purveiaunce° of God or of Fortune   *against, foresight*
That yeveth hem° ful ofte in many a gyse°   *gives them, way*
Wel bettre than they kan hemself° devyse?   *themselves*
1255 Som man desireth for to han° richesse   *have*
That cause is of his moerdre° or greet siknesse.   *murder*
And som man wolde out of his prisoun fayn°   *would gladly [get]*
That in his hous is of his meynee° slayn.°   *his [own] retinue, slain*
Infinite harmes been in this mateere.°   *matter*
1260 We witen nat° what we preyen heere.°   *know not, pray for*
We faren° as he that dronke° is as a mous.°   *behave, drunken, mouse*
A dronke man woot° wel that he hath an hous,°   *knows, house*
But he noot° which the righte wey° is thider.°   *does not know, way, there*
And to a dronke man the wey is slider.°   *slippery*
1265 And certes in this world so faren° we,   *fare*
We seken° faste° after felicitee,°   *seek, determinedly, happiness*
But we goon° wrong ful° often trewely.   *go, very*
Thus may we seyn° alle and namely° I,   *see, especially*
That wende° and hadde a greet opinioun   *expected*
1270 That if I myghte escapen from prisoun,
Thanne hadde I been in joye and parfit heele°   *perfect well-being*
That now I am exiled fro my wele,°   *happiness*
Syn° that I may nat° seen you, Emelye.   *Since, not*
I nam° but deed! Ther nys° no remedye!"   *am not, is not*
1275 UPON that oother syde° Palamon,   *side*

Whan that he wiste° Arcite was agon,°   knew, gone
Swich sorwe° he maketh that the grete tour   Such sorrow
Resouned° of his youlyng° and clamour.   resounded, yowling
The pure fettres° on his shynes° grete°   very chains, shins, swollen
1280   Weren° of his bittre salte teeres wete.°   were, wet
"Allas," quod he, "Arcita, cosyn° myn!   cousin
Of al oure strif,° God woot,° the fruyt° is thyn.   strife, knows, fruit
Thow walkest now in Thebes at thy large,°   freely
And of my wo thow yevest° litel charge.°   give, little care
1285   Thou mayst syn° thou hast wisdom and manhede°   since, manhood
Assemblen alle the folk of oure kynrede°   kindred
And make a werre so sharpe on this citee
That by som aventure° or som tretee°   chance, treaty
Thow mayst have hire° to lady and to wyf°   her, wife
1290   For whom that I moste nedes° lese° my lyf.   must needs, lose
For as by wey of possibilitee,°   as a possibility
Sith° thou art at thy large° of prisoun free   since, at large
And art a lord, greet is thyn avauntage
Moore than is myn that sterve° here in a cage.   die
1295   For I moot° wepe and wayle whil I lyve   must
With al the wo that prison may me yeve°   give
And eek with peyne° that love me yeveth also   pain
That doubleth al my torment and my wo!"
Therwith the fyr° of jalousie up sterte°   fire, jumped
1300   Withinne his brest and hente° him by the herte   grabbed
So woodly° that he lyk° was to biholde°   madly, like, behold
The boxtree[1] or the asshen° dede° and colde.   ashes, dead
THANNE seyde he, "O crueel° goddes that governe   cruel
This world with byndyng° of youre word eterne°   binding, eternal
1305   And writen in the table of atthamaunt°   adamant (strong stone)
Youre parlement° and youre eterne graunt,°   decision, eternal decree
What is mankynde moore unto you holde
Than is the sheepe that rouketh° in the folde?   huddles
For slayn is man right as another beest
1310   And dwelleth eek in prison and arreest°   arrest
And hath siknesse and greet adversitee
And ofte tymes giltlees° pardee!°   guiltless, by God
WHAT governance is in this prescience
That giltlees tormenteth innocence?[2]
1315   And yet encresseth° this al my penaunce,   increases

---

1   The box tree is known for its light yellow wood. Palamon is as pale as ashes.
2   "What governing principle is in this foresight/that torments innocent people [who are] guilt-
    less?"

That man is bounden° to his observaunce   *under obligation*
For Goddes sake to letten of° his wille   *restrain*
Theras° a beest may al his lust° fulfille?   *whereas, desire*
And whan a beest is deed, he hath no peyne,
1320 But after his deeth man moot° wepe and pleyne,°   *must, complain*
Though in this world he have care and wo
Withouten doute° it may stonden so.   *doubt*
The answere of this lete° I to dyvynys,°   *leave, religious scholars*
But wel I woot° that in this world greet° pyne° ys.°   *know, great, pain, is*
1325 Allas, I se° a serpent or a theef°   *see, thief*
That many a trewe man hath doon° mescheef° true,   *done, harm*
Goon at his large° and where hym list may turne.°   *go freely, where he desires*
But I moot been° in prisoun thurgh° Saturne   *must be, through*
And eek thurgh Juno,[1] jalous° and eek wood,°   *jealous, crazy*
1330 That hath destroyed wel ny° al the blood   *very nearly*
Of Thebes with hise° waste° walles wyde,°   *its, wasted, wide*
And Venus sleeth° me on that oother syde°   *kills, other side*
For jalousie and fere° of hym Arcite."   *fear*
NOW wol I stynte° of Palamon a lite°   *stop [speaking], little*
1335 And lete° hym in his prisoun stille° dwelle   *allow, quietly*
And of Arcita forth I wol° yow telle.   *will*
THE sonne passeth, and the nyghtes longe
Encressen doublewise° the peynes stronge   *increase doubly*
Bothe of the lovere and the prisoner.
1340 I noot° which hath the wofuller° mester.°   *do not know, sadder, profession*
For shortly for to seyn,° this Palamoun   *say*
Perpetuelly is dampned° to prisoun   *condemned*
In cheynes° and in fettres to been deed,°   *chains, [until he is] dead*
And Arcite is exiled upon his heed°   *upon [pain of losing] his head*
1345 Forever mo° as out of that contree.°   *more, country*
Ne nevere mo he shal his lady see.
Yow loveres, axe° I now this questioun: *ask*
Who hath the worse, Arcite or Palamoun?
That oon° may seen his lady day by day,   *one*
1350 But in prison he moot dwelle alway.
That oother, wher hym list° may ride or go,   *where he desires*
But seen his lady shal he nevere mo.°[2]   *more*

---

1 In Roman mythology, Juno—wife of Jupiter, the king of the gods—was the goddess of the hearth and of domesticity, and was frequently jealous of Jupiter's love affairs. Juno hated Thebes because of Jupiter's love affairs with the Theban women Semele, mother of Bacchus, and Alcmena, mother of Hercules.
2 This is a typical "question of love" or *demande d'amour*, setting forth a problem in the aristocratic code of love for courtiers to debate.

Now demeth as you list,° ye that kan,°   *judge as you desire, can*
For I wol° telle forth as I bigan.   *will*

EXPLICIT PRIMA PARS SEQUITUR PARS SECUNDA[1]

1355 WHAN that Arcite to Thebes comen was,°   *had arrived*
      Ful ofte a day he swelte° and seyde, "Allas!"   *fainted*
      For seen his lady shal he nevere mo
      And shortly to concluden° al his wo,   *to summarize*
      So muche sorwe hadde nevere creature
1360 That is or shal° whil° that the world may dure.°   *shall be, while, endure*
      His slepe,° his mete,° his drynke is hym biraft.°   *sleep, food, taken away*
      That lene° he wexeth° and drye as is a shaft.°   *lean, grows, arrow*
      Hise eyen° holwe° and grisly° to biholde,   *eyes, hollow, grim*
      His hewe° falow° and pale as asshen° colde,   *complexion, yellow, ashes*
1365 And solitarie he was and evere allone
      And waillynge al the nyght, makynge his mone.°   *moan*
      And if he herde song or instrument,
      Thanne wolde he wepe. He myghte nat be stent.°   *silenced*
      So feble eek° were hise° spiritz° and so lowe   *also, his, spirits*
1370 And chaunged so that no man koude° knowe   *could*
      His speche nor his voys,° though men it herde,   *voice*
      And in his geere° for al the world he ferde,°   *manner, fared*
      Nat° oonly lik° the loveris maladye   *not, like*
      Of hereos[2] but rather lyk° manye°   *like, mania*
1375 Engendred of humour malencolik[3]
      Biforn° his owene° celle fantastik.[4]   *before, own*
      And shortly, turned was al up so doun,°   *upside down*
      Bothe habit and eek disposicioun,
      Of hym this woful lovere daun Arcite.°   *Sir Arcite*
1380 WHAT sholde I al day of his wo endite,°   *write*
      Whan he endured hadde a yeer or two
      This crueel torment and this peyne and wo.
      At Thebes in his countree,° as I seyde,   *country*
      Upon a nyght in sleepe as he hym leyde,°   *lay*

---

1   This Latin passage reads, "Here ends the first part. The second part follows."

2   *Hereos* or *amor heroes* was the name given for the "disease" of love. There is a marginal Latin gloss
    noting that here there is a reference to a mania or mental aberration.

3   "Melancholic humor" is one of the four humors of the body according to classical and medi-
    eval medicinal theory. The other humors are the choleric, the phlegmatic, and the sanguine.
    Melancholic humor, of course, makes one sad—hence our word "melancholy."

4   The "fantastic cell" was thought to be the portion of the brain where the imagination resided.
    The other two "cells" were those of memory and reason.

1385 Hym thoughte° how that the wynged° god Mercurie[1] — *it seemed, winged*
Biforn° hym stood and bad hym° to be murie.° — *before, commanded him, merry*
His slepy yerde° in hond he bar° uprighte — *sleep-producing staff, bore*
An hat he werede° upon° hise heris° brighte. — *wore, MS up, hairs*
Arrayed° was this god, as I took keepe,°[2] — *dressed, as I noticed*
1390 As he was whan that Argus[3] took his sleepe
And seyde hym thus: "To Atthenes shaltou wende.° — *shall you go*
Ther is thee shapen° of thy wo an ende." — *for you ordained*
And with that word Arcite wook° and sterte.° — *woke, got up*
"Now trewely, hou soore that me smerte,"° — *however sorely I suffer*
1395 Quod he, "to Atthenes right now wol° I fare.° — *will, travel*
Ne° for the drede° of deeth shal I nat spare° — *nor, dread, not avoid*
To se my lady that I love and serve.
In hire presence I recche nat° to sterve!" — *care not*
AND with that word he caughte° a greet mirour° — *seized, mirror*
1400 And saugh° that chaunged was al his colour — *saw*
And saugh his visage° al in another kynde.° — *face, nature*
And right anon° it ran hym° in his mynde — *immediately, him*
That sith° his face was so disfigured — *since*
Of maladye, the which he hadde endured,
1405 He myghte wel, if that he bar hym lowe,° — *acted humbly*
Lyve in Atthenes everemoore unknowe° — *unknown*
And seen his lady wel ny day by day.° — *nearly every day*
And right anon° he chaunged his array° — *immediately, dress*
And cladde° hym as a povre° laborer. — *clothed, poor*
1410 And al allone save only a squier
That knew his privetee° and al his cas° — *secret, situation*
Which was disgised povrely° as he was — *poorly*
To Atthenes is he goon° the nexte way,° — *gone, shortest way*
And to the court he wente upon a day,
1415 And at the gate he profreth° his servyse — *offered*
To drugge° and drawe° what so men wol devyse.° — *drudge, draw [water], demand*
And shortly of this matere for to seyn,° — *say*
He fil° in office with a chamberleyn° — *fell, chamberlain*
The which that dwellynge was with Emelye.
1420 For he was wys° and koude soone espye° — *wise, see*
Of every servaunt which that serveth here.° — *her*
Wel koude he hewen° wode and water bere,° — *cut, carry*

---

1   In Roman mythology, Mercury was the messenger of the gods.
2   The line is often emended to read "as he took keepe," referring to Arcite's noticing Mercury's
    appearance.
3   In Roman mythology, Argus had a hundred eyes and bore watch over Io, whom Jupiter loved.
    Mercury put him to sleep with his staff and then killed him.

For he was yong° and myghty for the nones.°   *young, for the occasion*
And therto he was long° and big of bones   *tall*
1425 To doon° that° any wight° kan° hym devyse.°   *do, whatever, person, can, devise*
A yeer or two he was in this servyse,
Page° of the chambre° of Emelye the brighte,   *young servant, chamber*
And Philostrate[1] he seyde that he highte.°   *was named*
But half so wel biloved° a man as he   *beloved*
1430 Ne° was ther nevere in court of his degree.   *not*
He was so gentil° of condicioun   *noble*
That thurghout al the court was his renoun.°   *renown*
They seyden that it were a charitee°   *would be an act of charity*
That Theseus wolde enhauncen his degree°   *promote him*
1435 And putten hym in worshipful servyse°   *honorable service*
Theras° he myghte his vertu excercise.°   *where, show his qualities*
And thus withinne a while his name is spronge°   *spread about*
Bothe of hise dedes° and his goode tonge,°   *deeds, elegant speech*
That Theseus hath taken hym so neer°   *close to himself*
1440 That of his chambre[2] he made hym a squier
And gaf° hym gold to mayntene° his degree.°   *gave, maintain, rank*
And eek men broghte hym out of his contree
From yeer to yeer ful pryvely° his rente.[3]   *secretly*
But honestly and slyly° he it spente,   *discreetly*
1445 That no man wondred how that he it hadde.
And thre yeer° in this wise° his lif he ladde°   *years, way, led*
And bar hym° so in pees° and eek in werre.°   *conducted himself, peace, war*
Ther was no man that Theseus hath derre.°   *held more dear*
And in this blisse lete° I now Arcite   *leave*
1450 And speke I wole° of Palamon a lite.°   *will, little*
IN derknesse and horrible and strong prisoun
Thise seven yeer hath seten° Palamoun   *remained*
Forpyned,° what for wo and for distresse.   *tormented*
Who feeleth double soor° and hevynesse°   *soreness, heaviness*
1455 But Palamon that love destreyneth° so,   *afflicts*
That wood° out of his wit he goth° for wo?   *crazy, goes*
And eek therto he is a prisoner

---

1   "Philostrate" in Greek means "one knocked down by love."
2   Medieval English kings relied heavily on knights of their chamber for administrative duties
    of government. Originally servants who performed various domestic functions, these people
    had honorific titles implying these duties (such as steward or butler) but took on the duties of
    governmental administration instead.
3   The "rent" referred to here is not something Arcite must pay but what is owed to him instead.
    Medieval lords possessed land and were owed various rents and services from those allowed its
    use. A high lord like Arcite would have had much income from such sources.

Perpetuelly, noght oonly for a yer.
WHO koude ryme° in Englyssh proprely   *rhyme*
1460 His martirdom? Forsothe° it am nat° I!   *in truth, not*
Therfore I passe as lightly° as I may.   *quickly*
IT fel° that in the seventhe yer in May   *happened*
The thridde° nyght, as olde bookes seyn,°   *third, say*
That al this storie tellen° moore pleyn,°   *tell, plainly*
1465 Were it° by aventure° or destynee,°   *whether it were, chance, destiny*
As whan a thyng is shapen° it shal be,   *ordained*
That soone after the mydnyght Palamoun
By helpyng of a freend° brak° his prisoun   *friend, escaped*
And fleeth° the citee faste as he may go.   *flees*
1470 For he hadde yeve° his gayler° drynke so   *given, jailor*
Of a clarree° maad° of a certeyn° wyn   *spiced drink, made, certain*
Of nercotikes° and opie° of Thebes fyn°¹   *narcotics, opium, fine*
That al that nyght thogh that men wolde him shake,
This gayler sleepe;° he myghte nat awake.   *slept*
1475 AND thus he fleeth as faste as evere he may.
The nyght was short and faste by the day°   *it was almost day*
That nedes cost° he moot° hymselven hyde,   *necessarily, must*
And til° a grove faste therbisyde°   *to, nearby*
With dredeful° foot thanne stalketh° Palamon,   *fearful, walks quietly*
1480 For shortly, this was his opinion
That in that grove he wolde° hym hyde al day,   *would*
And in the nyght thanne wolde he take his way
To Thebesward,° his freendes for to preye°   *towards Thebes, ask*
On Theseus to helpe hym to werreye.°   *make war*
1485 And shortly outher° he wolde lese° his lif°   *either, lose, life*
Or wynnen° Emelye unto his wyf.   *win*
This is th'effect and his entente pleyn.°   *plain intent*
NOW wol I turne to Arcite ageyn,°   *again*
That litel wiste° how ny° that was his care,   *knew, near*
1490 Til that Fortune had broght him in the snare.
THE bisy larke,° messager° of day,   *lark, messenger*
Salueth° in hir song the morwe gray,   *salutes*
And firy Phebus² riseth up so brighte
That al the orient° laugheth of the lighte   *east*
1495 And with hise stremes° dryeth° in the greves°   *his beams, dries, branches*
The silver dropes hangynge on the leves.°   *leaves*
And Arcita that is in the court roial

---

1 There is a Latin gloss in the margin "Opium Theabicum," Theban opiate.
2 Phoebus is another name for Apollo, in Roman mythology god of the sun.

With Theseus, his° squier principal,[1]   [as] his
Is risen and looketh on the myrie° day.   merry
1500 And for to doon° his observaunce to May,[2]   do
Remembrynge on the poynt° of his desir,°   object, desire
He on a courser° startlynge° as the fir,°   warhorse, prancing, fire
Is riden into the feeldes° hym to pleye.   fields
Out of the court were it a myle or tweye°   mile or two
1505 And to the grove of which that I yow° tolde   you
By aventure° his wey° he gan to holde°   chance, way, held
To maken hym a gerland° of the greves,°   garland, branches
Were it of wodebynde° or hawethorn leves.°   woodbind, hawthorn leaves
And loude he song ayeyn the sonne shene,°   in the bright sunshine
1510 "May, with alle thy floures° and thy grene,°   flowers, green
Welcome be thou, faire, fresshe May,
In hope that I som grene° gete may."   something green
And from his courser° with a lusty herte°   warhorse, spirited heart
Into a grove ful hastily he sterte,°   jumped
1515 And in a path he rometh° up and doun°   roams, down
Theras° by aventure° this Palamoun   where, chance
Was in a bussh that no man myghte hym se,°   see
For soore aferd° of his deeth° thanne was he.   sore afraid, death
Nothyng ne knew° he that it was Arcite.   did not know
1520 God woot,° he wolde° have trowed° it ful lite!°   knows, would, believed, very little
But sooth° is seyd, so sithen° many yeres,°   truth, after, years
That "Feeld° hath eyen° and the wode° hath eres."°   field, eyes, wood, ears
It is ful fair a man to bere hym evene,
For al day meeteth men at unset stevene.[3]
1525 Ful litel woot° Arcite of his felawe   knew
That was so ny° to herknen° al his sawe,°   near, listen to, speech
For in the bussh he sitteth now ful stille.°   very quietly
WHAN that Arcite hadde romed° all his fille   roamed
And songen° al the roundel[4] lustily   sang
1530 Into a studie° he fil° al sodeynly   meditative mood, fell
As doon° thise loveres° in hir queynte° geres.°   do, lovers, curious, customs
Now in the crope,° now doun° in the breres,°   treetop, down, briars
Now up, now doun as boket° in a welle.   bucket
Right as the Friday, soothly° for to telle,   truly

---

1   Some manuscripts read "is squire principal."
2   The custom was for courtly people to rise early in mornings in May and roam about in the countryside to enjoy the good weather that had recently returned.
3   "It is very desireable for a man to behave with restraint,/for every day people meet at an unexpected time (*unset stevene*).
4   A roundel was a popular type of song in both France and England in the fourteenth century. It was characterized by repeated phrases of both music and words.

1535 Now it shyneth, now it reyneth° faste: *rains*
     Right so kan° geery° Venus overcaste   *can, fickle*
     The hertes of hir folk. Right as hir day[1]
     Is gereful,° right so chaungeth she array.°   *fickle, appearance*
     Selde° is the Friday al the wowke ylike.°   *seldom, like the rest of the week*
1540 WHAN that Arcite had songe,° he gan° to sike°   *sung, began, sigh*
     And sette hym doun° withouten any moore.   *set himself down*
     "Allas," quod he, "that day that I was bore!
     How longe, Juno, thurgh thy crueltee
     Woltow° werreyen° Thebes the citee?   *will you, make war [on]*
1545 Allas, ybroght° is to confusioun   *brought*
     The blood roial° of Cadme and Amphioun[2]—   *royal*
     Of Cadmus which that was the firste man
     That Thebes bulte,° or first the toun bigan,   *built*
     And of the citee first was crouned° kyng.   *crowned*
1550 Of his lynage° am I and his ofspryng   *lineage*
     By verray ligne° as of the stok roial,°   *true lineage, royal stock*
     And now I am so caytyf° and so thral,°   *captive, enslaved*
     That he that is my mortal enemy
     I serve hym as his squier povrely.°   *poorly*
1555 And yet dooth Juno me wel moore° shame,   *much more*
     For I dar° noght biknowe° myn owene name!   *dare, reveal*
     But theras I was wont to highte° Arcite,   *accustomed to be called*
     Now highte I Philostrate, noght worth a myte.°   *mite (small coin)*
     Allas, thou felle° Mars,[3] allas, Juno!   *cruel*
1560 Thus hath youre ire° oure kynrede°[4] al° fordo,°   *anger, kindred, always, destroyed*
     Save oonly me and wrecched° Palamoun   *wretched*
     That Theseus martireth° in prisoun.   *martyrs*
     And over al this to sleen° me outrely,°   *kill, completely*
     Love hath his firy dart so brennyngly°   *burningly*
1565 Ystiked° thurgh my trewe,° careful° herte,   *stuck, true, sorrowful*
     That shapen° was my deeth° erst° than my sherte.°[5]   *ordained, death, before, shirt*
     Ye sleen° me with youre eyen,° Emelye!   *kill, eyes*
     Ye been° the cause wherfore° that I dye!   *are, why*
     Of al the remenant of myn oother care,
1570 Ne sette I nat° the montance° of a tare,°   *I do not set, value, weed*

---

1 The days of the week were originally devoted to the various gods and goddesses, as our names
   for them still attest (Saturn's day = Saturday; Thor's day = Thursday). Venus's day was Friday
   (*Veneris dies*) in the Romance languages; the Germanic goddess most resembling Venus was
   named Freya.
2 They were earlier kings of Thebes. There is a gloss in the margin "Cadmus."
3 In Roman mythology, Mars was the god of war.
4 Hengwrt has "oure lynage," our lineage.
5 The reference here is probably to the first shirt made for Arcite when he was a baby.

So that I koude° doon aught° to youre plesaunce."°   *could, something, pleasure*
And with that word he fil° doun in a traunce   *fell*
A longe tyme, and after he up sterte.°   *jumped*
THIS Palamoun that thoughte that thurgh his herte
1575 He felte a coold swerd sodeynliche° glyde,   *suddenly*
For ire° he quook.° No lenger wolde° he byde.°   *anger, shook, would, wait*
And whan that he had herd Arcites tale,
As he were wood,° with face deed° and pale,   *crazy, dead*
He stirte hym up° out of the buskes° thikke°   *jumped up, bushes, thick*
1580 And seide, "Arcite, false traytour wikke,°   *wicked*
Now artow° hent° that lovest my lady so,   *are you, caught*
For whom that I have al this peyne and wo!
And art my blood° and to my conseil° sworn,   *[of] my blood, counsel*
As I ful ofte° have seyd thee heer biforn°   *often, before*
1585 And hast byjaped° heere Duc Theseus   *mocked*
And falsly chaunged hast thy name thus,
I wol be deed or elles° thou shalt dye!   *else*
Thou shalt nat love my lady Emelye.
But I wol love hire oonly and namo,°   *no more*
1590 For I am Palamon, thy mortal foo.°   *foe*
And though that I no wepene have in this place,
But out of prison am astert° by grace,   *escaped*
I drede noght° that outher° thow shalt dye   *fear not, either*
Or thow ne shalt nat loven Emelye!
1595 Chees° which thou wolt,° or thou shalt nat asterte."°1   *choose, wish, not escape*
THIS Arcite, with ful despitous° herte,   *relentless*
Whan he hym knew° and hadde his tale herd,   *recognized*
As fiers as leoun pulled out his swerd
And seyd thus: "By God that sit above,
1600 Nere it° that thou art sik° and wood° for love,   *were it not, sick, crazy*
And eek that thow no wepne° hast in this place,   *weapon*
Thou sholdest nevere out of this grove pace.°   *escape*
That thou ne sholdest dyen of myn hond!°   *should not die by my hand*
For I defye° the seurete° and the bond   *defy, promise*
1605 Which that thou seist that I have maad° to thee.   *made*
What, verray° fool, thynk wel that love is free,   *true*
And I wol° love hire° maugree° al thy myght!   *will, her, despite*
But for as muche° thou art a worthy knyght   *since*
And wilnest to darreyne hire by bataille,²
1610 Have heer° my trouthe:° tomorwe I wol nat faille   *here, vow*

---

1   Both Ellesmere and Hengwrt have "or thou shalt not asterte," but some manuscripts have "for thou shalt not asterte," which makes better sense.

2   "And wish to vindicate his right to her ('darreyne') by battle."

Withoute wityng° of any oother wight,°   *the knowledge, person*
That heere I wol° be founden as a knyght   *will*
And bryngen harneys° right ynough° for thee   *armor, enough*
And chese° the best and leve° the worste for me.   *choose, leave*
1615 And mete° and drynke this nyght wol I brynge   *food*
Ynough° for thee and clothes for thy beddynge.   *enough*
And if so be that thou my lady wynne°   *win*
And sle° me in this wode ther I am inne,°   *kill, in*
Thow mayst wel have thy lady as for me."
1620 THIS Palamon answerde, "I graunte it thee!"
And thus they been departed til amorwe,°   *separated until the next day*
Whan ech of hem had leyd his feith to borwe.°   *given his word as a pledge*
O CUPIDE,¹ out of all charitee!°   *charity*
O regne,° that wolt no felawe° have with thee!   *reign, equal*
1625 Ful sooth° is seyd that love ne° lordshipe   *very true, nor*
Wol noght, hir thankes, have no felaweshipe.²
Wel° fynden° that Arcite and Palamoun.   *well, find*
Arcite is riden anon° unto the toun,   *immediately*
And on the morwe er° it were dayes light   *before*
1630 Ful prively° two harneys° hath he dight,°   *secretly, suits of armor, prepared*
Bothe suffisaunt° and mete° to darreyne°   *sufficient, fitting, decide*
The bataille in the feeld bitwix hem tweyne.°   *between the two of them*
And on his hors allone as he was born
He carieth al the harneys hym biforn.
1635 And in the grove at tyme and place yset,°   *appointed*
This Arcite and this Palamon ben° met.   *are*
To chaungen° gan° the colour in hir° face,   *change, began, their*
Right as the hunters in the regne of Trace°   *kingdom of Thrace in Greece*
That stondeth at the gappe° with a spere,°   *gap, spear*
1640 Whan hunted is the leoun and the bere°   *bear*
And hereth° hym° come russhyng° in the greves°   *hear, them, rushing, branches*
And breketh° bothe bowes and the leves   *break*
And thynketh, "Heere cometh my mortal enemy!
Withoute faille, he moot° be deed or I.   *must*
1645 For outher° I moot° sleen° hym at the gappe°   *either, must, kill, gap*
Or he moot sleen me if that me myshappe."°   *I make a mistake*
So ferden° they in chaungyng° of hir hewe   *fared, appearance*
As fer as everich of hem oother knewe.°   *knew the other*

---

1   In Roman mythology, Cupid, son of Venus, was the god of love.
2   "Truly it is said that [neither] love nor lordship/will willingly (*hir thankes*) have equals (fellowship)." Hengwrt reads "his thankes." Since the sentence has a compound subject (love and lordship), the plural "hir" is appropriate, although the subject is strictly singular because of the "ne."

THER nas no° good day ne no° saluyng,°   *was neither, nor, saluting*
1650 But streight° withouten word or rehersyng°   *immediately, conversation*
Everich of hem heelpe for to armen oother°   *Each of them helps the other to arm*
As freenly° as he were his owene brother.   *friendly*
And after that with sharpe speres stronge
They foynen° ech at oother wonder° longe.   *thrust, wonderfully*
1655 Thou myghtest wene° that this Palamoun   *think*
In his fightyng were a wood° leoun.   *crazy*
And as a crueel tigre was Arcite.
As wilde bores gonne° they to smyte,   *began*
That frothen whit as foom for ire wood.[1]
1660 Up to the anclee° foghte they in hir° blood,   *ankle, their*
AND in this wise° I lete hem fightyng dwelle°   *manner, leave them still fighting*
And forth I wole° of Theseus yow telle.   *will*
THE destinee,° ministre° general   *destiny, agent*
That executeth in the world over al
1665 The purveiaunce° that God hath seyn° biforn,   *foresight, seen*
So strong it is that though the world had sworn
The contrarie of a thyng by ye° or nay,°   *yes or no*
Yet somtyme it shal fallen° on a day   *happen*
That falleth nat eft° withinne a thousand yeere.°   *not again, years*
1670 For certeinly oure appetites heere,
Be it of werre or pees° or hate or love,   *war or peace*
Al is this reuled° by the sighte above.   *ruled*
THIS mene° I now by myghty Theseus,   *mean*
That for to hunten° is so desirus,°   *hunt, eager*
1675 And namely at the grete hert° in May,   *great deer*
That in his bed ther daweth° hym no day   *dawns*
That he nys clad° and redy° for to ryde   *is not clothed, ready*
With hunte and horn and houndes hym bisyde,
For in his huntyng hath he swich delit°   *such pleasure*
1680 That it is al his joye and appetit°   *desire*
To been hymself the grete hertes bane.°   *slayer*
For after Mars he serveth now Dyane.[2]
CLEER° was the day, as I have toold° er° this,   *clear, told, before*
And Theseus with alle joye and blis°   *bliss*
1685 With his Ypolita the faire queene
And Emelye clothed al in grene
On huntyng° be they riden° roially.   *a-hunting, are they riding*
And to the grove that stood ful faste by°   *very nearby*

---

1   "That froth [at the mouth], white as foam, crazy for anger."
2   In Roman mythology, Diana was the goddess of the hunt. She and the women devoted to her
    refused marriage and the domination by men.

In which ther was an hert° as men hym tolde,   deer
1690 Duc Theseus the streighte wey° hath holde.°   straight road, has held
And to the launde° he rideth° hym ful right,°   land, rides, directly
For thider° was the hert wont° have his flight.   there, accustomed
And over a brook and so forth in his weye,
This duc wol han° a cours° at hym or tweye°   will have, run, two
1695 With houndes swiche as hym list comaunde.°   such as it pleases him to command
AND whan this duc was come unto the launde
Under the sonne° he looketh. And anon°   sun, immediately
He was war° of Arcite and Palamon°   aware, MS Palamoun
That foughten breme° as it were bores° two.   boldly, boars
1700 The brighte swerdes wenten to and fro
So hidously that with the leeste strook°   least stroke
It semed as it wolde fille° an ook!°   fell, oak
But what they were, nothyng he ne woot.[1]
This duc his courser° with his spores° smoot,°   warhorse, spurs, struck
1705 And at a stert° he was bitwix hem two   instantly
And pulled out a swerd and cride, "Hoo!°   Whoa!
Namoore° upon peyne° of lesynge° of youre heed!   no more, pain, losing
By myghty Mars, he shal anon° be deed   immediately
That smyteth° any strook° that I may seen.   strikes, stroke
1710 But telleth me what mystiers men ye been[2]
That been° so hardy° for to fighten here   are, bold
Withouten juge° or oother officere   judge (referee)
As it were in a lystes° roially."°   jousting station, royally
THIS Palamon answerde hastily
1715 And seyde, "Sire, what nedeth wordes mo?
We have the deeth disserved bothe two.
Two woful wrecches° been we, two caytyves°   woeful wretches, captives
That been encombred[3] of oure owene lyves.
And as thou art a rightful lord and juge,
1720 Ne yeve° us neither mercy ne refuge.   do not give
But sle° me first, for seinte charitee.   slay
But sle my felawe eek as wel as me.
Or sle hym first! For though thow knowest it lite,°   little
This is thy mortal foo.° This is Arcite   foe

---

1 "He did not know anything about who they were."
2 Hengwrt reads "myster." The line means: "But tell me what occupation you follow," that is, what kind of men they are. "Mystiers" is cognate with "mystery," which in the Middle Ages meant a trade or occupation and gave the name to the religious plays the trade guilds put on in various cities—"mystery plays."
3 "Encumbered" here means that they deserve death because of the terms of their conditional sentence: Palamon must stay in prison or die, while Arcite must remain in exile or die.

1725	That fro° thy lond is banysshed on his heed,[1]	*from*
	For which he hath deserved to be deed.	
	For this is he that cam unto thy gate	
	And seyde that he highte° Philostrate.	*was named*
	Thus hath he japed° thee ful° many a yer,°	*fooled, very, year*
1730	And thou hast maked hym thy chief squire,	
	And this is he that loveth Emelye.	
	For sith° the day is come that I shal dye,	*since*
	I make pleynly° my confessioun	*fully*
	That I am thilke° woful Palamoun	*the same*
1735	That hath thy prisoun broken° wikkedly.	*escaped*
	I am thy mortal foo, and it am I	
	That loveth so hoote° Emelye the brighte,	*hotly*
	That I wol dye,° present in hir sighte.	*will die*
	Wherfore I axe° deeth and my juwise.°	*ask, sentence*
1740	But sle° my felawe° in the same wise,°	*slay, companion, way*
	For bothe han° we deserved to be slayn!"	*have*
	THIS worthy duc answerde anon° agayn°	*immediately, again*
	And seyde, "This is a short conclusioun!°	*quick decision*
	Youre owene° mouth by youre confessioun	*own*
1745	Hath dampned° yow, and I wol° it recorde.	*damned, will*
	It nedeth noght to pyne yow with the corde:[2]	
	Ye shal be deed, by myghty Mars the rede!"°	*red*
	THE queene anon for verray° wommanhede°	*true, womanhood*
	Gan° for to wepe and so dide Emelye	*began*
1750	And alle the ladyes in the compaignye.	
	Greet pitee was it as it thoughte hem alle,°	*it seemed to them*
	That evere swich° a chaunce° sholde falle.°	*such, event, happen*
	For gentil° men, they were of greet estaat,°	*noble, rank*
	And no thyng but for love was this debaat,°	*quarrel*
1755	And saugh° hir blody woundes wyde and soore	*saw*
	And alle crieden° bothe lasse and moore,°	*cried, the lesser and the greater*
	"Have mercy, lord, upon us wommen alle!"	
	And on hir bare knees adoun they falle	
	And wolde have kist° his feet theras° he stood,	*kissed, where*
1760	Til at the laste aslaked° was his mood.	*calmed*
	For pitee° renneth° soone in gentil herte.	*pity, runs*
	And though he first for ire° quook° and sterte,°	*anger, shook, moved suddenly*
	He hath considered shortly° in a clause°	*briefly, briefly*
	The trespas° of hem bothe and eek the cause.	*crime*

---

1   "Banished on [with the consequence of losing] his head."
2   "There is no need to torture you with a rope" (which would be twisted about the prisoner's head).

1765 And although that his ire hir gilt° accused,   *their guilt*
     Yet in his resoun° he hem bothe excused   *reason*
     As thus: he thoghte wel that every man
     Wol° helpe hymself in love if that he kan°   *would, can*
     And eek delivere hymself out of prisoun.
1770 And eek his herte hadde compassioun
     Of wommen, for they wepen° evere in oon.°   *weep, in unity*
     And in his gentil herte he thoughte anon°   *immediately*
     And softe unto hymself he seyde, "Fy°   *shame*
     Upon a lord that wol have no mercy[1]
1775 But been a leoun bothe in word and dede°   *deed*
     To hem that been in repentaunce and drede°   *fear*
     As wel as to a proud, despitous° man   *scornful*
     That wol mayntene° that he first bigan.   *will try to justify*
     That lord hath litel of discrecioun
1780 That in swich cas° kan° no divisioun   *case, knows*
     But weyeth° pride and humblesse after oon."°   *weighs, equally*
     And shortly, whan his ire is thus agoon,°   *gone*
     He gan° to looken up with eyen° lighte   *began, eyes*
     And spak thise same wordes al on highte:°   *aloud*
1785 "THE god of love,[2] a benedicite,°[3]   *bless you*
     How myghty and how greet a lord is he!
     Ayeyns° his myght ther gayneth none obstacles.°   *against, no obstacle can prevail*
     He may be cleped° a god for hise myracles.°   *called, his miracles*
     For he kan° maken at his owene gyse°   *can, in his own way*
1790 Of everich herte as that hym list divyse.°   *as he wishes to arrange*
     Lo heere this Arcite and this Palamon,
     That quitly° weren out of my prisoun   *freely*
     And myghte han° lyved in Thebes roially°   *have, royally*
     And witen° I am hir mortal enemy   *know*
1795 And that hir deth lith° in my myght also,   *lies*
     And yet hath love maugree hir° eyen two[4]   *despite their*
     Broght hem hyder° bothe for to dye.   *them here*
     Now looketh: is nat° that an heigh° folye?°   *not, great, folly*
     WHO may been a fool but if he love?°   *unless he who loves*
1800 Bihoold,° for Goddes sake that sit above.   *behold*
     Se how they blede! Be they noght wel arrayed?°   *decorated*

---

1   There is a Latin gloss in the margin, "Note dominum," i.e., note that this is good advice for a lord.
2   That is, Cupid.
3   "Benedicite," bless us, was in Chaucer's English an almost meaningless interjection like our "my, my" or "golly." Chaucer often uses it as a line filler to get a rhyme.
4   The expression "maugree hir eyen" or "despite their eyes" means despite anything they could do.

Thus hath hir lord, the god of love, ypayed° — *paid*
Hir wages and hir fees for hir servyse!
And yet they wenen for to been ful wyse° — *consider [themselves] very wise*
1805 That serven love, for aught that may bifalle.° — *anything that may happen*
But this is yet the beste gam° of alle, — *game*
That she for whom they han° this jolitee° — *have, amusement*
Kan° hem therfore as muche thank as me. — *owes*
She woot namoore° of al this hoote° fare,° — *knows no more, hot, business*
1810 By God, than woot a cokkow° of an hare!¹ — *knows cuckoo*
But al moot° been assayed,° hoot and coold. — *must, tried*
A man moot been a fool or yong or oold.²
I woot° it by myself ful yore agon,° — *know, very long ago*
For in my tyme a servant³ was I oon,° — *one*
1815 And therfore syn° I knowe of loves peyne — *since*
And woot hou soore° it kan a man distreyne,° — *how painfully, afflict*
As he that hath been caught ofte in his laas,° — *trap*
I yow° foryeve° al hoolly° this trespass — *you, forgive, completely*
At requeste of the queene that kneleth heere° — *kneels here*
1820 And eek of Emelye, my suster deere.° — *sister[-in-law]*
And ye shul° bothe anon° unto me swere — *shall, immediately*
That nevere mo° ye shal my contree° dere° — *more, country, harm*
Ne° make werre° upon me nyght ne day — *nor, war*
But been my freendes in al that ye may.
1825 I yow foryeve this trespas every deel."° — *completely*
And they hym sworen° his axyng° faire and weel° — *swore, asking, well*
And hym of lordshipe° and of mercy preyde, — *begged him to be their lord*
And he hem graunteth grace,° and thus he seyde: — *grants his favor*
"To speke of roial lynage° and richesse, — *royal lineage*
1830 Though that she were a queene or a princesse,
Ech of you bothe is worthy doutelees° — *doubtless*
To wedden whan tyme is doutelees.⁴
I speke as for my suster Emelye,
For whom ye have this strif° and jalousye. — *strife*
1835 Ye woot° yourself she may nat wedden two — *know*
Atones,° though ye fighten everemo.° — *at once, forever*
That oon° of you, al be hym looth or lief,° — *one, whether he likes it or not*
He moot pipen in an yvy leef.° — *pipe in an ivy leaf (go whistle)*
This is to seyn, she may nat now han° bothe, — *have*

---

1 Many editors prefer the reading "or a hare," which is found in many manuscripts, but "less than a cuckoo knows about a hare" also makes sense.
2 "A man must be a fool, either when he is young or when he is old."
3 A servant, that is, of Cupid, the god of love.
4 Many manuscripts, including Hengwrt, have "natheless" (nevertheless). The repetition of "doubtless" is almost certainly a scribal error.

1840 Al be° ye never so jalouse ne° so wrothe.°   *although, nor, angry*
     And forthy° I yow putte° in this degree,°   *therefore, put, situation*
     That ech of yow shal have his destynee°   *destiny*
     As hym is shape° and herkneth in what wyse.°   *as is ordained for him, way*
     Lo heere° youre ende of that I shal devyse.°   *here [is], devise*
1845 "My wyl° is this for plat° conclusioun,   *will, plain*
     Withouten any repplicacioun:°   *reply*
     If that you liketh, take it for the beste,
     That everich° of you shal goon° where hym leste°   *each, go, where he wants*
     Frely° withouten raunson° or daunger,   *freely, ransom*
1850 And this day fifty wykes fer ne ner[1]
     Everich of you shal brynge an hundred knyghtes
     Armed for lystes° up at alle rightes,[2]   *arena*
     Al redy° to darreyne° hire by bataille.   *ready, win*
     And this bihote° I yow withouten faille°   *command, fail*
1855 Upon my trouthe° and as I am a knyght,   *truth*
     That wheither of yow° bothe that hath myght,   *whichever of you*
     This is to seyn,° that wheither he or thow   *say*
     May with his hundred as I spak° of now   *spoke*
     Sleen° his contrarie° or out of lystes dryve,   *kill, opponent*
1860 Thanne shal I yeve° Emelya to wyve   *give*
     To whom that Fortune yeveth so fair a grace.
     The lystes shal I maken in this place,
     And God so wisly° on my soule rewe,°   *wisely, have mercy*
     As I shal evene juge° been° and trewe,°   *a fair judge, be, true*
1865 Ye shul noon oother ende° with me maken,   *shall no other resolution*
     That oon of yow ne shal be° deed° or taken.°   *one shall not, dead, captured*
     And if yow thynketh this is weel ysayd,°   *well said*
     Seyeth° youre avys° and holdeth you apayd.°   *say, opinion, satisfied*
     This is youre ende and youre conclusioun."
1870 Who looketh lightly now but Palamoun?
     Who spryngeth up for joye but Arcite?
     Who kouthe° telle or who kouthe endite°   *could, write*
     The joye that is maked in the place
     Whan Theseus hath doon so fair a grace?°   *behaved so graciously*
1875 But doun on knees wente every maner wight°   *manner of person*
     And thonken hym with al hir herte° and myght,   *their heart*
     And namely° the Thebans often sithe.°   *especially, many times*
     And thus with good hope and with herte blithe°   *happy heart*

---

1 "Fifty weeks from this day, neither more nor less."
2 Lists were the spaces fenced off for a medieval tournament, in which knights fought in two groups, and for individual jousts. The description of the lists set up by Theseus in the lines below, however, is based on accounts of Roman arenas, like the Colliseum in Rome.

They taken hir leve° and homward gonne° they ride	*leave, began*
1880 To Thebes with hise° olde walles wyde.°	*its, wide*

EXPLICIT SECUNDA PARS SEQUITUR PARS TERTIA[1]

I TROWE° men wolde deme° it necligence	*believe, would judge*
If I foryete° to tellen the dispence°	*forget, expense*
Of Theseus that gooth° so bisily°	*who goes, busily*
To maken up the lystes° roially	*arena*
1885 That swich a noble theatre° as it was,	*ampitheater*
I dar wel seyn° in this world ther nas.°	*dare well say, there was not*
The circuit a myle was aboute,	
Walled of stoon° and dyched° al withoute.	*stone, ditched*
Round was the shape, in manere of compas,	
1890 Ful of degrees, the heighte° of sixty pas,°	*height, paces*
That whan a man was set on o° degree,	*one*
He lette nat° his felawe for to see.	*hindered not*
ESTWARD ther stood a gate of marbul° whit,	*marble*
Westward right swich another in the opposit.	
1895 AND shortly to concluden, swich a place	
Was noon° in erthe° as in so litel space,	*none, earth*
For in the lond ther was no crafty° man	*skillful*
That geometrie° or ars metrik° kan,°	*geometry, arithmetic, knew*
Ne portreitour,° ne kervere° of ymages°	*portrait-painting, carver, statues*
1900 That Theseus ne yaf° mete° and wages	*did not give, food*
The theatre° for to maken and devyse.°	*amphitheater, make and plan*
And for to doon° his ryte° and sacrifise	*do, ceremonies*
He estward hath upon the gate above	
In worshipe of Venus, goddesse of love,	
1905 Doon make° an auter° and an oratorie,°	*has made, altar, chapel*
And on the westward in memorie	
Of Mars, he maked hath right swich° another,	*just such*
That coste largely of gold a fother.[2]	
And northward in a touret° on the wal	*turret*
1910 Of alabastre° whit and reed° coral	*alabaster, red*
An oratorie riche for to see	
In worshipe of Dyane of chastitee	
Hath Theseus doon wroght° in noble wyse.°	*has made, manner*
BUT yet hadde I foryeten° to devyse°	*forgotten, describe*
1915 The noble kervyng° and the portraitures,°	*carving, portraits*

---

1   "Here ends the second part. The third part follows."
2   "That cost many a cartload of gold."

The shape, the contenaunce,° and the figures | *face*
That weren° in thise oratories thre.° | *were, three chapels*
FIRST, in the temple of Venus maystow se° | *you may see*
Wroght° on the wal ful pitous° to biholde° | *Made, very pitiful, behold*
1920 The broken slepes° and the sikes° colde, | *sleeps, sighs*
The sacred teeris° and the waymentynge,° | *tears, lamentation*
The firy strokes and the desirynge
That loves servantz° in this lyf° enduren,° | *love's servants, life, endure*
The othes° that hir° covenantz° assuren,° | *oaths, their, agreements, assure*
1925 Plesaunce° and Hope, Desir,° Foolhardynesse, | *Pleasure, Desire*
Beautee and Youthe, Bauderie,° Richesse, | *Bawdiness*
Charmes and Force, Lesynges,° Flaterye,° | *Lies, Flattery*
Despense,° Bisyness,° and Jalousye,° | *Spending, Anxiety, Jealousy*
That wered° of yelewe° gooldes° a gerland° | *wore, yellow, marigolds, garland*
1930 And a cokkow° sittynge on hir hand.[1] | *cuckoo*
Festes,° instrumentz,° caroles,[2] daunces, | *Feasts, [musical] instruments,*
Lust,° and array,° and all the circumstaunces | *pleasure, dress*
Of love, whiche that I rekned° have and rekne° shal, | *reckoned, reckon*
By ordre weren peynted° on the wal, | *were painted*
1935 And mo than I kan make of mencioun.° | *can make mention*
For soothly,° al the Mount of Citheroun[3] | *truly*
Ther° Venus hath hir principal dwellynge, | *where*
Was shewed on the wal in portreyynge° | *painting*
With al the gardyn and the lustynesse.° | *pleasure*
1940 Nat° was forgyeten the porter Ydelnesse[4] | *not*
Ne° Narcisus[5] the faire of yore agon,° | *nor, days of old*
And yet the folye° of Kyng Salomon,[6] | *folly*
And eek the grete strengthe of Ercules,° | *Hercules*
Th'enchauntementz of Medea and Circes,[7]

---

1   In keeping with a well-established literary tradition, best known through *The Romance of the Rose*, Chaucer here personifies the various aspects of a love affair and the qualities that are required to pursue one.

2   The word "carol" is known today primarily in the phrase "Christmas carol." Medieval carols were dances performed to the accompaniment of singing, and they could take place at any time, not just Christmas.

3   In Roman mythology, Venus rose from the sea fully formed at the island of Cythera. In a number of medieval texts, including the Knight's Tale, Mount Cithaeron is confused with this island.

4   In *The Romance of the Rose*, Idleness is the gatekeeper of the Garden of Love, indicating that a refined love affair was only possible for those with leisure.

5   The story of how Narcissus fell in love with his own image when he saw it in a spring is best known through Ovid's *Metamorphoses*.

6   In the Bible, King Solomon, previously depicted as the wisest of men, fell into folly under the influence of the many wives and concubines in his harem.

7   In Roman mythology, Medea and Circe were both sorceresses, in love with Jason and Odysseus respectively.

1945 Ne° of Turnus[1] with the hardy fiers° corage,°   *Nor, fierce, courage*
     The riche Cresus,[2] kaytyf° in servage.°   *captive, servitude*
     Thus may ye seen° that wysdom ne° richesse,   *see, nor*
     Beautee ne° sleighte,° strengthe, hardynesse°   *nor, trickery, boldness*
     Ne may° with Venus holde champartie.°   *may not, equal partnership*
1950 For as hir list,° the world than° may she gye.°   *as she desires, then, rule*
     Lo, alle thise folk so caught were in hir las,°   *snare*
     Til° they for wo ful ofte° seyde, "Allas!"   *until, very often*
     Suffiseth° heere ensamples° oon or two,   *There suffices, examples*
     And though I koude rekene° a thousand mo.   *reckon*
1955 THE statue of Venus glorious for to se
     Was naked, fletynge° in the large see,°   *floating, sea*
     And fro° the navele° doun° al covered was   *from, navel, down*
     With wawes° grene and brighte as any glas.   *waves*
     A citole[3] in hir right hand hadde she,
1960 And on hir heed,° ful semely° for to se,   *her head, very beautiful*
     A rose gerland° fressh and wel smellynge,°   *garland, sweet smelling*
     Above hir heed hir dowves° flikerynge.°   *doves, flittering*
     Biforn hire° stood hir sone Cupido.°   *before her, son Cupid*
     Upon his shuldres wynges hadde he two,
1965 And blynd° he was as it was often seene.   *blind*
     A bowe he bar° and arwes° brighte and kene.°   *carried, arrows, sharp*
     WHY sholde I noght° as wel eek telle yow al   *not*
     The portreiture° that was upon the wal   *painting*
     Withinne the temple of myghty Mars the rede?°   *red*
1970 Al peynted was the wal in lengthe and brede°   *breadth*
     Lyk° to the estres° of the grisly° place   *like, interior, horrible*
     That highte° the grete temple of Mars in Trace°   *was called, Thrace*
     In thilke° colde, frosty regioun   *the same*
     Theras° Mars hath his sovereyn° mansioun.[4]   *where, chief*
1975 FIRST on the wal was peynted a forest
     In which ther dwelleth° neither man ne best,   *there lives*
     With knotty, knarry,° bareyne° trees olde,   *gnarled, barren*
     Of stubbes° sharpe and hidouse° to biholde,   *stumps, hideous*
     In which ther ran a rumbel° and a swough°   *rumble, rush [of wind]*
1980 As though a storm sholde bresten° every bough.   *should break*

---

1   In the later books of Virgil's *Aeneid*, Turnus is Aeneas's main antagonist and opposes his marriage to Lavinia.
2   In Roman mythology, Croesus, king of Lydia, was fabulously rich but died a wretched death, captured by Cyrus. His relevance here is somewhat obscure.
3   A citole is a musical instrument that had a fingerboard and was plucked with a plectrum. It was a distant descendant of the classical lyre.
4   A "mansion" of a god/planet was, in astrological terms, its appropriate region in the sky, but here the reference is to Mars's greatest temple, in Thracia in northern Greece.

And dounward° from an hille under a bente,°   *downward, slope*
Ther stood the temple of Mars Armypotente,°   *powerful in arms*
Wroght° al° of burned° steel of which the entree°   *made, all, polished, entrance*
Was long and streit° and gastly° for to see.   *narrow, ghastly*
1985 And therout cam a rage° and swich a veze,°   *roar of wind, blast*
Thatit made al the gate for to rese.°   *shake*
The northren lyght in at the dores° shoon,   *doors*
For wyndowe on the wal ne was ther noon°   *there was none*
Thurgh which men myghten° any light discerne.°   *might, see*
1990 The dore was al of adamant° eterne,°   *strong stone, eternal*
Yclenched° overthwart° and endelong°   *supported, crosswise, lengthwise*
With iren° tough, and for to make it strong   *iron*
Every pyler° the temple to sustene   *pillar*
Was tonne-greet° of iren° bright and shene.°   *big as a barrel, iron, shining*
1995 THER saugh° I first the dirke ymaginyng°   *saw, dark plotting*
Of Felonye° and the compassyng,°   *Crime, scheming*
The crueel° Ire,° reed° as any gleede,°   *cruel, Anger, red, ember*
The pykepurs° and the pale Drede,°   *pick-pocket, Dread*
The smylere° with the knyf° under the cloke,°   *smiler, knife, cloak*
2000 The shepne° brennynge° with the blake smoke,   *stable, burning*
The tresoun of the mordrynge° in the bedde,°   *murdering, bed*
The open werre° with woundes al bibledde,°   *war, bloody*
Contek° with blody knyf and sharpe manace,°   *Conflict, menace*
Al ful of chirkyng° was that sory° place.[1]   *groaning, sorry*
2005 THE sleere of hymself° yet saugh° I ther: *suicide, saw*
His herte blood hath bathed al his heer,°   *hair*
The nayl° ydryven° in the shode° anyght,°   *nail, driven, temple, at night*
The colde deeth with mouth gapyng upright.
Amyddes° of the temple sat Meschaunce°   *in the middle, Misfortune*
2010 With disconfort° and sory contenaunce.°   *discomfort, sorry face*
YET saugh I Woodnesse° laughynge in his rage,   *Madness*
Armed Compleint,° Outhees,° and fiers Outrage,°   *Grievance, Outcry, fierce Violence*
The careyne° in the busk° with throte ycorve,°   *corpse, forest, cut throat*
A thousand slayn° and nat oon° of qualm ystorve,°   *killed, not one, killed by plague*
2015 The tiraunt° with the pray° by force yraft,°   *tyrant, prey, seized*
The toun° destroyed: ther was nothyng laft.°   *town, left*
YET saugh I brent° the shippes hoppesteres,°   *burned, dancing ships*
The hunte° strangled° with the wilde beres,°   *hunter, killed, by the wild bears*
The sowe° freten° the child right in the cradel,°   *sow, having eaten, cradle*
2020 The cook yscalded° for al his longe ladel.°   *scalded, ladle*
NOGHT was foryeten° by the infortune° of Marte:°   *forgotten, adverse influence, Mars*

---

1   The images and statues on the walls of the temple of Mars show the planet's influence, which causes not only war but other sorts of violence and catastrophe.

The cartere° overryden° with his carte. — *carter, run over by*
Under the wheel ful lowe° he lay adoun. — *very low*
THER were also of Martes divisioun° — *company*
2025 The laborer and the bocher° and the smyth° — *butcher, smith*
That forgeth sharpe swerdes° on his styth.°[1] — *swords, anvil*
AND al above depeynted° in a tour° — *painted, tower*
Saugh° I Conquest sittynge in greet honour — *saw*
With the sharpe swerd over his heed
2030 Hangynge by a soutil twynes threed.° — *thin twine's thread*
DEPEYNTED° was the slaughtre° of Julius, — *painted, assassination*
Of grete Nero and of Antonius.[2]
Al° be that thilke tyme° they were unborn,° — *although, the same time, not yet born*
Yet was hir deth° depeynted ther biforn° — *their death, painted before*
2035 By manasynge° of Mars, right by figure.° — *menacing, by horoscope*
So was it shewed° in that protreiture — *shown*
As is depeynted in the certres°[3] above — *certainties*
Who shal be slayn° or elles° deed° for love. — *killed, else, dead*
Suffiseth° oon ensample° in stories olde. — *suffices, one example*
2040 I may nat rekene hem alle,° though I wolde.° — *count them all, wanted to*
THE statue of Mars upun a carte° stood, — *upon a chariot*
Armed and looked grym° as he were wood.° — *looking grim, crazy*
And over his heed ther shynen° two figures — *shone*
Of sterres° that been cleped in scriptures,° — *stars, called in writings*
2045 Than oon° Puella, that oother° Rubeus.[4] — *one, other*
This god of armes was arrayed thus:
A wolf ther stood biforn° hym at his feet — *before*
With eyen rede° and of a man he eet.° — *red eyes, ate*
With soutil pencel° was depeynted this storie — *subtle or thin brush*
2050 In redoutynge° of Mars and of his glorie.° — *honor, glory*
NOW to the temple of Dyane the chaste
As shortly as I kan I wol me haste
To telle yow al the descripsioun.
Depeynted been the walles up and doun

---

1   These trades, which all use sharp tools, are under the protection of Mars.
2   Julius Caesar, the Emperor Nero, and Marc Antony all met violent deaths.
3   Ellesmere and Hengwrt read "certres" and "sertres" here, though most modern editions emend to "sterres," i.e., stars. There are a number of variants among the other manuscripts—"sertres," "circles," "septres," "storyes" among them—indication of some confusion among medieval readers of this line. "Written in the stars" makes the most obvious sense, and this actually argues against it being Chaucer's original intention, for the tendency is for scribes to simplify rather than make something more difficult. "Depicted in the [astrological] certainties" is likely Chaucer's meaning here.
4   Puella and Rubeus were patterned figures used in the method of predicting the future known as geomancy—a method of arranging dots into columns according to chance.

2055 Of huntyng and of shamefast° chastitee. — modest
THER saugh I how woful Calistopee,[1]
Whan that Diane agreved° was with here,° — angry, her
Was turned from a womman til° a bere.° — into, bear
And after was she maad° the loode sterre.°[2] — made, pole star
2060 Thus was it peynted. I kan° sey you no ferre.° — can, further
Hir sone°[3] is eek a sterre,° as men may see. — son, star
THER saugh I Dane[4] yturned° til a tree. — turned
I mene° nat° the goddesse Diane — mean, not
But Penneus doghter° which that highte° Dane. — Penneus's daughter, who was named
2065 THER saugh I Attheon[5] an hert° ymaked° — deer, made
For vengeaunce that he saugh Diane al naked.
I saugh how that hise houndes° have hym caught — dogs
And freeten° hym for that they knewe hym naught.° — eaten, did not know him
YET peynted a litel forthermoor° — a little further away
2070 How Atthalante[6] hunted the wilde boor° — boar
And Meleagree[7] and many another mo,
For which Dyane wroghte hym° care and wo. — fashioned for him
THER saugh I many another wonder° storie, — wonderful
The whiche me list nat drawen to memorie.[8]
2075 THIS goddesse on an hert° ful wel hye seet,° — deer, sat very high
With smale houndes al aboute hir feet.
And undernethe hir° feet she hadde a moone.° — her, moon
Wexynge° it was and sholde wanye° soone. — waxing, wane
In gaude grene° hir statue clothed was, — yellow-green
2080 With bowe in honde and arwes° in a cas.° — arrows, quiver
Hir eyen caste she ful lowe adoun
Ther° Pluto[9] hath his derke regioun. — where

---

1 Callisto, as Ovid recounts, was changed by Jupiter into a bear. When her son Arcas was about to kill her mistakenly in a hunt, Jupiter changed her into the constellation Ursa Major, the Great Bear.

2 A Latin gloss notes "Ursa maior" here. In fact the pole star, Polaris, is located in Ursa Minor, not Ursa Major.

3 Calisto's son is Arcas, whom Jupiter transformed into the constellation Ursa Minor, the Little Bear.

4 This is Daphne, who, as Ovid recounts, was chased by the god Apollo. At her request, the gods turned her into a laurel tree to protect her from him.

5 Actaeon saw the naked Diana taking a bath. She changed him into a deer to punish him and he was killed by his own hunting dogs.

6 Atalanta was a maiden and a hunter who, to avoid marriage, required her suitors to compete with her in a race. Hippomenes won the race, but he lacked gratitude to Venus, who changed him and Atalanta into lions.

7 Meleager was awarded Atalanta after the hunt for the Calydonian boar, occasioning jealousy between him and his family.

8 "Which I do not wish to call to memory."

9 In Greek mythology, Pluto was the god of the Underworld, the realm of the dead.

A WOMMAN travaillynge° was hire biforn,° — *laboring, before her*
But for° hir° child so longe was unborn. — *because, her*
2085 Ful pitously,° "Lucyna!"[1] gan she calle° — *very pitifully, began to call*
And seyde, "Helpe! For thow mayst best° of alle!" — *you may best [help]*
Wel koude° he peynten° lifly° that it wroghte.° — *could, paint, lifelike, made*
With many a floryn° he the hewes° boghte.° — *gold coin, colors, bought*
Now been the lystes° maad° and Theseus — *arena, made*
2090 That at his grete cost arrayed° thus — *arranged*
The temples and the theatre every deel,° — *part*
Whan it was doon, hym lyked wonder weel.° — *it pleased him very well*
But stynte° I wole of Theseus a lite° — *wish to stop speaking, little*
And speke of Palamon and of Arcite. —
2095 THE day approcheth° of hir retournynge — *approaches*
That everich sholde an hundred knyghtes brynge
The bataille° to darreyne° as I yow° tolde. — *battle, decide, you*
And til Atthenes,° hir covenantz° for to holde, — *to Athens, their agreement*
Hath everich of hem broght an hundred knyghtes
2100 Wel armed for the werre° at alle rightes.° — *war, in all aspects*
And sikerly,° ther trowed° many a man — *surely, believed*
That nevere sithen° that the world bigan — *ever since*
As for to speke of knyghthod° of hir hond, — *deeds of knighthood*
As fer as God hath maked see or lond
2105 Nas° of so fewe° so noble a compaignye. — *there was not, few*
For every wight° that lovede chivalrye — *person*
And wolde his thankes° han° a passant° name — *gladly, have, surpassing*
Hath preyd° that he myghte been of° that game. — *prayed, [part] of*
And wel was hym that therto chosen was,° — *chosen for it*
2110 For if ther fille° tomorwe swich a cas,° — *befell, such a chance*
Ye knowen wel that every lusty° knyght — *vigorous*
That loveth paramours° and hath his myght, — *who loves passionately*
Were it° in Engelond or elleswhere, — *if it were*
They wolde hir thankes° wilnen° to be there — *gladly, wish*
2115 To fighte for a lady, benedicitee.° — *bless you*
It were a lusty° sighte for to see! — *pleasant*
AND right so ferden° they with Palamon. — *did*
With hym ther wenten knyghtes many on.° — *one*
Som wol ben° armed in an haubergeon° — *One would be, mail-coat*
2120 And in bristplate° and in light gypon.° — *breastplate, over-garment*
And somme woln have a paire plates°[2] large — *plate armor*
And somme woln have a Pruce-sheeld° or a targe.° — *Prussian shield, shield*

---

1 Lucina is another name for Diana. Diana was not only the goddess of the hunt but also the goddess of childbirth.
2 Plate armor, as opposed to chain-mail armor, was a fairly recent invention in Chaucer's day.

Somme woln ben armed on hir legges° weel° — *legs, well*
And have an ax and somme a mace[1] of steel.
2125 There is no newe gyse° that it nas° old. — *new fashion, was not*
Armed were they as I have yow told,
Everych° after his opinioun. — *everyone*
Ther maistow seen comynge° with Palamon — *may you see coming*
Lygurge[2] hymself, the grete kyng of Trace.° — *Thrace*
2130 Blak was his berd, and manly was his face.
The cercles of hise eyen in his heed,
They gloweden° bitwixen yelow° and reed.° — *glowed, yellow, red*
And lik a grifphon[3] looked he aboute,
With kempe heeris° on hise browes stoute,° — *shaggy hairs, his large brows*
2135 Hise lymes° grete, his brawnes° harde and stronge, — *his limbs, muscles*
His shuldres brode,° hise armes rounde and longe. — *shoulders broad*
And as the gyse° was in his contree, — *fashion*
Ful hye° upon a chaar° of gold stood he — *very high, chariot*
With foure white boles° in the trays.° — *bulls, harness*
2140 Instede of cote armure° over° his harnays,° — *coat of arms, on, armor*
With nayles° yelewe° and brighte as any gold, — *nails, yellow*
He hadde a beres skyn,° col blak for old.° — *bear's skin, coal-black with age*
His longe heer was kembd° bihynde his bak. — *combed*
As any ravenes fethere,° it shoon° for blak. — *raven's feather, shone*
2145 A wrethe° of gold, arm-greet° of huge wighte° — *wreath, arm thick, weight*
Upon his heed set ful of stones° brighte, — *jewels*
Of fyne rubyes° and of dyamauntz.° — *fine rubies, diamonds*
Aboute his chaar° ther wenten white alauntz,° — *chariot, wolfhounds*
Twenty and mo, as grete as any steer
2150 To hunten at the leoun or° the deer, — *MS repeats or*
And folwed hym with mosel° faste ybounde,° — *muzzle, bound*
Colered° of gold and tourettes° fyled° rounde. — *collared, leash rings, filed*
An hundred lordes hadde he in his route,° — *company*
Armed ful wel with hertes stierne° and stoute. — *stern*
2155 WITH Arcite in stories as men fynde
The grete° Emetreus[4] the kyng of Inde° — *great, India*
Upon a steede bay,° trapped in steel, — *bay-colored horse*
Covered in clooth° of gold, dyapred[5] weel° — *cloth, well*

---

1 Originally, in Old English, a synonym for "sword," "mace" had come to mean a spiked metal club.
2 Lycurgus was the king of Sparta, in Greece, known for his austere militarism.
3 The gryphon (or griffin) was a mythological beast with a lion's hindquarters and an eagle's torso and head.
4 King Emetreus is not attested in classical mythology nor is he to be found in Chaucer's sources.
5 "Diapered" is a technical term drawn from the world of medieval manuscript illumination indicating the diamond-shaped patterns used as the background for many paintings in medieval

Cam ridynge lyk the god of armes, Mars.

2160　His cotearmure° was of clooth° of Tars,° — *cloth tunic, cloth, Tartary (China)*

Couched° with perles° white and rounde and grete. — *decorated, pearls*

His sadel° was of brend° gold newe ybete.°[1] — *saddle, burnished, polished*

A mantel° upon his shulder hangynge — *tunic*

Bratful° of rubyes rede as fyr sparklynge, — *full to the brim*

2165　His crispe heer° lyk rynges was yronne,° — *curly hair, curled*

And that was yelow and glytered° as the sonne. — *glittered*

His nose was heigh,° hise eyen bright citryn,° — *high, his eyes, lemon-colored*

Hise lippes° rounde, his colour was sangwyn.° — *lips, red*

A fewe frakenes° in his face yspreynd,° — *freckles, sprinkled*

2170　Bitwixen yelow and somdel blak° ymeynd.° — *somewhat black, mixed*

And as a leoun he his lookyng caste.° — *he looked about*

Of fyve and twenty yeer° his age I caste.° — *years, guess*

His berd° was wel bigonne° for to sprynge.° — *beard, begun, grow*

His voys was as a trompe thondrynge.° — *thundering trumpet*

2175　Upon his heed he wered° of laurer° grene — *wore, laurel leaves*

A gerland° fressh and lusty° for to sene.° — *garland, pleasant, see*

Upon his hand he bar° for his deduyt° — *carried, pleasure*

An egle° tame as any lilye whyt.° — *eagle, white lily*

An hundred lordes hadde he with hym there,

2180　Al armed save hir heddes° in al hir gere,° — *except their heads, armor*

Ful richely in alle maner thynges.

For trusteth wel that dukes, erles,° kynges — *earls*

Were gadered° in this noble compaignye — *gathered*

For love and for encrees° of chivalrye. — *increase*

2185　Aboute this kyng ther ran on every part° — *on every side*

Ful° many a tame leoun and leopard, — *very*

And in this wise° thise lordes alle and some — *way*

Been on the Sonday to the citee come,

Aboute pryme° and in the toun° alight.° — *morning, town, arrived*

2190　THIS Theseus, this duc, this worthy knyght,

Whan he had broght hem into his citee

And inned hem° everich in his degree,° — *lodged them at an inn, everyone according to his rank*

He festeth° hem and dooth° so greet labour — *feasts, does*

To esen° hem and doon hem al honour,° — *refresh, do them every honor*

2195　That yet man weneth° that no maner wit — *imagines*

Of noon estaat° ne koude° amenden it.° — *no estate, could, make it better*

THE mynstralcye,° the service at the feeste, — *musical performances*

---

books. King Emetreus's horse wears a decorative cloth covered with this type of pattern. War-horses in Chaucer's time often wore large, brightly colored decorative cloths.

1　"Newly beaten" refers to how a goldsmith works gold-plate jewelry into pleasing patterns by beating it with a small hammer.

The grete yiftes° to the meeste and leeste,° — *gifts, most and least [important]*
The riche array° of Theseus paleys, — *decoration*
2200 Ne who sat first ne° last° upon the deys,° — *nor, last, dais (high table)*
What ladyes fairest been or best daunsynge,
Or which of hem kan dauncen best and synge,° — *can best dance and sing*
Ne° who moost felyngly speketh° of love, — *nor, feelingly speak*
What haukes° sitten on the perche° above, — *hawks, perch*
2205 What houndes liggen° in the floor adoun,° — *lie, down*
Of al this make I now no mencioun,° — *mention*
But al th'effect° that thynketh me° the beste.[1] — *only the general effect, seems to me*
Now cometh the point, and herkneth if yow leste.° — *if you wish*
THE Sonday nyght er day bigan to sprynge,° — *dawn*
2210 Whan Palamon the larke herde synge,
Although it nere nat° day by houres two, — *were not*
Yet song° the larke and Palamon also. — *sang*
With hooly° herte and with an heigh corage° — *holy, high spirit*
He roos° to wenden° on his pilgrymage — *rose, go*
2215 Unto the blisful Citherea° benigne.° — *Venus, kind*
I mene Venus, honurable and digne.° — *worthy*
And in hir houre[2] he walketh forth a pas° — *slowly*
Unto the lystes° ther° hire° temple was, — *arena, where, her*
And doun he kneleth° with ful humble cheere° — *kneels, facial expression*
2220 And herte soor,° and seyde in this manere: — *sore heart*
"FAIRESTE of faire, O lady myn, Venus,[3]
Doughter to Jove and spouse of Vulcanus,[4]
Thow gladere[5] of the mount of Citheron,[6]
For thilke° love thow haddest to° Adoon,[7] — *the same, you had for*
2225 Have pitee of my bittre° teeris smerte° — *bitter, painful tears*
And taak° myn humble preyere at thyn herte.° — *take, to your heart*
Allas, I ne have no langage to telle° — *do not have any language to tell*
Th'effectes ne° the tormentz of myn helle!° — *nor, my hell*

---

1 Here Theseus offers an example of *occupatio*, the rhetorical figure in which one lists at great length the things one is not going to describe, thus describing them.

2 According to astrology, each hour of the day is devoted in succession to one of the gods/planets.

3 Here there is a gloss in the margin: "The preyere of Palamoun to Venus goddesse of love."

4 In Roman mythology, lame Vulcan was the blacksmith of the gods. Venus preferred her lover Mars to her husband Vulcan.

5 "Gladderer": Venus makes people glad because, in the old astrology, she, with Jupiter, is one of the two planets who uniformly bring good fortune. The two who bring bad luck are Saturn and Mars.

6 See page 61, note 3.

7 Adonis was a youth whom Venus loved. He was killed by a boar, and Venus transformed his blood into a flower.

Myn herte may myne harmes nat biwreye.°   *not reveal my wrongs*
2230 I am so confus,° that I kan noght seye°   *bewildered, can not say*
But 'Mercy!' Lady bright, that knowest weele°   *knows well*
My thought and seest what harmes° that I feele,   *wrongs*
Considere al this and rewe° upon my soore,°   *have mercy, pain*
As wisly° as I shal for everemore,   *as surely as*
2235 Emforth° my myght thy trewe servant be,   *according to*
And holden werre° alwey with chastitee,   *be at war*
That make I myn avow,° so ye me helpe,°   *promise, if you help me*
I kepe noght° of armes for to yelpe.°   *do not care, boast*
Ne I ne axe° nat tomorwe to have victorie   *nor do I ask*
2240 Ne° renoun° in this cas° ne veyneglorie°   *nor, fame, event, pride*
Of pris° of armes blowen up and doun.°   *reputation, made widely known*
But I wolde have fully possessioun
Of Emelye and dye in thy servyse.
Fynd thow the manere hou° and in what wyse.°   *means how, way*
2245 I recche nat but° it may bettre be   *do not care whether*
To have victorie of hem or they of me,
So that I have my lady in myne armes!
For though° so be that Mars is god of armes,   *For although*
Youre vertu° is so greet in hevene above,   *power*
2250 That if yow list,° I shal wel have my love.   *if you wish*
THY temple wol I worshipe everemo,°   *evermore*
And on thyn auter° where° I ride or go,   *your altar, wherever*
I wol doon° sacrifice and fires beete.°   *make, kindle fires [of sacrifice]*
And if ye wol nat so,° my lady sweete,   *you will not [do] so*
2255 Thanne preye° I thee tomorwe with a spere   *pray*
That Arcita me thurgh the herte bere!°   *pierce*
Thanne rekke° I noght whan I have lost my lyf,   *care*
Though that Arcita wynne hire to his wyf.°   *win her as his wife*
This is th'effect and ende of my preyeye.°   *prayer*
2260 Yif° me my love, thow blisful° lady deere."   *give, blissful*
WHAN the orison° was doon° of Palamon,   *prayer, done*
His sacrifice he dide and that anon°   *immediately*
Ful pitously° with alle circumstaunce,°   *very pitifully, ritual*
Al° telle I noght° as now° his observaunce.   *although, not, for now*
2265 But atte laste the statue of Venus shook
And made a signe wherby that he took
That his preyere accepted was that day.
For thogh the signe shewed° a delay,   *showed*
Yet wiste he wel° that graunted° was his boone.°   *knew he well, granted, request*
2270 And with glad herte he wente hym hoom ful° soone.   *very*

THE thridde° houre inequal[1] that Palamon — *third*
Bigan° to Venus temple for to gon,° — *began, go*
Up roos the sonne, and up roos Emelye,
And to the temple of Dyane gan hye.° — *went*
2275 Hir maydens,° that she thider with hire ladde,° — *ladies-in-waiting, led*
Ful redily with hem the fyr° they hadde.°[2] — *fire [for sacrifice], carried*
Th'encens,° the clothes, and the remenant al — *the incense*
That to the sacrifice longen shal,° — *pertained to the sacrifice*
The hornes° fulle of meeth,° as was the gyse.° — *drinking horns, mead, custom*
2280 Ther lakked noght to doon hir° sacrifise. — *nothing to do her*
SMOKYNGE° the temple ful of clothes faire,° — *incensing, cloth hangings*
This Emelye with herte debonaire,° — *gentle*
Hir body wessh° with water of a welle. — *washed*
But hou° she dide hir ryte,° I dar nat° telle, — *how, rite, dare not*
2285 But it be anythyng in general.° — *except in general terms*
And yet it were a game° to heeren° al. — *joy, hear*
To hym that meneth wel,° it were no charge,° — *means well, burden*
But it is good a man been at his large.° — *free [to speak]*
HIR° brighte heer° was kembd,° untressed° al. — *her, hair, combed, unbraided*
2290 A coroune° of a grene ook° cerial[3] — *crown, oak*
Upon hir heed was set ful fair and meete.° — *fitting*
Two fyres on the auter° gan she beete° — *altar, kindled*
And dide hir thynges° as men may biholde — *performed her duties*
In Stace[4] of Thebes and thise bookes olde.
2295 Whan kyndled° was the fyr, with pitous cheere° — *kindled, pitiful expression*
Unto Dyane she spak as ye may heere:
"O CHASTE goddesse of the wodes grene,[5]
To whom bothe hevene and erthe and see° is sene,° — *sea, seen*
Queene of the regne° of Pluto derk° and lowe, — *reign, dark*
2300 Goddesse of maydens° that myn herte hast knowe° — *maidens, known*
Ful many a yeer, and woost° what I desire, — *knows*
As keepe me fro° thy vengeaunce and thyn ire,° — *to keep me from, your anger*

---

1 In Chaucer's day there were two ways of dividing up time into hours. "Artificial" hours are those we use today, where both day and night are divided into twelve hours equal in amount. "Unequal" hours, the older system used in an age that did not have the clocks that made the artificial hours possible, was the division of the daylight time into twelve hours and the time of dark into twelve. The length of these unequal hours would of course change according to the seasons. They were the same as the artificial hours only at the spring and autumn equinoxes. Each hour of the day was devoted to one of the gods/planets.
2 Ellesmere repeats the word "ladde" from the previous line, but the reading in Hengwrt, "hadde" makes more sense as well as avoiding a rhyme on the same word.
3 "Cerial" specifies this as a distinct species of oak, *quercus cerris*.
4 On the Latin poet Statius, see p. 33, note 1.
5 There is a gloss in the margin: "The preyere of Emelye to Dyane, goddesse of maydens."

That Attheon[1] aboughte° cruelly. — paid for
Chaste goddesse, wel wostow° that I — well you know
2305 Desire to ben° a mayden al my lyf. — be
Ne° nevere wol° I be no love ne wyf! — nor, will
I am, thow woost,° yet of thy compaignye, — you know
A mayde, and love huntynge° and venerye° — hunting, hunting
And for to walken in the wodes wilde
2310 And noght° to ben° a wyf° and be with childe.° — not, be, wife, be pregnant
Noght° wol° I knowe the compaignye of man. — by no means, will
Now helpe me, lady, sith° ye may and kan,° — since, can
For tho° thre formes°[2] that thou hast in thee. — those, attributes
And Palamon that hath swich love to me
2315 And eek Arcite that loveth me so soore,
This grace I preye thee withoute moore:° — without any more [words]
And sende love and pees° bitwixe° hem° two, — peace, between, them
And fro° me turne awey hir hertes° so, — from, their hearts
That al hire hoote° love and hir desir — hot
2320 And al hir bisy° torment and hir fir° — intense, fire
Be queynt° or turned in another place. — quenched
And if so be thou wolt do me no grace,° — you will not grant my request
And if my destynee° be shapen° so — destiny, shaped
That I shal nedes° have oon of hem two, — must have
2325 As sende me hym that moost° desireth me. — most
Bihoold,° goddesse of clene° chastitee, — behold, pure
The bittre teeris° that on my chekes° falle! — tears, cheeks
Syn° thou art mayde and kepere° of us alle, — since, keeper
My maydenhede° thou kepe and wel conserve.° — virginity, preserve
2330 And whil° I lyve,° a mayde I wol° thee serve."[3] — while, live, will
THE fires brenne° upon the auter cleere° — burn, bright
Whil Emelye was thus in hir preyere.
But sodeynly she saugh a sighte queynte.° — curious sight
For right anon oon° of the fyres queynte° — one, went out
2335 And quyked agayn,° and after that anon° — kindled again, immediately
That oother fyr was queynt° and al agon.° — quenched, completely gone
And as it queynte, it made a whistlynge
As doon° thise wete° brondes° in hir brennynge.° — do, wet, sticks, burning
And at the brondes ende out ran anon
2340 As it were blody dropes° many oon,° — bloody drops, many a one

---

1   See p. 65, note 5.
2   The three attributes Emelye mentions here are Diana's being the goddess of the hunt, of the moon (as Luna), and of the underworld (as Proserpina).
3   The comma, like all the punctuation, has been supplied by modern editors. Here the meaning shifts slightly if it is placed after "mayde."

For which so soore° agast° was Emelye,   *sorely, appalled*
That she was wel ny mad° and gan to crye,°   *almost crazy, began to cry*
For she ne wiste° what it signyfied.   *did not know*
But oonly for the feere° thus hath she cried   *fear*
2345 And weepe that it was pitee° for to heere.°   *pity, hear*
And therwithal° Dyane gan appeere°   *with all of this, appeared*
With bowe° in honde,° right as an hunteresse   *bow, hand*
And seyde, "Doghter,° stynt° thyn hevynesse!°[1]   *daughter, stop, complaining*
AMONG the goddes hye,° it is affermed°   *high, affirmed*
2350 And by eterne° word writen and confermed: *eternal*
Thou shalt ben° wedded unto oon° of tho°   *you will be, one, those*
That han° for thee so muchel° care and wo.   *have, much*
But unto which of hem, I may nat telle.
Farwel, for I ne may no lenger dwelle.°   *may no longer stay*
2355 The fires whiche that on myn auter brenne°   *burn*
Shulle° thee declaren,° er that thou go henne,°   *shall tell, MS declare, away*
Thyn aventure° of love as in this cas."°   *fortune, situation*
And with that word, the arwes in the caas°   *quiver*
Of the goddesse clateren° faste and rynge,°   *clatter, ring*
2360 And forth she wente and made a vanysshynge,°   *vanished*
For which this Emelye astoned° was   *astonished*
And seyde, "What amounteth this,° allas?   *What does this mean*
I putte me in thy proteccioun,
Dyane, and in thy disposicioun."°   *under your care*
2365 And hoom she goth° anon° the nexte weye.   *goes, immediately*
This is th'effect. Ther is namoore to seye.
THE nexte houre of Mars folwynge this,
Arcite unto the temple walked is
Of fierse° Mars to doon° his sacrifise   *fierce, do*
2370 With alle the rytes° of his payen wyse.°   *rites, pagan customs*
With pitous herte° and heigh° devocioun   *pitiful heart, high*
Right thus to Mars he seyde° his orisoun:°   *said, prayer*
"O STRONGE god that in the regnes° colde[2]   *reigns*
Of Trace° honoured art and lord yholde°   *Thrace, considered lord*
2375 AND hast° in every regne and every lond°   *have, land*
Of armes al the brydel in thyn hond,[3]
And hem fortunest° as thee lyst devyse,°   *give fortune to them, wish to arrange*
Accepte° of me my pitous° sacrifise.   *accept, pitiful*
If so be that my youthe may deserve

---

1   There is a gloss in the margin: "The answere of Dyane to Emelye."
2   There is a gloss in the margin: "The orisoun [prayer] of Arcite to Mars, god of Armes."
3   Mars has complete control (has the bridle, or as might be said now, the reins) of all matters relating to arms.

2380 And that my myght° be worthy for to serve	strength
Thy godhede,° that I may been° oon of thyne,°	divinity, be, one of yours
Thanne° preye I thee to rewe° upon my pyne.°	Then, have pity, pain
For thilke peyne° and thilke hoote fir°	the same pain, hot fire
In which thow whilom° brendest° for desir°	once, burned, desire
2385 Whan that thow usedest° the beautee	used
Of faire, yonge, fresshe Venus fre°	noble
And haddest hire in armes at thy wille	
(Although thee ones° on a tyme° mysfille°	once, time, had a misfortune
Whan Vulcanus hadde caught thee in his las°	trap
2390 And foond° thee liggynge° by his wyf,° allas!)¹	found, lying, wife
For thilke sorwe° that was in thyn herte,	sorrow
Have routhe° as wel° upon my peynes smerte!°	pity, well, sore pains
I am yong° and unkonnynge,° as thow woost,°	young, unknowing, know
And, as I trowe,° with love offended° moost	believe, injured
2395 That evere was any lyves creature.°	any creature alive
For she that dooth° me al this wo endure°	does, enduring woe
Ne reccheth° nevere wher° I synke° or fleete!°	does not care, whether, sink, float
And wel I woot er° she me mercy heete,°	well I know before, promise
I moot° with strengthe wynne hire° in the place.	must, win her
2400 And wel I woot withouten helpe or grace	
Of thee ne may° my strengthe noght availle.°	may not, succeed
Thanne helpe me, lord, tomorwe in my bataille.	
For thilke fyr that whilom brente° thee	once burned
As wel as thilke fyr° now brenneth° me,	just as the same fire, burns
2405 And do° that I tomorwe have victorie.	cause it
Myn° be the travaille° and thyn° be the glorie.	mine, trouble, yours
Thy sovereyn° temple wol° I moost° honouren	chief, will, most
Of any place and alwey° moost labouren	always
In thy plesaunce° and in thy craftes² stronge.	pleasure
2410 And in thy temple I wol° my baner° honge.°	will, banner, hang
And alle the armes of my compaignye	
And evere mo unto that day I dye,	
Eterne fir° I wol° biforn thee fynde,°	Eternal fire, will, provide
And eek to this avow° I wol° me bynde:°	promise, will, bind
2415 My beerd,° myn heer° that hongeth° long adoun°	beard, my hair, hangs, down
That nevere yet ne felte offensioun°	felt offense (was cut)
Of rasour° nor of shere° I wol° thee yeve°	razor, scissors, will, give

---

1   Arcite refers here to the story of Vulcan's jealousy over the affair his wife, Venus had with Mars.
     As the greatest of smiths, he fashioned an invisible net, which he dropped upon Mars and Venus
     when they were in bed together, trapping them for all the gods to see their shame.
2   Mars's handicrafts, of course, are those that belong to war—wielding the sword and lance and
     horsemanship foremost among them.

And ben° thy trewe servant whil I lyve.   *be*
Now, lord, have routhe° upon my sorwes soore.°   *pity, sore sorrows*
2420 Yif° me the victorie. I aske thee namoore."°   *give, no more*
THE preyere stynt° of Arcita the stronge.   *ends*
The rynges° on the temple dore° that honge,°   *rings, door, hung*
AND eek the dores clatereden° ful° faste,   *clattered, very*
Of which Arcita somwhat hym agaste.°   *was somewhat surprised*
2425 The fyres brenden° upon the auter° brighte,   *burned, altar*
That it gan al the temple for to lighte.°   *lit all the temple*
And sweete smel the ground anon up yaf.°   *immediately gave*
And Arcita anon his hand up haf.°   *raised*
And moore encens° into the fyr he caste°   *incense, threw*
2430 With othere rytes° mo. And atte laste   *rites*
The statue of Mars bigan° his hauberk° rynge,   *began, mail-coat*
And with that soun° he herde° a murmurynge°   *sound, heard, murmuring*
Full lowe and dym,° and seyde thus: "Victorie,"   *very low and dim*
For which he yaf° to Mars honour and glorie.   *gave*
2435 And thus with joye and hope wel° to fare,   *well*
Arcite anon° unto his in° is fare°   *immediately, inn, has gone*
As fayn° as fowel° is of the brighte sonne.   *happy, bird*
AND right anon swich strif° ther is bigonne°   *such strife, begins*
For thilke grauntyng° in the hevene above.   *this granting [of answers to prayers]*
2440 Bitwixe° Venus the goddesse of love   *between*
And Mars the stierne° god armypotente,°   *stern, strong in arms*
That Juppiter was bisy° it to stente,°   *busy, stop it*
Til that the pale Saturnus the colde
That knew so manye of aventures° olde   *adventures*
2445 Foond° in his olde experience and art   *found*
That he ful soone° hath plesed° every part.°   *very soon, pleased, each side*
As sooth° is seyd,° elde° hath greet avantage.°   *true, said, age, advantage*
In elde is bothe wysdom and usage.°   *experience*
Men may the olde atrenne° and noght atrede.°   *outrun, not out-advise*
2450 Saturne anon, to stynten strif and drede,°   *stop strife and fear*
Albeit° that it is agayn° his kynde,°   *although, against, nature*
Of al this strif he gan remedie fynde.°   *found a remedy*
"MY deere° doghter, Venus," quod Saturne,   *dear*
"My cours° that hath so wyde° for to turne   *course [across the sky], wide*
2455 Hath moore power than woot° any man.[1]   *knows*
Myn is the drenchyng° in the see° so wan.°   *drowning, sea, dark*
Myn is the prison° in the derke cote.°   *imprisonment, dark cell*

---

1 Saturn, in the Middle Ages the farthest known planet from the sun, was believed to have a cold and harmful influence. The following speech of Saturn enumerates disasters that he as god and astrological planet typically causes.

Myn is the stranglyng and hangyng by the throte,°   *throat*
The murmure° and the cherles rebellyng,°   *murmur, peasants' rebellion*
2460 The groynynge° and the pryvee empoysonyng.°   *groaning, secret poisoning*
I do vengeance and pleyn correccioun°   *full punishment*
Whil I dwelle in signe of the leoun.°[1]   *lion*
Myn is the ruyne° of the hye° halles,   *ruin, high*
The fallynge of the toures° and of the walles   *towers*
2465 Upon the mynour° or the carpenter.[2]   *miner*
I slow° Sampsoun shakynge the piler.°[3]   *killed, pillar*
And myne be the maladyes colde,[4]
The derke tresons° and the castes° olde.   *treasons, plots*
My lookyng is the fader° of pestilence.°   *father, plague*
2470 Now weepe namoore.° I shal doon diligence°   *no more, shall take care*
That Palamon, that is thyn owene knyght
Shal have his lady as thou hast hym hight.°   *promised*
Though Mars shal helpe his knyght, yet nathelees°   *nevertheless*
Bitwixe yow° ther moot° be somtyme° pees,°   *between you, must, sometime, peace*
2475 Al° be ye noght of o compleccioun.°   *although, one temperament*
That causeth al day swich divisioun.°   *such disagreement*
I am thyn aiel,° redy at thy wille.   *your grandfather*
Weepe now namoore. I wol thy lust fulfille."°   *will satisfy your desire*
Now wol I stynten° of the goddes above,   *stop speaking*
2480 Of Mars and of Venus, goddesse of love,
And telle yow as pleynly° as I kan   *plainly*
The grete effect° for which that I bygan.   *result*

EXPLICIT TERCIA PARS SEQUITUR PARS QUARTA[5]

GREET was the feeste in Atthenes that day,
And eek the lusty seson° of that May   *pleasant season*
2485 Made every wight to been° in swich plesaunce,°   *be, enjoyment*
That al that Monday justen° they and daunce°   *joust, dance*
And spenten it in Venus heigh servyse.°   *Venus's high service*
And by the cause° that they sholde ryse°   *because, had to rise*

---

1 Saturn is most harmful when he is in the powerful astrological house of Leo.
2 The types of miners and carpenters here meant are probably military men who helped dig tunnels under besieged walls of towns and castles. The walls would be shored up with timber, and then, at the right time for an attack to start, the timbers would be set on fire, thus insuring the collapse of the walls. The disaster envisioned here is that which would occur if the miners and carpenters did not leave the tunnel in time before the walls collapsed.
3 The reference here is to Judges 23–31, in which Sampson, blinded and enslaved by his enemies, pulls down the pillars supporting their temple, killing them all and himself as well.
4 Diseases caused by a preponderance of the cold humor. See General Prologue, p. 16, note 7.
5 "Here ends the third part. The fourth part follows."

Eerly° for to seen the grete fight,   *early*
2490 Unto hir reste wenten they at nyght,
And on the morwe whan that day gan sprynge,°   *began to dawn*
Of hors° and harneys,° noyse° and claterynge°   *horse, equipment, noise, clattering*
Ther was in hostelryes° al aboute,   *inns*
And to the paleys° rood° ther many a route°   *palace, rode, crowd*
2495 Of lordes upon steedes and palfreys.°   *warhorses and everyday horses*
Ther maystow seen° divisynge of harneys°   *may you see, preparation of gear*
So unkouth° and so riche and wroght so weel°   *unusual, made so well*
Of goldsmythrye,° of browdynge,° and of steel,   *goldsmithery, embroidering*
The sheeldes brighte, testeres,° and trappures,°   *armor for horses' heads, horse-armor*
2500 Gold-hewen° helmes,° hauberkes,° cote-armures,°   *golden, helmets, mail-coats, tunics*
Lordes in parementz° on hir courseres,°   *robes, warhorses*
Knyghtes of retenue° and eek squieres°   *in service, squires*
Nailynge the speres° and helmes bokelynge,°   *nailing spears, buckling helmets*
Giggynge of sheeldes° with layneres lacynge°   *setting straps, lacing straps*
2505 (Thereas° nede° is, they weren° nothyng ydel°),   *where, need, were, idle*
The fomy° steedes on the golden brydel°   *foamy (with sweat), bridle*
Gnawynge,° and faste° the armurers° also   *gnawing, quickly, armorers*
With fyle° and hamer prikynge° to and fro,   *file, galloping*
Yemen° on foote and communes° many oon°   *yeomen, commoners, many a one*
2510 With shorte staves thikke° as they may goon,°   *densely, go*
Pypes,° trompes,° nakerers,° clariounes,°   *pipes, trumpets, drums, bugles*
That in the bataille blowen° blody sounes,°   *blow, bloody sounds*
The paleys ful of peples up and doun,
Heere thre, ther ten, holdynge° hir questioun,   *debating*
2515 Dyvynynge of° thise° Thebane knyghtes two.   *guessing about, these*
Somme seyden thus; somme seyde it shal be so;
Somme helden with° hym with the blake° berd;   *sided with, black*
Somme with the balled,° somme with the thikke herd;°   *bald, thick-haired*
Somme seyde he looked grymme° and he wolde fighte;°   *fierce, wanted to fight*
2520 "He hath a sparth° of twenty pound of wighte!"°   *axe, weight*
Thus was the halle ful of divynynge°   *guessing*
Longe after that the sonne gan to sprynge.°   *began to rise*
THE grete Theseus that of his sleepe awaked
With mynstralcie° and noyse that was maked°   *music, made*
2525 Heeld yet the chambre° of his paleys° riche   *stayed indoors, palace*
Til that the Thebane knyghtes bothe yliche°   *equally*
Honured were into the paleys fet.°   *fetched*
Duc Theseus was at a wyndow set,
Arrayed° right as he were a god in trone.°   *dressed, on [his] throne*
2530 The peple preesseth thiderward° ful° soone   *crowd towards there, very*
Hym for to seen and doon heigh reverence°   *do high honor*
And eek to herkne his heste° and his sentence.   *listen to his command*

AN heraud° on a scaffold made an "Oo!"°   *herald, Whoa!*
Til al the noyse of peple was ydo.°   *stopped*
2535 And whan he saugh the noyse of peple al stille,
Tho° shewed he the myghty dukes wille.   *Then*
"THE lord hath of his heigh discrecioun
Considered that it were destruccioun
To gentil° blood to fighten in the gyse°   *noble, in the manner*
2540 Of mortal bataille now in this emprise.°   *enterprise*
Wherfore° to shapen° that they shal nat dye,°   *therefore, ensure, die*
He wolde° his firste purpos modifye.°   *would, modify*
No man therfore up peyne of los of lyf°   *upon pain of loss of life*
No maner shot,° polax,° ne° short knyf°   *arrow, battle-axe, nor, knife*
2545 Into the lystes sende ne thider brynge,°   *bring there*
Ne short swerd for to stoke° with poynt bitynge.°   *stab, biting point*
Ne man ne drawe ne bere° by his syde.   *carry*
Ne no man shal unto his felawe° ryde   *against his opponent*
But o° cours° with a sharpe ygrounde spere.°   *one, turn, sharpened spear*
2550 Foyne, if hym list, on foote hymself to were.[1]
And he that is at meschief° shal be take°   *in trouble, taken*
And noght slayn,° but be broght unto the stake   *not killed*
That shal ben ordeyned° on either syde.   *be ordained*
But thider° he shal° by force and there abyde.   *to that place, shall [go] stay*
2555 AND if so be the chieftayn° be take°   *leader, taken*
On outher syde or elles sleen his make,°   *else his opponent (the opposing leader) killed*
No lenger° shal the turneiynge° laste.   *longer, tourneying*
God spede you! Gooth forth and ley° on faste!   *lay*
With long swerd and with maces fighteth youre fille.
2560 Gooth now youre wey. This is the lordes wille.
THE voys° of peple touched the hevene,°   *voice, sky*
So loude cride they with murie stevene,°   *merry voice*
"GOD save swich a lord that is so good!
He wilneth° no destruccion of blood."   *wills*
2565 Up goon° the trompes° and the melodye,°   *go, trumpets, melody*
And to the lystes rit° the compaignye,   *rides*
By ordinance° thurghout the citee large,   *by rank*
Hanged with clooth of gold and nat° with sarge.°   *not, serge (plain cloth)*
FUL lik a lord this noble duc gan ryde,°   *rode*
2570 Thise two Thebans upon either syde.
And after rood° the queene and Emelye,   *rode*
And after that another compaignye

---

1 "Let him parry, if he wishes, to protect himself when he is on foot." Knights who had been dismounted in a tournament would often continue to fight on foot. Although set in an arena and conducted under the eyes of the Roman gods, the tournament will follow the customs of Chaucer's own day.

Of oon and oother° after hir degree. — *one and another*
And thus they passen thurghout° the citee. — *through*
2575 And to the lystes come they by tyme.° — *in time*
It nas nat° of the day yet fully pryme[1] — *was not*
Whan set was Theseus ful riche and hye,
Ypolita the queene, and Emelye,
And othere ladys in degrees aboute.
2580 Unto the seetes° preesseth° al the route.° — *seats, press, crowd*
And westward thurgh the gates under Marte,°[2] — *Mars*
Arcite, and eek the hondred of his parte° — *party*
With baner° reed is entred right anon. — *banner*
AND in that selve° moment Palamon — *same*
2585 Is under Venus estward° in the place — *eastward*
With baner whyt° and hardy chiere and face.° — *white banner, facial expression*
In al the world to seken° up and doun° — *seek, down*
So evene, withouten variacioun,° — *variation*
Ther nere° swiche compaignyes° tweye! — *were not two, companies*
2590 For ther was noon° so wys° that koude seye — *no one, wise*
That any hadde° of oother° avauntage° — *had, [the] other, advantage*
Of worthynesse ne of estaat° ne age, — *worthiness nor of rank*
So evene were chosen for to gesse.° — *guess*
And in two renges° faire they hem dresse.° — *ranks, arrange themselves*
2595 WHAN that hir° names rad° were everichon° — *their, read, everyone*
That in hir nombre° gyle° were ther noon. — *number, trickery*
Tho° were the gates shet° and cried was loude: — *then, shut*
"Do now youre devoir,° yonge° knyghtes proude!" — *duty, young*
THE heraudes° lefte hir prikyng° up and doun.° — *heralds, galloping, down*
2600 Now ryngen trompes loude and clarioun.° — *loud trumpets and bugle*
Ther is namoore to seyn° but west and est — *to say*
In goon° the speres° ful sadly° in arrest.° — *go, spears, firmly, holder*
In gooth° the sharpe spore° into the syde.° — *go, spur, side*
Ther seen men who kan° juste° and who kan ryde. — *know how, joust*
2605 Ther shyveren° shaftes upon sheeldes thikke.° — *shiver, thick shields*
He feeleth° thurgh the herte-spoon° the prikke.° — *feels, breast, point*
Up spryngen° speres° twenty foot on highte.° — *spring, spears, height*
Out gooth° the swerdes° as the silver brighte. — *go, swords*
The helmes° they tohewen° and toshrede.° — *helmets, cut up, shred up*
2610 Out brest° the blood with stierne° stremes rede.° — *bursts, stern, red streams*
With myghty maces° the bones they tobreste.° — *metal clubs, break up*
He thurgh the thikkeste of the throng° ganth reste.° — *thickest of the crowd, began to thrust*
Ther semblen° steedes stronge, and doun° gooth al! — *there stumble, down*

---

1 Prime was the time for early morning prayer at the monasteries and churches.
2 There is a Latin gloss "under Mars" written above the line.

	He rolleth under foot as dooth a bal.°	*ball*
2615	He foyneth° on his feet with his tronchon.°	*parries, spear shaft*
	And he hym hurtleth° with his hors adoun.	*knocks down*
	He thurgh the body is hurt and sithen ytake,°	*afterwards captured*
	Maugree his heed,° and broght unto the stake.	*despite all he could do*
	As forward was,° right there he moste abyde.°	*as was the agreement, stay*
2620	Another lad° is on that oother syde.	*led*
	AND somtyme dooth hem° Theseus to reste,	*causes them*
	Hem to fresshen° and drynken if hem leste.°	*take refreshment, if they wanted*
	Ful ofte° a day han° thise Thebanes two	*very often, have*
	Togydre ymet° and wroght° his felawe wo.	*met together, caused*
2625	Unhorsed hath ech oother° of hem tweye.°	*each other, them two*
	Ther nas no° tygre° in the vale° of Galgopheye[1]	*was not, tiger, valley*
	Whan that hir whelpe° is stole° whan it is lite°	*cub, stolen, little*
	So crueel on the hunte as is Arcite	
	For jelous herte° upon this Palamoun.	*heart*
2630	Ne in Belmarye[2] ther nys so fel leoun°	*is not so fierce a lion*
	That hunted is or for his hunger wood°	*crazy*
	Ne° of his praye° desireth so the blood	*nor, prey*
	As Palamoun to sleen° his foo Arcite.	*kill*
	The jelous strokes on hir helmes° byte.°	*helmets, bite*
2635	Out renneth° blood on bothe hir sydes rede.°	*runs, their red sides*
	SOMTYME an ende ther is of every dede,°	*deed*
	For er° the sonne unto the reste wente,	*before*
	The stronge Kyng Emetreus gan hente°	*captured*
	This Palamon as he faught with Arcite	
2640	And made his swerd depe in his flessh to byte.	
	And by the force of twenty is he take°	*taken*
	Unyolden° and ydrawe° unto the stake.	*not yielding, drawn*
	And in the rescus° of this Palamon	*rescue*
	The stronge Kyng Lygurge is born adoun,°	*knocked down*
2645	And Kyng Emetreus for al his strengthe	
	Is born° out of his sadel° a swerdes lengthe,°	*carried, saddle, sword's length*
	So hitte° hym Palamoun er° he were take.°	*hit, before, taken*
	But al for noght.° He was broght to the stake.	*nothing*
	His hardy herte myghte hym helpe naught.°	*by no means*
2650	He moste abyde° whan that he was caught	*had to stay*
	By force and eek by composicioun.°	*agreement*
	WHO sorweth now but woful Palamoun,	
	That moot namoore goon agayn° to fighte?	*must no more go again*
	And whan that Theseus hadde seyn° this sighte,	*seen*

---

1   Galgophia is a valley in Greece.
2   Benmarin is a region of Morocco. In the General Prologue, we find that the Knight has fought
    there.

2655	Unto the folk that foghten° thus echon,°	fought, each one
	He cryde, "Hoo!° Namoore! For it is doon!	Whoa!
	I WOL be trewe juge and no partie.°	partisan
	Arcite of Thebes shal have Emelie,	
	That by his fortune hath hire faire ywonne."°	won fairly
2660	Anon° ther is a noyse of peple bigonne°	immediately, begun
	For joye of this. So loude and heighe withalle	
	It semed, that the lystes° sholde falle.	arena
	WHAT kan now faire Venus doon° above?	do
	What seith she now? What dooth this queene of love	
2665	But wepeth so for wantynge° of hir wille°	lack, will
	Til that hir teeres in the lystes fille?	
	She seyde, "I am ashamed doutelees!"°	doubtless
	SATURNUS seyde, "Doghter, hoold thy pees!°	hold your peace
	Mars hath his wille. His knyght hath al his bonne.°	request
2670	And by my heed,° thow shalt been esed° soone!"	head, be eased
	THE trompes° with the loude mystralcie,°	trumpets, music
	The heraudes° that ful° loude yolle° and crie	heralds, very, yell
	Been in hire° wele° for joye of Daun° Arcite.	their, prosperity, Sir
	But herkneth me,° and stynteth° now a lite°	listen to me, keep quiet, a little
2675	Which a myracle° ther bifel° anon.°	miracle, happened, immediately
	THIS fierse Arcite hath of his helm ydon,°	removed his helmet
	And on a courser for to shewe° his face	show
	He priketh° endelong° the large place,	gallops, from end to end of
	Lokynge° upward upon Emelye.	looking
2680	And she agayn° hym caste a freendlich° eye[1]	towards, friendly
2683	And was al his chiere° as in his herte.	facial expression
	OUT of the ground a furie infernal sterte,°	infernal fury arose
2685	From Pluto sent at requeste of Saturne,	
	For which his hors for fere° gan° to turne	fear, began
	And leepe° aside and foundred° as he leepe.°	leap, stumbled, leapt
	And er° that Arcite may taken keepe,°	before, take care
	He pighte° hym on the pomel° of his heed,[2]	knocked himself, crown
2690	That in the place he lay as he were deed.°	dead
	His brest° tobrosten° with his sadel° bowe,	breast, broken up, saddle
	As blak° he lay as any cole° or crowe,	black, coal
	So was the blood yronnen° in his face.	run

---

1 The following lines occur in most editions of *The Canterbury Tales* after this one: "For wommen, as to speken in comune,/Thei folwen alle the favour of Fortune." Ellesmere and Hengwrt both omit these lines. They are found in Oxford, Corpus Christi College MS 198. Dated c. 1410–20, this manuscript, like Ellesmere and Hengwrt, is a very early witness to the text of *The Canterbury Tales*. We omit the lines here but retain, for convenience's sake, the numbering found in most editions, for it has become traditional and is followed in all criticism of the poem.

2 There is a Latin gloss in the margin: "Note the danger."

Anon° he was yborn° out of the place   *immediately, carried*
2695 With herte soor° to Theseus paleys.   *sore*
Tho° was he korven° out of his harneys°   *then, cut, armor*
And in a bed ybrought° ful° faire and blyve,°   *brought, very, quickly*
For he was yet in memorie° and alyve°   *conscious, alive*
And alwey criynge° after Emelye.   *crying*
2700 DUC Theseus with al his compaignye
Is comen hoom to Atthenes his citee
With alle blisse and greet solempnitee.°   *ceremony*
Albeit that this aventure° was falle,°   *mishap, had happened*
He nolde noght° disconforten hem alle.°   *would not, distress them all*
2705 Men seyde eek that Arcite shal nat dye.°   *not die*
He shal been heeled° of his maladye.   *be healed*
AND of another thyng they weren as fayn,°   *glad*
That of hem alle° was ther noon yslayn.°   *them all, none killed*
Al° were they soore yhurt° and namely oon°   *although, sorely hurt, especially one*
2710 That with a spere was thirled° his brest boon.°   *pierced, breastbone*
To othere woundes and to broken armes
Somme hadden salves, and somme hadden charmes.[1]
Fermacies° of herbes and eek save°   *medicines, sage*
They dronken,° for they wolde hir lymes have.°   *drank, wanted to save their limbs*
2715 For which this noble duc, as he wel kan,
Conforteth and honoureth every man
And made revel al the longe nyght
Unto the straunge° lordes as was right.   *foreign*
Ne ther was holden no disconfitynge
2720 But as a justes or a tourneiynge.[2]
For soothly,° ther was no disconfiture.°   *truly, dishonor*
For fallyng nys nat° but an aventure,°   *is not, mischance*
Ne° to be lad° by force unto the stake   *nor, led*
Unyolden° and with twenty knyghtes take,   *unyielded*
2725 O° persone allone withouten mo,   *one*
And haryed° forth by arm, foot, and too,°   *dragged, toe*
And eek his steede° dryven° forth with staves,°   *horse, driven, clubs*
With footmen, bothe yemen° and eek knaves.°   *yeomen, boys*
It nas arretted° hym no vileynye.°[3]   *was not attributed, dishonor*
2730 Ther may no man clepen° it cowardye.°   *call, cowardice*
FOR which anon Duc Theseus leet crye°   *proclaimed*

---

1 "Some had salves and some had charms." Herbal medicine and medicinal magic were widely
  practiced in the Middle Ages.
2 "Nor was it considered a defeat [for anyone]/Except of the kind appropriate to a joust or tourna-
  ment."
3 "It was not attributed to him [as] no dishonor," i.e., as any dishonor, another example of the
  Middle English double negative.

To stynten° alle rancour° and envye,   *stop, disagreement*
The gree° as wel° of o° syde as of oother,° *victory, well, one, [the] other*
And eyther syde ylik° as ootheres brother,   *either side like*
2735 And yaf hem yiftes° after hir degree   *gave them gifts*
And fully heeld° a feeste dayes three°   *held, feast [for] three days*
And convoyed° the kynges worthily   *accompanied*
Out of his toun a journee° largely.   *day's ride*
And hoom went every man the righte way.
2740 Ther was namoore but "Farewel! Have good day!"
Of this bataille I wol namoore endite°[1]   *write*
But speke of Palamoun and of Arcite.
SWELLETH° the brest° of Arcite, and the soore° *swells, breast, sore*
Encreesseth° at his herte moore and moore.   *increases*
2745 The clothered° blood for any lechecraft° *clotted, skill in medicine*
Corrupteth° and is in his bouk° ylaft,°   *corrupts, chest, left*
That neither veyne-blood ne ventusynge[2]
Ne drynke of herbes may ben° his helpynge.° *may be, helping*
The vertu expulsif[3] or animal
2750 Fro thilke vertu° cleped° natural[4]   *power, called*
Ne may the venym° voyden° ne° expelle.   *poison, purge, nor*
The pipes of his longes° gonne° to swelle,   *lungs, began*
And every lacerte° in his brest° adoun°   *muscle, breast, down*
Is shent° with venym° and corrupcioun.   *destroyed, poison*
2755 Hym gayneth neither,° for to gete° his lif, *It helps him, preserve*
Vomyt° upward ne dounward laxatif.°   *vomit, laxative*
Al is tobrosten° thilke° regioun.   *broken apart, this same*
Nature hath now no dominacioun.
And certeinly ther° nature wol nat wirche,° *where, will not work*
2760 Farewel phisik!° Go ber° the man to chirche!° *medicine, carry, church*
This al and som° that Arcita moot dye,° *This briefly [means], must die*
For which he sendeth after Emelye
And Palamon, that was his cosyn deere.°   *dear cousin*
Thanne° seyde he thus, as ye shal after heere: *then*
2765 "NAUGHT° may the woful° spirit in myn herte *by no means, woeful*
Declare o° point of alle my sorwes smerte° *one, painful sorrows*
To yow, my lady that I love moost.

---

1 An apparent slip, since the Knight is telling, not writing the story. The Franklin uses the same
  expression at line 1550 of his tale.
2 "Vein-blood" is blood-letting, and "ventusing" is cupping, two medieval medical procedures.
3 This term refers to the power of the body to expel unhealthy humors, medieval medicine's
  version of modern immune theory. "Animal" was a term applied to this power, which was
  supposed to reside in one's brain.
4 "Natural power" in medieval medicine was supposed to reside in the liver, and it too helped
  combat illness.

But I biquethe the servyce of my goost.°   spirit
To yow aboven every creature,
2770 Syn° that my lyf may no lenger dure,°   since, no longer last
Allas the wo! Allas the peynes stronge
That I for yow have suffred and so longe!
Allas the deeth! Allas, myn Emelye!
Allas, departynge of oure compaignye!°   companionship
2775 Allas, myn hertes queene! Allas my wyf,[1]
Myn hertes lady, endere of my lyf!°   one who ends my life
What is this world? What asketh men to have?
Now with his love, now in his colde grave,
Allone withouten any compaignye.
2780 Farewel, my sweete foo, myn Emelye!
And softe, taak° me in youre armes tweye°   take, two
For love of God, and herkneth° what I seye.   listen to
I HAVE heer with my cosyn Palamon
Had strif and rancour many a day agon°   past
2785 For love of yow and for my jalousye.
And Juppiter so wys° my soule gye°   wise, guide
To speken of a servaunt° proprely   a servant [of love]
With alle circumstances trewely.
That is to seyn,° trouthe, honour, knyghthede,°   say, knighthood
2790 Wysdom, humblesse,° estaat,° and heigh kynrede,°   humility, estate, high kindred
Fredom,° and al that longeth° to that art.   generosity, pertains
So Juppiter have of my soule part
As in this world right now ne knowe I non°   I know none
So worthy to ben° loved as Palamon,   be
2795 That serveth yow and wol doon° al his lyf.   will do
And if that evere ye shul ben° a wyf,   shall be
Foryet nat° Palamon, the gentil° man."   forget not, noble
And with that word his speche faille gan,°   speech began to fail
And from his herte up to his brest was come
2800 The coold of deeth, that hadde hym overcome.
And yet moreover,° for in hise armes two   and that is not all
The vital strengthe° is lost and al ago.°   power of life, gone
Oonly° the intellect withouten moore   only
That dwelled in his herte° syk° and soore,°   heart, sick, sore
2805 Gan faillen° whan the herte felte deeth.[2]   began to fail
Dusked° hise eyen° two, and failled breeth.°   darkened, eyes, breath
But on his lady yet caste he his eye.

---

1   Arcite may simply be thinking of Emelye as the woman who would have been his wife, but in
    Boccaccio's *Teseida*, Chaucer's immediate source, Arcite actually marries her on his death-bed.
2   "Only" refers to "whan." "Only when the heart felt death did the intellect begin to fail."

His laste word was "Mercy, Emelye!"
His spirit chaunged hous° and wente ther° — *changed its dwelling, went where*
2810 As I can nevere.° I kan nat tellen° wher. — *can never know, can not tell*
Therfore I stynte.° I nam no divinistre.° — *am silent, am no theologian*
Of soules fynde° I nat° in this registre,° — *find, not, list*
Ne me ne list° thilke° opinions to telle — *I do not wish, these*
Of hem° though that they writen wher they dwelle.[1] — *them (other writers)*
2815 Arcite is coold. Ther Mars his soule gye!° — *guide*
Now wol I speken forth of Emelye.

SHRIGHTE° Emelye, and howleth° Palamon! — *shrieks, howls*
And Theseus his suster took anon,° — *immediately*
Swownynge° and baar° hire fro the corps° away. — *fainting, carried, corpse*
2820 What helpeth it to tarien forth° the day — *delay*
To tellen how she weepe bothe eve and morwe?° — *evening and morning*
For in swich cas° wommen have swich sorwe — *such a situation*
Whan that hir housbond is from hem ago,° — *gone*
That for the moore part they sorwen° so — *sorrow*
2825 Or ellis° fallen in swich maladye° — *else, malady*
That at the laste certeinly they dye.
INFINITE been the sorwes and the teeres
Of olde folk and eek of tendre° yeeres° — *[those of] tender, years*
In al the toun for deeth of this Theban.
2830 For hym ther wepeth bothe child and man.
So greet a wepyng was ther noon, certayn,° — *certainly*
Whan Ector[2] was ybroght° al fressh yslayn° — *brought, freshly killed*
To Troye. Allas, the pitee that was ther,
Cracchynge° of chekes,° rentynge° eek° of heer!° — *scratching, cheeks, tearing, also, hair*
2835 "Why woldestow° be deed,"° thise wommen crye, — *would you, dead*
"And haddest gold ynough° and Emelye?" — *enough*
No man myghte gladen Theseus° — *might make Theseus glad*
Savynge° his olde fader° Egeus, — *except for, father*
That knew this worldes transmutacioun,° — *changing*
2840 As he hadde seyn° it up and doun— — *seen*
Joye after wo and wo after gladnesse—
And shewed hem ensamples and liknesse.° — *showed them examples and analogies*
"RIGHT as ther dyed° nevere man," quod he, — *died*
"That he ne lyvede° in erthe° in som degree, — *did not live, earth*
2845 Right so ther lyvede never man," he seyde,[3]

---

1 Chaucer omits the discussion in the *Teseida* of Arcite's journey through the stars after his death.
2 Hector was the greatest of Trojan warriors, killed by the Greek Achilles, as recounted first in Homer's *Iliad*.
3 There is a Latin gloss in the margin, "Argument," indicating that a moral comment is being made.

"In al this world that somtyme he ne deyde.°   *did not die*
This world nys° but a thurghfare° ful of wo,   *is not, thoroughfare*
And we been pilgrymes passynge to and fro.
Deeth is an ende of every worldes soore,"°   *sorrow*
2850   And over al this yet seyde he muchel more
To this effect, ful° wisely to enhorte°   *very, exhort*
The peple that they sholde hem reconforte.°   *comfort themselves*
Duc Theseus with al his bisy cure°   *anxious care*
Cast° now wher that the sepulture°   *considered, grave*
2855   Of goode Arcite may best ymaked be°   *best be made*
And eek moost° honurable in his degree.°   *most, according to his rank*
And at the laste he took conclusioun
That theras° first Arcite and Palamoun   *since*
Hadden for love the bataille hem bitwene°   *between them*
2860   That in that selve° grove swoote° and grene°   *same, sweet, green*
Theras° he hadde hise amorouse° desires,   *where, amorous*
His compleynte,° and for love hise hoote° fires,   *lament, his hot*
He wolde° make a fyr° in which the office°   *would, fire, ceremony*
Funeral he myghte° al accomplice,°   *might, accomplish*
2865   And leet comande° anon° to hakke and hewe°   *ordered, immediately, cut*
The okes° olde and leye hem° on a rewe°   *oaks, lay them, row*
In colpons° wel arrayed° forto brenne.°   *pieces, arranged, to burn*
Hise officers with swifte feet they renne°   *run*
And ryden° anon at his comandement.°   *ride, commandment*
2870   And after this Theseus hath ysent°   *has sent*
After a beere,° and it al overspradde°   *bier, spread over it*
With clooth of gold, the richeste that he hadde.
And of the same suyte° he cladde° Arcite.   *material, clothed*
Upon his hondes hadde he gloves white,
2875   Eek on his heed a coroune° of laurer° grene,   *crown, laurel*
And in his hond a swerd ful bright and kene.°   *sharp*
He leyde hym,° bare the visage,° on the beere,   *laid him, bare-faced*
Therwith° he weepe that pitee° was to heere.°   *thus, pity, hear*
And for the peple sholde seen hym alle,
2880   Whan it was day, he broghte hym to the halle,
That roreth° of the criyng and the soun.°   *roars, sound*
Tho° cam° this woful° Theban Palamoun   *then, came, woeful*
With flotery° berd° and rugged, asshy heeres°[1]   *fluttering, beard, hairs*
In clothes blake,° ydropped° al with teeres,°   *black, wet, tears*
2885   And passynge othere° of wepynge,° Emelye,   *surpassing others, weeping*
The rewefulleste° of al the compaignye.   *most pitiful*
Inasmuche as the servyce sholde° be   *should*

---

1   To throw ashes on one's hair is an ancient form of mourning.

The moore noble and riche in his degree,
Duc Theseus leet forth thre steedes brynge,[1]
2890 That trapped° were in steel al gliterynge°   *equipped, all glittering*
And covered with the armes° of Daun Arcite.°   *coat of arms, Sir Arcite*
Upon thise steedes grete and white.
Ther sitten° folk of whiche oon° baar° his sheeld.   *sit, one, carried*
Another his spere in his hondes heeld.
2895 The thridde° baar with hym his bowe Turkeys.°   *third, Turkish bow*
(Of brend° gold was the caas° and eek the harneys°)   *polished, quiver, gear*
And riden forth a paas° with sorweful cheere°   *pace, sorrowful expression*
Toward the grove, as ye shul° after heere.   *shall*
The nobleste of the Grekes that ther were
2900 Upon hir shuldres° caryeden° the beere°   *shoulders, carried, bier*
With slak paas° and eyen rede and wete   *slow pace*
Thurghout the citee by the maister strete,°   *main street*
That sprad° was al with blak, and wonder hye°   *spread, wonderfully high*
Right of the same is the strete ywrye.°[2]   *draped [with funeral cloths]*
2905 Upon the right hond wente olde Egeus,
And on that oother syde Duc Theseus
With vessel° in hir hand of gold ful fyn,°   *jar, very fine*
Al ful of hony,° milk, and blood, and wyn,°   *honey, wine*
Eek Palamon with ful greet compaignye.°   *very great company*
2910 And after that cam woful Emelye
With fyr in honde as was that tyme the gyse°   *custom*
To do the office of funeral servyse.°   *service*
HEIGH° labour and ful greet apparaillynge°   *high, preparation*
Was at the service and the fyr makynge,°   *making of the fire*
2915 That with his grene° tope° the hevene raughte°[3]   *green, top, reached*
And twenty fadme° of brede° the armes straughte.° *fathoms, breadth, stretched*
This is to seyn, the bowes° weren so brode.°   *boughs, broad*
Of stree° first ther was leyd° ful many a lode.°   *straw, laid, load*
But how the fyr was maked upon highte°[4]   *high*
2920 Ne° eek the names that the trees highte°—   *nor, were named*

---

1   "Duke Theseus commanded that three horses be brought out."
2   The walls of the houses along the main street have been draped high with black cloth, a standard practice in the late Middle Ages for the funerals of great nobles.
3   The huge pile of trees, with its branches still green, reaches to the sky and is 120 feet (twenty fathoms) wide. Ellesmere omits "raughte." It is supplied by Hengwrt and of course initiates the rhyme. Chaucer draws his description of the funeral from Boccaccio's *Teseida* (Book 11) and also probably from Statius's *Thebiad* (6:98–106), which in turn draws on Virgil's *Aeneid*. Unlike the warfare, courtship, and tournament in the Knight's Tale, the funeral rituals are those of classical antiquity, not Chaucer's own day.
4   As Vincent J. DiMarco notes, lines 2919–62 form the longest sentence in Chaucer's poetry. The passage is another example of *occupatio*, described on p. 69, note 1.

As ook, firre, birch, aspe, alder, holm, popeler,
Wylugh, elm, plane assh, box, chasteyn, lynde, laurer,
Mapul, thorn, bech, hasel, ew, whippeltree[1]—
How they weren fild° shal nat° be toold for me,   *cut down, not*
2925 Ne hou° the goddes ronnen° up and doun,°   *Nor how, run, down*
Disherited° of hire° habitacioun°   *disinherited, their, dwelling*
In whiche they woneden° in reste and pees°—   *lived, peace*
Nymphus,° fawnes,° and amadrides°[2]—   *nymphs, fawns, hamadryads*
Ne hou the beestes and the briddes° alle   *birds*
2930 Fledden° for fere° whan the wode° was falle,°   *fled, fear, wood, cut down*
Ne how the ground agast was° of the light   *was frightened*
That was nat° wont° to seen the sonne bright,   *not, customarily*
Ne how the fyr was couched° first with stree°   *made, straw*
And thanne with drye stokkes cloven athre°   *sticks cut in three*
2935 And thanne with grene wode and spicerye°   *spices*
And thanne with clooth of gold° and with perrye°   *golden cloth, jewels*
And gerlandes° hangynge with ful many a flour,   *garlands*
The mirre,° th'encens,° withal so greet odour,°   *myrrh, the incense, great odor*
Ne how Arcite lay among al this,
2940 Ne what richesse aboute his body is,
Ne how that Emelye, as was the gyse,°   *custom*
Putte in the fyr of funeral servyse,°   *service*
Ne how she swowned° whan men made fyr,   *fainted*
Ne what she spak, ne what was hir desir,
2945 Ne what jeweles men in the fyre caste
Whan that the fyr was greet and brente faste,
NE how somme caste hir sheeld° and somme hir spere   *some threw in their shield*
And of hire vestimentz° whiche that they were°   *clothing, were [wearing]*
And coppes° fulle of wyn and milk and blood   *cups*
2950 Into the fyr that brente° as it were wood,°   *burned, crazy*
Ne how the Grekes with an huge route°   *crowd*
Thries° riden al the place about   *three times*
Upon the left hand° with a loud shoutynge   *i.e., counter clockwise*
And thries with hir speres claterynge°   *clattering*
2955 And thries how the ladyes gonne crye°   *cried*
And how that lad° was homward Emelye,   *led*
Ne how Arcite is brent° to asshen° colde,   *burned, ashen*
Ne how that lych-wake° was yholde°   *funeral wake, held*

---

1   Catalogues of trees are a feature of several epic poems from ancient times. The trees here listed are oak, fir, birch, aspen, alder, holm-oak, poplar, willow, elm, ash, boxtree, chestnut, linden, laurel, maple, thorn, beech, hazel, yew, and dogwood.

2   In Roman mythology, lesser gods and goddesses like those listed here lived in the woods and fields. Since the grove is cut down for the funeral, the gods and goddesses normally inhabiting it no longer have a home.

Al thilke° nyght,° ne° how the Grekes pleye° — *that same, night, nor, play*

2960 The wake-pleyes,° ne kepe I nat to seye° — *funeral games, I care not to say*

What° wrastleth° best naked with oille enoynt,° — *who, wrestles, anointed with oil*

Ne who that baar° hym best in no disjoynt.° — *carries, difficulty*

I wol nat tellen° eek how that they goon° — *will not tell, go*

Hoom til Atthenes° whan the pley° is doon,° — *home to Athens, games, done*

2965 But shortly to the point thanne wol I wende° — *turn*

And maken of my longe tale an ende.

By processe° and by lengthe of certeyn yeres, — *in due course*

Al stynted° is the moornynge° and the teres — *made quiet, mourning*

Of Grekes by oon° general assent, — *one*

2970 Thanne semed me° ther was a parlement° — *Then it seemed to me, parliament*

At Atthenes upon certein pointz° and caas,° — *points, cases*

Among the whiche pointz yspoken° was — *spoken*

To have with certein contrees° alliaunce° — *countries, alliance*

And have fully of Thebans obeisaunce,° — *obedience*

2975 For which this noble Theseus anon° — *immediately*

Leet senden° after gentil Palamon, — *had sent*

Unwist of hym° what was the cause and why. — *unknown by him*

But in hise blake clothes sorwefully

He cam at his comandement in hye.° — *in haste*

2980 Tho° sente Theseus for Emelye — *then*

Whan they were set and hust° was al the place. — *quieted*

And Theseus abiden° hadde a space — *waited*

Er° any word cam fram° his wise brest.° — *before, from, breast*

Hise eyen° sette he theras was his lest,° — *his eyes, where he wished*

2985 And with a sad visage° he siked stille,° — *serious expression, sighed quietly*

And after that right thus he seyde his wille:° — *will*

"THE Firste Moevere°[1] of the cause above, — *mover*

Whan he first made the faire cheyne° of love, — *chain*

Greet was th'effect and heigh was his entente.° — *intent*

2990 Wel wiste° he why and what therof he ment.° — *knew, meant*

For with that faire cheyne of love he bond° — *bound*

The fyr, the eyr, the water, and the lond[2]

In certeyn boundes, that they may nat flee.

That same prince and that same Moevere," quod he,

2995 "Hath stablissed° in this wrecched° world adoun° — *established, wretched, below*

---

1 The "First Mover" is an expression ancient philosophers sometimes used to speak of God. According to Aristotle, it is the first principle that sets all other things into motion. The idea that love unites all the elements, each of which is linked to the others in a hierarchical order ("the great chain of being"), goes back to Plato and is described in Boethius's *Consolation of Philosophy* (Book 2, meter 8), on which this passage is based (see Appendix, p. 389–90).

2 In ancient science, earth, air, fire, and water are the four elements from which everything is made.

Certeyne dayes and duracioun°   *duration*
To al that is engendred° in this place,   *born*
Over the which day they may nat pace,°   *not go beyond*
Al mowe° they yet tho° dayes wel abregge.°   *although, those, shorten*
3000 Ther nedeth noght noon auctoritee allegge,[1]
For it is preeved° by experience.   *proven*
But that me list declaren my sentence.°   *I wish to give my judgment*
Thanne may men by this ordre° wel discerne   *order*
That thilke° Moevere stable is and eterne.°   *the same, eternal*
3005 Wel may men knowe, but it be° a fool,   *unless [the man] is*
That every part dirryveth° from his hool.°   *derives, its wholeness*
For Nature hath taken his bigynnyng°   *its beginning*
Of no partie° or of cantel° of a thyng.   *part, portion*
But of a thyng that parfit° is and stable,   *perfect*
3010 Descendynge° so til it be corrumpable.°   *descending, corruptible*
And therfore of his wise purveiaunce,°   *foresight*
He hath so wel biset° his ordinaunce,°   *well established, laws*
That speces° of thynges and progressiouns°   *species, natural processes*
Shullen enduren° by successiouns,°   *shall last, one after another*
3015 And nat eterne,° withouten any lye.°   *not [be] eternal, lie*
This maystow° understonde and seen at eye.°[2]   *may you, see with your eye*
Loo, the ook° that hath so long a norisshynge°[3]   *oak, growing*
From tyme that it first bigynneth sprynge°   *begins to grow*
And hath so long a lif, as we may see,
3020 Yet at the laste wasted is the tree.
CONSIDERETH eek how that the harde stoon
Under oure feet on which we trede° and goon,°   *tread, go*
Yet wasteth it° as it lyth by the weye.°   *it wastes, lies along the road*
The brode ryver° somtyme wexeth dreye.°   *broad river, sometimes dries up*
3025 The grete toures° se° we wane and wende.° *towers, see, diminishing and changing*
Thanne may ye se that al this thyng hath ende.°   *has an end*
Of man and womman seen we wel also
That nedeth in oon° of thise termes two.   *one*
This is to seyn° in youthe or elles° age   *say, else*
3030 He moot° be deed°—the kyng as shal a page: *must, die*
Som in his bed, som in the depe see,
Som in the large feeld,° as men may see.   *field*
Ther helpeth noght.° Al goth that ilke weye.° *nothing can help, goes the same way*
Thanne may I seyn° al this thyng moot deye.°   *say, must die*

---

1   "There is no need to cite authority."
2   Ellesmere reads "it" here; the emendation is from Hengwrt.
3   There is a Latin gloss "Exemplum" in the margin, noting a general moral example, and another
    at line 3021.

3035 WHAT maketh this° but Juppiter the kyng,[1]   *who does this*
    That is prince and cause of alle thyng,
    Convertynge al unto his propre welle,°   *own source*
    From which it is dirryved,° sooth to telle?°   *derived, to tell the truth*
    And heer agayns no creature on lyve
3040 Of no degree availleth for to stryve.[2]
    THANNE° is it wysdom, as it thynketh me°   *then, it seems to me*
    To maken vertu of necessitee°   *make a virtue of a necessity*
    AND take it weel° that we may nat eschue,°   *well, avoid*
    And namely° that to us alle is due.   *especially*
3045 And who so gruccheth° ought, he dooth° folye°   *complains at all, does, folly*
    And rebel is to hym° that al may gye.°   *him, who may guide all (Jupiter)*
    And certeinly a man hath moost honour
    To dyen° in his excellence and flour°   *die, flower*
    Whan he is siker° of his goode name.   *sure*
3050 Thanne hath he doon° his freend ne hym° no shame.   *he has done, friend nor himself*
    And gladder oghte° his freend been of his deeth,   *ought*
    Whan with honour up yolden° is his breeth°   *yielded up, breath*
    Than whan° his name apalled° is for age,   *when, faded*
    For al forgeten is his vassellage.°   *service in arms*
3055 Thanne is it best as for a worthy fame
    To dyen whan that he is best of name.
    THE contrarie° of al this is wilfulnesse.°   *contrary, willfulness*
    Why grucchen° we? Why have we hevynesse°   *complain, sadness*
    That goode Arcite of chivalrie flour°   *flower*
3060 Departed is with duetee° and honour   *duty*
    Out of this foule prisoun of this lyf?
    Why grucchen heere his cosyn and his wyf
    Of his welfare, that loved hem so weel?
    Kan he hem thank? Nay, God woot, never a deel,°   *not a bit*
3065 That bothe his soule and eek hemself offende,°   *harm*
    And yet they mowe° hir lustes nat° amend.   *must, not*
    WHAT may I concluden of this longe serye,°   *series of arguments*
    But after wo I rede° us to be merye°   *advise, merry*
    And thanken Juppiter of al his grace.
3070 And er° that we departen from this place,   *before*
    I rede° we make of sorwes two   *advise*
    O° parfit° joye, lastynge everemo.   *one, perfect*
    And looketh now, wher° moost sorwe is herinne,°   *where, in [this matter]*
    Ther wol° we first amenden° and bigynne.   *will, amend*
3075 "SUSTER," quod he, "this is my fulle assent°   *desire*

---

1   Theseus here identifies Jupiter, as the senior of the classical gods, with the First Mover.
2   "And against this it is of no use for any living creature, of whatever rank, to struggle."

With al th'avys° heere° of my parlement,°   *advice, here, council*
That gentil Palamon, thyn owene° knyght   *your own*
That serveth yow with wille,° herte, and myght   *[all his] will*
And evere hath doon° syn° that ye first hym knewe,   *done, since*
3080 That ye shul of youre grace upon hym rewe°   *have pity upon him*
And taken hym for housbonde and for lord.
Lene me youre hond,° for this is oure accord.   *Give me your hand*
Lat se° now of youre wommanly pitee.°   *Let [us] see, pity*
He is a kynges brother sone,° pardee.°   *son, by God*
3085 And though he were a povre bacheler,°   *poor young knight*
Syn he hath served yow so many a yeer
And had for yow so greet adversitee,
It moste been° considered, leeveth me.°   *must be, believe me*
For gentil mercy oghte to passen right."°   *ought to prevail over justice*
3090 THANNE seyde he thus to Palamon ful right:[1]
"I trowe ther nedeth litel sermonyng°   *needs few words*
To make yow assente to this thyng.
Com neer,° and taak youre lady by the hond!"   *come near*
Bitwixen hem was maad° anon° the bond   *made, immediately*
3095 That highte matrimoigne° or mariage,   *matrimony*
By al the conseil° and the baronage.°   *council, company of barons*
And thus with alle blisse and melodye
Hath Palamon ywedded Emelye.
And God that al this wyde world hath wroght°   *made*
3100 Sende hym his love that it deere aboght.°   *who purchased it dearly*
For now is Palamon in alle wele,°   *good fortune*
Lyvynge° in blisse,° in richesse, and in heele.° *living, happiness, health*
And Emelye hym loveth so tendrely,
And he hire serveth so gentilly,°   *nobly*
3105 That nevere was ther no word hem bitwene
Of jalousie or any oother teene.°   *discord*
Thus endeth Palamon and Emelye.
And God save al this faire compaignye! Amen.

HEERE IS ENDED THE KNYGHTES TALE

---

1 "Right" means directly or exactly; "ful right" (most or very directly) is an empty phrase used
   to fill out the line. Hengwrt reads "the knyght," rather than "ful right."

THE MILLER'S PROLOGUE AND TALE

Opening page to *The Miller's Tale*. Ellesmere Manuscript EL 26 C9 f. 34v. Reprinted by permission of The Huntington Library.

THE MILLER'S PROLOGUE

HERE FOLWEN THE WORDES BITWENE THE HOOST AND THE
MILLERE

WHAN that the Knyght hath thus his tale ytoold,°   *told*
3110 In al the route° ne was ther° yong ne° oold   *company, there was not, nor*
That he ne seyde° it was a noble storie   *did not say*
And worthy for to drawen to memorie,°   *learn by heart*
And namely° the gentils° everichon.°   *especially, gentlefolk, everyone*
Oure Hoost lough° and swoor,° "So moot° I gon,   *laughed, swore, might*
3115 This gooth aright!° Unbokeled° is the male.°   *goes well, unbuckled, purse*
Lat se,° now, who shal telle another tale?   *Let's see*
For trewely, the game is wel bigonne.
Now telleth on, Sire Monk, if that ye konne,°   *if you can*
Somwhat to quite with° the knyghtes tale."   *pay back*
3120 THE Millere, that for dronken° was al pale   *being very drunk*
So that unnethe° upon his hors he sat,   *scarcely*
He nolde° avalen° neither hood ne hat   *would not, take off*
Ne abyde° no man for his curteisie,°   *nor wait for, courtesy*
But in Pilates[1] voys° he gan° to crie   *voice, began*
3125 And swoor, "By armes and by blood and bones,[2]
I kan° a noble tale for the nones°   *know, for the occasion*
With which I wol now quite° the Knyghtes tale!"   *pay back*
Oure Hoost saugh° that he was dronke of ale   *saw*
And seyde, "Abyd,° Robyn, my leeve° brother,   *wait, dear*
3130 Som bettre man shal telle us first another.
Abyde, and lat° us werken° thriftily."°   *let, work, respectably*
"By Goddes soule," quod he, "that wol° nat I.   *will*
For I wol speke or elles° go my wey."°   *else, way*
Oure Hoost answerde, "Tel on a devele wey!°   *in the devil's name*
3135 Thou art a fool! Thy wit is overcome!"
"Now herkneth,"° quod the Millere, "alle and some.°   *listen, one and all*
But first I make a protestacioun°   *protest*
That I am dronke; I knowe it by my soun.°   *sound*
And therfore if that I mysspeke or seye,°   *say something wrong*
3140 Wyte it° the ale of Southwerk, I preye.°   *blame it on, pray*
For I wol tell a legende and a lyf[3]

---

1   Pontius Pilate was the Roman judge who condemned Jesus to be crucified. In medieval religious plays he was depicted as a loud, rampaging villain.
2   Swearing during the Middle Ages and Renaissance often involved taking oaths on various parts of God's body—here God's arms, blood, and bones.
3   "Legend" and "life" normally refer to a "saint's life," or biography of a Christian saint.

Bothe of a carpenter and of his wyf,

How that a clerk° hath set the wrightes cappe."[1]   *student*

THE Reve answerde and seyde, "Stynt thy clappe!°   *shut your mouth*

3145 Lat be thy lewed,° dronken° harlotrye!°   *ignorant, drunken, bawdiness*

It is a synne° and eek° a greet° folye°   *sin, also, great, folly*

To apeyren° any man or hym° defame°   *harm, him, slander*

And eek to bryngen wyves in swich° fame.°   *such, (dis)honor*

Thou mayst ynogh° of othere thynges seyn."°   *enough, speak*

3150 THIS dronke° Millere spak° ful° soone agayn°   *drunken, spoke, very, again*

And seyde, "Leve brother Osewold,

Who hath no wyf, he is no cokewold.[2]

But I sey nat therfore that thou art oon.°   *one*

Ther been ful° goode wyves many oon   *very*

3155 And evere a thousand goode ayeyns° oon badde.°   *against, bad*

That knowestow wel thyself,° but if thou madde.°   *you know well, unless you are mad*

Why artow° angry with my tale now?   *are you*

I have a wyf, pardee,° as wel as thow,   *by God*

Yet nolde° I for the oxen in my plogh°   *would not, plow*

3160 Take upon me moore than ynogh,°   *enough*

As demen° of myself that I were oon.°   *judge, one (i.e., a cuckold)*

I wol bileve° wel° that I am noon.°   *believe, well, none*

An housbonde shal nat been inquisityf°   *inquisitive*

Of Goddes pryvetee° nor of his wyf,   *secrets*

3165 So he may fynde° Goddes foyson° there,   *find, abundance*

Of the remenant nedeth nat enquere!"°   *he need not inquire*

WHAT sholde I moore seyn, but this Millere,

He nolde° his wordes for no man forbere,°   *would not, forego*

But tolde his cherles° tale in his manere.°   *boor's, manner*

3170 M'athynketh° that I shal reherce° it heere,   *I regret, repeat*

And therfore every gentil wight° I preye,°   *noble person, pray*

For Goddes love demeth° nat° that I seye°   *judge, not, speak*

Of yvel entente,° but that I moot reherce°   *evil intent, repeat*

Hir° tales, all be they° bettre or werse   *their, although they be*

3175 Or elles° falsen° som of my mateere.°   *else, falsify, matter*

And therfore whoso° list° it nat° yheere,°   *whoever, wishes, not, hear*

Turne over the leef,° and chese° another tale.   *page, choose*

For he shal fynde° ynowe,° grete° and smale,°   *find, enough, great, small*

Of storial° thyng that toucheth gentillesse°   *historical, nobility*

3180 And eek moralitee° and hoolynesse.°   *morality, holiness*

Blameth nat me if that ye chese amys.°   *choose wrongly*

The millere is a cherl.° Ye knowe wel this.   *boor*

---

1   This expression means to "make a fool of."

2   A "cuckold" is a husband whose wife has had an affair with another man.

So was the Reve and othere manye mo,°   more
And harlotrie° they tolden bothe two.   bawdiness
3185   Avyseth yow;° putteth me out of blame,   be advised
And eek men shal nat maken ernest° of game.°   seriousness, joke

THE MILLER'S TALE

HEERE BIGYNNETH THE MILLERE HIS TALE

WHILOM° ther was dwellynge° at Oxenford°   once, living, Oxford
A riche gnof° that gestes° heeld to bord,[1]   house   fellow, guests
And of his craft° he was a carpenter.   profession
3190   With hym ther was dwellynge a povre° scoler°   poor, student
Hadde lerned° art, but al his fantasye°   learned, interest
Was turned for to lerne° astrologye,   learn
And koude a certeyn of conclusiouns[2]
To demen° by interrogaciouns°   judge, questions
3195   If that men asked hym in certein° houres[3]   certain
Whan that men sholde have droghte° or elles shoures°   drought, rain
Or if men asked hym what sholde bifalle°   happen
Of every thyng. I may nat rekene° hem° all.   count up, them
THIS clerk was cleped° hende° Nicholas.   Secret love he knew   named, handy
3200   Of deerne° love he koude° and of solas,°   secret, knew, pleasure
And therto he was sleigh° and ful privee°   sly, very secretive
And lyk° a mayden meke° for to see.   gentel   like, meek
A chambre° hadde he in that hostelrye,°   room, lodging
Allone° withouten any compaignye.   alone
3205   Ful fetisly° ydight° with herbes[4] swoote,°   fashionably, decorated, sweet
And he hymself as swete as is the roote°   root
Of lycorys° or any cetewale.[5]   licorice
His *Almageste*[6] and bookes grete and smale,
His astrelabie[7] longynge° for his art,   pertaining to

---

1   "Held to board" means "rented out rooms." There is a picture of the Miller with his bagpipes
    in the margin.
2   This expression means "knew some [astrological] calculations."
3   "Hours" here means astrological hours—times when certain planets exerted certain influence.
4   The medieval custom was to spread dried and sweet smelling herbs on the floors of rooms.
5   The spice zedoary, similar to ginger.
6   The *Almagest* was the basic textbook for medieval astronomy. It was the work of Claudius
    Ptolemy (second century AD), who gives his name to the Ptolemaic system, in which the sun
    revolves around the earth. According to Ptolemy, the heavens comprised nine concentric crystal
    spheres which revolved and on which the planets and stars were affixed.
7   An astrolabe was a scientific instrument used to measure angles of heavenly bodies. Chaucer
    wrote *The Treatise on the Astrolabe*, a prose work that is one of the first pieces of technical writing
    in the English language.

3210 Hise augrym stones¹ layen° faire apart°	lay, somewhat away
On shelves couched° at his beddes heed,°	arranged, bed's head
His presse° ycovered° with a faldyng° reed,°	cupboard, covered, cloth, red
And al above ther lay a gay sautrie°	psaltery (musical instrument)
On which he made a nyghtes° melodie°	at night, melody
3215 So swetely that al the chambre rong.°	rang
And *Angelus ad virginem*² he song.°	sang
And after that he song *The Kynges Noote,*³	
Full often blessed was his myrie° throte!°	merry, throat
And thus this sweete clerk° his tyme spente	student
3220 After his freendes fyndyng⁴ and his rente.°	income
THIS carpenter hadde wedded newe° a wyf	newly married
Which that he lovede moore than his lyf.	
Of eighteteene° yeer she was of age.	MS xviij
Jalous° he was and heeld hire narwe° in cage,°	jealous, closely, in a cage
3225 For she was yong and wylde and he was old	
And demed° hymself been° lik° a cokewold.°	guessed, to be, likely, cuckold
He knew nat Catoun,⁵ for his wit° was rude,°	intelligence, unformed
That bad° man sholde wedde his simylitude.°	advised, equal
Men sholde wedden after hire estaat,°	condition
3230 For youthe and elde° is often at debaat.°	age, in dispute
But sith° that he was fallen in the snare:°	since, trap
He moste endure° as oother folk his care.°	had to endure, sorrow
FAIR was this yonge wyf and therwithal	
As any wezele° hir body gent° and smal.	weasel, delicate
3235 A ceynt° she werede° ybarred° al of silk,	girdle, wore, striped
A barmclooth° as whit° as morne° milk	apron, white, morning
Upon hir lendes° ful of many a goore.°	hips, pleat
Whit was hir smok° and broyden° al bifoore°	undergarment, embroidered, in front
And eek bihynde on hir coler° aboute	collar
3240 Of col-blak° silk withinne and eek withoute.	coal-black
The tapes° of hir white voluper°	ribbons, cap
Were of the same suyte° of hir coler.	pattern

[marginalia: his wife and his jealous]

[marginalia: allison]

---

1 Augrim stones had numbers on them and were used for making mathematical calculations.
2 This piece of music is an antiphon used in liturgical service. It was originally in Latin Gregorian chant but by Chaucer's day it had been translated into English and several polyphonic versions of it had been composed. The song depicts the conversation between the angel Gabriel and the Virgin Mary about the coming birth of Jesus.
3 This song has not survived—unless it is Chaucer's name for "Gabriel from Heaven King," the English translation of *Angelus ad virginem*.
4 "According to what his friends gave him."
5 The *Distichs*, a widely circulated collection of proverbs and wise sayings in verse couplets, often used for teaching Latin in schools, were ascribed in the Middle Ages to the Roman writer Dionysius Cato.

Hir filet° brood° of silk and set ful hye.° — headband, broad, high
And sikerly° she hadde a likerous° eye.   certainly, flirtatious
3245 Ful smale ypulled° were hire browes° two,   plucked, eyebrows
And tho° were bent and blake° as any sloo.°   then, black, sloeberry (fruit)
She was ful moore blisful° on to see   much more pleasant
Than is the newe perejonette tree°   pear tree
And softer than the wolle° is of a wether.°   wool, male sheep
3250 And by hir girdel° heeng a purs of lether°   belt, hung a purse of leather
Tasseled with grene° and perled° with latoun.°   green, decorated, brass
In al this world to seken° up and doun   seek
Ther nas° no man so wys° that koude thenche°   was not, wise, imagine
So gay a popelote° or swich° a wenche.°   puppet, such, peasant girl
3255 Full brighter was the shynyng° of hir hewe°   shining, complexion
Than in the Tour° the noble° yforged° newe.¹   tower, gold coin, forged
BUT of hir song, it was as loude and yerne°   lively
As any swalwe° sittynge on a berne.°   swallow, barn
Therto she koude skippe° and make game°   dance, play
3260 As any kyde° or calf folwynge his dame.°   kid (young goat), mother
Hir mouth was sweete as bragot° or the meeth°   ale, mead (fermented honey)
Or hoord° of apples leyd° in hey° or heeth.°   hoard, stored, hay, heather
Wynsynge° she was as is a joly° colt,   skittish, pretty
Long as a mast and uprighte as a bolt.°   straight as an arrow
3265 A brooch she baar° upon hir loue coler°   wore, low collar
As brood° as is the boos² of a bokeler.°   broad, boss of a shield
Hir shoes were laced on hir legges hye.°   laced high on her legs
She was a prymerole,° a piggesnye°   primrose, pig's eye (flower)
For any lord to leggen° in his bedde   lay
3270 Or yet for any good yeman to wedde.   yeoman
NOW sire° and eft° sire, so bifel° the cas°   sir, again, befell, event
That on a day this hende° Nicholas   handy
Fil° with this yonge wyf to rage° and pleye°   fell, romp, play
Whil that hir housbonde was at Oseneye,³
3275 As clerkes been ful subtile° and ful queynte,°   very subtle, clever
And prively° he caughte hire by the queynte°⁴   secretly, elegant thing (genitals)
And seyde, "Ywis,° but if° ich° have my wille   indeed, unless, I

---

1 The Tower of London was in Chaucer's day an important mint where gold coins were forged.
2 A shield's boss was its center bulge, occasionally used to injure an enemy.
3 Oseney was a small town just to the west of Oxford (now part of the modern city) where there
   was an abbey.
4 A rhyme on two homonyms (such as blue/blew or guest/guessed), near homonyms (such as seke/
   seke, i.e., seeke and sick in the General Prologue, lines 18–19) or on two different meanings of the
   same word, as here with queynte, was known as "rime riche" and was much valued by the French
   court poets of Chaucer's day. The modern term "rich rhyme" has a slightly narrower meaning
   and is confined to rhymes on homonyms.

[handwritten marginal note: Nicholas begs her to sleep with him]

For deerne° love of thee, lemman,° I spille,"°　　*secret, sweetheart, die*
And heeld hire harde by the haunche bones°　　*thighs*

3280 And seyde,° "Lemman,° love me al at ones°　　*said, sweetheart, immediately*
Or I wol dyen,° also° God me save!"　　*will die, as*
And she sproong° as a colt dooth° in the trave,°　　*sprang, does, stall*
And with hir heed she wryed° faste awey.　　*twisted*
She seyde, "I wol nat kisse thee, by my fey!°　　*faith*

3285 Why, lat be, quod ich,°¹ lat be, Nicholas,　　*I say*
Or I wol crie 'Out, harrow, and allas!'²
Do wey° youre handes, for youre curteisye!"°　　*let go, courtesy*
THIS Nicholas gan mercy for to crye°　　*began to cry for mercy*
And spak so faire and profred° hire so faste　　*urged*

3290 That she hir love hym graunted atte last°　　*at last*
And swoor hir ooth,° "By Seint Thomas of Kent,"°　　*oath, St. Thomas a Becket*
That she wol° been at his comandement　　*would*
Whan that she may hir leyser° wel° espie.°　　*leisure, well, see*
"Myn housbonde is so ful of jalousie

3295 That but° ye wayte° wel and been privee,°　　*unless, wait, secretive*
I woot° right wel I nam° but deed," quod she.　　*know, am not*
"Ye moste° been ful deerne° as in this cas."°　　*must, very secretive, business*
"NAY, therof care thee noght,"° quod Nicholas,　　*have no care*
"A clerk hadde lutherly biset his whyle³

3300 But if° he koude a carpenter bigyle."°　　*unless, trick*
And thus they been accorded° and ysworn°　　*agreed, sworn*
To wayte a tyme° as I have told biforn.°　　*wait [for] a time, before*
WHAN Nicholas had doon° thus everideel°　　*done, every bit*
And thakked° hire aboute the lendes° weel,°　　*patted, loins, well*

3305 He kiste hire sweete and taketh his sawtrie°　　*psaltery*
And pleyeth° faste and maketh melodie.　　*plays*
THANNE fil it° thus that to the paryssh chirche　　*it happened*
Cristes owene werkes° for to wirche,°　　*works, perform (i.e., to pray)*
This goode wyf wente on an haliday.°⁴　　*holy day*

3310 Hir forheed° shoon° as bright as any day,　　*forehead, shone*
So was it wasshen° whan she leet° hir werk.°　　*washed, left, work*
NOW was ther of that chirche° a parissh clerk°⁵　　*church, parish clerk*

[handwritten marginal note: Nicholas begs again and she agrees]

---

1 Both Ellesmere and Hengwrt read "ich" here, yet modern editors emend to "she," under the assumption that Chaucer is here slipping in and out of direct discourse. The manuscript readings can be defended on the basis of her uttering these words: "Let me be, I said, let me be, Nicholas ... !"

2 "Out, harrow, and alas!" were common cries of alarm to summon assistance.

3 "Lutherly beset his while" means "wasted his time."

4 A holy day was a saint's day or the day of a major religious celebration.

5 Absolon is an assistant to the parish priest. He is a member of the clergy and probably in minor orders and might, in due course, be ordained as a priest himself.

The which that was ycleped° Absolon.[1]   *Churchclerk* — called
Crul° was his heer and as the gold it shoon — curled
3315 And strouted° as a fanne° large and brode,° — stretched out, fan, broad
Ful streight and evene lay his joly shode.° — the parting of his hair
His rode° was reed,° hise eyen° greye as goos,° — complexion, red, eyes, goose
With Poules wyndow[2] corven° on his shoos.° — carved, shoes
In hoses° rede° he wente fetisly.° — stockings, red, fashionably
3320 Yclad° he was ful smal° and proprely — clothed, very tightly
Al in a kirtel° of a lyght waget.° — tunic, blue
Ful° faire and thikke° been the poyntes° set, — very, thick, laces
And therupon he hadde a gay surplys° — surplice (liturgical garment)
As whit as is the blosme upon the rys.° — twig
3325 A myrie° child° he was, so God me save. — merry, young man
Wel koude° he laten blood° and clippe and shave[3] — could, let blood
And maken a chartre° of lond° or acquitaunce.° — contract, land, quit-claim
In twenty manere koude° he trippe and daunce — could
After the scole° of Oxenford tho,° — school, then
3330 And with his legges casten to and fro
And pleyen songes on a smal rubible.° — rebec (bowed stringed instrument)
Therto he song somtyme a loud quynyble,° — falsetto
And as wel koude he pleye on his giterne.° — gittern (plucked stringed instrument)
In al the toun° nas° brewhous ne taverne — town, was not
3335 That he ne visited° with his solas° — did not visit, comfort
Ther any gaylard tappestere° was. — merry barmaid
But sooth to seyn, he was somdeel squaymous° — somewhat squeamish
Of fartyng and of speche daungerous.° — fastidious
This Absolon that jolif° was and gay — jolly
3340 Gooth° with a sencer° on the haliday,°[4] — goes, censer, holy day
Sensynge° the wyves° of the parisshe faste. — incensing, wives
And many a lovely look on hem° he caste, — them
And namely° on this carpenteris wyf. — especially
To looke on hire hym thoughte a myrie° lyf. — merry
3345 She was so propre and sweete and likerous,° — wanton
I dar wel seyn° if she hadde been a mous° — dare well say, mouse

---

1   The biblical Absolon, son of King David, was famous for his beauty. See 2 Samuel 14:25–26.

2   Fancy shoes were sometimes cut to produce a lattice pattern, which Chaucer compares to the stained glass rose window at St. Paul's Cathedral, London, which burned down in the disastrous fire in 1666.

3   Medieval barbers not only worked on one's hair but also did minor surgery like letting blood. This procedure, which involved opening a vein and allowing blood to flow out, was considered important in keeping the body's four humors (one of which was blood) in balance, thus insuring good health.

4   It was and is the custom in liturgical churches to burn incense in a metal container called a "censer," which hung from a chain and was swung about by a cleric called a "thurifer."

And he a cat, he wolde° hire° hente° anon.°   *would, her, grab, immediately*
THIS parissh clerk, this joly° Absolon   *merry*
Hath in his herte swich a love longynge
3350 That of no wyf took he noon offrynge.°   *no offering*
For curteisie,° he seyde, he wolde noon.°   *courtesy, wanted none*
The moone, whan it was nyght, ful brighte shoon,
And Absolon his gyterne° hath ytake,°   *gittern, taken*
For paramours° he thoghte for to wake.°   *love's sake, stay awake*
3355 And forth he gooth,° jolif° and amorous,   *goes, jolly*
Til he cam to the carpenteres hous
A litel after cokkes hadde ycrowe°   *roosters had crowed*
And dressed° hym up by a shot-wyndowe°   *approached, shuttered window*
That was upon the carpenteris wal.°   *wall*
3360 He syngeth in his voys° gentil° and smal,°   *voice, refined, high-pitched*
"Now deere lady, if thy wille be,
I pray yow that ye wole thynke on me,"
Ful wel acordaunt° to his gyternynge.°   *in accord, playing of the gittern*
This carpenter awook and herde synge
3365 And spak unto his wyf and seyde anon,°   *immediately*
"What, Alison, herestow nat° Absolon   *don't you hear*
That chaunteth° thus under oure boures° wal?"   *who sings, bedroom's*
And she answerde hir housbonde therwithal,
"Yis, God woot,° John! I heere it every deel."°   *God knows, every bit*
3370 THIS passeth forth. What wol ye bet than weel?°   *What more do you want?*
Fro day to day[1] this joly Absolon
So woweth° hire that hym is wobigon.°   *woos, filled with woe*
He waketh al the nyght and al the day.
He kembeth° hise lokkes° brode and made hym gay.   *combs, hair*
3375 He woweth° hire by meenes° and brocage°   *woos, go-betweens, agents*
And swoor he wolde been hir owene page.°   *young servant*
He syngeth brokkynge° as a nyghtyngale.   *twittering*
He sent hire pyment,° meeth,° and spiced ale   *spiced wine, mead*
And wafres pipyng hoot° out of the gleede,°   *hot, fire*
3380 And for she was of towne, he profreth meede.°   *money*
For som folk wol ben wonnen° for richesse   *won*
And somme for strokes° and somme for gentillesse.°[2]   *force, nobility*
SOMTYME to shewe° his lightnesse° and maistrye°   *show, agility, ability*

---

1   Ellesmere adds another "to day," which Hengwrt lacks. The meter supports the reading from
    Hengwrt.
2   A Latin gloss in the margin notes, "Hence Ovid [writes that] peasants [are to be persuaded] by
    blows," but the quotation is not found in Ovid. No precise source has been identified, but the
    general idea is found in the *De honeste amandi* or *Art of Courtly Love* of Andreas Capellanus (c.
    1174–1233 AD).

He playeth Herodes[1] upon a scaffold° hye.°   *stage, high*

3385 But what availleth° hym as in this cas?°   *helps, situation*

She loveth so this hende° Nicholas   *handy*

That Absolon may blowe the bukkes° horn.[2]   *buck's*

He ne hadde° for his labour but a scorn.   *did not have*

And thus she maketh Absolon hire ape

3390 And al his ernest° turneth til a jape.°   *seriousness, joke*

Ful sooth° is this proverbe, it is no lye,°   *true, lie*

Men seyn right thus: "Alwey the nye slye°   *near sly one*

Maketh the ferre° leeve° to be looth."°   *far, loved one, hated*

For though that Absolon be wood° or wrooth,°   *crazy, angry*

3395 Bycause that he fer° was from hire sighte,   *far*

This nye Nicholas stood in his lighte.

Now bere° thee wel, thou hende Nicholas,   *bear*

For Absolon may waille° and synge "Allas!"   *complain*

And so bifel it° on a Saterday   *it happened*

3400 This carpenter was goon° til Osenay,°   *gone, to Oseney*

And hende Nicholas and Alisoun

Acorded° been to this conclusioun   *agreed*

That Nicholas shal shapen° hym a wyle°   *fabricate, scheme*

This sely,° jalous housbonde to bigyle,°   *simple, to trick*

3405 And if so be the game wente aright,

She sholde slepen° in his arm al nyght.   *sleep*

For this was his desir and hire° also,   *hers*

And right anon° withouten wordes mo   *immediately*

This Nicholas no lenger° wolde° tarie,°   *longer, would, delay*

3410 But dooth ful softe° unto his chambre carie°   *quietly, carry*

Bothe mete° and drynke for a day or tweye°   *food, two*

And to hire housbonde bad hire for to seye°   *asked her to say*

If that he axed° after Nicholas   *asked*

She sholde seye she nyste° where he was.   *did not know*

3415 Of al that day she saugh° hym nat° with eye.   *saw, not*

She trowed° that he was in maladye,°   *believed, sickness*

For° for°[3] no cry hir mayde koude° hym calle.   *Because, with, could*

He nolde° answere for thyng° that myghte falle.°   *would not, anything, happen*

This passeth forth° al thilke° Saterday,   *this continues, that same*

3420 That Nicholas stille° in his chambre lay   *quietly*

And eet° and sleepe° or dide what hym leste°   *ate, slept, what he wanted*

[handwritten: thru the carpenter]

---

1 King Herod, who ordered all the children in Bethlehem to be killed in hopes of thus killing the Messiah foretold by the Magi, was, like Pilate referred to in line 3124, depicted in medieval drama as loud and excessively violent.

2 The expression "blow the buck's horn" more or less means "go whistle."

3 Ellesmere and Hengwrt both repeat "for."

Til Sonday that the sonne gooth° to reste.   *goes*
THIS sely carpenter hath greet merveyle°   *wondered greatly*
Of Nicholas or what thyng myghte hym eyle°   *ail (trouble)*
3425 And seyde, "I am adrad° by Seint Thomas   *afraid*
It stondeth nat aright° with Nicholas.   *not right*
God shilde° that he deyde° sodeynly!°   *forbid, died, suddenly*
This world is now ful tikel,° sikerly.°   *uncertain, certainly*
I saugh° today a cors° yborn° to chirche°   *saw, body, carried, church*
3430 That now on Monday last I saugh hym wirche!°   *work*
Go up," quod he unto his knave° anoon,°   *serving boy, immediately*
"Clepe° at his dore° or knokke with a stoon.   *call, door*
Looke how it is and tel me boldely."
THIS knave gooth hym up° ful sturdily   *up to him*
3435 And at the chambre dore whil° that he stood,   *room's door while*
He cride and knokked as that he were wood,°   *crazy*
"What how! What do ye, maister Nicholay?
How may ye slepen al the longe day?"
BUT al for noght. He herde nat a word.
3440 An hole he foond° ful lowe upon a bord°   *found, board*
Theras° the cat was wont° in for to crepe,°   *where, used to, creep*
And at that hole he looked in ful depe°   *right in*
Til at the laste he hadde of hym a sighte.
This Nicholas sat capyng evere uprighte°   *gaping upwards*
3445 As he had kiked° on the newe moone.   *looked*
Adoun° he gooth° and tolde his maister soone   *down, goes*
In what array° he saugh that ilke° man.   *condition, same*
THIS carpenter to blessen[1] hym bigan°   *began*
And seyde, "Help us, Seinte Frydeswyde![2]
3450 A man woot° litel what hym shal bityde!°   *knows, what shall happen to him*
This man is falle° with his astromye°   *fallen, astronomy*
In som woodnesse° or in som agonye.°   *madness, fit*
I thoghte ay° wel how that it sholde be.   *I always thought*
Men sholde nat knowe of Goddes pryvetee.°   *secrets*
3455 Ye, blessed° be alwey° a lewed° man   *blessed, always, uneducated*
That noght but oonly° his Bileve[3] kan!°   *nothing other than, knows*
So ferde° another clerk° with astromye:°   *it happened, scholar, astronomy*
He walked in the feeldes° for to prye°   *fields, pry (study foolishly)*

---

1 "To bless oneself" in the Middle Ages meant to trace the sign of the cross with the right thumb
  on the forehead, lips, and heart.
2 The Anglo-Saxon St. Frideswide, a young noblewoman who was persecuted for her desire to
  be a nun, is the patron saint of the town of Oxford. She was abbess of a monastery that was on
  the site of the present Christ Church, Oxford.
3 Carpenter John's "Believe" is his Creed—the Apostle's Creed, which, along with the Lord's
  Prayer, was considered the minimum that every Christian must memorize.

Upon the sterres,° what ther sholde bifalle,° — *stars, happen*
3460 Til he was in a marleput[1] yfalle.° — *fallen*
He saugh nat° that! But yet by Seint Thomas, — *not*
Me reweth° soore of hende Nicholas. — *I have pity*
He shal be rated° of his studiyng — *scolded for*
If that I may by Jhesus hevene° kyng! — *heaven's*
3465 GET me a staf° that I may underspore,° — *staff, pry*
Whil that thou, Robyn, hevest of the dore.° — *heave off the door*
He shal out of his studiyng, as I gesse."° — *guess*
And to the chambre dore° he gan hym dresse.° — *door, approached*
His knave° was a strong carl° for the nones,° — *servant, fellow, for the occasion*
3470 And by the haspe° he haaf it of° atones. — *hinge, heaved it off*
Into° the floor the dore° fil° anon. — *onto, door, fell*
This Nicholas sat ay° as stille as stoon° — *ever, stone*
And evere caped° upward into the eir.° — *gaped, air*
This carpenter wende° he were in despeir° — *believed, despair*
3475 And hente° hym by the sholdres° myghtily — *grabbed, shoulders*
And shook hym harde and cride spitously,° — *loudly*
"What Nicholay! What how! What! Looke adoun!
Awake and thenk° on Cristes Passioun! — *think*
I crouche° thee from elves and fro wightes."° — *sign with the cross, evil creatures*
3480 Therwith the nyght spel° seyde he anonrightes° — *night [magic]-spell, right away*
On foure halves° of the hous aboute — *four corners*
And on the thresshfold° of the dore° withoute.° — *threshold, door, outside*
"Jhesu Crist and Seint Benedight[2]
Blesse this hous from every wikked wight° — *evil creature*
3485 For nyghtes nerye° the white Pater Noster:°[3] — *save, Lord's Prayer*
Where wentestow° Seint Petres soster?"° — *where did you go, sister*
AND atte laste this hende Nicholas
Gan° for to sike° soore and seyde, "Allas! — *began, sigh*
Shal al this world be lost eftsoones° now?" — *immediately*
3490 THIS carpenter answerde, "What seystow?° — *What do you say?*
What! Thynk on God as we doon, men that swynke."[4]

---

1 A marl pit is a ditch on a farm for keeping marl, a type of soil rich in clay used for fertilizing the fields.

2 St. Benedict of Nursia was an early sixth-century abbot who wrote the famous Rule that organized most monasteries in the following years.

3 Following Skeat, most editions of this tale read "nerye" as "verye," since in minim-based scribal hands u, v, and n are identical. As E. Talbot Donaldson pointed out in *Speaking of Chaucer*, p. 132, "nerye" is the subjunctive of the now obsolete word "nerian," to save. The line is a spell roughly meaning, "May the White Lord's Prayer save us from the night." The next line seems meaningless, John's muddled version of white magic.

4 "Men who labor." John is making the old distinction between the three estates here. The first estate comprises those who pray (the profession for which Nicholas is studying), the second those who fight (the nobility), and the third those who work and thus provide the food for all three estates.

THIS Nicholas answerde, "Fecche me° drynke   *get me*
And after wol I speke in pryvetee
Of certeyn° thyng that toucheth me and thee.   *[a] certain*
3495 I wol° telle it noon oother° man certeyn."   *will, [to] no other*
THIS carpenter goth doun and comth ageyn°   *comes again*
And broghte of myghty ale a large quart.
And whan that ech of hem° had dronke his part,   *them*
This Nicholas his dore faste shette°   *shut*
3500 And doun the carpenter by hym he sette.
HE seyde, "John, myn hoost, lief° and deere,°   *beloved, dear*
Thou shalt upon thy trouthe swere° me here   *swear*
That to no wight thou shalt this conseil° wreye,°   *counsel, betray*
For it is Cristes conseil that I seye.
3505 And if thou telle man,° thou art forlore,°   *someone, lost*
For this vengeaunce thou shalt han° therfore:°   *have, for it*
That if thou wreye° me, thou shalt be wood."°   *betray, crazy*
"NAY, Crist forbede° it for his hooly blood!"   *forbid*
Quod tho this sely° man, "I nam no labbe.°   *simple, am no blabber*
3510 Ne, though I seye,° I am nat lief to gabbe.°   *say, not accustomed to gab*
Sey what thou wolt, I shal it nevere telle
To child ne wyf by hym that harwed° helle!"[1]   *harrowed*
"NOW John," quod Nicholas, "I wol nat lye.
I have yfounde° in myn astrologye   *found*
3515 As I have looked in the moone bright
That now a Monday next° at quarter nyght[2]   *next Monday*
Shal falle a reyn° and that so wilde and wood°   *rain, crazy*
That half so greet° was nevere Noees° Flood.   *great, Noah's*
This world," he seyde, "in lasse° than an hour   *less*
3520 Shal al be dreynt,° so hidous° is the shour.°   *drowned, hideous, downpour*
Thus shal mankynde drenche° and lese hir lyf."°   *drown, lose their life*
THIS carpenter answerde, "Allas my wyf!
And shal she drenche? Allas, myn Alisoun!"
For sorwe° of this he fil° almoost adoun   *sorrow, fell*
3525 And seyde, "Is ther no remedie in this cas?"°   *situation*
"WHY, yis, for Gode," quod hende Nicholas.
"If thou wolt werken° after loore° and reed,°   *act, teaching, advice*
Thou mayst nat werken° after thyn owene heed,°   *not act, head (intelligence)*
For thus seith Salomon[3] that was ful trewe,

---

1. The Harrowing of Hell (another subject of medieval religious drama) was the victorious entry Christ made into Hell between his death and resurrection to save the righteous souls held in limbo.
2. "Quarter night" means one fourth of the way through the night.
3. Solomon, the ancient king of Israel, was known for his wisdom and was thought to be the author of several books of the Hebrew Bible. The reference here is to Ecclesiasticus 32:24. Nicholas

3530 'WERK° al by conseil° and thou shalt nat rewe!'°   Do, advice, regret
      And if thou werken wolt by good conseil,
      I undertake withouten mast and seyl,°   sail
      Yet shal I saven hire° and thee and me.   save her
      Hastou nat herd° hou saved was Noe°   have you not herd, Noah
3535 Whan that oure Lord hadde warned hym biforn°   before
      That al the world with water sholde be lorn?"°   lost
      "YIS," quod this carpenter, "ful yoore ago."°   very long ago
      "HASTOU nat herd," quod Nicholas, "also,
      The sorwe of Noe with his felaweshipe
3540 Er° that he myghte brynge his wyf to shipe?°¹   before, on board
      Hym hadde be levere,° I dar° wel undertake,°   he had rather, dare, affirm
      At thilke tyme° than alle hise wetheres blake°   at the same time, black sheep
      That she hadde had a shipe hirself° allone.   a ship to herself
      And therfore woostou° what is best to doone?   do you know
3545 This asketh° haste and of an hastif thyng°   requires, urgent business
      Men may nat preche° or maken tariyng.°   not preach, make delay
      ANON,° go gete us faste into this in°   immediately, house
      A knedyng trogh° or ellis a kymelyn°   kneading pot, tub
      For ech° of us—but looke that they be large—   each
3550 In whiche we mowe swymme° as in a barge.   may float
      And han therinne vitaille suffissant°   have in it enough food
      But for a day. Fy on° the remenant!   disregard
      The water shal aslake° and goon away   ebb
      Aboute pryme° upon the nexte day.   prime (an early hour of prayer)
3555 But Robyn may nat wite° of this, thy knave.°   know, servant
      Ne eek° thy mayde Gille I may nat° save.   nor also, not
      Axe nat° why, for though thou aske me,   ask not
      I wol nat tellen Goddes pryvetee.°   secrets
      Suffiseth thee,° but if thy wittes madde°   let it suffice, go crazy
3560 To han° as greet a grace as Noe hadde.   have
      Thy wyf shal I wel saven, out of doute.°   doubtless
      Go now thy wey, and speed thee heer aboute.°   have success in this matter
      BUT whan thou hast for hire and thee and me
      Ygeten° us thise knedyng tubbes thre,   gotten
3565 Thanne shaltow hange hem° in the roof ful hye°   shall you hang them, very high
      That° no man of oure purveiaunce° spye.   so that, preparations
      And whan thou thus hast doon as I have seyd
      And hast oure vitaille° faire in hem yleyd°   food, laid

---

      makes a mistake here: Ecclesiasticus, part of the Greek Old Testament considered apocryphal by
      Protestants or deuterocanonical by Catholics, was written by Jesus ben Sirach, not Solomon, as
      Saint Augustine, among others, noted.
    1 Noah's difficulty in persuading his wife to board the Ark is depicted in medieval drama.

And eek an ax to smyte the corde° atwo°   *rope, in two*
3570 Whan that the water comth that we may go,
And broke an hole anheigh° up on the gable   *on high*
Unto the gardynward° over the stable   *towards the garden*
That we may frely° passen forth oure way   *freely*
Whan that the grete shour° is goon away,   *great shower*
3575 Thanne shal I swymme° as myrie,° I undertake,°   *swim, merry, expect*
As dooth the white doke° after hire drake.   *duck*
Thanne wol I clepe,° 'How, Alison! How John!   *call*
Be myrie, for the flood wol passe anon!'
And thou wolt seyn, 'Hayl° maister Nicholay,   *Hail*
3580 Good morwe! I se thee wel, for it is day.'
And thanne shul° we be lordes al oure lyf   *shall*
Of al the world as Noe and his wyf.
But of o° thyng I warne thee ful right:°   *one, in particular*
Be wel avysed° on that ilke nyght°   *advised, that same night*
3585 That we ben entred° into shippes bord   *entered*
That noon° of us ne speke nat a word   *none*
Ne clepe° ne crie but been in his preyere,°   *nor call, prayers*
For it is Goddes owene heeste° deere.°   *commandment, dear*
Thy wyf and thou moote° hange fer° atwynne,°   *must, far, apart*
3590 For that bitwixe yow° shal be no synne°   *between you, sin*
Namoore° in lookyng than ther shal in deede.   *no more*
This ordinance° is seyd. Go, God thee speede!   *commandment*
Tomorwe at nyght whan folk ben alle aslepe
Into oure knedyng tubbes wol° we crepe°   *will, creep*
3595 And sitten there abidyng° Goddes grace.   *awaiting*
Go now thy wey. I have no lenger space°   *no more time*
To make of this no lenger° sermonyng.°   *no longer, speech*
Men seyn thus: 'Sende the wise and sey nothing.'
Thou art so wys, it nedeth thee nat to preche.°   *preach*
3600 Go save oure lyf, and that I the biseche."°   *implore*
This sely carpenter goth forth his wey.
Ful ofte he seith "Allas!" and "Weylawey!"
And to his wyf he tolde his pryvetee.°   *secret*
And she was war° and knew it bet° than he   *aware, better*
3605 What al this queynte cast° was for to seye.   *unusual scheme*
But nathelees° she ferde as° she wolde deye   *nevertheless, acted as if*
And seyde, "Allas! Go forth thy wey anon.
Help us to scape° or we been lost echon!°   *escape, everyone*
I am thy trewe, verray° wedded wyf.   *faithful*
3610 Go, deere spouse, and help to save oure lyf!"

Lo, which a greet° thyng is affeccioun!¹   *what a great*
Men may dyen° of ymaginacioun,°   *die, imagination*
So depe° may impressioun be take.°   *deep, taken*
This sely carpenter bigynneth quake.°   *begins to shake*
3615 Hym thynketh verraily° that he may see   *It truly appears to him*
Noees° Flood come walwynge° as the see   *Noah's, surging*
To drenchen° Alisoun his hony deere.°   *drown, honey-dear*
He wepeth, weyleth,° maketh sory cheere.°   *wails, makes a sorry face*
He siketh° with ful many a sory swogh.°   *sighs, groan*
3620 He gooth and geteth hym a knedyng trogh
And after that a tubbe and a kymelyn.°   *tub and bucket*
And pryvely he sente hem to his in°   *house*
And heng hem in the roof in pryvetee.°   *secrecy*
His owene hand made laddres thre
3625 To clymben by the ronges° and the stalkes°   *rungs, shafts*
Into the tubbes hangynge in the balkes°   *beams*
And hem vitailleth° bothe trogh and tubbe   *provides food for them*
With breed and chese and good ale in a jubbe,°   *jug*
Suffisynge° right ynogh° as for a day.   *sufficing, enough*
3630 But er° that he hadde maad al this array°   *before, made all these preparations*
He sente his knave° and eek his wenche° also   *serving boy, serving girl*
Upon his nede° to London for to go.   *need*
And on the Monday whan it drow to nyght,°   *approached night*
He shette° his dore withoute candel lyght   *shut*
3635 And dresseth° alle thyng as it shal be.   *arranged*
And shortly, up they clomben° alle thre.°   *climbed, three*
They sitten stille,° wel a furlong way.²   *quietly*
Now, "Pater Noster clom!"° seyde Nicholay.   *be quiet*
And "Clom," quod John. And "Clom," seyde Alisoun.
3640 This carpenter seyde his devocioun,°   *his prayers*
And stille he sit and biddeth his preyere,°   *says his prayers*
Awaitynge on the reyn, if he it heere.°   *hear*
The dede° sleepe, for wery° bisynesse   *dead, weary*
Fil° on this carpenter right as I gesse°   *fell, guess*
3645 About corfew° tyme or litel moore.³   *curfew*
For travaille° of his goost° he groneth soore   *labor, spirit*
And eft° he routeth,° for his heed° myslay.°   *also, snores, head, lay wrong*

---

1 There is a Latin gloss in the margin, "Auctor," which may imply that the glossator considers this
   to be the author's judgment or just a useful and authoritative moral comment.
2 "For the time it takes to walk a furlong" (about an eighth of a mile).
3 Curfew, from the French for "cover your fire," announced the time, often around 8 p.m., when
   all fires had to be covered and houses were shut up for the night.

Doun of the laddre stalketh Nicholay,
And Alisoun ful softe adoun she spedde.°   *hastens*
3650 Withouten wordes mo they goon to bedde
Theras° the carpenter is wont to lye.°   *where, is accustomed to lie*
Ther was the revel° and the melodye.   *fun*
And thus Alison and Nicholas
In bisynesse of myrthe° and of solas°   *mirth, comfort*
3655 Til that the belle of laudes¹ gan° to rynge   *began*
And freres° in the chauncel² gonne synge.°   *friars, began to sing*
THIS parissh clerk, this amorous Absolon
That is for love alwey so wobigon°   *sorrowful*
Upon the Monday was at Oseneye
3660 With a compaignye hym to disporte and pleye°   *play and have fun*
And axed upon cas° a cloistrer°   *asked by chance, monk*
Ful prively° after John the carpenter.   *very secretly*
And he drough hym apart° out of the chirche°   *drew him aside, church*
And seyde, "I noot. I saugh hym heere nat wirche
3665 Syn° Saterday.³ I trowe° that he be went°   *since, believe, is gone*
For tymber ther° oure abbot hath hym sent.   *timber where*
For he is wont° for tymber for to go   *accustomed*
And dwellen° at the grange° a day or two.⁴   *stay, farmhouse*
Or elles he is at his hous certeyn.
3670 Where that he be, I kan nat soothly seyn."°   *truly say*
THIS Absolon ful joly was and light
And thoghte, "Now is tyme [to] wake° al nyght,   *to stay awake*
For sikirly,° I saugh hym nat stirynge°   *certainly, not stirring*
Aboute his dore syn° day bigan to sprynge.°   *since, dawn*
3675 So moot° I thryve,° I shall at cokkes crowe   *might, thrive*
Ful pryvely knokke at his wyndowe
That stant ful° lowe upon his boures wal.°   *very, bedroom's wall*
To Alison now wol° I tellen al   *will*
My love-longynge. For yet I shal nat mysse
3680 That at the leeste wey° I shal hire kisse.   *very least*
Som maner° confort shal I have parfay.°   *kind of, in faith*
My mouth hath icched° al this longe day.   *itched*
That is a signe of kissyng atte leeste.
Al nyght me mette° eek I was at a feeste.°   *I dreamed, feast*
3685 Therfore I wol goon slepe° an houre or tweye°   *go sleep, two*
And al the nyght thanne° wol I wake and pleye."   *then*

---

1   Lauds is the monastic hour of prayer that occurs in the middle of the night.
2   The chancel area of a church or chapel is near the altar.
3   "I do not know. I have not seen him work here since Saturday."
4   Abbeys usually had outlying estates, such as this one where John the carpenter is working.

WHAN that the firste cok° hath crowe anon,   rooster
Up rist° this joly lovere Absolon   rose
And hym arraieth° gay at poynt devys.¹   dresses
3690 But first he cheweth greyn° of lycorys°   a grain, licorice
To smellen sweete er° he hadde kembd° his heer.°   before, combed, hair
Under his tonge° a trewe-love² he beer,°   tongue, carried
For therby wende he to ben gracious.°   expected to be attractive
He rometh° to the carpenteres hous,   roams
3695 And stille he stant° under the shot-wyndowe.°   stands, shuttered window
Unto his brist° it raughte,° it was so lowe.   breast, reached
And softe he knokketh with a semy soun.°   quiet sound
"What do ye, honycomb, sweete Alisoun,
My faire bryd,° my sweete cynamone?°   bird, cinnamon
3700 Awaketh, lemman myn,° and speketh to me.   my sweetheart
Wel litel° thynken ye upon my wo   very little
That for youre love I swete° ther° I go.   sweat, where
No wonder is thogh° that I swelte° and swete.   is it though, faint
I moorne° as dooth° a lamb after the tete.°   mourn, does, teat
3705 Ywis,° lemman,° I have swich° love longynge   indeed, sweetheart, such
That lik° a turtel° trewe is my moornynge.°   like, turtledove, mourning
I may nat ete° namoore° than a mayde."   not eat, anymore
"Go fro° the wyndow, Jakke fool,"° she sayde.   from, Jack-fool
"As help me God, it wol nat be 'com pa me.'°³   come kiss me
3710 I love another, and elles° I were to blame,   else
Wel bet° than thee, by Jhesu, Absolon.   better
Go forth thy wey or I wol caste a ston.°   throw a stone
And lat me slepe a twenty devel wey!"°   for the sake of twenty devils
"ALLAS,"° quod Absolon, "and weylawey,   alas
3715 That trewe° love was evere so yvel biset!°   true, ill bestowed
Thanne kys° me, syn° it may be no bet,°   kiss, since, better
For Jhesus love and for the love of me."
"WILTOW° thanne go thy wey?" quod she.   will you
"YE, certes, lemman," quod this Absolon.
3720 "THANNE make thee redy," quod she. "I come anon."
And unto Nicholas she seyde stille,°   quietly
"Now hust,° and thou shalt laughen al thy fille."   shush
THIS Absolon doun° sette° hym on his knees   down, set
And seyde, "I am lord at alle degrees,°   in every way

---

1 "At point devise" means "perfectly."
2 A "true-love" is a four-leaf clover.
3 "Come pa me" or "Come kiss me" sounds like either an idiomatic expression, a refrain from a
   song, or a form of baby talk. No other use of this precise expression has been found although
   Skeat provides some suggestive analogues.

3725 For after this I hope ther cometh moore.°   *there will come more*

Lemman, thy grace and sweete bryd,° thyn oore!"°   *bird, favor*

THE wyndow she undoth° and that in haste.   *unlatched*

"Have do," quod she. "Com of and speed the faste,[1]

Lest that oure neighebores thee espie."°   *see you*

3730 THIS Absolon gan wype° his mouth ful drie.°   *wiped, very dry*

Dirk° was the nyght as pich° or as the cole,°   *dark, pitch, coal*

And at the wyndow out she pitte° hir hole.   *put*

And Absolon hym fil° no bet° ne wers,°   *fell, better, worse*

But with his mouth he kiste° hir naked ers°   *kissed, ass*

3735 Ful savourly° er° he was war° of this.   *with relish, before, aware*

ABAK° he stirte° and thoughte it was amys,°   *backwards, jumped, wrong*

For wel° he wiste° a womman hath no berd.°   *well, knew, beard*

He felte a thyng al rough and longe yherd°   *long-haired*

And seyde, "Fy!° Allas! What have I do?"°   *fie, done*

3740 "TEHEE,"° quod she and clapte° the wyndow to.   *Ha ha, slammed*

And Absolon gooth forth a sory° pas.°   *sorry, step*

"A BERD,° a berd!" quod hende Nicholas.   *beard*

"By Goddes corpus,° this goth° faire and weel!"°   *body, goes, well*

THIS sely° Absolon herde° every deel°   *innocent, heard, part*

3745 And on his lippe° he gan for anger byte,°   *lip, began to bite*

And to hymself he seyde, "I shall thee quyte!"°   *repay*

WHO rubbeth now, who froteth° now his lippes   *wipes*

With dust, with sond, with straw, with clooth, with chippes°   *chips (of wood)*

But Absolon, that seith ful ofte, "Allas!

3750 My soule bitake° I unto Sathanas°   *commit, Satan*

But me were levere° than al this toun," quod he,   *rather*

"Of this despit° awroken° for to be.   *insult, avenged*

Allas," quod he, "Allas, I ne hadde ybleynt!"°   *had not restrained [myself]*

His hoote love was coold and al yqueynt.°   *quenched*

3755 For fro° that tyme° that he hadde kist° hir ers,°   *from, time, kissed, ass*

Of paramours° he sette nat a kers,°   *love, watercress (cared nothing)*

For he was heeled° of his maladie.   *healed*

Ful ofte paramours° he gan deffie°   *passionate love, denounced*

And weepe as dooth° a child that is ybete.°   *does, beaten*

3760 A softe paas° he wente over the strete°   *quiet step, street*

Until° a smyth° men cleped Daun° Gerveys,   *unto, blacksmith, Master*

That in his forge smythed plough° harneys.   *plow*

He sharpeth shaar° and kultour° bisily.   *plowshare, plow blade*

This Absolon knokketh al esily°   *quietly*

3765 And seyde, "Undo,° Gerveys, and that anon."   *open up*

"WHAT! Who artow?"° "I am heere, Absolon."   *Who are you?*

---

1 "'Hurry up,' she said, 'make haste and be quick.'"

"What! Absolon, for Cristes sweete tree,°   *cross*
Why rise ye so rathe?° Ey, benedicitee!°   *early, Ah, bless you!*
What eyleth° yow? Som gay gerl,° God it woot,°   *ails, girl, knows*
3770 Hath broght yow thus upon the viritoot.[1]
By Seinte Note,[2] ye woot wel° what I mene."°   *know well, mean*
THIS Absolon ne roghte nat a bene°   *did not care a bean*
Of al his pley. No word agayn° he yaf.°   *again, gave*
He hadde moore tow° on his distaf[3]   *flax*
3775 Than Gerveys knew and seyde, "Freend, so deere,°   *[be] so kind*
That hoote° kultour° in the chymenee heere,   *hot, plow blade*
As lene° it me. I have therwith to doone,°   *lend, do*
And I wol brynge it thee agayn ful soone."
GERVEYS answerde, "Certes, were it gold
3780 Or in a poke° nobles° alle untold,°   *bag, gold coins, unnumbered*
Thou sholdest have,° as I am trewe° smyth.   *have [it], true*
Ey, Cristes foo,° what wol ye do therwith?"   *foe*
"THEROF," quod Absolon, "be as be may.
I shal wel° telle it thee tomorwe day,"   *well*
3785 And caughte the kultour° by the colde stele.°   *plow blade, handle*
Ful softe out at the dore he gan to stele°   *began to steal*
And wente unto the carpenteris wal.
He cogheth° first and knokketh therwithal   *coughs*
Upon the wyndowe right° as he dide er.   *just*
3790 THIS Alison answerde, "Who is ther
That knokketh so? I warante it a theef."°   *thief*
"WHY, nay," quod he, "God woot, my sweete leef,°   *loved one*
I am thyn Absolon, my deerelyng.°   *darling*
Of gold," quod he, "I have thee broght a ryng.
3795 My mooder yaf° it me, so God me save.   *gave*
Ful fyn° it is and therto wel ygrave.°   *fine, engraved*
This wol° I yeve° thee if thou me kisse."   *will, give*
THIS Nicholas was risen for to pisse
And thoughte he wolde amenden° al the jape.   *make better*
3800 He sholde kisse his ers°[4] er° that he scape."°   *ass, before, escape*
And up the wyndowe dide° he hastily,   *opened*
And out his ers he putteth pryvely°   *secretly*
Over the buttok to the haunche bon.°   *thigh*
And therwith spak this clerk, this Absolon:
3805 "Spek, sweete bryd,° I noot nat° where thou art."   *bird, do not know*

---

1 "Viritoot" is unattested elsewhere, so no one knows exactly what it means.
2 St. Neot was a ninth-century monk from Glastonbury who became a hermit.
3 A distaff was a tool used in making thread to be spun into cloth.
4 Ellesmere omits "ers"; it is supplied from Hengwrt.

This Nicholas anon leet fle° a fart   *let fly*
As greet as it had been a thonder dent,°   *thunderclap*
That with the strook he was almoost yblent.°   *blinded*
And he was redy with his iren hoot,°   *hot iron*
3810 And Nicholas amydde [the]¹ ers° he smoot.°   *in the middle of the ass, struck*
Of gooth° the skyn° an hande brede° about.   *off goes, skin, a hand-breadth*
The hoote kultour brende° so his toute,°   *burned, rear*
And for the smert° he wende° for to dye.°   *pain, expected, die*
As he were wood for wo, he gan to crye,°   *began to cry*
3815 "Help, water, water, help, for Goddes herte!"
This carpenter out of his slomber° sterte°   *slumber, jumped*
And herde oon crien,° "Water!" as he were wood   *heard one cry*
And thoughte, "Allas, now comth Nowelis Flood!"
He sit hym up° withouten wordes mo,   *sits up*
3820 And with his ax he smoot the corde° atwo,°   *rope, in two*
And doun° gooth al! He foond neither to selle,   *down*
Ne breed ne ale til he cam to the celle²
Upon the floor, and there aswowne° he lay.   *in a faint*
Up stirte° hire Alison and Nicholay,   *jumped*
3825 And criden, "Out!" and "Harrow!" in the strete.
The neighebores bothe smale and grete°   *small and big*
In ronnen° for to gauren on° this man   *ran in, gape at*
That yet aswowne° he lay, bothe pale and wan.°   *in a faint, colorless*
For with the fal° he brosten hadde° his arm.   *fall, had broken*
3830 But stonde he moste unto his owene harm.³
For whan he spak, he was anon bore doun°   *shouted down*
With° hende Nicholas and Alisoun.   *by*
They tolden every man that he was wood.°   *crazy*
He was agast° so of "Nowelis" Flood   *aghast*
3835 Thurgh fantasie° that of his vanytee°   *fantasy, folly*
He hadde yboght° hym knedyng tubbes thre   *brought*
And hadde hem hanged in the rove° above,   *roof*
And that he preyde° hem for Goddes love   *asked*
To sitten in the roof par compaignye.°   *for company*
3840 The folk gan laughen° at his fantasye.   *began to laugh*
Into the roof they kiken° and they cape°   *stare, gape*
And turned al his harm unto a jape.°   *joke*
For what° so that this carpenter answerde,   *whatever*

---

1   The word is supplied by Hengwrt.
2   "He did not find bread or ale to sell until he came to the flooring (*celle*) on the ground (*floor*),"
     i.e., he did not stop on his way down.
3   This idiomatic expression has been interpreted differently. John the Carpenter must endure
     (or put up with or take responsibility for) his own injury, or he must stand up for himself even
     though it turned out badly.

It was for noght.° No man his reson herde.°   *nothing, would listen to his explanation*
3845 With othes° grete he was so sworn adoun°   *oaths, shouted down*
That he was holde° wood° in al the toun,   *held, crazy*
For every clerk° anonright heeld° with oother.   *scholar, agreed*
They seyde, "The man was wood, my leeve° brother."   *dear*
And every wight gan laughen° of this stryf.°   *began to laugh, strife*
3850 Thus swyved° was this carpenteris wyf   *made love to*
For al his kepyng° and his jalousye.°   *guarding, jealousy*
And Absolon hath kist° hir nether° eye,   *kissed, lower*
And Nicholas is scalded in the towte.°   *rear*
This tale is doon, and God save al the rowte!°   *company*

HEERE ENDETH THE MILLERE HIS TALE

THE REEVE'S PROLOGUE AND TALE

3855 WHAN folk had laughen° at this nyce cas°	laughed, silly matter
Of Absolon and hende° Nicholas,	handy
Diverse° folk diversly° they seyde,°	different, differently, said
But for the moore part° they loughe and pleyde.°	for the most part, played
Ne° at this tale I saugh° no man hym greve,°	nor, saw, become angry
3860 But° it were oonly° Osewold the Reve.	except, only
Bycause he was of carpenteris craft,	
A litel° ire° is in his herte° ylaft.°	little, anger, heart, left
He gan to grucche° and blamed it a lite.°	complain, little
"So theek,"° quod he, "ful wel koude° I yow quite°	As I thrive, very well could, requite
3865 With bleryng° of a proud milleres eye,	blearing
If that me liste speke of ribaudye.°	If I wanted to speak of bawdiness
But ik° am oold. Me list° no pley° for age.	I, I desire, play
Gras-tyme° is doon.° My fodder is now forage.[1]	grass-time, done
This white tope writeth° myne° olde yeris.°	declare, my, years
3870 Myn herte° is mowled° also as myne heris.°	my heart, grown moldy, my hairs
But if I fare as doth an open-ers.	
That ilke° fruyt° is ever leng the wers,°	same, fruit, gets ever worse
Til it be roten° in mullok° or in stree.°[2]	rotten, garbage, straw
We olde men, I drede,° so fare we	fear
3875 Til we be roten,° kan° we nat° be rype.°	rotten, can, not, ripe
We hoppen° ay° whil that the world wol° pype.°	dance, always, will, pipe (play music)
For in oure wyl° ther stiketh° evere° a nayl,°[3]	will, sticks, MS eve, nail
To have an hoor heed° and a grene tayl°	gray head, green tail
As hath a leek.[4] For thogh oure myght be goon,°	gone
3880 Oure wyl desireth folie° evere° in oon.	folly, always
For whan we may nat doon,° than wol° we speke,°	not do, will, speak
Yet in oure asshen° olde is fyr° yreke.°	ashes, fire, raked over
FOURE gleedes° han° we whiche I shal devyse:°	embers, have, describe
Avauntyng,° liyng,° anger, coveitise.°	boasting, lying, coveting
3885 Thise foure sparkles° longen° unto eelde.°	sparks, belong, age
Oure olde lemes° mowe° wel° been unweelde,°	limbs, must, well, weak
But wyl° ne shal nat faillen,° that is sooth.°	will, shall not fail, truth
And yet ik° have alwey a coltes° tooth[5]	I, colt's
As many a yeer° as it is passed henne°	year, away

---

1 My time in the pasture is over and now I am like a horse in the stable in winter who eats hay.

2 The medlar (a kind of plum) was known as an "open-ass" because it has a strong purgative effect. It only becomes edible when it is rotten.

3 I.e., we are always goaded by desire. A goad is a stick, often with a sharp metal point, used to drive animals.

4 "Green tail" is an expression, possibly proverbial, suggesting sexual activity. The image is also found in Boccaccio's *Decameron* in the introduction to the fourth day.

5 A proverbial expression for having the sexual desires of a young creature. Cf. Wife of Bath's prologue, line 602.

3890 Syn° that my tappe° of lif° bigan to renne.°	*since, tap, life, run*
For sikerly,° whan I was bore,° anon°	*surely, born, immediately*
Deeth drough the tappe of lyf and leet it gon[1]	
And ever sithe° hath so the tappe° yronne°	*since, tap, run*
Til that almoost al empty is the tonne.°	*tun (barrel)*
3895 The streem° of lyf° now droppeth° on the chymbe.°	*stream, life, drops, rim*
The sely° tonge may wel rynge° and chymbe°[2]	*silly, ring, chime*
Of wrecchednesse° that passed is ful yoore.°	*wretchedness, very long ago*
With olde folke, save dotage, is namoore."°	*no more*
WHAN that oure hoost hadde herd° this sermonyng,°	*heard, this sermonizing*
3900 He gan° to speke° as lordly as a kyng.	*began, speak*
He seide,° "What amounteth° al this wit?	*said, amounts*
What, shul we speke al day of hooly writ?°	*holy scriptures*
The devel° made a reve° for to preche°	*devil, reeve, preach*
And of a soutere,° shipman or a leche!°[3]	*cobbler, physician*
3905 Sey° forth thy tale, and tarie nat° the tyme.°	*say, tarry not, time*
Lo, Depeford, and it is half wey pryme![4]	
Lo, Grenewych,[5] ther° many a shrewe° is inne!°	*where, scoundrel, in*
It were al tyme° thy tale to bigynne!"°	*about time, begin*
"Now, sires," quod this Osewold the Reve,	
3910 "I pray yow all that ye nat yow greve°	*you do not take offense*
Thogh° I answere and somdeel° sette his howve.°[6]	*though, somewhat*
For leveful is with force force of showve.[7]	
THIS dronke° Millere hath ytoold° us heer°	*drunken, told, here*
How that bigyled° was a carpenteer—	*fooled*
3915 Paraventure° in scorn, for I am oon.	*Perhaps*
And by youre leve,° I shal hym° quite° anoon.°	*leave, him, requite, immediately*
Right in his cherles termes° wol I speke.	*churl's terms*
I pray to God his nekke mote breke!°	*neck might break*
He kan wel in myn eye seen a stalke,°	*sliver*
3920 But in his owene he kan nat seen a balke."°[8]	*beam*

---

1 "Death drew the tap of life and let it run." The image is of a large barrel whose spigot has been turned open by Death, so that the beer or wine runs out.

2 The old man's babbling tongue is like the splashing of the beer or wine on the rim of the barrel.

3 I.e., the devil, who made a reeve preach, also made a shipman or doctor (leech) from a cobbler. Hengwrt reads "Or of a soutere, a shipman, or a lech," which makes more sense and better meter.

4 Deptford is a town about three miles from Southwark on the road to Canterbury. Prime is an hour for prayer in the early morning.

5 Greenwich is about half a mile further on the road to Canterbury. Chaucer probably lived in Greenwich between about 1385 and 1398.

6 "Set his hood," is an expression that means "make him a fool."

7 There is a Latin gloss in the margin, "To repel force with force," referring to this well known legal principle.

8 These two lines paraphrase Matthew 7:3.

THE REEVE'S TALE

HEERE BIGYNNETH THE REVES TALE

At Trumpyngtoun, nat fer fro° Cantebrigge,[1]	*far from*
Ther gooth° a brook and over that a brigge,°	*runs, bridge*
Upon the which brook ther stant° a melle.°	*stands, mill*
And this is verray° sooth° that I yow telle.	*true, truth*

3925 A millere was ther dwellynge many a day.

As any pecok° he was proud and gay.	*peacock*
Pipen° he koude and fisshe and nettes beete°	*play the bagpipe, mend (fishing) nets*
And turne coppes[2] and wel wrastle° and sheete.°	*wrestle, shoot (arrows)*
And by his belt° he baar° a long panade,°	*on his belt, carried, short sword*

3930 And of a swerd° ful° trenchant° was the blade.   *sword, very, sharp*

A joly poppere° baar° he in his pouche.	*pretty dagger, carried*
Ther was no man for peril° dorste hym° touche.	*dared, him*
A Sheffeld thwitel° baar° he in his hose.°[3]	*knife, carried, stockings*
Round was his face and camuse° was his nose.	*snub*

3935 As piled° as an ape was his skulle.°   *bald, skull*

He was a market-betere° atte fulle.°	*street fighter, utterly*
Ther dorste° no wight° hand upon hym legge,°	*dared, person, lay*
That he ne swoor he sholde anon abegge.[4]	
A theef he was of corn° and eek° of mele,°	*grain, also, meal*

3940 And that a sly and usaunt° for to stele.   *accustomed*

His name was hoote° deynous° Symkyn.	*was called, arrogant*
A wyf he hadde ycomen° of noble kyn.°	*come, kindred*
The person° of the toun hir fader° was.	*parson, her father*
With hire he yaf ful many a panne of bras,[5]	

3945 For that Symkyn sholde° in his blood allye.°   *should, ally*

She was yfostred° in a nonnerye,°[6]	*brought up, convent of nuns*
For Symkyn wolde° no wyf, as he sayde,	*wanted*
But if° she were wel ynorissed° and a mayde,°	*unless, well brought up, virgin*
To saven° his estaat° of yomanrye.°	*preserve, estate, yeomanry*

3950 And she was proud and peert° as is a pye.°   *impudent, magpie*

A ful fair sighte was it upon hem° two	*them*
On haly dayes° biforn hire wolde° he go	*holy days, before her would*

---

1 Trumpington is about three miles south of Cambridge, and there was a mill there in medieval times. There is a picture of the Reeve in the margin.
2 "Turn cups" probably refers to drinking an alcoholic drink in one gulp.
3 Sheffield, in northern England, is still famous for its high-quality steel.
4 "That he did not swear that he should immediately pay for it."
5 The parson gave a large dowry (brass pans) because his daughter was illegitimate. Priests were not allowed to marry and were expected to be chaste.
6 Convents often served as schools for girls from well-off families.

With his typet° bounde aboute his heed,°   *scarf, head*
And she cam° after in a gyte° of reed.°   *came, gown, red*
3955 And Symkyn hadde hosen° of the same.   *stockings*
Ther dorste° no wight° clepen hire° but "Dame."   *dared, person, call her*
Was noon° so hardy that wente by the weye,°   *none, along the road*
That with hire dorste rage° or ones° pleye,°   *romp, once, flirt*
But if° he wolde be slayn° of Symkyn   *unless, wished to be killed by*
3960 With panade° or with knyf or boidekyn.°   *sword, dagger*
For jalous° folk been perilous° everemo.°   *jealous, dangerous, always*
Algate they wolde hire wyves wenden so.[1]
And eek,° for she was somdel° smoterlich,°[2]   *also, since, somewhat soiled*
She was as digne° as water in a dich,°   *haughty, ditch*
3965 As[3] ful of hoker° and of bismare.°   *contempt, scorn*
Hir thoughte that a lady sholde hire spare,[4]
What for hire kynrede° and hir nortelrie,°   *her kindred, nurture*
That she hadde lerned° in the nonnerie.°   *learned, convent*
A DOGHTER hadde they bitwexe hem° two,   *between them*
3970 Of twenty yeer,° withouten any mo,°   *years old, more*
Savynge° a child that was of half yeer° age.   *except, year*
In cradel° it lay and was a propre page.°   *cradle, handsome boy*
This wenche° thikke° and wel ygrowen° was,   *girl, thick, well-grown*
With kamuse° nose and eyen° greye as glas,°   *snub, eyes, glass*
3975 Buttokes brode° and brestes rounde and hye.   *buttocks broad*
But right° fair was hire heer,° I wol nat lye.°   *truly, her hair, not lie*
THIS person of the toun, for° she was feir,°   *because, fair*
In purpos was to maken hire his heir,°   *intended to make her his heir*
Bothe of his catel° and his mesuage.°   *belongings, household*
3980 And straunge° he made it of hir mariage.°   *difficult, her marriage*
His purpos was for to bistowe hire hye°   *bestow her high*
Into som° worthy blood of auncetrye,°   *some, ancestry [=nobility]*
For Hooly Chirches good moot been despended
On Hooly Chirches° blood that is descended.[5]   *Holy Church's*
3985 Therfore he wolde° his hooly° blood honoure,°   *wanted, holy, to honor*
Though that he Hooly Chirche sholde devoure.°   *should devour*
GREET sokene°[6] hath this millere, out of doute,°   *great monopoly, without doubt*

---

1   "At any rate they want their wives to think so."
2   She is "soiled" because she is the illegitimate daughter of a priest.
3   Hengwrt reads "And." This reading is followed in most editions.
4   Probably, "She thought that a lady [like herself] should be reserved," or possibly, "She thought that a lady should treat her with respect" (although this would be an unusual use of "spare").
5   "For the belongings of Holy Church must be spent on those who are descended from its blood" (i.e., the children of the clergy).
6   "Soken" was a term referring to a monopoly granted by a king or lord over a certain right or transaction.

With whete° and malt of al the land aboute.   *wheat*
And nameliche° ther° was a greet° collegge°   *namely, there, great, college*
3990 Men clepen° the Soler Halle¹ at Cantebregge.°   *call, Cambridge*
Ther was hir° whete and eek° hir malt ygrounde.°   *their, also, ground up*
And on a day it happed° in a stounde,°   *happened, once*
Sik° lay the maunciple°² on a maladye.°   *sick, manciple, illness*
Men wenden° wisly that he sholde dye,   *expected*
3995 For which this millere stal° bothe mele° and corn° *stole, meal (coarsely ground grain), grain*
An hundred tyme moore than biforn.
For therbiforn° he stal but curteisly,°   *before, courteously (discreetly)*
But now he was a theef outrageously,°   *thief blatantly*
For which the wardeyn° chidde° and made fare.°   *warden, complained, made a fuss*
4000 But therof° sette the millere nat a tare³   *about this*
And craketh boost° and swoor° it was nat° so.   *cracks a boast, swore, not*
THANNE were ther yonge povre clerkes° two   *poor students*
That dwelten° in this halle of which I seye.°   *lived, spoke*
Testif° they were and lusty° for to pleye°   *headstrong, energetic, play*
4005 And oonly for hire° myrthe° and reverye.°   *just for their, mirth, wildness*
Upon the wardeyn bisily° they crye°   *eagerly, cry*
To yeve hem leve° but a litel stounde°   *give them leave, a little while*
To goon to mille and seen hir corn ygrounde.
And hardily they dorste leye hir nekke°   *dared wager their neck*
4010 The millere sholde not stele hem° half a pekke°   *[from] them, peck*
Or corn by sleighte° ne by force hem° reve.°   *trickery, them, rob*
And at the laste the wardeyn yaf hem leve.
John highte° that oon° and Aleyn heet that oother.°   *was called, one, other*
Of o toun were they born that highte Strother,⁴
4015 Fer° in the north, I kan nat telle° where.   *far, cannot tell*
THIS Aleyn maketh redy° al his gere,°   *ready, equipment*
And on an hors the sak° he caste anon.°   *sack, threw immediately*
Forth goth Aleyn the clerk and also John
With good swerd and bokeler° by hir syde.°   *shield, side*
4020 John knew the wey; hem neded no gyde.°   *they did not need a guide*
And at the mille the sak adoun° he layth.°   *down, lays*
Aleyn spak first: "Al hayl,° Symond, yfayth!°   *hello, in faith*
Hou fares thy faire doghter and thy wyf?"
"ALEYN, welcome," quod Symkyn, "by my lyf!

---

1 Solar Hall is probably King's Hall, Cambridge, which had numerous solars or sun-rooms, upper
   rooms with large windows.
2 The manciple is responsible for the general upkeep of the college while the warden or master is
   a senior academic and the equivalent of a modern principal or president.
3 "Did not care at all." A "tare" is a weed, something of no value.
4 There is no town of this name in England, but there was a powerful Strother family in
   Northumbria.

4025	And John also. How now! What do ye heer?"°	here
	"Symond," quod John, "by God, nede has na peer!¹	
	Hym boes° serve hymselve that has na swayn,°	he must, no servant
	Or elles° he is a fool, as clerkes° sayn.°	else, scholars, say
	Oure manciple—I hope° he wil be deed—	expect
4030	Swa werkes ay the wanges° in his heed,°	so ache ever the teeth, head
	And forthy° is I come and eek° Alayn	therefore, also
	To grynde oure corn and carie° it ham agayn.°	carry, home again
	I pray yow spede° us heythen° that ye may."	help, hence
	"It shal be doon,"° quod Symkyn, "by my fay!°	done, faith
4035	What wol ye doon° whil° that it is in hande?"	will you do, while
	"By God, right by the hopur² wil I stande,"	
	Quod John, "and se how that the corn gas° in.	goes
	Yet saugh° I never by my fader kyn°	saw, father's kin
	How that the hopur wagges til and fra."°	hopper wags to and fro
4040	Aleyn answerde, "John, wiltow swa?°	will you so
	Thanne wil I be byneth,° by my croun,°	beneath, crown (of head)
	And se how that the mele° falles doun°	meal, falls down
	Into the trough. That sal° be my disport,°	shall, amusement
	For, John, yfaith,° I may been° of youre sort.	in faith, be
4045	I is as ille° a millere as ar ye!"°	ill, as are you
	This millere smyled of° hir nycetee°	smiled about, foolishness
	And thoghte,° "Al° this nys doon° but for a wyle.°	thought, all, is not done, trick
	They wene° that no man may hem° bigyle.°	think, them, trick
	But by my thrift, yet shal I blere hir eye°	make their eye bleary
4050	For al° the sleighte° in hir° philosophye.	all, trickery, their
	The moore° queynte crekes° that they make,	more, clever tricks
	The moore wol I stele° whan I take.	steal
	Instide of flour, yet wol I yeve° hem° bren.°	give, them, bran
	'The gretteste clerkes been noght° wisest men,'	greatest scholars are not
4055	As whilom° to the wolf thus spak° the mare.³	once, spoke
	Of al° hir° art counte I noght a tare."°	all, their, care not at all
	Out at the dore° he gooth° ful pryvely°	door, goes, very secretly
	Whan that he saugh his tyme° softely.°	opportunity, quietly
	He looketh up and doun til he hath founde	

---

1 "'Simon,' said John, 'by God, need has no peer (equal).'" Here Chaucer would normally write "hath." The students, from far in the north, speak a northern dialect of Middle English, often using *a* where Chaucer's southern English uses *o* (e.g., *ham* for *hom*) and ending the third-person indicative in *s* rather than in *th*.

2 The hopper is the mechanism that feeds the grain into the mill to be ground.

3 The story, which is found in Aesop's *Fables* and has several medieval versions, is that when the wolf offered to buy the mare's foal, she told him that the price was written on her hoof and that if he was a scholar he could come and read it. The wolf drew the moral after being kicked by the mare.

4060 The clerkes hors° ther° as it stood ybounde°	students' horse, where, tied
Bihynde° the mille under a lefsel.°	behind, arbor
And to the hors he goth hym faire and wel.	
He strepeth° of the brydel° right anon°	strips, bridle, right away
And whan the hors was laus° he gynneth° gon	loose, went
4065 Toward the fen° ther° wilde mares renne,°	swamp, where, run
And forth with "Wehee"° thurgh thikke and thurgh thenne.°	whinny, thick and thin
THIS millere gooth agayn. No word he seyde,	
But dooth° his note° and with the clerkes pleyde°	does, business, joked
Til that hir corn was faire and weel ygrounde.	
4070 And whan the mele° is sakked° and ybounde,°	meal, put into sacks, bound
This John goth° out and fynt° his hors away	goes, finds
And gan° to crie,° "Harrow and weylaway!"[1]	began, cry
Oure hors is lorn,° Alayn, for Goddes banes!°	lost, bones
Stepe on thy feet! Com° out, man, al atanes!°	come, all at once
4075 Allas, our wardeyn° has his palfrey° lorn!"°	warden, horse, lost
This Aleyn al forgat° bothe mele° and corn.°	all forgot, meal, grain
Al was out of his mynde° his housbondrie.°	mind, stewardship
"What! Whilk° way is he geen?"° he gan° to crie.	which, has he gone, began
THE wyf cam° lepynge inward° with a ren.°	came, running up, rein
4080 She seyde, "Allas, youre hors goth° to the fen°	goes, swamp
With wilde mares as faste as he may go!	
Unthank° come on his hand that boond hym° so	a curse, bound him
And he that bettre° sholde han knyt° the reyne!"°	better, should have tied, rein
"ALLAS!" quod Aleyn, "For Cristes peyne,°	pain
4085 Lay doun thy swerd,° and I wil myn alswa!°	sword, also
I is ful wight,° God waat,° as is a raa!°	strong, knows, roe (deer)
By God herte,° he sal nat scape° us bathe!°	God's heart, shall not escape, both
Why nadtow pit the capul in the lathe?[2]	
Ilhayl,° by God, Alayn, thou is a fonne!"°	bad luck, you are a fool
4090 THIS sely clerkes° han° ful° faste yronne°[3]	silly students, have, very, run
Toward the fen, bothe Aleyn and eek John.	
AND whan the millere saugh that they were gon,	
He half a busshel of hir° flour hath take°	their, taken
And bad° his wyf, "Go knede° it in cake."°	commanded, knead, into a loaf of bread
4095 He seyde, "I trowe° the clerkes were aferd,°	believe, afraid
Yet kan a millere make a clerkes berd[4]	
For al his art. Now lat hem goon hir weye.°	let them go their way
Lo, wher they goon! Ye, lat the children pleye.	

---

1 "Harrow and welaway" is the cry to raise help in an emergency.
2 "Why did you not put the horse in the barn?"
3 Ellesmere reads "yrenne." The emendation is from Hengwrt.
4 "Make a beard" is an expression for "make a fool of."

They gete hym nat so lightly, by my croun!"°   crown
4100 THISE sely clerkes rennen° up and doun   run
With "Keepe!° Keepe! Stand! Stand! Jossa!° Warderere!°   Down here!, Whoa!, Watch out!
Ga° whistle thou, and I shal kepe° hym here."°   go, keep, him here
But¹ shortly til that it was verray° nyght,   true
They koude nat thogh they do al hir myght°   . their might
4105 Hir capul cacche.° He ran alwey so faste,   their horse catch
Til in a dych° they caughte hym atte laste.°   ditch, at last
WERY° and weet° as beest° is in the reyn°   weary, wet, beast, rain
Comth° sely° John and with hym comth Aleyn.   comes, silly
"Allas," quod John, "the day that I was born!
4110 Now are we dryve til hethyng and til scorn.°   held up to mockery
Oure corn° is stoln! Men° wil us fooles calle,   grain, MS Me
Bathe° the wardeyn° and oure felawes° alle,   both, warden, fellows
And namely the millere, weylaway!"°   alas
THUS pleyneth° John as he gooth by the way°   laments, along the road
4115 Toward the mille and Bayard² in his hond.
The millere sittynge by the fyr he fond,°   found
For it was nyght and forther° myghte they noght.°   further, not [go]
But for the love of God they hym° bisoght°   him, requested
Of herberwe° and of ese° as for hir peny.°³   lodging, food, penny
4120 THE millere seyde° agayn, "If ther be eny,°   replied, any
Swich° as it is yet shal° ye have youre part.   such, shall
Myn hous is streit° but ye han lerned° art.⁴   my house is small, have learned
Ye konne° by argumentz make a place   know how
A myle° brood,° of twenty foot of space.   mile, broad
4125 Lat se° now if this place may suffise   let's see
Or make it rowm° with speche° as is youre gise."°   roomy, speech, custom
"Now, Symond," seyde John, "by Seint Cutberd,⁵
Ay° is thou myrie° and this is faire answerd.   ever, merry
I have herd seyd, 'Man sal taa° of twa thynges°   shall take, two things
4130 Slyk° as he fyndes or taa° slyk as he brynges.'°   such, take, brings
But specially, I pray thee, hoost deere,°   dear host
Get us som mete° and drynke° and make us cheere,°   food, drink, welcome

---

1   Ellesmere has a hole in the parchment after this word, one evidently present before the scribe
     worked on it since no word is missing from the text, as attested by Hengwrt.
2   Bayard was a typical name for a horse in the Middle Ages.
3   Since there were relatively few inns in the Middle Ages, residents of private homes often lodged
     travelers for money.
4   The sense of Symon's comment here is that the students have studied at the university, so they
     are practiced in logical argument, which can make something seem what it is not. A small house
     thus can seem big enough for two extra people.
5   The Anglo-Saxon Saint Cuthbert, who lived in the seventh century, was particularly venerated
     in the northern parts of England, which were home to Aleyn and John, as their accents reveal.

And we wil payen trewely atte fulle.°   *will pay truly the full amount*

With empty hand men may none haukes° tulle.°   *hawks, lure*

4135 Loo, heere° oure silver, redy° for to spende."   *here, ready*

THIS millere into toun his doghter sende

For ale and breed and rosted hem° a goos   *roasted them*

And boond° hire hors. It sholde nat goon loos.°   *tied up, not go loose*

And in his owene chambre° hem made a bed[1]   *own room*

4140 With sheetes and with chalons° faire yspred.°   *blankets, spread*

Noght from his owene bed ten foot or twelve

His doghter hadde a bed al by hirselve,

Right in the same chambre by and by.°   *nearby*

It myghte° be no bet° and cause why:°   *might, better, [this is the] reason why*

4145 Ther was no roumer herberwe° in the place.   *larger room*

They soupen° and they speke hem to solace°   *eat supper, to comfort themselves*

And drynke evere strong ale atte beste.°   *of the best*

Aboute mydnyght wente they to reste.

WEL hath this millere vernysshed° his heed.°[2]   *varnished, head*

4150 Ful° pale he was for dronken° and nat reed.°   *very, drinking, not red*

He yexeth,° and he speketh thurgh the nose   *burps*

As he were on the quakke or on the pose.°   *hoarse or had a cold*

To bedde he goth and with hym goth his wyf.

As any jay she light was and jolyf,°   *jolly*

4155 So was hir joly whistle wel ywet.°[3]   *wet*

The cradel° at hir beddes feet° is set   *cradle, foot of her bed*

To rokken° and to yeve the child to sowke.°   *rock, breast-feed*

And whan that dronken al was in the crowke,°   *jug*

To bedde wente the doghter right anon.°   *immediately*

4160 To bedde wente Aleyn and also John.

Ther nas namoore; hem neded no dwale.[4]

This millere hath so wisely bibbed° ale   *sipped*

That as a hors° he fnorteth° in his sleepe.   *horse, snores*

Ne of his tayl° bihynde° he took no keepe.   *tail, behind*

4165 His wyf bar° hym a burdon[5] a ful° strong.   *bore, very*

Men myghte° hir rowtyng° heere° two furlong.[6]   *might, snoring, hear*

The wenche° rowteth eek° par compaignye.°   *girl, also, for company's sake*

---

1   All family members in peasant households in the Middle Ages commonly slept in a home's main room.

2   "Varnished one's head" seems to have been an expression for getting drunk.

3   "Wetting one's whistle" is still today an expression for having a drink.

4   "They did not need for themselves any sleeping potion."

5   The burden of a medieval carol was its refrain, a line or phrase sung at the beginning and after each successive verse.

6   A furlong was a measure of distance 220 yards (or ⅛ mile). Originally, it was the length of the typical furrow made in the common fields by peasants when they ploughed.

ALEYN the clerk that herde this melodye,
He poked John and seyde, "Slepestow?°   *Do you sleep?*
4170 Herdtow evere° slyk° a sang° er now?°   *Did you ever hear, such, song, before*
Lo, whilk a cowplyng°¹ is ymel hem alle.°   *what a compline, among them all*
A wilde fyr° upon thair bodyes falle!   *wildfire (painful skin disease)*
Wha herkned° evere slyk° a ferly° thyng?   *who heard, such, marvelous*
Ye,° they sal° have the flour° of il° ending.   *yes, shall, flower (the best), ill*
4175 This lange nyght ther tydes me na reste.°   *long night there is no sleep for me*
But yet na fors,° al sal° be for the beste.   *it does not matter, shall*
For John," seyde he, "als° evere moot° I thryve,°   *as, might, thrive*
If that I may, yon° wenche wil° I swyve.°   *yonder, will, have sex with*
Som esement° has lawe° yshapen° us,   *some easement, law, shaped for*
4180 For, John, ther is a lawe that says thus:
That gif° a man in a point° be ygreved,°   *if, matter, injured*
That in another he sal° be releved.°   *shall, relieved*
Oure corn° is stoln.° Shortly is ne nay,°   *grain, stolen, no denying [it]*
And we han° had an il° fit al this day.   *have, ill*
4185 And syn° I sal° have neen amendement°   *since, shall, no pay-back*
Agayn° my los,° I wil° have esement.   *against, loss, will*
By God[es] sa[u]le,°² it sal° neen° other bee!"°   *God's soul, shall, no, be*
THIS John answerde, "Alayn, avyse° thee!   *be careful*
The millere is a perilous° man," he seyde,   *dangerous*
4190 "And gif° that he out of his sleepe abreyde,°   *if, awakes*
He myghte doon° us bathe° a vileynye."°   *might do, both, harm*
ALEYN answerde, "I counte hym nat a flye."°   *not [worth] a flea*
And up he rist,° and by the wenche he crepte.°   *he gets up, crawled*
This wenche lay upright° and faste slepte,   *on her back*
4195 Til he so ny° was, er° she myghte espie,°   *near, before, see*
That it had been to° late for to crie.°   *too, cry*
And shortly for to seyn,° they were aton.°   *say, united*
Now pley,° Aleyn, for I wol speke of John.   *play*
THIS John lith stille° a furlong wey or two,³   *lies quietly*
4200 And to hymself he maketh° routhe° and wo.°   *makes, pity, woe*
"Allas," quod° he, "this is a wikked jape!°   *said, wicked joke*
Now may I seyn that I is but an ape.
Yet has my felawe° somwhat° for his harm.   *companion, something*
He has the milleris doghter in his arm.
4205 He auntred° hym and has his nedes sped,°   *took a chance, need's success*

---

1   The normal spelling in Middle English for compline, the sung prayers of monks and nuns in
    the late evening hours, would have been "complyn." Aleyn evidently mispronounces the word,
    mixing it up with "coupling," a word that could refer to the act of sex, unless the error is simply
    that of the scribe Adam Pinkhurst.
2   The emendation is from Hengwrt.
3   For the time it takes to walk a furlong (220 yards or ⅛ of a mile).

And I lye° as a draf,[1] sek° in my bed.   *lie, sick*
And whan this jape° is tald° another day,   *joke, told*
I sal° been halde° a daf,° a cokenay.[2]   *shall, be considered, weakling*
I wil arise° and auntre° it by my fayth!°   *get up, risk, faith*
4210 'Unhardy is unseely.'[3] Thus men sayth."
And up he roos,° and softely° he wente   *rose, quietly*
Unto the cradel and in his hand it hente°   *grasped*
And baar° it softe unto the beddes feet.   *carried*
SOONE after this the wyf hir rowtyng leet°   *stopped snoring*
4215 And gan awake° and wente hire° out to pisse   *awoke, herself*
And cam agayn° and gan hir cradel mysse°   *came back, missed her cradle*
And groped heer and ther. But she foond noon.
"Allas," quod she, "I hadde almoost mysgoon.°   *made a mistake*
I hadde almoost goon° to the clerkes° bed!   *had almost gone, students'*
4220 Ey, benedicite,° thanne° hadde I foule ysped!"°   *Oh bless [me], then, done badly*
And forth she gooth til she the cradel fond.
She gropeth alwey forther° with hir hond   *further*
And foond° the bed and thoghte noght° but good,   *found, thought nothing*
Bycause that the cradel by it stood,
4225 And nyste wher° she was, for it was derk.°   *did not know where, dark*
But faire and wel° she creepe into° the clerk   *well, creeps towards*
And lith ful stille° and wolde han caught a sleepe.°   *lies very quietly, wanted to fall asleep*
Withinne° a while this John the clerk up leepe,°   *Within, jumped*
And on this goode wyf he leith on soore.°   *lays on vigorously*
4230 So myrie° a fit° hadde she nat ful yoore.°   *merry, episode, not for a long time*
He priketh harde° and soore as he were mad.°   *pierces vigorously, crazy*
This joly lyf° han° thise two clerkes lad°   *life, have, led*
Til that the thridde° cok bigan to synge.°   *third, cock began to crow*
ALEYN wax wery° in the dawenynge,°   *grew weary, dawn*
4235 For he had swonken° al° the longe nyght,   *labored, all*
And seyde,° "Fareweel,° Malyne, sweete wight,°   *said, farewell, person*
The day is come. I may no lenger byde.°   *no longer stay*
But everemo° wherso° I go or ryde,°   *ever more, wherever, ride*
I is thyn awen° clerk, swa° have I seel!"°   *your own, so, good luck*
4240 "Now, deere lemman,"° quod she, "go fare weel.°   *sweetheart, farewell*
But er° thow go, o thyng° I wol thee telle.   *before, one thing*
Whan that thou wendest homward by the melle,°   *you go homewards by the mill*

---

1   "Draf" is chaff, the waste material left over from grinding grain into flour, but "a draf" (a chaff) is an odd idiom. Hengwrt reads "draf sack" (a sack for chaff or refuse), which also makes better sense, since John is clearly not sick.

2   A "cockney" is a cock's egg. Folklore held that cocks did occasionally lay eggs but only tiny ones of no value.

3   The proverb John quotes roughly means, "The fearful one is the unhappy one."

Right at the entree° of the dore° bihynde°   entrance, door, behind
Thou shalt a cake of half a busshel fynde
4245 That was ymaked° of thyn owene mele°   made, meal
Which that I heelpe my fader for to stele.°   steal
And, goode lemman,° God thee save and kepe!"°   sweetheart, keep
And with that word almoost she gan to wepe.°   began to weep
ALEYN up rist° and thoughte, "Er° that it dawe,°   rose up, Before, dawns
4250 I wol go crepen in by my felawe,"
And fond the cradel with his hand anon."°   immediately
"By God," thoughte he, "Al wrang° I have mysgon!°   wrong, gone wrong
Myn heed° is toty° of my swynk° tonyght   head, dizzy, work
That maketh me that I go nat aright.°   not right
4255 I woot wel° by the cradel° I have mysgo.°   know well, cradle, gone wrong
Heere lith° the millere and his wyf also."   here lies
And forth he goth a twenty devel way¹
Unto the bed theras° the millere lay.   where
He wende have cropen° by his felawe John.   expected [to] have crept
4260 And by the millere in he creepe° anon   creeps in
And caughte hym by the nekke. And softe° he spak.   quietly
He seyde, "Thou John, thou swynes heed!° Awak,°   pig's head, awake
For Cristes saule,° and heer° a noble game!   soul, hear
For by that lord that called is Seint Jame,°   St. James
4265 As I have thries° in this shorte nyght   three times
Swyved° the milleres doghter bolt upright°   had sex with, lying on her back
Whil thow hast° as a coward° been agast!"   while you have, afraid
"YE° false harlot!"° quod the millere, "hast?°   yes, villain, have [you]
A, false traitour, false clerk," quod he,
4270 "Thow shalt be deed,° by Goddes dignitee!°   dead, dignity
Who dorste° be so boold° to disparage°   dares, bold, dishonor
My doghter that is come of swich lynage!"°   such lineage
And by the throte bolle° he caughte Alayn,   Adam's apple
And he hente hym despitously agayn,°   (Aleyn) grabbed him fiercely in return
4275 And on the nose he smoot hym° with his fest.°   hit him, fist
Doun ran the blody streem° upon his brest,°   bloody stream, breast
And in the floor with nose and mouth tobroke°   broken
They walwe° as doon° two pigges° in a poke.°   wallow, do, pigs, bag
And up they goon° and doun agayn° anon   go, down again
4280 Til that the millere sporned at° a stoon.°   stumbled on, stone
And doun he fil bakward upon his wyf,
That wiste nothyng° of this nyce stryf,°   who knew nothing, ludicrous strife
For she was falle aslepe° a lite wight°   had fallen asleep, a short time

---

1   This cliché means "in the name of twenty devils."

	With John the clerk that waked hadde° al nyght.	*who had been awake*
4285	And with the fal out of hir sleepe she breyde,°	*awoke*
	"Help, hooly croys° of Bromholm,"¹ she seyde,°	*holy cross, said*
	"In manus tuas, Lord, to thee I calle!²	
	Awak,° Symond, the feend° is on us falle!°	*awake, fiend, fallen*
	Myn herte° is broken. Help! I nam but deed!°	*my heart, I am as good as dead*
4290	Ther lyth oon° upon my wombe° and on myn heed.	*lies someone, stomach*
	Helpe, Symkyn, for the false clerkes fighte!"	
	THIS John stirte up° as soone as ever he myghte	*jumped up*
	And graspeth by the walles° to and fro	*gropes along the walls*
	To fynde a staf.° And she stirte up° also	*stick, got up*
4295	And knew the estres° bet° than dide° this John.	*interior, better, did*
	And by the wal a staf she foond° anon	*found*
	And saugh° a litel shymeryng° of a light,	*saw, little shimmering*
	For at an hole in shoon the moone bright.	
	And by that light she saugh hem bothe two.	
4300	But sikerly° she nyste° who was who,	*surely, did not know*
	But as° she saugh a whit thyng° in hir eye.	*except that, white thing*
	And whan she gan the white thyng espye,°	*saw the white thing*
	She wende° the clerk hadde wered° a volupeer,°	*thought, had worn, nightcap*
	And with the staf she drow ay neer and neer°	*drew ever nearer*
4305	And wende han hit° this Aleyn at the fulle°	*intended to hit, fully*
	And smoot° the millere on the pyled skulle.°	*hit, bald skull*
	And doun he gooth and cride,° "Harrow!³ I dye!"°	*cried, die*
	Thise clerkes beete hym weel° and lete hym lye°	*beat him well, let him lie*
	And greythen° hem and tooke° hir hors anon	*get dressed, took*
4310	And eek° hir mele,° and on hir wey° they gon.	*also, meal, their way*
	And at the mille yet they tooke hir cake°	*their loaf*
	Of half a busshel flour ful wel ybake.°	*very well baked*
	THUS is the proude millere wel ybete°	*well beaten*
	And hath ylost° the gryndynge° of the whete°	*lost, grinding, wheat*
4315	And payed° for the soper° everideel°	*paid, supper, every bit*
	Of Aleyn and of John that bette hym weel.°	*beat him well*
	His wyf is swyved° and his doghter als.°	*has had sex, as well*
	Lo, swich° it is a millere to be fals!°	*such [is the result], false*
	And therfore this proverbe is seyd° ful sooth:°	*said, in full truth*
4320	"Hym thar nat wene wel that yvele dooth."⁴	

---

1 This was a famous shrine in Bromholm, in Norfolk, which claimed to have a piece of the true cross.

2 "Into your hands, Lord, to you I call." The Latin is a quotation from Luke 23:46, words that Jesus utters immediately before death on the cross.

3 "Harrow" is a word used to raise help in an emergency.

4 "He who does evil should not expect good."

A gylour° shal hymself bigyled° be.   *trickster, tricked*
And God that sitteth heighe in Trinitee°   *who sits high in Trinity*
Save al this compaignye° grete and smale!°   *company, great and small*
Thus have I quyt° the Millere in my tale.   *requited*

HEERE IS ENDED THE REVES TALE

THE COOK'S PROLOGUE AND TALE

THE COOK'S PROLOGUE

4325 THE Cook of Londoun, whil° that the Reve spak,   *while*
    For ioye° him thoughte° he clawed him on the bak.[1]   *joy, it seemed to him*
    "Ha, ha," quod he, "for Cristes passioun,
    This millere hadde a sharpe conclusioun
    Upon his argument of herbergage!°   *lodging*
4330 Wel seyde° Salomon in his langage,°   *well said, language*
    'Ne brynge nat° every man into thyn hous,°   *do not bring, your house*
    For herberwynge° by nyghte° is perilous!'°   *lodging [someone], night dangerous*
    Wel oghte° a man avysed° for to be   *ought, advised*
    Whom that he broghte into his pryvetee.°   *privacy*
4335 I pray to God, so yeve° me sorwe° and care,   *give, sorrow*
    If evere sitthe° I highte° Hogge of Ware[2]   *since, was named*
    Herde° I a millere bettre yset awerk!°   *heard, set to work*
    He hadde a jape° of malice in the derk.°   *joke, dark*
    But God forbede° that we stynte° heere.°   *forbid, stop, here*
4340 And therfore if ye vouchesauf° to heere°[3]   *promise, hear*
    A tale of me that am a povre° man,   *poor*
    I wol yow telle° as wel° as evere I kan°   *will tell you, well, can*
    A litel jape° that fil° in oure citee."°[4]   *joke, happened, city*
    OURE Hoost answerde and seide, "I graunte it thee.
4345 Now telle on, Roger. Looke that it be good.
    For many a pastee° hastow laten blood°[5]   *pie, let blood*
    And many a Jakke of Dovere[6] hastow soold°   *have you sold*
    That hath been twies hoot and twies coold.°   *twice hot and twice cold*
    Of many a pilgrym hastow° Cristes curs°   *have you, curse*
4350 For of thy percely° yet they fare the wors,°   *parsley, worse*
    That they han eten° with thy stubbel° goos.°[7]   *have eaten, stubble, goose*
    For in thy shoppe is many a flye° loos.°   *fly, loose*

---

1   Scratching someone on the back is a favor; the Cook enjoys the Reeve's Tale so much, that he perceives it as a personal favor.

2   Hodge is an old nickname for Roger. Ware is a town in Hertfordshire, about thirty miles northeast of London.

3   This and the preceding line both end with "heere," a homonym in Middle English with identical spellings. To clarify matters the scribe has written over the first "here" the Latin word "hic" (here) and over the second the Latin "audire" (hear).

4   That is, London.

5   The pie referred to is a meat pie, and letting blood here means that the Cook has drained the gravy off to prevent it from becoming soggy so that he can still sell it.

6   A Jack of Dover is probably some type of meat pie.

7   A "stubble goose" is one that has been fattened on stubble rather than quality feed.

Now telle on, gentil° Roger by thy name.   *noble*
But yet I pray thee be nat° wroth° for game.°   *not, angry, for [this] joke*
4355 A man may seye ful sooth° in game and pley."°   *complete truth, play*
"THOU seist ful sooth," quod Roger, "by my fey.°   *faith*
But 'Sooth pley, quaad pley,' as the Flemyng seith!¹
And therfore, Herry Bailly, by thy feith,°²   *faith*
Be thou nat° wrooth° er° we departen heer,°   *MS na, not angry, before, from here*
4360 Though that my tale be of an hostileer.°   *innkeeper*
But nathelees° I wol nat° telle it yit.°³   *nevertheless, will not, yet*
But er° we parte, ywis,° thou shalt be quit."°   *before, indeed, requited*
And therwithal he lough° and made cheere°   *laughed made a [pleasant] face*
And seyde his tale as ye shul° after heere.°   *shall, hear*

THE COOK'S TALE

HEERE BIGYNNETH THE COOKES TALE

4365 A PRENTYS° whilom dwelled in oure citee°⁴   *apprentice, city (London)*
And of a craft of vitailliers° was hee.°   *food merchants, he*
Gaillard° he was as goldfynch° in the shawe,°   *merry, goldfinch, woods*
Broun° as a berye,° a propre° short felwe°   *brown, berry, fine, fellow*
With lokkes° blake° ykembd° ful fetisly.°   *hair, black, combed, elegantly*
4370 Dauncen° he koude° so wel° and jolily   *dance, could, well*
That he was cleped° Perkyn Revelour.°   *called, Party-Goer*
He was as ful of love and paramour°   *lovemaking*
As is the hyve° ful of hony° sweete.   *hive, honey*
Wel was the wenche° with hym myghte meete.°   *girl, who might meet him*
4375 At every bridale° wolde° he synge° and hoppe.°   *wedding, would, sing, dance*
He loved bet° the taverne than the shoppe.°   *better, shop*
For whan ther any ridyng° was in Chepe,°⁵   *procession, Cheapside*
Out of the shoppe thider° wolde° he lepe.°   *there, would, leap*
Til that he hadde° al the sighte yseyn°   *had, seen*
4380 And daunced wel, he wolde° nat come° ayeyn.°   *would, not return*
And gadered° hym a meynee° of his sort   *gathered, company*

---

1   "'True play, bad play,' (or a true joke is a bad joke) as the Fleming says." The line mimics the accent of one from Flanders and might be a Flemish proverb. Fleming cloth merchants were numerous in Chaucer's London. There was much resentment against them, and several were killed during the Rising of 1381.

2   Here we learn for the first time the Host's name. There actually was an innkeeper called Henry Bailley in Southwark in Chaucer's day.

3   The Host's original plan called for each pilgrim to tell two tales on the way to Canterbury and two on the way back.

4   There is a picture of the Cook in the margin.

5   Cheapside (the street for cheapening, which originally meant bargaining) was the major commercial street in London.

To hoppe° and synge° and maken swich disport.°   *dance, sing, such sport*
And ther they setten stevene° for to meete,°   *agreed, meet*
To pleyen° at the dys° in swich° a streete.   *play, dice, such*
4385 For in the toun nas° ther no prentys°   *was not, apprentice*
That fairer koude caste a paire of dys°   *could throw a pair of dice*
Than Perkyn koude. And therto he was free°   *generous*
Of his dispense° in place of pryvetee.°   *spending, secret place*
That fond° his maister wel° in his chaffare.°   *found, well, business*
4390 For often tyme he foond° his box ful bare.°   *found, completely empty*
For sikerly° a prentys revelour°   *surely, party-goer*
That haunteth° dys,° riot,° or paramour,°   *haunts, dice, rowdy living lovemaking*
His maister shal it in his shoppe abye,°   *pay for*
Al° have he no part of the mynstralcye.°   *though, music*
4395 For thefte° and riot,° they been convertible,°   *theft, rowdy living, interchangeable*
Al konne he pleye on gyterne or ribible.[1]
Revel° and trouthe° as in a lowe degree,   *rowdy living, truth*
They been ful wrothe° al day, as men may see.[2]   *are very angry*
THIS joly prentys with his maister bood°   *lived*
4400 Til he were ny out of his prentishood.°   *nearly done with his apprenticeship*
Al° were he snybbed° bothe erly° and late,   *although, criticized, early*
And somtyme lad° with revel° to Newegate.[3]   *led, rowdy living*
But atte laste° his maister hym bithoghte°   *at last, thought*
Upon a day whan he his papir°[4] soghte,°   *paper, sought*
4405 Of a proverbe that seith this same word:
"Wel bet° is roten° appul° out of hoord°   *very much better, rotten, apple, hoard*
Than that it rotie° al the remenaunt!"°   *rots, all the rest*
So fareth it by a riotous° servaunt.   *rowdy*
It is wel lasse° harm to lete hym pace°   *much less, let him go*
4410 Than he shende° alle the servantz in the place.   *ruin*
Therfore his maister yaf hym acquitance°   *gave him notice to leave*
And bad hym go° with sorwe° and with meschance.°   *ordered him to go, sorrow, bad luck*
And thus this joly prentys hadde° his leve.°   *had, leave*
Now lat hym riote al the nyght or leve.[5]
4415 And for° ther° is no theef° withoute a lowke°   *because, there, thief, accomplice*

---

1   "He" probably refers to the master, who takes no part in the revelry even though he knows how to play a gittern or a rebec. The gittern was a plucked instrument with a fingerboard, the "ribible" or rebec a bowed instrument.

2   "Rowdy living and truth (or honesty) are incompatible in one of low rank."

3   Newgate was a prison in London. The custom was to lead those accused of disorderly behavior through the streets accompanied by musicians so as to attract a large crowd and increase the shame.

4   I.e., when Perkin asked for his early release. This paper is the contract the master has with his apprentice, unless it refers to the master's accounts, which would show how much of his money is being wasted.

5   "Now let him be rowdy all the night or leave [being rowdy]."

That helpeth hym to wasten° and to sowke°   *waste [money] suck (spend money)*
Of that he brybe kan or borwe may,°   *can bribe or borrow*
Anon° he sente his bed and his array°   *immediately, belongings*
Unto a compier° of his owene° sort   *companion, own*
4420 That lovede dys° and revel° and disport°   *loved dice, rowdiness, sport*
And hadde° a wyf that heeld for contenance°   *kept, appearance*
A shoppe,° and swyved for hir sustenance.[1]   *shop*

---

1 "Had sex, i.e., worked as a prostitute, to make her (or their) living." The Ellesmere scribe normally uses "hir" for "their" and either "hire" or "hir" for "her." The tale ends at this point. The Ellesmere scribe (now identified as Adam Pinkhurst) wrote twenty-six lines on this page (folio 47v), leaving twenty-two ruled lines empty. There follow two blank pages (or one folio) before the Man of Law's Prologue begins, suggesting that Pinkhurst believed that Chaucer had written more to the tale and was leaving space to copy it when he found it. When he copied Hengwrt, however, the scribe (also now identified as Adam Pinkhurst) finished the fragment on the thirtieth line of a normally forty-line page and left the rest of the page blank, adding "Of this cokes tale made Chaucer na moore." There are no subsequent blank pages. The Cook reappears in the Prologue to the Manciple's Tale, where the Host says that the Cook "shall tell a tale" (9:13) as if he has not already done so.

THE WIFE OF BATH'S PROLOGUE AND TALE

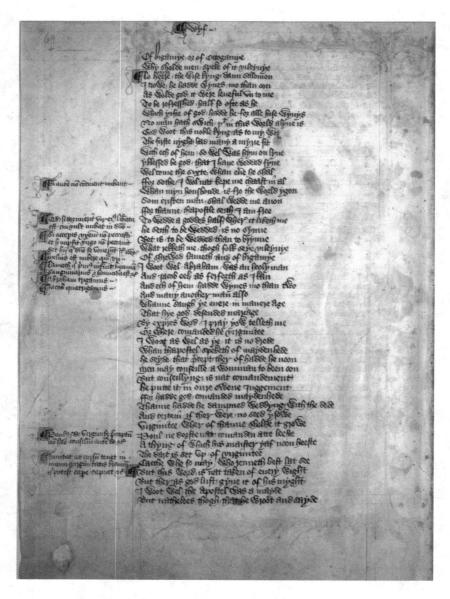

The Wife of Bath's Prologue with accompanying glosses. Ellesmere Manuscript EL 26 C9 f. 63r. Reprinted by permission of The Huntington Library.

THE WIFE OF BATH'S PROLOGUE

THE PROLOGUE OF THE WYVES TALE OF BATHE

"EXPERIENCE, though noon auctoritee
Were in this world, were right ynogh to me[1]
To speke° of wo° that is in mariage. — *speak, woe*
For lordynges,° sith° I twelve° yeer was of age, — *lords, since, MS xij*
5 Ythonked° be God that is eterne on lyve,° — *thanked, eternally alive*
Housbondes at chirche dore° I have had fyve.° — *church door, five*
For I so ofte have ywedded° bee.°[2] — *wedded, been*
And alle were worthy men in hir° degree. — *their*
But me was toold certeyn° nat longe agoon° is, — *certainly, not long ago*
10 That sith that Crist ne wente° nevere but onis° — *did not go, once*
To weddyng in the Cane° of Galilee[3] — *Cana*
By the same ensample° thoughte me°[4] — *example, it seemed to me*
That I ne sholde° wedded be but ones.°[5] — *should not, once*
Herkne eek° which a sharpe word for the nones° — *listen also, for the occasion*
15 Biside° a welle Jhesus, God and man, — *beside*
Spak° in repreeve° of the Samaritan;[6] — *spoke, rebuke*
'THOU hast yhad° fyve housbondes,' quod° he, — *have had, said*
'And that man the which that hath now thee° — *who now has you*
Is noght thyn housbonde.' Thus seyde he certeyn.
20 What that he mente therby,° I kan nat seyn.° — *meant by this, cannot say*
But that I axe,° why that the fifthe man — *ask*
Was noon housbonde to the Samaritan?
How manye myghte she have in mariage?[7]
Yet herde I nevere tellen° in myn age — *never heard told*
25 Upon this nombre° diffinicioun.° — *number, definition*

---

1 "Experience, even if there were no written authority in the world, would be quite enough for me ..." Authority, in this sense, refers to the writings of learned men, especially the Fathers of the Church, such as Saint Jerome, or ancient philosophers.

2 Many manuscripts have "If I so ofte myghte have ywedded be," i.e., if these multiple marriages were indeed lawful.

3 The attendance of Christ at the wedding in Cana is recounted in John 2:1–11. A Latin gloss in the margin notes "In Cana Galilee."

4 Hengwrt reads "taughte me," which follows what Jerome says in *Against Jovinian*.

5 There is a Latin gloss in the margin quoting Saint Jerome's *Against Jovinian*: "For by going once to a marriage he taught that one should be married only once." This work is one of Chaucer's major sources for the Wife of Bath's Prologue and forms part of the book that her fifth husband reads to her (see line 675).

6 Christ's rebuke of the Samaritan woman who had been wedded five times is recounted in John 4:1–42.

7 There is a Latin gloss in the margin from Jerome: "The number of wives is not defined, since, according to Paul, those who have wives [i.e., many wives] are as if they did not have them [i.e., were not truly married]." The gloss cites 1 Corinthians 7:29 in support.

Men may devyne° and glosen°[1] up and doun,°		*guess, gloss, down*
But wel I woot° expres° withoute lye,°		*well I know, clearly, lie*
God bad° us forto wexe and multiplye.°[2]		*commanded, to increase and multiply*
That gentil° text kan° I understonde!		*noble, can*
30 Eek wel I woot, he seyde myn housbonde		
Sholde lete fader and mooder° and take me.		*should leave father and mother*
But of no nombre° mencioun made he°		*number, did he make mention*
Of bigamye° or of octogamye.°		*bigamy, marriage to eight spouses*
Why sholde° men speke° of it vileynye?°		*should, speak, villainy*
35 Lo heere°[3] the wise kyng Daun° Salamon.		*hear, Master*
I trowe° he hadde wyves mo° than oon.°[4]		*believe, more, one*
As wolde God,° it were leveful° unto me		*if God allowed it, lawful*
To be refresshed° half so ofte° as he,		*refreshed, often*
Which yifte° of God hadde he for alle hise wyvys.°		*gift, wives*
40 No man hath swich° that in this world alyve° is.		*has such, alive*
God woot,° this noble kyng, as to my wit,°		*God knows, as far as I know*
The first nyght° had many a myrie° fit		*night, merry*
With ech° of hem,° so wel was hym° on lyve.		*each, them, he was so lucky*
Yblessed be God that I have wedded five![5]		
45 Welcome the sixte, whanevere he shal.°		*whenever he shall [arrive]*
Forsothe,° I wol nat kepe me chaast in al°[6]		*in truth, entirely chaste*
Whan myn housbonde is fro° the world ygon.°		*from, gone*
Som° Cristen° man shal wedde me anon,°		*some, Christian, immediately*
For thanne° th'apostle seith°[7] I am free		*then, the apostle says*

---

1 Since crucial points in the Bible, and other religious, philosophical, or legal texts were explained in glosses (comments written in the margins or between the lines), glossing became a general term for interpreting.

2 God's commandment to increase and multiply is found in Genesis 1:28, as a Latin gloss in the margin notes.

3 The scribe has written "audi" (*hear* in Latin) above "here."

4 According to the Bible (1 Kings 11:33) King Solomon had seven hundred wives and three hundred concubines.

5 Some manuscripts contain the following six line passage:

"Of whiche I have pyked out the beste
Bothe of here nether purs° and of here cheste.°   *their lower purse (testicles), money box*
Diverse scoles° maken parfyt clerkes°   [*Studying at*] *different universities, perfect scholars*
And diverse practyk° in many sondry werkes   *practice*
Maken the workman parfit sekirly
Of five husbandes scoleiyng° am I."   *schooling*

John Manly and Edith Rickert suggest that these lines are "a late Chaucerian insertion," i.e., part of a late rough draft of the poem.

6 There is a Latin gloss in the margin: "If, however, they cannot be chaste, let them marry" from 1 Corinthians 7:28.

7 St. Paul in 1 Corinthians 7:25–38 offers his views about the wisdom of marrying.

50 To wedde, a Goddes half, where it liketh me.[1]
    He seith to be wedded is no synne.°   *sin*
    'Bet° is to be wedded than to brynne.'°[2]   *better, burn*
    What rekketh me,° thogh folk seye° vileynye°   *what do I care, say, villainy*
    Of shrewed° Lameth[3] and of bigamye?°   *cursed, bigamy*
55 I woot wel° Abraham[4] was an hooly° man   *know well, holy*
    And Jacob eek, as ferforth as I kan,°   *as far as I know*
    And ech of hem° hadde wyves mo than two   *them*
    And many another man also.
    Whanne° saugh° ye evere in manere age°   *when, saw, in any age*
60 That hye° God defended° mariage   *high, forbade*
    By expres° word? I pray yow, telleth me.   *specific*
    Or where comanded he virginitee?°   *virginity*
    I woot as wel as ye,° it is no drede,[5]   *know as well as you*
    Whan th'apostel° speketh of maydenhede.°   *the apostle (Paul), virginity*
65 He seyde that precept° therof° hadde he noon.°[6] *commandment, about, none*
    Men may conseille° a womman to been oon,°   *counsel, single*
    But conseillyng is nat comandement.
    He putte it in oure owene juggement.°   *left it to our own judgment*
    For hadde° God comanded maydenhede,   *had*
70 Thanne° hadde he dampned° weddyng with the dede.°   *then, damned, in the act*
    And certein,° if ther were no seed ysowe°   *certainly, sown*
    Virginitee, wherof thanne° sholde° it growe?   *how then, should*
    Poul° ne dorste nat° comanden atte leeste° *Paul, dared not, command at least*
    A thyng of which his maister° yaf° noon heeste.°   *master, gave, no command*
75 The dart[7] is set up of virginitee:
    Cacche whoso may. Who renneth best, lat see![8]

---

1   "To wed, by God's permission, wherever I wish." There is a Latin gloss in the margin: "For if
    the husband dies, the wife is free to marry whom she wishes."
2   This quotation is from 1 Corinthians 7:9. There is a Latin gloss in the margin citing the line.
3   Lamech was the first to marry two wives. See Genesis 4:19.
4   The patriarch Abraham, as recounted in the book of Genesis, was favored by God, yet he had
    more than one wife, as did his grandson Jacob. A Latin gloss in the margin notes: "Lamach,
    who first entered into bigamy, was a bloody and murderous man; Abraham was the first to enter
    trigamy; Jacob quatrigamy."
5   "It is no dread" is a filler here meaning roughly, "do not doubt it."
6   As the Latin gloss in the margin at line 73 notes, Paul admits that he could find no justification
    for his view in the Old Testament, but gave his judgment in its support. This statement is found
    in 1 Corinthians 7:25.
7   Apparently a spear was sometimes given as a prize for a race in England in the Middle Ages.
    Many editors prefer the reading "for virginity" (found in many other manuscripts), which
    makes virginity the competitor rather than the prize.
8   "Let whoever can catch it. Let's see who runs best." A Latin gloss in the margin cites the descrip-
    tion of virginity as a prize in a race from Jerome's *Against Jovinian*.

But this word is nat taken of every wight.°	*does not apply to everyone*
But theras God lust gyve it of his myght.¹	
I woot wel the apostel was a mayde.°	*virgin*
80 But nathelees,° thogh° that he wroot° and sayde	*nevertheless, though, wrote*
He wolde° that every wight° were swich° as he,²	*wished, person, such*
Al nys but conseil° to virginitee.	*is not but advice*
And for to been° a wyf he yaf° me leve°	*be, gave, leave*
Of indulgence,° so it is no repreve°	*by permission, reproach*
85 To wedde me if my make° dye°	*mate, should die*
Withouten excepcioun° of bigamye.°	*objection, bigamy*
Al° were it good no womman for to touche,³	*Although*
He mente° as in his bed or in his couche.°	*meant, couch*
For peril is bothe fyr° and tow° t'assemble.°	*fire, flax (flammable material), to mix*
90 Ye knowe what this ensample° may resemble.	*example*
This is al and som,° that virginitee	*the whole matter*
Moore profiteth than weddyng in freletee.⁴	
Freletee° clepe I° but if° that he and she	*weakness, I call it, unless*
Wolde lede° al hir lyf° in chastitee.	*would lead, their life*
95 I graunte° it wel I have noon envie,°	*grant, no envy*
Thogh maydenhede preferre bigamye.⁵	
Hem liketh° to be clene,° body and goost.°	*they prefer, pure, spirit*
Of myn estaat° I nyl nat° make no boost.°	*my condition, will not, boast*
For wel ye knowe, a lord in his houshold,	
100 He nath nat° every vessel al of gold.	*does not have*
Somme been of tree° and doon° hir° lord servyse.	*some are of wood, do, their*
God clepeth° folk to hym in sondry wyse.°	*calls, in different ways*
And everich hath° of God a propre yifte°⁶—	*everyone has, particular gift*
Som this, som that, as hym liketh shifte.°	*as he pleases to give*
105 Virginitee is greet perfeccioun⁷	
And continence eek with devocioun.°	*[religious] devotion*
But Crist that of perfeccioun° is welle°	*perfection, well (source)*
Bad° nat° every wight° sholde° go selle	*commanded, not, person, should*
Al that he hadde and gyve° it to the poore	*give*
110 And in swich wise° folwe hym° and his foore.°⁸	*such a manner, follow him, footsteps*

---

1 "Except where God wishes, through his might, to impose this principle [of virginity]."

2 There is a Latin gloss in the margin quoting 1 Corinthians 7:7: "I wish, however, all men to be as myself."

3 There is a Latin gloss in the margin quoting 1 Corinthians 7:1: "It is good for a man not to touch a woman."

4 "Remaining a virgin is better than marrying through weakness."

5 "Though virginity be preferred to bigamy."

6 There is a Latin gloss in the margin quoting 1 Corinthians 7:7.

7 There is a Latin gloss in the margin quoting Revelation 14:1–4.

8 The unusual word "foore" caused many scribes trouble and "i. [e.], steppes" is written above.

He spak to hem that wolde lyve parfitly.°　　　*would live perfectly*
And, lordynges, by youre leve,° that am nat I!　　　*leave*
I wol bistowe° the flour° of myn° age　　　*will bestow, flower, my*
In the actes and in fruyt° of mariage.　　　*fruit*
115　TELLE me also, to what conclusioun
Were membres ymaad° of generacioun?[1]　　　*made*
And for what profit° was a wight ywroght?°[2]　　　*purpose, person made*
Trusteth° right wel, they were nat maad° for noght.°　　　*believe me, not made, nothing*
Glose whoso wole and seye bothe up and doun,[3]
120　That they were maad° for purgacioun°　　　*made, releasing*
Of uryne° and oure bothe thynges smale°[4]　　　*urine, our two small things (sexual organs)*
And eek° to knowe° a femele° from a male　　　*also, distinguish, female*
And for noon oother cause, sey° ye no?　　　*say*
The experience° woot wel° it is noght so.　　　*experience (in general) knows well*
125　So that the clerkes° be nat° with me wrothe,°　　　*theologians, not, angry*
I sey yis,° that they beth maked° for bothe.　　　*say yes, are made*
That is to seye,° for office and for ese°　　　*say, pleasure*
Of engendrure,°[5] ther we nat God displese.°　　　*conception, where do not displease*
Why sholde men elles° in hir bookes sette°　　　*otherwise, set down*
130　That a man shal yelde° to his wyf hire dette.°[6]　　　*yield, her debt*
Now, wherwith° sholde° he make his paiement°　　　*with what, should, payment*
If he ne used° his sely° instrument?　　　*did not use, innocent*
Thanne were they maad° upon a creature　　　*made*
To purge uryne° and for engendrure.°　　　*release urine, conception*
135　BUT I seye noght° that every wight° is holde°　　　*say not, person, obligated*
That hath swich harneys,° as I of tolde,　　　*such equipment*
To goon° and usen hem° in engendrure.　　　*go, them*
They shul° nat take of chastitee no cure.°[7]　　　*shall, attention*
Crist was a mayde° and shapen° as a man,　　　*virgin, formed*
140　And many a seint sith° the world bigan,°　　　*since, began*
Yet lyved they evere in parfit° chastitee.　　　*perfect*

1　"Members of generation" refers here to sexual organs. A Latin gloss in the margin notes "Questio" to show that there is a question for debate here.
2　For this line Hengwrt reads, "And of so parfit wys a wight ywroght" (And in such a perfect manner a human being is made). Other manuscripts have "wright" instead of "wight" (made by such a perfect wright or artisan).
3　"Let whoever wishes to do so offer an interpretation and say both up and down."
4　Ellesmere reads "Of urine bothe and thynges smale," which makes no sense. The emendation is from Hengwrt.
5　The phrase "office and ease of engendrure" means for a purpose (that is, conceiving children) and pleasure of procreation.
6　Yielding one's spouse a debt was a euphemism for having sex and acknowledged that both partners owed each other a certain sexual fulfillment, lest sexual frustration drive one of them to adultery. The line is a quotation from 1 Corinthians 7:3.
7　For this line Hengwrt reads, "Thanne sholde men take of chastitee no cure."

I nyl nat envye° no virginitee.°   *will not envy*

Lat hem° be breed° of pured whete° seed,   *let them, bread, refined wheat*

And lat° us wyves hoten° barly breed.   *let, be called*

145 And yet with barly breed, Mark[1] telle kan,

Oure Lord refresshed° many a man.   *gave food to*

In swich° estaat° as God hath cleped us°[2]   *such, condition, has called us*

I wol persevere.° I nam nat precius.°   *will remain, am not fastidious*

In wyfhode I wol use myn instrument°   *sexual organ*

150 As frely° as my makere hath it sent.   *freely*

If I be daungerous,° God yeve° me sorwe.°   *standoffish, give, sorrow*

Myn housbonde shal it have bothe eve and morwe.

Whan that hym list com forth and paye his dette.[3]

An housbonde I wol have, I nyl nat lette,°   *will not stop*

155 Which shal° be bothe my dettour° and my thral°[4] *who shall, debtor, slave*

And have his tribulacioun° withal°   *tribulation, also*

Upon his flessh whil I am his wyf.

I have the power durynge° al my lyf   *during*

Upon his propre° body and noght he.   *own*

160 Right thus the apostel[5] tolde it unto me

And bad° oure housbondes for to love us weel.° *commanded, well*

Al this sentence me liketh every deel."[6]

Up stirte° the Pardoner and that anon.°   *jumped, immediately*

"Now, Dame," quod he, "by God and by Seint John,

165 Ye been° a noble prechour° in this cas!°   *are, preacher, matter*

I was aboute to wedde a wyf, allas!

What sholde I bye it on my flessh so deere?[7]

Yet hadde I levere° wedde no wyf to yeere!"°   *rather, this year*

"Abyde,"° quod she, "my tale is nat bigonne.°   *wait, not begun*

170 Nay, thou shalt drynken° of another tonne°   *drink, cask (of wine)*

Er° that I go, shal savoure wors° than ale! *before, [that] shall taste worse*

---

1   The reference here is to John 6:9 and the miracle of the loaves and fishes, not to a passage in the Gospel of Mark.

2   The line echoes 1 Corinthians 7:20, as noted by a Latin gloss in the margin.

3   "When he wishes to come forth and pay his debt." For the sexual nature of the "debt," see above, p. 145, note 6.

4   There are two Latin glosses in the margin quoting Jerome's *Against Jovinian*. The first is at line 155: "He who has a wife is said to a be a debtor and to be uncircumcised, and a servant of his wife, and like a bad servant he is bound." The second is at 158: "And also, if you are a servant to your wife, do not be sad for this reason. Again, if you have married you have not sinned but those who do will have sorrow in the flesh. Again, a man does not have power over his own body, but his wife does. Again, men, love your wives."

5   The apostle here referred to is St. Paul, whose insights on marriage the Wife of Bath has been mentioning since she began to speak. In addition to the passage referred to above, p. 146, note 2, Paul's other major pronouncement on marriage is Ephesians 5:21–33.

6   "I like all this lesson [of Scripture], every part [of it]."

7   "Why should I pay so dearly for it with my flesh."

And whan that I have toold forth my tale
Of tribulacioun that is in mariage,
Of which I am expert in al myn age,°   *throughout my life*
175 This to seyn,° myself have been the whippe,°   *say, whip*
Than maystow chese wheither° thou wolt sippe°   *you can choose whether, will sip*
Of that tonne that I shal abroche.°   *open*
Bewar of it er° thou to ny° approche.°   *before, too near, approach*
For I shal telle ensamples° mo° than ten.   *examples, more*
180 Whoso that wol nat bewar by othere men[1]
By hym° shul° othere men corrected be.   *him, shall*
The same wordes writeth Protholomee.°   *Ptolemy*
Rede° it in his *Almageste* and take it there!"[2]   *read*
"DAME, I wolde praye° if youre wyl° it were,"   *would ask, will*
185 Seyde this Pardoner, "as ye bigan
Telle forth youre tale. Spareth° for no man,   *spare*
And teche us yonge men of youre praktike!"°   *practice*
"GLADLY, sires,° sith it may yow like.°   *sirs, it may please you*
But yet I praye° to al this compaignye,   *ask*
190 If that I speke after my fantasye,°   *fancy*
As taketh it nat agrief° that° I seye,   *take it not wrong, what*
For myn entente° is but for to pleye.°   *my intent, play*
NOW sire, now wol I telle forth my tale.[3]
As evere moote° I drynken wyn or ale,   *might*
195 I shal seye sooth° of tho housbondes that I hadde,   *say [the] truth*
As thre of hem were goode and two were badde.
The thre men were goode and riche and olde.
Unnethe° myghte° they the statut° holde   *scarcely, might, regulation*
In which that they were bounden° unto me.[4]   *bound*
200 Ye woot wel what I meene° of this, pardee.°   *mean, by God*
As help me God, I laughe whan I thynke
How pitously anyght° I made hem swynke!°   *at night, work*
And by my fey,° I tolde of it no stoor.°   *faith, set no store by it*
They had me yeven° hir° gold and hir tresoor.°   *given, their, treasure*
205 Me neded nat do lenger diligence[5]
To wynne hir love or doon hem reverence.°   *honor them*

---

1   "The one who will not be warned [by examples offered] by others."
2   The aphorism is not found in the *Almagest*, the great astrological treatise of Claudius Ptolemy (second century AD), who gives his name to the Ptolemaic system, in which the sun revolves around the earth, but in the preface to one of the translations of his work.
3   There is an English gloss in the margin: "Bihoold how this goode wyf served hir iij firste housbondes which were goode olde men."
4   In other words, the three old husbands could not fulfill their obligation to pay the marriage debt. There is a Latin gloss in the margin from Jerome's *Against Jovinian*, 1:49: "Also the high priests of Athens, even to this day, emasculate themselves by taking hemlock."
5   "I did not need to make any more effort."

They loved me so wel, by God above,
That I ne tolde no deyntee of hir love.° — *did not put any value on their love*
A wys° womman wol sette hire evere in oon° — *wise, will always determine*
210 To gete hire° love theras° she hath noon.° — *get herself, where, has none*
But sith I hadde hem° hoolly° in myn hond — *them, wholly*
And sith they hadde me yeven al hir lond, — *given, all their land*
What sholde° I taken heede° hem for to plese,° — *why should, bother, please*
But if° it were for my profit and myn ese?° — *unless, pleasure*
215 I sette hem so a werk,° by my fey,° — *to work, faith*
That many a nyght they songen° 'Weilawey!'° — *sang, alas*
The bacon was nat° fet° for hem, I trowe,° — *not, fetched, believe*
That som° men han° in Essex at Dunmowe.¹ — *some, have*
I governed hem so wel after my lawe,
220 That ech° of hem was ful blisful° and fawe° — *each, very happy, eager*
To brynge me gaye thynges° fro the fayre.° — *pretty things, fair*
They were ful glad whan I spak to hem faire,° — *nicely*
For, God it woot,° I chidde hem spitously!° — *knows, scolded them spitefully*
Now herkneth° hou° I baar me° proprely, — *listen, how, bore myself*
225 Ye wise wyves that kan understonde.
THUS shul ye speke and beren hem on honde.²
For half so boldely kan ther no man
Swere° and lye° as kan a womman. — *swear, lie*
I sey nat this by° wyves that been wyse, — *about*
230 But if° it be whan they hem mysavyse.° — *unless, give themselves bad advice*
A wys wyf, if that she kan hir good,° — *knows what is good for her*
Shal bere° hym on hond the cow is wood°³ — *shall deceive, crazy*
And take witnesse of hir owene mayde° — *own maid*
Of hir° assent, but herkneth° how I sayde:° — *her, listen [to], how I spoke*
235 'SIRE° olde kaynard,° is this thyn array?° — *Sir, dotard, behavior*
Why is my neighebores wyf so gay?° — *well dressed*
She is honoured over al ther she gooth.° — *wherever she goes*
I sitte at hoom.° I have no thrifty clooth.° — *home, proper clothing*
What dostow° at my neighebores hous? — *are you doing*
240 Is she so fair? Artow° so amorous? — *are you*
What rowne° ye with oure mayde,° benedicite?° — *whisper, maid, bless you*
Sire olde lecchour,° lat° thy japes° be! — *sir old lecher, let, tricks*
And if I have a gossib° or a freend,° — *confidant, friend*

---

1   The reference here is to a custom in the village of Dunmow of awarding a side of bacon to a
     married couple who did not quarrel for a year.
2   The expression "beren hem on honde" can mean either "to deceive them" or "to accuse them
     falsely." The Wife does both to her husbands.
3   "A wise woman can convince her husband that a tale-telling cowbird (a kind of jackdaw) [who
     tells him she has been unfaithful] is mad and use her own maid as a witness."

Withouten gilt,° thou chidest° as a feend!°   *guilt, complain, fiend*
245 If that I walke or pleye unto his hous,
    Thou comest hoom as dronken as a mous[1]
    And prechest° on thy bench, with yvel preef!°   *preach, bad luck to you*
    Thou seist° to me it is a greet meschief°   *you say, great misfortune*
    To wedde a povre° womman for costage.°   *poor, expense*
250 And if she be riche and of heigh parage,°   *high lineage*
    Thanne° seistow° it is a tormentrie°   *then, you say, torment*
    To suffren° hire pride and hire malencolie.°   *endure, sadness*
    And if she be fair, thou verray knave,°   *you true villain*
    Thou seyst that every holour° wol hire have.°   *lecher, will have her*
255 She may no while in chastitee° abyde°   *chastity, remain*
    That is assailled° upon ech a syde.°   *attacked, each side*
    THOU seyst that som folk desiren us for richesse,
    Somme for oure shape, somme for oure fairnesse
    And som for she kan synge and daunce°   *can sing and dance*
260 And som for gentillesse° and som for daliaunce,°   *nobility, flirtation*
    Som for hir handes and hir armes smale.°   *her slender arms*
    Thus goth° al to the devel,° by thy tale!   *goes, devil*
    Thou seyst men may nat kepe° a castel wal,°   *not keep, wall*
    It may so longe assailled been overal.
265 AND if that she be foul, thou seist that she
    Coveiteth° every man that she may se.°   *covets, see*
    For as a spaynel° she wol on hym lepe,°   *spaniel, leap*
    Til that she fynde° som man hire to chepe.°   *find, to buy her*
    Ne noon so grey goos gooth in the lake
270 As, seistow, wol been withoute make.[2]
    And seyst° it is an hard thyng° for to welde,°   *you say, thing, control*
    A thyng that no man wole his thankes helde.°   *willingly hold*
    Thus seistow, lorel,° whan° thow goost° to bedde   *fool, when, go*
    And that no wys man nedeth° for to wedde,   *needs*
275 Ne° no man that entendeth unto hevene.°   *nor, intends [to go] to Heaven*
    With wilde thonder dynt° and firy levene°   *wild thunderclaps, fiery lightning*
    Moote° thy welked nekke° be tobroke!°   *may, withered neck, broken*
    THOW seyst° that droppyng° houses and eek smoke   *you say, drippy*
    And chidyng° wyves maken men to flee   *nagging*
280 Out of hir owene houses. A, benedicitee,°   *bless you*
    What eyleth° swich an old man for to chide?°   *ails, complain*
    THOW seyst° that we wyves wol° oure vices hide   *you say, will*

---

1   It is not clear why mice are thought to be drunk, but the expression was common in medieval
    England. Cf. modern "drunk as a skunk."
2   "There is no goose in the lake, no matter how grey, who does not have a mate." Another
    proverb.

Til we be fast° and thanne we wol hem shewe.° *secure, show*
Wel° may that be a proverbe of a shrewe!° *well, villain*
285 THOU seist that oxen, asses, hors,° and houndes, *horses*
They been assayd° at diverse stoundes.° *tried, different times*
Bacyns,° lavours° er° that men hem bye,° *basins, bowls, before, buy them*
Spoones and stooles and al swich housbondrye,° *household equipment*
And so been° pottes,° clothes,° and array. *are, pots, clothing*
290 But folk of wyves maken noon assay° *do not try [them] out*
Til they be wedded. Olde dotard° shrewe! *old foolish*
Thanne seistow we wol oure vices shewe.
THOU seist also that it displeseth° me *displeases*
But if° that thou wolt preyse° my beautee *unless, will praise*
295 And but thou poure° alwey° upon my face *gaze, always*
And clepe° me 'faire dame!' in every place, *call*
And but° thou make a feeste° on thilke day° *unless, feast, the same*
That I was born and make me fressh and gay,
And but° thou do to my norice°¹ honour° *unless, nurse, honor*
300 And to my chambrere° withinne my bour° *chambermaid, bedroom*
And to my fadres° folk° and his allyes: *father's, relatives*
Thus seistow, olde barel° ful of lyes!° *barrel, lies*
AND yet of oure apprentice Janekyn,²
For his crispe heer° shynynge° as gold so fyn° *curly hair, shining, fine*
305 And for he squiereth° me bothe up and doun, *escorts*
Yet hastow° caught a fals° suspecioun.° *you have, false, suspicion*
I wol° hym noght,° though thou were deed° tomorwe!° *want, not, dead, tomorrow*
BUT tel me, why hydestow° with sorwe° *do you hide, with sorrow [to you]*
The keyes° of my cheste° awey fro° me? *keys, chest (safety box), from*
310 It is my good° as wel as thyn,° pardee!° *possession, yours, by God*
What wenestow to make an ydiot of oure dame?³
Now by that lord that called is Seint Jame,° *Saint James*
Thou shalt nat° bothe, thogh° thou were wood,° *'not, though, crazy*
Be maister° of my body and of my good!° *master, possessions*
315 That oon thou shalt forgo, maugree thyne eyen!⁴
What nedeth° thee° of me to enquere° or spyen?° *needs, you, inquire, spy*
I trowe° thou woldest° loke° me in thy chiste!°⁵ *believe, would, lock, chest*
Thou sholdest seye, 'Wyf, go wher thee liste.'⁶

---

1 Wealthy medieval people were attended to in their childhood by wet nurses, who often became
 for a time surrogate mothers.
2 A Latin gloss in the margin notes the line from Jerome's *Against Jovinian* 1.47: "There is an estate
 manager with curly hair." Jerome says that the title "estate manager" is "a cloak for adultery."
3 "What, do you expect to make an idiot of our lady?" "Oure dame" here is the Wife of Bath's
 reference to herself in the third person in her role of the lady of her old husband's household.
4 "You must give up one of them, despite your eyes!," i.e., despite anything you can do.
5 Medieval merchants used large locked chests to lock up their coins and their valuables.
6 "You should say, 'Wife, go wherever you want.'"

Taak° youre disport!° I wol leve° no talys.° — take, enjoyment, will believe, tales
320 I knowe yow for a trewe wyf, Dame Alys!'
We love no man that taketh kepe° or charge — takes keep
Wher that we goon.° We wol ben° at oure large.° — go, will be, free
OF alle men, blessed moot° he be, — might
The wise astrologien° Daun Protholome° — astronomer, Master Ptolemy
325 That seith this proverbe in his *Almageste*,
'Of alle men his wysdom is the hyeste° — highest
That rekketh° nevere who hath the world in honde.'°[1] — who cares, who possesses the world
By this proverbe thou shalt understonde:
Have thou ynogh, what thar thee recche or care[2]
330 How myrily° that othere folkes fare?° — merrily, behave
For certeyn,° olde dotard,° by youre leve,° — certain, old fool, leave
Ye shul° have queynte[3] right ynogh° at eve!° — shall, enough, at night
He is to greet° a nygard° that wolde werne° — too great, skinflint, would refuse
A man to lighte his candle at his lanterne.
335 He shal have never the lasse° light, pardee!° — less, by God
Have thou ynogh, thee thar nat pleyne thee.[4]
THOU seyst also that if we make us gay
With clothyng and with precious array,° — expensive adornment
That it is peril of oure chastitee.° — a danger to our chastity
340 And yet with sorwe thou most enforce thee° — you must support yourself
And seye thise wordes° in the Apostles[5] name. — say these words
'In habit° maad° with chastitee and shame — clothing, made
Ye wommen shul apparaille yow,'° quod he. — dress yourselves
'And noght° in tressed heer° and gay perree,° — not, braided hair, jewels
345 As perles° ne with gold ne° clothes riche.' — pearls, nor
After thy text° ne after thy rubriche° — your quotation, rubric
I wol nat wirche° as muchel as a gnat![6] — work
THOU seydest this, that I was lyk° a cat. — like
For whoso° wolde senge° a cattes skyn, — whoever, would singe
350 Thanne wolde the cat wel dwellen in his in.° — lodgings
And if the cattes skyn° be slyk° and gay, — cat's skin, sleek

---

1 There is a gloss in the margin giving a version of this saying from a Latin translation of Ptolemy's *Almagest*.
2 "If you have enough, why do you need to bother yourself or care?"
3 "Queynte" (elegant, clever, or pleasing thing) is a medieval euphemism for the female sexual organs. Cf. the Wife's use of "quonyam" (line 608), "bele chose" (lines 447, 510), and "chambre of Venus" (line 618).
4 "If you have enough, you do not need to complain for yourself."
5 The apostle here is again St. Paul. The following quotation comes from 1 Timothy 2:9 and is given in the Latin gloss in the margin.
6 "I will not follow ('work after') in the smallest way" or possibly, "any more than a gnat would." In medieval service books and books of devotion, rubrics (whose name comes from the red ink in which they were written) were directions about how to use the texts to which they referred either in communal worship or private devotion.

She wol nat dwelle° in house half a day,   *will not remain*
But forth she wole° er any° day be dawed°   *will [go], before, dawned*
To shewe hir skyn and goon° a caterwawed.[1]   *go*
355 This is to seye, if I be gay, sire shrewe,°   *sir villain*
I wol renne° out my borel° for to shewe!   *will run, cheap clothing*
SIRE olde fool, what eyleth° thee to spyen,°   *ails, spy*
Thogh thou preye° Argus[2] with hise° hundred eyen°   *ask, his, eyes*
To be my wardecors,° as he kan° best.   *bodyguard, can*
360 In feith,° he shal nat kepe° me but [me] lest!°   *faith, not keep, unless I want*
Yet koude° I make his berd,° so moot° I thee!°[3]   *could, fool him, might, thrive*
THOU seydest eek° that ther been thynges thre,°[4]   *also, there are three things*
The whiche thynges troublen° al this erthe   *trouble*
And that no wight° may endure the ferthe.°   *no person, fourth*
365 O leeve sire shrewe!° Jhesu shorte° thy lyf!°   *dear sir villain, shorten, life*
Yet prechestow° and seyst° an° hateful wyf   *you preach, say, MS and*
Yrekned is for oon° of thise meschances.°   *is counted as one, these misfortunes*
Been ther none othere° resemblances   *there are no other*
That ye may likne° youre parables to,   *liken*
370 But if a sely° wyf be oon° of tho?°   *innocent, one, those*
THOU liknest° wommenes love to helle,[5]   *liken*
To bareyne lond° ther° water may nat° dwelle.   *barren land, where, not*
THOU liknest it also to wilde fyr:[6]
The moore° it brenneth,° the moore it hath desir°   *more, burns, desires*
375 To consumen° everythyng that brent wole be.°   *consume, will be burned*
Thou seyst, right as wormes° shendeth° a tree,[7]   *grubs, harm*
Right so a wyf destroyeth hire housbond.
This knowe they that been to wyves bonde.°   *are bound*
LORDYNGES, right thus as ye have understonde[8]
380 Baar I stifly myne olde housbondes on honde,[9]
That thus they seyden° in hir dronkenesse.   *said*
And al was fals,° but that I took witnesse   *false*

---

1 Caterwauling is the loud noise cats make while they are mating.
2 Argus, in Greek mythology, was the hundred-eyed guardian of Zeus's mistress Io and spy for Zeus's wife Hera. He was killed by Hermes.
3 "So mote I thee" or "So may I thrive" means little more than "indeed" or "by my word."
4 There is a Latin gloss in the margin from *Against Jovinian*, 1:28: "Also a hateful wife, if she has a good husband, [is the worst of all things that trouble the earth]."
5 There is a Latin gloss in the margin from *Against Jovinian* 1:28, quoting a sentence beginning "A woman's love is compared to hell."
6 Greek fire, a mixture consisting largely of naptha, was used in naval warfare.
7 There is a Latin gloss in the margin from *Against Jovinian*, 1:28, quoting Proverbs 25:20, "like a worm in wood, so a wicked woman destroys her husband."
8 There is a Latin gloss in the margin from *Against Jovinian*, 1:28, "No one can know what a wife or a woman is unless he has endured her."
9 "I bore witness (*baar ... on honde*) firmly to my old husbands that they said this when they were drunk."

On Janekyn and on my nece° also.   *niece*
O Lord, the pyne° I dide hem° and the wo,°   *pain, [to] them, woe*
385 Ful giltlees,° by Goddes sweete pyne!°   *completely guiltless, pain*
For as an hors° I koude byte and whyne.°   *horse, whine*
I koude pleyne° thogh° I were in the gilt,°   *complain, though, guilty*
Or elles° oftentyme° hadde I been spilt.°   *else, often, destroyed*
Whoso comth° first to mille,° first grynt.°   *whoever comes, mill, grinds*
390 I pleyned first, so was oure werre° ystynt.°   *war, stifled*
They were ful glad to excuse hem° blyve°   *them, quickly*
Of thyng of which they nevere agilte hir lyve.[1]
Of wenches° wolde I beren hym on honde,°   *girls, accuse him*
Whan that for syk° unnethes° myghte he stonde.   *sickness, scarcely*
395 Yet tikled° it his herte,° for that° he   *tickled, heart, because*
Wende° that I hadde of hym° so greet° chiertee.°   *thought, for him, great, love*
I swoor° that al my walkynge° out by nyghte°   *swore, walking, night*
Was for t'espye° wenches that he dighte.°   *spy, had sex with*
Under that colour° hadde I many a myrthe,°   *excuse, mirth*
400 For al swich thyng was yeven° us in oure byrthe.°   *given, birth*
Deceite, wepyng, spynnyng° God hath yeve°   *spinning, given*
To wommen kyndely° whil° that they may lyve.°   *naturally, while, live*
And thus of o° thyng I avaunte° me: *one, boast*
Atte ende,° I hadde the bettre° in ech degree°   *at the end, better, each instance*
405 By sleighte,° or force, or by som maner thyng,°   *deceit, manner [of] thing*
As by continueel murmure° or grucchyng.°   *continual murmur, complaining*
Namely° abedde° hadden they meschaunce.°   *especially, in bed, misfortune*
Ther wolde I chide° and do hem no plesaunce.°   *nag, pleasure*
I wolde no lenger° in the bed abyde°   *longer, remain*
410 If that I felte° his arm over my syde°   *felt, side*
Til he had maad his raunsoun unto me.
Thanne wolde I suffre hym do his nycetee.°[2]   *foolishness*
And therfore every man this tale I telle:
Wynne° whoso° may, for al is for to selle.°   *win, whoever, for sale*
415 With empty hand men may none° haukes° lure,   *no, hawks*
For wynnyng° wolde° I al his lust endure   *profit, would*
And make me a feyned° appetit.   *pretended*
And yet in bacon[3] hadde I nevere delit.°   *delight*
That made me that evere I wolde hem chide,
420 For thogh° the Pope hadde seten hem biside,°   *though, sat beside them*
I wolde nat spare hem at hir owene bord.°   *table*
For by my trouthe, I quitte hem,° word for word,   *requited them*

---

1   "Of a thing that they had never been guilty of in their lives."
2   "[Not] until he had paid his ransom (given me his money) would I allow him to do his foolishness (have sex with me)."
3   Bacon, of course, is old meat preserved by salting it.

As helpe me verray° God omnipotent!° — *true, almighty*
Though I right now sholde make my testament,
425 I ne owe hem° nat a word that it nys quit.° — *did not owe them, was not paid back*
I broghte° it so aboute, by my wit, — *brought*
That they moste yeve it up° as for the beste — *had to give it up*
Or elles° hadde we nevere been in reste.° — *else, at rest*
For thogh° he looked as a wood leoun,° — *although, crazy lion*
430 Yet sholde he faille of his conclusion.° — *intent*
THANNE wolde I seye, 'Goodlief, taak keepe
How mekely° looketh° Wilkyn oure sheepe.[1] — *meekly, looks*
Com neer,° my spouse. Lat me ba thy cheke.° — *come near, kiss your cheek*
Ye sholde been al pacient and meke° — *meek*
435 And han° a sweete, spiced conscience,° — *have, delicate conscience*
Sith ye so preche° of Jobes pacience.° — *preach, Job's patience*
Suffreth alwey,° syn ye so wel kan preche, — *endure always*
And but° ye do, certein° we shal yow teche° — *unless, certainly, teach you*
That it is fair to have a wyf in pees.° — *peace*
440 Oon° of us two moste bowen,° doutelees,° — *one, must bow, doubtless*
And sith a man is moore resonable
Than womman is, ye moste been suffrable.° — *you must be patient*
What eyleth yow,° to grucche° thus and grone?° — *ails you, complain, groan*
Is it for ye wolde have my queynte° allone?° — *female sexual organs, alone*
445 Wy,° taak° it al! Lo, have it everydeel!° — *Why, take, every bit*
Peter, I shrewe yow but ye love it weel![2]
For if I wolde selle my bele chose,
I koude walke as fressh° as is a rose.[3] — *fresh*
But I wol kepe it for youre owene tooth.° — *own taste (pleasure)*
450 Ye be° to blame, by God, I sey yow sooth!'° — *you are, say you [the] truth*
SWICHE manere wordes hadde we on honde.[4]
Now wol° I speken° of my fourthe housbonde. — *will, speak*
My fourthe housbonde was a revelour.°[5] — *party-goer*
This is to seyn,° he hadde a paramour.° — *say, lover*
455 And I was yong° and ful of ragerye,° — *young, high spirits*
Stibourne° and strong and joly° as a pye.° — *stubborn, pretty, magpie*
Wel koude I daunce to an harpe smale° — *small harp*
And synge,° ywis,° as any nyghtyngale° — *sing, indeed, nightingale*

---

1   "Then would I say, 'Sweetheart, note well, how meekly Willie, our sheep (i.e., her husband) looks.'"
2   "Peter" here is not the old man's name; it is an oath: "By St. Peter!, I curse you unless you love it well," i.e., do you ever love it well.
3   In other words, if I sold myself sexually, I could dress myself beautifully with the proceeds.
4   "We were occupied (had in hand) by this kind of conversation."
5   There is an English gloss in the margin: "Of the condicioun of the fourthe housbonde of the goode wyf and how she served hym."

·Whan I had dronke a draughte° of sweete wyn.°   *drunk a draught, wine*
460 Metellius,¹ the foule cherl, the swyn,°   *swine*
That with a staf° birafte° his wyf hir lyf,   *club, stole from*
For° she drank wyn, thogh I hadde been his wyf,   *because*
He sholde nat han daunted me fro drynke!²
And after wyn, on Venus³ moste° I thynke.°   *must, think*
465 For also siker° as cold engendreth° hayl,°   *as sure, causes, hail*
A likerous° mouth moste han° a likerous tayl.°   *lecherous, must have, tail*
In wommen vinolent is no defence.⁴
This knowen lecchours° by experience.   *lechers*
But, Lord Crist, whan that it remembreth me°   *when I remember*
470 Upon my yowthe° and on my jolitee,°   *youth, jollity*
It tikleth° me aboute myn herte roote.°   *tickles, heart's root*
Unto this day it dooth myn herte boote°   *does my heart good*
That I have had my world as in my tyme.°   *time*
But age, allas, that al wole envenyme,°   *will poison all*
475 Hath me biraft° my beautee and my pith.°   *stolen from me, strength*
Lat° go! Farewel! The devel° go therwith!°   *let, devil, with it*
The flour° is goon.° Ther is namoore° to telle.   *flour, gone, no more*
The bren° as I best kan° now moste° I selle.°   *bran, can, must, sell*
But yet to be right myrie° wol° I fonde.°   *merry, will, try*
480 Now wol I tellen of my fourthe housbonde.
I seye I hadde in herte° greet despit°   *heart, great anger*
That he of any oother° had delit.°   *any other [woman], delight*
But he was quit,° by God and by Seint Joce!⁵   *punished*
I made hym of the same wode° a croce.°   *wood, cross*
485 Nat° of my body in no foul manere°   *not, manner*
But certein I made folk swich cheere,°   *hospitality*
That in his owene grece° I made hym° frye°   *own grease, him, fry*
For angre° and for verray jalousie.°   *anger, true jealousy*
By God, in erthe I was his purgatorie,°   *purgatory*
490 For which I hope his soule be in glorie.
For God it woot,° he sat ful ofte° and song   *knows it, very often*
Whan that his shoo° ful bitterly hym wrong.°   *shoe, hurt him very bitterly*

---

1 This reference is to an old story dating back to ancient Rome. A Latin gloss in the margin quotes the line "Metellius killed his own wife, whom he struck with his staff because she had drunk wine" and provides the reference to book 6 of Valerius Maximus (first century AD), i.e., to his *Facta et dicta memorabilia* (*Memorable Facts and Deeds*), a collection of short stories for orators.
2 "He should not have prevented me from drink."
3 In Roman mythology, Venus was the goddess of love. Here the Wife just means that once she was a little drunk she turned her mind to sex.
4 "There is no defense in drunken women," i.e., they are defenseless.
5 St. Judoc (St. Joyce) was a seventh-century prince in Brittany who gave up his succession to the throne to become a priest. He was also famous for going on a pilgrimage to Rome.

Ther was no wight° save God and he that wiste°   *person, who knew*
In many wise° how soore° I hym twiste.°   *ways, sorely, tormented him*
495 He deyde° whan° I cam fro° Jerusalem   *died, when, came from*
And lith ygrave° under the roode beem.°¹   *lies buried, beam of the cross*
Al is his tombe° noght° so curyus°   *tomb, not, elaborate*
As was the sepulcre° of hym° Daryus,°   *tomb, him, Darius*
Which that Appeles wroghte° subtilly.°²   *made, subtly*
500 It nys° but wast to burye° hym preciously.°   *is not, bury, expensively*
Lat hym° farewel! God yeve° his soule reste.   *let him, give*
He is now in his grave and in his cheste.°   *coffin*
Now of my fifthe housbonde wol I telle.³
God lete° his soule nevere come in Helle!   *let*
505 And yet was he to me the mooste shrewe.°   *most villainous*
That feele° I on my ribbes° al by rewe°   *feel, ribs, in a row*
And evere shal unto myn endyng day.⁴
But in oure bed he was ful fressh and gay.
And therwithal so wel koude° he me glose,°   *could, flatter*
510 Whan that he wolde han° my bele chose,⁵   *would have*
That thogh° he hadde me bet° on every bon,°   *though, beaten, bone*
He koude wynne agayn° my love anon.°   *win again, immediately*
I trowe° I loved hym° best for that he   *believe, him*
Was of his love daungerous° to me.   *standoffish*
515 We wommen han,° if that I shal nat lye,°   *have, shall not lie*
In this matere° a queynte fantasye.°   *matter, quaint fantasy*
Wayte,° what° thyng we may nat lightly° have,   *know [that], whatever, easily*
Therafter wol° we crie° al day and crave!   *after it will, cry*
Forbede° us thyng,° and that desiren° we.   *forbid, [a] thing, desire*
520 Preesse° on us faste, and thanne wol we fle.°   *press, then we will escape*
With daunger oute we al oure chaffare;
Greet prees at market maketh deere ware.⁶

---

1   By this the Wife of Bath means that her fourth husband was buried inside the local parish church under the crossbeam of the cross near the high altar, a place reserved for only the most influential members of a parish.

2   The legendary tomb of Darius the Mede, fashioned by the Jewish sculptor Appeles, was famous for its beauty. A Latin gloss in the margin notes: "Appeles made a marvelous work in the tomb of Darius," and provides the source, Walter of Chatillon's twelfth-century epic on Alexander the Great, the *Alexandreid*.

3   There is an English gloss in the margin: "Of the fifthe housbonde of this wyf and hou she bar hire ayens hym" (bore herself against him).

4   I.e., he beat her, as she makes clear further on.

5   See p. 151, note 3.

6   Either "Where [we are greeted with] scorn, we [put] out all our goods (i.e., are anxious to sell)" or "We [put] out all our goods with [a show of] scorn (i.e., as if we did not care if anyone bought them)." The following lines provide the reason for doing this: "A great crowd at the market makes for expensive goods."

And to greet cheepe° is holde° at litel prys.°   *too much merchandise, held, little price*
This knoweth every womman that is wys.
525 MY fifthe housbonde, God his soule blesse,
Which that I took for love and no richesse,
He somtyme° was a clerk° of Oxenford°   *once, student, Oxford*
And hadde left scole° and wente at hom° to bord°   *school, home, to rent a room*
With my gossib,° dwellynge in oure toun.   *confidant*
530 God have hir soule! Hir name was Alisoun.
She knew myn herte and eek my privetee°   *secrets*
Bet° than oure parisshe preest, as moot° I thee!°   *better, may, thrive*
To hire° biwreyed° I my conseil° al.   *her, revealed, counsel*
For hadde myn housbonde pissed on a wal°   *wall*
535 Or doon a thyng that sholde han° cost his lyf,   *should have*
To hire and to another worthy wyf
And to my nece,° which that I loved weel,°   *niece, well*
I wolde han toold° his conseil° everydeel.°   *would have told, counsel, every bit*
And so I dide ful often, God it woot!°   *God knows it*
540 That made his face ful often reed and hoot°   *hot*
For verray° shame, and blamed hymself, for he   *true*
Had toold to me so greet a pryvetee.
AND so bifel° that ones° in a Lente,°1   *it happened, once, Lent*
So oftentymes° I to my gossyb° wente.   *often, confidant*
545 For evere yet I loved to be gay
And for to walke in March, Averill,° and May   *April*
Fro hous to hous to heere sondry talys.°   *various tales*
That Jankyn clerk° and my gossyb Dame Alys   *student*
And I myself into the feeldes° wente.   *fields*
550 Myn housbonde was at Londoun al the Lente.
I hadde the bettre leyser° for to pleye   *better opportunity*
And for to se° and eek for to be seye°   *see, be seen*
Of lusty folk. What wiste I wher my grace
Was shapen for to be or in what place?2
555 Therfore I made my visitaciouns°   *visits*
To vigilies and to processiouns,3
To prechyng° eek and to thise pilgrimages,   *preaching*
To pleyes° of myracles and to mariages°   *plays, marriages*
And wered° upon my gaye scarlet gytes.°   *wore, red robes*

---

1   Lent is the period in the late winter to early spring when Christians prepare for Easter with fasting and penance.
2   "How could I know where or in what place my good luck was destined to be?" or possibly (to avoid the redundancy) "How could I know whether (*wher* can mean either *where* or *whether*) I was destined to have good luck, or where?"
3   "To vigils and to processions." Vigils were church services held on the evening before the feast day of a saint. Ceremonial processions formed part of the service on the day itself.

560 Thise wormes, ne° thise motthes,° ne thise mytes°   nor, moths, mites
Upon my peril frete° hem never a deel.°   eat, never a bit
And wostow° why? For they were used weel.°   do you know, well
Now wol I tellen forth what happed me.°   happened [to] me
I seye that in the feeldes walked we
565 Til trewely° we hadde swich° daliance,°   truly, such, flirtation
This clerk and I, that of my purveiance°   foresight
I spak to hym and seyde° hym how that he,   said [to]
If I were wydwe,° sholde° wedde me.   widowed, should
For certeinly I sey for no bobance,°   pride
570 Yet was I nevere withouten purveiance
Of mariage n'of° othere thynges° eek.   nor of, affairs
I holde a mouses herte° nat worth a leek   mouse's heart
That hath but oon hole forto sterte to,°   escape to
And if that faille,° thanne is al ydo.°¹   should fail, completely done for
575 I BAR hym on honde° he hadde enchanted me.   convinced him
My dame° taughte me that soutiltee.°   mother, trick
And eek I seyde I mette° of hym al nyght   dreamed
He wolde han slayn° me as I lay upright,°   have killed, lay on my back
And al my bed was ful of verray° blood.   true
580 But yet I hope that he shal do me good,
For blood bitokeneth° gold, as me° was taught.²   signifies, to me
And al was fals!° I dremed° of it right naught.°   false, dreamed, not at all
But I folwed ay° my dammes loore,°   followed ever, mother's teaching
As wel° of this as othere thynges° moore.°   well, matters, more
585 BUT now sire, lat me se° what I shal seyn.°   let me see, say
Aha! By God, I have my tale ageyn!°   again
WHAN that my fourthe housbonde was on beere,°   bier
I weepe° algate° and made sory cheere,°   wept, continuously, sorry face
As wyves mooten,° for it is usage,°   must, custom
590 And with my coverchief° covered my visage.°   kerchief, face
But for that° I was purveyed of° a make,°   because, provided with, mate
I wepte° but smal,° and that I undertake.°   wept, little, attest
To chirche° was myn housbonde born amorwe,°   church, in the morning
With neighebores° that for hym maden sorwe.°   neighbors, sorrow
595 And Jankyn oure clerk was oon of tho.°   one of those
As help me God, whan° that I saugh° hym go   when, saw
After the beere,° me thoughte° he hadde a paire   bier, I thought
Of legges and of feet so clene° and faire,°   neat, attractive
That al myn herte I yaf° unto his hoold.°   gave, possession

---

1   The mouse who has only one hole to escape to appears in the *Romance of the Rose* (line 13150),
whose character La Vielle, the old woman who knows all about love, is one of the models for
the Wife of Bath, and various proverbs. "Not worth a leek" means worth nothing at all.
2   Blood could serve as a token or symbol of gold, which was often described as red.

600 He was, I trowe,° a twenty wynter oold.   *believe*
And I was fourty, if I shal seye sooth.°   *say the truth*
And yet I hadde alwey° a coltes° tooth.   *always, colt's (youthful)*
Gat-tothed° I was, and that bicam me weel.°   *gap-toothed, appeared to my favor*
I hadde the prente° of Seint Venus seel.°   *imprint, seal*
605 As help me God, I was a lusty oon
And faire and riche and yong and wel bigon.°   *well established*
And trewely, as myne housbondes tolde me,
I hadde the beste "quonyam"° myghte° be.   *sexual organ, might*
For certes, I am al venerien[1]
610 In feelynge,° and myn herte is marcien.[2]   *feeling*
Venus me yaf° my lust, my likerousnesse,°   *gave, lecherousness*
And Mars yaf me my sturdy hardynesse.°   *courage*
Myn ascendent was Taur, and Mars therinne.[3]
Allas! Allas! That evere love was synne!°   *sin*
615 I folwed ay° myn inclinacioun°   *followed ever, inclination*
By vertu° of my constellacioun,°   *power, constellation*
That made me I koude noght withdrawe°   *could not withhold*
My chambre of Venus° from a good felawe.°   *sexual organ, fellow*
Yet have I Martes° mark upon my face—   *Mars's*
620 And also in another privee° place.   *private*
For God so wys° be my savacioun,°   *wise, salvation*
I ne loved nevere° by no discrecioun   *never loved*
But evere folwed° myn appetit,°   *ever followed, appetite*
Al° were he short or long° or blak or whit.   *whether or not, tall*
625 I took no kepe,° so that he liked me,°   *did not care, pleased me*
How poore° he was ne eek° of what degree.   *poor, nor also*
WHAT sholde I seye, but at the monthes ende,
This joly° clerk Jankyn that was so hende°   *pretty, handy*
Hath wedded me with greet solempnytee.°   *ceremony*
630 And to hym yaf° I al the lond° and fee°   *gave, land, property*
That evere° was me yeven° therbifoore.°   *ever, given, before this*
But afterward repented me ful soore!°   *I regretted it sorely*
He nolde suffre nothyng of my list.[4]
By God, he smoot° me ones° on the lyst,°   *hit, once, ear*
635 For that° I rente° out of his book a leef,°   *because, tore, page*

---

1   In astrology, one who is influenced by the planet Venus—in other words, prone to love.
2   In astrology, one who is influenced by the planet Mars—in other words, warlike.
3   At the moment when the wife was born the constellation of stars known as Taurus (the Bull) was coming over the horizon ("ascendant") along with the planet Mars. There is a Latin gloss in the margin beginning at line 609 explaining that if a woman is born with Venus and Mars ascending together she will be unchaste. The gloss gives the source as *Mansor Amphorisoun*, i.e., a little-known astrological treatise identified by Skeat as *Aphorismorum*, or *Aphorisms* of Almansor, which survives in a seventeenth-century edition.
4   "He would not allow anything I desired."

That of the strook° myn ere wax al deef.° — *stroke, ear grew completely deaf*
Stibourne° I was as is a leonesse° — *stubborn, lioness*
And of my tonge° a verray jangleresse.° — *tongue, true ceaseless talker*
And walke I wolde° as I had doon biforn° — *would, done before*
640 From hous to hous, although he had it sworn.° — *forbidden*
For which he often tymes wolde preche° — *often times would preach*
And me of olde Romayn geestes°[1] teche° — *Roman stories, teach*
How he, Symplicius Gallus, lefte his wyf
And hire forsook° for terme of al his lyf,° — *abandoned, the rest of his life*
645 Noght but for open heveded, he hir say,[2]
Lookynge° out at his dore° upon a day. — *looking, door*
ANOTHER Romayn tolde he me by name,
That, for° his wyf was at a someres game° — *because, summer's entertainment*
Withouten his wityng,° he forsook hire eke.° — *knowledge, also*
650 And thanne wolde he upon his Bible seke° — *seek*
That ilke° proverbe of Ecclesiaste[3] — *same*
Where he comandeth and forbedeth faste° — *forbids firmly*
Man shal nat suffre° his wyf go roule° aboute. — *not allow, wander*
Thanne wolde he seye right thus, withouten doute:° — *doubt*
655 'WHOSO that buyldeth his hous al of salwes[4]
And priketh° his blynde hors° over the falwes° — *spurs, blind horse, fields*
AND suffreth° his wyf to go seken° halwes° — *allows, seek, shrines*
Is worthy to been° hanged on the galwes.'°[5] — *be, gallows*
But al for noght! I sette° noght an hawe° — *valued, hawthorn berry*
660 Of his proverbes n'of° his olde lawe. — *nor of*
Ne° I wolde nat° of hym° corrected be. — *nor, would not, by him*
I hate hym that my vices telleth me,° — *tells me [about]*
And so doo° mo,° God woot,° of us than I. — *do, more, God knows*
This made hym with me wood° al outrely,° — *crazy, entirely*
665 I nolde noght° forbere° hym° in no cas. — *would not, endure, him*
Now wol I seye yow sooth,° by Seint Thomas,[6] — *tell you the truth*

---

1 Like the reference to Metellius above in line 460, the following are old misogynistic or anti-matrimonial stories dating back to ancient Rome. There is a Latin gloss in the margin at line 643 referring to the source for the story of Symplicius Gallus, Valerius Maximus (see p. 155, note 1).
2 "Just because he saw her bare-headed."
3 The reference is to Ecclesiasticus, 25:34.
4 "Whoever builds his house of all willow branches." A Latin gloss in the margin notes that this is a proverb.
5 A Latin gloss in the margin cites Ecclesiasticus 25:34: "Do not give ... to a woman the indulgence of gadding about."
6 There are three possible candidates for this St. Thomas: Thomas the Apostle, mentioned in the gospels; St. Thomas Aquinas, the thirteenth-century theologian (though his second name was more often used than not); and St. Thomas Becket, whose shrine the Canterbury pilgrims are journeying to visit. Thomas the Apostle was often referred to as "Thomas of India." Becket is the likely reference.

Why that I rente° out of his book a leef,°   tore, page
For which he smoot° me so that I was deef.°   hit, deaf
HE hadde a book that gladly, ·nyght and day,
670 For his desport° he wolde rede alway.°   fun, read always
He cleped° it *Valerie and Theofraste*,[1]   called
At which book he lough alwey ful faste.°   laughed always very much
AND eek° ther was somtyme° a clerk° at Rome,   also, once, theologian
A cardinal that highte° Seint Jerome,[2]   was named
675 That made a book,[3] *Agayn Jovinian*,
In which book eek ther was Tertulan,
Crisippus, Trotula, and Helowys
That was abbesse nat fer fro Parys,°   not far from Paris
And eek the *Parables of Salomon*,
680 Ovides° *Art*, and bookes many on.°   Ovid's, many another book
And alle thise° were bounden in o° volume.   these, bound into one
And every nyght and day was his custume°   habit
Whan° he hadde leyser° and vacacioun°   when, had leisure, opportunity
From oother° worldly occupacioun°   other, occupation
685 To reden° on this *Book of Wikked Wyves*.[4]   read
He knew of hem mo legendes and lyves°   stories and biographies
Than been° of goode wyves in the Bible.   than are
For, trusteth wel,° it is an inpossible°   trust well, it is impossible
That any clerk° wol speke° good of wyves   theologian, will speak
690 But if it be of hooly seintes lyves.°   holy saints' lives
Ne noon oother° womman never the mo.°   nor any other, more
Who peynted° the leoun,[5] tel me who?   painted

---

1   The Wife of Bath is actually referring to two separate works, often bound together into one volume
    in the Middle Ages—the *Dissuasio Valerii ad Rufinum* by the English scholar and courtier Walter Map
    (c. 1140–c. 1208) and the *Golden Book of Marriages* by Theophrastus, a supposed disciple of Aristotle.
    Theophrastus's work survives only in the lengthy quotations in Jerome's *Against Jovinian*. All three
    books were full of stories attacking women and discouraging men from marrying.
2   St. Jerome lived in the late fourth and early fifth centuries and was a major theologian who
    wrote many influential works, including the one referred to here. Jerome's greatest work was
    translating the Bible into Latin.
3   Like Jankyn's *Valerie and Theofraste*, this book is a composite of several different works. Tertullian was
    an early third-century theologian who wrote several treatises about the value of virginity. Crisippus
    was mentioned in Jerome's treatise referred to in line 671, but none of his works survive. Trotula
    was a female doctor who taught medicine at the University of Salerno in the eleventh century and
    wrote a treatise about gynecology. Heloise tried to persuade her lover Abelard not to marry her,
    giving typical anti-matrimonial reasons. She eventually became the abbess of the Paraclete, a convent
    of nuns near Paris. Her arguments against marriage are preserved in Abelard's *Historia calamitatum*
    or *History of My Misfortunes* and in their letters, but Chaucer probably knew her only through *The
    Romance of the Rose*. Solomon's *Parables* is the book of Proverbs from the Bible. Ovid's *Art of Love*
    concludes with a long argument about why it is prudent to avoid love.
4   This is the title for the whole compendium volume mentioned above.
5   In medieval versions of the fable of Aesop, a man and a lion were having a dispute about who
    was the stronger. For proof, the man showed the lion a picture of a man killing a lion, and the

By God, if wommen hadde writen stories
As clerkes han° withinne hire oratories,°   *have, inside their chapels*
695 They wolde han writen of men moore° wikkednesse°   *more, wickedness*
Than al the mark of Adam° may redresse.°   *all the male gender, compensate for*
The children of Mercurie and Venus°   *i.e., scholars and lovers*
Been in hir wirkyng ful contrarius.[1]
Mercurie loveth° wysdam° and science,°   *loves, wisdom, knowledge*
700 And Venus loveth ryot° and dispence.°   *parties, squandering money*
And for hire diverse disposicioun,°   *their diverse natures*
Ech falleth in otheres exaltacioun.°[2]   *exaltation*
And thus, God woot,° Mercurie is desolat°   *God knows, desolate*
In Pisces,° wher Venus is exaltat.°   *Pisces (Zodiac sign), exalted*
705 And Venus falleth ther° Mercurie is reysed.°[3]   *falls where, raised*
Therfore no womman of no clerk° is preysed.   *theologian*
The clerk, whan he is oold° and may noght° do   *old, not*
Of Venus werkes° worth his olde sho,°   *Venus's works (sex), shoe*
Thanne sit he doun and writ in his dotage°   *old age*
710 That wommen kan nat kepe hir mariage.°   *marriage*
BUT now to purpos° why I tolde thee   *to the reason*
That I was beten° for a book, pardee.°   *beaten, by God*
Upon a nyght Jankyn that was oure sire°   *our [household's] master*
Redde° on his book as he sat by the fire   *read*
715 Of Eva° first, that for hir wikkednesse   *Eve*
Was al mankynde broght to wrecchednesse,
For which Crist hymself was slayn,°   *killed*
That boghte° us with his herte blood agayn.°   *who bought, again*
Lo heere,° expres° of womman may ye fynde,   *hear, specifically*
720 That womman was the los° of al mankynde.   *loss*
THO° redde° he me how Sampson[4] loste hise heres°   *there, read, his hairs*
Slepynge.° His lemman° kitte° it with hir sheres,°   *sleeping, lover, cut, scissors*
Thurgh° which tresoun° loste he bothe hise eyen.°   *through, betrayal, eyes*

---

     lion then asked the man who painted the lion. The implication is that the painting was biased
     and a different picture, painted by a lion, would look different. Then the lion ate the man. A
     Latin gloss in the margin asks "Who painted the lion?"

1   In addition to influencing the body's humors (see General Prologue, lines 413 ff), the planets
     were thought to govern various parts of the body and various trades. Mercury was the planet
     of scholars and merchants, so "the children of Mercury" here just means scholars, who, in their
     ways of doing things are completely at odds with lovers.

2   A Latin gloss in the margin notes "Each one falls where the other is exalted." A second gloss
     three lines later explains the astrological concept of "exaltation," the sign of the zodiac in which
     one planet's influence is strongest and that of an opposing planet is weakest, quoting Almansor's
     Aphorisms (see p. 159, note 3).

3   A Latin gloss above the word "reysed" notes "that is, in [the sign of] Virgo."

4   The reference is to Judges 16:15–22.

THO redde° he me, if that I shal nat lyen,°   *then read, not lie*
725 Of Hercules and of his Dianyre,[1]
That caused hym to sette hymself afyre.°   *on fire*
NOTHYNG forgat he° the sorwe and wo   *he did not at all forget*
That Socrates hadde with hise wyves two,
How Xantippa caste pisse° upon his heed.°   *threw urine, head*
730 This sely° man sat stille° as he were deed.°   *innocent, quietly, dead*
He wiped his heed. Namoore dorste he seyn°   *No more dared he say*
But, 'Er that thonder stynte, comth a reyn.'°   *Before thunder stops comes rain*
OF Phasifpha, that was the queene of Crete,
For shrewednesse° hym thoughte° the tale swete.°   *nastiness, he thought, sweet*
735 Fy!° Spek namoore!° It is a grisly° thyng,   *Fie, speak no more, horrible*
Of hire horrible lust° and hir likyng![2]   *pleasure*
OF Clitermystra,[3] for hire lecherye,
That falsly° made hire housbonde for to dye,°   *falsely, die*
He redde it with ful good devocioun.°   *much devotion*
740 HE tolde me eek for what occasioun°   *occasion*
Amphiorax at Thebes loste his lyf.[4]
Myn housbonde hadde a legende° of his wyf,   *story*
ERIPHILEM, that for an ouche° of gold   *brooch*
Hath prively° unto the Grekes° told   *secretly, Greeks*
745 Wher that hir housbonde hidde hym° in a place,   *hid himself*
For which he hadde at Thebes sory° grace.   *sorry*
OF Lyvia tolde he me and of Lucye.[5]
They bothe made hir housbondes for to dye°—   *caused their husbands to die*
That oon° for love, that oother was for hate.   *one*
750 Lyvia hir housbonde upon an even° late   *evening*
Empoysoned° hath,[6] for° that she was his fo.°   *poisoned, because, foe*
Lucia likerous° loved hire housbonde so,   *lustfully*
That, for he sholde° alwey° upon hire thynke,   *so that he should, always*

---

1   Deianira was the wife of Hercules and inadvertently caused his death by giving him a poisoned shirt that she thought would keep him faithful.

2   In Greek mythology, Queen Pasiphae of Crete had sex with a bull and gave birth to the monster Minotaur.

3   Clytemnestra and her lover Aegisthus murdered her husband Agamemnon when he returned from the Trojan war.

4   Amphiaraus hid so he would not have to fight in war, but his hiding place was betrayed by his wife Eriphyle, and he was killed in battle. There is a Latin gloss in the margin quoting the reference to Pasiphae, Clytemnestra, and Eriphyle in Jerome's *Against Jovinian*.

5   Livia was either Augustus's wife, who poisoned several prominent Romans (including her own husband) for political gain; or Livilla, Livia's granddaughter, who poisoned her husband at the instigation of her lover Sejanus. Lucilla poisoned her husband, the Roman philosopher Lucretius (c. 99–c. 55 BC), author of *On the Nature of Things*, with a love potion intended to increase his desire for her.

She yaf hym° swich a manere love drynke°   *gave him, type of love potion*
755 That he was deed° er° it were by the morwe.°   *dead, before, morning*
And thus algates° housbondes han sorwe.°   *always, have sorrow*
THANNE tolde he me how that oon° Latumyus[1]   *one*
Compleyned unto his felawe° Arrius   *friend*
That in his gardyn growed swich a tree
760 On which he seyde how that hise wyves thre
Hanged hemself° for herte despitus.°   *themselves, cruel heart*
'O leeve° brother,' quod this Arrius,   *dear*
'Yif° me a plante° of thilke° blissed° tree,   *give, seedling, that, blessed*
And in my gardyn planted it shal bee!'°   *shall be*
765 OF latter date of wyves hath he red,
That somme han slayn hir housbondes in hir bed
And lete hir lecchour dighte hire al the nyght[2]
Whan that the corps° lay in the floor upright.   *body*
AND somme han dryve nayles° in hir brayn°[3]   *have driven nails, their brain*
770 Whil that they slepte, and thus they han hem slayn.
SOMME han hem yeve poysoun in hire drynke.[4]
He spak moore harm than herte may bithynke.°   *consider*
And therwithal° he knew of mo proverbes   *with all this*
Than in this world ther growen gras or herbes.
775 'Bet° is,' quod he, 'thyn habitacioiun°   *better, your dwelling place*
Be with a leoun or a foul dragoun
Than with a womman usynge for to chyde.°   *who is accustomed to nag*
Bet is,' quod he, 'hye° in the roof abyde°   *high, live*
Than with an angry wyf doun in the hous.
780 They been° so wikked and contrarious.°   *are, disagreeable*
They haten that hir housbondes loveth ay.'[5]
He seyde, 'A womman cast° hir shame away   *throws*
Whan she cast of hir smok. And forthermo,[6]
A fair womman but° she be chaast° also   *unless, chaste*
785 Is lyk° a gold ryng in a sowes° nose.'[7]   *like, pig's*
Who wolde leeve or who wolde suppose°   *would believe*
The wo that in myn herte was and pyne?°   *pain*
AND whan I saugh he wolde nevere fyne°   *stop*
To reden on this cursed book al nyght,

---

1   The incident related below is another misogynistic story from ancient Rome, for which
    Chaucer's source is probably Walter Map's *Dissuasio Valerii* (see p. 161, note 1).
2   "And let her lover have sex with her all night."
3   The reference here is perhaps to Judges 4:17–22.
4   "Some have given them poison in their drink."
5   "They always hate what their husbands love."
6   "When she throws off her undergarment. And furthermore."
7   There is a Latin gloss in the margin quoting the original saying from Proverbs 11:22.

790 Al sodeynly° thre leves° have I plyght°	*suddenly, pages, torn*
Out of his book, right as he radde. And eke	
I with my fest° so took° hym on the cheke,°	*fist, hit, cheek*
That in oure fyr he fil bakward adoun.°	*fell down backwards*
And he up stirte° as dooth° a wood leoun,°	*jumps, does, crazy lion*
795 And with his fest° he smoot° me on the heed,°	*fist, hit, head*
That° in the floor° I lay as I were deed.°	*so that, on the floor, dead*
And whan he saugh how stille° that I lay,	*quietly*
He was agast° and wolde han fled his way.°	*afraid, have fled away*
Til atte laste° out of my swogh° I breyde.°	*at the last, faint, awoke*
800 'O hastow slayn° me, false theef?'° I seyde.	*have you killed, thief*
'And for my land thus hastow° mordred° me!	*have you, murdered*
Er I be deed,° yet wol I kisse thee.'	*before I am dead*
AND neer° he cam and kneled faire° adoun	*near, kneeled pleasantly*
And seyde, 'Deere suster° Alisoun,	*dear sister*
805 As help me God, I shal thee nevere smyte!	
That I have doon,° it is thyself to wyte.°	*what I have done, to blame*
Foryeve° it me, and that I thee biseke.'°	*forgive, beg you*
And yet eftsoones° I hitte hym on the cheke	*once more*
And seyde, 'Theef, thus muchel° am I wreke.°	*much, avenged*
810 Now wol I dye. I may no lenger speke.'	
But atte laste° with muchel° care and wo,	*at the last, much*
We fille acorded° by usselven° two.	*came to an agreement, ourselves*
He yaf° me al the bridel° in myn hond°	*gave, bridle, my hand*
To han° the governance° of hous° and lond°	*have, control, house, land*
815 And of his tonge° and his hond also,	*tongue*
And made hym brenne his book anon° right tho.°	*immediately, there*
And whan that I hadde geten° unto me	*had gotten*
By maistrie° al the soveraynetee,°	*mastery, sovereignty*
And that he seyde, 'Myn owene trewe wyf,	
820 Do as thee lust to terme of al thy lyf.[1]	
Keepe thyn honour and keepe eek myn estaat.'°	*my estate*
After that day we hadden never debaat.°	*never had disagreement*
God helpe me so, I was to hym as kynde	
As any wyf from Denmark unto Ynde°	*India*
825 And also trewe, and so was he to me.	
I prey° to God that sit in magestee,°	*pray, who sits in majesty*
So blesse his soule° for his mercy deere.°	*soul, dear*
Now wol I seye° my tale, if ye wol heere."°	*tell, will hear*

---

1   "Do as you wish as long as you live."

BIHOLDE THE WORDES BITWENE THE SOMONOUR AND THE
FRERE[1]

THE Frere° lough° whan he hadde herd al this.   *Friar, laughed*
830 "Now Dame," quod he, "so have I joye or blis,°   *bliss*
This is a long preamble° of a tale!"   *preamble (prologue)*
And whan the Somonour herde the Frere gale,°   *speak up*
"Lo," quod the Somonour, "Goddes armes two![2]
A frere wol entremette hym evere mo![3]
835 Lo, goode men, a flye° and eek a frere   *fly*
Wol falle in every dyssh and mateere![4]
What spekestow of preambulacioun?°   *what do you say of preambling*
What! Amble or trotte° or pees° or go sit doun!°   *trot, pace, down*
Thou° lettest° oure disport° in this manere."°   *you, spoil, fun, manner*
840 "YE, woltow so,° sire Somonour?" quod the Frere.   *will you [say] so*
"Now by my feith,° I shal° er° that I go   *faith, shall, before*
Telle of a somonour swich a tale or two,
That alle the folk shal laughen in this place!"
"Now elles,° Frere, I bishrewe° thy face!"   *otherwise, curse*
845 Quod this Somonour, "and I bishrewe me
But° if I telle tales two or thre°   *unless, three*
Of freres er° I come to Sidyngborne![5]   *before*
That I shal make thyn herte for to morne,°   *be sorry*
For wel I woot° thy pacience° is gon."°   *well I know, patience, gone*
850 OURE Hoost cride, "Pees,° and that anon!"°   *peace, immediately*
And seyde, "Lat the womman telle hire tale.
Ye fare° as folk that dronken were of ale!   *you behave*
Do, Dame, telle forth youre tale, and that is best."
"ALREDY,° sire,"° quod she, "right as yow lest,°   *ready, sir, you wish*
855 If I have licence of this worthy Frere."
"YIS, dame," quod he, "tel forth, and I wol heere."

HEERE ENDETH THE WYF OF BATHE HIR PROLOGE AND
BIGYNNETH HIR TALE[6]

---

1   "Behold the words between the Summoner and the Friar."
2   "God's two arms." This is an oath like those uniformly condemned by the Church.
3   "A friar will always put himself in the middle [of things]."
4   "Will fall into every dish and matter."
5   Sittingbourne is a small town about forty miles from London on the road to Canterbury.
6   "Here ends the Wife of Bath's Prologue and [here] begins her tale."

THE WIFE OF BATH'S TALE

In th'olde° dayes of Kyng Arthour, — *the old*
Of which that Britons speken greet honour,
Al was this land fulfild° of fairye.[1] — *filled up with*
860 The Elf Queene with hir joly compaignye° — *jolly company*
Daunced ful ofte° in many a grene mede.° — *very often, green meadow*
This was the olde opinion as I rede.° — *read*
I speke of manye hundred yeres ago.
But now kan° no man se none elves mo.° — *can, no more elves*
865 For now the grete charitee and prayeres° — *charity and prayers*
Of lymytours[2] and othere hooly freres° — *holy friars*
That serchen° every lond° and every streem° — *search, land, stream*
As thikke as motes° in the sonne beem,° — *dust particles, sunbeam*
Blessynge° halles, chambres,° kichenes,° boures,° — *blessing, rooms, kitchens, bedrooms*
870 Citees, burghes,° castels, hye toures,° — *fortified cities, high towers*
Thropes,° bernes,° shipnes,° dayeryes°— — *villages, barns, stables, dairies*
This maketh° that ther been° no fairyes. — *causes it, there are*
For theras° wont° to walken° was an elf, — *where, accustomed, walk*
Ther walketh now the lymytour° hymself — *friar*
875 In undermeles and in morwenynges,° — *late and early mornings*
And seyth° his matyns° and his hooly thynges° — *says, morning service, prayers*
As he gooth° in his lymytacioun.° — *goes about, limited area*
Wommen may go saufly° up and doun° — *safely, down*
In every bussh or under every tree.
880 Ther is noon oother° incubus[3] but he. — *no other*
And he ne wol doon hem but dishonour.° — *will do them [nothing] but dishonor*
And so bifel° that this Kyng Arthour — *it happened*
Hadde° in hous° a lusty bacheler° — *had, house, young knight*
That on a day cam ridynge° fro ryver° — *came riding, from [a] river*
885 And happed° that allone° as he was born, — *happened, alone*
He saugh a mayde° walkynge hym biforn,° — *maid, walking in front of him*
Of which mayde anon, maugree hir heed,° — *against her will*
By verray° force birafte hire maydenhed,° — *true, stole from her her virginity*
For which oppressioun° was swich° clamour° — *oppression, such, outcry*
890 And swich pursute° unto the Kyng Arthour, — *appeal*

---

1 "Fairye" is a term which here loosely refers to the supernatural beings from the mythical Otherworld known as elves or fairies. Though they have no place in the dominant medieval Christian ideology, such beings maintained a hold on people's imaginations through folktale and legend.

2 A "lymytour," as the word partially suggests, was a friar who was licensed to preach in a limited area in a parish or county.

3 In folklore, an incubus was a devilish spirit who would appear to women in dreams and thereby impregnate them.

es of kyng Arthour
t Britons speken greet honour
And fulfild of fairye
ne With his wyf compaignye
a grene mede
as yede
yeres ago
one elues no
And prayeres
hooly freres
o euery streem
comune beem
kichenes boures
e tounes
Ayeryes
no fairyes
was an elf
my hym self
cuyuges
his hooly thynges
n
us oon
tree
us but he
t disshonour
Arthour
yster

Detail, opening page of *The Wife of Bath's Tale*. Ellesmere Manuscript EL 26 C9 f. 72r. Reprinted by permission of The Huntington Library.

That dampned° was this knyght for to be deed°   *condemned, dead*
By cours° of lawe, and sholde han° lost his heed.   *course, should have*
Paraventure° swich was the statut° tho,°   *by chance, law, then*
But that the queene and othere ladyes mo
895 So longe preyden° the kyng of grace,°   *requested, mercy*
Til he his lyf hym graunted° in the place   *granted*
And yaf° hym to the queene al at hir wille°   *gave, will*
To chese° wheither° she wolde hym save or spille.°   *choose, whether, kill*
THE queene thanketh the kyng with al hir myght
900 And after this thus spak she to the knyght
Whan that she saugh hir tyme° upon a day,   *saw her time*
"Thou standest yet," quod she, "in swich array,°   *condition*
That of thy lyf yet hastow° no suretee.°   *have you, certainty*
I grante thee lyf if thou kanst° tellen me   *can*
905 What thyng is it that wommen moost desiren.
Bewar° and keepe thy nekke boon° from iren!°   *beware, neckbone, iron*
And if thou kanst nat tellen° it anon,   *cannot tell*
Yet shal I yeve° thee leve° for to gon°   *give, leave, go*
A twelf month° and a day to seche° and leere°   *for a year, seek, learn*
910 An answere suffisant° in this mateere.°   *sufficient, matter*
And suretee° wol I han er° that thou pace°—   *guarantee, will I have before, leave*
Thy body for to yelden° in this place."   *yield (i.e., return)*
Wo° was this knyght, and sorwefully he siketh,°   *sad, sighs*
But he may nat do al as hym liketh.°   *as he wishes*
915 And at the laste he chees° hym for to wende°   *chooses, go*
And come agayn° right at the yeres° ende   *again, year's*
With swich answere as God wolde° hym purveye°   *would, provide him*
And taketh his leve and wendeth° forth his weye.   *goes*
HE seketh every hous and every place
920 Whereas° he hopeth for to fynde° grace   *where, find*
To lerne what thyng wommen loven moost.
But he ne koude arryven° in no coost,°   *arrive, region*
Wheras he myghte fynde in this mateere
Two creatures accordynge° in feere.°   *agreeing, together*
925 SOMME seyde° wommen loven best richesse.   *some said*
Somme seyde honour. Somme seyde jolynesse,°   *jollity*
Somme riche array.° Somme seyden lust abedde°   *clothing, in bed*
And oftetyme° to be wydwe° and wedde.°   *often, widowed, married*
SOMME seyde that oure hertes been moost esed°   *most refreshed*
930 Whan that we been yflatered° and yplesed.°[1]   *are flattered, pleased*
HE gooth ful ny the sothe, I wol nat lye![2]

---

1   A Latin gloss in the margin notes "Titus Liveus," indicating that this opinion can be found in
     the writings of Titus Livius (59 BC–17 AD), presumably in his famous *History of Rome*.
2   "He gets very near the truth, I will not lie."

A man shal wynne° us best with flaterye°   *shall win, flattery*
And with attendance° and with bisynesse,   *attention*
Been we° ylymed[1] bothe moore and lesse.   *we are*

935 AND somme seyn that we loven best
For to be free and so do right as us lest°   *just as we wish*
And that no man repreve us° of oure vice   *complain to us*
But seye that we be wise and nothyng nyce.°   *not foolish*
For trewely, ther is noon° of us alle   *none*

940 If any wight° wol° clawe° us on the galle°   *person, will, claw, a sore*
That we nel kike,° for he seith° us sooth.°   *will not kick, says, truth*
Assay° and he shal fynde it that so dooth.°   *try, does so*
For be° we never so vicious° withinne,°   *are, wicked, within*
We wol been holden wise° and clene of synne.°   *wish to be considered, free of sin*

945 AND somme seyn that greet delit° han° we   *great delight, have*
For to been holden° stable and eek secree,°   *considered, also discreet*
And in o° purpos stedefastly° to dwelle   *one, steadfastly*
And nat biwreye° thyng° that men us telle.   *not betray, something*
But that tale is nat worth a rake-stele!°   *handle of a rake*

950 Pardee, we wommen konne nothyng hele![2]
Witnesse on Myda.[3] Wol ye heere the tale?
OVYDE° amonges° othere thyngs smale°   *Ovid, among, small works*
Seyde Myda° hadde° under his longe heres°   *Midas, had, hairs*
Growynge° upon his heed two asses eres,°   *growing, ears*

955 The which vice he hydde° as he best myghte°   *hid, might*
Ful subtilly° from every mannes sighte,°   *very carefully, man's sight*
That save his wyf, ther wiste° of it namo.°   *knew, no more*
He loved hire moost and triste° hire also.   *trusted*
He preyde° hire that to no creature   *asked*

960 She sholde tellen° of his disfigure.°   *would tell, disfigurement*
SHE swoor° hym nay° for al this world to wynne.°   *swore, no, gain*
She nolde° do that vileynye° or synne°   *would not, villainy, sin*
To make hir housbonde han° so foul a name.   *have*
She nolde nat° telle it for hir owene shame.   *would not*

965 But nathelees,° hir thoughte that she dyde,°   *nevertheless, she thought would die*
That she so longe sholde° a conseil° hyde.°   *should, secret, hide*
Hir thoughte it swal so soore aboute hir herte[4]
That nedely som word hire moste asterte.[5]

---

1   "Limed." Lime was used to form a sticky paste that was spead on sticks to catch birds.
2   "By God, we women know nothing about how to hold [a secret]."
3   Midas's story, which the Wife of Bath recounts below, is found in Ovid's *Metamorphoses*, Book
     11, although in Ovid's version it is the king's barber, not his wife, who whispers the secret.
4   "It seemed to her that it became so sorely swollen around her heart."
5   "That by necessity some word had to blurt out from her."

And sith° she dorste° telle it to no man,   *since, dare*
970 Doun to a mareys° faste by° she ran,   *marsh, close by*
Til she cam there° hir herte was afyre.°   *where, on fire*
And as a bitore° bombleth° in the myre,°   *bittern (small heron), calls, mud*
She leyde° hir mouth unto the water doun.   *laid*
"Biwreye° me nat, thou water, with thy soun,"°   *betray, sound*
975 Quod she, "To thee I telle it and namo.°   *nobody else*
Myn housbonde hath longe asses erys° two!   *asses' ears*
Now is myn herte al hool.° Now is it oute.   *whole*
I myghte no lenger kepe it out of doute."°   *without doubt*
Heere may ye se thogh we a tyme° abyde,°   *for a time, wait*
980 Yet out it moot.° We kan no conseil hyde.   *must [go]*
The remenant of the tale if ye wol heere,
Redeth Ovyde,° and ther ye may it leere.°   *Ovid, learn*
THIS knyght of which my tale is specially,
Whan that he saugh he myghte nat° come therby,   *might not*
985 This is to sey, what wommen love moost,
Withinne his brest ful sorweful° was the goost.°   *very sorrowful, spirit*
But hoom he gooth.° He myghte nat sojourne.°   *goes, not delay*
The day was come that homward moste° he tourne.°   *must, turn*
And in his wey it happed° hym to ryde   *happened*
990 In al this care under a forest syde
Wheras° he saugh° upon a daunce°[1] go   *where, saw, dance*
Of ladyes foure and twenty and yet mo,
Toward the which daunce he drow ful yerne°   *drew very eagerly*
In hope that som wysdom sholde° he lerne.   *should*
995 But certeinly er° he cam fully there,   *before*
Vanysshed was this daunce he nyste° where.   *did not know*
No creature saugh he that bar lyf,°   *bore life*
Save on the grene° he saugh sittynge° a wyf.   *green (meadow), sitting*
A fouler wight° ther may no man devyse.°   *uglier person, imagine*
1000 Agayn° the knyght this olde wyf gan ryse°   *towards, rose*
And seyde, "Sire Knyght, heer forth ne lith° no wey.°   *lies, road*
Tel me what that ye seken by youre fey.°   *faith*
Paraventure° it may the bettre° be.   *perhaps, better*
Thise° olde folk kan muchel thyng,"° quod she.   *these, know many things*
1005 "My leeve mooder,"° quod this knyght certeyn,°   *dear mother, certainly*
"I nam° but deed but if° that I kan seyn°   *am not, unless, can say*
What thyng it is that wommen moost desire.
Koude ye me wisse, I wolde wel quite youre hire."[2]

---

1   One traditional way mortals encounter elves is in the woods at night, where they are performing a ritual dance.

2   "If you could inform me, I would pay you back well."

"PLIGHT° me thy trouthe° heere° in myn hand," quod she.   *pledge, word, here*

1010 "The nexte thyng that I requere thee,°   *ask of you*

Thou shalt it do if it lye in thy myght,°   *your might*

And I wol telle it yow° er it be nyght."   *to you*

"HAVE heer° my trouthe," quod the knyght. "I grante."   *here*

"THANNE," quod she, "I dar° me wel avante.°   *dare, well boast*

1015 Thy lyf is sauf,° for I wol stonde therby.°   *safe, by it*

Upon my lyf the queene wol seye as I.

Lat se° which is the proudeste of hem alle   *let's see*

That wereth° on a coverchief° or a calle°   *wears, kerchief, hairnet*

That dar seye nay° of that I shal thee teche.°   *dare says no, teach*

1020 Lat us go forth withouten lenger speche."°   *longer speech*

Tho° rowned° she a pistel° in his ere°   *then, whispered, lesson, ear*

And bad hym° to be glad and have no fere.°   *commanded him, fear*

WHAN they be comen° to the court, this knyght   *they have arrived*

Seyde he had holde° his day as he hadde hight°   *kept, had promised*

1025 And redy was his answere, as he sayde.

Full° many a noble wyf and many a mayde   *very*

And many a wydwe,° for that they been° wise,   *widow, are*

The queene° hirself sittynge as justise,°   *[with] the queen, sitting as a judge*

Assembled been° his answere for to heere.   *are gathered*

1030 And afterward this knyght was bode appeere.°   *commanded to appear*

To every wight comanded was silence

And that the knyght sholde° telle in audience°   *should, in [their] hearing*

What thyng that worldly wommen loven best.

This knyght ne stood nat stille° as doth a best,°   *did not stand quietly, beast*

1035 But to his questioun anon° answerde   *immediately*

With manly voys° that al the court it herde.   *voice*

"MY lige° lady generally," quod he,   *sovereign*

"Wommen desiren have sovereynetee°   *desire to have sovereignty*

As wel° over hir housbond as hir love   *well*

1040 And for to been in maistrie hym above.°   *to be in control over him*

This is youre mooste desir,° thogh ye me kille.   *greatest desire*

Dooth as yow list.° I am at youre wille."   *do as you wish*

IN al the court ne was ther° wyf ne mayde   *there was neither*

Ne wydwe° that contraried that° he sayde   *widow, disagreed with what*

1045 But seyden° he was worthy han his lyf.°   *said, have his life*

AND with that word up stirte° the olde wyf   *up jumped*

Which that the knyght saugh sittynge in the grene.°   *meadow*

"Mercy," quod she, "my sovereyn° lady queene!   *sovereign*

Er° that youre court departe, do me right.   *before*

1050 I taughte this answere unto the knyght,

For which he plighte° me his trouthe° there.   *promised, word*

The firste thyng I wolde° hym requere,°   *would, require of him*

He wolde it do if it lay in his myght.
Bifore the court thanne preye° I thee, Sire Knyght," | ask
1055 Quod she, "that thou me take unto thy wyf.
For wel thou woost° that I have kept° thy lyf. | you know, saved
If I seye fals,° sey nay,° upon thy fey!"° | say false, no, faith
THIS knyght answerde, "Allas° and weylawey! | Alas
I woot° right wel that swich was my biheste.° | know, promise
1060 For Goddes love, as chees° a newe requeste! | choose
Taak° al my good,° and lat° my body go!" | take, possessions, let
"NAY thanne,"° quod she, "I shrewe° us bothe two, | no then, curse
For thogh° that I be foul, oold, and poore, | though
I nolde° for al the metal° ne for oore° | would not, [precious] metal, ore
1065 That under erthe° is grave° or lith° above | earth, buried, lies
But if thy wyf I were and eek thy love!"
"MY love!" quod he. "Nay, my dampnacioun!° | damnation
Allas, that any of my nacioun° | family
Sholde evere so foule disparaged° be!" | badly shamed
1070 But al for noght!° Th'end° is this: that he | nothing, the end
Constreyned° was. He nedes moste hire wedde° | compelled, had to marry her
And taketh his olde wyf and gooth to bedde.
NOW wolden som men seye paraventure° | perhaps
That for my necligence° I do no cure° | negligence, do not care
1075 To tellen yow the joye and al th'array° | the arrangements
That at the feeste° was that ilke° day | feast, same
To which thyng shortly answere I shal.
I seye ther nas no° joye ne feeste at al. | was no
Ther nas° but hevynesse and muche sorwe.° | was nothing, depression,
1080 For prively he wedded hire on a morwe,° | morning
And al day after hidde hym° as an owle.° | hid himself, owl
So wo° was hym,° his wyf looked so foule. | sorrowful, him
GREET was the wo the knyght hadde in his thoght
Whan he was with his wyf abedde ybroght.°[1] | brought to bed
1085 He walweth,° and he turneth to and fro. | writhes about
His olde wyf lay smylynge° evere mo | smiling
And seyde, "O deere housbonde, benedicitee!° | bless you
Fareth° every knyght thus with his wyf as ye? | behaves
Is this the lawe of Kyng Arthures hous?
1090 Is every knyght of his so dangerous?° | standoffish
I am youre owene love and youre wyf.
I am she which that saved hath youre lyf.
And certes, yet ne dide° I yow nevere unright.° | did not, unjustice

---

1 In medieval weddings, it was the custom for the guests to escort the bride and groom to their bedroom.

Why fare° ye thus with me this firste nyght?   *behave*
1095 Ye faren° lyk a man had lost his wit.   *behave*
What is my gilt?° For Goddes love, tel it,   *guilt*
And it shal been amended° if I may."   *fixed*
"AMENDED!" quod this knyght. "Allas, nay! Nay!
It wol nat been amended nevere mo.°   *forever more*
1100 Thou art so loothly° and so oold° also   *ugly, old*
And therto comen° of so lough° a kynde,°   *come, low, lineage*
That litel wonder is thogh° I walwe° and wynde.°   *though, writhe, twist about*
So wolde God myn herte wolde breste!"°   *burst*
"Is this," quod she, "the cause of youre unreste?"
1105 "YE, certeinly," quod he, "no wonder is!"
"NOW sire," quod she, "I koude amende° al this   *could fix*
If that me liste° er° it were dayes thre,°   *if I wished, before, three days*
So wel ye myghte bere yow unto me.[1]
BUT for ye speken° of swich gentillesse°[2]   *you speak, such nobility*
1110 As is descended out of old richesse,
That therfore sholden° ye be gentilmen,   *should*
Swich arrogance is nat° worth an hen!   *not*
Looke who that is moost vertuous alway,
Pryvee° and apert° and moost entendeth ay°   *private, open, always tries most*
1115 To do the gentil dedes° that he kan.°[3]   *noble deeds, can*
Taak hym° for the grettest gentilman.   *take him*
Crist wole° we clayme° of hym oure gentillesse,   *will, claim*
Nat of oure eldres° for hire old richesse.   *ancestors*
For thogh they yeve us al hir° heritage,   *their*
1120 For which we clayme° to been° of heigh parage,°   *claim, be, high lineage*
Yet may they nat biquethe° for nothyng°   *not bequeath, nothing*
To noon° of us hir° vertuous lyvyng.°   *none, their, living*
That made hem° gentilmen ycalled be°   *them, be called*
And bad us folwen hem° in swich° degree.   *requested us to follow them, such*
1125 WEL kan° the wise poete of Florence   *well can*
That highte Dant° spoken in this sentence.°   *is named Dante, matter*
Lo, in swich maner rym° is Dantes tale: *such a kind of rhyme*
'Ful selde° up riseth° by his branches smale°   *seldom, rises, small*
Prowesse° of man.[4] For God of his goodnesse   *strength*

---

1   "Provided that you might behave yourself well towards me."
2   "Gentillesse" is the quality that makes someone a gentleman or woman. In the Middle Ages it normally implied distinguished birth but also refined manners and moral virtue. There is a Latin gloss in the margin "About generosity."
3   "Look for whoever is always most virtuous in private and in public and always strives to do the most noble deeds."
4   "The excellence of a man seldom extends to the further branches [of his family tree]," i.e., the sons are seldom worthy of the father. Dante said something similar to the old woman's comment in his *Convivio*, 4 and in *Purgatorio* 7:121.

1130 Wole° that of hym we clayme° oure gentillesse.'   wishes, claim
For of oure eldres° may we nothyng clayme   ancestors
But temporel thyng° that man may hurte and mayme.°   temporal things, maim
EEK every wight woot° this as wel as I.   every person knows
If gentillesse were planted natureelly°   implanted by nature
1135 Unto a certeyn lynage° doun the lyne,°   particular lineage, down the line [of generations]
Pryvee nor apert thanne wolde they nevere fyne°   stop
To doon° of gentillesse the faire office.¹   do
They myghte do no vileynye° or vice.   villainy
TAAK° fyr° and ber° it in the derkeste° hous   take, fire, carry, darkest
1140 Bitwix° this and the mount of Kaukasous°   between, Caucasus
And lat men shette° the dores° and go thenne,°   shut, doors, go away
Yet wole° the fyr as faire lye° and brenne°   will, blaze, burn
As twenty thousand men myghte it biholde.°   behold
His° office natureel ay° wol it holde,   its, ever
1145 Up peril of my lyf, til that it dye.²
HEERE may ye se wel how that genterye³
Is nat annexed° to possessioun,   linked
Sith folk ne doon hir operacioun°   do not behave
Alwey as dooth the fyr, lo, in his kynde.°   according to its nature
1150 For God it woot,° men may wel° often fynde°   God knows it, well, find
A lordes sone° do shame and vileynye,°   son, villainy
And he that wole han° pris° of his gentrye,   will have, honor
For he was born of a gentil hous°   noble house
And hadde hise eldres° noble and vertuous   his ancestors
1155 And nel hymselven° do no gentil dedis°   will not himself, deeds
Ne folwen° his gentil auncestre that deed° is.   nor follow, dead
He nys nat° gentil be he duc° or erl,°   is not, duke, earl
For vileyns° synful dedes° make a cherl.°   villainous, sinful deeds, churl
For gentillesse nys° but renomee°   is not, renown
1160 Of thyne auncestres for hire heigh bountee,°   their high goodness
Which is a strange thyng to thy persone.°   thing alien to your person
Thy gentillesse cometh fro God allone.
Thanne comth oure verray gentillesse of grace.
It was nothyng biquethe us° with oure place.   by no means bequeathed to us
1165 THENKETH how noble as seith Valerius
Was thilke° Tullius Hostillius,⁴   that
That out of poverte roos° to heigh noblesse.   rose

---

1   "Then they would never stop [fyne] doing the fair office of gentle deeds, either in private or in
     public."
2   "Upon my life, it will always perform its natural function (i.e., burn) until it dies."
3   A Latin gloss in the margin notes "Exemplum," showing that here there is a moral example.
4   Tullius Hostillius in ancient Rome started life as a peasant and rose to become king. The story is told
     by the Roman writer Valerius Maximus (see p. 155, note 1).

Reed Senek° and redeth eek Boece.°¹	*Seneca, Boethius*
Ther shul ye seen expres° that no drede° is	*specifically, doubt*
1170 That he is gentil that dooth gentil dedis.	
And therfore, leeve° housbonde, I thus conclude,	*dear*
Al° were it that myne auncestres weren rude,°	*although, of low birth*
Yet may the hye° God—and so hope I—	*high*
Grante me grace to lyven° vertuously.	*live*
1175 Thanne am I gentil whan that I bigynne°	*begin*
To lyven° vertuously and weyve synne.°	*live, avoid sin*
AND theras° ye of poverte me repreeve,°²	*since, reproach*
The hye° God on whom that we bileeve°	*high, believe*
In wilful poverte° chees° to lyve his lyf.	*voluntary poverty, chose*
1180 And certes, every man, mayden, or wyf	
May understonde that Jhesus Hevene kyng°	*king of Heaven*
Ne wolde nat chesen° vicious° lyvyng.	*would not choose, evil*
Glad° poverte is an honeste° thyng, certeyn.³	*joyful, virtuous*
This wole° Senec and othere clerkes° seyn.°	*will, writers, say*
1185 Whoso that halt hym payd of his poverte,⁴	
I holde hym° riche, al° hadde he nat a sherte.°	*consider him, though, shirt*
He that coveiteth° is a povere wight,°	*covets, poor person*
For he wolde han that° is nat in his myght.	*would have what*
But he that noght hath ne coveiteth have°	*has nothing and does not covet*
1190 Is riche, although ye holde hym° but a knave.	*consider him*
VERRAY poverte,° it syngeth° properly.	*true poverty, sings*
Juvenal⁵ seith of poverte myrily,°	*merrily*
'The povre man, whan he goth by the weye,°	*goes along the road*
Bifore the theves° he may synge and pleye.'	*thieves*
1195 Poverte is hateful good and, as I gesse,⁶	
A ful greet bryngere° out of bisynesse,°	*very great remover, anxiety*
A greet amendere° eek of sapience°	*improver, wisdom*
To hym that taketh° it in pacience.°	*takes, patience*
Poverte is this, although it seme° alenge,°	*seem, wretched*
1200 Possessioun° that no wight° wol chalenge.°	*possession, person, will claim*

---

1   See Boethius's *Consolation of Philosophy*, book 3, prose 6 and meter 3.

2   There is a Latin gloss in the margin: "On poverty."

3   A Latin gloss in the margin quotes the saying and notes that it comes from the epistles of Seneca, the Stoic philosopher (c. 5 BC–65 AD).

4   "Whoever considers himself satisfied with his poverty." There is a Latin gloss in the margin that closely follows lines 1186–90 and notes a similar moral in Revelation 3:17. The source for this Latin passage has not been identified, and it may in fact be based directly on Chaucer's own text.

5   There is a Latin gloss in the margin that quotes and identifies Chaucer's source, the *Satires* of the Roman poet Juvenal (first century AD).

6   A Latin gloss in the margin cites a discussion of poverty attributed to the Roman philosopher Secundus that is found in the thirteenth-century encyclopedia of Vincent of Beauvais, beginning "poverty is a hateful good."

Poverte ful ofte° whan a man is lowe   *very often*
Maketh° his God and eek hymself to knowe.[1]   *causes*
Poverte a spectacle is, as thynketh me,°   *as it seems to me*
Thurgh° which he may hise° verray freendes° see.   *through, his, true friends*
1205 And therfore sire, syn that I noght yow greve,°   *do not grieve you*
Of my poverte namoore° ye me repreve.°   *no more, reproach*
Now sire, of elde° ye repreve me,[2]   *old age*
And certes, sire, thogh noon auctoritee
Were in no book, ye gentils° of honour   *nobles*
1210 Seyn that men sholde an oold wight doon favour°   *do honor*
And clepe° hym fader for youre gentillesse.   *call*
And auctours° shal I fynden,° as I gesse.   *authors, find*
Now ther° ye seye that I am foul° and old.[3]   *where, ugly*
Than drede° you noght° to been a cokewold.°   *fear, not, cuckold*
1215 For filthe° and eelde,° also moot I thee,°   *ugliness, old age, might I thrive*
Been grete wardeyns upon chastitee.°   *guardians of chastity*
But nathelees,° syn I knowe youre delit,°   *nevertheless, delight*
I shal fulfille youre worldly appetit.°   *appetite*
CHESE° now," quod she, "oon of thise thynges tweye:°   *choose, these two things*
1220 To han° me foul and old til that I deye°   *have, until I die*
And be to yow a trewe, humble wyf
And nevere yow displese° in al my lyf,   *displease you*
Or elles° ye wol han° me yong and fair   *else, will have*
And take youre aventure° of the repair°   *chance, visiting*
1225 That shal be to youre hous bycause of me
Or in som oother place may wel be.[4]
Now chese yourselven wheither that yow liketh."°   *whichever pleases you*
THIS knyght avyseth° hym and sore siketh.°   *considers, sorely sighs*
But atte laste° he seyde in this manere,   *at the last*
1230 "My lady and my love and wyf so deere,
I put me in youre wise governance.
Cheseth youreself which may be moost plesance°   *most pleasant*
And moost honour to yow and me also.
I do no fors° the wheither of the two,   *I do not care*
1235 For as yow liketh, it suffiseth me."
"THANNE have I gete° of yow maistrie," quod she,   *gotten*
"Syn I may chese and governe as me lest?"°   *as I wish*

---

1   There is a Latin gloss in the margin that refers to the story of the Stoic philosopher Crates of
    Thebes, who threw his gold into the sea lest it destroy him. The story comes from Jerome's
    Against Jovinian 2:9.
2   There is a Latin gloss in the margin: "On old age."
3   There is a Latin gloss in the margin: "On foulness."
4   "And take your chances (*aventure*) of the visiting (*repair*) [i.e., by lovers] at your house, or perhaps
    in some other places, in order to see me."

"Ye° certes, wyf," quod he, "I holde it best."　　　　　　　　*yes*
"Kys me," quod she, "we be no lenger wrothe.°　　　　　　*no longer angry*
1240　For by my trouthe,° I wol be to yow bothe.　　　　　　　*truth*
This is to seyn, ye bothe° fair and good.　　　　　　　　　*indeed both*
I prey° to God that I moote° sterven wood°　　*pray, might, die crazy*
But° I to yow be also good and trewe　　　　　　　　　　*unless*
As evere was wyf, syn that the world was newe.
1245　And but° I be tomorn° as fair to seene°　　　*unless, tomorrow, see*
As any lady, emperice,° or queene　　　　　　　　　　*empress*
That is bitwixe° the est° and eke the west,　　　*between, east*
Dooth° with my lyf and deth right as yow lest.°　*do, just as you wish*
Cast up the curtyn.° Looke how that it is."　　　　　　　*curtain*
1250　And whan the knyght saugh veraily al this,
That she so fair was and so yong therto,
For joye he hente hire° in hise armes two.　　　　　　　　*held her*
His herte° bathed in a bath of blisse.　　　　　　　　　　*heart*
A thousand tyme arewe° he gan hire kisse.°　　*in a row, kissed her*
1255　And she obeyed hym in everythyng
That myghte doon hym plesance or likyng.°　*do him pleasure or enjoyment*
And thus they lyve unto hir lyves ende
In parfit° joye. And Jhesu Crist us sende　　　　　　　　*perfect*
Housbondes meeke,° yonge, and fressh abedde°　　　*meek, in bed*
1260　And grace to t'overbyde hem° that we wedde.　　　　*control them*
And eek I pray Jhesu shorte hir lyves°　　　　　*shorten their lives*
That nat wol be° governed by hir wyves.　　　　　　　*will not be*
And olde and angry nygardes° of dispence,°　　*skinflints, spending*
God sende hem soone verray pestilence!°　　　　　　*true plague*

HEERE ENDETH THE WYVES TALE OF BATHE[1]

1　"Here ends the Wife of Bath's Tale."

The Friar (179)

THE FRIAR'S PROLOGUE AND TALE

THE PROLOGE OF THE FRERES TALE

1265 THIS worthy lymytour,[1] this noble Frere,° — *friar*
He made alwey° a maner louryng chiere° — *always, kind of scowling expression*
Upon the Somonour. But for honestee° — *decency*
No vileyns° word as yet to hym° spak° he. — *villainous, him, spoke*
But atte laste,° he seyde unto the Wyf,° — *at the last, Wife [of Bath]*
1270 "Dame," quod he, "God yeve° yow right good lyf.° — *give, life*
Ye han heer° touched, also moot I thee,° — *have here, might I thrive*
In scole-matere greet difficultee.[2]
Ye han seyd muche thyng right wel, I seye.[3]
But dame, heere as we ryde by the weye° — *along the road*
1275 Us nedeth nat to speken but of game[4]
And lete auctoritees on Goddes name° — *leave authorities in God's name*
To prechyng° and to scole of clergye.° — *preaching, clergy*
And if it lyke to this compaignye,° — *if it is pleasing to this company*
I wol° yow of a somonour telle a game.° — *will, tell a joke*
1280 Pardee° ye may wel knowe by the name — *By God*
That of a somonour may no good be sayd.
I praye that noon of you be yvele apayd.[5]
A somonour is a rennere° up and doun° — *runner, down*
With mandementz° for fornicacioun° — *summonses, fornication*
1285 And is ybet° at every townes ende."[6] — *beaten*
OURE Hoost tho° spak, "A sire, ye sholde be hende° — *then, should be polite*
And curteys° as a man of youre estaat° — *courteous, rank*
In compaignye. We wol have no debaat.° — *quarreling*
Telleth youre tale and lat° the Somonour be." — *let*
1290 "Nay," quod the Somonour, "lat hym seye to me
Whatso hym list.° Whan it comth° to my lot,° — *whatever he wishes, comes, turn*
By God, I shal hym quiten° every grot!° — *have revenge on him groat (coin)*
I shal hym tellen which a greet honour° — *what a great honor*
It is to be a flaterynge lymytour° — *flattering friar*
1295 And of many another manere cryme,° — *kind of crime*

---

1 A "lymytour" was a friar who was licensed to preach in a limited area in a parish or county.
2 "School-matere" is subject matter for scholastic debate. In the medieval universities, commonly called schools, students were taught logic and also theology through debating difficult problems. From the latter part of the thirteenth century through the fourteenth, friars were the most influential teachers in the schools.
3 "You have said many things very well, I say."
4 "We need not speak of anything except [for the purpose of] fun."
5 "I ask that none of you be displeased."
6 In other words, the summoners were often attacked when entering the towns they visited.

Which nedeth nat rehercen° for this tyme.   *needs not be repeated*
And his office I shal hym telle ywis."°   *indeed*
OURE Hoost answerde, "Pees!° Namoore° of this!"   *Peace, No more*
And after this he seyde unto the Frere,
1300 "Tel forth youre tale, leeve maister deere."°   *dear master dear*

THE FRIAR'S TALE

HEERE BIGYNNETH THE FRERES TALE

WHILOM° ther was dwellynge° in my contree   *once, living*
An erchedekene,°¹ a man of heigh degree°   *archdeacon, high rank*
That boldely dide execucioun°   *boldly imposed sentences*
In punysshynge° of fornicacioun,°   *punishing, fornication*
1305 Of wicchecraft° and eek° of bawderye,°   *witchcraft, also, soliciting sex*
Of diffamacioun° and avowtrye,°   *slander, adultery*
Of chirche reves° and of testamentz,°²   *robbing of churches, wills*
Of contractes° and eek° of lakke° of sacramentz,³   *contracts, also, not observing*
Of usure and of symonye also.⁴
1310 But certes,° lecchours° dide he grettest wo.°   *certainly, lechers greatest woe*
They sholde syngen° if that they were hent.°   *had to sing (= cry), arrested*
And smale tytheres°⁵ weren foule yshent,°   *small tithers, severely punished*
If any persoun° wolde upon hem pleyne.°   *parson (parish priest), complain*
Ther myghte asterte hym no pecunyal peyne.⁶
1315 For smale° tithes and smal offrynge°   *small offering [at church services]*
He made the peple° pitously° to synge.°   *people, pitifully, complain*
For er the bisshope caughte hym with his hook,⁷
They were in the erchedeknes book.

---

1   The archdeacon of a diocese would help the bishop attend to administrative matters, including
     directing the church courts that disciplined parishioners for their sins. There is a picture of the
     Friar in the margin.
2   "Robbing wills" might have included ignoring their provisions, which often included dona-
     tions to the Church.
3   "Not observing the sacraments," which would mean, in particular, not confessing at Easter. The
     word "eek" appears in both Hengwrt and Ellesmere but produces an unmetrical line and is not
     needed for sense.
4   "Of usury and of simony." Usury was lending money and charging interest for it, a practice
     basic to modern economics but roundly condemned in the Bible and in Church law. Simony
     was paying money to procure a position in the Church.
5   It was law that a person had to pay one tenth of all earnings, both money and material goods
     (including crops), to the Church. The Church courts enforced this law with particular vigor.
6   "No monetary pain (i.e., fine) could escape from him." In other words, as the *Riverside Chaucer*
     notes, "he never failed to impose fines rather than other penances."
7   The bishop's crozier, or staff of office, is shaped like a shepherd's crook to symbolize his pastoral
     role, guarding and guiding the people in his diocese.

And thanne hadde he thurgh his jurisdiccioun° — *jurisdiction*
1320 Power to doon on hem correccioun.° — *impose on them punishment*
He hadde a somonour redy° to his hond, — *ready*
A slyer boye° nas noon° in Engelond. — *slyer knave, there was none*
For subtilly° he hadde his espiaille° — *slyly, spies*
That taughte hym wher hym myghte availle.° — *might succeed*
1325 He koude° spare of lecchours° oon° or two — *could, lechers, one*
To techen hym° to foure and twenty mo.° — *direct him to, more*
For thogh° this somonour wood° was as an hare,° — *though, crazy, rabbit*
To telle his harlotrye° I wol nat° spare. — *wickedness, will not*
For we been° out of his correccioun.° — *we (i.e., friars) are, jurisdiction*
1330 They han of us no jurisdiccioun,[1]
Ne nevere shullen,° terme of hir lyves."° — *shall, for all their lives*
"PETER!° So been wommen of the styves,"° — *By St. Peter!, brothels*
Quod the Somonour, "yput° out of my cure!"° — *put, authority*
"PEES° with myschance° and with mysaventure!"° — *peace, misfortune, bad luck*
1335 Thus seyde oure Hoost, "and lat hym telle his tale.
Now telleth forth, thogh° that the Somonour gale.° — *though, complain loudly*
Ne spareth nat,° myn owene maister deere." — *do not stop*
THIS false theef, this somonour, quod the Frere,
Hadde alwey bawdes redy to his hond° — *pimps ready at hand*
1340 As any hauk° to lure[2] in Engelond, — *hawk*
That tolde hym° al the secree° that they knewe. — *him, secrets*
For hire aqueyntance° was nat come of newe.° — *their acquaintance, not recent*
They weren hise approwours prively.° — *his agents privately*
He took hymself a greet° profit therby.° — *great, by this*
1345 His maister° knew nat° alwey what he wan.° — *master, not, gained*
Withouten mandement a lewed man
He koude somne on peyne of Cristes curs.[3]
And they were glade for to fille his purs° — *purse*
And make hym grete feestes atte nale.° — *entertain him at an alehouse*
1350 And right as Judas[4] hadde purses smale° — *small purses*
And was a theef,° right swich° a theef was he. — *thief, such*
His maister hadde but half his duetee.° — *what was owed him*
He was, if I shal yeven hym his laude,° — *give him his praise*
A theef and eek a somnour and a baude.

---

1 Friars were officially answerable to the Pope, not to the local bishop; thus they were not subject to the authority of the archdeacons and their summoners.
2 In the sport of falconry, hawks were brought back to their handlers' wrists after hunting by means of lures.
3 "He could summon a layman on pain of excommunication (Christ's curse) without a written command."
4 According to John 12:6, Judas carried the money for the use of Christ and the apostles.

1355 He hadde eek wenches at his retenue°	*girls in his service*
That, wheither° that Sir Robert or Sir Huwe°	*whether, Hugh*
Or Jakke° or Rauf° or whoso° that it were	*Jack, Ralph, whoever*
That lay by hem,° they tolde it in his ere.°	*them, ear*
THUS was the wenche and he of oon assent.°	*in agreement*
1360 And he wolde fecche° a feyned mandement°	*fetch, false summons*
And somne hem° to chapitre° bothe two	*summon them, court*
And pile° the man and lete the wenche° go.	*rob, girl*
THANNE wolde he seye, "Freend, I shal for thy sake	
Do striken hire out° of oure lettres blake.	*cross out her [name]*
1365 Thee thar namoore as in this cas travaille.¹	
I am thy freend° ther° I thee may availle."°	*friend, where, help*
Certeyn, he knew of bribryes° mo°	*extortions, more*
Than possible is to telle in yeres two.	
For in this world nys dogge for the bowe°²	*a hunting dog*
1370 That kan° an hurt deer from an hool° knowe	*can, healthy one*
Bet° than this somnour knew a sly lecchour°	*better, lecher*
Or an avowtier° or a paramour.°	*adulterer, mistress*
And for that was the fruyt of al his rente,³	
Therfore on it he sette al his entente.°	*intent*
1375 AND so bifel° that ones° on a day	*it happened, once*
This somnour evere waityng° on his pray°	*always waiting for, prey*
For to somne° an old wydwe,° a ribibe,°⁴	*summon, widow, rebec*
Feynynge° a cause for he wolde brybe.°	*falsifying, would extort*
Happed° that he saugh bifore hym ryde	*It happened*
1380 A gay yeman° under a forest syde.°	*carefree yeoman, close to a forest*
A bowe he bar° and arwes° brighte and kene.°	*carried, arrows, sharp*
He hadde° upon a courtepy° of grene°	*had, jacket, green*
An hat upon his heed° with frenges° blake.°	*head, tassles, black*
"SIRE," quod this somnour, "hayl° and wel atake!"°	*hail, well met*
1385 "WELCOME," quod he, "and every good felawe!	
Wher rydestow under this grene wode shawe?"⁵	
Seyde this yeman, "Wiltow fer° today?"	*Will you [go] far*
THIS somnour hym answerde and seyde, "Nay.	
Heere faste by,"° quod he, "is myn entente	*here close by*
1390 To ryden° for to reysen° up a rente°	*ride, raise, fee*

---

1   "You need trouble yourself no more in this matter."
2   According to Skeat, the expression "dog for the bow" refers to "a dog used to accompany an archer, to follow up a stricken deer."
3   "From that came all the best part (the fruit) of his income."
4   A rubible or rebec was a small, pear-shaped stringed musical instrument played with a bow. It had a high, nasal sound, thus occasioning the metaphor here to describe the old widow: she doubtless has a whining voice.
5   "Where do you ride under this greenwood thicket?"

That longeth° to my lordes duetee."°   *belongs, dues*
"ARTOW thanne° a bailly?"[1] "Ye," quod he.   *Are you then*
He dorste nat° for verray filthe° and shame   *dared not, true filth*
Seye that he was a somonour for the name.°   *because the name itself [was so shameful]*
1395 "DEPARDIEUX,"° quod this yeman, "deere broother,   *By God*
Thou art a bailly and I am another!
I am unknowen as in this contree.
Of thyn aqueyntance I wolde praye thee°   *would ask you for*
And eek of bretherhede if that yow leste.°   *if you wish*
1400 I have gold and silver in my cheste,
If that° thee happe to comen° in oure shire°   *if, happen to come, into our region*
Al shal be thyn,° right as thou wolt desire."°   *yours, just as you would like*
"GRANTMERCY,"° quod this somonour, "by my feith!"°   *thank you, faith*
Everych° in ootheres° hand his trouthe° leith°   *each, the other's, trust, places*
1405 For to be sworn bretheren til they deye.°   *die*
In daliance° they ryden° forth hir weye.°   *playfulness, ride, way*
THIS somonour that was as ful of jangles°   *useless talk*
As ful of venym° been° thise waryangles°[2]   *venom, are, these shrikes*
And evere enqueryng upon° everythyng,   *asking about*
1410 "BROTHER," quod he, "where is now youre dwellyng,
Another day if that I sholde yow seche?"°   *should look for you*
This yeman hym answerde in softe speche,°   *quiet speech*
"BROTHER," quod he, "fer in the north contree,[3]
Whereas° I hope somtyme I shal thee see.°   *where, look for you*
1415 Er° we departe° I shal thee so wel wisse,°   *before, part, shall know you so well*
That of myn hous ne shaltow nevere mysse."°   *you shall never fail to find my house*
"NOW brother," quod this somonour, "I yow preye,°   *ask*
Teche° me whil that we ryden by the weye,   *teach*
Syn that ye been° a baillif° as am I,   *since you are, bailiff*
1420 Som subtiltee,° and tel me feithfully   *some trick*
In myn office° how I may moost wynne.°   *my job, most profit*
And spareth nat° for conscience ne synne,°   *spare not, sin*
But as my brother tel me how do ye."
"NOW by my trouthe, brother deere," seyde he,
1425 "As I shal tellen thee a feithful° tale,   *faithful*
My wages been° ful streite and ful smale.°   *are, very little*
My lord is hard to me and daungerous,°   *haughty*
And myn office is ful laborous.°   *laborious*

---

1 A bailey or bailiff was one who managed a lord's estate.
2 The "waryangle" is a northern English name for the shrike, also known as the butcher bird, so called because it impales insects and small birds on thorns and then pulls them apart. T.P. Harrison notes that according to medieval lore, the thorns then became poisonous.
3 In Isaiah 14.13, Lucifer is said to have set his throne above God and in the north.

And therfore by extorcions° I lyve.   *extortions*
1430 Forsothe,° I take al that men wol me yeve,°   *in truth, will give*
Algate° by sleyghte° or by violence.   *anyhow, trickery*
Fro yeer° to yeer I wynne° al my dispence.°   *year, gain, expenses*
I kan no bettre° telle feithfully."   *better*
"Now certes,"° quod this somonour, "so fare I.   *certainly*
1435 I spare nat to taken, God it woot,°   *God knows it*
But if it be to hevy° or to hoot,°[1]   *too heavy, too hot*
What° I may gete° in conseil° prively.°   *whatever, get, counsel, privately*
No maner° conscience of that have I.   *kind of*
Nere myn extorcioun I myghte nat lyven,[2]
1440 Nor of swiche japes° wol° I nat be shryven.°   *such tricks, will, not be confessed*
Stomak ne° conscience ne knowe I noon.°   *compassion nor, none*
I shrewe thise shrifte-fadres everychoon![3]
Wel be we met,° by God and by Seint Jame!   *well are we met*
But, leeve brother, tel me thanne thy name,"
1445 Quod this somonour. In this meenewhile°   *the meanwhile*
This yeman gan° a litel° for to smyle.°   *began, little, smile*
"BROTHER," quod he, "wiltow that I thee telle?°   *do you want me to tell you?*
I am a feend.° My dwellyng is in Helle,   *fiend*
And heere I ryde aboute my purchasyng,°   *profit-taking*
1450 To wite wher° men wolde me yeven° anythyng.   *know whether, would give*
My purchas is th'effect of al my rente.[4]
Looke how thou rydest for the same entente.°   *intent*
To wynne good° thou rekkest° nevere how.   *goods, care*
Right so fare I, for ryde I wolde° right now   *would*
1455 Unto the worldes ende° for a preye."°   *world's end, prey*
"A,"° QUOD this somonour, "benedicite!° What sey° ye?   *Ah, bless you, say*
I wende° ye were a yeman, trewely!°   *thought, truly*
Ye han° a mannes shape° as wel° as I.   *have, man's form, well*
Han ye° figure° thanne determinat°   *have you, form, determined*
1460 In Helle, ther ye been° in youre estat?"°   *where you are, normal condition*
"NAY, certeinly," quod he, "ther have we noon.°   *none*
But whan us liketh,° we kan take us oon°   *when we wish, one*
Or elles° make yow seme° we been shape°   *else, seem to you, are formed*
Somtyme lyk° a man or lyk an ape.[5]   *sometimes like*

---

1   Cf. the modern expression "too hot to hold."
2   "If it were not for my extortion, I could not live."
3   "I curse every one of these priests who give penance."
4   "What I gain from my activities (*purchas*) provides the total of my income (*rente*)."
5   Chaucer here echoes the opinion of authorities such as Vincent of Beauvais. According to
    Vincent's *Speculum naturale* (*Mirror of Nature*) "The general opinion is that demons are not
    aethereal spirits but impure incorporeal spirits and that in keeping with their nature they are

1465 Or lyk an angel kan I ryde° or go.° — *ride, walk*
It is no wonder thyng° thogh it be so. — *wonderful thing*
A lowsy° jogelour° kan deceyve° thee, — *lousy, conjurer, deceive*
And, pardee,° yet kan° I moore craft° than he!" — *by God, know, more skill*
"WHY," quod this somonour, "ryde ye thanne or goon° — *walk*
1470 In sondry shape° and nat° alwey in oon?" — *different shapes, not*
"FOR we," quod he, "wol° us swiche° formes make — *will, such*
As moost able° is oure preyes° for to take." — *is best, prey*
"WHAT maketh° yow to han° al this labour?"° — *causes, have, labor*
"FUL many a cause, leeve sire somonour,"
1475 Seyde this feend, "but all thyng hath tyme.° — *everything has time*
The day is short, and it is passed pryme,° — *prime (hour for morning prayer)*
And yet ne wan I nothyng° in this day. — *I have gained nothing*
I wol entende° to wynnen° if I may — *will try, profit*
And nat entende oure wittes° to declare.¹ — *our clever devices*
1480 For, brother myn,° thy wit is al to° bare — *my brother, too*
To understonde, althogh I tolde hem thee.° — *them to you*
But for thou axest° why labouren we, — *you ask*
For somtyme° we been Goddes instrumentz° — *sometimes, are God's instruments*
And meenes° to doon hise comandementz° — *the means, do his commandments*
1485 Whan that hym list° upon his creatures, — *he wishes*
In divers art and in diverse figures.° — *different ways and means*
Withouten hym, we have no myght,° certayn,° — *power, certainly*
If that hym list to stonden° ther agayn. — *he wishes to prevent it*
And somtyme at oure prayere° han° we leve° — *request, have, leave*
1490 Oonly the body and nat° the soule greve.° — *not, torment*
Witnesse on Job, whom° that we diden wo.° — *to whom, caused sorrow*
And somtyme han we myght of bothe° two. — *have power over both*
This is to seyn, of soule and body eke.
And somtyme be we suffred° for to seke° — *allowed, disturb*
1495 Upon a man and doon his soule° unreste° — *soul, discomfort*
And nat his body, and al is for the beste.²
Whan he withstandeth oure temptacioun
It is cause of his savacioun,° — *salvation*
Albeit° that it was nat° oure entente° — *although, not, intent*
1500 He sholde be sauf but that we wolde hym hente.° — *but rather we wished to seize him*
And somtyme° be° we servant unto man, — *sometimes, are*

---

invisible to us, but that when they appear to men they assume from the air in which they live [the appearance] of bodies" (Chapter 125, "Whether Demons Have Bodies?"; quoted by Pauline Aiken, "Vincent of Beauvais and the Green Yeoman's Lecture on Demonology," *Studies in Philology* 35 [1938]: 1-9).
1 Ellesmere has "hir wittes." The emendation is from Hengwrt.
2 Ellesmere has "And nat his soule." The emendation is from Hengwrt.

As to the bisshope, Seint Dunstan.[1]
And to the apostles servant eek was I."
"YET tel me," quod the somonour "feithfully,°   *truthfully*
1505 Make ye yow newe bodies thus alway
Of elementz?"° The feend° answerde, "Nay.   *elements, fiend*
Somtyme we feyne,° and somtyme we aryse°   *pretend, arise*
With dede bodyes° in ful sondry wyse°   *dead bodies, very many ways*
And speke° as renably° and faire and wel   *speak, readily*
1510 As to the Phitonissa dide Samuel.
And yet wol som men seye it was nat he.[2]
I do no fors of° youre dyvynytee.°   *do not care about, theology*
But o thyng° warne I thee; I wol nat jape.°   *one thing, will not joke*
Thou wolt algates wite° how we been shape.°   *You will certainly know, are formed*
1515 Thou shalt herafterwardes,° my brother deere,   *after this*
Come there° thee nedeth nat° of me to leere.°   *where, you need not, learn*
For thou shalt, by thyn owene experience,
Konne in a chayer rede of this sentence[3]
Bet° than Virgile[4] while he was onlyve°   *better, alive*
1520 Or Dant also. Now lat° us ryde° blyve,°   *let, ride, quickly*
For I wole° holde compaignye° with thee   *will, company*
Til it be so that thou forsake me."
"NAY," quod this Somonour, "that shal nat bityde.°   *not happen*
I am a yeman, knowen° is ful wyde.°   *known, far and wide*
1525 My trouthe° wol° I holde° as in this cas,°   *promise, will, keep, case*
For though thou were the devel Sathanas,°   *devil Satan*
My trouthe wol I holde to my brother
As I am sworn, and ech° of us til oother,°   *each, to the other*
For to be trewe, brother, in this cas.°   *matter*
1530 And bothe we goon abouten oure purchas,°   *go about our business*
Taak° thou thy part what that men wol thee yeve,   *take*
And I shal myn,° and thus may we bothe lyve.   *shall [take] mine*
And if that any of us have moore than oother,
Lat hym° be trewe° and parte° it with his brother."   *let him, true, share*

---

1   St. Dunstan was a tenth-century Archbishop of Canterbury and a leader of monastic reform.
His saint's life recounts several incidents in which he defeated the temptations and harassments
of devils, in one case catching the devil's nose with red-hot tongs.

2   The Phitonissa here is the Witch of Endor, who raised up the spirit of the prophet Samuel
at King Saul's request. See 1 Samuel 28:3–25. Opinion was divided in the Middle Ages as to
whether it was Samuel himself who appeared, or a devil who took on his form, or a hallucina-
tion in Saul's mind. See *Catholic Encyclopedia* 10.36.

3   "For you will be able, based on your own experience, to lecture from a chair on this subject."
The chair here refers to that of a professor of theology at a university.

4   Both Virgil and Dante (mentioned in the next line) recounted visits to Hell in *The Aeneid*, Book
VI, and *The Divine Comedy*, respectively.

1535 "I GRAUNT,"° quod the devel, "by my fey!"°   grant, faith
     And with that word they ryden forth hir wey.
     And right at the entryng° of the townes ende   entrance
     To which this somonour shoope hym for to wende,°   intended go
     They saugh° a cart that charged° was with hey,°   saw, loaded, hay
1540 Which that a cartere° droof° forth in his wey.°   carter, drove, way
     Deepe° was the wey° for which° the carte stood.   deep [in mud], way, on which
     This cartere smoot° and cryde as he were wood,°   struck [his horses], mad
     "Hayt, Brok! Hayt, Scot!¹ What spare ye° for the stones?   spare yourselves
     The feend," quod he, "yow fecche,° body and bones,   fetch
1545 As forthly° as evere were ye foled,°   as sure as, you were born (foaled)
     So muche wo° as I have with yow tholed!°   woe, endured
     The devel have al, bothe hors and cart and hey!"
     THIS somonour seyde, "Heere shal we have a pley!"°   amusement
     And neer the feend he drough as noght ne were²
1550 Ful prively° and rowned° in his ere,°   very secretly, whispered, ear
     "Herkne,° my brother, herkne, by thy feith.°   listen, faith
     Herestow nat° how that the cartere seith?   Do you not hear
     Hent° it anon,° for he hath yeve it thee,°   grab, immediately, given it to you
     Bothe hey and cart and eek hise caples thre."°   his three horses
1555 "NAY," quod the devel, "God woot,° never a deel.°   God knows, not at all
     It is nat his entente, truste me weel.
     Axe hym thyself if thou nat trowest° me,   do not believe
     Or elles stynt° a while and thou shalt see."   else be quiet
     THIS cartere taketh his hors° on the croupe,°   horses, hindquarters
1560 And they bigonne drawen and to stoupe.°   pull and stoop (lean against the harness)
     "Heyt now!" quod he ther. "Jhesu Crist yow blesse,
     And al his handwerk,° bothe moore° and lesse!°   handiwork, more, less
     That was wel° twight,° myn° owene lyard° boy!   well, pulled, my, dappled
     I pray God,³ save thee and Seint Loy!⁴
1565 Now is my cart out of the slow,° pardee."°   mud, by God
     "LO, brother," quod the feend, "what tolde I thee?
     Heere may ye se, myn owene deere brother,
     The carl° spak oon° but he thoghte another.   fellow, spoke one [thing]
     Lat us go forth abouten oure viage.°   journey
1570 Heere wynne I nothyng upon cariage."⁵

---

1   "Hayt" is a word to encourage the horses to move, and Brock and Scot are the horses' names.
2   "And he drew near the fiend as if it were nothing (i.e., as if nothing were happening)."
3   Ellesmere reads, "I pray to God." The emendation is from Hengwrt.
4   St. Loy is another name for St. Eligius, a seventh-century Merovingian goldsmith and artist who
    became Bishop of Noyon and was the patron saint of carters. The Prioress also appeals to Saint
    Loy (see General Prologue, line 120).
5   "Cariage" was the right of a lord to use a peasant's cart and horse when needed.

WHAN that they coomen somwhat out of towne,
This somonour to his brother gan° to rowne.°   *began, whisper*
"Brother," quod he, "heere woneth° an old rebekke°¹   *lives, rebec*
That hadde almoost as lief to lese hire nekke°   *almost as willing to lose her neck*
1575 As for to yeve° a peny° of hir good.°   *give, penny, belongings*
I wol han° twelf pens,° though that she be wood,°   *will have, pennies, crazy*
Or I wol sompne hire° unto oure office.°   *summon her, court*
And yet, God woot, of hire knowe I no vice.
But° for thou kanst° nat as in this contree   *because, you cannot*
1580 Wynne thy cost,° taak heer ensample of me."   *cover your expenses*
THIS somonour clappeth° at the wydwes° gate.   *knocks, widow's*
"Com° out," quod he, "thou old virytrate!°   *come, hag*
I trowe° thou hast som frere° or preest° with thee!"   *believe, some friar, priest*
"WHO clappeth?" seyde this wyf. "Benedicitee!°   *Bless you*
1585 God save yow, sire. What is youre sweete wille?"
"I HAVE," quod he, "of somonce° a bille.°   *summons, writ*
Upon peyne° of cursyng,° looke that thou be   *pain, excommunication*
Tomorn° bifore° the erchedeknes° knee   *tomorrow, before, archdeacon's*
T'answere° to the court of certeyn thynges."°   *to answer, certain things*
1590 "NOW lord," quod she, "Crist Jhesu, kyng of kynges,
So wisly° helpe me as I ne may!°   *wisely, may not*
I have been syk° and that ful° many a day.   *sick, very*
I may nat go so fer," quod she, "ne ryde,
But I be deed,° so priketh° it in my syde!   *without it killing me, hurts*
1595 May I nat axe° a libel,° sire Somonour   *not ask [for], written summons*
And answere there by my procutour°   *representative*
To swich thyng° as men wole° opposen° me?"   *such thing, will, accuse*
"YIS," quod this somonour, "pay anon°—lat se°—   *immediately, let [us] see*
Twelf pens° to me, and I wol thee acquite.   *pennies*
1600 I shal° no profit han therby° but lite.°   *shall have, from it, little*
My maister hath the profit and nat I.
Com of and lat me ryden° hastily.   *ride*
Yif° me twelf° pens. I may no lenger tarye."°   *give, MS xij, longer wait*
"TWELF pens!" quod she. "Now lady Seinte Marie
1605 So wisly help me God out of care and synne!°   *sin*
This wyde° world, thogh that I sholde wynne,°   *wide, should win*
Ne have I nat twelf° pens withinne myn hoold.°   *MS xij, my possession*
Ye knowen wel that I am povre and oold.
Kithe° youre almesse° on me, povre wrecche!"   *make known, charity*
1610 "NAY thanne," quod he, "the foule feend me fecche°   *fetch*
If I th'excuse, though thou shul be spilt!"°   *shall die*

---

1   See p. 184, note 4.

"ALLAS!" quod she, "God woot, I have no gilt!"°   *guilt*

"PAY me," quod he, "or by the sweete Seinte Anne,[1]

As I wol bere awey° thy newe panne°   *will carry away, pan*

1615 For dette,° which that thou owest me of old,   *debt*

Whan that thou madest thyn housbonde cokewolde.°   *cuckold*

I payde at hoom for thy correccioun."[2]

"THOU lixt!"° quod she, "By my savacioun,°   *lie, salvation*

Ne was I nevere° er° now, wydwe ne wyf,   *Nor was I ever, before*

1620 Somoned unto youre court in al my lyf!

Ne nevere I nas but of my body trewe.[3]

Unto the devel° blak° and rough of hewe°   *devil, black, rough in appearance*

Yeve° I thy body and my panne° also!"   *give, pan*

AND whan the devel herde° hire° cursen° so,   *heard, her, curse*

1625 Upon hir knees he seyde in this manere,

"Now Mabely, myn owene° mooder° deere,   *own, mother*

Is this youre wyl° in ernest° that ye seye?"°   *will, seriousness, say*

"THE devel," quod she, "so fecche hym° er° he deye°—   *fetch him, before, dies*

And panne and al, but he wol hym repente!"

1630 "NAY,° olde stot,° that is nat myn entente,"°   *no, cow, my intent*

Quod this somonour, "for to repente me

For anythyng that I have had of thee.

I wolde° I hadde thy smok° and every clooth."°   *wished, underclothes, cloth*

"Now, brother," quod the devel, "be nat wrooth.°   *not angry*

1635 Thy body and this panne been myne by right.

Thou shalt with me to Helle yet tonyght,

Where thou shalt knowen of° oure privetee°   *know about, secrets*

Moore° than a maister° of dyvynytee."°   *more, master, theology*

And with that word this foule feend hym hente.°   *took*

1640 Body and soule he with the devel wente

Whereas that somonours han hir heritage.°   *their inheritance*

And God that made after his ymage°   *image*

Mankynde save and gyde° us alle and some°   *guide, one and all*

And leve° thise° somonours goode men bicome!°   *allow, these, to become*

1645 LORDYNGES, I koude han toold yow, quod this Frere,

Hadde I had leyser,° for this Somnour heere°   *leisure, here*

After the text of Crist, Poul, and John

And of oure othere doctours° many oon°   *theologians, many a one*

Swiche peynes° that youre herte myghte agryse,°   *such pains, might terrify your heart*

1650 Albeit° so no tonge° may it devyse,°   *although, tongue, describe*

---

1 St. Anne was the mother of the Virgin Mary.

2 The summoner claims that he paid the widow's fine (*correcioun*) himself when he returned to the archdeacon's court.

3 "Nor was I ever anything other than true with my body."

Thogh that I myghte a thousand wynter° telle | winters
The peynes° of thilke° cursed hous° of Helle. | pains, that, house
But for to kepe° us fro° that cursed place, | keep, from
Waketh° and preyeth° Jhesu for his grace | keep awake, pray to
1655 So kepe° us fro° the temptour° Sathanas. | keep, from, tempter
Herketh° this word: Beth war° as in this cas!°[1] | listen to, be wary, situation
The leoun° sit in his awayt° alway° | lion, waiting, always
To sle° the innocent, if that he may. | kill
Disposeth° ay° youre hertes° to withstonde | set, ever, hearts
1660 The feend that yow wolde° make thral° and bonde.° | would, slave, bound
He may nat tempte yow over youre myght.° | beyond your power
For Crist wol be youre champion and knyght.
And prayeth that thise somonours hem° repente | themselves
Of hir mysdedes° er° that the feend hem hente.° | misdeeds, before, take them

HEERE ENDETH THE FRERES TALE

---

1   There is a Latin gloss in the margin "[The wicked man] lies in ambush with wealthy men," a version of Psalm 10.8, "[The wicked man] lies in ambush near the villages."

THE SUMMONER'S PROLOGUE AND TALE

THE SUMMONER'S PROLOGUE

1665 THIS Somonour in his styropes° hye° stood.	*stirrups, high*
Upon this Frere° his herte° was so wood,°	*Friar, heart, angry*
That lyk an aspen leef° he quook° for ire.°	*leaf, shook, anger*
"Lordynges," quod he, "but o thyng I desire.	
I yow biseke° that of youre curteisye,°	*request, courtesy*
1670 Syn° ye han herd° this false Frere lye,°	*since, have heard, lie*
As suffreth me° I may my tale telle.	*allow me*
This Frere bosteth° that he knoweth Helle.	*boasts*
And God it woot,° that it is litel wonder!	*God knows it*
Freres and feendes been° but lyte asonder!°	*are, little apart*
1675 For pardee,° ye han ofte° tyme herd° telle	*by God, have often, heard*
How that a frere° vanysshed° was to Helle	*friar, vanished*
In spirit ones° by a visioun.°	*once, vision*
And as an angel ladde hym° up and doun°	*led him, down*
To shewen hym° the peynes° that ther were	*show him, pains*
1680 In al the place, saugh° he nat a frere.	*saw*
Of oother° folk he saugh ynowe° in wo.°	*other, enough, woe*
Unto this angel spak° the frere tho.°	*spoke, then*
'Now sire,' quod he, 'han° freres swich° a grace	*have, such*
That noon of hem° shal come to this place?'	*them*
1685 'YIS,'° quod this angel, 'many a millioun.'°	*yes, million*
And unto Sathanas° he ladde hym doun.°	*Satan, led him down*
'And now hath Sathanas,' seith he, 'a tayl°	*tail*
Brodder° than of a carryk° is the sayl.°	*broader, ship, sail*
Hoold up thy tayl, thou Sathnas,' quod he.	
1690 'Shewe forth thyn ers° and lat° the frere se°	*your ass, let, see*
Where is the nest of freres in this place.'	
And er that half a furlong¹ wey of space,	
Right so as bees out swarmen° from an hyve,°	*swarm, hive*
Out of the develes ers° ther gonne dryve°	*devil's ass, began to fly*
1695 Twenty thousand freres in a route.°	*crowd*
And thurghout° Helle swarmeden° aboute	*throughout, swarmed*
And comen agayn° as faste as they may gon.°	*again, go*
And in his ers they crepten everychon.°	*every one*
He clapte° his tayl agayn and lay ful stille.°	*clapped, very quietly*
1700 This frere whan he hadde looke° al his fille	*had looked*
Upon the tormentz° of this sory° place,	*torments, miserable*
His spirit God restored of his grace	

---

1 Two or three minutes, i.e., the time taken to walk a furlong or 220 yards.

Unto his body agayn,° and he awook.°	*again, awoke*
But natheles° for fere° yet he quook.°	*nevertheless, fear, shook*
1705 So was the develes ers° ay° in his mynde.°	*devil's ass, ever, mind*
That is his heritage of verray kynde.°	*true nature*
God save yow alle, save° this cursed Frere!	*except*
My prologe wol I ende in this manere."	

THE SUMMONER'S TALE

HEERE BIGYNNETH THE SOMONOUR HIS TALE

LORDYNGES, ther is in Yorkshire, as I gesse,°	*guess*
1710 A merssh contree° called Holdernesse,[1]	*marsh country*
In which ther wente a lymytour°[2] aboute	*friar*
To preche° and eek° to begge.°[3] It is no doute.°	*preach, also, beg, doubt*
And so bifel° that on a day this frere	*it happened*
Hadde preched° at a chirche in his manere.	*preached*
1715 And specially aboven everythyng	
Excited he the peple° in his prechyng	*people*
To trentals[4] and to yeve° for Goddes sake	*give*
Wherwith° men myghte° hooly° houses make,[5]	*that with which, might, holy*
Theras° divine servyce is honoured,	*where*
1720 Nat theras° it is wasted and devoured,[6]	*not where*
Ne ther° it nedeth nat° for to be yeve°	*nor where, needs not, given*
As to possessioners[7] that mowen lyve,°	*might live*
Thanked be God, in wele° and habundaunce.°	*wealth, abundance*
"Trentals," seyde he, "deliveren fro° penaunce°	*from, punishment (in hell)*
1725 Hir freendes soules as wel olde as yonge.°	*both old and young*
Ye, whan that they been hastily ysonge,°[8]	*are sung without delay*

---

1   Holderness is a flat area in the southeast of Yorkshire, near Hull. There is a picture of the Summoner in the margin.

2   A "lymytour" was a friar who was licensed to preach in a limited area in a parish or county.

3   Friars traditionally begged for a living.

4   Trentals are prayer services of thirty masses said for souls in Purgatory.

5   Although the friars were not supposed to own anything personally, they used the income from donations to build large churches, with elaborate stained-glass windows. In England these churches fell into ruin after the religious orders of monks, nuns, and friars were abolished in the sixteenth century.

6   The scribe has squeezed in "as" after "ther" between the lines.

7   Friars swore oaths of poverty, though their institutional poverty was much relaxed in Chaucer's day. From their point of view, the other clergy, monks and parish priests, with whom they were often in competition, were "possessioners"—that is, clergy who could gain morally problematic wealth.

8   Medieval church services were usually sung rather than spoken. The friars could sing all thirty masses in a single day, whereas a parish priest would only have the time to sing a few each day.

	Nat° for to holde° a preest° joly° and gay.	not, maintain, priest, jolly
	He syngeth nat but o masse° in a day.	one mass
	Delivereth out," quod he, "anon the soules.[1]	
1730	Ful° hard it is with flesshhook or with oules°[2]	very, awls
	To been yclawed° or to brenne° or bake.	be clawed, burn
	Now spede° yow hastily, for Cristes sake!"	speed
	And whan this frere had seyd al his entente,°	intent
	With *qui cum patre*[3] forth his wey he wente.	
1735	WHAN folk in chirche had yeve° him what hem leste,°	given, what they wished
	He wente his wey°—no lenger wolde° he reste°—	way, would, stay
	With scrippe and tipped staf ytukked hye.[4]	
	In every hous he gan° to poure° and prye°	began, look about, pry
	And beggeth mele° and chese° or elles° corn.°	meal (grain), cheese, else, grain
1740	His felawe° hadde a staf tipped with horn,	companion
	A peyre° of tables° al of yvory,°	pair, [wax writing] tablets, ivory
	And a poyntel° polysshed fetisly,°[5]	stylus, polished carefully
	And wroot° the names alwey° as he stood	wrote, always
	Of alle folk that yaf hym° any good,°	gave him, goods
1745	Ascaunces° that he wolde for hem preye.°	as if, would pray for them
	"Yif° us[6] a busshel whete,° malt, or reye,°	give, [of] wheat, rye
	A Goddes kechyl or a trype of chese[7]	
	Or elles° what yow lyst°—we may nat cheese°—	else, what you wish, choose
	A Goddes halfpeny or a masse peny,[8]	
1750	Or yif us of youre brawn° if ye have eny,°	meat, any
	A dagoun° of youre blanket, leeve dame.°	piece, dear lady
	Oure suster deere—lo, here I write youre name—	
	Bacoun or boef° or swich thyng° as ye fynde."°	beef, such thing, find
	A STURDY harlot° wente ay hem bihynde,°	servant, ever behind them
1755	That was hir hostes man,° and bar° a sak.°	their innkeeper's servant, carried, bag

---

1 "'Deliver out [of Purgatory],' he said, 'the souls immediately.'"

2 Medieval pictures of Purgatory and treatises about visionary journeys there often depict devils using meathooks, awls, and similar implements to torment the souls kept there.

3 This is a Latin phrase often used in church services. It means "who with the Father," and is always followed with "and the Son and the Holy Spirit, who lives and reigns now and forever, Amen."

4 "With [his] bag and walking stick tipped [with metal to preserve its point against the continual contact with the ground] and [his robe] tucked high [so it does not drag along the ground]."

5 In an age before the ready availability of paper, writing of a temporary nature was done on wax tablets that were easy to erase once what was written had no longer any use. A stylus, which was simply a pointed stick or quill, was used to write on the soft wax.

6 Ellesmere reads "Yif hym." The emendation is from Hengwrt.

7 "A God's cake or a small piece of cheese." A God's cake was a cake given in charity to the poor.

8 A God's half-penny was given in charity to the poor, usually in a collection box at church. A mass-penny was money given as an offering at a church service.

	And what men yaf hem leyde° it on his bak.°	*laid, back*
	And whan that he was out at dore° anon,°	*door, immediately*
	He planed awey° the names everichon°	*erased away, every one*
	That he biforn° had writen in his tables.°	*before, wax tablets*
1760	He served hem° with nyfles° and with fables.°	*them, trifles, lies*
	"NAY, ther thou lixt,° thou Somonour!" quod the Frere.	*you lie there*
	"PEES,"° quod oure Hoost, "for Cristes mooder deere!	*Peace*
	Tel forth thy tale and spare it nat at al!"	
	"So thryve I," quod this Somonour, "so I shal!"	
1765	So longe he wente hous by hous til he	
	Cam til an hous ther° he was wont° to be	*came to a house where, accustomed*
	Refresshed moore than in an hundred placis.°	*places*
	Syk° lay the goode man whos the place is.	*sick*
	Bedrede° upon a couche lowe he lay.	*bedridden*
1770	*Deus hic,*"° quod he. "O Thomas, freend,° good day!"	*God [be] here, friend*
	Seyde this frere, curteisly° and softe.°	*courteously, softly*
	"Thomas," quod he, "God yelde° yow! Ful ofte°	*reward, very often*
	Have I upon this bench faren ful weel.°	*done very well*
	Heere° have I eten many a myrie meel."°	*here, merry meal*
1775	And fro the bench he droof awey° the cat	*drove away*
	And leyde adoun° his potente° and his hat	*laid down, walking staff*
	And eek his scrippe° and sette hym° softe° adoun.°	*bag, himself, softly, down*
	His felawe was go walked° into toun	*had walked*
	Forth with his knave° into that hostelrye°	*servant, inn*
1780	Whereas he shoope° hym thilke nyght° to lye.°	*intended, that night, lie*
	"O DEERE maister," quod this sike° man,	*sick*
	"How han ye fare° sith° that March bigan?°	*have you been, since, began*
	I saugh° yow noght this fourtnyght° or moore.	*saw, these two weeks*
	God woot,"° quod he, "laboured I have ful soore.°	*God knows, very sorely*
1785	And specially for thy savacioun°	*your salvation*
	Have I seyd many a precious orisoun.°	*valuable prayer*
	And for oure othere freendes, God hem° blesse,	*them*
	I have today been at youre chirche° at messe°	*church, mass*
	And seyd a sermoun after my° symple° wit,	*according to, simple*
1790	Nat° al after° the text of hooly writ.°	*not, according to, the Bible*
	For it is hard to yow,° as I suppose,	*difficult for you [to understand]*
	And therfore wol° I teche° yow al the glose.°	*will, teach, commentary*
	Glosynge is a glorious thyng, certeyn,[1]	

---

1   "Making commentary [on the Bible] is a glorious thing, certainly." Glosses were explanatory
    notes between the lines or in the margins of texts, originally written by university masters to
    explain difficulties in the works they were teaching. By Chaucer's day the glossing of the Bible
    had come to be associated with self-interested misinterpretation and was sharply criticized by
    reformers, such as John Wycliffe, and satirists, such as William Langland.

For lettre sleeth,°¹ so as thise clerkes seyn.° — *letter kills, these theologians say*
1795 There have I taught hem to be charitable
And spend hir good° ther° it is resonable.° — *goods, where, reasonable*
And there I saugh oure dame.° A, where is she?" — *the lady of your house*
"YOND° in the yerd,° I trowe° that she be," — *yonder, yard, believe*
Seyde this man, "and she wol come anon."° — *immediately*
1800 "EY,° maister, welcome be ye by Seint John," — *Oh*
Seyde this wyf. "How fare ye° hertely?"° — *how are you, heartily*
THE frere ariseth up ful curteisly° — *rises up very courteously*
And hire embraceth in his armes narwe° — *embraces her tightly in his arms*
And kiste hire sweete° and chirteth° as a sparwe° — *kissed her sweetly, chirps, sparrow*
1805 With his lyppes.° "Dame," quod he, "right weel,° — *lips, very well*
As he that is youre servant every deel.° — *completely*
Thanked be God that yow yaf° soule and lyf! — *gave you*
Yet saugh I nat this day so fair a wyf
In al the chirche, God so save me!"
1810 "YE, God amende defautes,° sire," quod she. — *improve [our] faults*
"Algates° welcome be ye, by my fey."° — *always, faith*
"GRAUNTMERCY,° Dame, this have I founde alwey.° — *Thank you, always*
But of youre grete goodnesse, by youre leve,
I wolde prey yow° that ye nat yow greve.° — *ask you, do not grieve*
1815 I wole with Thomas speke a litel throwe.° — *speak a little while*
Thise curatz°² been ful necligent° and slowe — *parish priests, very negligent*
To grope tendrely° a conscience — *inspect tenderly*
In shrift.° In prechyng° is my diligence — *confession, preaching*
And studie in Petres wordes and in Poules.³
1820 I walke and fisshe Cristen mennes soules° — *Christian people's souls*
To yelden° Jhesu Crist his propre rente.° — *give to, proper due*
To sprede° his word is set al myn entente."° — *spread, all my intent*
"Now, by youre leve, o deere sire," quod she,
"Chideth hym weel° for Seinte Trinitee!° — *rebuke him well, holy Trinity*
1825 He is as angry as a pissemyre,° — *ant (honey-pisser)*
Though that he have° al that he kan° desire. — *if he has, can*
Though I hym wrye a nyght° and make hym warm — *cover him at night*
And on hym° leye° my leg outher° myn arm, — *him, lay, or*
He groneth° lyk° oure boor° lith° in oure sty. — *groans, like, pig, [which] lies*

---

1   The reference here is to 2 Corinthians 3:6b: "For the letter [of the law] kills, but the [Holy] Spirit gives life." There is a Latin gloss in the margin: "The letter kills." In the Middle Ages this line was often understood to refer to the need to read the Bible for its deeper spiritual or allegorical meaning rather than just literally.

2   There was a bitter rivalry between the friars and the parish priests. "Curate" here means a priest who is taking care of the parish for a salary from another, usually better connected, priest who has the right to the parish's income.

3   The apostles Peter and Paul both wrote epistles that are included in the New Testament.

1830	Oother desport° right noon° of hym° have I.	*fun, none, him*
	I may nat plese hym in no maner cas."°	*please him in no way*
	"O THOMAS, *je vous dy*,° Thomas, Thomas,[1]	*I say to you*
	This maketh the feend!° This moste ben amended!°	*fiend, must be fixed*
	Ire° is a thyng° that hye° God defended.°	*anger, thing, high, forbade*
1835	And therof wol I speke a word or two."	
	"Now maister," quod the wyf, "er that I go,	
	What wol ye dyne?° I wol go theraboute."°	*will you eat, go and get it ready*
	"Now dame," quod he, "now *je vous dy sanz doute*.°	*I tell you without a doubt*
	Have I nat of a capoun° but the lyvere°	*capon (small chicken), liver*
1840	And of youre softe breed° nat° but a shyvere°	*soft bread, not, little piece*
	And after that a rosted pigges heed°—	*roasted pig's head*
	But that I nolde° no beest for me were deed°—	*would not [have], beast killed*
	Thanne hadde I with yow hoomly suffisaunce.°	*simple sufficiency*
	I am a man of litel sustenaunce.°	*[who needs] little sustenance*
1845	My spirit hath° his fostryng° in the Bible.	*has, nurturing*
	The body is ay so redy and penyble	
	To wake, that my stomak is destroyed.[2]	
	I prey yow, dame, ye be nat anoyed°	*[that] you are not annoyed*
	Though I so freendly yow my conseil° shewe.°	*counsel, show*
1850	By God, I wolde nat telle it but a fewe!"°	*except to a few people*
	"Now sire," quod she, "but o word er I go:	
	My child is deed° withinne thise wykes two,°	*dead, these two weeks*
	Soone after that ye wente out of this toun."	
	"His deeth saugh I by revelacioun,"°	*revelation*
1855	Seith this frere, "at hoom° in oure dortour.°	*home, our dormitory*
	I dar wel seyn° that er° that half an hour	*dare well say, before*
	After his deeth I saugh hym born° to blisse°	*saw him carried, bliss*
	In myn avisioun,° so God me wisse!°	*my vision, guide*
	So dide oure sextayn° and oure fermerer,[3]	*sacristan*
1860	That han been trewe freres fifty yeer.°	*true friars for fifty years*
	They may now, God be thanked of his loone,°	*gift*
	Maken hir jubilee° and walke allone.°[4]	*celebrate their anniversary, alone*
	And up I roos° and al oure covent eke°	*rose up, also*
	With many a teere° triklyng° on my cheke,	*tear, trickling*
1865	Withouten noyse° or claterynge of belles.°	*noise, clattering of bells*

---

1 Friar John speaks a little French to show how genteel he is.
2 "[My] body is always so ready and so inured to the pain of keeping vigil that my digestion is destroyed."
3 A sacristan is responsible for the care of church property and liturgical vestments. A fermerer is in charge of an infirmary.
4 The custom was for friars always to walk about with another friar as a companion. Apparently those who had been friars for fifty years were trusted to walk alone.

Te deum[1] was oure song and nothyng elles,°   *nothing else*
Save that to Crist I seyde an orisoun°   *a prayer*
Thankynge hym of his revelacioun.
For sire and dame, trusteth me right weel,°   *trust me very well*
1870 Oure orisons been° wel moore effectueel°   *are, more effective*
And moore we seen° of Cristes secree thynges°   *see, secret things*
Than burel folk,° although° they weren° kynges. *laypeople, even if, are*
We lyve in poverte and in abstinence
And burell folk in richesse and despence°   *spending [on]*
1875 Of mete and drynke and in hir° foul delit.°   *their, pleasure*
We han this worldes lust° al in despit.°   *world's pleasure, contempt*
Lazar and Dives[2] lyveden diversly,°   *lived differently*
And diverse gerdoun° hadden they therby.   *different reward*
Whoso wol preye,° he moot° faste and be clene° *whoever will pray, must, pure*
1880 And fatte° his soule and make his body lene.°[3]   *fatten, skinny*
We fare as seith th'apostle.° Clooth° and foode[4] *the apostle [Paul], clothing*
Suffisen° us, though they be nat ful goode.° *are enough for, not very good*
The clennesse° and the fastynge° of us freres   *purity, fasting*
Maketh° that Crist accepteth oure preyeres.°   *Causes, prayers*
1885 Lo, Moyses° fourty dayes and fourty nyght[5]   *Moses*
Fasted er° that the heighe° God of myght°   *before, high, might*
Spak° with hym in the Mount of Synay.°[6]   *spoke, Sinai*
With empty wombe° fastynge many a day   *stomach*
Receyved he the Lawe° that was writen   *Ten Commandments*
1890 With Goddes fynger.° And Elye° wel ye witen° *God's finger, Elijah, know*
In Mount Oreb° er° he hadde any speche°   *Horeb, before, speech*
With hye° God that is oure lyves leche,°   *high, life's physician*
He fasted longe and was in contemplaunce.°[7]   *contemplation*
Aaron, that hadde the temple in governaunce,°   *in his control*
1895 And eek that othere preestes everichon°   *everyone*

---

1 *Te deum* ("you, God") were the first words and thus the title of an important chant sung in church services. It is a song of praise which depicts all creatures praising God.

2 The story of Lazarus and the "rich man" (in Latin, *dives*, which was in the Middle Ages interpreted as a proper name) is found in Luke 16:19–26. Lazarus, a poor man, dies and goes to Heaven, where he rests in Abraham's bosom, while Dives dies and goes to Hell. Tormented by the flames, Dives pleads with Abraham to let Lazarus ease him in his suffering, and Abraham rebukes him.

3 There is a Latin gloss in the margin: "It is better to fatten the soul than the body" from Jerome's *Against Jovinian* 2.6.

4 There is a Latin gloss in the margin quoting 1 Timothy 6:8, "[If we have] food and clothing, we shall be content."

5 There is a Latin gloss in the margin: "About prayers and fasting."

6 The reference here is to Exodus 34:28.

7 The reference here is to 1 Kings 19:8.

Into the temple whan they sholde gon
To preye for the peple and do servyse,°   *perform the service*
They nolden° drynken in no maner wyse°   *would not, in no way*
No drynke, which that myghte hem dronke make.°   *make them drunk*
1900 But there in abstinence preye and wake,°   *keep a vigil*
Lest that they deyden.° Taak heede° what I seye,   *they died, take heed*
But° they be sobre° that for the peple° preye.°   *unless, sober, people, pray*
War that I seye namoore, for it suffiseth.[1]
OURE Lord Jhesu, as hooly writ devyseth,°   *the Bible relates*
1905 Yaf° us ensample° of fastynge and preyeres.° *gave, example, fasting and prayers*
Therfore we mendynantz,° we sely° freres,   *beggars (friars), innocent*
Been° wedded to poverte° and continence,°   *are, poverty, abstinence*
To charite,° humblesse,° and abstinence,   *charity, humility*
To persecucioun for rightwisnesse,°   *righteousness*
1910 To wepynge, misericorde,° and clennesse.°   *mercy, purity*
And therfore may ye se that oure preyeres—
I speke of us, we mendynantz, we freres—
Been to the hye God moore acceptable
Than youres with youre feestes at the table.
1915 Fro Paradys first, if I shal nat lye,°   *shall not lie*
Was man out chaced° for his glotonye.°   *chased, gluttony*
And chaast° was man in Paradys, certeyn.   *chaste*
BUT herkne, Thomas, what I shal seyn:
I ne have no text of it as I suppose,
1920 But I shal fynde it in a maner glose,°   *some kind of commentary*
That specially oure sweete Lord Jhesus
Spak° this by freres° whan° he seyde thus: *spoke, about friars, when*
'BLESSED be they that povere° in spirit been,'°[2]   *poor, are*
And so forth, al the gospel may ye seen,° *you can check all the Gospels*
1925 Wher° it be likker° our professioun°   *whether, more like, profession*
Or hirs[3] that swymmen° in possessioun.°   *swim, possessions*
Fy° on hire pompe and hire glotonye,   *Fie*
And for hir lewednesse° I hem diffye!°   *ignorance, defy them*
ME thynketh° they been lyk° Jovinyan,[4]   *It seems to me that, like*
1930 Fat as a whale and walkynge as a swan,° *walking like a swan (i.e., strutting)*
Al vinolent° as botel° in the spence.°   *full of wine, bottle, pantry*
Hir preyere° is of ful greet° reverence   *their prayer, very great*
Whan they for soules seye the psalm of Davit.°   *David*

---

1   "Understand that I say no more, for it is enough."
2   Matthew 5:3.
3   "Theirs" here refers to the curates mentioned in line 1816 above.
4   Jovinian was the adversary of St. Jerome to whom Jerome addressed his *Against Jovinian*, mentioned in line 675 of the Wife of Bath's Prologue. Jovinian had maintained that abstinence was not necessary for the Christian life. *Against Jovinian* 1.40 describes him as fat.

Lo, "Buf,"° they seye, "*cor meum eructavit.*"[1] — *burp*

1935 Who folweth° Cristes gospel and his foore° — *follows, path*

But we that humble been° and chaast° and poore,° — *are, chaste, poor*

Werkeris° of Goddes word, nat auditours.° — *workers, not listeners*

Therfore, right as° an hauk° up at a sours° — *just as, hawk, soaring [upwards]*

Up spryngeth° into th'eir° right, so prayeres — *springs up, the air*

1940 Of charitable and chaste, bisy° freres — *busy*

Maken hir sours° to Goddes eres° two. — *soaring, ears*

Thomas, Thomas, so moote° I ryde° or go, — *might, ride*

And by that lord that clepid° is Seint Yve,[2] — *called*

Nere° thou oure brother sholdestou nat° thryve.°[3] — *were not, you should not thrive*

1945 In oure chapitre° praye we day and nyght — *chapter (daily meeting)*

To Crist that he thee sende heele° and myght° — *send you health, might*

Thy body for to weelden° hastily." — *govern*

"GOD woot,"° quod he, "nothyng therof feele° I, — *God knows, feel no benefit*

As help me Crist, as in a fewe yeres.

1950 I han° spent upon diverse manere[4] freres° — *have, different types of friars*

Ful° many a pound,° yet fare I never the bet!° — *very, pound (money), better*

Certeyn,° my good° I have almoost biset.° — *Certainly, goods, given away*

Farwel° my gold, for it is al ago!"° — *Farewell, gone*

THE frere answerde, "O Thomas, dostow so?

1955 What nedeth yow diverse freres seche?° — *to seek out*

What nedeth hym that hath a parfit leche° — *perfect doctor*

To sechen othere leches in the toun?

Youre inconstance° is youre confusioun. — *inconstancy, [the cause of]*

Holde ye° thanne° me or elles oure covent° — *do you think, then, convent*

1960 To praye for yow been insufficient?° — *insufficient*

Thomas, that jape° nys nat worth a myte.° — *joke, is not worth a mite*

Youre maladye° is for° we han to lyte.° — *sickness, because, too little*

A, yif° that covent° half a quarter otes!° — *give, convent, oats*

A, yif that covent foure and twenty° grotes!° — *MS xxij, groats (coins)*

1965 A, yif that frere a peny, and lat hym go!

Nay, nay, Thomas, it may nothyng be so.

What is a ferthyng° worth, parted in twelve? — *farthing (coin)*

---

1   Ellesmere reads "But" for "Buf." The emendation is from Hengwrt. The nonsense word imitates the sound of a burp. "My heart is stirring," is a quotation from the opening verse of Psalm 45. The Latin verb also meant "to burp," so this psalm was a constant source of merriment for the less devout monks who would sing it in their regular cycle of prayers, evidently occasionally accompanying it with the appropriate sound effects.

2   St. Ivo of Brittany was a thirteenth-century lawyer famous for his fasting and abstinence.

3   Thomas is a member of a third order or lay-confraternity that is attached to Friar John's house. The third orders, established in the thirteenth century, allowed laymen and women to maintain a close connection to the friars while remaining married and working in society.

4   There were four major orders of friars—the Franciscan, the Dominican, the Augustinian, and the Carmelite.

Lo, ech thyng° that is oned° in itselve°¹   *each thing, whole, itself*
Is moore° strong than whan° it is toscatered.°   *more, when, divided*
1970 Thomas, of me thou shalt nat been yflatered.°   *not be flattered*
Thou woldest han° oure labour al for noght.°   *would have, all for nothing*
The hye God that al this world hath wroght°   *has made*
Seith° that the werkman° worthy is his hyre.°²   *says, workman, hire*
Thomas, noght° of youre tresor° I desire   *nothing, treasure*
1975 As for myself, but that al oure covent
To preye for yow is ay° so diligent,   *ever*
And for to buylden° Cristes owene Chirche.°   *build, own Church*
Thomas, if ye wol lernen° for to wirche°   *will learn, work*
Of buyldynge° up of chirches, may ye fynde,°   *building, find*
1980 If it be good, in Thomas lyf of Inde.³
Ye lye° heere° ful of anger, of ire,°   *lie, here, anger*
With which the devel° set youre herte° afyre°   *devil, heart, on fire*
And chiden° heere° the sely° innocent,   *scolded, here, simple*
Youre wyf, that is so meke° and pacient.°   *meek, patient*
1985 And therfore, Thomas, trowe° me if thee leste.°   *trust, if you wish*
Ne stryve nat° with thy wyf as for thy beste,°   *do not struggle, best*
And ber° this word awey now, by thy feith,   *carry*
Touchynge this thyng. Lo, what the wise° seith: *wise man*
'WITHINNE thyn hous° ne be thou no leoun°   *your house, lion*
1990 To thy subgitz.° Do noon oppressioun.°   *your subjects, no oppression*
Ne° make thyne aqueyntances° nat° for to flee.'⁴   *nor, your acquaintances, not*
And, Thomas, yet eftsoones° I charge thee: *once more*
Bewar from hire° that in thy bosom slepeth.°   *beware of her, sleeps*
Bewar fro the serpent that so slily° crepeth°   *slyly, creeps*
1995 Under the gras° and styngeth° subtilly.°⁵   *grass, stings, secretly*
Bewar, my sone,° and herkne paciently,°   *son, listen patiently*
That twenty thousand men han lost hir lyves
For stryvyng° with hir lemmans° and hir wyves.   *struggling, their sweethearts*
Now sith° ye han so hooly° meke° a wyf,   *since, wholly, meek*
2000 What nedeth yow,° Thomas, to maken stryf?°   *why do you need, make strife*
Ther nys,° ywys,° no serpent so cruel   *is not, indeed*

---

1   A gloss in the margin gives the Latin version of this saying, which Jill Mann has traced to the metaphysical work the *Liber de causis* (*Book of Causes*), which in the Middle Ages was often attributed to Aristotle.

2   The reference here is to Luke 10:7. The verse is quoted in a Latin gloss in the margin.

3   "In the life of St. Thomas of India." St. Thomas of India was the apostle Thomas, "Doubting Thomas," who needed to touch Christ's wounds to believe he was risen (John 20:26–29). According to medieval legend he used the money he had been given by a king so that he could build a palace to build churches instead.

4   The line is a paraphrase of Ecclesiasticus 4:35, which is cited in the Latin gloss in the margin.

5   John here echoes the *Romance of the Rose*, lines 16323 ff and 9800–04 on the dangers of sharing secrets with one's wife and of marrying an argumentative woman.

What man tret° on his tayl ne half so fel° — *steps, nor so dangerous*
As womman is whan she hath caught an ire.° — *an anger*
Vengeance is thanne al that they desire.
2005 Ire is a synne,° oon of the grete of sevene,[1] — *sin*
Abhomynable° unto the God of Hevene. — *abominable*
And to hymself it is destruccioun.° — *destruction*
This every lewed viker° or parsoun — *ignorant vicar*
Kan seye,° how ire engendreth homycide.° — *can say, causes murder*
2010 Ire is in sooth° executour° of pryde.° — *truth, cause, pride*
I koude° of ire seye° so muche sorwe,° — *could, say, sorrow*
My tale sholde laste til tomorwe.
And therfore preye I God bothe day and nyght,
An irous° man, God sende hym litel myght! — *angry*
2015 It is greet° harm and eek° greet pitee° — *great, also, pity*
To sette an irous man in heigh degree.
WHILOM° ther was an irous potestat,° — *once, potentate*
As seith Senek,° that durynge° his estaat°[2] — *Seneca, during, reign*
Upon a day out ryden° knyghtes two. — *ride out*
2020 And as fortune wolde° that it were so, — *would*
That oon of hem° cam hoom,° that oother noght.° — *one of them, came home, not*
Anon° the knyght bifore° the juge° is broght, — *immediately, before, judge*
That seyde thus: 'Thou hast thy felawe slayn,
For which I deme° thee to the deeth, certayn.' — *judge*
2025 And to another knyght comanded he,
'Go lede hym° to the deeth, I charge thee.' — *lead him*
And happed° as they wente by the weye — *it happened*
Toward the place ther° he sholde deye, — *where*
The knyght cam which men wenden° had be deed.° — *thought, been dead*
2030 Thanne thoughte they it was the beste reed° — *plan*
To lede hem° bothe to the juge agayn. — *lead them*
They seiden, 'Lord, the knyght ne hath nat slayn
His felawe. Heere he standeth hool° alyve!'° — *whole, alive*
'Ye shul be deed,' quod he, 'so moot I thryve!'° — *might I prosper*
2035 That is to seyn, bothe oon and two and thre.'
And to the firste knyght right thus° spak° he: — *just like this, spoke*
'I dampned° thee. Thou most algate° be deed, — *condemned, at any rate*
And thou also most nedes lese thyn heed,° — *must needs lose your head*
For thou art cause why thy felawe deyth.'
2040 And to the thridde knyght right thus he seith:

---

1 The reference is to the Seven Deadly Sins—pride, sloth, envy, anger, greed, gluttony, and lust.
2 There is a Latin gloss in the margin: "About a certain angry potentate." The three stories illustrating the dangers of anger that follow can all be found in the *Dialogues* of the Roman stoic philosopher Seneca (c. 4 BC–c. 65 AD), but Chaucer's source was probably the thirteenth-century *Communiloqium* of John of Wales.

'Thou hast nat doon that I comanded thee.'

And thus he dide doon sleen hem alle thre.°   *caused to be killed all three of them*

IROUS° Cambises¹ was eek dronkelewe°   *angry, prone to be drunk*

And ay delited hym° to been° a shrewe.°   *ever delighted himself, be, villain*

2045 And so bifel° a lord of his meynee°   *it happened that, troop*

That loved vertuous moralitee°   *morality*

Seyde on a day bitwene hem° two right thus:°   *between them, just like this*

'A LORD is lost if he be vicius,°   *depraved*

And dronkenesse is eek a foul record°   *reputation*

2050 Of any man and namely° in a lord.   *especially*

Ther is ful° many an eye and many an ere°   *very, ear*

Awaityng° on a lord, and he noot° where.   *waiting for, does not know*

For Goddes love, drynk moore attemprely!°   *more temperately*

Wyn maketh man to lesen° wrecchedly°   *lose, wretchedly*

2055 His mynde and hise lymes° everichon.°   *his limbs, everyone*

'THE revers shaltou se,'° quod he anon,   *You shall see the reverse*

'And preeve° it by thyn owene° experience   *test, your own*

That wyn ne dooth° to folk no swich° offence.   *wine does not, such*

Ther is no wyn bireveth° me my myght°   *[that] robs, [of] my might*

2060 Of hand ne foot ne of myne eyen sight.'°   *my eyes' sight*

And for despit° he drank ful muchel moore,°   *spite, very much more*

An hondred part° than he hadde bifoore.°   *a hundred times, had before*

And right anon this irous, cursed wrecche°   *wretch*

Leet° this knyghtes sone° bifore° hym fecche,°   *caused, son, before, be fetched*

2065 Comandynge hym he sholde bifore hym stonde.²

And sodeynly he took his bowe° in honde,°   *bow, hand*

And up the streng° he pulled to his ere,°   *string, ear*

And with an arwe° he slow° the child right there.   *arrow, killed*

'Now wheither have I a siker° hand or noon?'°   *sure, none*

2070 Quod he, 'is al my myght and mynde° agon?°   *mind, gone*

Hath wyn bireft° me myne eyen sight?'°   *stolen from, my eyes' sight*

WHAT sholde° I telle th'answere of the knyght?   *why should*

His sone was slayn.° Ther is namoore° to seye.   *killed, no more*

Beth war° therfore with lordes how ye pleye.°   *be wary, deal*

2075 Syngeth° placebo,°³ and I shal if I kan,   *Sing, "it will be well"*

But° if it be unto° a povre° man.   *except, to, poor*

To a povre man men sholde hise vices telle,°   *tell his vices*

But nat to a lord, thogh he sholde go to Helle.

---

1   Cambises succeeded his father, Cyrus, king of Persia.

2   "Commanding him that he should stand before him."

3   *Placebo* ("I will please") from Psalm 116:9, in older versions of the Bible, was sung as part of the Office of the Dead, but the word means "to flatter." Cf. the courtier Placebo in the Merchant's Tale, lines 1476 ff.

Lo, irous Cirus,[1] thilke Percien,°   *that Persian*
2080 How he destroyed the ryver° of Gysen,   *river*
For that an hors of his was dreynt therinne°   *drowned in it*
Whan that he wente Babiloigne to wynne.°   *to conquer Babylon*
He made that the ryver was so smal
That wommen myghte wade it overal.°   *over it*
2085 Lo, what seyde he that so wel teche kan?°   *can teach*
'Ne be no felawe° to an irous man   *do not be a companion*
Ne with no wood man° walke by the weye,   *crazy man*
Lest thee repent.' Ther is namoore to seye.
Now Thomas, leeve brother, lef thyn ire.°   *leave your anger*
2090 Thou shalt me fynde as just as is a squyre.
Hoold nat the develes knyf ay at thyn herte.[2]
Thyn angre dooth thee al to soore smerte.[3]
But shewe° to me al thy confessioiun."°   *show, your confession*
"NAY," quod the sike° man, "by Seint Symoun![4]   *sick*
2095 I have be shryven° this day at my curat.°   *been confessed, by my parish priest*
I have hym toold hoolly al myn estat.°   *told him completely my condition*
Nedeth namoore to speken of it, seith he,[5]
"But if me list of myn humylite."[6]
"YIF° me thanne° of thy gold to make oure cloystre,"°   *give, then, cloister*
2100 Quod he, "for many a muscle° and many an oystre,°   *mussel, oyster*
Whan othere men han ben ful wel at eyse,°   *have been very well at ease*
Hath been oure foode,° oure cloystre for to reyse.°   *food, raise (=build)*
And yet, God woot,° unnethe° the fundement°   *God knows, scarcely, foundation*
Parfourned° is ne° of oure pavement   *completed, is not*
2105 Nys nat° a tyl° yet withinne oure wones.°   *is not, tile, dwellings*
By God, we owen° fourty pound° for stones.   *owe, forty pounds*
Now help, Thomas, for hym that harwed Helle![7]
For elles° moste° we oure bookes selle.°   *else, must, sell our books*
And if ye lakke° oure predicacioun,°   *lack, preaching*

---

1 Cyrus II, the Great, King of Persia, defeated the Babylonians in the sixth century BC. The story of how Cyrus diverted the river Gyndes, a tributary of the Tigris, is found in both Seneca's *On Anger* and the *Communiloqium* of John of Wales.

2 "Do not hold the devil's knife always at your heart."

3 "Your anger causes you all too sore a pain."

4 There are several saints who were named Simon. Which one Thomas means is unclear.

5 "'There is no need anymore to speak of it,' says he." The placing of the quotation marks here is based on the assumption that "he" refers to Thomas's parish priest, not to Thomas.

6 "Unless I wish to, because of my humility." In other words, Thomas can confess the same sins for a second time as a devotional exercise meant to increase his humility, but there is no need to do so, since he has already received absolution from his parish priest.

7 The Harrowing of Hell is the event mentioned in the Creed and depicted in medieval religious drama in which Christ descends to Hell after the Crucifixion to rescue the righteous souls imprisoned there.

2110 Thanne goth the world al to destruccioun.
  For whoso wolde us fro this world bireve,°   *whoever would take us from*
  So God me save, Thomas, by youre leve,°   *leave*
  He wolde bireve° out of this world the sonne!°   *would take, sun*
  For who kan teche° and werchen° as we konne?° *can teach, work, know how*
2115 And that is nat of litel tyme,"° quod he,   *not recent*
  "But syn° Ennok was or Elise[1]   *since*
  Han° freres been. That fynde° I of record   *have, find*
  In charitee, ythanked° be oure Lord.   *thanked*
  Now Thomas, helpe, for Seinte Charitee!"°   *holy charity*
2120 And doun anon he sette hym° on his knee.   *set himself*
  THIS sike man wax wel ny wood° for ire.   *grew almost crazy*
  He wolde that the frere had been on fire,
  With his false dissymulacioun.°   *pretense*
  "Swich thyng° as in my possessioun,"   *such a thing*
2125 Quod he, "that may I yeven° and noon oother.   *give*
  Ye sey me thus, that I am youre brother."[2]
  "YE certes," quod the frere, "trusteth weel°   *trust well*
  I took oure dame oure lettre° and oure seel."°   *letter, seal*
  "Now wel," quod he, "and somwhat shal I yeve
2130 Unto youre hooly covent whil I lyve.
  And in thyn hand thou shalt it have anon,
  On this condicioun and oother noon,
  That thou departe° it so, my leeve brother,   *distribute*
  That every frere have also muche° as oother.   *just as much*
2135 This shaltou° swere on thy professioun°   *you shall, religious vows*
  Withouten fraude° or cavillacioun."°   *fraud, argument*
  "I SWERE it," quod this frere, "by my feith!"
  And therwithal his hand in his he leith.°   *lays*
  "Lo, heer my feith.° In me shal be no lak."°   *faith, lack*
2140 "Now thanne, put in thyn hand doun by my bak,"
  Seyde this man, "and grope wel bihynde.
  Bynethe° my buttok° ther shaltow fynde° *beneath, buttocks, shall you find*
  A thyng° that I have hyd° in pryvetee."°   *thing, hid, secret*
  "A,"° THOGHTE this frere, "this shal go with me!" *Ah*
2145 And doun his hand he launcheth° to the clifte° *launches, crack*
  In hope for to fynde there a yifte.
  And whan this sike man felte this frere

---

1 Enoch, the father of Methuselah, is briefly mentioned in Genesis 5:18–24. He was taken away by God without experiencing death. Elisha was the prophet who succeeded Elijah; his career is recounted in 2 Kings 2–9. Hengwrt gives the two names as "Elie" and "Elize"—Elijah and Elisha—and most editions follow this reading. The Carmelite friars claimed Elijah as their founder, thus gaining priority over the other orders of friars. Chaucer's point is probably that the friar of this tale is confused about the origins of his order.

2 Thomas is a member of a lay confraternity. See note to line 1944.

Aboute his tuwel° grope there and heere,°　　　*anus, here and there*
Amydde° his hand he leet° the frere a fart.　　　*in the middle of, let*
2150　Ther nys no° capul° drawynge° in a cart　　　*is no, horse, pulling*
That myghte have lete a fart of swich a soun!°　　　*sound*
THE frere up stirte° as dooth a wood leoun.°　　　*jumped up, crazy lion*
"A, fals cherl,"° quod he, "for Goddes bones,　　　*villain*
This hastow for despit doon for the nones!¹
2155　Thou shalt abye° this fart, if that I may!"　　　*pay for*
HIS meynee,° whiche that herden° this affray,°　　　*group of servants, heard, dispute*
Cam lepynge° in and chaced° out the frere,　　　*came leaping, chased*
And forth he gooth with a ful angry cheere°　　　*very angry expression*
And fette° his felawe° theras° lay his stoor.°　　　*fetches, companion, where, hoard*
2160　He looked as it were a wilde boor.°　　　*wild boar*
He grynte° with his teeth, so was he wrooth.°　　　*grinds, angry*
A sturdy paas° doun to the lordes court he gooth,　　　*at a furious pace*
Whereas woned° a man of greet° honour,　　　*lived, great*
To whom that he was alwey° confessour.°　　　*always, confessor*
2165　This worthy man was lord of that village.
This frere cam as he were° in a rage　　　*as if he were*
Whereas° this lord sat etyng° at his bord.°　　　*to where, eating, table*
Unnethes° myghte the frere speke a word,　　　*scarcely*
Til atte laste he seyde, "God yow see!"°　　　*look after you*
2170　THIS lord bigan to looke and seide, "Benedicitee!°　　　*Bless you*
What, Frere John, what maner world is this?
I trowe° som maner thyng ther is amys.°　　　*believe, is wrong here*
Ye looken as the wode° were ful of thevys.°　　　*woods, thieves*
Sit doun anon and tel me what youre grief is,
2175　And it shal been amended,° if that I may."　　　*remedied*
"I HAVE," quod he, "had a despit° this day,　　　*insult*
God yelde° yow, adoun in youre village,　　　*reward*
That in this world is noon° so povre° a page°　　　*none, poor, boy servant*
That he nolde° have abhomynacioun°　　　*would not, loathing*
2180　Of that I have receyved° in youre toun.　　　*received*
And yet greveth° me nothyng so soore°　　　*grieves, sore*
As that this olde cherl° with lokkes hoore°　　　*villain, gray hair*
Blasphemed hath oure hooly covent eke."°　　　*holy convent also*
"Now maister," quod this lord, "I yow biseke."°　　　*plead with you [to tell me]*
2185　"No maister," quod he, "but servitour,°　　　*servant*
Thogh I have had in scole swich honour.²
God liketh nat° that 'raby'° men us calle,³　　　*likes not, rabbi (teacher)*
Neither in market ne in youre large halle."

1　"This have you done for spite for the occasion."
2　"Though I have had that honor in university." Master was the title given a professor.
3　The reference here is to Matthew 23:5–7.

"No fors,"° quod he, "but tel° me al youre grief."   *it does not matter, tell*
2190 "SIRE,"° quod he, "an odious° meschief   *Sir, hateful*
This day bityd is° to myn ordre° and me.   *has happened, my order [of friars]*
And so *per consequens*° in ech degree   *consequently*
Of Hooly Chirche.° God amende it soone!"°   *Holy Church, make it soon better*
"SIRE," quod the lord, "ye woot° what is to doone.°   *you know, to be done*
2195 Distempre yow noght.° Ye be my confessour.°   *do not be upset, confessor*
Ye been the salt of the erthe° and the savour.°   *earth, taste*
For Goddes love, youre pacience ye holde.
Tel me youre grief." And he anon hym tolde
As ye han herd biforn. Ye woot wel° what.   *know well*
2200 THE lady of the hous al stille° sat   *completely quietly*
Til she had herd what the frere sayde.
"Ey,° Goddes mooder," quod she, "blisful mayde!°   *Ah, blissful maid*
Is ther oght elles? Telle me feithfully."
"MADAME," quod he, "how thynke ye herby?"°   *what do you think of this*
2205 "HOW that me thynketh," quod she, "so God me speede,°   *so God give me success*
I seye a cherl hath doon a cherles dede.°   *deed*
What sholde I seye? God lat hym° nevere thee!°   *let him, thrive*
His sike heed° is ful of vanytee.°   *sick head, foolishness*
I holde hym° in a manere frenesye."°   *him, [as if] in a kind of madness*
2210 "MADAME," quod he, "by God, I shal nat lye,°   *shall not lie*
But° I on hym oother weyes° be wreke!°   *unless, in another way, avenged*
I shal disclaundre hym overal ther I speke[1]—
This false blasphemour that charged me
To parte that wol nat departed be°—   *divide what will not be divided*
2215 To every man yliche° with meschaunce!"°   *equally, misfortune*
THE lord sat stille° as he were in a traunce,°   *quietly, trance*
And in his herte° he rolled up and doun°   *heart, down*
How hadde the cherl° this ymaginacioun°   *boor, imagination*
To shewe swich a probleme° to a frere.   *to pose such a problem*
2220 "Nevere erst er° now herde I of swich mateere.   *before*
I trowe° the devel° putte it in his mynde.°   *believe, devil, mind*
In ars metrik° shal° ther° no man fynde°   *arithmetic, shall, there, find*
Biforn° this day of swich° a questioun.   *before, such*
Certes,° it was a shrewed° conclusioun,   *certainly, clever*
2225 That every man sholde° have yliche° his part   *should, equally*
As of the soun° or savour° of a fart.   *sound, smell*
O vile, proude cherl, I shrewe° his face!   *curse*
Lo, sires," quod the lord, "With harde grace!°   *what bad luck!*
Who herde evere of swich a thyng er now?
2230 To every man ylike,° tel me how?   *equally*

---

1   "I shall slander him over all [this matter] of which I speak."

It is an inpossible.° It may nat be. *logically impossible*
Ey, nyce° cherl, God lete° thee nevere thee!° *foolish, let, thrive*
The rumblynge° of a fart and every soun° *rumbling, sound*
Nis° but of eir reverberacioun.° *is not, reverberation of air*
2235 And evere it wasteth° litel° and litel awey.° *wastes, little, away*
Ther is no man kan deemen,° by my fey,° *can judge, faith*
If that it were departed° equally. *divided*
What lo, my cherl, lo, yet how shrewedly° *cleverly*
Unto my confessour today he spak.° *spoke*
2240 I holde hym certeyn a demonyak.° *demoniac (crazy)*
Now ete° youre mete,° and lat° the cherl go pleye.° *eat, food, let, play*
Lat hym go honge hymself° a devel weye!"° *hang himself, in the devil's name*

THE WORDES OF THE LORDES SQUIER AND HIS KERVERE FOR DEPARTYNGE OF THE FART ON TWELVE[1]

Now stood the lordes squier at the bord,° *table*
That karf° his mete and herde word by word *who carved*
2245 Of alle thynges whiche that I have sayd.
"My lord," quod he, "beth nat yvele apayd.° *be not displeased*
I koude° telle for a gowne clooth°[2] *could, cloth gown*
To yow, sire frere, so ye be nat wroth,° *not angry*
How that this fart evene delt shal be° *shall be divided evenly*
2250 Among youre covent, if it lyked me."° *if I wanted to*
"Tel," quod the lord, "and thou shalt have anon
A gowne clooth, by God and by Seint John."
"My lord," quod he, "whan that the weder° is fair *weather*
Withouten wynd° or perturbynge° of air, *wind, disturbance*
2255 Lat brynge° a cartwheel into this halle. *have brought in*
But looke that it have his spokes alle.° *all of its*
Twelve spokes hath a cartwheel comunly.° *commonly*
And bryng me thanne twelve° freres. Woot ye why? *MS xij*
For twelve is a covent, as I gesse.°[3] *guess*
2260 The confessour heere for his worthynesse
Shal parfourne° up the nombre of his covent. *complete*
Thanne shal they knele doun° by oon assent° *kneel down, one accord*
And to every spokes° ende in this manere *spoke's*
Ful sadly° leye° his nose shal° a frere. *devoutly, lay, shall*

---

1 "The words of the lord's squire and his carver [of meat at the table] for the dividing of the fart into twelve [parts]."

2 The members of noble households were often paid for their services with gifts of clothing, as the young Geoffrey Chaucer was when he was a page in the household of the Countess of Ulster. In fact, the earliest known record of his life is one that records such a gift.

3 Often houses of monks or friars would have twelve members plus an abbot or prior in imitation of the number of Christ and the apostles in the gospels.

2265 Youre noble confessour there, God hym save,
    Shal holde his nose upright under the nave.°   *hub*
    Thanne shal this cherl with bely° stif° and toght°   *belly, stiff, taut*
    As any tabour been hyder ybroght.°   *as is any drum brought here*
    And sette hym° on the wheel right of this cart   *set him*
2270 Upon the nave,° and make hym° lete° a fart.   *hub, him, let [go]*
    And ye shal seen up peril of my lyf°   *on peril of my life*
    By preeve° which that is demonstratif°   *proof, demonstrable*
    That equally the soun° of it wol wende°   *sound, will go*
    And eke° the stynk° unto the spokes ende,   *also, stink*
2275 Save° that this worthy man, youre confessour,   *except*
    Bycause he is a man of greet honour,
    Shal have the firste fruyt,° as resoun is,°   *first fruit, reasonable*
    As yet the noble usage° of freres is.   *custom*
    The worthy men of hem shul first be served.
2280 And certeinly, he hath it weel disserved.°   *well deserved*
    He hath today taught us so muche good
    With prechyng in the pulpit ther° he stood,   *where*
    That I may vouchesauf,° I sey for me,   *guarantee*
    He hadde the firste smel° of fartes thre.°   *smell, three farts*
2285 And so wolde° al the covent hardily.   *would*
    He bereth° hym so faire and hoolily."°   *behaves, devoutly*
    THE lord, the lady, and alle men save° the frere   *except*
    Seyde that Jankyn spak in this matere
    As wel as Euclude or Protholomee.[1]
2290 Touchynge° this cherl, they seyde, subtiltee°   *touching, cleverness*
    And heigh° wit made hym speke as he spak.   *high*
    He nys° no fool ne° no demonyak.°   *is no, nor, madman*
    And Jankyn hath ywonne° a newe gowne.°   *has won, new gown*
    My tale is doon.° We been almoost at towne.°   *done, are at [the] town*

HEERE ENDETH THE SOMONOUR'S TALE

---

1   Euclid was a great mathematician and Ptolemy a great astronomer.

THE CLERK'S PROLOGUE AND TALE

THE CLERK'S PROLOGUE

"Sire Clerk of Oxenford,"° oure Hoost sayde,   *Oxford*
"Ye ryde° as coy° and stille° as dooth a mayde°   *ride, shy, quietly, maid*
Were newe spoused, sittynge at the bord.[1]
This day ne herde° I of youre tonge° a word.   *did not hear, tongue*
5 I trowe° ye studie° aboute som sophyme.°   *believe, study, some sophism*
But Salomon seith everythyng hath tyme.°[2]   *has time*

For Goddes sake, as beth of bettre cheere!°   *be of better disposition*
It is no tyme for to studien° heere.   *study*
Telle us som myrie° tale by youre fey.°   *merry, faith*
10 For what° man that is entred in a pley,°   *whatever, started to play*
He nedes moot unto the pley assente.°   *necessarily must agree with the rules*
But precheth° nat as freres° doon° in Lente[3]   *preach, friars, do*
To make us for oure olde synnes wepe,°   *weep*
Ne° that thy tale make us nat to slepe!°   *nor, sleep*

15 Telle us som murie thyng° of aventures.°   *merry thing, adventures*
Youre termes, youre colours, and youre figures,[4]
Keepe hem° in stoor° til so be that ye endite°   *keep them, store, write*
Heigh° style as whan that men to kynges write.   *high*
Speketh so pleyn° at this tyme, we yow preye,°   *plainly, ask you*
20 That we may understonde what ye seye."

This worthy Clerk benignely answerde,°   *mildly answered*
"Hoost," quod he, "I am under youre yerde.°   *yardstick (control)*
Ye han° of us as now the governance.   *have*
And therfore wol° I do yow obeisance,°   *will, obedience*
25 As fer° as resoun axeth° hardily.   *far, reason requires*
I wol yow telle a tale which that I
Lerned° at Padwe° of a worthy clerk,°   *learned, Padua, scholar*
As preved° by his wordes and his werk.°   *proved, work*
He is now deed° and nayled° in his cheste.°   *dead, nailed, coffin*
30 I prey° to God so yeve° his soule reste.   *pray, give*

---

1   "Who is newly married, sitting at the [banquet] table."
2   The reference is to Ecclesiastes 3:1. In Ellesmere, the prologue is divided up into stanzas of six to ten lines and at the end of each line the scribe has written "pausacio," i.e., pause or break.
3   Lent is the season in the Christian year devoted to fasting and penance.
4   Terms, colors, and figures here refer to figures of speech taught by rhetoricians to make a speech, a letter, or a poem effective.

FRAUNCEYS Petrak,[1] the lauriat poete,°   *poet laureate*
Highte° this clerk whos rethorik° sweete   *was named, whose rhetoric*
Enlumyned° al Ytaille° of poetrie,   *illumined, Italy*
As Lynyan[2] dide° of philosophie   *did*
35 Or lawe or oother art particuler.°   *particularly*
But deeth that wol nat dwellen heer,[3]
But as it were a twynklyng° of an eye,   *twinkling*
Hem bothe hath slayn.° And alle shul we dye!°   *Has killed them both, shall die*

BUT forth to tellen of this worthy man
40 That taughte me this tale as I bigan,
I seye that first with heigh stile° he enditeth°   *style, writes*
Er° he the body of his tale writeth   *Before*
A prohemye° in the which discryveth° he   *prologue, describes*
Pemond°[4] and of Saluces° the contree   *Piedmont, Saluzzo*
45 And speketh of Appenyn° the hilles hye   *Apennines*
That been the boundes° of west Lumbardye,°   *boundaries, Lombardy*

AND of Mount Vesulus° in special,°   *Monte Viso, in particular*
Whereas the Poo° out of a welle smal°   *river Po, small well*
Taketh his firste spryngyng° and his sours,°   *first spring, source*
50 That estward ay encresseth° in his cours°   *increases, course*
To Emeleward,° to Ferrare° and Venyse,°   *towards Emilia, Ferrara, Venice*
The which a long thyng were to devyse.°   *describe*
And trewely,° as to my juggement,   *truly*
Me thynketh° it a thyng impertinent,°   *it seems to me, irrelevancy*
55 Save° that he wole convoyen° his mateere.°   *Unless, will introduce, subject*
But this his tale, which that ye may heere."

---

1   Ellesmere reads "Perak." The emendation is from Hengwrt. Francis Petrarch was a great four-
    teenth-century Italian writer, famous, among other things, for his sonnets. He translated from
    Italian into Latin a version of the story of Griselda in Giovanni Boccaccio's *Decameron*. The
    Clerk's Tale follows Petrarch's Latin text closely, even word for word, in many places, as the
    glosses indicate. Chaucer also drew on an anonymous French prose translation, but the glosses
    only refer to the more prestigious Latin text.
2   Giovanni da Lignano (d. 1383) was a law professor at the university in Bologna.
3   "But death, that will not [allow us to] remain here."
4   This and the following places named are all found in northern Italy. Beginning at line 40 there is
    a Latin gloss in the margin which quotes the opening lines from Petrarch's prologue, describing
    the area.

THE CLERK'S TALE

HEERE BIGYNNETH THE TALE OF THE CLERK OF OXENFORD

THER is at the west syde° of Ytaille°¹   *side, Italy*
Doun° at the roote° of Vesulus° the colde   *down, root, Monte Viso*
A lusty playne,° habundant of vitaille°²   *pleasant plain, abundant with food*
60 Where many a tour° and toun thou mayst biholde°   *tower, see*
That founded were in tyme of fadres olde
And many another delitable° sighte.   *delightful*
And Saluces° this noble contree highte.°   *Saluzzo, was named*

A MARKYS³ whilom° lord was of that lond,   *once*
65 As were hise worthy eldres hym bifore.°   *ancestors before him*
And obeisant° and redy° to his hond°   *obedient, ready, hand*
Were alle hise liges° bothe lasse and moore.°   *noble subjects, less and more*
Thus in delit° he lyveth and hath doon yoore,°   *delight, done from old*
Biloved° and drad° thurgh favour of Fortune,   *beloved, feared*
70 Bothe of his lordes and of his commune.°   *commoners*

THERWITH° he was, to speke° as of lynage,°   *thus, speak, lineage*
The gentilleste° yborn° of Lumbardye,⁴   *noblest, born*
A fair° persone and strong and yong of age   *attractive*
And ful of honour⁵ and of curteisye,°   *courtesy*
75 Discreet ynogh° his contree for to gye,°   *discreet enough, guide*
Save that in somme thynges that he was to blame.
And Walter was this yonge lordes name.

I BLAME hym thus: that he considereth noght
In tyme comynge what hym myghte bityde,°   *might happen to him*
80 But in his lust° present was al his thoght,°   *pleasure, thought*
As for to hauke°⁶ and hunte on every syde.   *hawk*
Wel ny° alle othere cures° leet° he slyde,°   *very near, cares, let, slide*

---

1 There is a Latin gloss in the margin quoting Petrarch's reference to Vesuvius and the region of Saluzzo.

2 There is a Latin gloss in the margin giving Petrarch's Latin ("grata planicies") for "lusty plain."

3 A marquis is a high-ranking nobleman, roughly equivalent to a duke. There is a picture in the margin of the Clerk on his lean horse with a book in his hand.

4 The reference to Lombardy, a region of northern Italy centered around Milan, is not found in Petrarch or Boccaccio. In Chaucer's day, Lombardy was notorious for its tyrants, such as Bernabò Visconti, Duke of Milan, whose fall is recounted in the Monk's Tale, lines 2703–10.

5 Ellesmere reads "ful honour." The emendation is from Hengwrt.

6 Hawking, or hunting small birds with predator hawks, was the most popular sport of the Middle Ages.

And eek° he nolde°—and that was worst of alle—   *also, would not*
Wedde no wyf° for noght° that may bifalle.°   *wife, nothing, happen*

85 OONLY that point his peple° bar so soore°   *people, took it so hard*
That flokmeele° on a day they to hym wente,°[1]   *in small groups, went to him*
And oon of hem° that wisest was of loore°—   *them, learning*
Or elles that the lord best wolde assente°   *would agree*
That he sholde telle hym what his peple mente°   *meant*
90 Or elles° koude° he shewe° wel swich mateere°—   *else, could, show, such matter*
He to the markys° seyde as ye shul heere.°   *marquis, shall hear*

"O NOBLE markys, youre humanitee[2]
Asseureth° us to yeve° us hardinesse°   *assures, give, courage*
As ofte as tyme is of necessitee,
95 That we to yow mowe° telle oure hevynesse.°   *might, sadness*
Accepteth,° lord, now for youre gentillesse°   *accept, nobility*
That° we with pitous herte° unto yow pleyne,°   *what, pitiful heart, complain to you*
And lat° youre eres° nat my voys desdeyne.°   *let, ears, disdain my voice*

"Al° have I noght to doone° in this mateere°   *although, nothing to do, matter*
100 Moore than another man hath in this place,
Yet forasmuche° as ye, my lord so deere,°   *in so far as, dear*
Han alwey shewed° me favour and grace,   *have always shown*
I dar° the bettre° aske of yow a space   *dare, better*
Of audience to shewen° oure requeste   *show*
105 And ye, my lord, to doon right as yow leste.°   *just as you please*

FOR certes,° lord, so wel us liketh yow°   *certainly, you please us*
And al youre werk and evere han doon, that we
Ne koude nat us-self devysen° how .   *could not ourselves devise*
We myghte lyven in moore felicitee,°   *more happiness*
110 Save o thyng, lord, if youre wille be,
That for to been a wedded man yow leste.°   *desired*
Thanne were youre peple in sovereyn hertes° reste.   *supreme heart's*

BOWETH° youre nekke° under that blisful yok°   *bend, neck, yoke*
Of soveraynetee,° noght of servyse,°   *sovereignty, service*
115 Which that men clepeth spousaille° or wedlok,°   *marriage, wedlock*
And thenketh, lord, among youre thoghtes wyse,
How that oure dayes passe in sondry wyse.°   *different manners*

---

1 There is a Latin gloss in the margin "cateruatim," Petrarch's Latin for "flockmeele."
2 There is a Latin gloss in the margin quoting Petrarch's reference to the humanity of the
   Marquis.

For thogh we slepe or wake or rome° or ryde, — *roam*
Ay fleeth the tyme.° It nyl no man abyde.° — *Ever the time passes, will not await*

120 AND thogh youre grene youthe floure as yit,° — *your green youth still flowers*
In crepeth° age alwey,° as stille° as stoon,° — *creeps, always, quiet, stone*
And deeth manaceth° every age and smyt° — *death threatens, strikes*
In ech estaat,° for ther escapeth noon.° — *each estate, no one*
And al so certein as we knowe echoon° — *everyone*
125 That we shul deye,° as uncerteyn we alle — *die*
Been° of that day whan deeth shal on us falle. — *are*

ACCEPTETH° thanne of us the trewe entente° — *accept, true intent*
That nevere yet refuseden thyn heeste.° — *refused your command*
And we wol, lord, if that ye wole assente,
130 Chese° yow a wyf, in short tyme atte leeste,° — *choose, at the least*
Born of the gentilleste° and of the meeste° — *noblest, greatest [family]*
Of al this land, so that it oghte seme° — *ought to seem*
Honour to God and yow, as we kan deeme.° — *can determine*

DELIVERE us out of al this bisy° drede,° — *anxious, fear*
135 And taak a wyf, for hye Goddes sake.
For if it so bifelle,° as God forbede,° — *happened, forbid*
That thurgh° youre deeth youre lyne° sholde slake° — *through, lineage, fail*
And that a straunge successour° sholde take — *strange successor*
Youre heritage, o,° wo° were us alyve!° — *oh, woe, alive*
140 Wherfore° we pray yow hastily to wyve."° — *therefore, to marry*

HIR meeke preyere° and hir pitous cheere° — *their meek request, pitiful expression*
Made the markys herte° han pitee.° — *heart, have pity*
"Ye wol," quod he, "myn owene peple deere,
To that I nevere erst° thoughte streyne me.° — *never before, to constrain myself*
145 I me rejoysed of my liberte
That seelde° tyme is founde° in mariage. — *seldom, found*
Ther° I was free I moot been° in servage.° — *where, must be, servitude*

BUT nathelees,° I se° youre trewe entente — *nevertheless, see*
And truste upon youre wit° and have doon ay.° — *intelligence, ever done*
150 Wherfore of my free wyl I wole assente° — *will agree*
To wedde me as soone as evere I may.
But theras° ye han profred° me this day — *since, have offered*
To chese° me a wyf, I yow relesse° — *choose, release*
That choys° and prey° of that profre° cesse.° — *choice, ask, offer, cease*

155 FOR God it woot° that children ofte been°   God knows it, often are
     Unlyk° hir worthy eldres° hem bifore.°   unlike, ancestors, before them
     Bountee comth° al of God, nat° of the streen°   goodness comes, not, strain
     Of which they been engendred and ybore.°   conceived and born
     I truste in Goddes bontee,° and therfore   goodness
160 My mariage and myn estaat° and reste   my estate
     I hym bitake.° He may doon as hym leste.°   leave to him, as he wishes

     LAT° me allone° in chesynge° of my wyf.   let, alone, choosing
     That charge upon my bak° I wole endure.   back
     But I yow preye° and charge upon youre lyf,   ask
165 What° wyf that I take ye me assure   whatever
     To worshipe hire° whil that hir lyf° may dure°   honor her, while her life, endure
     In word and werk bothe heere and everywheere
     As she an emperoures doghter° weere.   emperor's daughter

     AND forthermoore, this shal ye swere: that ye
170 Agayn° my choys° shul° neither grucche° ne   against, choice, shall, complain
        stryve.°   struggle
     For sith° I shal forgoon° my libertee   since, give up
     At youre requeste as evere moot I thryve,°   might I thrive
     Theras myn herte is set, ther wol I wyve.°   marry
     And but° ye wole assente in this manere,°   unless, to this arrangement
175 I prey yow, speketh namoore of this matere."

     WITH hertely wyl° they sworen° and assenten°   hearty will, swore, agreed
     To al this thyng. Ther seyde no wight° nay,°   person, no
     Bisekynge hym of° grace er° that they wenten   asking him for, before
     That he wolde graunten hem° a certein° day   would grant them, certain
180 Of his spousaille° as soone as evere he may.   marriage
     For yet alwey the peple somwhat dredde°   feared
     Lest that the markys no wyf wolde wedde.

     HE graunted hem a day, swich as hym leste,°   such as he desired
     On which he wolde be wedded sikerly°   certainly
185 And seyde he dide al this at hir requeste.
     And they with humble entente° buxomly°   intent, obediently
     Knelynge° upon hir knees ful° reverently   kneeling, very
     Hym thonken alle.° And thus they han° an ende   all thank him, have
     Of hire entente,° and hoom agayn they wende.°   their purpose, turn

190 AND heerupon° he to hise officeres°   with this, his officers
     Comanndeth° for the feste° to purveye°   commands, feast, provide

And to hise privee¹ knyghtes and squieres°   *squires*
Swich° charge yaf° as hym liste° on hem leye.°   *such, gave, as he wished, to lay on them*
And they to his comandement° obeye,°   *commandment, obey*
195 And ech of hem dooth al his diligence°   *makes a great effort*
To doon° unto the feeste° reverence.°   *do, feast, respect*

EXPLICIT PRIMA PARS. INCIPIT SECUNDA PARS²

NOGHT fer fro thilke paleys honurable°³   *Not far from this honorable palace*
Theras° this markys shoope° his mariage,   *where, planned*
There stood a throope° of site delitable°   *village, delightful*
200 In which that povre folk of that village
Hadden hir beestes° and hir herbergage°   *kept their beasts, dwellings*
And of hire labour° tooke hir sustenance   *their labor*
After that the erthe yaf hem habundance.°   *gave them abundance*

AMONGES thise povre folk ther dwelte a man
205 Which that was holden° povrest of hem alle.   *who was considered*
But hye° God somtyme senden kan°   *high, sometimes can send*
His grace into a litel oxes stalle.°⁴   *little ox's stall*
Janicula men of that throope° hym calle.°   *village, call him*
A doghter hadde he, fair ynogh° to sighte,   *pretty enough*
210 And Grisildis this yonge mayden highte.°   *maiden was named*

BUT for to speke of vertuous bountee,°⁵   *virtuous goodness*
Thanne was she oon the faireste° under sonne.°   *fairest, sun*
For povreliche° yfostred up° was she.   *in poverty, brought up*
No likerous lust° was thurgh hire herte° yronne.° *lecherous desire, through her heart, ran*
215 Wel ofter° of the welle° than of the tonne°   *more often, well, barrel of wine or ale*
She drank. And for° she wolde° vertu plese,°   *since, wanted, to please virtue*
She knew wel labour but noon ydel ese.°   *no idle ease*

BUT thogh this mayde tendre° were of age,   *tender*
Yet in the brest° of hire virginitee°   *breast, her virginity*
220 Ther was enclosed rype° and sad corage,°   *ripe, constant heart*

---

1   The reference is to the knights and squires of the "privy" chamber, or private chamber. These
    people would attend the king or duke, living at close quarters with him. They often were his
    closest advisors.
2   "Here ends the first part. The second part begins."
3   There is a Latin gloss in the margin quoting Petrarch's line "Not far from the palace, etc."
4   The reference is to the baby Jesus being laid in a manger because there was no room at the inn.
    See Luke 2:7.
5   Hengwrt reads "beautee" here.

And in greet reverence and charitee
Hir olde, povre° fader fostred° shee.   poor, cared for
A fewe sheepe, spynnynge,° on feeld° she kepte.[1]   spinning, field
She wolde noght been ydel° til she slepte.   would not be idle

225 AND whan she homward cam, she wolde brynge
Wortes° or othere herbes° tymes ofte,°   vegetables, herbs, often times
The whiche she shredde° and seeth° for hir lyvynge°   shreds, boils, her living
And made hir bed ful harde° and nothyng softe.°   very hard, by no means soft
And ay° she kepte hir fadres lyf° on lofte°   always, life, flourishing
230 With everich obeisaunce° and diligence°   every obedience, effort
That child may doon to fadres reverence.°   to honor a father

UPON Grisilde, this povre creature,
Ful ofte° sithe° this markys caste his eye   very often, ago
As he on huntyng° rood° paraventure,°   a-hunting, rode, by chance
235 And whan that it fil° that he myghte hire espye,° happened, might see her
He noght° with wantowne lookyng° of folye°   not, flirtatious, folly
Hise eyen° caste on hire but in sad wyse.°   eyes, respectful manner
Upon hir chiere° he gan° hym° ofte° avyse,° face, began, him, often, to contemplate

COMMENDYNGE° in his herte hir wommanhede°   commending, womanhood
240 And eek hir vertu passynge° any wight°   surpassing, person
Of so yong age as wel in chiere° as dede.°   expression, deed
For thogh the peple hadde no greet insight
In vertu,[2] he considered ful° right   very
Hir bountee° and disposed° that he wolde   her goodness, decided
245 Wedde hire oonly,° if evere he wedde sholde.°   only her, he should marry

THE day of weddyng cam, but no wight kan
Telle what womman that it sholde be,
For which merveille° wondred many a man   marvel
And seyden whan that they were in privetee,°   private
250 "Wol nat oure lord yet leve° his vanytee?°   leave, foolishness
Wol he nat wedde? Allas, allas, the while!
Why wole he thus hymself° and us bigile?"°   himself, trick

BUT nathelees° this markys hath doon make°   nevertheless, caused to be made
Of gemmes° set in gold and in asure°   jewels, lapis lazuli (gem)
255 Brooches and rynges for Grisildis sake,
And of hir clothyng took he the mesure
By a mayde lyk to hire stature,°   similar to her in height

---

1   That is, she doubled her labor by spinning thread while she watched her sheep.
2   "For although the common people (i.e., Walter's subjects) are slow to recognize virtue ..."

And eek of othere aornementz° alle   *ornaments*
That unto swich a weddyng sholde falle°   *should be fitting*

260 THE time of undren° of the same day   *dawn*
Approcheth° that this weddyng sholde° be,   *approaches, should*
And al the paleys put was in array,°   *palace was decorated*
Bothe halle and chambres, ech in his degree.°   *each according to its importance*
Houses of office° stuffed with plentee°   *side-buildings, plenty*
265 Ther maystow seen° of deyntevous vitaille,°   *may you see, gourmet food*
That may be founde as fer° as last Ytaille.°   *far, furthest Italy*

THIS roial° markys richely arrayed°   *royal, dressed*
Lordes and ladyes in his compaignye,
The whiche that to the feeste weren yprayed,°   *were invited*
270 And of his retenue° the bachelrye°   *followers, young knights*
With many a soun° of sondry melodye,°   *sound, different [types of] music*
Unto the village of the which I tolde
In this array the righte wey° han holde.°   *way, have held (gone)*

GRISILDE of this, God woot,° ful innocent,°   *God knows, completely ignorant*
275 That for hire shapen° was al this array,   *made*
To fecchen water at a welle° is went°   *well, has gone*
And comth hoom as soone as ever she may.
For wel she hadde herd seyd that thilke° day   *that same*
The markys sholde wedde. And if she myghte,
280 She wolde fayn han seyn° som of that sighte.   *gladly have seen*

SHE thoghte, "I wole with othere maydens stonde,[1]
That been my felawes° in oure dore, and se   *friends*
The markysesse.° And therfore wol I fonde°   *marquessa, will attempt*
To doon° at hoom as soone as it may be   *do*
285 The labour which that longeth° unto me.   *belongs*
And thanne I may at leyser° hire biholde°   *leisure, see her*
If she this wey° unto the castel° holde."°   *way, castle, goes*

AND as she wolde over hir thresshfold° gon,   *her threshold*
The markys cam and gan hire for to calle.°   *called her*
290 And she set doun hir water pot anon°   *immediately*
Biside the thresshfold° in an oxes° stalle,   *threshold, ox's*
And doun upon hir knes° she gan to falle°   *her knees, fell*
And with sad contenance° kneleth stille°   *serious expression, quietly*
Til she had herd what was the lordes wille.

---

1   There is a Latin gloss in the margin quoting the opening sentence of the equivalent passage from Petrarch.

295 THIS thoghtful° markys spak unto this mayde[1]   *pensive*
     Ful sobrely° and seyde in this manere.°   *gravely, manner*
     "Where is youre fader, o Grisildis?" he sayde.
     And she with reverence in humble cheere°   *manner*
     Answerede, "Lord, he is alredy heere."°   *already here*
300 And in she gooth withouten lenger lette,°   *longer delay*
     And to the markys she hir fader fette.°   *fetched*

     HE by the hand thanne took this olde man
     And seyde thus, whan he hym hadde asyde,
     "Janicula, I neither may ne kan°   *can*
305 Lenger the plesance° of myn herte° hyde.°   *pleasure, my heart, hide*
     If that thou vouchesauf° what so bityde,°   *promise, whatever happens*
     Thy doghter wol I take er° that I wende°   *before, turn to go*
     As for my wyf unto hir lyves° ende.   *her life's*

     THOU lovest me—I wot it wel° certeyn°—   *know it well, certainly*
310 And art my feithful° lige° man ybore.°   *faithful, liege, born*
     And al that liketh me,° I dar wel seyn.°   *pleases me, dare well say*
     It liketh thee° and specially° therfore   *pleases you, in particular*
     Tel me that poynt° that I have seyd bifore,°   *point, said before*
     If that thou wolt° unto that purpos drawe,°   *you will, agree*
315 To take me as for thy sone-in-lawe."

     THIS sodeyn cas° this man astonyed° so,   *sudden chance, astonished*
     That reed he wax° abayst° and al quakyng°   *he grew red, embarrassed, trembling*
     He stood. Unnethes° seyde he wordes mo   *scarcely*
     But oonly thus: "Lord," quod he, "my willynge°   *will*
320 Is as ye wole,° ne ayeyns° youre likynge°   *will, nor against, desire*
     I wol nothyng. Ye be my lord so deere.
     Right as yow lust,° governeth this mateere."°   *desire, arrange this matter*

     "YET wol I," quod this markys softely,
     "That in thy chambre I and thou and she
325 Have a collacioun.° And wostow° why?   *meeting, do you know*
     For I wol axe if it hire wille be
     To be my wyf and reule hire after me.°   *obey me*
     And al this shal be doon in thy presence.
     I wol noght speke out of thyn audience."°   *your hearing*

330 AND in the chambre whil they were aboute
     Hir tretys° which as ye shal after heere,°   *their bargaining, hear*

---

1   Here, and also at lines 337 and 344, there are Latin glosses in the margin quoting the beginning
    of the equivalent passages from Petrarch.

The peple cam unto the hous withoute°   *outside*
And wondred hem° in how honeste manere   *were amazed*
And tentifly° she kepte° hir fader deere.   *attentively, kept*
335 But outrely° Grisildis wondre myghte,°   *extremely, might wonder*
For nevere erst° ne saugh° she swich° a sighte.   *before, saw, such*

No wonder is, thogh° she were astoned,°   *though, astonished*
To seen so greet a gest° come in that place.   *guest*
She nevere was to swiche gestes woned,°   *accustomed*
340 For which she looked with ful pale face.
But shortly forth this tale for to chace,°   *continue*
Thise arn° the wordes that the markys sayde   *are*
To this benigne,° verray, feithful° mayde: *kind, true*

"GRISILDE," he seyde, "ye shal wel understonde
345 It liketh° to youre fader and to me   *pleases*
That I yow wedde. And eek° it may so stonde,°   *also, stand*
As I suppose ye wol that it so be.
But thise demandes° axe I first," quod he,   *conditions*
"That sith° it shal be doon° in hastif° wyse,   *since, done, hastily*
350 Wol ye assent or elles yow avyse?¹

I SEYE this: be ye redy with good herte
To al my lust, and that I frely may,²
As me best thynketh, do yow laughe or smerte,³
And nevere ye to grucche it,° nyght° ne day.   *complain about it, night*
355 And eek whan I sey ye ne sey nat nay,°   *yes you do not say no*
Neither by word ne frownyng contenance.°⁴   *frowning face*
Swere this, and heere I swere yow alliance."

WONDRYNGE upon this word, quakynge° for drede,⁵   *trembling*
She seyde, "Lord, undigne° and unworthy   *undeserving*
360 Am I to thilke honour° that ye me beede.°   *that honor, offer*
But as ye wole youreself, right so wol I,
And heere I swere that nevere willyngly
In werk ne thoght I nyl° yow disobeye,   *will not*
For to be deed,⁶ though me were looth to deye."°   *though I would rather not die*

---

1   "Will you agree, or do you wish to think about it?" Skeat notes that this was "really a delicate
    way of expressing refusal," as in the formula "le roy s'avisera" (the king will think about it),
    which was used to refuse proposed laws.
2   "To [do] all my desire and what I freely may [desire]."
3   "As it seems best to me, whether it pleases or displeases you."
4   There is a Latin gloss in the margin quoting the equivalent expression from Petrarch.
5   There is a Latin gloss in the margin quoting Griselda's vow from Petrarch.
6   "Even if I were to be dead (i.e., condemned to die) ..."

365 "THIS is ynogh, Grisilde myn," quod he,
And forth he gooth with a ful sobre cheere.°   *serious face*
Out at the dore and after that cam she,
And to the peple he seyde in this manere.
"Ths is my wyf," quod he, "That standeth heere.
370 Honoureth hire and loveth hire, I preye,
Whoso me loveth.° Ther is namoore to seye."   *Whoever loves me*

AND for that nothyng of hir olde geere°[1]   *belongings*
She sholde brynge° into his hous,° he bad°   *should bring, house, ordered*
That wommen sholde dispoillen hire° right theere.°   *should undress her, there*
375 Of which thise ladyes were nat right glad°   *not very happy*
To handle hir clothes wherinne° she was clad.°   *in which, clothed*
But nathelees,° this mayde bright of hewe°   *nevertheless, color*
Fro° foot to heed° they clothed han al newe.   *from, head*

HIR heris° han they kembd° that lay untressed°   *hairs, have combed, unbraided*
380 Ful rudely,° and with hir fyngres smale°   *roughly, their small fingers*
A corone° on hire heed they han ydressed°   *nuptial garland, have placed*
And sette hire ful of nowches° grete and smale.   *adorned her with brooches*
Of hire array, what sholde I make a tale?[2]
Unnethe° the peple hir knew for hire fairnesse   *scarcely*
385 Whan she translated° was in swich richesse.   *transformed*

THIS markys hath hire spoused° with a ryng   *has married her*
Broght° for the same cause and thanne hire sette°   *brought, then set her*
Upon an hors snow whit° and wel amblyng,°   *white, trotting well*
And to his paleys er° he lenger lette,°   *before, longer delayed*
390 With joyful peple that hire° ladde° and mette,°   *her, led, met*
Convoyed° hire, and thus the day they spende her   *escorted*
In revel° til the sonne gan descende.°   *celebrating, sun began to go down*

AND shortly forth this tale for to chace,°   *continue*
I seye that to this newe markysesse
395 God hath swich favour sent hire of his grace,
That it ne semed nat by liklynesse°   *did not seem likely*
That she was born and fed in rudenesse,°   *poverty*
As in a cote° or in an oxe stalle,   *cottage*
But norissed° in an emperoures halle.   *brought up*

---

1   There is a Latin gloss in the margin quoting the equivalent passage from Petrarch.
2   "Why should I make a long story about her clothes."

400 To every wight° she woxen° is so deere°¹   *person, grown, dear*
    And worshipful, that folk ther° she was bore°   *where, born*
    And from hire birthe knewe hire yeer by yeere,
    Unnethe trowed° they—but dorste han swore°—   *scarcely believed, dared have sworn*
    That she to Janicle of which I spak bifore
405 She doghter were, for as by conjecture°   *inference*
    Hem thoughte° she was another creature.   *It seemed to them*

    For though that evere vertuous was she,°   *had always been*
    She was encressed° in swich° excellence   *increased, such*
    Of thewes° goode yset° in heigh bountee°   *morals, well set, high goodness*
410 And so discreet and fair of eloquence
    So benigne° and so digne of reverence°   *kind, worthy of honor*
    And koude so the peples herte° embrace,   *people's heart*
    That ech hire lovede that looked on hir face.

    Noght oonly° of Saluces in the toun   *not only*
415 Publiced° was the beautee of hir name,   *made public*
    But eek biside° in many a regioun,   *round about*
    If oon seide wel° another seyde the same.   *one said well*
    So spradde° of hire heighe bountee the name,   *spred*
    That men and wommen as wel yonge as olde
420 Goon° to Saluce upon hire to biholde.°   *go, to see her*

    Thus Walter lowely°—nay° but roially°²—   *lowly, no, royally*
    Wedded with fortunat honestetee.°   *fortunate honor*
    In Goddes pees° lyveth ful esily°   *peace, lives very well*
    At hoom. And outward grace ynogh° had he.³   *enough*
425 And for he saugh° that under lowe⁴ degree   *saw*
    Was vertu° hid, the peple hym heelde°   *virtue, considered him*
    A prudent man, and that is seyn ful seelde!°   *seen very seldom*

    Nat oonly° this Grisildis thurgh hir wit°   *not only, intelligence*
    Koude° al the feet° of wyfly humblenesse°   *knew, duties, humility*
430 But eek, whan that the cas° required it,   *situation*
    The commune° profit koude° she redresse.°   *common, could, promote*
    Ther nas° discord, rancour,° ne hevynesse°   *was not, rancor, sadness*

---

1   There is a Latin gloss in the margin quoting the equivalent passage from Petrarch.
2   There is a Latin gloss in the margin quoting the equivalent passage from Petrarch.
3   That Walter had "outward grace" means either that he appeared gracious or benevolent on the
    surface or that he did so in public, outside his home.
4   Ellesmere reads "heigh"; the emendation is from Hengwrt. Lines 425, 428, and 435 have mar-
    ginal glosses quoting equivalent passages from Petrarch.

In al that land that she ne koude apese°   *appease*
And wisely brynge hem alle° in reste and ese.°   *bring them all, rest and quiet*

435 THOUGH that hire housbonde absent were, anon,°   *at once*
If gentilmen° or othere of hire contree   *noblemen*
Were wrothe,° she wolde bryngen hem aton.°   *angry, would get them to agree*
So wise and rype° wordes hadde she   *mature*
And juggementz° of so greet equitee,°   *judgments, fairness*
440 That she from Hevene° sent was, as men wende,°   *Heaven, thought*
Peple to save and every wrong t'amende.°   *to amend*

NAT longe tyme after that this Grisild
Was wedded, she a doghter hath ybore.°   *has given birth to*
Al had hire levere have born a man-child,[1]
445 Glad was this markys and the folk therfore.°   *for this*
For though a mayde-child coome al bifore,°   *girl comes before*
She may unto a man-child° atteyne°   *boy, attain*
By liklihede,° syn° she nys nat bareyne.°   *probability, since, is not barren*

EXPLICIT SECUNDA PARS. INCIPIT TERCIA PARS[2]

THER fil,° as it bifalleth tymes mo,°[3]   *it happened, it happens frequently*
450 Whan that this child had souked° but a throwe,°   *suckled, short time*
This markys in his herte longeth° so   *desires*
To tempte his wyf, hir sadnesse° for to knowe,   *constancy*
That he ne myghte out of his herte throwe°   *could not expell from his heart*
This merveillous desir° his wyf t'assaye.°   *marvelous desire, to try*
455 Nedelees, God woot, he thoghte hire for t'affraye.[4]

HE hadde assayed hire ynogh bifore°   *enough before*
And foond° hire evere good. What neded it°   *found, why was it necessary*
Hire for to tempte and alwey moore and moore,
Though som men preise it for a subtil wit?°   *clever idea*
460 But as for me, I seye that yvele° it sit   *evil*
To assaye a wyf whan that it is no nede
And putten hire in angwyssh° and in drede.°   *anguish, fear*

FOR which this markys wroghte° in this manere: *behaved*
He cam allone° anyght° theras she lay[5]   *came alone, at night*

---

1 "Although she would have preferred to have given birth to a male child."
2 "Here ends the second part. The third part begins."
3 There is a Latin gloss in the margin quoting the equivalent passage from Petrarch.
4 "Needlessly, God knows, he thought to frighten her."
5 It was the custom in the Middle Ages for rulers and their wives to have separate living quarters.

465 With stierne° face and with ful trouble cheere°   *stern, very ominous expression*
And seyde thus, "Grisilde," quod he, "that day
That I yow took out of youre povere array°   *poor clothing*
And putte yow in estaat° of heigh noblesse,   *estate*
Ye have nat° that forgeten° as I gesse.°   *not, forgotten, guess*

470 I SEYE, Grisilde, this present dignitee°   *dignity*
In which that I have put yow, as I trowe,°   *believe*
Maketh yow nat foyetful° for to be   *forgetful*
That I yow took in povre estaat ful lowe,°   *poor estate very low*
For any wele° ye moot youreselven knowe.°   *luck, might*
475 Taak heed° of every word that y yow° seye.   *take heed, to you*
Ther is no wight° that hereth° it but we tweye.°   *person, hears, two*

YE wot° youreself wel how that ye cam heere   *know*
Into this hous. It is nat longe ago.
And though to me that ye be lief° and deere°   *beloved, dear*
480 Unto my gentils,° ye be nothyng so.°   *nobles, not so*
They seyn to hem° it is greet shame and wo°   *them, woe*
For to be subgetz° and to been in servage°   *subjected, be in servitude*
To thee, that born art of a smal village.

AND namely,° sith° thy doghter was ybore°   *especially, since, born*
485 Thise° wordes han° they spoken doutelees.°   *these, have, doubtless*
But I desire as I have doon bifore°   *done before*
To lyve my lyf with hem° in reste and pees.°   *them, peace*
I may nat in this caas° be recchelees.°   *situation, reckless*
I moot doon° with thy doghter for the beste,   *must do*
490 Nat as I wolde but as my peple leste.°   *people desire*

AND yet, God woot,° this is ful looth° to me,   *God knows, very hateful*
But nathelees° withoute youre wityng°   *nevertheless, knowledge*
I wol nat doon° but this wol I," quod he,   *not do*
"That ye to me assente° as in this thyng.°   *agree, matter*
495 Shewe° now youre pacience° in youre werkyng°   *show, patience, behavior*
That ye me highte and swore° in youre village   *promised*
That day that maked was oure mariage."

WHAN she had herd al this she noght ameved°   *by no means moved*
Neither in word or chiere° or contenaunce.°¹   *face, expression*
500 For as it semed,° she was nat agreved.°   *seemed, not grieved*
She seyde, "Lord, al lyth° in youre plesaunce.°   *lies, pleasure*

---

1   There is a Latin gloss in the margin quoting the equivalent phrase from Petrarch.

My child and I with hertely obeisaunce°   *hearty obedience*
Been youres al, and ye mowe save and spille°   *might save and kill*
Youre owene thyng. Werketh after° youre wille.°   *do according to, will*

505 THER may nothyng, God so my soule save,
Liken to yow that may displese° me.   *please*
Ne I ne desire° nothyng for to have ·   *do not desire*
Ne drede° for to leese,° save oonly° thee.   *fear, lose, except only*
This wyl is in myn herte, and ay° shal be.   *ever*
510 No lengthe of tyme or deeth may this deface°   *change*
Ne chaunge my corage° to another place."   *heart*

GLAD was this markys of hire answeryng,
But yet he feyned° as he were nat so.   *pretended*
Al drery° was his cheere° and his lookyng   *grim, face*
515 Whan that he sholde out of the chambre go.
Soone after this a furlong¹ wey° or two   *away*
He prively° hath toold° al his entente°   *privately, has told, intent*
Unto a man and to his wyf hym sente.

A MANER sergeant° was this privee° man,   *kind of officer, secret*
520 The which that feithful° ofte° he founden hadde°   *faithful, often, had been found*
In thynges grete,° and eek swich folk wel kan   *great matters*
Doon execucioun° on thynges badde.°   *put into practice, bad things*
The lord knew wel that he hym loved and dradde,°   *feared him*
And whan this sergeant wiste° the lordes wille,   *knew*
525 Into the chambre he stalked° hym ful stille.°   *walked, very quietly*

"MADAME," he seyde, "ye moote foryeve° it me   *must forgive*
Though I do thyng° to which I am constreyned.°   *[a] thing, constrained*
Ye been so wys° that ful wel° knowe ye   *wise, very well*
That lordes heestes° mowe nat been yfeyned.°   *commandments, disregarded*
530 They mowe° wel been biwailled and compleyned.°   *may, wept for and lamented*
But men moote nede° unto hire lust° obeye,   *necessarily must, their desire*
And so wol I. Ther is namoore to seye.

THIS child I am comanded for to take."
And spak namoore but out the child he hente°   *took*
535 Despitously° and gan a cheere make°   *cruelly, assumed an expression*
As though he wolde han slayn° it er he wente.   *have killed*
Grisildis moot al suffren and consente,°   *must endure all and consent*

---

1 A furlong, originally the length of a plowed furrow, was 220 yards.

And as a lamb she sitteth meke° and stille°   meek, quietly
And leet° this crueel sergeant doon° his wille.   lets, do

540 SUSPECIOUS° was the diffame° of this man,[1]   ominous, bad reputation
Suspect° his face, suspect his word also,   ominous
Suspect the tyme in which he this bigan,°   began
Allas! Hir doghter that she loved so,
She wende° he wolde han slawen° it right tho.°   thought, would have killed, there
545 But nathelees,° she neither weepe ne syked,°   nevertheless, nor sighed
Consentynge hire to that the markys lyked.°   desired

BUT atte laste to speken she bigan,
And mekely° she to the sergeant preyde,°   meekly, prayed
So as he was a worthy, gentil° man,   noble
550 That she moste kisse° hir° child er° that it deyde.°   might kiss, her, before, died
And in hir barm° this litel child she leyde°   her lap, laid
With ful sad face° and gan° the child to kisse   very grave face, began
And lulled it and after gan it blisse.°   began to bless it

AND thus she seyde in hire benigne voys,°   kind voice
555 "Fareweel, my child. I shal thee nevere see.
But sith° I thee have marked with the croys°   since, cross
Of thilke° fader, blessed moote° he be,   that, may
That for us deyde° upon a croys° of tree,°   died, cross, wood
Thy soule, litel child, I hym bitake,°   give over to him
560 For this nyght shaltow dyen° for my sake."   shall you die

I TROWE° that to a norice° in this cas°   believe, nurse, situation
It had been hard this reuthe° for to se.°   pity, see
Wel myghte a mooder thanne han cryd "Allas!"
But nathelees, so sad° and stidefast° was she,   constant, steadfast
565 That she endured al adversitee
And to the sergeant mekely she sayde,
"Have heer agayn youre litel, yonge mayde.°   young maid

"GOOTH now," quod she, "and dooth my lordes heeste.
But o thyng wol I prey° yow of youre grace,   one thing will I ask
570 That but° my lord forbad yow, atte leeste°   unless, at the least
Burieth° this litel body in som place   bury
That beestes ne no briddes° it to race.°""   beasts nor birds, tear to pieces

---

1   There is a series of Latin glosses in the margin quoting the equivalent expressions ("A man of sinister reputation," etc.) from Petrarch.

But he no word wol to that purpos seye
But took the child and wente upon his weye.

575 THIS sergeant cam unto his lord ageyn,
And of Grisildis wordes and hire cheere°   *her expression*
He tolde hym point for point in short and pleyn°   *plain*
And hym presenteth with° his doghter deere.   *gives him*
Somwhat this lord hath routhe° in his manere,°   *pity, manner*
580 But nathelees his purpos heeld° he stille   *held*
As lordes doon whan they wol han hir wille°   *will have their will*

AND bad° his sergeant that he pryvely°   *commanded, secretly*
Sholde this child softe wynde° and wrappe°   *softly wind, wrap*
With alle circumstances tendrely°   *tenderly*
585 And carie° it in a cofre° or in a lappe,°   *carry, box, pouch*
But upon peyne his heed of° for to swappe°   *on pain of his head, swipe off*
That no man sholde knowe of his entente
Ne whenne ne whider° that he wente,   *nor when nor where*

BUT at Boloigne° to his suster deere,   *Bologna (Italian city)*
590 That thilke tyme° of Pavik¹ was countesse,°   *that time, countess*
He sholde it take and shewe hire this mateere,°   *explain to her this matter*
Bisekynge° hire to doon hire bisynesse°   *asking, take eager care*
This child to fostre° in alle gentillesse.°   *raise up, nobility*
And whos child that it was he bad hym hyde°   *commanded him to hide*
595 From every wight° for oght that may bityde.°   *person, whatever might happen*

THE sergeant gooth and hath fulfild° this thyng.°   *fulfilled, task*
But to this markys now retourne we,
For now gooth he ful faste ymaginyng°   *very firmly imagining*
If by his wyves cheere° he myghte se   *expression*
600 Or by hire word aperceyve° that she   *perceive*
Were chaunged.° But he nevere hire koude fynde   *changed*
But evere in oon ylike,° sad° and kynde.°   *the same, constant, kind*

As glad, as humble, as bisy° in servyse,°²   *busy, service*
And eek° in love as she was wont° to be   *also, accustomed*
605 Was she to hym in every maner° wyse.   *in every type of situation*
Ne of hir doghter noght a word spak she.

---

1   This region does not exist except in the fiction of this story. Giovanni Boccaccio, the story's first
    author, gave the name as Panago, while Petrarch, whom the Clerk alludes to as his source, gives
    it as Panico. Chaucer may have spelled the name Panik in the exemplar from which the scribe
    Adam Pinkhurst copied.
2   There is a Latin gloss in the margin quoting the equivalent passage from Petrarch.

Noon accident° for noon adversitee°   *no outward sign, adversity*
Was seyn in hire, ne nevere hir doghter name
Ne nempned° she in ernest nor in game.°   *named, seriously or in jest*

EXPLICIT TERCIA PARS. SEQUITUR PARS QUARTA[1]

610 IN this estaat° ther passed been foure yeer[2]   *condition*
Er° she with childe was.° But as God wolde,   *before, was pregnant*
A man-child° she bar° by this Walter,   *male child, bore*
Ful gracious and fair for to biholde.
And whan that folk it to his fader tolde,
615 Nat oonly° he but al his countree merye°   *not only, merry*
Was for this child, and God they thanke and herye.°   *praise*

WHAN it was two yeer old and fro° the brest°   *from, breast*
Departed of his norice,°[3] on a day   *nurse*
This markys caughte yet another lest°   *desire*
620 To tempte his wyf yet ofter° if he may.   *more often*
O nedelees° was she tempted in assay!°   *needless, trial*
But wedded men ne knowe no mesure°   *any measure*
Whan that they fynde a pacient° creature.   *patient*

"WYF," quod this markys, "ye han herd er° this   *before*
625 My peple sikly berth oure mariage,°[4]   *take our marriage ill*
And namely° sith my sone yborn° is.   *especially, born*
Now is it worse than evere in al oure age.
The murmure sleeth° myn herte° and my corage,   *kills, heart*
For to myne eres° comth the voys° so smerte,°   *my ears, voice, painful*
630 That it wel ny destroyed hath° myn herte.   *almost has destroyed*

NOW sey they thus, 'Whan Walter is agon,°   *gone*
Thanne shal the blood of Janicle succede°   *succeed*
And been oure lord, for oother have we noon.'°   *none*
Swiche wordes seith my peple, out of drede.°   *without doubt*
635 Wel oughte I of swich° murmur taken heede.°   *such, take heed*
For certeinly I drede° swich sentence°   *fear, such meaning*
Though they nat pleyn° speke in myn audience.°   *do not plainly, hearing*

---

1 "Here ends the third part. The fourth part follows."
2 There is a Latin gloss in the margin quoting the equivalent passage from Petrarch.
3 Because it was not the custom in medieval high-status households for a mother to nurse her own baby, the child would be given to a wet-nurse, who would feed it with her own milk.
4 There is a Latin gloss in the margin, copied by the main scribe, Adam Pinkhurst, quoting the equivalent passage from Petrarch. A second and later hand has copied the gloss out again.

I WOLDE lyve in pees if that I myghte.
Wherfore° I am disposed outrely°   *Therefore, utterly*
640 As I his suster served by nyghte,
Right so thenke I to serve hym pryvely.°   *secretly*
This warne° I yow: that ye nat° sodeynly°   *warn, not, suddenly*
Out of youreself for no wo° sholde outreye.°   *woe, should have a breakdown*
Beth pacient,° and therof° I yow preye."°   *be patient, for this, ask*

645 "I HAVE," quod she, "seyd thus and evere shal:
I wol nothyng ne nyl° nothyng certayn°   *will not, certainly*
But as yow list.° Naught greveth° me at al   *desire, grieves*
Though that my doughter and my sone be slayn
At youre comandement. This is to sayn,
650 I have noght° had no part of children tweyne°   *not, two*
But first siknesse° and after wo° and peyne.°   *sickness, woe, pain*

YE been oure lord. Dooth with youre owene thyng°   *own property*
Right as yow list.° Axeth° no reed° at me.°   *desire, ask, counsel, from me*
For as I lefte° at hoom al my clothyng   *left*
655 Whan I first cam to you, right so," quod she,
"Lefte I my wyl° and al my libertee   *will*
And took youre clothyng. Wherfore I yow preye,
Dooth youre plesaunce.° I wol youre lust obeye.°   *do your pleasure, desire obey*

AND certes,° if I hadde prescience°   *certainly, foresight*
660 Youre wyl to knowe er° ye youre lust° me tolde,   *before, pleasure*
I wolde° it doon° withouten necligence.°   *would, do, negligence*
But now I woot° youre lust and what ye wolde,°   *know, willed*
Al youre plesance° ferme° and stable° I holde.   *pleasure, firmly, stably*
For wiste I° that my deeth wolde do yow ese,°¹   *if I knew, ease*
665 Right gladly wolde I dyen yow to plese.°   *die to please you*

DETH may noght make no comparisoun
Unto youre love." And whan this markys say°   *saw*
The constance° of his wyf, he caste adoun°   *constancy, cast down*
Hise eyen° two and wondreth that° she may   *his eyes, wonders how*
670 In pacience suffre° al this array.°   *suffer, treatment*
And forth he goth with drery contenance,°   *sad expression*
But to his herte it was ful greet plesance.°   *very great pleasure*

THIS ugly sergeant in the same wyse°   *way*
That he hire doghter caughte, right so he,

---

1   There is a Latin gloss in the margin quoting the equivalent passage from Petrarch.

675 Or worse—if men worse kan devyse,°— *can imagine*
Hath hent hire sone° that ful was of beautee. *has taken her son*
And evere in oon° so pacient was she *in every circumstance*
That she no chiere° maade° of hevynesse° *[bad] expression, made, sadness*
But kiste hir° sone and after gan it blesse.° *kissed her, blessed him*

680 SAVE this: she preyde° hym that if he myghte *asked*
Hir litel sone he wolde in erthe° grave° *earth, bury*
His tendre lymes° delicaat° to sighte° *tender limbs, delicate, sight*
Fro foweles° and fro beestes for to save. *from birds*
But she noon answere of hym myghte have.
685 He wente his wey as hym° nothyng° ne roghte.° *him, nothing, did not care*
But to Boloigne° he tendrely° it broghte.° *Bologna, tenderly, brought*

THIS markys wondred evere lenger the moore° *ever more and more*
Upon hir pacience° and if that he *patience*
Ne hadde soothly knowen ther bifoore° *not truly known before this*
690 That parfitly° hir children loved she, *perfectly*
He wolde have wend° that of som subtiltee° *thought, some treachery*
And of malice or for crueel corage° *cruel heart*
That she hadde suffred this with sad visage.° *constant expression*

BUT wel he knew that next hymself,° certayn,° *next to himself, certainly*
695 She loved hir children best in every wyse.° *way*
But now of wommen wolde I axen fayn° *gladly ask*
If thise assayes° myghte nat suffise.° *these trials, might not suffice*
What koude a sturdy° housbonde moore devyse° *harsh, more imagine*
To preeve° hir wyfhod° or hir stedefastnesse?° *prove, wifehood, steadfastness*
700 And he continuynge evere in sturdinesse?° *cruelty*

BUT ther been folk of swich condcioun,° *such condition*
That whan they have a certein° purpose take° *certain, taken*
They kan nat stynte° of hire entencioun.° *stop, their intention*
But right as they were bounden to that stake *tied*
705 They wol nat° of that firste purpos slake.° *not, desist*
Right so this markys fulliche hath purposed° *fully had intended*
To tempte his wyf as he was first disposed.

HE waiteth° if by word or contenance° *watches, expression*
That she to hym was changed of corage.° *heart*
710 But nevere koude he fynde° variance.° *find, a change*
She was ay oon° in herte and in visage,° *ever the same, face*
And ay the forther° that she was in age, *ever the more*
The moore trewe, if that it were possible,
She was to hym in love and moore penyble.° *more attentive*

715 FOR which it semed° thus, that of hem° two   *seemed, them*
Ther nas° but o wyl,° for as Walter leste,°   *was not, one will, desired*
The same lust was hire plesance also.
And, God be thanked, al fil for the beste.°   *all was for the best*
She shewed wel, for no worldly unreste
720 A wyf, as of hirself, nothyng ne sholde
Wille, in effect, but as hir housbonde wolde.¹

THE sclaundre° of Walter ofte° and wyde spradde,°²   *slander, often, widely spread*
That of a crueel herte he wikkedly,
For he a povre womman wedded hadde,
725 Hath mordred° bothe his children prively.°   *murdered, secretly*
Swich murmure° was among hem° communly.°   *such murmur, them, commonly*
No wonder is, for to the peples ere°   *people's ear*
Ther cam no word but that they mordred were.

FOR which whereas his peple therbifore°   *before this*
730 Hadde loved hym wel, the sclaundre° of his diffame°   *slander, bad reputation*
Made hem that they hym hated therfore.°   *because of it*
To been a mordrere° is an hateful name.   *murderer*
But nathelees, for ernest ne for game,°   *seriously or in jest*
He of his crueel purpos° nolde stente.°   *purpose, would not cease*
735 To tempte° his wyf was set al his entente.   *test*

WHAN that his doghter twelf yeer was of age,
He to the court of Rome, in subtil° wyse   *cleverly*
Enformed° of his wyl,° sente his message,   *informed, will*
Comaundynge hem swiche bulles to devyse°   *to compose such [papal] bulls (decrees)*
740 As to his crueel purpose may suffyse,°   *suffice*
How that the Pope as for his peples° reste   *people's*
Bad° hym to wedde another if hym leste.°   *commanded, if he wished*

I SEYE he bad they sholde countrefete°   *counterfeit*
The Popes bulles,° makynge mencioun°   *decrees, making mention*
745 That he hath leve° his firste wyf to lete,°   *leave, leave*
As by the Popes dispensacioun,°   *dispensation*
To stynte° rancour° and dissencioun°   *stop, ill will, dissent*
Bitwixe his peple and hym. Thus seyde the bulle,
The which they han publiced° atte fulle.°   *have published, in full*

---

1 "She clearly showed [that] no wife, despite any worldly misfortune, should, for her own sake,
   will anything, in fact, but as her husband wills it."
2 There is a Latin gloss in the margin quoting the equivalent passage from Petrarch.

750 THE rude peple° as it no wonder is   *commoners*
    Wenden° ful wel° that it hadde be right so,   *thought, very well*
    But whan thise tidynges° cam to Grisildis,   *this news*
    I deeme° that hire herte was ful wo!°   *judge, woe*
    But she ylike sad° forevere mo°   *likewise constant, more*
755 Disposed was, this humble creature,
    The adversitee of Fortune al t'endure,°   *to endure*

    ABIDYNGE° evere his lust and his plesance°   *enduring, will and pleasure*
    To whom that she was yeven° herte and al,   *given*
    As to hire° verray° worldly suffisance.°   *her, true, sustenance*
760 But shortly, if this storie I tellen shal,
    This markys writen hath in special°   *specially*
    A lettre° in which he sheweth° his entente°   *letter, shows, intent*
    And secreely he to Boloigne it sente.

    To the Erl° of Pavyk, which that hadde tho°   *earl, then*
765 Wedded his suster, preyde° he specially   *asked*
    To bryngen hoom agayn hise children two
    In honurable estaat° al openly.   *honorable condition*
    But o thyng he hym preyde outrely,°   *with all his force*
    That he to no wight,° though men wolde enquere,°   *person, inquire*
770 Sholde nat telle whos children that they were,

    BUT seye the mayden sholde ywedded be°   *should be married*
    Unto the Markys of Saluce anon.°   *immediately*
    And as this erl was preyd, so dide he,
    For at day-set° he on his wey° is goon°   *sunset, way, gone*
775 Toward Saluce, and lordes many oon°   *many a one*
    In riche array° this mayden for to gyde,°   *dress, guide*
    Hir yonge brother ridynge hire bisyde.°   *beside her*

    ARRAYED° was toward hir mariage   *dressed*
    This fresshe mayde ful of gemmes cleere,°   *bright jewels*
780 Hir brother, which that seven° yeer was of age   *MS .vij.*
    Arrayed eek ful fressh° in his manere.   *dressed also very attractively*
    And thus in greet noblesse and with glad cheere°   *expression*
    Toward Saluces shapynge hir journey°   *making their journey*
    Fro day to day they ryden in hir wey.

EXPLICIT QUARTA PARS. SEQUITUR PARS QUINTA[1]

---

1   "Here ends the fourth part. The fifth part follows."

785 AMONG al, this, after his wikke usage,   *test*
 This markys yet his wyf to tempte° moore   *test*
 To the outtreste preeve° of hir corage,°   *furthest proof, heart*
 Fully to han° experience and loore°   *have, learning*
 If that she were as stidefast° as bifoore,°   *steadfast, before*
790 He on a day in open audience°   *open hearing*
 Ful boistously° hath seyd hire this sentence:°   *very loudly, statement*

 "CERTES, Grisilde, I hadde ynogh plesance
 To han yow to my wyf for youre goodnesse,
 As for youre trouthe,° and for youre obeisance,°   *truth, obedience*
795 Noght for youre lynage° ne for youre richesse.   *lineage*
 But now knowe I in verray soothfastnesse°   *true truthfulness*
 That in greet° lordshipe, if I wel avyse,°   *great, judge well*
 Ther is greet servitute in sondry wyse.°   *different ways*

 I MAY nat doon as every plowman may.
800 My peple me constreyneth° for to take   *constrain*
 Another wyf and crien day by day,
 And eek the Pope, rancour° for to slake.°   *anger, diminish*
 Consenteth° it that dar° I undertake   *consents, dare*
 And treweliche thus muche I wol yow seye:
805 My newe wyf is comynge by the weye.°   *along the road*

 BE strong of herte and voyde anon hir place,°   *leave her place immediately*
 And thilke dowere° that ye broghten me,   *the same dower*
 Taak it agayn. I graunte° it of my grace.   *grant*
 Retourneth to youre fadres hous," quod he.
810 "No man may alwey han prosperitee.°   *always have prosperity*
 With evene° herte I rede° yow t'endure°   *peaceful, advise, to endure*
 This strook° of Fortune or of aventure."°   *stroke, chance*

 AND she answerde agayn in pacience,
 "My lord," quod she, "I woot and wiste alway°   *knew always*
815 How that bitwixen° youre magnificence   *between*
 And my poverte no wight° kan° ne° may   *person, can, nor*
 Maken comparisoun. It is no nay.°   *it cannot be denied*
 I ne heeld° me nevere digne° in no manere°   *did not hold, worthy, manner*
 To be youre wyf—no, ne youre chambrere.°   *chambermaid*

820 AND in this hous ther° ye me lady maade,°   *where, made*
 The heighe God take I for my witnesse
 And also wysly he my soule glaade,°   *make glad*

I nevere heeld° me lady ne maistresse,°   held, mistress
But humble servant to youre worthynesse,
825 And evere shal whil that my lyf may dure,°   endure
Aboven every worldly creature.

THAT ye so longe of youre benignitee°   kindness
Han holden° me in honour and nobleys,°   have held, nobility
Whereas° I was noght worthy bee,°   where, to be
830 That thonke I God and yow, to whom I preye,
Foryelde it yow.° Ther is namoore to seye.   give it back to you
Unto my fader gladly wol I wende°   will I turn back
And with hym° dwelle unto my lyves° ende.   him, life's

THER I was fostred° of a child ful smal,°   brought up, very small
835 Til I be deed° my lyf ther wol° I lede,°   dead, will, lead
A wydwe° clene° in body, herte, and al.   widow, pure
For sith° I yaf° to yow my maydenhede°   since, gave, virginity
And am youre trewe wyf, it is no drede,°   it cannot be denied
God shilde° swich° a lordes wyf to take   shield, such
840 Another man to housbonde or to make.°   mate

AND of youre newe wyf, God of his grace
So graunte yow wele° and prosperitee.°   well-being, prosperity
For I wol gladly yelden hire° my place   yield her
In which that I was blisful wont to bee.°   accustomed to be happy
845 For sith it liketh° yow, my lord," quod shee,   pleases
"That whilom° weren al myn hertes reste,°   once, heart's ease
That I shal goon,° I wol goon whan yow leste.°   go, when you wish

BUT theras° ye me profre° swich dowaire°   since, offer, dower
As I first broghte,° it is wel° in my mynde°   brought, well, mind
850 It were my wrecched clothes, nothyng faire,°   not attractive
The whiche to me were hard now for to fynde.°   find
O goode God, how gentil° and how kynde°   noble, kind
Ye semed° by youre speche and youre visage°   seemed, face
The day that maked° was oure mariage!   made

855 BUT sooth is seyd, algate I fynde it trewe[1]
For in effect it preeved° is on me,   proven
Love is noght oold as whan that it is newe.
But certes,° lord, for noon adversitee°   certainly, no adversity
To dyen in the cas,° it shal nat bee   even though I should die for it

---

1 "But it is truly said, at least, I find it is true …"

860 That evere in word or werk° I shal repente°　　　*deed, shall repent*
That I yow yaf° myn herte in hool entente.°　　　*gave you, whole intent*

My lord, ye woot that in my fadres place
Ye dide me streepe° out of my povre weede°　　　*made me strip, poor clothing*
And richely me cladden° of youre grace　　　*dressed*
865 To yow broghte I noght elles, out of drede,°　　　*it is no doubt*
But feith° and nakednesse and maydenhede.°　　　*faith, virginity*
And heere agayn my clothyng I restoore°　　　*restore*
And eek° my weddyng ryng foreveremoore.　　　*also*

The remenant of youre jueles° redy° be　　　*jewels, ready*
870 In with youre chambre, dar° I saufly sayn.°　　　*dare, safely say*
Naked out of my fadres hous," quod she,
"I cam, and naked moot I turne agayn.°¹　　　*return again*
Al youre plesance wol° I folwen fayn,°　　　*will, gladly follow*
But yet I hope it be nat youre entente
875 That I smoklees° out of youre paleys° wente.　　　*without an undergarment, palace*

Ye koude nat doon so dishoneste° a thyng　　　*dishonorable*
That thilke° wombe in which youre children leye°　　　*the same, lay*
Sholde biforn the peple in my walkyng
Be seyn° al bare. Wherfore° I yow preye,　　　*seen, therefore*
880 Lat° me nat° lyk° a worm go by the weye.²　　　*let, not, like*
Remembre yow, myn owene lord so deere,
I was youre wyf, though I unworthy weere.

Wherfore in gerdon of° my maydenhede　　　*as a reward for*
Which that I broghte and noght agayn° I bere,°　　　*not again, carry away*
885 As vouchethsauf to yeve° me to my meede°　　　*agree to give, reward*
But swich a smok as I was wont to were,°　　　*accustomed to wear*
That I therwith° may wrye° the wombe of here　　　*with it, cover*
That was youre wyf. And heer take I my leeve
Of yow, myn owene lord, lest I yow greve."°　　　*grieve you*

890 "The smok,"° quod he, "that thou hast on thy bak,　　　*undergarment*
Lat it be stille° and bere° it forth with thee."　　　*let it remain, carry*
But wel unnethes° thilke° word he spak°　　　*scarcely, that, spoke*
But wente his wey° for routhe° and for pitee.°　　　*way, pity, pity*
Biforn the folk hirselven strepeth° she.　　　*strips*

---

1 Griselda quotes here Job 1:21.
2 The phrase "naked as a worm" was proverbial.

895 And in hir smok with heed and foot al bare
Toward hir fader hous forth is she fare.°   *has she journeyed*

THE folk hire folwe, wepynge in hir weye,
And Fortune ay° they cursen° as they goon.°   *ever, curse, go*
But she fro wepyng kepte hire eyen dreye,°   *kept her eyes dry*
900 Ne in this tyme word ne spak she noon.
Hir fader, that this tidynge° herde anoon,°   *news, immediately*
Curseth° the day and tyme that nature   *curses*
Shoope hym° to been° a lyves° creature,   *destined for him, be, living*

FOR out of doute this olde, povre man
905 Was evere in suspect of hir mariage.°   *ever suspected her marriage*
For evere he demed° sith that it bigan   *thought*
That whan the lord fulfild hadde his corage,°   *desire*
Hym wolde thynke° it were a disparage°   *it would appear to him, dishonor*
To his estaat° so lowe for t'alighte°   *condition, to go down*
910 And voyden hire° as soone as ever he myghte.°   *get rid of her, might*

AGAYNS° his doghter hastiliche° goth he,   *towards, hastily*
For he by noyse of folk knew hire comynge.
And with hire olde coote,° as it myghte be,   *gown*
He covered hire, ful sorwefully wepynge.
915 But on hire body myghte he it nat brynge,°   *not put it*
For rude° was the clooth° and she moore of age°   *of poor quality, cloth, older*
By dayes fele° than at hire mariage.   *many*

THUS with hire fader for a certeyn space°   *certain while*
Dwelleth° this flour° of wyfly° pacience,   *lives, flower, wifely*
920 That neither by hire wordes ne hire face
Biforn the folk ne eek° in hire° absence   *nor also, her*
Ne shewed she that hire was doon offence.°   *she was offended*
Ne of hire heighe estaat no remembraunce,
Ne hadde she as by hire contenaunce.°   *her expression*

925 NO wonder is, for in hire grete estaat
Hire goost° was evere in pleyn humylitee.°   *spirit, plain humility*
No tendre mouth, noon herte delicaat,°   *no self-indulgent spirit*
No pompe, no semblant° of roialtee,°   *semblance, royalty*
But ful of pacient benyngnytee,°   *kindness*
930 Discreet, and pridelees,° ay° honurable,   *without pride, ever*
And to hire housbonde evere meke° and stable.   *meek*

MEN speke of Job and moost° for his humblesse,°   *especially, humility*
As clerkes whan hem list konne wel endite,[1]
Namely of men, but as in soothfastnesse,°   *truth*
935 Though clerkes° preise° wommen but a lite,°   *theologians, praise, little*
Ther kan° no man in humblesse° hym acquite°   *can, humility, acquit himself*
As womman kan ne been half so trewe
As wommen been, but it be falle of newe.°   *recently happened*

FRO Boloigne is this Erl of Pavyk come,
940 Of which the fame° up sprang° to moore and lesse,°   *news, rose up, more and less*
And in the peples eres° alle and some   *people's ears.*
Was kouth° eek that a newe markysesse°   *made known, marquessa*
He with hym broghte, in swich pompe and richesse,
That nevere was ther seyn with mannes eye
945 So noble array° in al West Lumbardye.   *display*

THE markys which that shoope° and knew al this,   *arranged*
Er that this erl was come sente his message
For thilke sely° povre Grisildis,   *that same innocent*
And she with humble herte and glad visage,°   *happy face*
950 Nat with no swollen thoght° in hire corage°   *thought, her heart*
Cam° at his heste° and on hire° knees hire sette,   *came, command, her*
And reverently and wisely she hym grette.

"GRISILDE," quod he, "my wyl is outrely°   *utterly*
This mayden that shal wedded been to me
955 Received be tomorwe as roially°   *royally*
As it possible is in myn hous to be
And eek° that every wight° in his degree   *also, person*
Have his estaat° in sittyng° and servyse°   *rank, sitting, service*
And heigh plesaunce,° as I kan° best devyse.°   *high pleasure, can, devise*

960 I HAVE no wommen suffisaunt,° certayn,   *skillful enough*
The chambres for t'arraye° in ordinaunce°   *to decorate, good order*
After my lust.° And therfore wolde I fayn°   *pleasure, would I gladly*
That thyn° were al swich° manere governaunce.°   *yours, such, [of] control*
Thow knowest eek of old al my plesaunce,
965 Thogh thyn array° be badde and yvel biseye.°   *your clothing, bad-looking*
Do thou thy devoir° at the leeste° weye."   *your duty, at the least*

"NAT oonly, lord, that I am glad," quod she,
"To doon youre lust,° but I desire also   *do your pleasure*

---

1   "As theologians, when they wish, can well write."

Yow for to serve and plese in my degree
970 Withouten feyntyng,° and shal everemo.   *fainting*
Ne nevere for no wele° ne no wo°   *well-being, woe*
Ne shal the goost° withinne myn herte stente°   *spirit, cease*
To love yow best with al my trewe entente."°   *true intent*

AND with that word she gan the hous to dighte°   *began to clean the house*
975 And tables for to sette° and beddes make   *set*
And peyned hire° to doon al that she myghte,   *took pains*
Preyynge° the chambreres° for Goddes sake   *Asking, chambermaids*
To hasten hem and faste swepe and shake.[1]
And she the moost servysable° of alle   *most serviceable*
980 Hath every chambre arrayed° and his halle.   *arranged*

ABOUTEN undren° gan this erl alighte,°   *mid-morning, arrived*
That with hym broghte thise noble children tweye,°   *two*
For which the peple ran to seen the sighte
Of hire array° so richely biseye.°   *their clothing, seen*
985 And thanne at erst amonges hem° they seye°   *among them, say*
That Walter was no fool, thogh° that hym leste°   *though, he desired*
To chaunge° his wyf, for it was for the beste.   *change*

FOR she is fairer, as they deemen° alle,   *judge*
Than is Grisilde and moore tendre° of age,   *more tender*
990 And fairer fruyt bitwene hem sholde falle°   *fruit between them should be born*
And moore plesant for hire heigh lynage.°   *her high lineage*
Hir brother eek so fair was of visage,°   *face*
That hem to seen° the peple hath caught plesaunce,   *to see them*
Commendynge° now the markys governaunce.   *commending*

995 "O STORMY peple, unsad° and evere untrewe,°[2]   *unconstant, untrue*
Ay undiscreet° and chaungynge° as a vane,°   *indiscreet, fickle, weathervane*
Delitynge° evere in rumbul° that is newe,   *delighting, rumor*
For lyk the moone° ay wexe° ye and wane!   *moon, wax*
Ay ful of clapping,° deere ynogh° a jane,°[3]   *chattering, dear enough, coin*
1000 Youre doom° is fals, youre constance° yvele° preeveth!   *judgment, constancy, evil*
A ful greet fool is he that on yow leeveth!"°   *believes you*

THUS seyden sadde° folk in that citee   *constant*
Whan that the peple gazed up and doun,

---

1 "To hurry themselves and quickly sweep and shake [drapery to remove dust]."
2 Lines 995–1008 are not found in Chaucer's sources. There is a Latin gloss in the margin, "Auctor," indicating that this passage offers a moral commentary.
3 "Expensive enough at half a penny." A jane is a small Genoese coin of little value.

For they were glad right° for the noveltee°   *very glad, novelty*
1005 To han a newe lady of hir toun.
He Namoore of this make I now mencioun,
But to Grisilde agayn wol° I me dresse°   *will, turn*
And telle hir constance° and hir bisynesse.°   *her constancy, her busyness*

FUL bisy was Grisilde in everythyng
1010 That to the feeste° was apertinent.°   *feast, appropriate*
Right noght was she abayst° of hire clothyng,   *not very concerned*
Thogh it were rude and somdeel eek torent,°   *also somewhat torn*
But with glad cheere° to the yate° is she went   *happy face, gate*
With oother folk to greete° the markysesse   *greet*
1015 And after that dooth forth hire bisynesse.°   *goes about her business*

WITH so glad chiere° hise gestes° she receyveth   *expression, his guests*
And so konnyngly° everich° in his degree,   *skillfully, everyone*
That no defaute° no man aperceyveth,°   *fault, perceives*
But ay they wondren what she myghte bee
1020 That in so povre array° was for to see°   *dress, to be seen*
And koude° swich° honour and reverence,   *knew, such*
And worthily they preisen° hire prudence.   *praise*

IN al this meenewhile° she ne stente°   *meanwhile, did not stop*
This mayde and eek hir brother to commende
1025 With al hir herte in ful benyngne entente°   *very kind intent*
So wel, that no man koude° hire pris amende.°   *could, improve her praise*
But atte laste° whan° that thise° lordes wende°   *at the last, when, these, turned*
To sitten doun to mete,° he gan to calle°   *sit down to the food, called*
Grisilde, as she was bisy in his halle.

1030 "GRISILDE," quod he, as it were in his pley,
"How liketh thee my wyf and hire beautee?"
"Right wel," quod she, "my lord, for in good fey°   *faith*
A fairer saugh° I nevere noon° than she.   *saw, none*
I prey to God yeve hire° prosperitee.   *give her*
1035 And so hope I that he wol to yow sende
Plesance ynogh unto youre lyves ende!°   *lives' end*

O THYNG biseke° I yow and warne° also,[1]   *ask, warn*
That ye ne prikke° with no tormentynge°   *prick, tormenting*
This tendre mayden as ye han doon mo,[2]

---

1   There is a Latin gloss in the margin quoting the equivalent passage from Petrarch.
2   "As you have done to more, [i.e., to others]." Skeat suggests the equivalent modern phrase would
    be "as you did to *somebody else*," a delicate hint.

1040 For she is fostred° in hire norissynge°   *brought up, her nourishing*
     Moore tendrely, and to my supposynge°   *supposing*
     She koude nat adversitee endure
     As koude a povre fostred° creature."   *brought up in poverty*

     AND whan this Walter saugh hire pacience,
1045 Hir glad chiere,° and no malice at al,   *face*
     And he so ofte had doon to hire offence,[1]
     And she ay sad and constant as a wal,°   *wall*
     Continuynge evere hire innocence overal,
     This sturdy markys gan his herte dresse°   *began to prepare his heart*
1050 To rewen° upon hire wyfly stedfastnesse.°   *have pity, her wifely steadfastness*

     "THIS is ynogh, Grisilde myn!" quod he.
     "Be now namoore agast° ne yvele apayed.°   *afraid, displeased*
     I have thy feith° and thy benyngnytee,°   *faith, kindness*
     As wel as evere womman was, assayed,
1055 In greet estaat and povreliche arrayed.[2]
     Now knowe I, goode wyf, thy stedfastnesse!"
     And hire in armes took and gan hire kesse.°   *kissed her*

     AND she for wonder took of it no keepe.°   *gave no notice to it*
     She herde nat° what thyng he to hire seyde.°   *heard not, said to her*
1060 She ferde° as she had stert° out of a sleepe,   *acted, started*
     Til she out of hir mazednesse° abreyde.°   *amazement, awaked*
     "Grisilde," quod he, "by God that for us deyde,
     Thou art my wyf. Noon oother I have
     Ne nevere hadde, as God my soule save!

1065 THIS is thy doghter, which thou hast supposed
     To be my wyf. That oother feithfully
     Shal be myn heir, as I have ay° supposed.   *ever*
     Thou bare hym° in thy body trewely.°   *gave birth to him, truly*
     At Boloigne have I kept hem prively.°   *secretly*
1070 Taak hem agayn; for now maystow nat seye
     That thou hast lorn noon of thy children tweye.[3]

     AND folk that ootherweys han seyd° of me,   *have said*
     I warne hem wel, that I have doon this deede

---

1   Ellesmere omits "offence." It is supplied, to mend the rhyme, from Hengwrt.
2   "In great estate and poorly dressed" (i.e., both in high and low places).
3   "Take him again, for you may see that you have lost neither of your two children." Middle
    English often uses double negatives, as in "nat ... none" here.

For no malice ne for no crueltee,
1075 But for t'assaye° in thee thy wommanheede°   *try, womanhood*
And nat to sleen° my children, God forbeede!   *kill*
But for to kepe hem pryvely° and stille°   *keep them secretly, quietly*
Til I thy purpos° knewe and al thy wille."   *purpose*

WHAN she this herde, aswowne° doun° she falleth   *in a faint, down*
1080 For pitous° joye. And after hire swownynge°   *pitiful, her faint*
She bothe hire yonge children unto hire° calleth,   *to herself*
And in hire armes pitously wepynge
Embraceth hem. And tendrely kissynge,
Ful lyk° a mooder with hire salte teeres,°   *just like, her salty tears*
1085 She bathed bothe hire visage° and hire heeres.°   *their face, their hair*

O WHICH a pitous thyng it was to se
Hir swownyng° and hire humble voys° to heere!   *fainting, voice*
"Grauntmercy, lord! That thanke I yow," quod she,
"That ye han saved me my children deere.
1090 Now rekke° I nevere to been deed right heere!   *care*
Sith I stonde in youre love and in youre grace,
No fors of deeth ne whan my spirit pace!"[1]

O TENDRE, o deere, o yonge children myne,
Youre woful mooder wende stedfastly°   *expected steadfastly*
1095 That crueel houndes° or som° foul vermyne°   *dogs, some, vermin*
Hadde eten yow! But God of his mercy
And youre benyngne° fader tendrely°   *kind, tenderly*
Hath doon yow kept!"° And in that same stounde°   *has kept you, moment*
Al sodeynly° she swapte adoun° to grounde.   *suddenly, fell down*

1100 AND in hire swough° so sadly° holdeth she   *her faint, steadfastly*
Hire children two, whan she gan hem t'embrace,°   *began to embrace them*
That with greet sleighte° and greet difficultee°   *great skill, great difficulty*
The children from hire arm they gonne arace.°   *began to take away*
O many a teere on many a pitous face
1105 Doun ran° of hem that stooden hire bisyde.°   *ran down, stood beside her*
Unnethe° abouten hire myghte° they abyde.°   *scarcely, might, remain*

WALTER hire gladeth and hire sorwe slaketh.[2]
She riseth up abaysed° from hire traunce,°   *confused, her trance*
And every wight° hire° joye and feeste maketh,[3]   *person, her*

---

1   "Death does not matter nor when my spirit passes [from this life]."
2   "Walter encourages her, and her sorrow diminishes."
3   "To make a feast" is an expression for "to give encouragement."

1110 Til she hath caught agayn° hire contenaunce.°   gained again, composure
     Walter hire dooth so feithfully plesaunce,°   faithfully give her pleasure
     That it was deyntee° for to seen° the cheere°   delightful, see, expression
     Bitwixe hem two, now they been met yfeere.°   have been reunited

     THISE ladyes, whan that they hir tyme say,°   saw their opportunity
1115 Han taken hire and into chambre gon
     And strepen hire° out of hire rude array,°   strip her, her rustic clothing
     And in a clooth of gold that brighte shoon,
     With a coroune° of many a riche stoon°   crown, stone (jewel)
     Upon hire heed,° they into halle hire broghte.   her head
1120 And ther she was honured as hire oghte.°   honored as she should be

     THUS hath this pitous day a blisful° ende.   blissful
     For every man and womman dooth his myght
     This day in murthe° and revel° to dispende,°   mirth, enjoyment, spend
     Til on the welkne° shoon° the sterres lyght,°   sky, shone, stars' light
1125 For moore solempne° in every mannes syght   splendid
     This feste° was and gretter of costage°   feast, greater of cost
     That was the revel° of hire mariage.   enjoyment

     FUL many a yeer in heigh prosperitee°   high prosperity
     Lyven° thise two in concord° and in reste,   live, harmony
1130 And richely his doghter maryed he°   he married off his daughter
     Unto a lord, oon of the worthieste°   one of the most worthy
     Of al Ytaille.° And thanne in pees° and reste   Italy, peace
     His wyves fader in his court he kepeth,°   keeps
     Til that the soule out of his body crepeth.°   creeps

1135 HIS sone succedeth° in his heritage   succeeds
     In reste and pees after his fader day
     And fortunat was eek in mariage,
     Al putte he nat his wyf in greet assay.°   great trial
     This world is nat so strong—it is no nay°—   it cannot be denied
1140 As it hath been of olde tymes yoore.°1   long ago
     And herkneth° what this auctour seith° therfoore.   listen to, author says

     THIS storie is seyd nat for that wyves sholde2
     Folwen° Grisilde as in humylitee,   follow
     For it were inportable° though they wolde,°   impossible, even if they wished to
1145 But for that every wight in his degree

---

1   The notion that the world was in decline was common in the Middle Ages.
2   There is a long Latin gloss in the margin quoting the first half of Petrarch's concluding para-
     graph.

Sholde be constant in adversitee°   *adversity*
As was Grisilde. Therfore Petrak° writeth   *Petrarch*
This storie, which with heigh stile° he enditeth.°   *high style, writes*

1150 FOR, sith a womman was so pacient
Unto a mortal man, wel moore° us oghte°   *even more, ought*
Receyven° al in gree° that God us sent.   *receive, graciously*
For greet skile is he preeve° that he wroghte,°   *there's a good reason he tests, made*
But he ne tempteth° no man that he boghte,°   *does not tempt, bought [from sin]*
As seith Seint Jame, if ye his pistel° rede.°¹   *epistle, read*
1155 He preeveth° folk al day—it is no drede°—   *test, it cannot be denied*

AND suffreth° us as for oure excercise°   *allows, discipline*
With sharpe scourges° of adversitee°   *sharp blows, adversity*
Ful ofte to be bete° in sondry wise,°   *beaten, various ways*
Nat for to knowe oure wyl,° for certes° he,   *our will, certainly*
1160 Er we were born, knew oure freletee.°   *frailty*
And for oure beste is al his governaunce.°   *governing*
Lat° us thanne lyve in vertuous suffraunce.°   *let, virtuous patience*

BUT o word, lordynges, herkneth er I go.
It were ful hard° to fynde° nowadayes   *very difficult, find*
1165 In al a toun Grisildis thre or two.
For if that they were put to swiche assayes,°   *such trials*
The gold of hem hath now so badde alayes°   *bad alloys*
With bras,° that though the coyne° be fair at eye,°   *brass, coin, to see*
It wolde rather breste atwo° than plye.°   *burst in two, bend*

1170 FOR which heere for the Wyves love of Bathe,°   *love of the Wife of Bath*
Whos lyf and al hire secte° God mayntene   *her sect (group)*
In heigh maistrie,° and elles were it scathe.°   *high mastery, a shame*
I wol with lusty° herte fressh and grene°   *vigorous, green*
Seyn yow a song to glade yow,° I wene.°   *to make you glad, expect*
1175 And lat° us stynte° of ernestful matere.°   *let, stop, serious matter*
Herkneth my song that seith in this manere:

---

1   The reference here is to James 1:13.

L'ENVOY DE CHAUCER[1]

GRISILDE is deed° and eek° hire pacience,   *dead, also*
And bothe atones buryed° in Ytaille,°   *at once buried, Italy*
For which I crie° in open audience.°   *cry, hearing*
1180 No wedded man so hardy be t'assaille°   *to try*
His wyves pacience in hope to fynde
Grisildis, for in certein° he shal faille.°   *certainly, fail*

O NOBLE wyves, ful of heigh° prudence,   *great*
Lat° noon humylitee youre tonge° naille,°   *let, tongue, nail*
1185 Ne lat no clerk° have cause or diligence   *theologian*
To write of yow a storie of swich mervaille°   *such marvel*
As of Grisildis, pacient and kynde,
Lest Chichivache yow swelwe in hire entraille![2]

FOLWETH Ekko,°[3] that holdeth no silence,°   *Echo, does not keep silent*
1190 But evere answereth at the countretaille.°   *in reply*
Beth nat bidaffed° for youre innocence,   *be not fooled*
But sharply taak° on yow the governaille.°   *take, governing*
Emprenteth° wel this lessoun in youre mynde,   *imprint*
For commune° profit, sith it may availle.°   *common, help*

1195 YE archiwyves,°[4] stondeth° at defense,   *arch-wives, stand*
Syn° ye be strong as is a greet camaille.°   *since, great camel*
Ne suffreth° nat that men yow doon offense.   *endure*
And sklendre° wyves, fieble° as in bataille,°   *slender, feeble, in battle*
Beth egre° as is a tygre° yond° in Ynde.°   *eager, tiger, yonder, India*
1200 Ay clappeth° as a mille,° I yow consaille.°   *clatter, mill, counsel*

NE dreed hem nat.° Doth hem no reverence,   *Do not fear them*
For though thyn housbonde° armed be in maille,°   *your husband, armor*

---

1 "The envoy of Chaucer." An *envoy* is normally a short conclusion addressed to the listener at the end of a ballade, a French form of lyric, as if to send the poem on its way. The rubric "L'envoy de Chaucer," which also appears in Hengwrt and many other manuscripts, might suggest that the Clerk has finished speaking and Chaucer is addressing us directly, or just that the envoy is Chaucer's original contribution. Skeat judged the words "unsuited to the coy Clerk," but others find it in character.

2 "In case Chichevache swallow you in its stomach." Chichevache was the legendary cow who fed only on patient wives and thus was very skinny.

3 The reference is to the nymph Echo in Ovid's *Metamorphoses*, whom Juno rendered incapable of saying anything except by repeating the last words of someone else.

4 An archbishop is a chief bishop and the Arch-poet was a legendary wandering scholar and poet in the twelfth century, so an arch-wife is a chief wife or wife of extraordinary powers, or, judging by the context, an especially domineering wife. Chaucer appears to have been the first to use the word.

The arwes° of thy crabbed° eloquence   *arrows, spiteful*
Shal perce° his brest° and eek° his aventaille.°   *pierce, breast, also, neck armor*
1205 In jalousie I rede° eek° thou hym bynde,°   *advise, also, bind him*
And thou shalt make hym couche° as doth° a quaille!°   *cower, does, quail*

If thou be fair, ther° folk been in presence,°   *where, are in [your] presence*
Shewe° thou thy visage° and thyn apparaille.°   *show, face, clothing*
If thou be foul, be fre° of thy dispence.°   *free, spending*
1210 To gete° thee freendes° ay do thy travaille.°   *get, friends, ever to do your will*
Be ay° of chiere° as light as leef° on lynde,°   *ever, manner, leaf, linden tree*
And lat° hym care and wepe° and wrynge° and waille!°*let, weep, wring [hands], wail*

BIHOOLD THE MURYE WORDES OF THE HOOST[1]

2012a THIS worthy Clerk,° whan° ended was his tale,   *scholar, when*
Oure Hoost seyde and swoor,° "Be Goddes bones!   *swore*
Me were levere° than a barel° ale   *I had rather, barrel of*
My wyf at hoom° had herd° this legende° ones!°   *home, heard, saint's life, once*
This is a gentil° tale for the nones!°   *noble, for the occasion*
As to my purpos:° Wiste° ye my wille?°   *purpose, know, will*
2012g But thyng that wol nat be, lat° it be stille.°   *let, quiet*

HEERE ENDETH THE TALE OF THE CLERK OF OXENFORD

---

1   "Behold the merry words of the Host." The following stanza is not present in many manuscripts
of *The Canterbury Tales* and is thus left out of the standard numbering of lines. Both Ellesmere
and Hengwrt include it.

THE MERCHANT'S PROLOGUE AND TALE

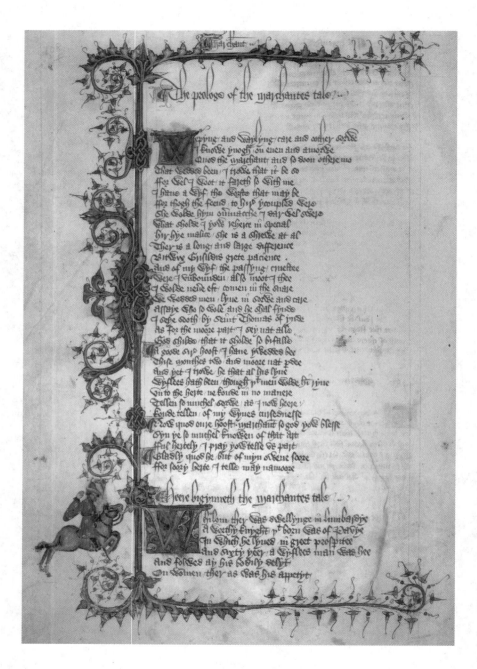

Opening page of *The Merchant's Tale*. Ellesmere Manuscript EL 26 C9 f. 102v. Reprinted by permission of The Huntington Library.

THE MERCHANT'S PROLOGUE

THE PROLOGE OF THE MARCHANTES TALE

"WEPYNG° and waylyng,° care and oother sorwe   *weeping, wailing*
   I knowe ynogh° on even and amorwe,"°   *enough, evening and morning*
1215 Quod° the marchant, "and so doon° othere mo°   *said, do, many others*
   That wedded been. I trowe° that it be so,   *believe*
   For wel I woot° it fareth° so with me.   *well I know, fares*
   I have a wyf, the worste that may be,
   For thogh the feend to hire ycoupled were,°   *were married to her*
1220 She wolde hym overmacche,° I dar wel swere!°   *overcome, swear*
   What° sholde I yow reherce° in special°   *why, describe, specially*
   Hir hye° malice? She is a shrewe° at al.   *extreme, nag*
   Ther is a long and large difference
   Bitwix Grisildis grete pacience°   *great patience*
1225 And of my wyf the passyng crueltee.°   *surpassing cruelty*
   Were I unbounden,° also moot I thee,°   *loosed, might I thrive*
   I wolde nevere eft comen° in the snare   *would never again come*
   We wedded men lyve in—sorwe and care.
   Assaye whoso wole,° and he shal fynde   *try who will*
1230 I seye sooth,° by Seint Thomas of Ynde!¹   *say truth*
   As for the moore part,° I sey nat° alle.   *most part, say not*
   God shilde° that it sholde° so bifalle!°   *prevent, should, happen*
   A,° good sire Hoost, I have ywedded bee°   *Ah, been married*
   Thise monthes two and moore nat, pardee,°   *by God*
1235 And yet I trowe° he that al his lyve°   *believe, life*
   Wyflees° hath been,° though that men wolde him ryve°   *without a wife, has been, stab*
   Unto the herte,° ne koude° in no manere°   *heart, could not, manner*
   Tellen so muchel° sorwe° as I now heere°   *much, sorrow, here*
   Koude tellen° of my wyves cursednesse!"   *could tell*
"NOW," quod oure Hoost, "Marchaunt, so God yow blesse,
1240 Syn° ye so muchel° knowen of that art,   *since, much*
   Ful hertely I pray yow, telle us part."
"GLADLY," quod he, "but of myn owene soore,
   For soory herte I telle may namoore."²

---

1 St. Thomas of India is the apostle Thomas in the gospels. His legend made him the evangelist of India.

2 "But I can tell no more of my own sorrow because of my sorrowful heart."

THE MERCHANT'S TALE

HEERE BIGYNNETH THE MARCHANTES TALE

1245	WHILOM° ther was dwellynge° in Lumbardye°	*once, living, Lombardy*
	A worthy knyght that born was of Pavye,°	*Pavia*
	In which he lyved in greet prosperitee.°	*great prosperity*
	And sixty yeer a wyflees man was hee	
	And folwed ay° his bodily delyt°	*always followed, delight*
1250	On wommen theras° was his appetyt,°	*where, appetite*
	As doon° thise° fooles that been seculeer.°	*do, these, worldly*
	And whan that he wes passed sixty yeer,	
	Were it° for hoolynesse° or for dotage,°	*whether it was, holiness, senility*
	I kan nat seye,° but swich° a greet corage°	*cannot say, such, desire*
1255	Hadde this knyght to been a wedded man,	
	That day and nyght he dooth al that he kan	
	T'espien° where he myghte° wedded be,	*to find out, might*
	Preyinge° oure Lord to graunten° him that he	*praying to, grant*
	Mighte ones° knowe of thilke blisful lyf°	*once, that happy life*
1260	That is bitwixe° an housbonde and his wyf	*between*
	And for to lyve under that hooly boond,°	*holy bond*
	With which that first God man and womman bond.°	*bound*
	"Noon oother lyf," seyde he, "is worth a bene,°	*bean*
	For wedlok° is so esy and so clene,°	*wedlock, pure*
1265	That in this world it is a Paradys."°	*paradise*
	Thus seyde this olde knyght, that was so wys.°	*wise*
	AND certeinly, as sooth° as God is kyng,	*true*
	To take a wyf, it is a glorious thyng!	
	And namely° whan a man is oold and hoor.°	*especially, old and gray*
1270	Thanne° is a wyf the fruyt° of his tresor.°	*then, best part, treasure*
	Thanne sholde he take a yong wyf and a feir,°	*fair*
	On which he myghte engendren hym° an heir	*might beget himself*
	And lede° his lyf in joye and in solas,°	*lead, comfort*
	Whereas° thise bacheleris synge° allas,	*where, young knights sing*
1275	Whan that they fynden° any adversitee°	*find, adversity*
	In love, which nys° but childyssh vanytee.°	*is not, childish foolishness*
	And trewely,° it sit wel° to be so	*truly, it is fitting*
	That bacheleris have often peyne° and wo.°	*pain, woe*
	On brotel° ground they buylde,° and brotelnesse°[1]	*brittle, build, brittleness*
1280	They fynde whan they wene° sikernesse.°	*expect, security*
	They lyve° but as a bryd° or as a beest—	*live, bird*

---

1 "They build on brittle (i.e., promiscuous) ground and they find brittleness when they expect security (i.e., fidelity)."

In libertee° and under noon arreest,°	liberty, no hindrance
Theras° a wedded man in his estaat°	where, condition
Lyveth a lyf blisful° and ordinaat,°	happy, ordered
1285 Under this yok° of mariage ybounde.°	yoke, bound
Wel may his herte in joye and blisse habounde,°	abound
For who kan° be so buxom° as a wyf?	can, obedient
Who is so trewe and eek so ententyf	
To kepe hym syk and hool as is his make?[1]	
1290 For wele° or wo,° she wole° hym nat forsake.	wellness, woe, will
She nys nat° wery° hym to love and serve,	is not, wearied
Thogh that he lye° bedrede° til he sterve.°	lie, bedridden, die
And yet somme clerkes° seyn° it nys nat° so,	some scholars, say, is not
Of whiche he, Theofraste,[2] is oon° of tho.°	one, those
1295 What force° though Theofraste liste lye?°	who cares, wants to lie
"Ne take no wyf," quod he, "for housbondrye°	economy
As for to spare in houshold thy dispence.°	expenses
A trewe servant dooth moore diligence°	takes more care
Thy good° to kepe° than thyn owene wyf.	possessions, preserve
1300 For she wol clayme° half part al hir lyf.°	will claim, her life
And if thou be syk,° so God me save,	sick
Thy verray freendes° or a trewe knave°	own friends, true servant
Wol kepe thee bet than she that waiteth ay	
After thy good and hath doon many a day.[3]	
1305 And if thou take a wyf unto thyn hoold,°	under your protection
Ful lightly° maystow been° a cokewold."°	easily, may you be, cuckold
This sentence and an hundred thynges° worse	things
Writeth° this man, ther° God his bones corse!°	writes, there, curse
But take no kepe° of al swich vanytee.°	take no heed, such folly
1310 Deffie° Theofraste and herke me.°	defy, listen to me
A wyf is Goddes yifte,° verraily.°[4]	gift, truly
Alle otherere maner yiftes° hardily,°	other kind of gifts, certainly
As londes, rentes, pasture, or commune,°	right to common land

---

1 "Who is as true and attentive as his partner to keep him when he is sick or healthy."

2 Theophrastus wrote a book attacking marriage, which Jerome quotes in his work *Against Jovinian*, mentioned by the Wife of Bath in her Prologue, line 671.

3 "Will keep you better than she who is always on the look out for [a way of getting] your possessions and has done so for many a day."

4 There is a Latin gloss in the margin quoting, not quite accurately, the biblical passage, Proverbs 19:14, "a prudent wife is from the Lord," but misattributing it to Ecclesiasticus. Chaucer's immediate source was the *Liber Consolationis et Consilii* (*The Book of Consolation and Counsel*), a work of moral guidance written in Latin by the thirteenth-century Italian judge, Albertano of Brescia for one of his sons. Curiously, the glosses reproduce Albertano's Latin text, although Chaucer for the most part drew on the fourteenth-century French translation, *Le Livre de Melibée et de Dame Prudence*, which he in turn translated into English as his *Tale of Melibee*, the second tale offered by his pilgrim narrator.

Or moebles° alle been yiftes of Fortune[1] — *movable property*
1315 That passen° as a shadwe° upon a wal. — *pass, shadow*
But dredelees,° if pleynly speke° I shal, — *doubtless, plainly speak*
A wyf wol laste and in thyn hous endure° — *your house remain*
Wel lenger° than thee list,° paraventure.° — *much longer, you wish, perhaps*
MARIAGE is a ful greet° sacrement.[2] — *very great*
1320 He which that hath no wyf, I holde hym shent!° — *consider him ruined*
He lyveth helplees and al desolat.° — *desolate*
I speke of folk in seculer estaat.°[3] — *worldly condition*
And herke° why. I sey nat this for noght:° — *listen to, nothing*
That womman is for mannes helpe ywroght.° — *created*
1325 The hye° God, whan he hadde Adam maked° — *high, made*
And saugh hym° al allone,° bely-naked,° — *saw him, alone, completely naked*
God of his grete goodnesse seyde than,
"Lat° us now make an helpe° unto this man — *let, helper*
Lyk to hymself."°[4] And thanne he made him Eve. — *like himself*
1330 Heere may ye se and heerby° may ye preve° — *by this, prove*
That wyf is mannes helpe and his confort,
His Paradys terrestre° and his disport.° — *earthly Paradise, enjoyment*
So buxom° and so vertuous is she, — *obedient*
They moste nedes° lyve in unitee.° — *necessarily must, unity*
1335 O flessh° they been,° and o flessh as I gesse,° — *one flesh, are, guess*
Hath but oon herte° in wele° and in distresse. — *only one heart, prosperity*
A° WYF—a, Seinte Marie, benedicite°— — *ah, bless you*
How myghte a man han° any adversitee° — *have, adversity*
That hath a wyf? Certes, I can nat seye.
1340 The blisse° which that is bitwixe hem tweye,° — *happiness, between the two of them*
Ther may no tonge° telle or herte° thynke.° — *tongue, heart, think*
If he be povre,° she helpeth hym° to swynke.° — *poor, him, work*
She kepeth° his good° and wasteth° never a deel.° — *keeps, possessions, wastes, bit*
Al that hire housbonde lust,° hire liketh weel.° — *desires, pleases well*
1345 She seith nat ones° nay whan he seith ye. — *not once*
"Do this," seith he. "Al redy, sire," seith she.
O, blisful order of wedlok precious,
Thou art so murye° and eek° so vertuous — *merry, also*
And so commended and appreved° eek, — *approved*

---

1   There is a Latin gloss in the margin "gifts of fortune."
2   This is a quotation of Paul's Letter to the Ephesians, 5:32, "sacramentum hoc magnum est," often translated "This is a great mystery." By the thirteenth century, marriage had come to be regarded as a sacrament by most Christian theologians.
3   As opposed to priests, who were forbidden to marry but, by implication, were not destroyed by celibacy.
4   Genesis 2:18. There is a Latin gloss in the margin citing the passage.

1350 That every man that halt hym worth a leek[1]
Upon his bare knees oughte al his lyf
Thanken his God that hym hath sent a wyf
Or elles° preye° to God hym for to sende   *else, pray*
A wyf to laste unto his lyves ende.
1355 For thanne his lyf is set in sikernesse.°   *security*
He may nat be deceyved,° as I gesse,   *deceived*
So° that he werke after° his wyves reede.°   *provided, follow, advice*
[Thanne may he boldely kepen° up his heed.°   *keep, head*
They been so trewe and therwith al so wyse,
1360 For which if thow wolt werken as the wyse,°   *you will do as the wise*
Do alwey° so as wommen wol thee rede.°][2]   *always, will advise you*
Lo HOW that Jacob, as thise clerkes rede,°   *scholars recount*
By good conseil of his mooder° Rebekke,   *mother*
Boond the kydes skyn° aboute his nekke,°   *kid's skin, neck*
1365 Thurgh° which his fadres benysoun° he wan.°[3]   *through, father's blessing, won*
Lo Judith, as the storie eek° telle kan,°   *also, can tell*
By wys conseil° she Goddes peple° kepte°   *wise counsel, people, saved*
And slow° hym, Olofernus, whil he slepte.[4]   *killed*
Lo Abigayl, by good conseil, how she[5]
1370 Saved hir housbonde Nabal whan that he
Sholde han be slayn.°[6] And looke, Ester° also   *should have been killed, Esther*
By good conseil delyvered out of wo°   *woe*
The peple of God and made hym, Mardochee,°   *Mordecai*
Of Assuere° enhaunced° for to be.[7]   *Ahasuerus [Xerxes], promoted*
1375 THER nys° nothyng in gree superlatyf,°   *is not, highest degree*
As seith° Senek,° above an humble wyf.[8]   *says, Seneca*

---

1   "Holds himself worth a leek," i.e., worth anything at all.
2   Lines 1358–61 are not included in Ellesmere. They are supplied chiefly from Hengwrt, with a few missing words supplied from John Manly and Edith Rickert, *The Text of the Canterbury Tales*.
3   This story is related in Genesis 27:5–29. There is a Latin gloss in the margin at line 1362, "Jacob, through the advice of his mother," etc. This example of woman's counsel, along with the following examples of Judith, Abigail, Esther, the saying misattributed to Seneca, the saying of Cato, and the passages from Paul's Letter to the Ephesians all appear in this order in Albertano da Brescia's *Book of Consolation and Counsel.*
4   This story is recounted in the book of Judith in the apocryphal portion of the Bible. There is a Latin gloss in the margin "Judith from the hands of Holofernes."
5   The story is recounted in 1 Kings 25. There is a Latin gloss in the margin: "Abigail, through her good counsel, freed her husband from the wrath of David."
6   This story is recounted in 1 Samuel 25.
7   This story is recounted in the book of Esther. There is a Latin gloss in the margin: "Esther etc. [saved] the Jews together with Mordecai in the reign of Ahasuerus."
8   There is a Latin gloss in the margin: "Seneca: Just as nothing is [better than] a mild wife, nothing is crueler than an aggressive one." The quotation actually comes from the *Mythologies* of Fabius Planciades Fulgentius, a late fifth-century Christian writer, known for his elaborate allegorical interpretation of classical writers such as Ovid and Virgil.

SUFFRE° thy wyves tonge,° as Catoun bit.°¹   *endure, tongue, Cato asked*
She shal comande, and thou shalt suffren° it.   *endure*
And yet she wole obeye of curteisye.°   *courtesy*
1380 A wyf is kepere° of thyn housbondrye.°²   *keeper, your household*
Wel° may the sike° man biwaille° and wepe,°   *well, sick, complain, weep*
Theras° ther nys° no wyf the hous to kepe.   *where, is no*
I warne thee if wisely thou wolt wirche,°   *will work*
Love wel thy wyf, as Crist loved his Chirche.°³   *Church*
1385 If thou lovest thyself, thou lovest thy wyf.
No man hateth his flessh, but in his lyf
He fostreth° it.⁴ And therfore bidde I thee°   *nurtures, ask you*
Cherisse° thy wyf, or thou shalt nevere thee.°   *cherish, thrive*
Housbonde and wyf, whatso men jape° or pleye,°   *whatever people say in joke, play*
1390 Of worldly folk holden the siker weye.°   *hold the sure way*
They been so knyt,° ther may noon° harm bityde°—   *joined together, no, happen*
And namely° upon the wyves syde.°   *especially, side*
For which this Januarie, of whom I tolde,
Considered hath, inwith hise dayes olde,°   *in his old age*
1395 The lusty lyf,° the vertuous quyete°   *vigorous life, quiet*
That is in mariage hony-sweete.°   *sweet as honey*
And for hise freendes on a day he sente
To tellen hem° th'effect° of his entente.°   *them, the substance, plan*
WITH face sad,° his tale he hath hem toold.°   *constant, told them*
1400 He seyde, "Freendes, I am hoor and oold°   *gray and old*
And almoost, God woot,° on my pittes brynke.°   *God knows, brink of my grave*
Upon the soule somwhat moste° I thynke.   *must*
I have my body folily despended.°   *foolishly spent*
Blessed be God that it shal been amended!°   *shall be made better*
1405 For I wol be, certeyn, a wedded man—
And that anoon° in al the haste I kan°   *immediately, can*
Unto som mayde° fair and tendre° of age.   *maid, tender*

---

1   Cato's *Distichs* 3.23. There is a Latin gloss in the margin: "Cato: Remember to put up with your wife's tongue if she is frugal." Dionysius Cato was reputed in the Middle Ages to be the author of a widely circulating collection of proverbs and wise sayings, often used for teaching Latin in schools.

2   There is a Latin gloss in the margin "A good wife is a faithful and good guardian of the home." The lines come from another work by Albertano da Brescia, his *De amore Dei* (*Of the Love of God*).

3   Ephesians 5:25. There is a Latin gloss in the margin citing the line "Love your wives as Christ loved his Church."

4   Ephesians 5:28–29, 33. There is a Latin gloss in the margin combining the lines: "Thus men ought to love their own wives as their own bodies, since he who loves his wife loves himself; nobody ever hates his own body but rather nourishes and cherishes it, and therefore everyone should love his wife as himself."

I prey yow,° shapeth° for my mariage°   *ask you, arrange, marriage*
Al sodeynly,° for I wol nat abyde.°   *quickly, will not wait*
1410 And I wol fonde t'espien° on my syde°   *attempt to find out, side*
To whom I may be wedded hastily.
But forasmuche° as ye been mo° than I,   *since, be more*
Ye shullen° rather swich° a thyng espyen°   *shall, such, find out*
Than I, and where me best were to allyen.°   *ally myself (through marriage)*
1415 BUT o thyng° warne° I yow, my freendes deere: *one thing, warn*
I wol noon oold° wyf han in no manere.°   *will have no old, no way*
She shal nat passe° twenty yeer,° certain.°   *exceed, years, certainly*
Oold fissh° and yong flessh° wolde I have fayn.°   *old fish, young flesh, gladly*
Bet° is," quod he, "a pyk° than a pykerel.°   *better, pike, pickerel (young pike)*
1420 And bet than olde boef° is the tendre veel.°   *beef, tender veal*
I wol no womman thritty° yeer of age.   *thirty*
It is but benestraw and greet forage.[1]
And eek thise olde wydwes,° God it woot,°   *widows, God knows it*
They konne° so muchel craft° on Wades boot,[2]   *know, much skill*
1425 So muchel broken harm whan that hem lest,°   *when they wish*
That with hem° sholde° I nevere lyve° in reste.   *them, should, live*
For sondry scoles maken sotile clerkis.[3]
Womman of manye scoles° half a clerk° is.   *schools, scholar*
But certeynly, a yong thyng may men gye°   *guide*
1430 Right as men may warm wex° with handes° plye.°   *wax, hands, manipulate*
Wherfore I sey yow pleynly° in a clause,   *plainly*
I wol noon oold wyf han.° For this cause: *have*
For if so were° that I hadde swich myschaunce,°   *if it were thus, such misfortune*
That I in hire ne koude han° no plesaunce,°   *could not have, pleasure*
1435 Thanne sholde I lede° my lyf in avoutrye°—   *spend, adultery*
And streight unto the devel whan I dye!°   *die*
Ne children sholde I none upon hire geten.°   *beget*
Yet were me levere° that houndes° had me eten°   *I would rather, dogs, eaten*
Than that myn heritage° sholde falle   *heritage (lands and property)*
1440 In straunge hand.° And this I telle yow alle: *into a strange hand*
I dote nat.° I woot° the cause why   *am not senile, know*
Men sholde wedde. And forthermore,° woot I   *furthermore*
Ther speketh many a man of mariage

---

1   "It is [nothing] but bean-straw and great fodder." In other words, marrying a woman older than
    January wishes is a waste.
2   "They have so much skill in Wade's boat; [they know] so much about how to cause (*broken*)
    harm." Wade was once a famous hero, but only passing references to him survive (including one
    in Chaucer's *Troilus and Criseyde*, 3.164). The significance of his boat remains obscure, despite
    much scholarly speculation.
3   "For different schools make subtle scholars."

That woot namoore of it than woot my page.°	*boy servant*
1445 For whiche causes, man sholde take a wyf,	
Siththe° he may nat lyven chaast° his lyf,°	*since, chaste, [all] his life*
Take hym a wyf with greet devocioun,°	*great devotion*
Bycause of leveful procreacioun°	*lawful procreation*
Of children to th'onour° of God above	*the honor*
1450 And nat oonly° for paramour° or love	*not only, sex*
And for they sholde leccherye eschue°	*avoid lechery*
And yelde° hir dettes° whan° that they ben due°¹	*yield, debts, when, are due*
Or for that ech° of hem° sholde° helpen oother°	*each, them, should, the other*
In meschief,° as a suster shal the brother,	*misfortune*
1455 And lyve in chastitee ful holily.°	*very devoutly*
But sires,° by youre leve,° that am nat I.°	*sirs, leave, I am not like that*
For God be thanked, I dar° make avaunt:°	*dare, boast*
I feele my lymes° stark° and suffisaunt°	*limbs, strong, capable*
To do al that a man bilongeth to.°	*is appropriate for a man*
1460 I woot° myselven best what I may do.	*know*
Though I be hoor,° I fare as dooth° a tree	*gray, does*
That blosmeth° er° that fruyt ywoxen bee.°	*blossoms, before, fruit is ripe*
And blosmy° tree nys° neither drye° ne deed.°	*blossom-filled, is not, dry, dead*
I feele° me nowhere hoor but on myn heed.°	*feel, my head*
1465 Myn herte and alle my lymes° been as grene°	*limbs, green*
As laurer° thurgh° the yeer° is for to sene.°	*laurel, throughout, year, seen*
And syn° that ye han herd° al myn entente,°	*since, have heard, my intention*
I prey° yow to my wyl ye wole assente."°	*ask, will agree*
DIVERSE° men diversely hym tolde	*different*
1470 Of mariage manye ensamples olde.°	*many old examples*
Somme° blamed it. Somme preysed° it, certeyn.°	*some, praised, certainly*
But atte laste,° shortly for to seyn,°	*at the last, say*
As al day falleth° altercacioun°	*falls, disagreement*
Bitwixen freendes° in disputisoun,°	*friends, debate*
1475 Ther fil° a stryf° bitwixe hise bretheren° two,	*fell, strife, his brothers*
Of whiche that oon° was cleped° Placebo;²	*one, named*
Justinus soothly° called was that oother.°	*truly, other*
PLACEBO seyde, "O Januarie brother,	
Ful litel nede° hadde ye, my lord so deere,	*very little need*
1480 Conseil to axe° of any that is heere,°	*ask, here*
But that ye been so ful of sapience°	*wisdom*

---

1 The reference here is to the marriage "debt" of having sex with one's spouse. Cf. Wife of Bath's Prologue, line 130.

2 This name in Latin means, "I will please." His brother's name in the line below implies a just or true opinion. The scribe has written either "Placebo" or "Justinus" in the margins at the beginning of each of their speeches.

That yow ne liketh° for youre heighe prudence° — *it does not please you, high wisdom*
To weyven fro° the word of Salomon.° — *depart from, Solomon*
This word seyde he unto us everychon:° — *everyone*
1485 'Wirk° alle thyng by conseil,' thus seyde he, — *work*
'And thanne shaltow nat repente° thee.'[1] — *shall you not regret*
But though that Salomon spak swich° a word, — *such*
Myn owene° deere brother and my lord, — *own*
So wysly° God my soule brynge at reste,° — *surely, bring to rest*
1490 I holde youre owene conseil is the beste.
For brother myn, of me taak° this motyf:° — *take, thought*
I have now been a court-man° al my lyf, — *courtier*
And God it woot,° though I unworthy be, — *God knows it*
I have stonden° in ful greet degree° — *stood, very high*
1495 Abouten lordes of ful heigh estaat.° — *very high rank*
Yet hadde I nevere with noon of hem° debaat.° — *them, disagreement*
I nevere hem contraried,° trewely. — *disagreed with them*
I woot wel that my lord kan moore° than I. — *knows more*
What° that he seith° I holde it ferme and stable.° — *whatever, says, firm and certain*
1500 I seye the same or elles° thyng semblable.° — *else, a similar thing*
A ful greet° fool is any conseillour° — *great, counselor*
That serveth° any lord of heigh° honour — *who serves, high*
That dar° presume or elles° thenken° it, — *dare, else, think*
That his conseil sholde passe° his lordes wit. — *should surpass*
1505 Nay, lordes been no fooles, by my fay!° — *faith*
Ye han° youreselven seyd° heer° today — *have, said, here*
So heigh sentence,° so holily and weel,° — *judgment, devoutly and well*
That I consente and conferme° everydeel° — *confirm, every part*
Youre wordes alle and youre opinioun.
1510 By God, ther nys° no man in al this toun — *is not*
Nyn Ytaille° that koude bet han sayd.° — *nor in Italy, have said better*
Crist halt hym of this conseil ful wel apayd.[2]
And trewely, it is an heigh corage° — *act of high courage*
Of any man that stapen is in age° — *stooped by age*
1515 To take a yong wyf, by my fader kyn.° — *father's kin*
Youre herte hangeth on a joly pyn.[3]
Dooth° now in the matiere° right as yow leste,° — *Do, matter, as you wish*
For finally, I holde it for the beste."° — *consider it the best*
JUSTINUS, that ay stille° sat and herde° — *ever quiet, heard*

---

1 This quotation is from the apocryphal or deuterocanonical book of Ecclesiasticus 32:24.
2 "Christ considers himself very well paid by this council," i.e., it is pious.
3 A pin is a wooden peg. The phrase seems to mean either that your heart is tuned cheerfully or that it is hung up conspicuously, in either case that it is merry.

1520 Right in this wise,° he to Placebo answerde,	*way*
"Now, brother myn, be pacient,° I preye,°	*patient, pray*
Syn ye han seyd,° and herkneth° what I seye.	*Since you have spoken, listen*
SENEK° among his othere wordes wyse°	*Seneca, wise*
Seith that a man oghte hym right wel avyse°	*be advised*
1525 To whom he yeveth° his lond° or his catel.°	*gives, land, possessions*
And syn I oghte avyse me right wel° ·	
To whom I yeve° my good° awey fro° me,	*give, possessions, away from*
Wel muchel moore° I oghte avysed be	*very much more*
To whom I yeve my body for alwey.°	*always*
1530 I warne° yow wel, it is no childes pley°	*warn, child's play*
To take a wyf withouten avysement.°	*advice*
Men moste enquere°—this is myn assent°—	*inquire, my counsel*
Wher° she be wys or sobre or dronkelewe°	*whether, drunken*
Or proud or elles° ootherweys° a shrewe,°	*else, otherwise, nag*
1535 A chidestere° or wastour° of thy good°	*nag, waster, possessions*
Or riche or poore or elles mannyssh wood.¹	
Albeit° so that no man fynden shal°	*although, shall find*
Noon° in this world that trotteth hool in al,²	*none*
Ne man ne beest° which as men koude devyse.°	*neither man nor beast, could imagine*
1540 But nathelees, it oghte ynough suffise°	*ought to be enough*
With any wyf, if so were that she hadde°	*if she had*
Mo° goode thewes° than hire vices badde.°	*more, customs, her bad vices*
And al this axeth leyser° for t'enquere.°	*requires time, to inquire*
For God it woot, I have wept many a teere°	*tear*
1545 Ful pryvely° syn I have had a wyf.	*privately, since*
Preyse° whoso wole,° a wedded mannes lyf,	*praise, whoever wishes to*
Certein, I fynde in it but cost and care	
And observances of alle blisses bare.°	*lacking all happiness*
And yet, God woot, my neighebores° aboute,	*neighbors*
1550 And namely of wommen many a route,°	*crowd*
Seyn° that I have the mooste stedefast° wyf	*say, steadfast*
And eek° the mekeste oon° that bereth lyf.°	*also, meekest one, bears life*
But I woot best where wryngeth° me my sho.°	*wrings, shoe*
Ye mowe for me right as yow liketh do.³	
1555 Avyseth° yow—ye been° a man of age—	*advise, are*
How that ye entren° into mariage,	*enter*
And namely° with a yong wyf and a fair.	*especially*
By hym that made water, erthe, and air,	

---

1 Man-mad, i.e., either as fiercely crazy as a man or, possibly, crazy for men.
2 "Trots perfectly in all respects." The metaphor is drawn from buying horses.
3 "You may, as far as I am concerned, do as you wish to do."

The yongeste man that is in al this route°   *crowd*
1560 Is bisy ynough° to bryngen it aboute   *hard pressed enough*
To han° his wyf allone,° trusteth me.°   *have, alone, trust me*
Ye shul nat plesen hire° fully yeres thre.°   *shall not please her, for three years*
This is to seyn, to doon hire ful plesaunce.°   *do her great pleasure*
A wyf axeth° ful many an observaunce.°   *asks, attention*
1565 I prey° yow that ye be nat yvele apayd."°   *pray, displeased*
"WEL," quod this Januarie, "and hastow ysayd?°   *have you spoken*
Straw for thy Senek° and for thy proverbes!   *Seneca*
I counte nat° a panyer° ful of herbes   *not, basket*
Of scole termes.[1] Wyser men than thow,
1570 As thou has herd,° assenteden° right now   *heard, agree*
To my purpos. Placebo, what sey° ye?"   *say*
"I SEYE it is a cursed man," quod he,
"That letteth matrimoigne,° sikerly."   *hinders matrimony*
And with that word they rysen sodeynly°   *rise suddenly*
1575 And been assented fully° that he sholde   *completely agreed*
Be wedded whanne hym liste° and where he wolde.°   *he wished, would*
HEIGH fantasye and curious bisynesse°   *elaborate concern*
Fro° day to day gan° in the soule impresse°   *from, began, impress*
Of Januarie aboute his mariage.
1580 Many fair shape and many a fair visage°   *face*
Ther passeth thurgh° his herte nyght by nyght,   *passes through*
As whoso tooke° a mirour° polisshed bryght°   *as if someone took, mirror, polished brightly*
And sette it in a commune° market place;   *common*
Thanne sholde he se° ful many° a figure pace°   *see, very many, pass*
1585 By his mirour, and in the same wyse°   *way*
Gan° Januarie inwith° his thoght° devyse°   *began, within, thought, imagine*
Of maydens° whiche that dwellen hym bisyde.°   *maidens, lived near him*
He wiste nat wher° that he myghte abyde,°   *knew not where, might settle*
For if that oon° have beaute in hir face,   *one*
1590 Another stant° so in the peples grace°   *stands, people's favor*
For hire sadnesse° and hire benyngnytee°   *constancy, kindness*
That of the peple grettest voys° hath she.   *greatest fame*
And somme° were riche and hadden badde name.°   *some, had a bad name*
But nathelees, bitwixe ernest and game,[2]
1595 He atte laste apoynted hym on oon°   *decided himself upon one*
And leet alle othere° from his herte goon°   *let all others, go*
And chees° hire of his owene auctoritee.°   *choose, own authority*
For love is blynd° alday° and may nat see.   *blind, all day (i.e., always)*

---

1   "School terms" refers to the type of debates engaged in at the universities.
2   "But nevertheless, between seriousness and jest."

And whan that he was in his bed ybroght,°   *brought*
1600 He purtreyed° in his herte and in his thoght   *imagined*
Hir fresshe beautee and hir age tendre,°   *tender age*
Hir myddel smal,° hire armes longe and sklendre,°   *slender waist, slender*
Hir wise governaunce,° hir gentillesse,°   *behavior, nobility*
Hir wommanly berynge° and hire sadnesse.°   *behavior, constancy*
1605 And whan that he on hire was condescended,°   *decided*
Hym thoughte his choys myghte nat ben amended.[1]
For whan that he hymself concluded hadde,°   *had decided*
Hym thoughte° ech oother mannes° wit so badde,°   *It seemd to him, man's, bad*
That inpossible it were to repplye°   *object*
1610 Agayn his choys.° This was his fantasye.°   *choice, delusion*
Hise freendes sente he to° at his instaunce°   *he sent for his friends, insistence*
And preyed hem° to doon° hym° that plesaunce°   *asked them, do, him, pleasure*
That hastily they wolden° to hym come.   *would*
He wolde abregge° hir° labour alle and some.°   *would shorten, their, one and all*
1615 Nedeth namoore° for hym to go ne ryde.°   *there is not need, nor ride*
He was apoynted° ther he wolde abyde.°   *had decided, would remain*
PLACEBO cam and eek° hise freendes soone,   *also*
And alderfirst° he bad hem° alle a boone,°   *at first, asked them, favor*
That noon of hem° none argumentz make   *none of them*
1620 Agayn the purpos° which that he hath take,   *purpose*
Which purpos was "plesant° to God," seyde he,   *pleasant*
And verray ground° of his prosperitee.   *true basis*
HE seyde ther was a mayden in the toun
Which° that of beautee hadde greet renoun,°   *who, beauty had great fame*
1625 Al° were it so she were of smal degree.°   *although, low-born family*
Suffiseth hym hir yowthe and hir beautee.[2]
Which mayde,° he seyde, he wolde han to his wyf,   *maid*
To lede° in ese° and hoolynesse° his lyf,°   *lead, ease, piety, life*
And thanked God that he myghte han hire al,°   *might have her all*
1630 That no wight° his blisse parten shal,°   *person, shall share*
And preyde hem° to laboure in this nede°   *asked them, need*
And shapen° that he faille nat to spede.°   *arrange, fail not to succeed*
For thanne, he seyde, his spirit was at ese.°   *ease*
"Thanne is," quod he, "nothyng may me displese,
1635 Save o thyng° priketh° in my conscience,   *one thing, bothers*
The which I wol reherce° in youre presence.   *will relate*
I HAVE," quod he, "herd seyd° ful yoore ago,°   *heard said, long ago*
Ther may no man han parfite blisses two.°   *two perfect happinesses*

---

1 "It seemed to him that his choice might not be bettered."
2 "Her youth and her beauty were enough for him."

This is to seye, in erthe and eek in Hevene.

1640 For though he kepe hym° from the synnes sevene°   *keep himself, seven (deadly) sins*
And eek° from every branche of thilke° tree,[1]   *also, that*
Yet is ther so parfit felicitee°   *perfect happiness*
And so greet ese° and lust° in mariage,   *great comfort, pleasure*
That evere I am agast° now in myn age°   *afraid, my (old) age*
1645 That I shal lede° now so myrie° a lyf,   *lead, merry*
So delicat° withouten wo and stryf,°   *delightful, strife*
That I shal have myn Hevene in earthe here.
For sith° that verray Hevene° is boght° so deere°   *since, Heaven itself, bought, dearly*
With tribulacioun° and greet penance,°   *trouble, penance*
1650 How sholde° I thane, that lyve° in swich plesaunce°   *should, who live, such pleasure*
As alle wedded men doon with hire° wyvys,   *their*
Come to the blisse° ther° Crist eterne° on lyve° ys?   *happiness, where, eternal, alive*
This is my drede,° and ye, my bretheren tweye,°   *fear, two brothers*
Assoilleth° me this questioun, I preye."°   *resolve, ask*
1655 JUSTINUS, which that hated his folye,   *folly*
Answerde anon° right in his japerye,°   *immediately, mockery*
And for he wolde his longe tale abregge,   *shorten*
He wolde noon auctoritee° allegge°   *no authors, quote*
But seyde, "Sire, so ther be noon obstacle
1660 Oother than this, God of his hygh myracle°   *high miracle*
And of his hygh mercy may so for yow wirche°   *work*
That er ye have youre right of Hooly Chirche,[2]
Ye may repente of wedded mannes lyf
In which ye seyn ther is no wo ne stryf.
1665 And elles, God forbe̍de° but° he sente   *forbid, unless*
A wedded man hym° grace to repente   *him*
Wel ofte,° rather° than a sengle° man.   *very often, sooner, single*
And therfore, sire—the beste reed I kan°—   *best advice I know*
Dispeire° yow noght but have in youre memorie,   *despair*
1670 Paraunter° she may be youre Purgatorie.   *perhaps*
She may be Goddes meene° and Goddes whippe.°   *means, whip*
Thanne shal youre soule up to Hevene skippe°   *skip*
Swifter than dooth° an arwe° out of the bowe.   *does, arrow*
I hope to God herafter° shul ye knowe   *after this*
1675 That ther nys° no so greet felicitee°   *is not, happiness*
In mariage ne° nevere mo shal bee,°   *nor, more shall be*
That yow shal lette of youre savacioun,°   *shall hinder your salvation*
So that ye use, as skil is and resoun,°   *reasonable and sensible*

---

1   The seven deadly sins were often described by preachers as the branches of a tree. Cf. Parson's Tale, line 387.

2   "Before you have your due (i.e., last rites and burial) from Holy Church."

The lustes° of youre wyf attemprely°	desires, temperately
1680 And that ye plese hire nat to° amorously	not too
And that ye kepe° yow eek from oother synne.°	keep, other sin
My tale is doon,° for my wit is thynne.°	done, thin
Beth nat agast herof,° my brother deere,	Be not afraid of this
But lat° us waden° out of this mateere!°	let, wade, matter
1685 The Wyf of Bathe,° if ye han understonde,°	Wife of Bath, you have understood
Of mariage, which ye have on honde,°	you have on hand
Declared hath° ful wel in litel space.	has declared
Fareth now wel!° God have yow in his grace!"	now farewell
And with this word this Justyn and his brother	
1690 Han take hir leve° and ech of hem° of oother.	their leave, each of them
For whan they saugh° that it moste be,	saw
They wroghten° so by sly and wys tretee°	made it happen, wise treaty
That she this mayden, which that Mayus highte,°	was named May
As hastily as evere that she myghte	
1695 Shal wedded be unto this Januarie.	
I trowe° it were to longe° yow to tarie°	believe, too long, delay
If I yow tolde of every scrit and bond°	contract and agreement
By which that she was feffed in his lond[1]	
Or for to herknen of° hir° riche array.	hear about, her
1700 But finally ycomen° is the day	come
That to the chirche° bothe be they went°	church, have they gone
For to receyve° the hooly sacrement.°	receive, holy sacrament (of marriage)
Forth comth the preest° with stole° aboute his nekke°	priest, scarf, neck
And bad hire be lyk to Sarra and Rebekke[2]	
1705 In wysdom and in trouthe° of mariage	constancy
And seyde hir orisons as is usage°	their prayers as is customary
And croucheth hem and bad God sholde hem blesse[3]	
And made al siker ynogh° with hoolynesse.°	certain enough, holiness
THUS been they wedded° with solempnitee,°	are they married, ceremony
1710 And at the feeste° sitteth he and she	feast
With othere worthy folk upon the deys.°	upon the high table
Al ful of joye and blisse is the paleys,°	palace
And ful of instrumentz° and of vitaille,°	[musical] instruments, food
The mooste deyntevous° of al Ytaille.°	choice, Italy

---

1   "By which she was enfeoffed into his landed possession." Being enfeoffed here means that she
     was given possession of some of his land. The term is a survival of the older medieval form of
     social arrangement known as feudalism, no longer fully in effect in Chaucer's day.
2   "And commanded her to be like Sarah and Rebecca"—two sometimes obedient wives in the
     book of Genesis. The actual ceremony of marriage is performed on the church steps and is fol-
     lowed by a nuptial mass inside.
3   "And blesses them with the sign of the cross and asked that God should bless them."

1715 Biforn hem stooden instrumentz of swich soun¹
      That Orpheus ne° of Thebes Amphioun²   *nor*
      Ne maden° nevere swich° a melodye.   *nor made, such*
      At every cours° thanne° cam° loud mynstralcye,°   *course, then, came, music*
      That nevere tromped° Joab³ for to heere°   *trumpeted, hear*
1720 Nor he Theodomas yet half so cleere°   *clear*
      At Thebes whan the citee was in doute.°⁴   *doubt*
      Bacus⁵ the wyn° hem° skynketh° al aboute,   *wine, them, pours*
      And Venus⁶ laugheth° upon every wight.°   *laughs, person*
      For Januarie was bicome° hire° knyght   *had become, her*
1725 And wolde° bothe assayen his corage°   *wanted, to attempt his vigor*
      In libertee° and eek in mariage   *liberty (i.e., as a bachelor)*
      And with hire fyr brond° in hire° hand aboute   *her fiery torch, her*
      Daunceth biforn° the bryde and al the route.°   *before, company*
      And certeinly, I dar° right wel seyn this: *dare*
1730 Ymeneus that God of weddyng is,⁷
      Saugh° nevere his lyf so myrie a wedded man.   *saw*
      Hoold° thou thy pees,° thou poete Marcian,⁸   *hold, peace*
      That writest° us that ilke° weddyng murie°   *writes, that same, merry*
      Of hire, Philologie, and hym, Mercurie
1735 And of the songes that the Muses song!⁹
      To° smal is bothe thy penne and eek thy tonge°   *too, tongue*
      For to discryven° of this mariage.   *describe*
      Whan tendre youthe hath wedded stoupyng° age   *stooping*
      Ther is swich myrthe° that it may nat be writen.   *such mirth*
1740 Assayeth° it youreself. Thanne may ye witen°   *try, know*
      If that I lye or noon° in this matiere.°   *not, matter*
      Mayus,° that sit with so benyngne a chiere,°   *May, kind a face*
      Hire to biholde,° it semed° fairye.°   *behold, seemed, magical*
      Queene Ester° looked nevere with swich° an eye   *Esther, such*

---

1 "Before them stood musical instruments of such sound."
2 In Greek mythology, Orpheus could charm beasts, rocks, and trees and was almost able to rescue his wife Eurydice from Hades by playing his lyre. King Amphion was a famous harper who helped build Thebes by using the magical power of his harp to assemble the stones.
3 Joab was King David's trumpeter, mentioned in 2 Samuel 2:28.
4 In Greek legend, Theodomas was a Theban prophet whose pronouncements were heralded by a trumpet.
5 In Greek mythology, Bacchus was the god of wine.
6 In Greek mythology, Venus was the goddess of sex and love.
7 In Greek mythology, Hymen was the god of marriage and wedding ceremonies.
8 The North African poet Martianus Capella (fifth century AD) wrote an allegorical account of the seven liberal arts, *The Marriage of Philology and Mercury*, i.e., the union of the science of language with eloquence, represented by the god Mercury.
9 In classical mythology, the Muses were the goddesses who controlled artistic expression.

1745 On Assuer,° so meke° a look hath she.¹   *Ahasuerus, meek*
     I may yow nat devyse° al hir beautee.   *not describe for you*
     But thus muche of hire beautee telle I may,
     That she was lyk the brighte morwe° of May,   *morning*
     Fulfild of° alle beautee and plesaunce.°   *filled with, pleasure*
1750 THIS Januarie is ravysshed° in a traunce°   *ravished, trance*
     At every tyme he looked on hir face.
     But in his herte he gan hire to manace,°   *began to menace her*
     That he that nyght° in armes wolde hire streyne°   *night, would constrain her*
     Harder than evere Parys dide Eleyne.²
1755 But nathelees,° yet hadde he greet pitee°   *nevertheless, great pity*
     That thilke nyght offenden hire moste he°   *same night he had to harm her*
     And thoughte, "Allas, o tendre creature!
     Now wolde° God ye myghte° wel° endure   *would, might, well*
     Al my corage,° it is so sharpe and keene!   *sexual prowess*
1760 I am agast° ye shul it nat susteene.°   *afraid, shall not sustain it*
     But God forbede that I dide al my myght!³
     Now wolde° God that it were woxen nyght°   *would, it were turned to night*
     And that the nyght wolde lasten everemo!°   *would last forever*
     I wolde° that al this peple° were ago!"°   *wish, people, gone*
1765 And finally he dooth al his labour°   *endeavors*
     As he best myghte, savyng° his honour,°   *saving, honor*
     To haste hem° fro° the mete° in subtil wyse.°   *hasten them, from, food, subtle way*
     THE tyme cam that resoun° was to ryse,°   *reasonable, rise*
     And after that men daunce and drynken faste,
1770 And spices al aboute the hous they caste.⁴
     And ful of joye and blisse is every man—
     Al but a squyer° highte° Damyan,   *squire, named*
     Which carf° biforn° the knyght ful many a day.°⁵   *carved, before, for a long time*
     He was so ravysshed° on his lady May,   *ravished*
1775 That for the verray peyne° he was ny wood.°   *true pain, nearly crazy*
     Almoost he swelte° and swowned° ther° he stood,   *died, fainted, where*
     So soore° hath Venus hurt hym with hire brond,°   *sorely, torch*
     As that she bar° it daunsynge° in hire hond.°   *carried, dancing, her hand*
     And to his bed he wente hym° hastily.   *himself*

---

1   The marriage of Queen Esther and King Ahasuerus (King Xerxes) is described in Esther 2.
2   Paris's rape of Helen and their subsequent flight to Troy occasioned the Trojan war.
3   "God forbid that I not perform as powerfully as I can."
4   An old marriage custom was to throw spices on the floor during a wedding feast. This symbol-
    ized the beginning of the marriage, because medieval floors were often bare dirt strewn with
    straw and herbs. The old material would be removed before the new was strewn about.
5   One of the duties of a squire was to carve the meat and serve his lord at dinner. Cf. General
    Prologue, line 100.

1780 Namoore° of hym at this tyme speke I,¹   *No more*
    But there I lete hym wepe ynogh and pleyne,²
    Til° fresshe May wol rewen° on his peyne.°   *until, have pity, pain*
    O PERILOUS fyr,° that in the bedstraw³ bredeth,°   *fire, breeds*
    O famulier foo,⁴ that his servyce° bedeth,°   *service, offers*
1785 O servant traytour,° false, hoomly hewe,°   *traitor, domestic servant*
    Lyk to the naddre° in bosom, sly, untrewe!   *snake*
    God shilde° us alle from youre aqueyntaunce!°   *shield, acquaintance*
    O Januarie, dronken° in plesance,°   *drunk, pleasure*
    In mariage se° how thy Damyan,   *see*
1790 Thyn owene squier and thy born man,⁵
    Entendeth° for to do thee vileynye.°   *intends, harm*
    God graunte° thee thyn° hoomly fo° t'espye.°   *grant, your, foe at home, to see*
    For in this world nys° worse pestilence   *is not*
    Than hoomly foo alday° in thy presence.   *every day*
1795 PARFOURNED° hath the sonne° his ark diurne.°⁶   *performed, sun, diurnal arc*
    No lenger° may the body of hym sojourne°   *longer, its body travel*
    On th'orisonte° as in that latitude.   *horizon*
    Night with his mantel° that is derk° and rude°   *robe, dark, rough*
    Gan oversprede° the hemysperie° aboute,   *began to spread over, hemisphere*
1800 For which departed is this lusty route°   *energetic crowd*
    Fro Januarie with thank on every syde.
    Hoom° to hir hous° lustily they ryde,   *home, their houses*
    Whereas they doon hir thynges as hem leste.⁷
    And whan they sye hir tyme goon to reste,°   *see their time to go*
1805 Soone after that this hastif° Januarie   *impatient*
    Wolde go to bedde. He wolde no lenger tarye.°   *longer wait*
    He drynketh ypocras, clarree, and vernage⁸
    Of spices hoote° t'encreessen his corage.°   *hot spices, increase his potency*
    And many a letuarie° hath° he ful fyn,°   *potion, has, very fine*
1810 Swiche° as the monk Daun Constantyn   *such*
    Hath writen in his book, *De Coitu.*⁹

---

1 Ellesmere lacks "I." It is supplied from Hengwrt.
2 "But there I leave him weeping enough and complaining."
3 Medieval mattresses were often filled with straw. There is a Latin gloss "Auctor" in the margin, implying that this is the author's (or possibly the narrator's) own judgment or just a useful moral.
4 The "familiar foe" is an enemy within the household.
5 "Your own man, born into your service."
6 The daily arc of the sun is, in mythology, the conveyance that takes it through the sky. This line is an elaborate way to say that the sun has set.
7 "Where they go about their affairs as they wish."
8 Hypocras, clary, and vernaccia were all types of spiced wine.
9 Constantine the African, who came from Carthage and converted to Christianity, wrote a medical treatise entitled *About Intercourse* which, among other things, recommends various remedies for impotence similar to those here consumed by January.

To eten hem alle° he nas nothyng eschu,°   *eat them all, he is not reluctant*
And to hise privee freendes° thus seyde he,   *his close friends*
"For Goddes love, as soone as it may be,
1815 Lat voyden° al this hous in curteys° wyse!"   *empty, courteously*
And they han doon° right° as he wol devyse.°   *have done [it], just, would have it*
Men drynken° and the travers° drawe anon.   *drink, curtains*
The bryde was broght abedde° as stille° as stoon.°   *brought to bed, quiet, stone*
And whan the bed was with the preest yblessed,°   *blessed by the priest*
1820 Out of the chambre hath every wight hym dressed.[1]
And Januarie hath faste° in armes take°   *has firmly, taken*
His fresshe° May, his Paradys, his make.°   *fresh, mate*
He lulleth hire.° He kisseth hire ful ofte.   *speaks softly to her*
With thilke brustles° of his berd unsofte°   *those bristles, rough beard*
1825 Lyk to the skyn of houndfyssh° sharpe as brere,°   *dogfish, briar*
For he was shave° al newe in his manere.°   *shaven, manner*
He rubbeth hire° aboute hir tendre face   *rubs her*
And seyde thus: "Allas, I moot trespace°   *must trespass*
To yow my spouse and yow greetly offende°   *greatly offend you*
1830 Er tyme come° that I wil doun° descende.   *before the time comes, down*
But nathelees,° considereth this," quod he,   *nevertheless*
"Ther nys no werkman° what so evere he be   *is no workman*
That may bothe werke wel and hastily.
This wol be doon at leyser,° parfitly.°   *leisure, perfectly*
1835 It is no fors° how longe that we pleye.°   *It does not matter, play*
In trewe wedlok° wedded be we tweye.°   *true wedlock, we two*
And blessed be the yok° that we been inne!°   *yoke, are in*
For in actes we mowe° do no synne.°   *may, sin*
A man may do no synne with his wyf
1840 Ne hurte hymselven° with his owene knyf.°   *hurt himself, own knife*
For we han leve° to pleye° us by the lawe."[2]   *have permission, play*
Thus laboureth° he til that the day gan dawe.°   *labors, began to dawn*
And thanne he taketh a sope in fyn clarree,[3]
And upright in his bed thanne sitteth he.
1845 And after that he sang ful loude and cleere°   *very loudly and clearly*
And kiste° his wyf and made wantowne cheere.°   *kissed, behaved flirtatiously*
He was al coltissh,° ful of ragerye°   *like a colt, full of lechery*
And ful of jargon° as a flekked pye.°   *chatter, spotted magpie*
The slakke° skyn aboute his nekke shaketh°   *slack, neck shakes*
1850 Whil that he sang, so chaunteth° he and craketh.°   *sings, croaks*

---

1 "Out of the room everyone has gone."
2 "The law permits us to enjoy ourselves." Church law, known as canon law, governed matters of sexual morality. It actually placed many restrictions on sexual activity within marriage.
3 "And then he takes a piece of bread [soaked] in fine wine."

But God wot° what that May thoughte in hir herte   *knows*
Whan she hym saugh up sittynge° in his sherte,°   *saw him sitting up, nightshirt*
In his nyght cappe,° and with his nekke lene.°   *nightcap, lean*
She preyseth nat° his pleyyng° worth a bene.°   *does not praise, playing, bean*
1855 Thanne seide he thus: "My reste wol I take.
Now day is come. I may no lenger° wake."   *longer*
And doun he leyde his heed and sleepe til pryme.[1]
And afterward, whan that he saugh° his tyme,°   *saw, time*
Up ryseth° Januarie. But fresshe May   *rises*
1860 Heeld hire chambre° unto the fourthe day,   *kept in her room*
As usage° is of wyves for the beste.   *custom*
For every labour somtyme moot han° reste,   *labor sometimes must have*
Or elles° longe may he nat endure.   *else*
This is to seyn, no lyves creature,°   *living creature*
1865 Be it of fyssh or bryd or beest or man.
Now wol I speke of woful° Damyan,   *woeful*
That langwissheth° for love, as ye shul heere.°   *languishes, shall hear*
Therfore I speke to hym° in this manere: *about him*
I SEYE, O sely° Damyan, allas.[2]   *foolish*
1870 Andswere° to my demaunde,° as in this cas.°   *answer, question, situation*
How shaltow° to thy lady, fresshe May,   *shall you*
Telle thy wo? She wole alwey seye nay.
Eek if thou speke, she wol° thy wo biwreye.°   *will, betray*
God be thyn helpe. I kan° no bettre seye.°   *can, say no better*
1875 THIS sike° Damyan in Venus fyr°   *sick, fire*
So brenneth,° that he dyeth° for desyr,°   *burns, dies, desire*
For which he putte his lyf in aventure.°   *danger*
No lenger° myghte he in this wise° endure.   *longer, way*
But prively a penner gan he borwe,[3]
1880 And in a lettre° wroot° he al his sorwe°   *letter, wrote, sorrow*
In manere of a compleynt or a lay[4]
Unto his faire, fresshe lady May.
And in a purs° of sylk heng° on his sherte°   *purse, silk, [which] hung, shirt*
He hath it put and leyde° it at his herte.   *laid*
1885 THE moone, that at noon was thilke day°   *that day*
That Januarie hath wedded fresshe May
In two of Tawr,[5] was into Cancre glyden,°   *glided*

---

1 "And down he placed his head and slept until [the time of] morning prayer [around 9 a.m.]."
2 There is another gloss, "Auctor," in the margin.
3 "But secretly he borrowed a pencase or box with writing materials." Pencases normally be-
   longed to scholars or clerics. Damyan is literate but does not write very often.
4 Complaints and lais were types of short poems, often expressing a lover's sorrow.
5 "The moon, that on noon of that day that January married May was in the second degree of [the
   sign of the zodiac] Taurus had moved into the second [degree] of [the sign of the zodiac] Cancer."

So longe hath Mayus in hir chambre° byden°   *bedroom, stayed*
As custume° is unto thise noble alle.°   *custom, for all these nobles*
1890 A bryde° shal nat eten° in the halle   *bride, not eat*
Til dayes foure° or thre dayes atte leeste°   *MS iij, until at the least*
Ypassed been.° Thanne lat hire go to feeste.   *are passed*
The fourthe day compleet° fro° noon to noon   *complete, from*
Whan that the heighe masse° was ydoon.°   *high mass, done*
1895 In halle sit this Januarie and May,
As fressh as is the brighte someres° day.   *summer's*
And so bifel° how that this goode man   *it happened*
Remembred hym upon this Damyan
And seyde, "Seynte Marie, how may this be
1900 That Damyan entendeth nat° to me?   *does not attend*
Is he ay syk?° Or how may this bityde?"°   *Is he sick? happen*
His squieres,° whiche that stooden° ther bisyde,   *squires, who stood*
Excused hym bycause of his siknesse,
Which letted hym° to doon° his bisynesse.°   *prevented him, do, duty*
1905 Noon oother° cause myghte° make hym tarye.°   *no other, might, him delay*
"THAT me forthynketh,"° quod this Januarie.   *grieves*
"He is a gentil° squier, by my trouthe!   *noble*
If that he deyde,° it were° harm and routhe.°   *died, would be, pity*
He is as wys, discreet, and as secree°   *private*
1910 As any man I woot° of his degree,   *know*
And therto manly and eek servysable°   *eager to serve*
And for to been° a thrifty° man right able.°   *be, successful, very qualified*
But after mete° as soone as evere I may   *food*
I wol myself visite hym, and eek May,
1915 To doon hym al the confort° that I kan."   *comfort*
And for that word hym blessed every man,°   *every man blessed him*
That of his bountee° and his gentillesse°   *bounty, nobility*
He wolde so conforten in siknesse
His squier, for it was a gentil dede.°   *noble deed*
1920 "Dame," quod this Januarie, "taak° good hede.°   *take, heed*
At afternoon ye with youre wommen alle,
Whan ye han been° in chambre° out of this halle,   *have been, the room*
That alle ye go se° this Damyan.   *see*
Dooth hym disport.° He is a gentil man.   *cheer him up*
1925 And telleth hym that I wol hym visite.
Have I nothyng but° rested me a lite.°   *when I have only, little*
And spede° yow faste, for I wole abyde°   *speed, will wait*
Til that ye slepe° faste by my syde."°   *sleep, side*
And with that word he gan° to hym° to calle   *began, him*
1930 A squier that was marchal° of his halle   *marshall (master of ceremonies)*

And tolde hym certeyn thynges° what he wolde.°   *certain things, wanted*
THIS fresshe May hath streight hir wey yholde°   *has immediately taken her way*
With alle hir wommen unto Damyan.
Doun by his beddes syde° sit she than,   *bed's side*
1935 Confortynge hym as goodly° as she may.   *well*
This Damyan, whan that his tyme he say,°   *saw his opportunity*
In secree wise° his purs° and eek his bille,°   *secret way, purse, letter*
In which that he ywriten hadde his wille,°   *had written his desire*
Hath put into hire hand withouten moore,°   *without more*
1940 Save° that he siketh° wonder depe° and soore,°   *except, sighs, deeply, sorely*
And softely to hire right thus seyde he:
"Mercy, and that ye nat discovere° me,   *betray*
For I am deed° if that this thyng be kyd!"°   *dead, known*
This purs° hath she inwith° hir bosom hyd°   *purse, inside, hidden*
1945 And wente hire wey. Ye gete namoore° of me.   *get no more*
But unto Januarie ycomen is she,°   *has she come*
That on his beddes syde sit ful softe,°   *sits very quietly*
And taketh hire and kisseth hire ful ofte,°   *very often*
And leyde hym° doun to slepe, and that anon.°   *lay himself, immediately*
1950 She feyned° hire as that she moste gon°   *pretended, had to go*
Theras° ye woot° that every wight moot neede,°   *where, know, person must need*
And whan she of this bille° hath taken heede,°   *letter, paid attention*
She rente° it al to cloutes° atte laste,°   *tore, pieces, at the last*
And in the pryvee° softely it caste.°   *privy, threw*
1955 WHO studieth° now but faire, fresshe May?   *considers*
Adoun by olde Januarie she lay,
That sleepe° til that the coughe° hath hym awaked.   *who sleeps, cough*
Anon he preyde hire° strepen° hire al naked.   *asked her, strip*
He wolde of hire, he seyde, han som plesaunce.°   *have some pleasure*
1960 He seyde hir clothes dide hym encombraunce.°   *got in his way*
And she obeyeth, be hire lief or looth.°   *whether she wished to or not*
But lest ye precious° folk be with me wrooth,°   *prudish, angry*
How that he wroghte,° I dar nat° to yow telle,   *acted, dare not*
Or wheither that hire thoughte it° Paradys or Helle.   *it seemed to her*
1965 But heere I lete hem° werken° in hir wyse°   *leave them, acting, their way*
Til evensong rong° and that they moste aryse.°   *evening service rang, had to rise*
Were it° by destynee° or by aventure,°   *whether it were, destiny, chance*
Were it by influence° or by nature°   *(astrological) influence, natural cause*
Or constellacioun,° that in swich estaat°   *constellation, condition*
1970 The hevene stood that tyme fortunaat[1]
Was for to putte a bille° of Venus werkes°—   *letter, Venus's works*

---

1   "The heavens stood in such an arrangement that time was fortunate," i.e., the planetary influences were favorable.

For alle thyng hath tyme, as seyn° thise clerkes°[1]— *say, scholars*
To any womman for to gete° hire love, *get*
I kan nat seye.° But grete God above, *cannot say*
1975 That knoweth° that noon act is causelees,° *who knows, without cause*
He deme of al,° for I wole° holde my pees.° *May he judge everything, will, peace*
But sooth° is this, how that this fresshe May *true*
Hath take° swich° impressioun that day *has taken, such*
For pitee° of this sike Damyan, *pity*
1980 That from hire herte she ne dryve kan° *cannot drive*
The remembrance for to doon hym ese.° *memory (thought) of comforting him*
"Certeyn," thoghte she, "whom that this thyng displese,
I rekke noght,° for heere° I hym assure *care not, here*
To love hym best of any creature,
1985 Though he namoore hadde° than his sherte."° *had no more [possessions], shirt*
Lo, pitee° renneth° soone in gentil herte! *pity, runs*
HEERE may ye se how excellent franchise° *generosity*
In wommen is whan they hem narwe avyse.° *consider [things] carefully*
Som tyrant° is, as ther be many oon,° *some cruel woman, many a one*
1990 That hath an herte as hard as any stoon,° *stone*
Which wolde han lat hym storven° in the place *have let him die*
Wel rather° than han graunted hym hire grace,° *much rather, have granted him her favor*
And hem rejoysen in hire crueel pryde[2]
And rekke nat to been an homycide.° *care not to be a murderer*
1995 THIS gentil May fulfilled of pitee,° *full of pity*
Right of hire hand a lettre made she,
In which she graunteth hym hire verray grace.° *grants him her true favor*
Ther lakketh noght° oonly but day and place, *lacks nothing*
Wher that she myghte unto his lust suffise,° *might satisfy his desire*
2000 For it shal be right as he wole devyse.° *just as he will determine*
And whan she saugh hir tyme° upon a day *saw her opportunity*
To visite this Damyan gooth May,
And sotilly° this lettre doun° she threste° *subtly, down, thrust*
Under his pilwe,° rede° it if hym leste.° *pillow, read, if he wishes*
2005 She taketh hym by the hand and harde hym twiste° *squeezes*
So secrely° that no wight° of it wiste° *secretly, person, knew*
And bad hym been al hool.° And forth he wente *asked him to be whole*
To Januarie whan that he for hym sente.
UP riseth° Damyan the nexte morwe.° *rises, morning*
2010 Al passed was his siknesse° and his sorwe.° *sickness, sorrow*
He kembeth hym.° He preyneth° hym and pyketh.° *combs himself, preens, cleans*

---

1 The scholar or learned man is Solomon in Ecclesiastes 3:1.
2 "And rejoice themselves in their cruel pride." Chaucer switches subjects from singular to plural in mid sentence.

He dooth° al that his lady lust and lyketh.° · · · · · · · · · · · · · · *wishes, likes*
And eek to Januarie he gooth as lowe° · · · · · · · · · · · · · · · · · *meekly*
As evere dide a dogge for the bowe.[1]
2015 He is so plesant unto every man—
For craft is al whoso that do it kan[2]—
That every wight° is fayn° to speke hym good.° · · · · · · · *person, glad, speak well of him*
And fully in his lady grace° he stood. · · · · · · · · · · · · · · · · · *lady's favor*
Thus lete° I Damyan aboute his nede, · · · · · · · · · · · · · · · · · *leave*
2020 And in my tale forth I wol procede.
SOMME clerkes° holden° that felicitee° · · · · · · · · *scholars, believe, happiness*
Stant° in delit,° and therfore certeyn° he, · · · · · · · · · *stands, delight, certainly*
This noble Januarie, with al his myght,° · · · · · · · · · · · · · · · *power*
In honeste wyse° as longeth to a knyght, · · · · · · · · · · · · · · · *manner*
2025 Shoope° hym to lyve° ful deliciously.° · · · · · · · *determined, live, very delightfully*
His housynge,° his array as honestly° · · · · · · · · · · · · · · *housing, honorably*
To his degree was maked° as a kynges.° · · · · · · · · · · · · · · *made, king's*
Amonges othere of hise honeste thynges,° · · · · · · · · · · · · *honorable things*
He made a gardyn walled al with stoon.
2030 So fair a gardyn woot I nowher noon.[3]
For out of doute,° I verraily suppose · · · · · · · · · · · · · · · *without doubt*
That he that wroot the *Romance of the Rose*[4]
Ne koude of it the beautee wel devyse!° · · · · · · · · · · · · · *well describe*
Ne Priapus[5] ne myghte nat suffise,° · · · · · · · · · · · · · · · *might suffice*
2035 Though he be god of gardyns, for to telle
The beautee of the gardyn and the welle° · · · · · · · · · · · · · · · *well*
That stood under a laurer alwey grene.° · · · · · · *laurel tree [that was] always green*
Ful ofte° tyme he Pluto and his queene · · · · · · · · · · · · · · · *very often*
Proserpina and al hire fairye°[6] · · · · · · · · · · · · · · · · · · *their fairies*
2040 Disporten hem° and maken° melodye · · · · · · · · · *enjoyed themselves, music*
Aboute that welle and daunced° as men tolde. · · · · · · · · · · · · · *danced*
THIS noble knyght, this Januarie the olde
Swich deyntee hath° in it to walke and pleye° · · · · · · · · · *has such delight, play*

---

1 A hunting dog trained to work with an archer.
2 "For cunning is all that matters, as whoever can practice it knows."
3 "I do not know of so fair a garden anywhere."
4 *The Romance of the Rose* is a thirteenth-century French poem begun by Guillaume de Lorris and completed by Jean de Meun. Its earlier part depicts the Garden of Love, where Cupid holds his court. Chaucer translated part of this very influential poem into English.
5 In Greek mythology, Priapus was the god of gardens. He was also associated with male sexual potency.
6 In Greek mythology, Pluto was the god of the Underworld. He abducted Proserpina and forcibly made her his queen. Her mother Ceres, the goddess of the earth, caused the world to suffer perpetual winter until her daughter was returned. Since Proserpina had eaten some seeds from a pomegranate while in the Underworld, however, she was forced to reside there for half the year. Her mother mourns when she is there, dooming the earth to winter.

	That he wol no wight suffren bere the keye°	*will allow no one to have the key*
2045	Save he hymself. For of the smale wyket°	*small wicket gate*
	He baar° alwey of silver a clyket,°	*carried, key*
	With which whan that hym leste he° it unshette.°	*he desired, unlocked*
	And whan he wolde° paye his wyf hir dette°	*wanted, marriage-debt*
	In somer sesoun° thider° wolde° he go	*summer season, there, would*
2050	And May his wyf and no wight° but they two.	*person*
	And thynges whiche that were nat doon abedde°	*not done in bed*
	He in the gardyn parfourned hem° and spedde.°	*performed them, succeeded*
	And in this wyse many° a murye° day	*manner, merry*
	Lyved° this Januarie and fresshe May.	*Lived*
2055	But worldly joye may nat alwey dure°	*not always last*
	To Januarie ne° to no creature.	*nor*
	O SODEYN hape!° O thou Fortune instable,°¹	*sudden chance, unstable*
	Lyk° to the scorpion so deceyvable°	*Like, deceptive*
	That flaterest° with thyn heed° whan thou wolt stynge!°²	*flatters, your head, sting*
2060	Thy tayl° is deeth thurgh° thyn envenymynge.°	*tail, through, poisoning*
	O brotil° joye, o sweete venym° queynte,°	*brittle, venom, odd*
	O monstre° that so subtilly kanst peynte°	*monster, subtly can paint*
	Thy yiftes° under hewe° of stidefastnesse°	*gifts, color, steadfastness*
	That thou deceyvest° bothe moore and lesse!°	*deceive, more and less*
2065	Why hastow° Januarie thus deceyved,°	*have you, deceived*
	That haddest hym for thy ful freend° receyved?°	*close friend, received*
	And now thou hast biraft hym° bothe hise eyen,°	*taken from him, eyes*
	For sorwe of which desireth he to dyen.°	*die*
	ALLAS, this noble Januarie free	
2070	Amydde° his lust° and his prosperitee°	*amidst, desire, prosperity*
	Is woxen blynd° and that al sodeynly!°	*grown blind, suddenly*
	He wepeth,° and he wayleth pitously.°	*weeps, wails pitifully*
	And therwithal° the fyr° of jalousie,°	*with this, fire, jealousy*
	Lest that his wyf sholde falle in swich folye,°	*such folly*
2075	So brente° his herte that he wolde fayn°	*burned, would gladly*
	That som man bothe hym and hire had slayn.°	*killed*
	For neither after his deeth nor in his lyf	
	Ne wolde he° that she were love° ne wyf	*he did not want, lover*
	But evere lyve as wydwe° in clothes blake,	*widow*
2080	Soul° as the turtle° that lost hath hire make.°	*single, turtledove, her mate*
	But atte laste,° after a monthe or tweye,°	*at the last, two*
	His sorwe gan aswage,° sooth° to seye.	*sorrow began to diminish, true*
	For whan he wiste° it may noon oother° be,	*knew, no other*
	He paciently° took his adversitee,°	*patiently, adversity*

---

1 There is a Latin gloss, "Auctor," in the margin.
2 Ellesmere reads "synge." The emendation is from Hengwrt.

2085 Save out of doute° he may nat forgoon°   doubt, not stop
     That he nas jalous everemoore in oon,[1]
     Which jalousye it was so outrageous
     That neither in halle n'yn noon oother hous°   nor in any other house
     N'yn noon other place° never° the mo°   nor in any other place, never, more
2090 He nolde suffre° hire for to ryde° or go   would not allow, ride
     But° if that he had hond° on hire alway.   unless, a hand
     For which ful ofte wepeth fresshe May,
     That loveth Damyan so benyngnely°   kindly
     That she moot outher dyen° sodeynly°   must either die, suddenly
2095 Or elles she moot han hym° as hir leste.°   have him, as she wished
     She wayteth whan hir herte wolde breste.°   expects that her heart would burst
     UPON that oother syde, Damyan
     Bicomen° is the sorwefulleste° man   has become, most sorrowful
     That evere was, for neither nyght ne day
2100 Ne myghte he speke° a word to fresshe May   he might not speak
     As to his purpos of no swich mateere°   no such matter
     But if° that Januarie moste it heere,°   except, must hear it
     That hadde an hand upon hire everemo.°   ever more
     But nathelees° by writyng° to and fro   nevertheless, writing
2105 And privee signes° wiste° he what she mente.   secret signs, knew
     And she knew eek° the fyn° of his entente.°   also, aim, intent
     O JANUARIE, what myghte it thee availle°   what may help you
     Thogh° thou myghtest se° as fer° as shippes saille?   although, see, far
     For as good is blynd° deceyved be°   blind, to be deceived
2110 As to be deceyved whan a man may se.°   see
     LO ARGUS,[2] which that hadde an hondred eyen,°   hundred eyes
     For al that evere he koude poure° or pryen,°   investigate, pry
     Yet was he blent.° And God woot,° so been° mo°   blinded, knows, are, more
     That wenen wisly that it be nat so.[3]
2115 Passe over is an ese.[4] I sey namoore.
     THIS fresshe May that I spak of so yoore°   spoke of so long ago
     In warm wex° hath emprented° the clyket°   wax, imprinted, key
     That Januarie bar° of the smale wyket,°   carried, wicket gate
     By which into his gardyn ofte he wente.
2120 And Damyan, that knew al hire entente,
     The cliket countrefeted pryvely.°   counterfeited secretly
     Ther nys namoore° to saye but hastily   is no more

---

1   "Being jealous forever in one [matter]."
2   In Greek mythology, Argus was the guardian of Jove's mistress Io; he was killed by Mercury.
3   "And God knows, so are many others, who believe firmly that it is not so" (i.e., that they are not
    being deceived).
4   "To pass over something is a comfort" or "is the best course" (i.e., what you don't know won't
    hurt you).

Som° wonder by this clyket shal bityde,°   *some, shall happen*
Which ye shul heeren° if ye wole abyde.°   *shall hear, wait*
2125 O NOBLE Ovyde,[1] ful sooth° seystou,° God woot,°   *truth, you say, God knows*
"What sleighte° is it thogh it be long and hoot,°   *trick, difficult*
That he nyl fynde° it out in som manere?"°   *will not find, some way*
By Piramus° and Tesbee° may men leere,°   *Pyramus, Thisbe, learn*
Thogh they were kept ful longe streit overal,°   *long guarded most carefully*
2130 They been accorded rownynge° thurgh a wal   *whispering*
Ther no wight koude han founde out swich a sleighte.[2]
BUT now to purpose. Er° that dayes eighte°   *before, eight days*
Were passed er° the monthe of Juyl bifille,°   *before, July arrived*
That Januarie hath caught so greet a wille,°   *desire*
2135 Thurgh eggyng° of his wyf, hym for to pleye   *incitement*
In his gardyn, and no wight but they tweye,°   *two*
That in a morwe° unto this May seith° he,[3]   *one morning, says*
"Rys up, my wyf, my love, my lady free!
The turtle voys° is herd, my dowve° sweete.   *turtledove's voice, dove*
2140 The wynter° is goon° with his reynes weete.°   *winter, gone, wet rains*
Com forth now with thyne eyen columbyn.°   *your dovelike eyes*
How fairer been thy brestes° than is wyn.°   *are your breasts, wine*
The gardyn is enclosed al aboute.
Com forth my white spouse, out of doute.°   *doubt*
2145 Thou hast° me wounded in myn herte, o wyf!   *have*
No spot° of thee ne knew° I al my lyf.   *fault, not knew*
Com forth, and lat us taken som disport.°   *pleasure*
I chees° thee for my wyf and my confort."   *choose*
SWICHE° olde, lewed[4] wordes used he.   *such*
2150 On° Damyan a signe made she   *to*
That he sholde go biforn with his cliket.
This Damyan thanne hath opened the wyket,
And in he stirte,° and that in swich manere   *jumps*
That no wight myghte it se neither yheere.°   *see nor hear*
2155 And stille° he sit under a bussh anon.°   *quietly, immediately*
THIS Januarie, as blynd° as is a stoon,°   *blind, stone*
With Mayus in his hand and no wight° mo°   *person, more*

---

1 The Roman poet Ovid wrote the following quotation in his *Metamorphoses*, Book 4.68, in his recounting of the star-crossed lovers, Pyramus and Thisbe. They were separated by their families, but could whisper through a crack in the wall that was between their houses. There is a Latin gloss, "Auctor," in the margin.
2 "There no one could have found out such a trick."
3 The following speech is a quotation of various passages from the Song of Solomon in the Bible.
4 The word "lewed" in Middle English normally just means ignorant or uneducated. Here it may also have the modern sense of lascivious.

Into his fresshe gardyn is ago°   *gone*
And clapte to° the wyket sodeynly.°   *slammed, suddenly*
2160 "Now wyf," quod he, "heere nys° but thou and I,   *here is not*
That art the creature that I best love.
For by that Lord that sit in Hevene above,
Levere ich° hadde° to dyen° on a knyf°   *rather I, had, die, knife*
Than thee offende, trewe, deere wyf!
2165 For Goddes sake, thenk° how I thee chees,°   *think, chose*
Noght for no coveitise,° doutelees,°   *greed, doubtless*
But oonly for the love I had to thee.
And though that I be oold and may nat see
Beth° to me trewe,° and I shal telle yow why.   *be, true*
2170 Thre thynges, certes, shal ye wynne° therby.°   *win, by this*
First, love of Crist and to youreself honour
And al myn heritage,° toun° and tour.°   *my property, town, tower*
I yeve it yow. Maketh chartres as yow leste.[1]
This shal be doon° tomorwe er sonne reste.°   *done, before sunset*
2175 So wisly° God my soule brynge in blisse,°   *surely, bring into bliss*
I prey° yow first in covenat° ye me kisse.°   *ask, [to seal the] covenant kiss*
And though that I be jalous,° wyte° me noght.°   *jealous, blame, not*
Ye been so depe enprented° in my thoght,   *deeply imprinted*
That whan I considere youre beautee
2180 And therwithal the unlikly elde° of me,   *unsuitable old age*
I may nat, certes, though I sholde dye
Forbere° to been° out of youre compaignye.   *bear, be*
For verray° love this is withouten doute.   *true*
Now kys me, wyf, and lat us rome° aboute."   *roam*
2185 This fresshe May, when she thise wordes herde,
Benyngnely° to Januarie answerde,   *kindly*
But first and forward she bigan° to wepe,°   *began, weep*
"I have," quod she, "a soule for to kepe°   *guard*
As wel as ye and also myn honour°   *my honor*
2190 And of my wyfhod thilke tendre flour°   *that tender flower*
Which that I have assured in youre hond°   *given over to your control*
Whan that the preest° to yow my body bond.°   *priest, bound*
Wherfore° I wole answere in this manere: *therefore*
By the leve° of yow, my lord so deere,   *leave*
2195 I prey° to God that nevere dawe° the day   *pray, dawn*
That I ne sterve,° as foule° as womman may,   *do not die, foully*
If evere I do unto my kyn° that shame   *my relatives*
Or elles° I empeyre° so my name   *else, damage*

---

1 "I give it to you. Make charters [legal documents] as you wish."

That I be fals. And if I do that lakke,°   *offense*
2200 Do strepe° me and put me in a sakke,°   *strip, sack*
And in the nexte ryver do me drenche.°   *drown*
I am a gentil womman and no wenche.°   *peasant girl or mistress*
Why speke ye thus? But men been evere untrewe,°   *are always untrue*
And wommen have repreve° of yow ay newe.°   *reproach, constantly*
2205 Ye han noon oother° contenance,° I leeve,°   *have no other, behavior, believe*
But speke to us of untrust° and repreeve!"°   *mistrust, reproach*
AND with that word she saugh wher Damyan
Sat in the bussh. And coughen she bigan,°   *began to cough*
And with hir fynger° signes° made she   *finger, signs*
2210 That Damyan sholde clymbe upon a tree
That charged was with fruyt.° And up he wente.   *was full of fruit*
For verraily,° he knew al hire entente.   *truly*
And every signe that she koude make,
Wel bet° than Januarie, hir owene make.°   *much better, her own mate*
2215 For in a lettre she had toold hym al
Of this matere, how he werchen shal.°   *what he should do*
And thus I lete hym sitte° upon the pyrie°   *leave him sitting, pear tree*
And Januarie and May romynge myrie.°   *roaming merrily*
BRIGHT was the day and blew° the firmament.°   *blue, sky*
2220 Phebus[1] hath of gold hise stremes doun ysent°   *sent down his beams*
To gladen° every flour° with his warmnesse.°   *make glad, flower, warmth*
He was that tyme in Geminis, as I gesse,°   *guess*
But litel fro his declynacioun
Of Cancer, Jovis exaltacioun.[2]
2225 And so bifel° that brighte morwetyde°   *it happened, morning*
That in that gardyn in the ferther syde°   *farther side*
Pluto, that is kyng of Fairye,[3]
And many a lady in his compaignye,°   *company*
Folwynge° his wyf, the queene Proserpyne,   *following*
2230 Ech° after oother, right as a lyne,°[4]   *each, line*
Whil that she gadered floures° in the mede.°   *gathered flowers meadow*

---

1 In classical mythology, Phoebus was god of the sun.
2 The sun (Phoebus) is in the sign of Gemini (often represented in the Middle Ages by a couple
   embracing). The sun has almost entered his maximum northern declination and will reach it a
   few days later when he moves into the astrological sign of Cancer. Cancer is the "exaltation" of
   Jupiter, i.e., the astrological sign in which he was considered to be most powerful.
3 Pluto, also known as Hades, the god of the Underworld in Greek mythology, is here made the
   king of the Celtic Otherworld, just as he is in the contemporary romance *Sir Orpheo*.
4 Hengwrt reads for this line, "Whos answere hath doon many a man pyne." Both readings are
   somewhat deficient in sense and have been added later to what were originally incomplete lines
   in the two manuscripts. Several other manuscripts read (with minor variations) "Which that
   he ravysshed out of Ethna." This line makes more sense but is deficient in rhyme unless the
   preceding line is changed to read "Proserpina."

In Claudyan[1] ye may the stories rede.°   *read*
And in his grisly carte° he hire sette,°   *gruesome chariot, placed her*
This kyng of Fairye, thanne adoun° hym sette°   *down, sat himself*
2235 Upon a bench of turves fressh and grene.[2]
And right anon° thus seyde he to his queene: *immediately*
"MY wyf," quod he, "ther may no wight seye nay.
Th'experience° so preveth° every day   *experience, proves*
The tresons° whiche that wommen doon° to man.   *treasons, do*
2240 Ten hondred thousand° tellen I kan   *a million*
Notable of youre untrouthe and brotilnesse.°   *unreliability*
O Salomon wys and richest of richesse,
Fulfild of sapience° and of worldly glorie,°   *full of wisdom, glory*
Ful worthy been thy wordes to memorie°   *to be memorized*
2245 To every wight that wit and reson kan.°   *who has wit and reason*
Thus preiseth° he yet the bountee° of man: *praises, goodness*
'AMONGES a thousand men yet foond° I oon,°   *found, one*
But of wommen alle foond I noon.'
THUS seith the kyng that knoweth youre wikkednesse.
2250 And Jhesus *filius* Syrak,[3] as I gesse,
Ne speketh° of yow but seelde° reverence.   *does not speak, seldom*
A wyldefyr°[4] and corrupt pestilence°   *wildfire, corrupt plague*
So falle upon youre bodyes° yet tonyght.   *bodies*
Ne se ye nat° this honurable knyght,   *Do you not see*
2255 Bycause,° allas, that he is blynd and old,   *because*
His owene man shal make hym cokewold?°   *cuckold*
Lo, heere he sit, the lechour,° in the tree!   *lecher*
Now wol I graunten° of my magestee°   *grant, majesty*
Unto this olde, blynde, worthy knyght
2260 That he shal have ayeyn° hise eyen syght°   *again, his eyesight*
Whan that his wyf wold doon hym vileynye.°   *would do him a wrong*
Thanne shal he knowen al hire harlotrye,°   *her wickedness*
Bothe in repreve° of hire and othere mo."°   *reproach, more*
"YE shal?" quod Proserpyne, "wol° ye so?   *will*
2265 Now by my moodres sires soule°[5] I swere°   *mother's father's soul, swear*
That I shal yeven hire suffisant° answere   *shall give her sufficient*

---

1   The Roman author Claudian (c. 400 AD), in his *Rape of Proserpina*, recounts the story of Pluto and his queen.
2   Medieval gardens often contained turf benches made by piling up earth and then growing grass on it.
3   Jesus, son of Sirach (not Jesus Christ) is the author of the apocryphal or deuterocanonical book of Ecclesiasticus.
4   Wildfire or erysipelas is a painful skin disease.
5   Proserpina was the daughter of Ceres, whose father Saturn was known for his wisdom but also for his destructive power (cf. The Knight's Tale, lines 2453 ff).

And alle wommen after for hir sake,
That though they be in any gilt° ytake,°   *guilt, taken*
With face boold° they shulle hemself excuse°   *bold, shall excuse themselves*
2270 And bere hem doun that wolden hem accuse!¹
For lakke° of answere noon° of hem° shal dyen,°   *lack, none, them, shall die*
Al hadde man seyn a thyng with bothe hise eyen!²
Yit° shul° we wommen visage it hardily°   *yet, shall, outface it boldly*
And wepe and swere° and chide°³ it subtilly,°   *swear, accuse, subtly*
2275 So that ye men shul been as lewed° as gees.°   *ignorant, geese*
What rekketh me of youre auctoritees?°   *what do I care for your authorities*
I woot wel° that this Jew, this Salomon,   *know well*
Foond of us wommen fooles many oon.⁴
But though that he ne foond no good womman,
2280 Yet that ther founde many another man.
Wommen ful trewe, ful goode and vertuous.
Witnesse on hem that dwelle in Cristes hous.⁵
With martirdom they preved° hire constance.°   *proved, their constancy*
The Romayn geestes° eek° maken remembrance°   *Roman stories, also, record*
2285 Of many a verray, trewe wyf also.
But sire, ne be nat wrooth° albeit so,°   *not angry, although it is so*
Though that he seyde he foond no good womman,
I prey yow, take the sentence° of the man.   *meaning*
He mente° thus: that in sovereyn bontee°   *meant, supreme goodness*
2290 Nis noon° but God, that sit in Trinitee.°   *is no one, Trinity*
Ey,° for verray° God, that nys° but oon.°   *Ah, true, is not, one*
What make ye so muche of Salomon?
What though he made a temple, Goddes hous?
What though he were riche and glorious?
2295 So made he eek a temple of false goddis.
How myghte he do a thyng that moore forbode° is?   *forbidden*
Pardee,° as faire as ye his name emplastre,⁶   *By God*
He was a lecchour° and an ydolastre!°   *lecher, idolater*
And in his elde° he verray° God forsook.   *old age, true*
2300 And if God ne hadde, as seith the book,
Yspared hym for his fadres sake, he sholde
Have lost his regne rather than he wolde.⁷

---

1   "And bear them down who would accuse them."
2   "Although a man had seen a thing with both of his eyes."
3   Ellesmere repeats "visage" here from the previous line. The emendation is taken from Hengwrt.
4   "Found many a one of us women [to be] fools."
5   Those who "dwell in Christ's house" are the martyrs, who are in Heaven.
6   To "emplastre" is to apply a medicinal plaster over a wound, hence to plaster over or gloss over.
7   "If God had not spared him for his father's sake, as the Bible says, he would have lost his
    kingdom sooner than he wished." See 1 Kings 11:12–13. Ellesmere lacks the word "hym." The
    emendation is from Hengwrt.

I sette right noght° of al the vileynye,°   *consider nothing, villainy*
That ye° of wommen write, a boterflye!°[1]   *you (men), butterfly*
2305 I am a womman. Nedes moot I speke°   *I must needs speak*
Or elles swelle til myn herte breke.°   *break*
For sithen he seyde that we been jangleresses,°   *are chatterboxes*
As evere hool I moote brouke my tresses,[2]
I shal nat° spare for no curteisye°   *not, courtesy*
2310 To speke hym harm that wolde us vileynye!"[3]
"DAME," quod this Pluto, "be no lenger wrooth!°   *no longer angry*
I yeve° it up. But sith° I swoor° myn ooth,   *give, since, swore*
That I wolde graunten hym his sighte ageyn,
My word shal stonde.° I warne yow certeyn°   *stand, certainly*
2315 I am a kyng. It sit me noght to lye!"°   *not to lie*
"AND I," quod she, "a queene of Fairye.
Hir answere shal she have, I undertake.
Lat us namoore wordes heerof° make.   *about this*
For sothe, I wol no lenger° yow contrarie."°   *longer, disagree with*
2320 NOW lat° us turne agayn to Januarie,   *let*
That in the gardyn with his faire May
Syngeth ful murier° than the papejay,°   *much more merrily, parrot*
"Yow love I best and shal and oother noon."
So longe aboute the aleyes° is he goon,   *alleys*
2325 Til he was come agayns thilke pyrie,°   *come upon that same pear tree*
Whereas° this Damyan sitteth ful myrie°   *where, very merrily*
An heigh° among the fresshe leves grene.   *on high*
THIS fresshe May that is so bright and sheene°   *shining*
Gan for to syke° and seyde, "Allas my syde!°   *began to sigh, side*
2330 Now sire," quod she, "for aught° that may bityde,°   *anything, may happen*
I moste han° of the peres° that I see,   *must have, pears*
Or I moot dye,° so soore longeth me°   *might die, sorely I desire*
To eten° of the smale peres grene!   *eat*
Help for hir love that is of Hevene queene![4]
2335 I telle yow wel,° a womman in my plit°[5]   *well, plight*
May han to fruyt° so greet an appetit   *have for fruit*
That she may dyen but° she of it have!"   *unless*
"ALLAS," quod he, "that I ne had heer a knave°   *did not have a servant here*
That koude clymbe!° Allas! Allas" quod he,   *could climb*
2340 "That I am blynd!" "Ye sire, no fors,"° quod she.   *it does not matter*
"BUT wolde ye vouchesauf° for Goddes sake   *promise*

---

1 "I do not at all think all the villainy you (i.e., men) write about women is worth a butterfly."
2 "As ever I enjoy my braids," i.e., as long as I am a woman.
3 "To say bad things about him who would [intend] villainy [towards us]."
4 The Queen of Heaven is the Virgin Mary.
5 The plight May obliquely refers to is pregnancy.

The pyrie° inwith° youre armes for to take.   *pear tree, in*
For wel I woot° that ye mystruste° me.   *well I know, mistrust*
Thanne sholde I clymbe wel ynogh,"° quod she,   *well enough*
2345 "So I my foot myghte sette upon youre bak."
"CERTES," quod he, "theron° shal be no lak,   *on this*
Mighte I yow helpen° with myn herte blood."   *If I might help you*
He stoupeth doun,° and on his bak she stood   *stoops down*
And caughte hire° by a twiste.° And up she gooth.   *raised herself, branch*
2350 Ladyes, I prey° yow that ye be nat wroth.°   *ask, be not angry*
I kan nat glose.° I am a rude° man.   *cannot speak indirectly, rough*
And sodeynly anon° this Damyan   *at once*
Gan pullen up the smok, and in he throng.[1]
AND whan that Pluto saugh this grete wrong,
2355 To Januarie he gaf agayn° his sighte   *back again*
And made hym se as wel as evere he myghte.
And whan that he hadde caught his sighte agayn,°   *gained his sight again*
Ne was° ther nevere man of thyng° so fayn,°   *was not, thing, glad*
But on his wyf his thoght was everemo.°   *ever more*
2360 Up to the tree he caste hise eyen two°   *cast his two eyes*
And saugh that Damyan his wyf had dressed°   *treated*
In swich° manere° it may nat been expressed   *such, manner*
But if I wolde speke uncurteisly.°   *uncourteously*
And up he yaf° a roryng° and a cry   *gave, roaring*
2365 As dooth the mooder° whan the child shal dye.°   *mother, shall die*
"Out! Helpe! Allas! Harrow!"[2] he gan° to crye.   *began*
"O stronge lady stoore,° what dostow?"°   *bold, what do you do*
AND she answerde, "Sire, what eyleth° yow?   *ails*
Have pacience and resoun in youre mynde.
2370 I have yow holpe on° bothe youre eyen blynde.°   *have helped you with, blind eyes*
Up peril° of my soule, I shal nat lyen.°   *on peril, shall not lie*
As me was taught° to heele° with youre eyen°   *as taught to me, heal, eyes*
Was nothyng bet° to make yow to see   *better*
Than strugle° with a man upon a tree.   *struggle*
2375 God woot,° I dide it in ful good entente!"°   *knows, completely good intent*
"STRUGLE?" quod he. "Ye, algate in it wente![3]
God yeve° yow bothe on shames deth° to dyen!°   *give, a shameful death, die*
He swyved thee!° I saugh it with myne eyen!   *had sex with you*
And elles be I hanged by the hals!"°   *neck*
2380 "THANNE is," quod she, "my medicyne fals.°   *false*

---

1 "Pulled up the undergarment, and in he thrust."
2 "Out! Help! Alas! Harrow!" is the cry to raise help when one is in trouble. It was referred to as the "hue and cry."
3 "'Struggle?' said he. 'Yes, it went all the way in!'"

For certeinly, if that ye myghte se,
Ye wolde nat seyn° thise wordes unto me.   *would not say*
Ye han som glymsyng° and no parfit sighte."°   *have some glimpsing, perfect sight*
"I SE," quod he, "as wel as evere I myghte,
2385 Thonked be God, with bothe myne eyen two.
And by my trouthe° me thoughte° he dide thee so!"   *truth, it seemed to me*
"YE maze,° maze, goode sire," quod she.   *you are dazed*
"This thank have I, for I have maad° yow see.   *made*
Allas," quod she, "that evere I was so kynde!"
2390 "Now dame," quod he, "lat° al passe° out of mynde.°   *let, pass, mind*
Com doun,° my lief,° and if I have myssayd,°   *come down, dear, said wrong*
God helpe me so as I am yvele apayd.°   *evilly paid back (I am sorry)*
But by my fader° soule, I wende han seyn°   *father's, thought to have seen*
How that this Damyan hadde by thee leyn°   *lain*
2395 And that thy smok° hadde leyn° upon his brest."°   *undergarment, had lain, chest*
"YE sire," quod she, "ye may wene as yow lest.°   *think as you wish*
But, sire, as man that waketh° out of his sleepe,   *wakes*
He may nat sodeynly° wel° taken keepe   *suddenly, well*
Upon a thyng ne seen it parfitly°   *perfectly*
2400 Til that he be adawed verraily.°   *truly awakened*
RIGHT so a man that longe hath blynd ybe°   *has been blind*
Ne may nat sodeynly so wel yse°   *see so well*
First whan his sighte is newe come ageyn°   *newly come again*
As he that hath a day or two yseyn.°   *seen for a day or two*
2405 Til that youre sighte ysatled be awhile°   *is settled for awhile*
Ther may ful° many a sighte yow bigile.°   *very, trick you*
Beth war,° I prey° yow, for by Hevene kyng,   *Beware, pray*
Ful many a man weneth° to seen a thyng,   *thinks*
And it is al another than it semeth.
2410 He that mysconceyveth° he mysdemeth."°   *misconceives, misjudges*
And with that word she leepe° doun fro the tree.   *leapt*
THIS Januarie, who is glad but he?
He kisseth hire and clippeth hire ful ofte,°   *hugs her very often*
And on hire wombe° he stroketh hire° ful softe.   *belly, strokes her*
2415 And to his palays° hoom° he hath hire lad.°   *palace, home, has led her*
Now goode men, I pray yow be glad.
Thus endeth heere my tale of Januarie.
God blesse us and his mooder, Seinte Marie!

HEERE IS ENDED THE MARCHANTES TALE OF JANUARIE

THE FRANKLIN'S PROLOGUE AND TALE

Opening page of *The Franklin's Tale*. Ellesmere Manuscript EL 26 C9 f. 123v. Reprinted by permission of The Huntington Library.

THE FRANKLIN'S PROLOGUE

"IN feith,° Squier, thow hast thee wel yquit° *faith, you have done well*
And gentilly.° I preise wel° thy wit," *nobly, praise well*
675 Quod° the Frankeleyn,[1] "considerynge thy yowthe.° *said, youth*
So feelyngly° thou spekest,° sire, I allowe the,° *sensitively, speak, I praise you*
As to my doom,° ther is noon° that is heere *judgment, no one*
Of eloquence that shal be thy peere° *shall be your equal*
If that thou lyve.° God yeve° thee good chaunce° *live, give, chance*
680 And in vertu° sende thee continuaunce!° *virtue, continuing*
For of thy speche I have greet deyntee.° *great delight*
I have a sone,° and by the Trinitee,° *son, Trinity*
I hadde levere° than twenty pound worth lond,[2] *rather*
Though it right now were fallen in my hond,° *had fallen into my hand*
685 He were a man of swich discrecioun° *such discretion*
As that ye been.° Fy° on possessioun,° *you are, fie, possession*
But if° a man be vertuous withal!° *unless, as well*
I have my sone snybbed,° and yet shal, *scolded*
For he to vertu listeth nat entende.[3]
690 But for to pleye° at dees° and to despende° *play, dice, spend*
And lese al° that he hath is his usage.° *lose all, custom*
And he hath levere talken° with a page° *rather talk, boy servant*
Than to comune° with any gentil wight,° *talk, noble person*
Where he myghte lerne gentillesse aright."°[4] *learn nobility properly*
695 "STRAW for youre gentillesse!" quod oure Hoost.
"What, Frankeleyn, pardee° sire,° wel thou woost° *by God, sir, well you know*
That ech of yow moot tellen atte leste° *each must tell at least*
A tale or two or breken his biheste."° *break his promise*
"THAT knowe I wel, sire," quod the Frankeleyn.
700 "I prey yow,° haveth me nat in desdeyn° *ask you, do not disdain me*
Though to this man I speke a word[5] or two."
"TELLE on thy tale withouten wordes mo."° *without more words*

---

1 Hengwrt has the Merchant, not the Franklin, utter these words and engage in the following
   dispute with the Host.
2 Twenty pounds worth of land is that which provides an annual income of twenty pounds—a
   considerable sum in the late fourteenth century, equal to half a yearly income for a well-off
   knight.
3 "Because he does not want (*listeth nat*) to pay attention to virtue." Ellesmere reads "listneth"; the
   emendation is from Hengwrt.
4 "Gentilesse" is the quality that makes someone a gentleman or woman. In the Middle Ages it
   normally implied distinguished birth but also refined manners and moral virtue.
5 Ellesmere omits "a word," but it has been added by a later hand in the margin.

"GLADLY, sire Hoost," quod he. "I wole obeye°   *will obey*
Unto youre wyl.° Now herkneth° what I seye.   *will, listen to*
705 I wol yow nat contrarien in no wyse,[1]
As fer° as that my wittes° wol suffyse.°   *far, wits, will suffice*
I prey to God that it may plesen yow.°   *please you*
Thanne woot° I wel that it is good ynow."°   *know, enough*

EXPLICIT[2]

THE PROLOGE OF THE FRANKELEYNS TALE

THISE olde, gentil° Britouns° in hir dayes°   *noble, Bretons, their days*
710 Of diverse aventures° maden layes,°   *various adventures, songs*
Rymeyed° in hir firste° Briton tonge,°   *rhymed, original, language*
Whiche layes° with hir instrumentz° they songe°   *songs, their instuments, sung*
Or elles redden hem° for hir plesaunce.°[3]   *read them, pleasure*
And oon of hem° have I in remembraunce,°   *one of them, memory*
715 Which I shal seyn° with good wyl° as I kan.°   *say, will, can*
BUT sires, bycause I am a burel° man,   *uneducated*
At my bigynnyng first I yow biseche,°   *I ask you*
Have me excused of my rude speche.°   *rough speech*
I lerned nevere rethorik,° certeyn.°   *never learned rhetoric, certainly*
720 Thyng that I speke,° it moot° be bare and pleyn.°   *what I speak, must, plain*
I sleepe° nevere on the Mount of Pernaso,°[4]   *slept, Parnassus*
Ne lerned° Marcus Tullius Scithero.[5]   *nor did I learn*
Colours[6] ne° knowe I none, withouten drede,°   *nor, without doubt*
But swiche colours as growen° in the mede,°   *grow, meadow*
725 Or elles swiche as men dye or peynte.°   *paint*

---

1 "I will not contradict you in any way."

2 "Here it ends."

3 The Bretons came from Brittany, the northwest corner of modern-day France. They were a Celtic people, many of whose ancestors had almost a thousand years earlier than Chaucer's time fled from Britain to escape the Anglo-Saxon invaders, joining the earlier Celtic inhabitants. The Breton lay, mentioned here by the Franklin and embodied in his tale, is originally an oral genre. It always involved love and the marvelous and was accompanied by a harp. The twelfth-century poet Marie de France composed in French the oldest, and by most accounts the best, of the surviving Breton *lais*. In fact, Chaucer's source is more likely to be Boccaccio, who tells the story twice, once in the *Decameron* and once in the *Filocolo*.

4 In classical mythology, Mount Parnassus was the home of the Muses, the goddesses of artistic achievement. There is a marginal Latin gloss quoting the ultimate source, three lines from the *Satires* of the Roman poet Persius (34–62 AD). As Joanne Rice notes in the *Riverside Chaucer*, the lines are slightly garbled, suggesting Chaucer, or whoever is ultimately responsible for the glosses, did not know Persius's work directly.

5 Marcus Tullius Scithero is Cicero (106–43 BC), the famous Roman orator who wrote, among other subjects, about rhetoric.

6 The "colors of rhetoric" were the stylistic devices and figures of speech recommended by rhetoricians for use in effective public speaking and writing. Despite the Franklin's protestation that he knows no rhetoric, his tale has several ornate passages that make heavy use of these rhetorical colors.

Colours° of rethoryk° been to queynte!° *colors, rhetoric, are too unusual*
My spirit feeleth noght° of swich mateere.° *understands nothing, such matter*
But if yow list,° my tale shul ye heere.° *if you wish, shall you hear*

THE FRANKLIN'S TALE

HEERE BIGYNNETH THE FRANKELEYNS TALE

In Armorik,° that called is Britayne,° *Armorica, Brittany*
730 Ther was a knyght that loved and dide his payne° *took pains*
To serve a lady in his beste wise.°[1] *manner*
And many a labour, many a greet emprise° *undertaking*
He for his lady wroghte° er° she were wonne.° *did, before, won*
For she was oon the faireste° under sonne° *one of the fairest, sun*
735 And eek° therto° comen° of so heigh kynrede° *also, in addition, come, high kindred*
That wel unnethes dorste° this knyght for drede° *scarcely dared, fear*
Telle hire his wo,° his peyne,° and his distresse. *woe, pain*
But atte laste, she for his worthynesse° *worth*
And namely° for his meke obeysaunce° *especially, meek obedience*
740 Hath swich a pitee° caught of his penaunce° *pity, penance*
That pryvely° she fil of his accord° *secretly, fell in agreement with him*
To take hym for hir housbonde and hir lord—
Of swich lordshipe as men han° over hir wyves.° *have, their wives*
And for to lede° the moore° in blisse° hir lyves,° *lead, more, happiness, their lives*
745 Of his free wyl° he swoor hire° as a knyght *will, swore to her*
That nevere in al his lyf° he, day ne nyght, *life*
Ne sholde° upon hym° take no maistrie° *he would not, him, control*
Agayn hir wyl° ne kithe° hire° jalousie *against her will, show, her*
But hire obeye and folwe hir° wyl in al *follow her*
750 As any lovere to his lady shal,
Save that° the name of soveraynetee,° *except, sovereignty*
That wolde° he have for shame of his degree.° *would, not to shame his rank*
She thanked hym and with ful greet humblesse° *humility*
She seyde, "Sire, sith° of youre gentillesse *since*
755 Ye profre° me to have so large a reyne,° *offer, rein*
Ne wolde nevere God bitwixe us tweyne,
As in my gilt, were outher werre or stryf.[2]
Sire, I wol be youre humble, trewe wyf.
Have heer my trouthe° til that myn herte breste."° *pledge, burst*
760 Thus been they bothe in quiete and in reste.
For o° thyng, sires, saufly dar° I seye, *one thing, safely dare*

---

1 There is a picture of the Franklin in the margin.
2 "God would never wish that there were ever [i.e., may there never be] any quarrel or strife between us two through any fault of mine."

That freendes everych oother moot obeye°   *must obey each other*
If they wol longe holden compaignye.°   *remain in company*
Love wol nat been constreyned° by maistrye.°   *not be constrained, control*
765 Whan maistrie comth,° the god of love anon   *comes*
Beteth hise wynges,° and, farewel, he is gon!   *beats his wings*
Love is a thyng—as any spirit—free.
Wommen of kynde° desiren libertee°   *by nature, desire liberty*
And nat to been constreyned° as a thral.°   *not to be constrained, slave*
770 And so doon° men, if I sooth° seyen shal.°   *do, truth, shall say*
Looke, who that is moost pacient in love,
He is at his advantage° al above.   *advantage, MS advantate*
Pacience is an heigh vertu,° certeyn,   *great virtue*
For it venquysseth,° as thise clerkes° seyn,   *vanquishes, theologians*
775 Thynges that rigour sholde nevere atteyne.°   *harshness could never achieve*
For every word men may nat chide or pleyne.°   *not nag or complain*
Lerneth° to suffre° or elles,° so moot I goon,[1]   *learn, endure, else*
Ye shul it lerne wherso° ye wole° or noon!°   *whether, will, not*
For in this world, certein, ther no wight° is   *person*
780 That he ne dooth° or seith som tyme° amys°   *does not, says sometime, wrong*
Ire,° siknesse,° or constellacioun,[2]   *anger, sickness*
Wyn,° wo,° or chaungynge° of complexioun[3]   *wine, woe, changing*
Causeth ful ofte° to doon amys or speken.°   *very often, do or speak wrong*
On every wrong a man may nat° be wreken.°   *not, avenged*
785 After the tyme moste be temperaunce[4]
To every wight that kan on governaunce.°   *knows about governing*
And therfore hath this wise, worthy knyght,
To lyve in ese, suffrance hire bihight.°   *promised her patience*
And she to hym ful wisly gan to swere°   *swore*
790 That nevere sholde ther be defaute° in here.°   *fault, her*
HEERE° may men seen° an humble, wys° accord.°   *here, see, wise, agreement*
Thus hath she take° hir servant and hir lord—   *has she taken*
Servant in love and lord in mariage.
Thanne° was he bothe in lordshipe and servage.°   *Then, service*
795 Servage? Nay, but in lordshipe above,
Sith he hath bothe his lady and his love—
His lady, certes, and his wyf also,
The which that lawe of love acordeth to.°   *agrees to*

---

1 "So moot I goon" (as I might go) is an idiomatic expression meaning roughly "By my word" or "I assure you."
2 "Constellation" here means by the influence of the stars and planets.
3 "Complexion" here means "temperament." Medieval medical theory maintained that what we now call "personality" was a function of the balance in the body of the four bodily fluids known as humors.
4 "Moderation must be suited to the time or occasion."

And whan° he was in this prosperitee,°   *when, prosperity*
800 Hoom° with his wyf he gooth to his contree,   *home*
Nat fer fro° Pedmark,[1] ther° his dwellyng was,   *not far from, where*
Whereas° he lyveth in blisse and in solas.°   *where, comfort*
WHO koude° telle, but he hadde wedded° be,   *could, he who had married*
The joye, the ese,° and the prosperitee°   *ease, well being*
805 That is bitwixe° an housbonde and his wyf?   *between*
A yeer and moore lasted this blisful lyf,
Til that the knyght of which I speke of thus,
That of Kayrrud[2] was cleped° Arveragus,   *called*
Shoope° hym to goon° and dwelle a yeer or tweyne°   *intended, go, year or two*
810 In Engelond, that cleped was eek Briteyne,°   *also was called Britain*
To seke° in armes worshipe° and honour.   *seek, knightly reputation*
For al his lust° he sette° in swich° labour   *pleasure, set, such*
And dwelled there two yeer. The book seith thus.
NOW wol° I stynten° of the Arveragus,   *will, cease speaking*
815 And speken I wole of Dorigene his wyf,
That loveth hire housbonde as hire hertes lyf.
For his absence wepeth° she and siketh,°   *weeps, sighs*
As doon° thise noble wyves whan hem liketh.°   *do, when they wish*
She moorneth, waketh, wayleth, fasteth, pleyneth![3]
820 Desir of his presence hire so destreyneth,°   *afflicts*
That al this wyde world she sette at noght.°   *set at nothing*
Hire freendes,° whiche that knewe hir hevy thoght,°   *her friends, her sad thoughts*
Conforten hire° in al that ever they may.   *comfort her*
They prechen hire.° They telle hire nyght and day   *preach to her*
825 That causelees° she sleeth hirself,° allas!   *without cause, kills herself*
And every confort° possible in this cas°   *comfort, case*
They doon to hire with al hire bisynesse,°   *their efforts*
Al for to make hire leve hire hevynesse.°   *leave her sadness*
BY proces,° as ye knowen everichoon,°   *gradually, everyone*
830 Men may so longe graven° in a stoon°   *engrave, stone*
Til som figure therinne emprented be.°   *some image be engraved on it*
So longe han° they conforted hire, til she   *have*
Receyved hath° by hope and by resoun°   *has received, reason*
The emprentyng° of hire consolacioun,°   *imprinting, their consolation*
835 Thurgh which hir grete sorwe gan aswage.°   *began to lessen*
She may nat alwey duren° in swich rage.°   *endure, passion*
AND eek Arveragus in al this care

---

1 Penmarch is a town in Brittany.
2 In modern Brittany there are several towns called Kerru (from the Celtic name for red fort), but none is near Penmarch.
3 "She mourns, lies sleepless, wails, fasts, complains."

Hath sent hire lettres hoom of his welfare
And that he wol come hastily agayn,
840 Or elles° hadde this sorwe hir herte slayn.   *else*
HIRE freendes sawe hir sorwe gan to slake°   *began to lessen*
And preyde hire° on knees, for Goddes sake   *asked her*
To come and romen° hire in compaignye°   *roam about, company*
Awey to dryve° hire derke fantasye.°   *to drive away, dark imaginings*
845 And finally she graunted that requeste,
For wel she saugh° that it was for the beste.   *saw*
NOW stood hire castel° faste° by the see,°   *castle, close, sea*
And often with hire freendes walketh shee
Hire to disporte° upon the bank an heigh,°   *to enjoy herself, on high*
850 Whereas° she many a shipe and barge seigh°   *where, sees*
Seillynge hir cours, whereas hem liste go.¹
But thanne was that a parcel° of hire wo,°   *part, her woe*
For to hirself ful ofte° "Allas!" seith she.   *very often*
"Is ther no shipe of so manye as I se°   *see*
855 Wol bryngen hom° my lord? Thanne were myn herte   *that will bring home*
Al warisshed° of hise bittre peynes smerte!"°   *cured, the hurt of its bitter pains*
ANOTHER tyme ther wolde she sitte and thynke
And caste hir eyen dounward fro the brynke.°   *eyes downward from the brink*
But whan she saugh the grisly rokkes blake,°   *horrible black rocks*
860 For verray feere° so wolde hir herte quake,   *true fear*
That on hire feet she myghte hire noght sustene.°   *might not sustain herself*
Thanne wolde she sitte adoun° upon the grene°   *sit down, green*
And pitously into the see biholde°   *pitifully look into the sea*
And seyn right thus with sorweful sikes colde,²
865 "ETERNE° God, that thurgh° thy purveiaunce°   *eternal, through, foresight*
Ledest° the world by certein governaunce,°   *leads, certain governing*
In ydel,° as men seyn,° ye nothyng make.   *vain, say*
But, Lord, thise grisly,° feendly° rokkes blake   *horrible, fiendish*
That semen° rather a foul confusioun   *seem*
870 Of werk° than any fair creacioun°—   *work, creation*
Of swich a parfit,° wys° God and a stable,°   *perfect, wise, unchanging*
Why han ye wroght° this werk unresonable?°³   *have you made, irrational work*
For by this werk south, north, ne° west, ne eest,   *nor*
Ther nys yfostred° man ne bryd° ne beest.°   *is not helped, bird, beast*
875 It dooth no good to my wit° but anoyeth.°   *understanding, harms*
Se ye nat, Lord, how mankynde it destroyeth?

---

1   "Sailing their course, where they wished to go."
2   "And say just like this with sorrowful, cold sighs."
3   Dorigen's questioning of how God, who forsees and controls all, could allow evil, echoes
     Boethius's *Consolation of Philosophy* Book 1, meter 5, lines 22 and Book 3, meter 9, lines 1–10,
     and Palamon's questioning in the Knight's Tale, lines 1303–24.

An hundred thousand bodyes° of mankynde — *bodies*
Han° rokkes slayn,° al° be they nat in mynde,° — *have, killed, although, not remembered*
Which mankynde is so fair part of thy werk,
880 That thou it madest lyk° to thyn owene merk.° — *made it like, your own image*
THANNE semed it ye hadde a greet chiertee° — *love*
Toward mankynde. But how thanne may it bee
That ye swiche meenes° make it to destroyen— — *means*
Whiche meenes do no good but evere anoyen?° — *harm*
885 I woot wel clerkes wol seyn as hem leste[1]
By argumentz° that al is for the beste, — *arguments*
Though I kan the causes nat yknowe.° — *cannot know the causes*
But thilke God that made wynd to blowe,
As kepe my lord! This my conclusioun.[2]
890 To clerkes° lete° I al this disputisoun.° — *theologians, leave, debate*
But wolde God that alle thise rokkes blake° — *these black rocks*
Were sonken° into Helle for his[3] sake! — *sunk*
Thise rokkes sleen myn herte for the feere!"° — *kill my heart for fear*
Thus wolde she seyn with many a pitous teere.° — *pitiful tear*
895 HIRE freendes sawe that it was no disport° — *comfort*
To romen° by the see° but disconfort° — *roam, sea, distress*
And shopen for° to pleyen° somwher elles.° — *arranged, play, somewhere else*
They leden hire° by ryveres° and by welles° — *led her, rivers, springs*
And eek° in othere places delitables.° — *also, delightful*
900 They dauncen, and they pleyen at ches° and tables.° — *chess, backgammon*
SO ON a day, right in the morwetyde,° — *morning*
Unto a gardyn that was ther bisyde,° — *nearby*
In which that they hadde maad hir ordinaunce° — *had made their arrangements*
Of vitaille° and of oother purveiaunce,° — *food, other provisions*
905 They goon° and pleye hem° al the longe day. — *go, enjoy themselves*
And this was in the sixte morwe° of May— — *sixth morning*
Which May hadde peynted° with his softe shoures° — *had painted, gentle rain*
This gardyn ful of leves and of floures
And craft of mannes hand so curiously° — *cleverly*
910 Arrayed° hadde this gardyn trewely,° — *arranged, truly*
That nevere was ther gardyn of swich prys° — *value*
But if it were the verray Paradys.° — *Paradise itself*
The odour° of floures and the fresshe sighte° — *odor, fresh sight*
Wolde han maked° any herte lighte — *would have made*
915 That evere was born, but if to greet siknesse° — *too great sickness*

---

1 "I know well that theologians will say as they wish."
2 "[May] thát same God that caused the wind to blow/take care of my lord. That is my conclusion." Dorigen closes her discussion of the theological question of God's foreknowledge by using the formal term for the end of a scholastic argument, conclusion.
3 "His" refers here to her husband Arveragus rather than to God.

Or to greet sorwe° helde it in distresse,   *too great sorrow*
So ful it was of beautee with plesaunce.°   *pleasure*
At after dyner° gonne they to daunce°   *dinner, began to dance*
And synge also—save° Dorigen allone,°   *except, alone*
920 Which° made alwey° hir compleint° and hir moone.°   *who, always, her lament, moan*
For° she ne saugh° hym on the daunce go   *because, saw*
That was hir housbonde and hir love also.
But nathelees,° she moste a tyme abyde°   *nevertheless, must wait for a time*
And with good hope lete hir sorwe slyde.°   *go away*
925 UPON this daunce, amonges othere men,
Daunced a squier° biforn° Dorigen   *squire, before*
That fressher was and jolyer° of array,°   *jollier, dress*
As to my doom,° than is the monthe of May.   *judgment*
He syngeth, daunceth passynge° any man   *surpassing*
930 That is or was sith that the world bigan.
Therwith° he was, if men sholde hym discryve,°   *for this, should describe him*
Oon° of the beste farynge° man onlyve°—   *one, behaving, alive*
Yong,° strong, right vertuous and riche and wys°   *young, wise*
And wel biloved° and holden in greet prys.°   *well liked, held in great value*
935 And shortly, if the sothe° I tellen shal,   *truth*
Unwityng of this,° Dorigen at al   *ignorant of this*
This lusty° squier,° servant to Venus,[1]   *vigorous, squire*
Which that ycleped was° Aurelius,   *was called*
Hadde loved hire best of any creature,
940 Two yeer and moore, as was his aventure.°   *chance*
But nevere dorste° he tellen hire° his grevaunce.°   *dared, tell her, grief*
Withouten coppe he drank al his penaunce.[2]
He was despeyred.° Nothyng dorste° he seye,   *in despair, dared*
Save° in his songes somwhat wolde he wreye°   *except, reveal*
945 His wo, as in a general compleynyng.°   *lamenting*
He seyde he lovede and was biloved nothyng.°   *not at all beloved*
Of swich matere made he manye layes,°   *songs*
Songes, compleintes,° roundels, virelayes,[3]   *laments*
How that he dorste nat° his sorwe telle   *dared not*
950 But langwissheth° as a Furye[4] dooth° in Helle.   *languishes, does*
And dye° he moste,° he seyde, as dide Ekko°   *die, must, Echo*

---

1 "Servant of Venus" here means that Aurelius, like Chaucer's Squire or Palamon in the Knight's
   Tale, is devoted to courtly love, which was conceived of as a form of service, demanding total
   loyalty and subservience to one's lady.
2 "He drank his penance without a cup." The expression may suggest he suffered intensely or even
   eagerly (without bothering with a cup) but its exact meaning is unclear.
3 These are all genres of song popular in fourteenth-century France and England.
4 In classical mythology, the three Furies were winged goddesses, their faces often encircled by
   snakes, who avenge wrongs.

For Narcisus,° that dorste nat° telle hir wo.[1]   Narcissus, dared not
In oother manere than ye heere me seye
Ne dorste he nat to hire his wo biwreye,°   reveal his woe to her
955 Save that° paraventure° somtyme at daunces   except, perhaps
Ther° yong folk kepen hir observaunces,°   where, keep their rituals
It may wel be he looked on hir face
In swich a wise° as man that asketh grace.°   such a way, favor
But nothyng wiste° she of his entente.°   knew, intent
960 Nathelees, it happed er they thennes wente,[2]
Bycause that he was hire neighebour
And was a man of worshipe° and honour   renown
And hadde yknowen hym of tyme yore,[3]
They fille° in speche,° and forth moore and moore   fell, speech
965 Unto° this purpos° drough° Aurelius,   towards, purpose, drew
And whan he saugh his tyme, he seyde thus:
"MADAME," quod he, "by God that this world made,
So that I wiste° it myghte youre herte glade,°   provided I knew, gladden your heart
I wolde that day that youre Arveragus
970 Wente over the see° that I, Aurelius,   sea
Hadde went ther nevere I sholde have come agayn,°   (i.e., had died)
For wel I woot,° my servyce is in vayn.°   well I know, vain
My gerdoun° is but brestyng° of myn herte.   reward, breaking
Madame, reweth° upon my peynes smerte,°   have pity, sharp pains
975 For with a word ye may me sleen° or save.   kill
Heere at youre feet God wolde that I were grave!°   buried
I ne have as now no leyser moore to seye.°   do not have leisure to say more
Have mercy, sweete, or ye wol do me deye!"°   will cause my death
SHE gan to looke° upon Aurelius.   looked
980 "Is this youre wyl?"° quod she. "And sey ye thus?   will
Nevere erst,"° quod she, "ne wiste° I what ye mente!°   before, knew not, meant
But now, Aurelie, I knowe youre entente.
By thilke° God that yaf° me soule and lyf,   that same, gave
Ne shal I nevere been untrewe wyf,
985 In word ne° werk,° as fer° as I have wit.   nor, deed, far
I wol been° his to whom that I am knyt.°   will be, knit
Taak° this for fynal° answere as of me."   take, final
But after that in pley thus seyde she:

---

1 In Greek mythology, Narcissus looked into a well, saw his image, and fell in love with him-
   self. Echo, who could only repeat the last words of others, loved him but died because he
   did not return her love, fading away until only her voice was left. A marginal Latin gloss
   "Metamorphosios" indicates that this story is told by the Roman poet Ovid (43 BC–18 AD) in
   his *Metamorphoses* 3:353–407.
2 "But nevertheless, it happened before they went from there."
3 "And [she] had known him for a long time."

"AURELIE," quod she, "by heighe° God above,   *high*
990   Yet wolde I graunte yow to been° youre love,   *grant you to be*
      Syn I yow se so pitously complayne.°   *pitifully complain*
      Looke what day¹ that endelong° Britayne   *all along*
      Ye remoeve° alle the rokkes, stoon by stoon,   *remove*
      That they ne lette° shipe ne boot° to goon,°   *hinder, nor boat, go*
995   I seye whan ye han maad° the coost° so clene°   *have made, coast, clear*
      Of rokkes, that ther nys no stoon ysene,°   *is no stone seen*
      Thanne wol I love yow best of any man.
      Have heer my trouthe in al that evere I kan."²
      "Is THER noon oother grace° in yow?" quod he.   *no other mercy*
1000 "NO, BY that Lord," quod she, "that maked me!°   *made me*
      For wel I woot° that it shal never bityde.°   *know, shall never happen*
      Lat swiche folies out of youre herte slyde!³
      What deyntee° sholde° a man han° in his lyf   *delight, should, have*
      For to go love another mannes wyf,
1005 That hath hir body whan so that hym liketh?"°   *whenever he wishes*
      AURELIUS ful ofte soore siketh.°⁴   *sighs sorely*
      Wo was Aurelie whan that he this herde,
      And with a sorweful herte he thus answerde:
      "MADAME," quod he, "this were an inpossible!°   *impossible [thing]*
1010 Thanne moot° I dye° of sodeyn° deth horrible!"   *must, die, sudden*
      And with that word he turned hym anon.°   *turned himself away immediately*
      Tho° coome hir° othere freendes, many oon,°   *then, their, many a one*
      And in the aleyes° romeden° up and doun,°   *alleys, roamed, down*
      And nothyng wiste° of this conclusioun°   *knew nothing, matter*
1015 But sodeynly bigonne revel newe,°   *suddenly began new revelry*
      Til that the brighte sonne loste his hewe.°   *color*
      For th'orisonte° hath reft° the sonne his light°—   *horizon, taken from, light*
      This is as muche to seye as it was nyght.
      And hoom they goon° in joye and in solas,°   *go, comfort*
1020 Save° oonly wrecche° Aurelius, allas!   *except, wretched*
      He to his hous is goon with sorweful herte.
      He seeth he may nat fro his deeth asterte.°   *not escape from his death*
      Hym semed that he felte his herte colde.⁵
      Up to the Hevene hise handes he gan holde,°   *raised*
1025 And on hise knowes bare° he sette hym doun,°   *bare knees, set himself down*

---

1   "Looke what day" is an idiomatic expression meaning "On whatever day."
2   "Have here my word, as far as I am able."
3   "Let such follies slide out of your heart."
4   The awkward position of line 1006, which seems an interruption, may be an error, but it is
    found in many manuscripts, including both Ellesmere and Hengwrt. Three manuscripts whose
    readings are on the whole considered less reliable have lines 999 and 1000 following after 1006,
    which removes the problem.
5   "It seemed to him that he felt his heart grow cold."

And in his ravyng° seyde his orisoun.°   *raving, prayer*
For verray wo out of his wit he breyde.°   *went out of his mind*
He nyste° what he spak. But thus he seyde   *did not know*
With pitous herte. His pleynt hath he bigonne°   *lament has he begun*
1030   Unto the goddes and first unto the sonne:°   *sun*
HE seyde, "Appollo, god and governour[1]
Of every plannte, herbe, tree, and flour
That yevest° after thy declinacioun°[2]   *gives, according to your declination*
To ech of hem his tyme and his sesoun,°   *season*
1035   As thyn herberwe° chaungeth° lowe or heighe,   *harbor, changes*
Lord Phebus,° cast thy merciable eighe°   *Phoebus Apollo, merciful eye*
On wrecche Aurelie, which am but lorn.°   *lost*
Lo, Lord, my lady hath my deeth ysworn°—   *sentenced me to death*
Withoute gilt.° But° thy benignytee,°   *guilt, unless, kindness*
1040   Upon my dedly herte° have som pitee,°   *deathly heart, some pity*
For wel I woot, Lord Phebus, if yow lest,°   *if you wish*
Ye may me helpen, save° my lady, best.°   *best help me, except for*
Now vouchethsauf° that I may yow devyse°   *grant, explain to you*
How that I may been holpen° and in what wyse.°   *be helped, what way*
1045   YOURE blisful suster° Lucina[3] the sheene,°   *sister, bright*
That of the see° is chief goddesse and queene—   *sea*
Though Neptunus have deitee° in the see,   *divine rule*
Yet emperisse° aboven hym is she—   *empress*
Ye knowen wel, Lord, that right as hir desir°   *just as her desire*
1050   Is to be quyked° and lightned° of youre fir,   *animated, illuminated*
For which she folweth yow ful bisily.°   *very eagerly*
Right so° the see desireth° naturelly   *just so, desires*
To folwen hire° as she that is goddesse,   *follow her*
Bothe in the see and ryveres moore and lesse.°   *greater and lesser*
1055   Wherfore,° Lord Phebus, this is my requeste: *therefore*
Do this miracle or do myn herte breste°—   *make burst*
That now next at this opposicioun,°   *opposition [of planets]*
Which in the signe° shal be of the leoun,°[4]   *sign, lion*
As preieth hire° so greet a flood to brynge°   *ask her, bring*

---

1   In Roman mythology, Phoebus Apollo was the god of the sun. There is a marginal English gloss: "The complaint of Aurelius to the goddess and the sonne."

2   In astrology, "declination" refers to a planet's angle from the celestial equator. As Skeat notes in his edition, "The change of season depends on the sun's change of position (called *herberwe* or 'harbour' in line 1035) to be high or low in the sky."

3   In Roman mythology, Lucina was another name for Diana, goddess of the moon, who is also identified with Proserpina, queen of the Underworld. A gloss above the name Lucina provides the more familiar "Luna."

4   This is a reference to the constellation Leo, part of the zodiac. The sun's influence is strongest in this sign, which is his house or mansion. When the sun and the moon are in opposition—i.e., 180° apart—their effect on the earth is strongest and the tides highest.

1060 That fyve fadme° at the leeste° it oversprynge°   *five fathoms (30 feet), least, overwhelm*
    The hyeste rokke° in Armorik Briteyne,°   *highest rock, Armorican Brittany*
    And lat this flood endure yeres tweyne.°   *last two years*
    Thanne, certes, to my lady may I seye,
    'Holdeth youre heste. The rokkes been aweye!'[1]
1065 LORD Phebus, dooth° this miracle for me!   *do*
    Preye hire she go° no faster cours° than ye.   *ask her that she go, orbit*
    I seye, preyeth youre suster° that she go   *sister*
    No faster cours than ye thise yeres two.°   *these two years*
    Thanne shal she been evene atte fulle alway,°[2]   *be completely even with you*
1070 And spryng° flood laste bothe nyght and day.   *spring*
    And but° she vouchesauf° in swich manere°   *unless, grant, such manner*
    To graunte° me my sovereyn° lady deere,°   *grant, sovereign, dear*
    Prey hire to synken° every rok adoun°   *sink, down*
    Into hir owene dirke regioun°   *her own dark region*
1075 Under the ground, ther° Pluto dwelleth° inne,[3]   *where, lives*
    Or neveremo° shal I my lady wynne.   *nevermore*
    Thy temple in Delphos[4] wol I barefoot seke.°   *seek*
    Lord Phebus, se° the teeris° on my cheke,°   *see, tears, cheek*
    And of my peyne have som compassioun.'
1080 And with that word in swowne° he fil adoun.°   *faint, fell down*
    And longe tyme he lay forth in a traunce.°   *trance*
    HIS brother, which° that knew of his penaunce,°   *who, grief*
    Up caughte hym,° and to bedde he hath hym broght.   *raised him up*
    Dispeyred° in this torment and this thoght   *despairing*
1085 Lete° I this woful creature lye.   *Leave*
    Chese he for me wheither he wol lyve or dye![5]
    ARVERAGUS, with heele° and greet honour,   *health*
    As he that was of chivalrie the flour,°   *flower*
    Is comen hoom and othere worthy men.
1090 O blisful artow° now, thou Dorigen,   *happy are you*
    That hast° thy lusty° housbonde in thyne armes!   *have, pleasant*
    The fresshe° knyght, the worthy man of armes   *vigorous*
    That loveth thee as his owene hertes lyf,
    Nothyng list hym to been ymaginatyf[6]
1095 If any wight hadde spoke whil° he was oute°   *while, abroad*

---

1   "Be true to your promise. The rocks are away."
2   Aurelius wishes the sun and moon to align in the sky for two years, thus causing abnormally high tides, a physical impossibility.
3   In Greek mythology Pluto was the god of the Underworld and husband of Persephone (Roman Proserpina), who was sometimes associated with the moon goddess, Luna.
4   Apollo's oracle at the temple at Delphi provided clues from the gods to help solve difficult problems.
5   "Let him choose, for all I care, whether he live or die."
6   "He by no means wishes to be inquisitive."

To hire of love. He hadde of it no doute.°   *doubt*
He noght entendeth° to no swich mateere°   *pays no attention, matter*
But daunceth, justeth, maketh hire good cheere.°   *treats her in a friendly way*
And thus in joye and blisse° I lete hem° dwelle,   *happiness, let them*
1100 And of the sike° Aurelius I wol yow telle.   *sick*
In langour and in torment furyus°   *extreme distress*
Two yeer and moore lay wrecche° Aurelyus   *wretched*
Er° any foot he myghte on erthe gon.°   *before, could walk*
Ne confort° in this tyme hadde he noon,°   *nor comfort, none*
1105 Save° of his brother, which that was a clerk.°   *except, student*
He knew of al this wo and al this werk,°   *effort*
For to noon oother° creature, certeyn,   *to no other*
Of this matere he dorste° no word seyn.°   *dared, say*
Under his brest° he baar° it moore secree°   *breast, carried, more secretly*
1110 Than evere dide Pamphilus for Galathee.[1]
His brest was hool withoute° for to sene,°   *healthy outside, to be seen*
But in his herte ay° was the arwe kene.°   *ever, sharp arrow*
As wel ye knowe that of a sursanure°   *a wound healed only on the outside*
In surgerye° is perilous° the cure,   *surgery, dangerous*
1115 But men myghte touche the arwe or come therby.[2]
His brother weepe and wayled pryvely,°   *wailed privately*
Til atte laste hym fil in remembraunce°   *he remembered*
That whiles he was at Orliens° in Fraunce[3]   *Orléans*
As yonge clerkes° that been° lykerous°   *students, are, eager*
1120 To reden° artz° that been curious,°   *read, sciences, exotic*
Seken° in every halke and every herne°   *seek, every nook and corner*
Particuler° sciences° for to lerne,   *specialized, types of knowledge*
He hym remembred that upon a day
At Orliens in studie° a book he say°   *[a hall of] study, saw*
1125 Of magyk natureel,°[4] which his felawe°   *natural magic, friend*
That was that tyme a bacheler of lawe,°   *student of law*
Al were he ther° to lerne another craft,°.   *although he was there, subject*
Hadde prively upon his desk ylaft,°   *left*
Which book spak° muchel° of the operaciouns,°   *spoke, much, operations*

---

1   The two were the main characters in the late twelfth-century Latin romance, *Pamphilus de amore* (*Pamphilus on Love*). A marginal Latin gloss refers to this work and quotes one line from it: "I am wounded and bear the shaft."

2   "A wound that has healed on the outside, but is still not healed beneath the surface, is hard to cure in medicine, unless one can find the arrow head."

3   The university at Orléans, south of Paris, was famous for law and had a more dubious reputation as a center for magic.

4   Natural magic, such as that of Chaucer's Physician (cf. General Prologue, line 416), is based on a knowledge of the powers of the planets and the physical world, as opposed to black magic, which makes use of spirits or devils.

1130 Touchynge the eighte and twenty mansiouns°   *pertaining to the 28 houses (in astrology)*
That longen° to the moone and swich folye,°   *belong, such folly*
As in oure dayes is nat° worth a flye.°   *not, fly*
For Hooly Chirches feith in oure bileve
Ne suffreth noon illusioun us to greve.[1]
1135 And whan this book was in his remembraunce,
Anon for joye his herte gan° to daunce,   *began*
And to hymself he seyde pryvely,
"My brother shal be warisshed° hastily,   *shall be healed*
For I am siker° that ther be sciences   *certain*
1140 By whiche° men make diverse apparences,°   *MS whce, illusions*
Swiche as thise subtile tregetours° pleye.[2]   *these clever magicians*
For ofte at feestes, have I wel herd seye,°   *said*
That tregetours withinne an halle large
Have maad come in a water and a barge
1145 And in the halle rowen up and doun.
Somtyme hath semed come a grym leoun,[3]
And somtyme floures sprynge° as in a mede,°   *flowers spring up, meadow*
Somtyme a vyne° and grapes white and rede,   *vine*
Somtyme a castel° al of lym° and stoon,   *castle, mortar*
1150 And whan hym lyked° voyded it anon.°   *he wished, it disappeared at once*
Thus semed° it to every mannes° sighte.   *seemed, man's*
Now thanne, conclude I thus: that if I myghte
At Orliens som oold felawe° yfynde°   *old friend, find*
That hadde this moones mansions° in mynde°   *moon's mansion, mind*
1155 Or oother magyk natureel° above,   *other natural magic*
He sholde wel make my brother han° his love.   *have*
For with an apparence a clerk may make
To mannes sighte° that alle the rokkes blake   *man's sight*
Of Britaigne weren yvoyded° everichon°   *were removed, everyone*
1160 And shippes by the brynke° comen and gon°   *shore, come and go*
And in swich forme° enduren a wowke° or two.   *such form, last a week*
Thanne° were my brother warisshed° of his wo.   *then, healed*
Thanne moste she nedes holden hire biheste,[4]
Or elles he shal shame hire atte leeste."°   *at the least*
1165 WHAT sholde° I make a lenger° tale of this?   *why should, longer*
Unto his brotheres bed he comen is,

---

1 "Because the faith in Holy Church [set out] in our creed does not allow any illusion to grieve us." The passage reminds us that the story ostensibly takes place in pagan times, even though the social customs are more or less those of Chaucer's day.
2 Tregetours produced special effects and illusions, often for banquets.
3 "Sometimes a fierce lion seems to come."
4 "Then must she necessarily keep her promise."

And swich confort° he yaf hym° for to gon°   *comfort, gave him, go*
To Orliens, that he up stirte anon,°   *got up right away*
And on his wey forthward° thanne is he fare°   *forward, gone*
1170 In hope for to been lissed° of his care.   *relieved*
WHAN they were come almoost to that citee,
But if it were a two furlong¹ or thre,
A yong clerk romynge° by hymself they mette,°   *roaming, met*
Which that in Latyn° thriftily hem grette.°   *Latin, appropriately greeted them*
1175 And after that he seyde a wonder° thyng.   *wonderful*
"I knowe," quod he, "the cause of youre comyng."
And er they ferther any foote wente,
He tolde hem al that was in hire entente.°   *their intent*
THIS Briton clerk hym asked of felawes,°   *about friends*
1180 The whiche that he had knowe in olde dawes,°   *days*
And he answerde hym that they dede° were,   *dead*
For which he weep ful ofte° many a teere.   *wept very often*
DOUN of his hors Aurelius lighte anon,°   *dismounted immediately*
And with this magicien° forth is he gon°   *magician, gone*
1185 Hoom to his hous and maden hem° wel at ese.°   *them, ease*
Hem lakked no vitaille that myghte hem plese,²
So wel arrayed hous as ther was oon
Aurelius in his lyf saugh nevere noon.³
HE shewed° hym er° he wente to sopeer°   *showed, before, supper*
1190 Forestes, parkes ful of wilde deer.
Ther saugh he hertes° with hir hornes hye,°   *harts (deer), high horns*
The gretteste that evere were seyn with eye.
He saugh of hem° an hondred slayn with houndes°   *them, killed by dogs*
And somme with arwes° blede° of bittre° woundes.   *arrows, bleeding, bitter*
1195 HE saugh, whan voyded° were thise wilde deer,   *gone*
Thise fauconers° upon a fair ryver,   *these falconers*
That with hir haukes° han° the heroun slayn.°   *their hawks, have, killed*
THO saugh he knyghtes justyng° in a playn.°   *jousting, plain*
And after this he dide hym° swich plesaunce°   *gave him, pleasure*
1200 That he hym shewed his lady on a daunce,°   *at a dance*
On which hymself he daunced° as hym thoughte.   *at which he himself danced*
And whan this maister° that this magyk wroughte°   *Master [of Arts], performed*
Saugh it was tyme, he clapte° hise handes two,   *clapped*
And, farewel, al oure revel° was ago!°   *revelry, gone*
1205 And yet remoeved° they nevere out of the hous   *moved*
Whil they saugh al this sighte merveillous,°   *marvelous sight*

---

1   A furlong is 220 yards.
2   "They lacked no food that might please them."
3   "Aurelius, in his life, never saw any house so well arranged [or supplied] as the one that was there."

But in his studie thereas° hise bookes be   *where*
They seten stille° and no wight° but they thre.   *sat quietly, no one*
To HYM this maister called his squier°1   *squire*
1210 And seyde hym thus: "Is redy° oure soper?   *ready*
Almoost an houre it is, I undertake,°   *I suppose*
Sith° I yow bad° oure soper for to make,   *since, commanded*
Whan that thise worthy men wenten° with me   *went*
Into my studie, theras my bookes be."°   *where my books are*
1215 "SIRE," quod this squier, "whan it liketh yow,°   *when you wish*
It is al redy, though ye wol right now."
"Go we thanne soupe,"° quod he, "as for the beste.   *then to eat*
This amorous folk somtyme moote han hir° reste!"   *lovers must have their*
AT after soper° fille they in tretee°   *after supper, began to negotiate*
1220 What somme° sholde this maistres gerdoun° be   *what sum, Master's payment*
To remoeven° alle the rokkes of Britayne   *remove*
And eek from Geround° to the mouth of Sayne.°   *Gironde, Seine (rivers)*
HE made it straunge° and swoor° so God hym save,   *made difficulties, swore*
Lasse than a thousand pound he wolde nat have,
1225 Ne° gladly for that somme° he wolde nat goon.°2   *nor, sum, would not go*
AURELIUS with blisful° herte anoon°   *happy, immediately*
Answerde thus: "Fy° on a thousand pound!   *Fie*
This wyde world which that men seye is round,3
I WOLDE it yeve° if I were lord of it.   *give*
1230 This bargayn is ful dryve,° for we been knyt.°   *fully made, agreed*
Ye shal be payed trewely, by my trouthe.°   *on my honor*
But looketh now, for no necligence° or slouthe°   *negligence, laziness*
Ye tarie us heere° no lenger° than tomorwe."   *keep us here, longer*
"NAY," quod this clerk, "have heer° my fieth° to borwe!"°   *here, faith, as a pledge*
1235 TO BEDDE is goon Aurelius whan hym leste,°   *when he wished*
And wel ny° al that nyght he hadde his reste.   *very nearly*
What for his labour and his hope of blisse,
His woful herte of penaunce° hadde° a lisse.°   *grief, had, break*
UPON the morwe whan that it was day
1240 To Britaigne tooke they the righte way,°   *direct road*
Aurelius and this magicien bisyde,°   *as well*
And been descended ther° they wolde abyde.°   *are arrived where, would stay*
And this was as thise bookes me remembre,°   *these books remind me*

---

1   The squire is not a knight in training but a personal servant. The title nevertheless suggests that his master is a man of consequence.
2   "Nor, at that price, would he not gladly refuse the job," i.e., it was the minimum he would accept.
3   Contrary to popular modern lore, educated people in the Middle Ages knew the world was round.

The colde, frosty sesoun of Decembre.

1245 PHEBUS wax° old and hewed lyk latoun,°   *The sun grew, colored like brass*

That in his hoote declynacioun°   *hot declination*

Shoon° as the burned° gold with stremes brighte.°   *shone, polished, bright streams*

But now in Capricorn adoun° he lighte,°¹   *down, alights*

Whereas° he shoon ful pale,° I dar wel seyn.   *where, very pale*

1250 The bittre frostes with the sleet and reyn°   *rain*

Destroyed hath the grene° in every yerd.°   *green, yard*

Janus² sit by the fyr with double berd°   *beard*

And drynketh of his bugle horn° the wyn.   *drinking horn*

Biforn hym stant° brawen° of the tusked swyn,°³   *stands, meat, boar*

1255 And "Nowel!"° crieth every lusty° man.   *Noel, energetic*

AURELIUS in al that evere he kan

Dooth to his maister chiere and reverence⁴

And preyeth hym° to doon his diligence°   *asks him, do his best*

To bryngen hym° out of his peynes smerte°   *bring him, sharp pains*

1260 Or with a swerd° that he wolde slitte° his herte.   *sword, pierce*

THIS subtil clerk° swich routhe° had of this man   *scholar, pity*

That nyght and day he spedde hym that he kan°   *tried as best he could*

To wayten° a tyme° of his conclusioun.°   *watch for, time, conclusion*

This is to seye, to maken illusioun

1265 By swich a apparence° of jogelrye°—   *such an appearance, trickery*

I ne kan no termes of astrologye°—   *know no astrological jargon*

That she and every wight sholde wene° and seye   *should think*

That of Britaigne the rokkes were aweye

Or ellis they were sonken under grounde.°   *sunk under the ground*

1270 So atte laste he hath his tyme yfounde°   *found*

To maken hise japes° and his wrecchednesse°   *tricks, wretchedness*

Of swich a supersticious cursednesse.

Hise tables *Tolletanes*⁵ forth he brought,

---

1 The declination is the distance above or below the equator. The hot declination is the sign of Cancer, which the sun enters in June. When it was in Cancer the sun shone hotly, but now in December it enters Capricorn, where it is at its lowest altitude and shines most faintly.

2 In Roman mythology, Janus was the double-faced god who represents the exit of the old year and the entrance of the new. The month of January is named after him. A marginal Latin gloss notes "Janus the double."

3 The roasted boar's head was the favorite meal during the twelve days of Christmas.

4 "Treats the magician in a friendly and respectful manner."

5 "Toledan tables" were the astrological tables drawn up for the latitude of Toledo, Spain, in the thirteenth century by King Alfonso the Wise. The tables allow the astronomer or astrologer to predict the motions of the planets relative to the earth. Lines 1273–80 contain many references to astrology which Chaucer explains in his *Treatise on the Astrolabe* (the instrument used for measuring the angles of various planets). The complete calculation required adding together figures for the planet's motion during the collect years (periods of twenty to 300 years), expanse

Ful wel° corrected ne° ther lakked nought,°   *very well, nor, lacked nothing*
1275 Neither his collect ne hise expans yeeris°   *collect [years] expanse-years*
Ne hise rootes° ne hise othere geeris,°   *roots (dates), equipment*
As been his centris° and his argumentz°   *centric table, arguments*
And hise proporcioneles convenientz°   *fitting proportionals*
For hise equacions° in everythyng.   *his equations*
1280 And by his eighte° speere in his wirkyng[1]   *MS 8*
He knew ful wel how fer Alnath[2] was shone°   *had shone*
Fro° the heed° of thilke fixe° Aries[3] above,   *from, head, that fixed*
That in the ninthe° speere° considered is.[4]   *ninth MS 9, sphere*
Ful subtilly° he hadde kalkuled° al this.   *cleverly, he had calculated*
1285 WHAN he hadde founde his firste mansioun,°   *first [planetary] mansion*
He knew the remenaunt° by proporcioun°   *the rest, proportion*
And knew the arisyng of his moone weel
And in whos face and terme[5] and everydeel°   *every part*
And knew ful weel the moones mansioun°   *moon's mansion*
1290 Acordaunt° to his operacioun°   *according, calculation*
And knew also hise othere observaunces,°   *observations*
For swich illusiouns and swiche meschaunces°   *evil practices*
As hethen° folk useden° in thilke dayes,°   *heathen, used, those days*
For which no lenger maked° he delayes,°   *made, delays*
1295 But thurgh his magik for a wyke or tweye,
It semed° that alle the rokkes were aweye.   *seemed*
AURELIUS, which that yet despeired is°   *is still in despair*
Wher° he shal han° his love or fare amys,°   *whether, have, lose out*
Awaiteth nyght and day on this myracle.
1300 And whan he knew that ther was noon obstacle,
That voyded° were thise rokkes everychon,   *gone*
Doun to hise maistres feet he fil anon
And seyde, "I, woful wrecche Aurelius,
Thanke yow, lord and lady myn Venus,

---

years (periods of one to twenty years), and fractions of years. Roots are quantities, such as dates or the longitude of a planet, which are used when consulting the tables. "Centris" are probably not parts of the astrolabe but rather centric tables of planetary distances, while "argumentz," are angles or arcs from which the planets' motions can be measured. Fitting proportionals are figures used when taking into account the passage of fractions of a year.

1 "And by the eighth sphere in his calculation." According to medieval cosmology, the universe was made up of nine concentric crystalline spheres on which the planets and stars were affixed and which moved them across the sky.

2 According to the Latin gloss in the margin, Alnath is the name of the first mansion, i.e., the astrological house, of the moon.

3 Aries is a constellation and a sign in the zodiac.

4 A marginal Latin gloss notes "in the ninth sphere." Despite the Franklin's protest that he knows nothing about astrology (line 1266), the highly technical terms are used correctly.

5 "Face" and "term" are subdivisions of a sign of the zodiac.

1305 That me han holpen° fro my cares colde!"°   *have helped, cold sorrows*
    And to the temple his wey° forth hath he holde,°   *way, has gone*
    Whereas° he knew he sholde his lady see.[1]   *where*
    And whan he saugh his tyme, anon right hee
    With dredful herte° and with ful humble cheere°   *fearful heart, very humble manner*
1310 Salewed hath° his sovereyn° lady deere.   *has greeted, sovereign*
    "MY righte lady," quod this woful man,
    "Whom I moost drede and love as I best kan°   *can*
    And lothest° were of al this world displese,°   *most unwilling, displease*
    Nere it° that I for yow have swich disese,°   *were it not, discomfort*
1315 That I moste dyen heere° at youre foot anon,   *must die here*
    Noght° wolde I telle how me is wobigon,°   *by no means, afflicted by woe*
    But certes, outher° moste° I dye° or pleyne.°   *either, must, die, lament*
    Ye sle° me giltlees° for verray peyne!°   *kill, guiltless, true pain*
    But of my deeth, thogh that ye have no routhe,°   *pity*
1320 Avyseth° yow er that ye breke youre trouthe.°   *consider, promise*
    Repenteth° yow, for thilke° God above,   *Repent, that*
    Er ye me sleen° bycause that I yow love.   *kill*
    For, madame, wel ye woot what ye han hight°—   *have promised*
    Nat that I chalange° anythyng of right   *claim*
1325 Of yow, my sovereyn lady, but youre grace°—   *favor*
    But in a gardyn yond,° at swich a place,   *over there*
    Ye woot right wel what ye bihighten° me   *promised*
    And in myn hand youre trouthe plighten ye°   *you gave your promise*
    To love me best. God woot,° ye seyde so,   *God knows*
1330 Al° be that I unworthy am therto.°   *although, of it*
    Madame, I speke it for the honor of yow
    Moore than to save myn hertes lyf right now.
    I have do° so as ye comanded me,   *done*
    And if ye vouchesauf,° ye may go see.   *grant it*
1335 Dooth as yow list.° Have youre biheste in mynde.   *Do as you wish*
    For quyk or deed,° right there ye shal me fynde.   *living or dead*
    In yow lith al to do me lyve or deye.[2]
    But wel I woot the rokkes been aweye."°   *are gone*
    HE taketh his leve, and she astoned° stood.   *stunned*
1340 In al hir face nas a drope° of blood.   *was not a drop*
    She wende nevere han come in swich a trappe.[3]

---

1   In the Middle Ages, lovers often used church services as an opportunity to meet. Chaucer here
    gives the social customs of his own day a pagan coloring by having Dorigen go to the temple.
    Chaucer frequently alternates between the simple past (Aurelius *knew*) and present or perfect
    forms (Aurelius *has gone* rather than *had gone*).
2   "In you lies everything to make me live or die."
3   "She never expected to come into such a trap."

"Allas," quod she, "that evere this sholde happe!°   *happen*
For wende I nevere by possibilitee°   *I never expected it possible*
That swich a monstre° or merveille° myghte bee.   *monstrosity, marvel*
1345 It is agayns the proces° of nature!"   *course*
And hoom she goth, a sorweful creature.
For verray feere° unnethe° may she go.   *true fear, scarcely*
She wepeth, wailleth° al a day or two   *wails*
And swowneth° that it routhe° was to see.   *faints, pity*
1350 But why it was to no wight tolde shee,°   *she told*
For out of towne was goon° Arveragus.   *gone*
But to hirself she spake and seyde thus,
With face pale and with ful sorweful cheere,°   *very sorrowful expression*
In hire compleynt,° as ye shal after heere:°   *lament, shall hear afterwards*
1355 "ALLAS," quod she, "on thee, Fortune, I pleyne,°[1]   *lament*
That unwar wrapped hast me in thy cheyne![2]
For which t'escape° woot° I no socour,°   *to escape, know, help MS scour*
Save oonly deeth° or dishonour.   *death*
Oon of thise two bihoveth me to chese.°   *I am compelled to choose*
1360 But nathelees,° yet have I levere to lese°   *nevertheless, rather lose*
My lif than of my body have a shame
Or knowe myselven fals or lese° my name.   *lose*
And with my deth I may be quyt,° ywis.°   *freed, indeed*
Hath ther nat° many a noble wyf er this   *has not*
1365 And many a mayde yslayn hirself,° allas,   *killed herself*
Rather than with hir body doon trespas?°   *do a wrong*
YIS, certes, lo thise stories beren witnesse:°   *bear witness*
Whan thritty° tirauntz° ful of cursednesse°   *thirty MS xxx, tyrants, wickedness*
Hadde slayn Phidoun[3] in Atthenes° at feste,°   *Athens, at a feast*
1370 They comanded hise doghtres for t'areste°[4]   *to be arrested*
And bryngen hem biforn° hem in despit°   *before, scorn*
Al naked to fulfille hir foul delit,°   *pleasure*
And in hir fadres° blood they made hem daunce   *father's*

---

1 There is a marginal English gloss: "The compleynt of Dorigene ayeyns fortune." On the role of fortune, see the Knight's Tale, p. 34, note 2.

2 "That have tangled me unawares in your chain."

3 The many examples of women in trouble that Dorigen cites below come from Jerome's *Against Jovinian* (see Appendix, p. 387), the book the Wife of Bath also mentions in her discussion of marriage in her Prologue. Thirty oligarchs ruled Athens briefly in 403 BC before being overthrown by the naval commander Thrasybulus.

4 A marginal Latin gloss summarizes the story from *Against Jovinian*, 1.41. There are similar Latin glosses at lines 1379, 1387, 1399, 1405, 1409, 1414, 1426, 1428, 1432, 1434, 1437, 1439, 1442, 1445, 1448, 1451, 1453, 1455, 1456, 1458, 1459, and 1462, so that the glosses fill most of the space on the side of the page. The last gloss sums up the matter: "The blessed Jerome tells these various stories and many others concerning this subject in the first book [of *Against Jovinian*]." Many of these glosses are also found in Hengwrt.

	Upon the pavement. God yeve hem myschaunce!°	*give them misfortune*
1375	For which thise woful° maydens ful of drede°	*these woeful, fear*
	Rather than they wolde lese hir maydenhede,°	*lose chastity*
	They prively° been stirt° into a welle°	*secretly, jumped, well*
	And dreynte° hemselven, as the bookes telle.	*drowned*
	THEY of Mecene° leet enquere° and seke°	*Messene, allow an inquiry, seek*
1380	Of Lacedomye° fifty maydens eke,	*Sparta*
	On whiche they wolden doon hir lecherye.°¹	*exercise their lust*
	But was ther noon of al that compaignye	
	That she nas slayn and with a good entente°	*willingly*
	Chees° rather for to dye than assente°	*choose, agree*
1385	To been oppressed° of hir maydenhede.	*raped*
	Why sholde I thanne to dye been in drede?°	*fear to die*
	LO EEK, the tiraunt Aristoclides,	
	That loved a mayden heet° Stymphalides,²	*named*
	Whan that hir fader slayn was on a nyght,	
1390	Unto Dianes° temple goth° she right°	*Diana's, goes, right away*
	And hente° the ymage° in hir handes two,	*grasped, image (statue)*
	Fro which ymage wolde° she nevere go.°	*would, [let] go*
	No wight ne myghte hir handes of it arace°	*pull away*
	Til she was slayn right in the selve° place.	*same*
1395	NOW sith that maydens hadden swich despit°	*contempt*
	To been defouled with mannes° foul delit,	*men's*
	Wel oghte° a wyf rather hirselven slee°	*ought, kill herself*
	Than be defouled,° as it thynketh me!°	*defiled, as it seems to me*
	WHAT shal I seyn of Hasdrubales wyf,	
1400	That at Cartage° birafte hirself hir lyf?°³	*Carthage, killed herself*
	For whan she saugh that Romayns° wan° the toun,	*Romans, conquered*
	She took hir children alle and skipte adoun°	*jumped down*
	Into the fyr and chees° rather to dye°	*chose, die*
	Than any Romayn dide hire vileynye.°	*should do her villainy*
1405	HATH nat Lucresse° yslayn hirself, allas,	*Lucretia*

---

1 According to Jerome, there was such close friendship between Sparta (Lacedaemonia) and Messene, in southern Greece, that they exchanged maidens for religious rituals.

2 According to Jerome, *Against Jovinian* 1.41, Aristoclides was a tyrant of Orchomenos who "fell in love with a virgin of Stymphalus" (virginem Stymphalidem). Both Chaucer and whoever composed the glosses to the Ellesmere manuscript (possibly Chaucer himself) take Stymphalos to be the woman's name.

3 Hasdrubal, king of Carthage, the North African empire that threatened Rome, committed suicide when the Romans took the city in 146 BC, although only after his wife had rebuked him for his cowardice. According to Jerome, she leapt into the fire with her little children (*Against Jovinian* 1.43). Chaucer alludes to the story in the Nun's Priest's Tale, lines 3363–65. (Two later Carthaginian generals who fought with Hannibal were also called Hasdrubal.)

At Rome whan she oppressed was
Of Tarquyn?[1] For hire thoughte° it was a shame   *it seemed to her*
To lyven whan she had lost hir name.°   *[good] name*
THE sevene maydens° of Melesie also   *seven maidens, Miletus*
1410 Han slayn hemself for drede and wo
Rather than folk of Gawle hem sholde oppresse.[2]
Mo than a thousand stories, as I gesse,
Koude I now telle as touchynge this mateere.
WHAN Habradate was slayn, his wyf so deere
1415 Hirselven slow° and leet hir blood to glyde°   *killed herself, flow*
In Habradates woundes depe and wyde
And seyde, 'My body at the leeste way
Ther shal no wight defoulen, if I may.'[3]
What° sholde I mo ensamples° heerof sayn,   *why, examples*
1420 Sith° that so manye han hemselven slayn,   *since*
Wel rather than they wolde defouled be?
I wol conclude that it is bet° for me   *better*
To sleen myself than been defouled thus.
I wol be trewe unto Arveragus
1425 Or rather sleen° myself in som manere!   *kill*
As DIDE Demociones doghter deere,°   *dear daughter*
Bycause that she wolde nat defouled be.[4]
O CEDASUS, it is ful greet pitee
To reden how thy doghtren deyde, allas,
1430 That slowe hemself for swich manere cas![5]   *such a situation*
As greet a pitee was it or wel moore°   *even more*
The Theban mayden that for Nichanore
Hirselven slow,° right for swich manere wo.[6]   *killed herself*
ANOTHER Theban mayden dide right so,°   *did the same*

---

1   Lucretia committed suicide after being raped by Tarquinus Sextus, prince of Rome. The people then rebelled and drove the Tarquins out (*Against Jovinian* 1.46). The story is told by Ovid in his *Fasti* 2.685–852 and by Chaucer in his *Legend of Good Women*.

2   Miletus, in Asia Minor (now Turkey) was conquered by the Galatians in 276 BC (*Against Jovinian* 1.41).

3   King Abradates of Susi was killed fighting the Egyptians and his wife Panthea killed herself on his body (*Against Jovinian* 1.45). Jerome takes the story from the Greek historian Xenophon's account of the life of Cyrus, the *Cyropaedia*.

4   According to Jerome, when she heard that her husband, the general Leosthenes, had been killed in battle, the daughter of Demotion committed suicide rather than remarry (*Against Jovinian* 1.41).

5   The marginal Latin gloss cites only the opening words, "With what words may we praise the daughters of Scedasus" from Jerome's account. The daughters offered hospitality to two youths who got drunk and raped them. The daughters then stabbed each other to death (*Against Jovinian* 1.41).

6   Nicanor, one of Alexander the Great's officers, fell in love with one of the captured Thebans after taking the city in 336 BC. She killed herself rather than submit to him (*Against Jovinian* 1.41).

1435 For oon° of Macidonye° hadde hire oppressed.   *because someone, Macedonia*
     She with hire deeth hir maydenhede redressed.[1]
     WHAT shal I seye of Nicerates wyf,
     That for swich cas° birafte° hirself hir lyf?[2]   *such a situation, took*
     HOW trewe eek was to Alcebiades
1440 His love, rather for to dyen chees°   *chose to die*
     Than for to sufre his body unburyed be.°[3]   *allow his body to be unburied*
     Lo, which a wyf° was Alceste!" quod she.   *what a wife*
     "WHAT seith Omer of goode Penalopee?
     Al Grece° knoweth of hire chastitee.[4]   *Greece*
1445 PARDEE,° of Lacedomya° is writen thus: *by God, Lacedoma*
     That whan at Troie was slayn Protheselaus,
     No lenger° wolde she lyve after his day.[5]   *longer*
     THE same of noble Porcia telle I may.
     Withoute Brutus koude° she nat lyve,   *could*
1450 To whom she hadde al hool° hir herte yeve.°[6]   *completely, given*
     THE parfit° wyfhod° of Arthemesie   *perfect, wifehood*
     Honored is thurgh al the Barbarie.°[7]   *Barbary Coast (n. Africa)*
     O TEUTA Queene, thy wyfly chastitee
     To alle wyves may a mirour° bee!°   *mirror, be*
1455 THE same thyng I seye of Bilyea,
     OF Rodogone and eek of Valeria."[8]

---

1 "She made up for [the loss of] her chastity with her death." According to Jerome this anony-
   mous Theban killed her rapist and then herself (*Against Jovinian* 1.41).

2 According to Jerome, the wife of Nicerates killed herself to escape the lust of the thirty oligarchs
   (the same ones that commanded Phidoun's daughters to dance before them) (*Against Jovinian*
   1.44).

3 Alcibiades, the friend of Socrates, was beheaded at the command of the Spartan general
   Lysander. His mistress risked her life to bury him (*Against Jovinian* 1.44).

4 The marginal Latin gloss quotes Jerome: "Fables say that Alcestis died willingly for her hus-
   band Admetus and Penelope's modesty (i.e., chastity) is [the subject] of Homer's song." (*Against
   Jovinian* 1.45). The story of Penelope, wife of Ulysses, and how she kept her unwanted suitors at
   bay is told by Homer and was known in the Middle Ages in various translations.

5 Protesilaus, the husband of Lacedomia (or Laodamia) was the first of the Greeks to be killed at
   the siege of Troy. At her entreaty he was brought briefly back to life and when he died a second
   time she died with him. Ovid tells the story in *Heroides* 13. Jerome says only that "her praises are
   sung by the poets" (*Against Jovinian* 1.45).

6 The marginal Latin gloss cites Jerome, "Portia could not live without Brutus" (*Against Jovinian*
   1.46). The story of Brutus joining the conspiracy against Julius Caesar and committing suicide
   when defeated by Marc Antony is now best known through Shakespeare's play, but was also
   popular in the Middle Ages.

7 Arthemesia built the famous mausoleum at Halicarnasus for her husband Mausolus, king of
   Caria, in what is now northern Greece. As Jerome notes, "to the present day all costly sepulchers
   are called after his name *mausoleums*" (*Against Jovinian* 1.44).

8 The marginal Latin gloss notes only "Teuta, queen of the Illyricans." According to Jerome
   "she owed her long sway over her brave warriors, and her frequent victories over Rome, to her

THUS pleyne[d]° Dorigene a day or tweye, *laments*
Purposynge° evere that she wolde deye. *intending*
BUT nathelees,° upon the thridde° nyght *nevertheless, third*
1460 Hoom cam° Arveragus, this worthy knyght, *came*
And asked hire why that she weepe so soore.° *wept so sorely*
And she gan wepen ever lenger the moore.° *began to weep more and more*
"ALLAS," quod she, "that evere I was born!
Thus have I seyd," quod she. "Thus have I sworn!"
1465 And toold hym al as ye han herd bifore.° *have heard before*
It nedeth nat reherce° it yow namoore.° *needs not be repeated, no more*
THIS housbonde with glad chiere° in freendly wyse° *expression, friendly way*
Answerde and seyde as I shal yow devyse.° *describe*
"Is ther oght elles,° Dorigen, but this?" *anything else*
1470 "NAY, nay," quod she, "God helpe me so, as wys
This is to muche, and it were Goddes wille!"[1]
"YE, wyf," quod he, "Lat slepen that is stille.° *Let alone what is quiet*
It may be wel paraventure° yet today. *perhaps*
Ye shul youre trouthe holden,° by my fay!° *keep your promise, faith*
1475 For God so wisly° have mercy upon me, *wisely*
I hadde wel levere ystiked for to be° *had much rather be stabbed*
For verray° love which that I to yow have, *true*
But if ye sholde youre trouthe kepe° and save! *keep*
Trouthe° is the hyeste° thyng that man may kepe." *truth, highest*
1480 But with that word he brast° anon to wepe° *burst out, weeping*
And seyde, "I yow forbede up peyne [of] deeth,° *forbid you on pain of death*
That nevere whil thee lasteth° lyf° ne breeth° *lasts, life, breath*
To no wight° telle thou of this aventure.° *no person, misfortune*
As I may best, I wol my wo endure.
1485 Ne make no contenance of hevynesse° *sad expression*
That folk of yow may demen harm or gesse."[2]
AND forth he cleped° a squier° and a mayde.° *called, squire, maid*
"Gooth forth° anon° with Dorigen," he sayde, *go out, immediately*
"And bryngeth hire° to swich a place anon!" *bring her*
1490 They take hir leve,° and on hir wey they gon. *take their leave*

---

marvelous chastity" (*Against Jovinian* 1.44). She assumed the throne of Illyria, on the Dalmatian coast, on the death of her husband in 231 BC. Bilyea's martyrdom consisted in enduring her husband's bad breath. When he reproached her for not having told him about it, she replied that she thought all men's breath was that foul (*Against Jovinian* 1.46). Rhodogune, daughter of Darius, king of Persia, killed her nurse for suggesting she remarry (*Against Jovinian* 1.44). The Roman Valeria also refused to remarry (*Against Jovinian* 1.46). Although Dorigen's list has seemed to many critics to be already comically long, the Latin glosses list several other examples from Jerome that Chaucer did not include. In his edition, Skeat, who assumes the glosses reflect Chaucer's own comments, suggests that he may have been contemplating adding them.

1 "God help me so, as certainly (*wis* means certainly, surely, or indeed) this is too much, even if it were God's will."

2 "That people may think or guess that there is anything wrong with you."

But they ne wiste° why she thider wente.°   *did not know, went there*
He nolde no wight tellen° his entente.   *would not tell anyone*
PARAVENTURE° an heepe° of yow, ywis,°   *perhaps, many, indeed*
Wol holden hym° a lewed° man in this,   *consider him, foolish*
1495 That he wol putte° his wyf in jupartie.°   *put, jeopardy*
Herkneth° the tale er° ye upon hire crie.°   *listen to, before, cry out against her*
She may have bettre fortune than yow semeth.°   *than it seems to you*
And whan that ye han herd° the tale, demeth.°   *have heard, judge*
THIS squier which that highte° Aurelius   *was named*
1500 On Dorigen that was so amorus,
Of aventure° happed hire to meete°   *by chance, happened to meet*
Amydde° the toun, right in the quykkest strete,°   *in the middle of, busiest street*
As she was bown to goon° the wey° forthright   *bound to go, way*
Toward the gardyn theras° she had hight.°   *where, promised*
1505 And he was to the gardynward° also,   *towards the garden*
For wel he spyed° whan she wolde go°   *saw, wanted to go*
Out of hir hous to any maner place.°   *kind of place*
But thus they mette° of aventure° or grace,°   *met, chance, fortune*
And he saleweth hire° with glad entente°   *greets her, intent*
1510 And asked of hire whiderward° she wente.   *where*
AND she answerde half as she were mad,
"Unto the gardyn, as myn housbonde bad,°   *commanded*
My trouthe° for to holde,° allas! Allas!"   *promise, keep*
AURELIUS gan wondren° on this cas°   *began to wonder, situation*
1515 And in his herte hadde greet compassioun°   *compassion*
Of hire and of hire lamentacioun
AND of Arveragus, the worthy knyght,
That bad hire holden al that she had hight,
So looth hym was his wyf sholde breke hir trouthe.[1]
1520 And in his herte he caughte of this greet routhe,°   *had great pity for this*
Considerynge° the beste° on every syde,   *considering, best*
That fro° his lust° yet were hym levere abyde°   *from, pleasure, he would rather abstain*
Than doon so heigh° a cherlyssh° wrecchednesse   *great, churlish*
Agayns franchise° and alle gentillesse.°   *generosity, all nobility*
1525 For which in fewe wordes seyde he thus:
"MADAME, seyeth to youre lord Arveragus
That sith I se his grete gentillesse
To yow and eek I se wel youre distresse,
That him were levere han shame°—and that were   *would rather have shame*
      routhe°—   *pity*
1530 Than ye to me sholde breke thus youre trouthe,
I have wel levere evere to suffre wo°   *suffer woe*

---

1 "Who had commanded her to keep all that she had promised,/So distasteful was it to him that
his wife should break her promise."

Than I departe° the love bitwix° yow two.   *separate, between*
I yow relesse, madame, into youre hond
Quyt every serement and every bond
1535 That ye han maad to me as heer biforn[1]
Sith thilke tyme° which that ye were born.   *since that time*
My trouthe° I plighte.° I shal yow never repreve°   *promise, give, reproach*
Of no biheste.° And heere I take my leve   *promise*
As of the treweste and the beste wyf
1540 That evere yet I knew in al my lyf.
But every wyf bewar of hire biheeste!°   *her promise*
On Dorigene remembreth, atte leeste.°   *at the least*
Thus kan a squier doon a gentil dede
As wel as kan a knyght, withouten drede."°[2]   *doubt*
1545 SHE thonketh hym upon hir knees al bare,
And hoom unto hir housbonde is she fare°   *has she gone*
And tolde hym al as ye han herd me sayd.
And be ye siker,° he was so weel apayd,°   *certain, well pleased*
That it were inpossible° me to wryte.[3]   *impossible*
1550 What sholde° I lenger° of this cas° endyte?°   *why should, longer, matter, write*
ARVERAGUS and Dorigene his wyf
In sovereyn blisse° leden forth hir lyf.°   *highest joy, spend their life*
Nevere eft° ne was ther angre hem bitwene.   *again*
He cherisseth° hire as though she were a queene,   *cherishes*
1555 And she was to hym trewe for everemoore.
Of thise folk ye gete° of me namoore.°   *get, no more*
AURELIUS, that his cost° hath al forlorn,°   *money, has lost all*
Curseth the tyme that evere he was born.
"Allas," quod he, "allas that I bihighte°   *promised*
1560 Of pured° gold a thousand pound of wighte°   *pure, weight*
Unto this philosophre!° How shal I do?   *wise man*
I se namoore° but that I am fordo.°   *see no more, ruined*
Myn heritage° moot° I nedes selle°   *inheritance, must, necessarily sell*
And been a beggere.° Heere may I nat dwelle°   *beggar, not live*
1565 And shamen° al my kynrede° in this place.   *shame, kindred*
But° I of hym may gete bettre grace.°   *unless, mercy*
But nathelees, I wole of hym assaye
At certeyn dayes yeer by yeer to paye[4]

---

1   "I release you, Madame, into your power [hand], discharged of every oath (*serement* from Latin *sacramentum*) and pledge that you have made to me before." Aurelius is using the language of a formal legal contract.

2   Most editors attribute lines 1541–44 to Aurelius and place the quotation marks accordingly. The lines could also be attributed to the Franklin. The medieval manuscripts leave the matter open, since they contain almost no punctuation.

3   An apparent slip, since the Franklin is telling, not writing, the story.

4   "But, nonetheless, I will try to get from him [an agreement] to pay back the money in fixed installments over the years."

And thanke hym of his grete curteisye.
1570 My trouthe wol I kepe. I wol nat lye."
     WITH herte soor he gooth unto his cofre°   *money chest*
     And broghte gold unto this philosophre,
     The value of fyve hundred pound, I gesse,
     And hym bisecheth° of his gentillesse°   *asks him, nobility*
1575 To graunte hym° dayes of the remenaunt°   *grant him, for the rest*
     And seyde, "Maister, I dar wel° make avaunt.°   *dare well, boast*
     I failled° nevere of my trouthe as yit.   *failed*
     For sikerly,° my dette shal be quyt°   *surely, shall be paid*
     Towardes yow, howevere that I fare
1580 To goon a begged° in my kirtel° bare.   *go as a beggar, shirt*
     But wolde ye vouchesauf° upon seuretee°[1]   *grant, security*
     Two yeer° or thre for to respiten me,°   *years, give me respite*
     Thanne° were I wel, for elles moot° I selle   *otherwise, must*
     Myn heritage.° Ther is namoore to telle."   *inheritance*
1585 THIS philosophre sobrely° answerde   *soberly*
     And seyde thus whan he thise wordes herde:
     "Have I nat holden covenant° unto thee?"   *not kept promise*
     "YES, certes, wel and trewely," quod he.
     "HASTOW nat had thy lady as thee liketh?"
1590 "NO, no!" quod he, and sorwefully he siketh.°   *sighs*
     "WHAT was the cause? Tel me, if thou kan."
     AURELIUS his tale anon bigan
     And tolde hym al as ye han herd bifoore.[2]
     It nedeth nat to yow reherce° it moore.   *repeat*
1595 HE seide, "Arveragus of gentillesse
     Hadde levere dye° in sorwe and in distresse   *had rather die*
     Than that his wyf were of hir trouthe fals."°   *her promise false*
     The sorwe of Dorigen he tolde hym als,°   *also*
     How looth hire° was to been° a wikked wyf   *unpleasant to her, be*
1600 And that she levere had° lost that day hir lyf   *had rather*
     And that hir trouthe she swoor° thurgh innocence.   *swore*
     She nevere erst hadde herd speke of apparence.[3]
     "That made me han of hire so greet pitee.
     And right as frely as he sente hire me,
1605 As frely sente I hire to hym ageyn!
     This al and som. Ther is namoore to seyn."
     THIS philosophre answerde, "Leeve° brother,   *dear*

---

1   In effect, Aurelius is here offering to mortgage his land in return for time to pay back the full
     thousand pounds of gold.
2   Ellesmere has "as he han herd bifoore," which makes no sense in this context. The emendation
     is from Hengwrt.
3   "Never before had she heard [someone] speak of illusion."

Everich of yow dide gentilly til oother.°   *each of you acted nobly to the other*
Thou art a squier, and he is a knyght.
1610 But God forbede° for his blisful myght   *forbid*
But if a clerk koude doon a gentil dede
As wel as any of yow, it is no drede!°   *doubt*
Sire, I releese thee° thy thousand pound,   *release you from*
As thou right now were cropen° out of the ground,   *had crept*
1615 Ne nevere er° now ne haddest° knowen me.   *before, had*
For sire, I wol nat taken a peny of thee
For al my craft° ne noght for my travaille.°   *skill, trouble*
Thou hast ypayed wel° for my vitaille.°   *paid well, food*
It is ynogh,° and farewell. Have good day!"   *enough*
1620 And took his hors° and forth he goth his way.   *horse*
LORDYNGES, this questioun thanne wolde I aske now:
Which was the mooste fre,° as thynketh yow?°[1]   *generous, do you think*
Now teleth° me er that ye ferther wende.°   *tell, go further*
I kan namoore.° My tale is at an ende.   *know no more*

HEERE IS ENDED THE FRANKELYNS TALE

---

1 Assuming that each of the characters has demonstrated the generosity of spirit that is crucial to
  gentilesse, the Franklin poses a "question of love" or *demande d'amour*, rather like the Knight's
  question of who suffers most, Palamon or Arcite (Knight's Tale, line 1347).

THE PARDONER'S PROLOGUE AND TALE

Opening page of *The Pardoner's Tale*. Ellesmere Manuscript EL 26 C9 f. 138r. Reprinted by permission of The Huntington Library.

THE PARDONER'S PROLOGUE

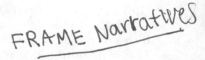

FRAME Narratives

HEERE FOLWETH THE PROLOGE OF THE PARDONERS TALE

RADIX MALORUM EST CUPIDITAS AD THIMOTHEUM 6

	"LORDYNGES,"° quod he, "in chirches° whan I preche,°	*lords, churches, preach*
330	I peyne me to han° an hauteyn speche°	*take pains to have, haughty speech*
	And rynge° it out as round° as gooth a belle,°	*ring, roundly, rings a bell*
	For I kan al by rote° that I telle.°	*know by memory, say*
	My theme[1] is alwey oon° and evere was:	*text, always one*
	Radix malorum est cupiditas.[2]	
335	FIRST I pronounce° whennes° that I come,	*say, from where*
	And thanne my bulles[3] shewe I alle° and some.	*show to everyone*
	Oure lige lordes[4] seel° on my patente,°	*seal, license*
	That shewe° I first, my body to warente,°	*show, protect*
	That no man be so boold,° ne preest ne clerk,[5]	*bold*
340	Me to destourbe° of Cristes hooly werk.°	*disturb, holy work*
	And after that thanne telle I forth my tales.	
	Bulles° of popes and of cardynales,°	*licenses, cardinals*
	Of patriarkes° and bisshopes° I shewe,	*patriarchs, bishops*
	And in Latyn° I speke a wordes fewe°	*Latin, speak a few words*
345	To saffron°[6] with my predicacioun°	*season, preaching*
	And for to stire hem° to devocioun.°	*stir them, devotion*
	Thanne shewe I forth my longe cristal stones,°	*glass cases*
	Ycrammed° ful of cloutes° and of bones.	*crammed, rags*
	Relikes° been° they, as wenen they echoon.°	*relics, are, as everyone believes*
350	Thanne have [I] in latoun° a sholder boon°	*brass, shoulder bone*
	Which that was of an hooly Jewes sheepe.°[7]	*holy Jew's sheep*
	"Goode men," I seye, "taak of my wordes keepe.°	*take heed*
	If that this boon be wasshe° in any welle,°	*washed, well*

promise

---

1   Medieval sermons were usually organized around a "theme," a short passage from the Bible.

2   "The root of evils is cupidity." This line is a quotation from 1 Timothy 6:10. "Cupidity" is often translated as "avarice" or "love of money," but, like the word "covetousness," it can also refer to any excessive or sinful love of earthly things.

3   These are papal bulls (written documents which put official policy into effect). Pardoners had licenses from the Pope to raise money for charitable causes by selling indulgences (certificates that reduce the number of years the buyer must serve in Purgatory after death).

4   The liege lord in question might be the bishop or possibly even the king.

5   The term "clerk" can refer to students, scholars, or assistants to priests (as in the Miller's Tale), so "neither priest nor clerk" means no member of the clergy at all. The parish clergy often regarded wandering preachers as interlopers.

6   Saffron was a very expensive spice imported from the East.

7   The reference here is possibly to one of the shepherds in the book of Genesis, perhaps Jacob, who stole sheep from his father-in-law, Laban.

If cow or calf or sheepe or oxe swelle°   swell
355 That any worm° hath ete° or worm ystonge,°   snake, eaten, stung
Taak water of that welle and wassh his tonge,
And it is hool° anon. And forthermoor,°   healthy, immediately
Of pokkes° and of scabbe° and every soor°   pocks, scab, sore
Shal every sheepe be hool that of this welle
360 Drynketh a draughte.° Taak kepe° eek° what I telle!   a drink, take heed, also
IF that the goode man that the beestes oweth°   owns the beasts
Wol° every wyke° er° that the cok hym croweth°   will, week, before, rooster crows
Fastynge° drynke of this welle a draughte,   while fasting
As thilke° hooly° Jew oure eldres° taughte,   that, holy, ancestors
365 Hise beestes° and his stoor° shal multiplie.°   his beasts, possessions, multiply
AND sire, also it heeleth jalousie.°   heals jealousy
For though a man be falle° in jalous rage,   fallen
Lat maken° with this water his potage,°   cause to be made, soup
And nevere shal he moore his wyf mystriste,°   mistrust
370 Though he the soothe° of hir defaute° wiste,°   truth, default, knew
Al had she taken preestes two or thre.[1]
HEERE is a miteyn° eek that ye may se.   mitten
He that his hand wol putte in this mitayn,
He shal have multipliyng of his grayn°   grain
375 Whan he hath sowen,° be it whete° or otes,°   has sown [it], wheat, oats
So that he offre pens or elles grotes.[2]
GOODE men and wommen, o° thyng warne° I yow: one, warn
If any wight° be in this chirche now   person
That hath doon synne horrible,° that he   committed a horrible sin
380 Dar nat° for shame of it yshryven° be,   dare not, confessed
Or any womman, be she yong or old,
That hath ymaked hir housbonde cokewold,°   made her husband a cuckold
Swich folk shal have no power ne no grace
To offren° to my relikes in this place.   make an offering
385 And whoso fyndeth hym out° of swich fame,°   finds himself free, such [ill]-repute
They wol come up and offre° on° Goddes name,   offer, in
And I assoille hem° by the auctoritee°   absolve them, authority
Which that by bulle° ygraunted° was to me.   license, granted
BY this gaude° have I wonne° yeer° by yeer   trick, gained, year
390 An hundred mark° sith° I was pardoner.[3]   marks, since
I stonde lyk° a clerk° in my pulpet,°   like, cleric, pulpit

---

1 "Even if she had taken [as lovers] two or three priests."
2 "Provided that he offers pennies or else groats" (a coin worth fourpence).
3 A hundred marks was worth over £66, making the Pardoner a wealthy man. In comparison, in
   1367 Chaucer was granted an annual pension of 20 marks.

And whan the lewed[1] peple° is doun yset,°   laypeople, settled down
I preche so as ye han herd bifoore°   have heard before
And telle an hundred false japes° moore.   tricks
395 Thanne peyne° I me to strecche° forth the nekke°   take pains, stretch, neck
And est and west upon the peple I bekke°   nod
As dooth a dowve° sittynge on a berne.°   dove, barn
Myne handes and my tonge goon° so yerne,°   go, eagerly
That it is joye to se° my bisynesse.°   see, busyness
400 Of avarice° and of swich cursednesse°   greed, cursedness
Ys° al my prechyng for to make hem free°   is, generous
To yeven hir pens°—and namely unto me.   give their pence
For myn entente° is nat but for to wynne°   my intent, profit
And nothyng° for correccioun of synne.   by no means
405 I rekke nevere° whan they been beryed,°[2]   do not care, buried
Though that hir soules° goon a blakeberyed!°   their souls, go picking blackberries
For certes,° many a predicacioun°   certainly, sermon
Comth ofte tyme of yvel entencioun°—   evil intent
Som° for plesance° of folk and flaterye°   some, pleasure, flattery
410 To been avaunced° by ypocrisye°   be advanced, hypocrisy
And som for veyneglorie° and som for hate.   pride
For whan I dar° noon oother weyes debate,°   dare, argue in no other way
Thanne wol I stynge hym°[3] with my tonge smerte°   sting him, sharp tongue
In prechyng, so that he shal nat asterte°   shall not escape
415 To been° defamed falsly if that he   be
Hath trespased° to my bretheren° or to me.   has harmed, brothers
For though I telle noght° his propre° name,   by no means, own
Men shal wel knowe that it is the same
By signes° and by othere circumstances.   signs
420 Thus quyte° I folk that doon° us displesances.°   pay back, do, displeasure
Thus spitte° I out my venym° under hewe°   spit, venom, guise
Of hoolynesse,° to semen° hooly and trewe.   holiness, seem
BUT shortly, myn entente I wol devyse:°   will describe
I preche of nothyng but for coveityse.°   covetousness
425 Therfore my theme is yet and evere was
Radix malorum est cupiditas.
Thus kan I preche agayn that same vice
Which that I use. And that is avarice.
But though myself be gilty in that synne,

---

1 "Lewed" generally means uneducated, illiterate in the medieval sense (i.e., unable to read Latin), or simple, but it can also refer to lay people in general. It does not have the modern meaning of sexually offensive.
2 Hengwrt reads "whan that they been beryed," producing a more regular metrical line.
3 Any opponent. Pardoners were much criticized by the parish clergy and by reformers.

430 Yet kan I maken oother folk to twynne°   *turn away*
     From avarice and soore° to repente.   *sorely*
     But that is nat my principal entente.
     I preche nothyng but for coveitise.
     Of this mateere° it oghte ynogh suffise.°   *matter, should be sufficient*
435 THANNE telle I hem° ensamples° many oon   *them, examples*
     Of olde stories longe tyme agoon.°   *ago*
     For lewed peple° loven tales olde.   *laypeople*
     Swiche thynges kan they wel reporte and holde.°   *remember*
     What? Trowe ye,° the whiles° I may preche   *Do you believe, while*
440 And wynne° gold and silver for I teche,°   *gain, because I teach*
     That I wol lyve in poverte wilfully?°   *willingly*
     Nay, nay! I thoghte it nevere, trewely.
     For I wol preche and begge° in sondry landes.°   *beg, different countries*
     I wol nat do no labour with myne handes
445 Ne make baskettes° and lyve therby,°   *baskets, live by it*
     Bycause° I wol nat beggen ydelly.°   *because, will not beg in vain*
     I wol noon° of the apostles[1] countrefete!°   *none, counterfeit*
     I wol have moneie,° wolle,° chese,° and whete,°   *money, wool, cheese, wheat*
     Al were° it yeven° of the povereste page°   *even if, given, poorest boy*
450 Or of the povereste wydwe° in a village,   *widow*
     Al sholde° hir children sterve° for famyne.°   *should, die, hunger*
     Nay, I wol drynke licour of the vyne°   *vine*
     And have a joly wenche° in every toun.   *pretty girl*
     But herkneth,° lordynges,° in conclusioun: *listen, lords*
455 YOURE likyng° is that I shal telle a tale.   *your pleasure*
     Now have I dronke a draughte of corny° ale,   *malty (strong)*
     By God, I hope I shal yow telle a thyng
     That shal by resoun° been° at youre liking.°   *with reason, be, pleasure*
     For though myself be a ful vicious man,
460 A moral tale yet I yow telle kan,°   *can tell you*
     Which I am wont° to preche for to wynne.°   *accustomed, gain*
     Now hoold° youre pees!° My tale I wol bigynne."   *hold, peace*

THE PARDONER'S TALE

HEERE BIGYNNETH THE PARDONERS TALE

     IN Flaundres° whilom° was a compaignye   *Flanders, once*
     Of yonge folk that haunteden folye°   *followed foolish living*
465 As riot,° hasard,° stywes,° and tavernes,   *loud parties, gambling, brothels*

---

1 In the gospels and the book of Acts, the apostles were enjoined to live in poverty so as to give
   surplus goods to the poor.

Whereas° with harpes, lutes, and gyternes°[1]   *where, gitterns*
They daunce and pleyen at dees° bothe day and nyght   *play at dice*
And eten° also and drynken over hir myght,°   *eat, their capacity*
Thurgh° which they doon the devel sacrifise°   *through, sacrifice to the devil*
470 Withinne that develes temple° in cursed wise°   *devil's temple (i.e., tavern), manner*
By superfluytee abhomynable.°   *terrible excess*
Hir othes been° so grete° and so dampnable°   *their oaths are, great, damnable*
That it is grisly° for to heere hem swere.°   *horrible, hear them swear*
Oure blissed° Lordes body they to-tere.°   *blessed, tear apart*
475 Hem thoughte that Jewes rente hym noght ynough!°[2]
And ech of hem° at otheres synne° lough.°   *them, the other's sin, laughed*
And right anon° thanne° comen tombesteres°   *right away, then, female acrobats*
Fetys° and smale° and yonge° frutesteres,°   *elegant, slender, young, fruit-sellers*
Syngeres° with harpes,° baudes,° wafereres,°   *singers, harps, pimps, pastry sellers*
480 Whiche been° the verray devels officeres°   *Who are, true devil's officers*
To kyndle° and blowe the fyr° of lecherye°   *kindle, fire, lechery*
That is annexed unto° glotonye.°   *allied with, gluttony*
The Hooly Writ° take I to my witnesse   *Bible*
That luxurie° is in wyn° and dronkenesse.°   *lust, wine, drunkenness*
485 Lo how that dronken° Looth[3] unkyndely°   *drunken, unnaturally*
Lay by hise doghtres two unwityngly!°   *two daughters unknowingly*
So dronke he was, he nyste what he wroghte.°   *did not know what he did*
HERODES,° whoso wel the stories soghte,[4]   *Herod*
Whan he of wyn was replest° at his feeste,°   *most filled, feast*
490 Right at his owene table he yaf° his heeste°   *gave, command*
To sleen° the Baptist John ful giltelees.°[5]   *kill, entirely guiltless*
SENEC° seith° a good word, doutelees.°   *Seneca, says, doubtless*
He seith he kan no difference fynde°   *can find*
Bitwix° a man that is out of his mynde   *between*
495 And a man which that is dronkelewe,°   *often drunk*
But that woodnesse,° fallen in a shrewe,°   *madness, occurring in a villain*
Persevereth lenger° than dooth dronkenesse.°[6]   *lasts longer*

---

1   Like the harp and the lute, the medieval gittern was a plucked stringed instrument.
2   "They thought that Jews did not tear him apart enough." The oaths figuratively tore God's body apart, according to the moralists. In the Middle Ages in Europe, Jews were usually blamed for Christ's crucifixion.
3   The story of how Lot, while drunk, made his daughters pregnant is recounted in Genesis 19:30–38. There is an English gloss in the margin: "Off glutonye and of leccherye" and a Latin gloss citing Ephesians 5:18: "Be not drunk with wine in which is excess."
4   "whoever consulted the stories carefully [can confirm]."
5   The story of how Herod ordered the death of John the Baptist is recounted in Matthew 14:1–12.
6   Seneca, whose name is written in the margin, compares drunkenness to insanity in his *Moral Epistles*.

O glotonye, ful of cursednesse,
O cause first of oure confusioun,[1]
500 O original° of oure dampnacioun,   *first [cause]*
Til Crist hadde boght° us with his blood agayn!   *has redeemed*
Lo how deere,° shortly for to seyn,°   *expensively, say*
Aboght° was thilke° cursed vileynye!°   *purchased, that, villainy*
Corrupt was al this world for glotonye.
505 ADAM oure fader and his wyf also
Fro Paradys° to labour and to wo°   *from Paradise, woe*
Were dryven° for that vice, it is no drede.°   *driven, doubt*
For whil° that Adam fasted, as I rede,°[2]   *while, read*
He was in Paradys, and whan that he
510 Eet° of the fruyt deffended° on the tree,   *ate, prohibited*
Anon° he was outcast° to wo and peyne.°   *immediately, cast out, pain*
O glotonye, on thee wel oghte° us pleyne!°   *ought, complain*
O, wiste a man° how manye maladyes°   *if one knew, diseases*
Folwen° of excesse° and of glotonyes,   *follow, excess*
515 He wolde been° the moore mesurable°   *would be, temperate*
Of his diete,° sittynge° at his table.   *diet, sitting*
Allas, the shorte throte,° the tendre° mouth   *throat, tender* MS tende
Maketh° that est and west and north and south,   *causes*
In erthe, in eir, in water man to swynke°   *labor*
520 To gete° a glotoun° deyntee° mete and drynke.   *get, glutton, delicious*
Of this matiere, O Paul, wel kanstow trete:°   *can you write*
"Mete° unto wombe° and wombe eek° unto mete: *food, stomach, also*
Shal° God destroyen° bothe," as Paulus seith.°[3]   *shall, destroy, says*
Allas, a foul thyng is it, by my feith,
525 To seye this word, and fouler is the dede°   *deed*
Whan man so drynketh of the white and rede,°   *white and red [wine]*
That of his throte he maketh his pryvee,°   *latrine*
Thurgh° thilke° cursed superfluitee.°   *through, that, excess*
THE apostel wepyng seith ful pitously,°   *very pitifully*
530 "Ther walken° manye of whiche yow toold have I.°   *walk, I have told you*
I seye it now wepyng with pitous voys:°   *pitiful voice*
Ther been° enemys° of Cristes croys°   *are, enemies, cross*
Of whiche the ende is deeth. Wombe° is hir° god."[4]   *stomach, their*

---

1 The reference here is to the role of gluttony in causing Adam and Eve to eat the forbidden fruit.
2 There is a Latin gloss in the margin from Jerome's *Against Jovinian*, 2.15: "So long as [Adam] fasted, he remained in Paradise; he ate and was cast out." This work is cited extensively in the Wife of Bath's Prologue and in the Franklin's Tale.
3 The reference here is to 1 Corinthians 6:12–13. A gloss in the margin cites the line from the Latin Bible.
4 As a Latin gloss in the margin notes, the Pardoner quotes the words of St. Paul in Philippians 3:18–19.

O wombe, o bely,° o stynkyng cod,°   *belly, stinking bag*
535 Fulfilled of donge° and of corrupcioun,   *filled with dung*
At either ende of thee foul is the soun!°   *sound*
How greet° labour and cost is thee to fynde.°   *great, provide for*
Thise cookes, how they stampe° and streyne° and grynde°   *pound, strain, grind*
And turnen° substaunce° into accident[1]   *turn, substance*
540 To fulfillen al thy likerous talent!°   *lecherous inclination*
Out of the harde bones knokke° they   *knock*
The mary,° for they caste noght awey°   *marrow, throw nothing away*
That may go thurgh the golet° softe and swoote.°   *throat, sweet*
Of spicerie° of leef° and bark and roote°   *spices, leaf, root*
545 Shal been his sauce ymaked,° by delit°   *made, through delight*
To make hym° yet a newer appetit.   *give him*
But certes, he that haunteth swiche delices°   *follows such delights*
Is deed whil that he lyveth° in tho° vices.[2]   *lives, those*
A LECHEROUS thyng is wyn, and dronkenesse[3]
550 Is ful of stryvyng° and of wrecchednesse.°   *argumentation, wretchedness*
O dronke man, disfigured is thy face.
Sour is thy breeth! Foul artow° to embrace!   *are you*
And thurgh thy dronke nose semeth the soun°   *seems [to come] the sound*
As though thou seydest ay° "Sampsoun, Sampsoun!"   *always said*
555 And yet, God woot,° Sampsoun drank nevere no wyn![4]   *God knows*
Thou fallest as it were a styked swyn.°   *stuck (i.e., speared) pig*
Thy tonge° is lost and al thyn honeste cure.°   *tongue, care*
For dronkenesse is verray sepulture°   *true tomb*
Of mannes° wit and his discrecioun.°   *man's, discretion*
560 In whom that drynke hath dominacioun,°   *has control*
He kan no conseil° kepe,° it is no drede.°   *counsel, keep, doubt*
Now kepe yow fro the white and fro the rede[5]
And namely fro the white wyn of Lepe°   *Lepe (Spanish town)*
That is to selle° in Fyssh Strete° or in Chepe.°[6]   *for sale, Fish Street, Cheapside*
565 This wyn of Spaigne° crepeth subtilly°   *Spain, creeps subtly*

---

1 This distinction between the basic food and the flavors given to it by the cooks draws on Aristotle's distinction between substance (essential inner reality) and its superficial qualities (accidents). This line could be read as an allusion to contemporary philosophical debates between Nominalists and Realists or to contemporary theological controversies concerning the process through which the bread and wine of the Eucharist are transformed into the body and blood of Christ.

2 There is a Latin gloss in the margin quoting 1 Timothy 5:6: "But she that lives in pleasure is dead while she lives."

3 There is a Latin gloss in the margin quoting the corresponding lines from Proverbs 20:1.

4 As recounted in Judges 13, which actually says that Samson's mother did not drink wine during her pregnancy.

5 "Now keep yourself from the white and red [wines]."

6 These two places were market districts in London. Chaucer's father was a wine merchant on Fish Street.

In othere wynes growynge faste by,°[1]   *growing nearby*
Of which ther ryseth° swich fumositee°   *there rises, vapors*
That whan a man hath dronken draughtes thre°   *three drinks*
And weneth° that he be at hoom° in Chepe,°   *thinks, is at home, Cheapside*
570 He is in Spaigne, right at the toune of Lepe—
Nat at the Rochele ne at Burdeux toun—
And thanne wol he seye, "Sampsoun, Sampsoun!"
But herkneth, lordes, o° word, I yow preye,°   *one, ask you*
That alle the sovereyn actes,° dar I seye,   *sovereign acts*
575 Of victories in the Olde Testament
Thurgh verray° God that is omnipotent   *true*
Were doon° in abstinence and in preyere.°   *done, prayer*
Looketh° the Bible, and ther ye may it leere.°   *look in, learn*
Looke, Attilla[2] the grete conquerour
580 Deyde° in his sleepe with shame and dishonour,   *died*
Bledynge° ay° at his nose in dronkenesse.   *bleeding, ever*
A capitayn° sholde lyve in sobrenesse.°   *leader, sobriety*
And over al° this avyseth yow right wel°   *besides this, consider carefully*
What was comaunded° unto Lamwel.[3]   *commanded*
585 Nat Samuel[4] but Lamwel, seye I.
Redeth° the Bible, and fynde it expresly°   *read, specifically*
Of wyn yevyng° to hem that han justise.°   *giving wine, legal power*
Namoore° of this, for it may wel suffise.°   *no more, is quite enough*
And now I have spoken of glotonye,
590 Now wol I yow deffenden° hasardrye.°[5]   *prohibit, gambling*
Hasard is verray mooder° of lesynges°   *true mother, lying*
And of deceite and cursed forswerynges,°   *perjury*
Blasphemyng of Crist, manslaughtre, and wast° also   *wasteful spending*
Of catel° and of tyme. And forthermo,°   *goods, furthermore*
595 It is repreeve° and contrarie of° honour   *reproach, contrary to*
For to ben holde° a commune hasardour.°   *be considered, common gambler*
And ever the hyer° he is of estaat°   *higher, condition*

---

1   Expensive French wines, shipped through Bordeaux and La Rochelle, were often surreptitiously
     mixed with cheaper, but stronger, Spanish wines.
2   Attila the Hun was a fifth-century nomadic chieftain who ravaged vast stretches of central
     Europe. According to medieval histories, such as those of Jordanes and Paul the Deacon, he died
     from drink on the night that he took a new bride.
3   Lemuel, King of Massa, is mentioned in Proverbs 31:4–5. A Latin gloss in the margin quotes the
     opening verse in which his mother warns him not to drink wine.
4   The prophet Samuel, much more famous than King Lemuel, is a main character in the book of
     1 Samuel.
5   There is an English gloss in the margin, "Of hasardrye," which is followed by a Latin reference
     to the *Policraticus*, a work of political theory by John of Salisbury, bishop of Chartres in the
     twelfth century, who lists gambling as a temptation and calls it "the mother of lies and perju-
     ries."

The moore is he holden° desolaat.°[1]   held, vile
If that a prynce useth hasardrye,°   prince frequently gambles
600 In alle governaunce° and policye°   governing, policy
He is as by commune opinioun°   common opinion
Yholde° the lasse° in reputacioun.   considered, less
STILBOUN,[2] that was a wys embassadour,°   wise ambassador
Was sent to Cornythe° in ful greet° honour   Corinth (Greek city), very great
605 Fro Lacidomye° to maken hire alliaunce,°   Sparta, alliance
And whan he cam, hym happed par chaunce[3]
That alle the gretteste° that were of that lond   greatest
Pleyynge atte hasard° he hem fond,°   gambling, found them
For which, as soone as it myghte be,
610 He stal hym hoom agayn° to his contree   secretly went home again
And seyde, "Ther wol I nat lese° my name!   not lose
Ne° I wol nat take on me so greet defame°   Nor, dishonor
Yow for to allie° unto none hasardours.°   ally, gamblers
Sendeth otherewise embassadours.°   Send other ambassadors
615 For by my trouthe,° me were levere dye°   truth, I would rather die
Than I yow sholde to hasardours allye.
For ye that been so glorious in honours
Shul nat allyen yow° with hasardours,   yourselves
As by my wyl,° ne° as by my tretee."°   will, nor, treaty
620 This wise philosophre thus seyde hee.
LOOKE eek° that the kyng Demetrius,   also
The kyng of Parthes,° as the book seith us,°[4]   Parthia, tells us
Sente him a paire of dees° of gold in scorn,   dice
For he hadde used hasard ther-biforn,°   often gambled before this
625 For which he heeld° his glorie or his renoun°   held, renown
At no value or reputacioun.
Lordes may fynden oother maner pley°   kinds of amusement
Honeste ynough° to dryve the day awey.°   honorable enough, pass the day
Now wol I speke of othes false and grete[5]
630 A word or two, as olde bookes trete.°   treat
Greet sweryng° is a thyng abhominable,°   swearing, terrible
And fals sweryng° is yet moore reprevable.°   perjury, disgraceful
The heighe God forbad sweryng at al.[6]

---

1 Many modern editors emend to "yholden" to give a more regular pentameter line, but both
   Ellesmere and Hengwrt have "holden."
2 This is an ambassador named Chilon, who is mentioned in John of Salisbury's *Policraticus*, 1.5.
3 "And when he came, it happened to him by chance."
4 King Demetrius of Parthia has not been securely identified, but John of Salisbury tells his story
   in the *Policraticus* immediately after that of Chilon.
5 There is an English gloss in the margin: "Of sweryng and forsweryng" (i.e., perjury).
6 There is a Latin gloss in the margin: "Do not swear at all," from Matthew 5:34.

Witnesse on Mathew,[1] but in special,° *specially*
635 Of sweryng seith the hooly Jeremye,° *holy Jeremiah*
"Thou shalt seye sooth thyne othes° and nat lye° *truly your oaths, lie*
And swere in doom° and eek in rightwisnesse."°[2] *judgment, righteousness*
But ydel sweryng° is a cursednesse. *idle swearing*
Bihoold and se° that in the firste table° *see, tablet (of Moses)*
640 Of heighe Goddes heestes honurable° *honorable commandments*
Hou that the seconde heeste of hym° is this *them*
"Take nat my name in ydel or amys."°[3] *in vain or amiss*
Lo, rather° he forbedeth swich sweryng *sooner*
Than homycide or any cursed thyng.
645 I seye° that as by ordre° thus it stondeth.° *say, order, stands*
This knowen that hise heestes understondeth,[4]
How that the seconde heeste° of God is that. *second commandment*
And forther over,° I wol thee telle al plat° *furthermore, plainly*
That vengeance shal nat parten° from his hous *depart*
650 That of his othes° is to outrageous.°[5] *oaths, too excessive*
"By Goddes precious herte!"° and "By his nayles"° *heart, nails*
And "By the blood of Crist that is in Hayles,[6]
Sevene° is my chaunce° and thyn° is cynk° and treye!"°[7] *seven, chance, yours, five, three*
By Goddes armes, if thou falsly pleye,
655 This daggere° shal thurghout thyn herte go!"° *dagger, pierce*
This fruyt cometh of the bicched bones° two[8]— *cursed bones*
Forsweryng,° ire,° falsnesse,° homycide. *perjury, anger, lying*
Now for the love of Crist that for us dyde,
Lete° youre othes, bothe grete and smale. *leave*
660 But sires, now wol I telle forth my tale.
→ THISE riotours° thre of whiche I telle *party-goers*
Longe erst er prime° rong° of any belle *before morning prayer, rang*
Were set hem° in a taverne to drynke. *themselves*

---

1   The reference here is to Matthew 5:33–36.
2   The Ellesmere scribe has repeated the words "in doom" and then underlined them with dots to indicate that they should be omitted. There is a Latin gloss in the margin indicating that the quotation is from Jeremiah 4:2.
3   Deuteronomy 5:7–21. As Skeat notes in his edition, in the Middle Ages the first two commandments were normally grouped as one, making what is now considered the third commandment the second, as it is here. The tenth commandment was then broken into two to make up the difference.
4   "Those who understand his commandments know this."
5   An allusion to the apocryphal or deuterocanonical book Ecclesiasticus 23:11.
6   This location is Hales Abbey in Gloucestershire, a monastery that claimed to have some of Christ's blood as a relic.
7   The modern game of craps is a version of medieval hazard, in which the player rolling the dice must call out the numbers he hopes to roll.
8   The cursed bones are the dice; dice were made of bone in the Middle Ages.

	And as they sat, they herde a belle clynke°	*ring*
665	Biforn a cors° was caried° to his grave.	*corpse, [that] was carried*
	That oon of hem° gan callen° to his knave,°	*them, called, servant*
	"Go bet,"° quod he, "and axe redily°	*Go quickly, ask eagerly*
	What cors is this that passeth heer forby.°	*passes by here*
	And looke that thou reporte his name weel."°	*well*
670	"Sire," quod this boy, "it nedeth never a deel.°	*it is not necessary*
	It was me toold er ye cam heer two houres.[1]	
	He was, pardee,° an old felawe° of youres.	*by God, friend*
	And sodeynly° he was yslayn° tonyght.	*suddenly, killed*
	For dronke[2] as he sat on his bench upright	
675	Ther cam° a privee theef° men clepeth Deeth,	*came, secret thief, call Death*
	That in this contree al the peple sleeth,°[3]	*kills all the people*
	And with his spere° he smoot° his herte atwo°	*spear, cut, in two*
	And wente his wey withouten wordes mo.	
	He hath a thousand slayn this pestilence.°	*[during] this epidemic*
680	And maister,° er° ye come in his presence,	*master, before*
	Me thynketh that it were necessarie	
	For to bewar° of swich an adversarie.	*beware*
	Beth redy° for to meete hym everemoore.°	*be ready, always*
	Thus taughte me my dame.° I sey namoore."°	*mother, say no more*
685	"By seinte Marie,"° seyde this taverner,°	*St. Mary, tavern keeper*
	"The child seith sooth,° for he hath slayn this yeer	*speaks truly*
	Henne° over a mile withinne a greet° village	*from here, large*
	Bothe man and womman, child and hyne° and page.°	*hired hand, boy servant*
	I trowe° his habitacioun° be° there.	*believe, dwelling, is*
690	To been° avysed° greet wysdom it were,	*be, warned*
	Er that he dide a man a dishonour."°	*lest he cause a man harm*
	"Ye, Goddes armes," quod this riotour,°	*party-goer*
	"Is it swich peril with hym for to meete?	
	I shal hym seke° by wey° and eek ...	*..., road, street*
695	I make avow° to Goddes digne° b...	*...mise, worthy*
	Herkneth,° felawes,° we thre been ...	*...three together*
	Lat ech° of us holde up his hand til oother,°	*each, to the other*
	And ech of us bicomen° otheres brother.	*become*

handwritten annotations: *they set out to find death* ; *they think death is a person so they go seek to take him down*

---

1 "It was told to me two hours ago, before you came here."

2 We have been guided by the manuscript, which has a space between "for" and "dronke" and punctuated accordingly. But medieval word division did not always follow modern norms and the word "fordronke" could mean simply "totally drunk." Most editors, going back to Thomas Tyrwhitt, take that meaning and insert a comma rather than a period after "tonight," so that the lines read "suddenly he was slain tonight as he sat, totally drunk, on the bench."

3 The reference here is doubtless to plague. The Black Death that spread from Italy across Europe hit England in 1348 and in the space of a year killed between a quarter and a half of the population. There were further outbreaks in 1361–62, 1369, and 1375–76.

And we wol sleen this false traytour,° Deeth!   *traitor*
700 He shal be slayn, which that so manye sleeth,°   *kills so many people*
     By Goddes dignitee° er° it be nyght!"   *dignity, before*
     TOGIDRES han thise thre° hir trouthes plight°   *together have these three, promised*
     To lyve and dyen ech of hem for oother
     As though he were his owene° yborn° brother.   *own, born*
705 And up they stirte° al dronken° in this rage.[1]   *jumped, drunk*
     And forth they goon° towardes that village   *go*
     Of which the taverner hadde spoke biforn.
     And many a grisly° ooth thanne han they sworn,   *horrible*
     And Cristes blessed body they torente.°   *tear apart (with their oaths)*
710 Deeth shal be deed, if that they may hym hente!°   *catch him*
     WHAN they han[2] goon° nat fully half a mile   *have gone*
     Right as they wolde han troden over a stile,[3]
     An oold man and a povre° with hem mette.°   *poor, encountered them*
     This olde man ful mekely° hem grette°   *meekly, greeted*
715 And seyde thus: "Now, lordes, God yow see!"°   *God watch over you*
     THE proudeste of thise riotours three
     Answerde agayn, "What, carl,° with sory grace!°   *peasant, bad luck to you*
     Why artow° al forwrapped,° save° thy face?   *are you, all wrapped up, except*
     Why lyvestow° so longe in so greet age?"   *live you*
720 THIS olde man gan looke° in his visage°   *looked, face*
     And seyde thus: "For° I ne kan nat fynde   *because*
     A man though that I walked into Ynde°   *India*
     Neither in citee nor in no village
     That wolde chaunge his youthe for myn age.
725 And therfore moot I han° myn age stille,   *I must have*
     As longe tyme as it is Goddes wille.
     NE deeth, allas, ne wol nat han my lyf.
     Thus walke I lyk a restelees° kaityf.°   *restless, wretch*
     And on the ground which is my moodres° gate   *mother's*
730 I knokke with my staf° bothe erly and late   *walking stick*
     And seye, 'Leeve Mooder,° leet me in!   *Dear Mother*
     Lo how I vanysshe°—flessh and blood and skyn!   *waste away*
     Allas, whan shul my bones been at reste?
     Mooder, with yow wolde I chaunge° my cheste°   *change, money box*
735 That in my chambre° longe tyme hath be,°   *room, time has been*
     Ye, for an heyre clowt°[4] to wrappe me.'°   *hair shirt, wrap around*

---

1 Ellesmere has "and dronken." The emendation is from Hengwrt.
2 Chaucer frequently alternates between the simple past (the rioters jumped up, the old man met
   with them) and the present or the perfect forms (the rioters *have gone* rather than *had gone* or *went*,
   which we would expect in modern English).
3 "Just as they were about to climb over a stile" (steps to get over a wall or fence).
4 Remorseful people in the Middle Ages sometimes wore shirts made of horse hair, which

But yet to me she wol nat do that grace,°   *favor*
For which ful pale° and welked° is my face.   *very pale, withered*
BUT sires, to yow° it is no curteisye°   *in you, courtesy*
740 To speken to an old man vileynye,°   *insults*
But° he trespasse° in word or elles in dede.°   *unless, offend, deed*
In Hooly Writ° ye may yourself wel rede°   *the Bible, well read*
'Agayns° an oold man hoor° upon his heed°   *in the presence of, gray, head*
Ye sholde arise.'[1] Wherfore° I yeve° yow reed:°   *therefore, give, advice*
745 Ne dooth unto an oold man noon harm now,[2]
Namoore° than that ye wolde° men did to yow[3]   *no more, would*
In age—if that ye so longe abyde.°   *live long enough*
And God be with yow, where° ye go° or ryde.   *wherever, walk*
I moot° go thider° as I have to go.'   *must, where*
750 "NAY, olde cherl, by God thou shalt nat so!"
Seyde this oother hasardour° anon.°   *second gambler, immediately*
"Thou partest nat° so lightly, by Seint John!   *do not get away*
Thou spak right now of thilke traytour° Deeth,   *that traitor*
That in this contree alle oure freendes sleeth.°   *kills*
755 Have heer my trouthe° as thou art his espye.°   *On my word, spy*
Telle where he is, or thou shalt it abye°   *you pay for it*
By God and by the hooly sacrement!°   *holy sacrament (the Eucharist)*
For soothly,° thou art° oon° of his assent°   *truly, are, one, his plot*
To sleen us yonge folk, thou false theef!"
760 "NOW sires," quod he, "if that ye be so leef,°   *if you wish*
To fynde Deeth, turne up this croked wey.°   *crooked way*
For in that grove I lafte hym, by my fey,°   *faith*
Under a tree. And there he wole abyde.°   *will wait*
Noght for youre boost he wole him nothyng hyde.[4]
765 Se ye that ook?° Right there ye shal hym fynde.   *oak*
God save yow that boghte° agayn mankynde   *who redeemed*
And yow amende!"° Thus seyde this olde man.   *make you better*
And everich° of thise riotours ran   *each*
Til he cam to that tree. And ther they founde
770 Of floryns° fyne of gold ycoyned° rounde   *florins (coins), coined*
Wel ny° an eighte° busshels, as hem thoughte.°   *very nearly, MS viij, they thought*

treasure!

---

irritated the body, expecting the pain to gain them spiritual benefit. Here the old man wishes to
be buried in such a shirt, exchanging it for the chest that holds his money.

1   The quotation is from Leviticus 19:32, and the opening words are given in a Latin gloss in the
margin.

2   "Do not do an old man none [i.e., any] harm." In Middle English multiple negatives reinforce
each other, rather than canceling each other out.

3   Compare the Golden Rule from Matthew 7:12: "So whatever you wish that men would do to
you, do so to them."

4   "He will not hide himself in any way because of your boasting."

No lenger° thanne after Deeth they soughte.   *longer*
But ech of hem so glad was of that sighte,
For that the floryns been so faire and brighte,
775 That doun° they sette hem° by this precious hoord.°   *down, sat themselves, hoard*
The worste of hem, he spak the firste word.
"BRETHEREN,"° quod he, "taak kepe° what I seye.   *brothers, pay attention to*
My wit is greet,° though that I bourde° and pleye.°   *large, joke, play*
This tresor° hath Fortune unto us yeven°   *treasure, given*
780 In myrthe and joliftee° oure lyf to lyven.°   *jollity, live*
And lightly as it comth,° so wol° we spende.   *comes, will*
Ey,° Goddes precious dignitee!° Who wende°   *ah, dignity, expected*
Today that we sholde han so fair a grace?°   *such good luck*
But myghte this gold be caried fro this place
785 Hoom to myn hous, or elles unto yours—
For wel ye woot° that al this gold is oures°—   *you know, ours*
Thanne were we in heigh felicitee.°   *great happiness*
But trewely, by daye it may nat bee.°   *not be*
Men wolde seyn° that we were theves stronge°   *would say, downright thieves*
790 And for oure owene tresor doon us honge.°   *cause us to be hanged*
This tresor moste ycaried be° by nyghte   *must be carried*
As wisely and as slyly° as it myghte.   *secretly*
Wherfore° I rede° that cut° among us alle   *therefore, advise, lots*
Be drawe° and lat se° wher the cut wol falle,[1]   *drawn, let see*
795 And he that hath the cut with herte blithe°   *happy*
Shal renne° to towne and that ful swithe°   *run, very quickly*
And brynge us breed° and wyn ful prively.°   *bread, very secretly*
And two of us shul kepen subtilly°   *shall guard cleverly*
This tresor wel. And if he wol nat tarie,°   *will not delay*
800 Whan it is nyght we wol this tresor carie°   *carry*
By oon assent° whereas us thynketh best."°   *in agreement, where we think best*
That oon of hem° the cut° broghte° in his fest°   *one of them, lots, brought, fist*
And bad hym drawe° and looke where it wol falle.°   *asked them to draw, will fall*
And it fil on° the yongeste of hem alle.   *fell to*
805 And forth toward the toun he wente anon.
And also soone° as that he was gon,   *as soon*
That oon spak thus unto that oother:
"Thow knowest wel thou art my sworn brother.
Thy profit° wol I telle thee anon.   *your advantage*
810 Thou woost wel° that oure felawe is agon.°   *well know, gone*
And heere is gold, and that ful greet plentee,°   *a great deal of it*
That shal departed been° among us thre.   *shall be divided*

---

1 The three rioters will draw straws, just as the Canterbury pilgrims did to see who would tell the first tale.

But nathelees,° if I kan shape it so,°   nevertheless, can cause it
That it departed were among us two,
815 Hadde I nat doon a freendes torn° to thee?"   friend's turn
THAT oother answerde, "I noot° hou that may be.   do not know
He woot° how that the gold is with us tweye.°   knows, two
What shal¹ we doon? What shal we to hym seye?"
"SHAL it be conseil?"° seyde the firste shrewe.°   our plan, villain
820 "And I shal tellen in a wordes fewe
What we shal doon and bryngen it wel aboute."
"I GRAUNTE,"° quod that oother, "out of doute,°   grant, without doubt
That by my trouthe° I shal thee nat biwreye."°   truth, not betray you
"Now," quod the firste, "thou woost wel we be tweye,
825 And two of us shul strenger be° than oon.   will be stronger
Looke whan that he is set, that right anoon°   right away
Arys° as though thou woldest with hym pleye,°   arise, would play with him
And I shal ryve hym° thurgh the sydes tweye°   stab him, two sides
Whil that thou strogelest° with hym as in game,°   struggle, jest
830 And with thy daggere, looke thou do the same.
And thanne shal al this gold departed° be,   divided
My deere freend, bitwixen me and thee.
Thanne may we bothe oure lustes° all fulfille   pleasures
And pleye at dees° right at oure owene wille."   dice
835 And thus acorded been° thise shrewes tweye°   are agreed, these two villains
To sleen° the thridde,° as ye han herd me seye.   kill, third
THIS yongeste, which° that wente unto the toun,   who
Ful ofte in herte he rolleth up and doun
The beautee of thise floryns newe and brighte.
840 "O Lord," quod he, "if so were that I myghte
Have al this tresor to myself allone,
Ther is no man that lyveth under the trone°   throne
Of God that sholde lyve so murye as I!"
And atte laste the feend° oure enemy   fiend
845 Putte in his thought that he sholde poyson beye,°   buy poison
With which he myghte sleen° hise felawes tweye.   kill
For why the feend foond hym in swich lyvynge
That he hadde leve hym to sorwe brynge.²
For this was outrely° his fulle entente,°   utterly, intent
850 To sleen hem bothe° and nevere to repent.   kill them
And forth he gooth—no lenger° wolde he tarie°—   longer, would he delay

---

1 For "What shal," Ellesmere provides "Whal." The emendation is from Hengwrt.
2 "Because the devil found him living in such a way [i.e., so sinfully] that he had permission [from
   God] to bring him to sorrow [i.e., damnation]." Ellesmere has "hem to sorwe brynge," i.e.,
   "bring them to sorrow." The emendation is from Hengwrt.

Into the toun unto a pothecarie°[1]   *apothecary*
And preyde hym° that he hym wolde selle   *asked him*
Som poysoun that he myghte hise rattes quelle.°   *kill his rats*
855 And eek ther was a polcat in his hawe,
That, as he seyde, hise capouns hadde yslawe.[2]
And fayn° he wolde wreke hym,° if he myghte,   *gladly, would avenge himself*
On vermyn° that destroyed° hym by nyghte.   *vermin, harmed*
THE pothecarie answerde, "And thou shalt have
860 A thyng that, also° God my soule save,   *as*
In al this world ther is no creature
That eten or dronken hath of this confiture°   *concoction*
Noght° but the montance° of a corn of whete,°   *nothing, size, grain of wheat*
That he ne shal his lif anon° forlete.°   *immediately, lose*
865 Ye, sterve he shal,° and that in lasse while°   *he shall die, less time*
Than thou wolt goon a paas° nat but a mile,   *go at a walking pace*
The poysoun is so strong and violent."
THIS cursed man hath in his hond yhent°   *hand taken*
This poysoun in a box, and sith° he ran   *afterwards*
870 Into the nexte strete° unto a man   *street*
And borwed hym large botels thre.°   *borrowed from him three bottles*
And in the two his poyson poured he.
The thridde he kepte clene° for his owene drynke.   *kept pure*
For al the nyght he shoope° hym for to swynke°   *intended, labor*
875 In cariynge° of the gold out of that place.   *carrying*
And whan this riotour with sory grace°   *wretched misfortune*
Hadde filled with wyn hise grete botels thre,
To hise felawes agayn repaireth° he.   *returns*
WHAT nedeth° it to sermone° of it moore?°   *needs, talk, more*
880 For right so° as they hadde cast° his deeth bifoore,   *just as, had determined*
Right so they han hym slayn,° and that anon.   *have killed him*
And whan that this was doon, thus spak that oon,°   *the first*
"Now lat° us sitte and drynke and make us merie,   *let*
And afterward we wol his body berie."°   *will bury his body*
885 And with that word it happed° hym° par cas°   *happened, to him, by chance*
To take the botel ther the poysoun was,
And drank and yaf his felawe drynke also,
For which anon they storven° bothe two.   *died*
BUT certes,° I suppose that Avycen[3]   *certainly*

---

1 Apothecaries sold herbal medicines.
2 "And also there was a polcat [a type of weasel] in his yard [*hawe*]/That, as he said, had killed his poultry."
3 Avicenna or Ibn Sina (980–1037 AD) was a Persian philosopher who wrote, among other things, a treatise about medicine entitled *Liber Canonis Medicinae* (*The Book of the Canon of Medicine*). The

890	Wroot° nevere in no *Canoun* ne in no fen°	*wrote, chapter*
	Mo wonder signes° of empoisonyng°	*wonderfully signs, poisoning*
	Than hadde thise wrecches two er hir endyng.[1]	
	Thus ended been thise° homycides° two	*these, murderers*
	And eek the false empoysonere also.	
895	O CURSED synne of alle cursednesse,[2]	
	O traytours° homycide, o wikkednesse,	*traitorous*
	O glotonye, luxurie,° and hasardrye,°	*lust, gambling*
	Thou blasphemour of Crist with vileynye°	*villainy*
	And othes grete° of usage° and of pride!	*great oaths, from habit*
900	Allas, mankynde, how may it bitide°	*happen*
	That to thy creatour, which that the wroghte°	*who made you*
	And with his precious herte blood° thee boghte,°	*heart's blood, bought you*
	Thou art so fals and so unkynde,° allas?	*unnatural*
	"Now goode men, God foryeve yow youre trespas°	*sin*
905	And ware yow fro° the synne of avarice!	*guard you from*
	Myn hooly° pardoun may yow all warice,°	*holy, save*
	So that° ye offre° nobles or sterlynges[3]	*provided that, offer*
	Or elles silver broches,° spoones,° rynges.°	*brooches, spoons, rings*
	Boweth youre heed° under this hooly bulle.°	*head, license*
910	Com up, ye wyves, offreth° of youre wolle.°	*offer, wool*
	Youre names I entre° heer° in my rolle° anon.°	*enter, here, list, immediately*
	Into the blisse of Hevene shul ye gon.	
	I yow assoille° by myn heigh power,	*pardon you*
	Yow that wol offre, as clene° and eek as cleer°	*pure, clear*
915	As ye were born. And lo, sires, thus I preche.[4]	
	And Jesu Crist that is oure soules leche°	*soul's physician*
	So graunte° yow his pardoun to receyve.°	*grant, receive*
	For that is best. I wol yow nat deceyve.°	*not deceive*
	BUT sires, o° word forgat I in my tale.	*one*
920	I have relikes° and pardoun° in my male°	*relics, pardons, purse*
	As faire as any man in Engelond,	
	Whiche were me yeven° by the Popes hond.°	*given, hand*
	If any of yow wole° of devocioun°	*will, in devotion*
	Offren and han myn absolucioun,°	*have my pardon*
925	Com forth anon, and kneleth° heere adoun,	*kneel*

Handwritten marginalia: "Pardoner", "saves pitch", "accepting payment".

---

word *Canon* in the next line refers to this book. It was divided into chapters called "fens" from the Arabic word for a part of a science.

1   "Than had these two wretches before their death."

2   There is a Latin gloss in the margin, "Auctor," suggesting that the scribe believes the author is offering his own moral comment here or perhaps just that this seemed a particularly useful moral.

3   Nobles and sterlings were both coins—nobles gold and sterlings silver.

4   Here the Pardoner ends his recreation of his typical sermon and addresses the pilgrims directly.

And mekely receyveth° my pardoun.   *meekly receive*
Or elles taketh pardoun as ye wende,°   *go*
Al newe and fressh° at every miles ende,°   *fresh, mile's end*
So that ye offren alwey newe° and newe   *always anew*
930 Nobles or pens,° whiche that be goode and trewe.°[1]   *pence, true*
It is an honour to everich° that is heer   *everyone*
That ye mowe° have a suffisant° pardoneer°   *may, capable, pardoner*
T'assoille° yow in contree° as ye ryde   *pardon, [the] country*
For aventures° whiche that may bityde.°   *accidents, happen*
935 Paraventure° ther may fallen° oon° or two   *perhaps, happen, one*
Doun of his hors and breke his nekke atwo.
Looke which a seuretee° is it to yow alle   *what a guarantee*
That I am in youre felaweshipe yfalle,°   *fallen into your company*
That may assoille yow° bothe moore and lasse°   *pardon you, greater and lesser (of rank)*
940 Whan that the soule shal fro the body passe.
I rede° that oure Hoost heere shal bigynne,°   *advise, begin*
For he is moost envoluped° in synne.   *wrapped up*
Com forth, sire Hoost, and offre first anon,
And thou shalt kisse my relikes everychon.
945 Ye, for a grote unbokele anon thy purs."[2]
"NAY, nay," quod he, "thanne have I° Cristes curs!°   *may I have, curse*
Lat be,"° quod he. "It shal nat be, so thee'ch!°   *Drop it, as I thrive*
Thou woldest make me kisse thyn olde breech°   *your old pants*
And swere it were a relyk of a seint—
950 Though it were with thy fundement° depeint!°   *anus, stained*
But by the croys which that Seint Eleyne[3] fond,
I wolde° I hadde thy coillons° in myn hond   *wish, testicles*
Instide° of relikes or of seintuarie!°   *instead, reliquaries*
Lat kutte hem of!° I wol with thee hem carie.°   *Let them be cut off, carry them*
955 They shul be shryned° in an hogges toord!"°   *enshrined, hog's turd*
THIS Pardoner answerde nat a word.
So wrooth° he was, no word ne wolde he seye.   *angry*
"NOW," quod oure Hoost, "I wol no lenger pleye°   *no longer joke*
With thee ne with noon oother° angry man!"   *nor no other*
960 But right anon° the worthy knyght bigan   *right away*
Whan that he saugh that al the peple lough,°   *laughed*
"N— — —° —th—l— For it is right ynough!°   *No more, quite enough*

[handwritten marginal note: Host / say hell / no.]

[handwritten note, lower left: host is mad → / Pardoners mad / he would say svch / things]

[footnotes, partially obscured:]
° coins (i.e., shaving off some of the silver or gold from the edges)
—er's day.
—in], unbuckle immediately your purse!"
—the Roman emperor Constantine in the early fourth century.
—the Holy Land and found there the true cross on which Christ

Sire Pardoner, be glad and myrie of cheere.°   *merry of face*
And ye, sire Hoost, that been to me so deere,
965 I prey° yow that ye kisse the Pardoner.   *ask*
And Pardoner, I prey thee, drawe thee neer,°   *come near*
And as we diden,° lat us laughe and pleye!"   *did*
Anon they kiste and ryden° forth hir weye.°   *rode, their way*

everyone makes up... kiss and make up!

HEERE IS ENDED THE PARDONERS TALE

— why would pardoner tell people his plan to their people and then use a plan?
— irony of this religous journey and the stories that all told... (Chaucer blends worldly and sacred matters)

Pope is living lavish and telling people to give $1 to rome and live frugal life
Corruption of Church

THE PRIORESS'S PROLOGUE AND TALE

Opening page of *The Prioress's Tale*. Ellesmere Manuscript EL 26 C9 f. 148v. Reprinted by permission of The Huntington Library.

THE PRIORESS'S PROLOGUE

DOMINE DOMINUS NOSTER[1]

"O LORD, oure Lord, thy name how merveillous°   *marvelous*
Is in this large world ysprad,"° quod° she.   *spread about, said*
455 "For noght oonly° thy laude° precious   *not only, praise*
Parfourned° is by men of dignitee°   *proclaimed, dignity*
But by the mouth of children thy bountee°   *goodness*
Parfourned is, for on the brest° soukynge°   *breast, sucking*
Somtyme° shewen° they thyn heriynge.°[2]   *sometimes, show, your praise*

460 Wherfore° in laude,° as I best kan° or may,   *therefore, praise, can*
Of thee and of the lylye flour,°   *lily flower*
Which that the bar°[3] and is a mayde° alway,°   *who bore thee, virgin, always*
To telle a storie I wol do my labour—
Nat° that I may encreessen° hir honour,°   *not, increase, her honor*
465 For she hirself is honour and the roote°   *root*
Of bountee next hir sone and soules boote.[4]

O mooder° mayde,° o mayde mooder free,°   *mother, maid, generous*
O bussh unbrent, brennynge in Moyses sighte,[5]
That ravysedest doun fro the Deitee,°   *snatched*
470 Thurgh thyn humblesse, the goost that in th'alighte,[6]
Of whos vertu, whan he thyn herte lighte,[7]
Conceyved° was the Fadres sapience,°[8]   *conceived, Father's wisdom (i.e., Christ)*
Helpe me to telle it in thy reverence.°   *for your honor*

---

1 "O Lord, our lord." These are the first words of Psalm 8, which the Prioress paraphrases in the
   first stanza of her Prologue.
2 "For sometimes, while [still] sucking on the breast, they show your praise."
3 In medieval iconography, the Virgin Mary is presented with a lily, a symbol of her purity, by the
   angel Gabriel during the Annunciation of the birth of Christ.
4 "Of goodness, next to her son, and the soul's help."
5 "O unburned bush, burning in Moses's sight." The reference is to the encounter Moses has in
   Exodus 3 with God in the form of a burning bush that is unconsumed by the fire. This became
   a popular image for Mary, who preserved her virginity despite being a mother.
6 "Who allured down from the Deity, through your humility, the spirit that alighted in you."
7 "Of whose power when he illumined your heart."
8 Although each member of the Christian Trinity is equal, they are often associated with particu-
   lar qualities. Christ, the Word or "Logos," is associated with wisdom; the Father with power;
   and the Holy Spirit with love.

	Lady, thy bountee,° thy magnificence,°	*goodness, majesty*
475	Thy vertu,° and thy grete humylitee	*power*
	Ther may no tonge° expresse in no science.°	*tongue, with no knowledge*
	For somtyme,° Lady, er° men praye to thee,	*sometimes, before*
	Thou goost biforn° of thy benyngnytee°	*you anticipate, goodness*
	And getest us thurgh° lyght° of thy preyere°	*through, light, prayer*
480	To gyden° us unto thy Sone° so deere.°	*guide, son, dear*

	My konnyng° is so wayk,° o blisful° queene,	*ability, weak, blessed*
	For to declare thy grete worthynesse,°	*great worth*
	That I ne may the weighte nat susteene.°	*may not sustain the weight*
	But as a child of twelf monthe oold or lesse°	*one year old or less*
485	That kan unnethe° any word expresse,°	*can scarcely, pronounce*
	Right so fare I. And therfore I yow preye,°	*pray you*
	Gydeth° my song that I shal of yow seye.°"	*guide, tell of you*

EXPLICIT[1]

THE PRIORESS'S TALE

HEERE BIGYNNETH THE PRIORESSES TALE

Anti Semetic tail...

	THER was in Asye°[2] in a greet citee°	*Asia, great city*
	Amonges Cristene° folk a Jewerye,°	*Christian, Jewish ghetto*
490	Sustened° by a lord of that contree°	*sustained, country*
	For foul usure° and lucre of vileynye,°[3]	*foul interest [rates], villainous profit*
	Hateful to Crist and to his compaignye.°	*company (i.e., Christians)*
	And thurgh this strete° men myghte ride or wende,°	*street, go*
	For it was free and open at eyther ende.	

495	A litel scole° of Cristen folk ther stood	*little school*
	Doun° at the ferther° ende, in which ther were	*down, farther*
	Children an heepe° ycomen° of Cristen blood,	*many children, come*
	That lerned° in that scole yeer by yere°	*who learned, year by year*

---

1   "Here it ends."
2   In the Middle Ages, the geographical term "Asia" meant Asia Minor, which today is the coun-
     try of Turkey and part of northern Greece. All Jews were expelled from England in 1290. In
     Chaucer's day there were some Jews living in France (from which they were expelled first in
     1306 and again in 1394), some in central and eastern Europe, the Balkans and Asia Minor, and
     significant Jewish communities in Spain, Italy, North Africa, and the Middle East.
3   In the Middle Ages, the Church prohibited Christians from lending money at interest. Such
     commerce, necessary for the economy of the time, was engaged in by the few non-Christian
     peoples of Europe, especially the Jews. There is a Latin gloss in the margin at line 491, "foul
     gain."

Swich manere doctrine° as men used there.   *such kind of teaching*
500 This is to seyn,° to syngen° and to rede,°   *say, sing, read*
As smale children doon° in hire childhede.°   *do, their childhood*

Among thise° children was a wydwes sone,°   *these, widow's son*
A litel clergeoun[1] seven yeer of age,
That day by day to° scole was his wone.°   *to [go to], custom*
505 And eek also whereas° he saugh° th'ymage°   *where, saw, the image*
Of Cristes mooder,° he hadde in usage,°   *mother, he had the habit*
As hym° was taught, to knele adoun° and seye°   *him, kneel down, say*
His *Ave Marie*[2] as he goth by the weye.°   *goes along the road*

Thus hath this wydwe hir litel sone ytaught°   *taught*
510 Oure blisful° lady, Cristes mooder deere,°   *blessed, dear mother*
To worshipe ay.° And he forgat it naught,°   *always, not*
For sely° child wol alday° soone leere,°   *innocent, all the time, learn*
But ay° whan° I remembre on this mateere,°   *ever, when, matter*
Seint Nicholas[3] stant° evere in my presence,   *stands*
515 For he so yong° to Crist° dide° reverence.   *young, Christ, did*

This litel child, his litel book lernynge,°   *learning*
As he sat in the scole at his prymer,°   *primer (school book)*
He *Alma redemptoris*[4] herde synge°   *heard being sung*
As children lerned hire° anthiphoner.[5]   *their*
520 And as he dorste,° he drough hym ner° and ner   *dared, drew himself nearer*
And herkned° ay the wordes and the noote°   *always listened [to], melody*
Til he the firste vers koude al by rote.°   *knew the first verse by heart*

Noght wiste he° what this Latyn° was to seye,°   *he did not know, Latin, meant*
For he so yong and tendre was of age.
525 But on a day his felawe gan he preye°   *he began to ask his friend*
T'expounden hym° this song in his langage°[6]   *to explain to him, language*

---

1   The term "clergeon" means pupil but can also refer to a choir boy. Young boys often served in choirs in exchange for education.
2   "Hail Mary" are the words of the angel Gabriel to the Virgin at the Annunciation. His speech was set to music and frequently sung in church services in the Middle Ages.
3   St. Nicholas became the patron saint of children. He was a fourth-century bishop of Myra in Asia Minor. His legend maintained that as an infant he fasted on Wednesdays and Fridays by refusing his mother's breast milk.
4   "Kindly Mother of the Redeemer." This song was an antiphon used in church services in the Middle Ages during Advent.
5   An antiphoner is a book containing the words and music of antiphons like *Alma Redemptoris*. It was used for church services in the Middle Ages.
6   The school boys can sing Latin but do not understand it. The younger one asks the older to explain the words in their own vernacular language (which is not specified).

Or telle hym why this song was in usage.
This preyde he hym to construe and declare°   *he asked him to translate*
Ful often tyme° upon hise knowes bare.°   *very often, his bare knees*

530 His felawe, which that elder° was than he,   *older*
Answerde hym thus: "This song, I have herd seye,°   *heard said*
Was maked of° oure blisful° lady free,°   *made for, blessed, noble*
Hir to salue° and eek hire for to preye°   *to honor her, pray*
To been oure helpe and socour° whan we deye.°   *aid, die*
535 I kan namoore expounde° in this mateere.   *can no more explain*
I lerne song. I kan° but smal grammeere."°   *know, little grammar*

"And is this song maked° in reverence°   *made, honor*
Of Cristes mooder?" seyde this innocent.
"Now, certes,° I wol do my diligence°   *certainly, will work hard*
540 To konne° it al er Cristemasse is went,°   *learn, before Christmas has passed*
Though that I for my prymer shal be shent[1]
And shal be beten° thries in an houre.°   *beaten, three times*
I wol it konne,° oure Lady for to honoure."   *will learn it*

His felawe taughte hym homward prively[2]
545 Fro day to day, til he koude it by rote.°   *knew it by heart*
And thanne he song° it wel and boldely   *sang*
Fro word to word,[3] acordynge with the note.°   *according to the melody*
Twies° a day it passed thurgh° his throte,°   *Twice, through, throat*
To scoleward° and homward whan he wente.   *Towards school*
550 On Cristes mooder set was his entente.°   *intent*

As I have seyd, thurghout° the Juerie°   *throughout, ghetto*
This litel child, as he cam to and fro,
Ful murily° wolde° he synge° and crie°   *merrily, would, sing, cry*
O *Alma redemptoris* everemo.°   *ever more*
555 The swetnesse° his herte perced° so   *sweetness, pierced*
Of Cristes mooder, that to hire to preye°   *pray*
He kan nat stynte° of syngyng° by the weye.   *cannot stop, singing*

OURE firste foo,° the serpent Sathanas,°[4]   *foe, Satan*
That hath in Jues herte° his waspes° nest   *Jewish hearts, wasp's*

---

1 "Although I shall be harmed for [neglecting] my school book." Corporal punishment was the norm in medieval schools for students who were slow at learning their lessons.
2 "On the way home, his friend taught him privately."
3 Ellesmere reads "Fro word to word to word," thus breaking the line's meter. The emendation is from Hengwrt.
4 There is a Latin gloss in the margin, "auctor," indicating that the author is offering a moral lesson.

560 Up swal° and seide, "O Hebrayk peple,° allas!   *swelled up, Hebrew people*
Is this to yow a thyng that is honest,°   *respectable*
That swich° a boy shal walken as hym lest°   *such, walk as he wishes*
In youre despit° and synge° of swich sentence°   *spite, sing, meaning*
Which is agayn° oure lawes reverence?"°[1]   *against, law's honor*

565 Fro thennes forth° the Jues han° conspired   *from this time on, Jews have*
This innocent out of this world to chace.°   *chase*
An homycide° therto han they hyred°   *murderer, have hired*
That in an aleye° hadde a privee° place.   *alley, secret*
And as the child gan forby for to pace,°   *began to pass by*
570 This cursed Jew hym hente° and heeld hym faste°   *grabbed him, held him firmly*
And kitte° his throte and in a pit hym caste.°   *cut, threw him*

I seye° that in a wardrobe° they hym threwe,   *say, latrine*
Whereas° thise Jewes purgen hire entraille.°   *where, these Jews defecate*
O cursed folk of Herodes°[2] al newe,   *Herod's*
575 What may youre yvel entente° yow availle?°   *evil intent, help you*
Mordre wol out! Certeyn, it wol nat faille,
And namely, ther th'onour of God shal sprede.[3]
The blood out crieth° on youre cursed dede!°   *cries out, deed*

O MARTIR° sowded° to virginitee,°   *martyr, united, virginity*
580 Now maystow syngen,° folwynge evere in oon°   *may you sing, following in unity*
The white Lamb celestial,°[4] quod she,[5]   *heavenly Lamb*
Of which the grete° evaungelist° Seint John   *great, evangelist*
In Pathmos wroot,[6] which seith that they that goon°   *go*
Biforn this Lamb and synge a song al newe
585 That nevere flesshly wommen they ne knewe.°[7]   *did not know*

THIS povre wydwe awaiteth° al that nyght   *waits*
After hir litel child. But he cam noght.°   *did not come*

---

1   Both Ellesmere and Hengwrt have "oure lawes," associating Satan with the Jews. Other manu-
    scripts have "youre lawes."
2   In Matthew 2:1–18, Herod causes all the children of the region to be murdered in his effort to
    kill the baby Jesus.
3   "Murder will come to light. Certainly, it will not fail, and especially in that place the honor of
    God shall spread."
4   The reference here is to Revelation 14:1–5.
5   "She said." This line filler breaks momentarily the fiction that the Prioress is telling this tale on
    the road to Canterbury.
6   The writer of Revelation identifies himself as John, who was exiled for his faith on the island
    of Patmos off the coast of Turkey, where he had the visions that form the basis of the book of
    Revelation.
7   The reference here is to the virginity of those who praise the Lamb. There is a Latin gloss
    "carnaliter" (carnally) over the word fleshly.

For which, as soone as it was dayes lyght°   *daylight*
With face pale of drede° and bisy thoght°   *for fear, hectic thoughts*
590 She hath at scole and elleswhere° hym soght,°   *elsewhere, sought him*
Til finally she gan so fer espie,°   *found out this much*
That he last seyn° was in the Juerie.°   *seen, ghetto*

With moodres pitee° in hir brest enclosed,   *mother's pity*
595 She gooth as she were half out of hir mynde
To every place where she hath supposed
By liklihede° hir litel child to fynde.   *it likely*
And evere on Cristes mooder meeke and kynde
She cride.° And atte laste thus she wroghte:°   *prayed, did*
Among the cursed Jues she hym soghte.°   *she looked for him*

600 She frayneth,° and she preyeth° pitously   *asks, begs*
To every Jew that dwelte in thilke place
To telle hire if hir child wente oght forby.°   *went at all by*
They seyde nay, but Jesu of his grace
Yaf in hir thoght inwith a litel space,[1]
605 That in that place after hir sone° she cryde,°   *her son, cried*
Where he was casten° in a pit bisyde.°   *thrown, nearby*

O GRETE God, that parfournest° thy laude°[2]   *proclaims, praise*
By mouth of innocentz,° lo heere° thy myght!   *innocents, behold here*
This gemme° of chastite, this emeraude°   *gem, emerald*
610 And eek of martirdom° the ruby bright,   *martyrdom*
Ther° he with throte ykorven° lay upright,°   *where, cut throat, on his back*
He *Alma redemptoris* gan to synge°   *began to sing*
So loude that al the place gan to rynge!°   *began to ring*

THE Cristene folk that thurgh° the strete wente   *through*
615 In coomen° for to wondre upon this thyng.   *came in*
And hastily they for the provost sente.[3]
He cam anon withouten tariyng°   *without delay*
And herieth° Crist that is of Hevene kyng   *praises*
And eek his mooder, honour of mankynde,
620 And after that the Jewes leet he bynde.°   *he commanded to be bound*

---

1   "Brought to her mind within a little while."
2   There is a second Latin gloss in the margin: "auctor."
3   A provost was a medieval judge who oversaw legal matters within a town.

THIS child with pitous lamentacioun
Up taken° was, syngynge° his song alway,°   *lifted up, singing, always*
And with honour of greet processioun°   *procession*
They carien° hym unto the nexte abbay.°   *carry, nearest monastery*
625 His mooder swownynge° by his beere° lay.   *fainting, bier*
Unnethe° myghte the peple° that was theere   *scarcely, people*
This newe Rachel[1] brynge° fro° his beere!   *bring, from*

WITH torment and with shameful deeth° echon,°   *death, each one*
This provost dooth° the Jewes for to sterve,°   *causes, die*
630 That of this mordre wiste° and that anon.   *knew*
He nolde no swich cursednesse observe.°   *allow such villainy*
Yvele° shal° he have that yvele wol° deserve!   *evil, shall, will*
Therfore with wilde hors° he dide hem drawe,°   *horses, caused them to be dragged*
And after that he heng° hem° by° the lawe.   *hung, them, according to*

635 UPON this beere° ay° lith° this innocent   *bier, ever, lies*
Biforn° the chief auter° whil° the masse laste.°   *before, altar, while, mass lasted*
And after that the abbot with his covent°   *group of monks*
Han sped hem° for to burien hym° ful faste.°   *have hurried, bury him, very fast*
And whan they hooly° water on hym caste,°   *holy, cast*
640 Yet spak° this child whan spreynd° was hooly water   *spoke, sprinkled*
And song° O alma redemptoris mater.   *sang*

THIS abbot, which that was an hooly man,
As monkes been° or elles° oghte be,°   *are, else, ought to be*
This yonge child to conjure he bigan°   *began to call upon*
645 And seyde, "O deere child, I halsen°[2] thee   *ask*
In vertu° of the Hooly Trinitee,°   *power, Holy Trinity*
Tel me what is thy cause for to synge,
Sith that thy throte is kut to my semynge."°   *as it seems to me*

"MY throte is kut unto my nekke boon,"°   *neckbone*
650 Seyde this child, "and as by wey° of kynde°   *way, nature*
I sholde have dyed, ye,° longe tyme agon.°   *yes, ago*
But Jhesu Crist, as ye in bookes fynde,
Wil° that his glorie laste and be in mynde.°   *wishes, remembered*
And for the worshipe of his mooder deere,
655 Yet may I synge O alma loude and cleere.

---

1 The reference is to Matthew 2:18, which quotes Jeremiah 31:15. Rachel, according to Matthew, is a
   metaphor for the Jewish mothers who have lost their children when Herod had them slaughtered.
2 Many editors emend to the standard singular form, "halse," but both Ellesmere and Hengwrt
   read "halsen."

THIS welle° of mercy, Cristes mooder sweete   *well (source)*
I loved alwey,° as after my konnynge.°   *always, according to my knowledge*
And whan that I my lyf sholde forlete,°   *should have lost*
To me she cam and bad° me for to synge   *commanded*
660 This anthephen° verraily° in my deyynge,°   *antiphon, truly, dying*
Me thoughte° she leyde° a greyn° upon my tonge.°   *I thought, laid, grain, tongue*

Wherfore° I synge, and synge I moot,° certeyn,°   *therefore, must, certainly*
In honour of that blisful° mayden free,°   *blessed, noble maiden*
665 Til fro° my tonge of taken° is the greyn.   *from, taken off*
And afterward thus seyde she to me:
'My litel child, now wol° I fecche thee°   *will, fetch you*
Whan that the greyn is fro thy tonge ytake.°   *taken*
Be nat agast.° I wol thee nat forsake!'"°   *afraid, will not forsake you*

670 THIS hooly monk, this abbot, hym meene I,°   *I mean him*
His tonge out caughte° and took awey the greyn,   *pulled out*
And he yaf° up the goost° ful softely.°   *gave, spirit, very quietly*
And whan this abbot hadde this wonder seyn,°   *seen this marvel*
Hise salte teeris trikled doun as reyn,[1]
675 And gruf he fil al plat° upon the grounde,   *on his face fell flat*
And stille° he lay as he had leyn° ybounde.°   *quietly, lain, bound*

The covent° eek lay on the pavement,   *group of monks*
Wepynge and herying° Cristes mooder deere.   *MS heryen, praising*
And after that they ryse° and forth been went°   *rise, gone away*
680 And tooken awey this martir from his beere.
And in a temple of marbul° stones cleere°   *marble, clear*
Enclosen° they his litel body sweete.   *enclose*
Ther he is now, God leve° us alle for to meete!°   *allow, meet [him]*

O YONGE° Hugh of Lyncoln,[2] slayn° also   *young, killed*
685 With cursed Jewes, as it is notable,°   *noteworthy*

---

1   "His salty tears trickled down as rain."
2   Hugh of Lincoln was a child supposedly murdered by Jews in 1255. He was one of the two
principal saints associated with Lincoln, a town midway up England's east coast. In 1386 Henry,
Earl of Derby (John of Gaunt's son by his first wife and the future Henry IV), became a mem-
ber of the fraternity of Lincoln cathedral, to which Edward III and John of Gaunt already
belonged. Chaucer's wife Philippa, who was a member of the household of John of Gaunt's
wife, Constance or Constanza of Castille, also became a member of the fraternity at the same
ceremony. Chaucer may have had a special interest in Hugh of Lincoln given this connection to
the cathedral's fraternity, although he was not a member of it himself.

For it is but a litel while ago,
Preye° eek for us, we synful folk unstable,   *pray*
That of his mercy God so merciable°   *merciful*
On us his grete mercy multiplie°   *multiply*
690 For reverence° of his mooder° Marie. Amen.   *honor, mother*

HEERE IS ENDED THE PRIORESSES TALE

— rise up and kill the Jews...

She is facinated by boy living and she overlooks over the racial attitudes...
anti semetic attitude?
@ time — normal tale

she is fascinated by bad living
and is oblivious over the social
attitudes...
on + semantic attitudes?
② true – natural form

THE NUN'S PRIEST'S PROLOGUE AND TALE

Opening page of *The Nun's Priest's Tale*. Ellesmere Manuscript EL 26 C9 f. 179r. Reprinted by permission of The Huntington Library.

THE NUN'S PRIEST'S PROLOGUE

HEERE STYNTETH THE KNYGHT THE MONK OF HIS TALE[1]

THE PROLOGE OF THE NONNES PREESTES TALE

"Hoo,"° quod the Knyght, "good sire, namoore° of° this! *Whoa, no more, MS omits of*
That ye han seyd is right ynough, ywis,[2]
And muchel moore,° for litel hevynesse° *much more, a little heaviness*
2770 Is right ynough to muche folk,° I gesse.° *many people, guess*
I seye for me it is a greet disese,° *great discomfort*
Whereas° men han been in greet welthe° and ese,° *where, wealth, ease*
To heeren° of hire sodeyn fal,° allas! *hear, their sudden fall*
And the contrarie° is joye and greet solas,° *contrary, comfort*
2775 As whan a man hath° been in povre estaat° *has, poor condition*
And clymbeth° up and wexeth fortunat° *climbs, grows fortunate*
And there abideth° in prosperitee.° *remains, prosperity*
Swich thyng is gladsom,° as it thynketh me,° *pleasant, as I think*
And of swich° thyng were goodly for to telle." *such*
2780 "YE," quod oure Hoost, "by Seint Poules belle,[3]
Ye seye right sooth.° This Monk, he clappeth lowde.° *truth, clatters loudly*
He spak how Fortune covered with a clowde°[4] *cloud*
I NOOT nevere° what. And also of a tragedie *do not know*
Right now ye herde,° and, pardee,° no remedie° *heard, by God, remedy*
2785 It is for to biwaille° ne° compleyne° *lament, nor, lament*
That that is doon,° and als° it is a peyne,° *That which is done, also, pain*
As ye han seyd,° to heere° of hevynesse.° *have said, hear, sadness*
SIRE Monk, namoore of this, so God yow blesse!
Youre tale anoyeth° al this compaignye. *annoys*
2790 Swich talkyng is nat° worth a boterflye!° *not, butterfly*
For therinne is ther no desport° ne° game. *sport, nor*
WHERFORE,° sire Monk, Daun Piers° by youre name, *therefore, Peter*
I pray yow hertely° telle us somwhat elles.° *heartily, something else*
For sikerly, nere° clynkyng° of youre belles *were it not for, clinking*
2795 That on youre bridel° hange on every syde, *bridle*
By Hevene Kyng° that for us alle dyde,° *the King of Heaven, died*
I sholde° er° this han fallen doun for sleepe, *should, before*
Althogh the slough° had never been so deepe. *mud*
Thanne hadde youre tale al be toold in veyn.° *vain*

---

1   "Here the Knight stops the Monk [telling] his tale."
2   "What you have said is quite enough, indeed."
3   The bell of St. Paul's Cathedral in London.
4   The Host appears to echo line 2677, the last line of the Monk's tale of Croesus, which in some
    manuscripts is the last tale the Monk tells.

2800 For certeinly, as that thise clerkes seyn,°   *these scholars say*
    Whereas° a man may have noon° audience,   *where, no*
    Noght helpeth it° to tellen his sentence.°   *It is of no use, meaning*
    And wel I woot, the substance is in me
    If anythyng shal wel reported be.[1]
2805 Sire, sey° somwhat of huntyng, I yow preye."   *tell us*
    "NAY," quod this Monk, "I have no lust° to pleye.°   *desire, play*
    Now lat° another telle as I have toold."   *let*
    THANNE spak oure Hoost with rude speche° and boold°   *rough speech, bold*
    And seyde unto the Nonnes Preest anon,
2810 "Com neer, thou Preest. Com hyder,° thou sire John![2]   *here*
    Telle us swich thyng as may oure hertes glade.°   *gladden*
    Be blithe,° though thou ryde upon a jade.°   *happy, bad horse*
    What thogh thyn hors be bothe foul and lene?°   *lean*
    If he wol serve thee, rekke nat a bene!°   *do not care a bean*
2815 Looke that thyn herte be murie° everemo."°   *merry, ever more*
    "YIS sire," quod he, "yis, Hoost, so moot I go.°   *as I may go*
    But° I be myrie, ywis,° I wol be blamed."   *unless, indeed*
    And right anon° his tale he hath attamed,°   *right away, has begun*
    And thus he seyde unto us everichon,°   *everyone*
2820 This sweete preest, this goodly man, sire John.

EXPLICIT[3]

THE NUN'S PRIEST'S TALE

HEERE BIGYNNETH THE NONNES PREESTES TALE OF THE COK
AND HEN, CHAUNTECLEER AND PERTELOTE

    A POVRE° wydwe° somdeel° stape° in age   *poor, widow, somewhat, advanced*
    Was whilom° dwellyng° in a narwe° cotage°   *once, living, small, cottage*
    Biside a grene[4] stondynge° in a dale.°   *standing, valley*
    This wydwe of which I telle yow my tale,
2825 Syn° thilke day that she was last a wyf   *since*

---

1 Either "I have the stuff (*substance*) in me [i.e., the power] to understand if a story is well told" or possibly "If a story is well told, I know when I have grasped the core (*substance*) of it."
2 The Host addresses the Nun's Priest with the familiar "thou," not the polite "you" that he uses for the Knight, the Monk, or most of the other gentle folk.
3 "Here it ends."
4 Hengwrt and modern editions read "grove" for Ellesmere's "grene." A "green" was a common area in a village used for pasturage or other agricultural pursuits not demanding the plowing of the green into a field. Villages also had woods in common, where peasants would drive their pigs in autumn to forage for acorns; this is the meaning of Hengwrt's "grove."

In pacience ladde° a ful° symple lyf.   *led, very*

For litel° was hir catel° and hir rente.°   *little, possessions, income*

By housbondrie° of swich° as God hire sente   *careful use, such*

She foond hirself and eek hir doghtren two.[1]

2830 Thre° large sowes° hadde she and namo,°   *three, pigs, no more*

Thre keen° and eek° a sheepe° that highte° Malle.   *cows, also, sheep, was named*

Ful sooty was hir bour° and eek hir halle°   *bedroom, hall*

In which she eet° ful many a sklendre meel.°   *ate, meager meal*

Of poynaunt° sauce hir neded never a deel.°   *spicy, she had no need*

2835 No deyntee° morsel passed thurgh hir throte.°   *dainty, through her throat*

Hir diete° was accordant to hir cote.°   *diet, in accord with her cottage*

Repleccioun° ne made hire nevere sik.   *eating too much*

Attempree diete° was al hir phisik°   *temperate diet, her medical remedy*

And excercise and hertes suffisaunce.°   *heart's content*

2840 The goute lette hire nothyng for to daunce,[2]

N'apoplexie shente nat hir heed.°   *nor stroke harmed not her head*

No wyn ne drank she, neither whit ne reed.

Hir bord° was served moost with whit and blak—   *table*

Milk and broun breed, in which she foond no lak,[3]

2845 Seynd bacoun° and somtyme an ey° or tweye.°   *smoked bacon, egg, two*

For she was, as it were, a maner deye.°   *a kind of dairy farmer*

A YEERD° she hadde enclosed al aboute   *yard*

With stikkes and a drye dych°[4] withoute,°   *dry ditch, outside of it*

In which she hadde a cok° heet° Chauntecleer.[5]   *rooster, named*

2850 In al the land of crowyng° nas° his peer.°   *crowing, was not, equal*

His voys° was murier° than the murie orgon°   *voice, merrier, organ*

On messedayes that in the chirche gon.[6]

Wel sikerer° was his crowing in his logge°   *more reliable, dwelling*

Than is a clokke or an abbey orlogge.°   *monastery clock*

2855 By nature he crew° ech ascencioun°   *crowed, each ascension*

Of the equynoxial[7] in thilke° toun.   *that same*

For whan degrees fiftene° weren° ascended,   *fifteen, were*

---

1   "She provided for herself and also her two daughters."

2   "The gout [a disease affecting the feet and brought on by over-eating or drinking] by no means hindered her from dancing."

3   "Lak" can mean either defect or lack, so either "In which she found no fault" or "of which she had no shortage."

4   A dry ditch contrasts with a moat, found at castles, which was normally filled with water.

5   Chauntecleer ("clear singer") is the name of the rooster in the *Romance of Renard*, which tells the adventures of a wily fox and contains one of the best known medieval versions of the story told by the Nun's Priest.

6   "That go [i.e., are played] in Church on Sundays." The organ, an instrument of many pipes, was considered grammatically plural.

7   The sense of this passage is that Chauntecleer crows when each hourly point of the celestial equator rises past the horizon.

Thanne crew he that it myghte nat been amended.°   might not be improved
His coomb° was redder than the fyn° coral   coxcomb, fine
2860 And batailled° as it were a castel wal.°¹   crenallated, castle's wall
His byle° was blak, and as the jeet it shoon.°   bill, jet (precious stone) shone
Lyk asure° were his legges and his toon.°   azure (blue gem), toes
Hise nayles° whitter° than the lylye flour°   nails, whiter, lily flower
And lyk the burned° gold was his colour.   polished
2865 This gentil cok° hadde in his governaunce°   noble rooster, control
Sevene hennes° for to doon° al his plesaunce,°   hens, do, pleasure
Whiche were hise sustres° and his paramours°   his sisters, lovers
And wonder lyk° to hym as of colours,   marvelously similar
Of whiche the faireste hewed° on hir throte°   colored, her throat
2870 Was cleped° faire damoysele° Pertelote.²   called, damsel
Curteys° she was, discreet,° and debonaire°   courteous, discreet
And compaignable,° and bar hyrself so faire°   gracious, friendly, behaved so well
Syn thilke day that she was seven nyght oold,°   nights old
That trewely, she hath the herte in hoold°   holds the heart
2875 Of Chauntecleer, loken° in every lith.°   locked, limb
He loved hire so, that wel was hym therwith.°   it made him all well
And swich a joye was it to here hem synge,
Whan that the brighte sonne bigan to sprynge,°   began to rise
In sweete accord,° "My Lief is Faren in Londe."³   harmony
2880 For thilke tyme,° as I have understonde,°   [at] that time, understood
Beestes° and briddes° koude speke and synge.   beasts, birds
AND so bifel° that in the dawenynge,°   it happened, at dawn
As Chauntecleer among hise wyves alle
Sat on his perche° that was in the halle   perch
2885 And next hym sat this faire Pertelote,
This Chauntecleer gan gronen° in his throte   began to groan
As man that in his dreem is drecched soore.°   sorely disturbed
AND whan that Pertelote thus herde hym roore,°   roar
She was agast° and seyde, "O herte deere,°   afraid, dear heart
2890 What eyleth° yow to grone in this manere?°   ails, manner
Ye been a verray slepere.° Fy!° For shame!"   are a good sleeper, Fie
AND he answerde and seyde thus: "Madame,
I pray° yow that ye take it nat agrief.°   beg, take it not wrong
By God, me thoughte° I was in swich meschief°   I thought, such trouble
2895 Right now, that yet myn herte is soore afright.°   sorely afraid

---

1   The crenelation on a castle's walls is the alternation of high, squared masonry with blank spaces.
    This would provide cover for the archers defending the castle against the arrows of the attackers.
2   Pertelote is described as a damsel, as if she were a heroine in a courtly romance.
3   "My dear one has traveled into [a foreign] land." This is the title of a popular song, one version
    of which has survived in a manuscript in Trinity College, Cambridge of c. 1500.

Now God," quod he, "me swevene recche aright[1]
And kepe° my body out of foul prisoun!°   *keep, prison*
Me mette° how that I romed° up and doun°   *I dreamed, roamed, down*
Withinnne oure yeerd, wheereas° I saugh° a beest   *where, saw*
2900 Was lyk an hound and wolde han maad areest°   *have captured*
Upon my body and han had me deed!°   *have had me dead*
His colour was bitwixe yelow and reed,
And tipped was his tayl° and bothe hise eeris,°   *tail, his ears*
With blak unlyk° the remenant of hise heeris,°   *unlike, his hairs*
2905 His snowte smal° with glowynge eyen tweye.°   *small nose, two glowing eyes*
Yet of his look, for feere° almoost° I deye.°   *fear, almost, die*
This caused me my gronyng, doutelees."°   *doubtless*
"*Avoy!*"° quod she. "Fy° on yow, hertelees!°   *Shame, Fie, coward*
Allas," quod she, "for by that God above,
2910 Now han ye lost myn herte and al my love.
I kan nat love a coward, by my faith!
For certes, whatso° any womman seith,   *whatever*
We alle desiren, if it myghte bee,°   *might be*
To han housbondes hardy,° wise, and free,°   *brave, and generous*
2915 And secree° and no nygard° ne° no fool,   *discreet, cheapskate, nor*
Ne hym that is agast° of every tool,°   *afraid, weapon*
Ne noon avauntour,° by that God above.   *nor any braggart*
How dorste° ye seyn, for shame, unto youre love   *dare*
That anythyng myghte make yow aferd?°   *afraid*
2920 Have ye no mannes herte,° and han° a berd?°[2]   *man's heart, have, beard*
ALLAS, and konne ye been agast° of swevenys?°   *be afraid, dreams*
Nothyng, God woot,° but vanitee° in swevene° is!   *knows, foolishness, [a] dream*
Swevenes engendren of replecciouns°   *are caused by overeating*
And ofte of fume° and of complecciouns[3]   *[stomach-] gas*
2925 Whan humours been to habundant in a wight.[4]
CERTES, this dreem which ye han met° tonyght   *have dreamed*
Cometh of greet superfluytee°   *great excess*
Of youre rede colera, pardee,[5]
Which causeth folk to dreden° in hir dremes   *fear*
2930 Of arwes° and of fyr° with rede lemes,°   *arrows, fire, red flames*
Of grete beestes that they wol hem byte,°   *will bite them*

---

1   "'Now God,' he said, 'interpret my dream correctly.'"
2   Pertelote describes Chauntecleer as if he were a mature man (and not a beardless youth), but as a rooster he also has wattles.
3   The "complexions" mentioned here are the four humors of medieval medical theory. They caused the four temperaments, or bodily types. If they were unbalanced, disease would result.
4   "When humors are too abundant in a person."
5   "Of your red choler, by God." Choler was one of the four bodily humours. The red choler was formed of yellow bile, which was hot and dry.

Of contek° and of whelpes grete and lyte.°   *conflict, large and small dogs*
Right as° the humour° of malencolie°¹   *just as, humor, melancholy*
Causeth ful many a man in sleepe to crie
2935 For feere of blake beres° or boles° blake   *black bears, bulls*
Or elles blake develes wole hem take.°   *devils will seize them*
Of othere humours koude I telle also
That werken° many a man in sleepe ful wo.°   *cause, much woe*
But I wol passe° as lightly as I kan.   *pass over*
2940 Lo Catoun,°² which that was so wys° a man,   *Cato, wise*
Seyde he nat thus: 'Ne do no fors of dremes'?³
Now sire," quod she, "whan ye flee fro° the bemes,°   *fly from, beams*
For Goddes love, as taak som laxatyf!°   *take some laxative*
Up peril° of my soule and of my lyf,   *upon peril*
2945 I conseille° yow the beste—I wol nat lye°—   *counsel, not lie*
That bothe of colere° and of malencolye°   *choler, melancholy*
Ye purge yow,° and for ye shal nat tarie,°   *purge yourself, so you do not delay*
Though in this toun is noon apothecarie,°   *no pharmacist*
I shal myself to herbes techen yow,°   *teach you about herbs*
2950 That shul been for youre heele° and for youre prow.°   *health, profit*
And in oure yeerd° tho herbes° shal I fynde,   *yard, those herbs*
The whiche han of hire propretee° by kynde°   *their property, nature*
To purge yow bynethe° and eek above.°   *beneath, also above*
Foryet nat this, for Goddes owene love!
2955 Ye been ful coleryk of compleccioun.°   *choleric of complexion*
Ware the sonne in his ascencioun
Ne fynde yow nat repleet of humours hoote.⁴
And if it do, I dar wel leye a grote°   *bet a groat (four pence)*
That ye shul° have a fevere terciane°⁵   *shall, tertian fever*
2960 Or an agu° that may be youre bane.°   *ague (fever), your cause of death*
A day or two ye shul have digestyves°   *stomach medicines*
Of wormes,° er ye take youre laxatyves   *worms*
Of lawriol,° centaure,° and fumetere°   *laurel, centaury, fumaria (all herbs)*
Or elles of ellebor,° that groweth there,   *hellebore (herb)*
2965 Of katapuce° or of gaitrys° beryis.   *euphorbia, rhamus (herbs)*

---

1   "Melancholy" was another of the four humors. It was formed of black bile, which was cold and dry.
2   The Roman Dionysius Cato was believed in the Middle Ages to be the author of a widely circulating collection of proverbs which was often used to teach basic Latin grammar.
3   "Said he not this: 'Do not pay attention to dreams'?"
4   "Beware that the sun when it is climbing [and therefore astrologically most powerful] does not find you when you are [already] full of hot humors." The movements of the planets affected a patient's balance of humors.
5   Medieval people classified the types of fevers they would contract by how frequently they recurred. This one would return every "third" day—meaning every other day, in which the first day is counted, as is the non-fever day and the recurring-fever day. The disease is possibly malaria.

Of herbe yve,° growyng in oure yeerd ther mery is.°[1] *herb-ivy, where it is merry*
Pekke hem up right as they growe, and ete hem yn.° *eat them up*
Be myrie, housbonde, for youre fader kyn!° *father's kin*
Dredeth no dreem. I kan sey yow namoore."
2970 "MADAME," quod he, "*graunt mercy* of youre loore!°[2] *advice*
But nathelees,° as touchyng° Daun Catoun,° *nevertheless, pertaining to, Master Cato*
That hath of wysdom swich a greet renoun,° *fame*
Though that he bad no dremes for to drede,° *fear*
By God, men may in olde bookes rede
2975 Of many a man moore of auctorite
Than evere Caton was, so moot I thee,° *so might I thrive*
That al the revers seyn of this sentence° *say completely the opposite meaning*
That han wel founden° by experience, *have found out well*
That dremes been significacrouns° *dreams are signs*
2980 As wel of joye as of tribulaciouns° *troubles*
That folk enduren° in this lif present. *endure*
Ther nedeth make° of this noon° argument. *needs to make, no*
The verray preeve° sheweth° it in dede.° *experience itself, shows, deed*
OON of the gretteste auctour°[3] that men rede *authors*
2985 Seith thus: that whilom° two felawes wente *once*
On pilgrimage in a ful good entente,° *with a very good intention*
And happed so° they coomen in a toun, *so it happened*
Wheras° ther was swich congregacioun° *where, such a gathering*
Of peple and eek so streit of herbergage,° *such a shortage of lodging*
2990 That they ne founde as muche as o cotage° *one cottage*
In which they bothe myghte logged bee.° *might be lodged*
Wherfore° they mosten of necessitee *for which reason*
As for that nyght departen compaignye.° *part company*
And ech of hem gooth° to his hostelrye° *each of them goes, lodging*
2995 And took his loggyng° as it wolde falle.° *lodging, would happen*
That oon of hem was logged in a stalle° *stall*
Fer° in a yeerd, with oxen of the plough. *far*
That oother man was logged wel ynough,
As was his aventure° or his fortune, *chance*
3000 That us governeth° alle as in commune.° *governs, in common*
AND so bifel° that, longe er° it were day, *it happened, long before*

---

1 While Pertelote's general diagnosis is in keeping with medieval medical theory, her remedies are extreme. Taken together, they would not only purge Chauntecleer violently, but endanger his life.

2 "Graunt mercy" from French "grand merci" or "much thanks." Chauntecleer, as an aristocrat, draws on French phrases.

3 The Roman orator and writer Cicero (106–43 BC) tells the story in *On Divination* and it is also found in the *Memorable Deeds and Sayings* of Valerius Maximus (see Wife of Bath's Prologue, line 460). There is a Latin gloss in the margin "Note [that this is about] dreaming."

This man mette in his bed theras° he lay,[1]   *where*
How that his felawe gan upon hym calle°   *began to call to him*
And seyde, 'Allas, for in an oxes stalle
3005 This nyght I shal be mordred ther I lye!°   *murdered where I lie*
Now helpe me, deere brother, or I dye.
In alle haste com to me,' he sayde.
THIS man out of his sleepe for feere abrayde,°   *woke up*
But whan that he was wakened of his sleepe,
3010 He turned hym° and took of it no keepe.°   *turned him over, notice*
Hym thoughte° his dreem nas° but a vanitee.°   *It seemed to him, was not, folly*
Thus twies° in his slepyng dremed hee,   *twice*
And atte thridde tyme° yet his felawe   *at the third time*
Cam as hym thoughte and seide, 'I am now slawe.°   *slain*
3015 Bihoold° my bloody woundes depe and wyde.   *behold*
Arys° up erly° in the morwe tyde,°   *arise, early, morning time*
And at the west gate of the toun,' quod he,
'A carte ful of donge° ther shaltow se°   *dung, shall you see*
In which my body is hid ful prively.°   *hidden very secretly*
3020 Do thilke carte arresten boldely.[2]
My gold caused my mordre, sooth to sayn,'°   *true to say*
And tolde hym every point° how he was slayn   *detail*
With a ful pitous° face, pale of hewe.°   *very pitiful, color*
And truste wel, his dreem he foond ful trewe.°   *very true*
3025 For on the morwe, as soone as it was day,
To his felawes in° he took the way,   *friend's inn*
And whan that he cam to this oxes stalle,
After his felawe he bigan to calle.
THE hostiler° answerde hym anon   *innkeeper*
3030 And seyde, 'Sire, youre felawe is agon.°   *gone*
As soone as day he wente out of the toun.'
THIS man gan fallen in suspecioun,°   *began to be suspicious*
Remembrynge on hise dremes that he mette.°   *dreamed*
And forth he gooth—no lenger° wolde he lette°—   *longer, would he delay*
3035 Unto the west gate of the toun and fond°   *found*
A dong-carte, as it were to donge lond°   *to manure a field*
That was arrayed in that same wise°   *way*
As ye han herd the dede man devyse.°   *describe*
And with an hardy herte° he gan to crye,°   *bold heart, began to cry*
3040 'Vengeance and justice of this felonye!°   *crime*
My felawe mordred is this same nyght,
And in this carte heere° he lith,° gapyng upright.°   *here, lies, on his back*

---

1 A roughly contemporaneous hand has written "i. [e.] dremed" above the word "mette."
2 "Cause that cart to be seized boldly."

I crye out on the ministres,'° quod he,   *magistrates*
'That sholden kepe° and reulen° this citee!   *care for, rule*
3045 Harrow! Allas!¹ Heere lith my felawe slayn!'
What sholde I moore unto this tale sayn?°   *about this story*
The peple out sterte° and caste° the cart to grounde,   *jumped up, threw*
And in the myddel of the dong they founde
The dede man that mordred was al newe.°   *was recently murdered*
3050 O BLISFUL° God that art so just and trewe,²   *blessed*
Lo how that thou biwreyest° mordre alway!°   *reveal, always*
Mordre wol out.° That se° we day by day.   *will [be found] out, see*
Mordre is so wlatsom° and abhomynable°   *repulsive, abominable*
To God that is so just and resonable,°   *reasonable*
3055 That he ne wol nat suffre° it heled° be,   *will not allow, concealed*
Though it abyde° a yeer or two or thre.   *wait*
Mordre wol out! This my conclusioun.
And right anon,° ministres° of that toun   *just then, magistrates*
Han hent° the cartere and so soore° hym pyned°   *arrested, sorely, tortured*
3060 And eek the hostiler so soore engyned,°   *tortured on a rack*
That they biknewe hire wikkednesse° anon   *confessed their wickedness*
And were anhanged° by the nekke bon.°   *hanged, neckbone*
HEERE may men seen that dremes been to drede.°   *are to be feared*
And certes,° in the same book I rede,   *certainly*
3065 Right in the nexte chapitre after this³—
I gabbe° nat, so have I joye or blis°—   *babble, bliss*
TWO men that wolde han° passed over see°   *would have, sea*
For certeyn° cause into a fer contree,°   *a certain, distant country*
If that the wynd ne hadde been contrarie,°   *had not been contrary*
3070 That made hem in a citee for to tarie°   *delay*
That stood ful myrie° upon an haven-syde.°   *very merrily, harborside*
But on a day agayn the eventyde,°   *towards evening*
The wynd gan chaunge° and blew right as hem leste.° *changed, blew just as they wanted*
Jolif° and glad, they wente unto hir reste°   *jolly, their rest*
3075 And casten hem ful erly for to saille.°   *decided to sail very early*
BUT herkneth: to that o man fil a greet mervaille,⁴
That oon of hem in slepyng as he lay

---

1 "Harrow and allas" were words used to call for help in emergencies.
2 There is a Latin gloss in the margin: "Auctor," implying that the scribe considers this Chaucer's
   own moral judgment or perhaps simply a particularly useful moral.
3 There is a Latin gloss in the margin at line 3065: "Here [there is more] about dreams," but nei-
   ther Cicero's *On Divination* nor the *Memorable Deeds and Sayings* of Valerius Maximus have more
   information in the following chapter. Chaucer may have been drawing on some other source
   that itself drew on Cicero or Valerius. Alternatively, Chauntecleer may have lost his reference
   and be deceiving Pertelote by making one up.
4 "But listen! To one man happened a great marvel."

Hym mette° a wonder dreem agayn the day.°   *dreamed, toward daybreak*
Hym thoughte° a man stood by his beddes syde   *It seemed to him*
3080 And hym comanded that he sholde abyde°   *should wait*
And seyde hym thus: 'If thou tomorwe wende,°   *go*
Thow shalt be dreynt.° My tale is at an ende.'   *drowned*
HE wook° and tolde his felawe what he mette   *woke*
And preyde hym his viage to lette.°   *begged him to delay his voyage*
3085 As for that day he preyde hym to byde.°   *to wait*
HIS felawe, that lay by his beddes syde,
Gan° for to laughe and scorned hym° ful faste.°   *began, mocked him, very much*
'No dreem,' quod he, 'may so myn herte agaste°   *frighten*
That I wol lette° for to do my thynges.°   *will delay, business*
3090 I sette nat a straw by thy dremynges!
For swevenes° been° but vanytees° and japes.°   *dreams, be, nonsense, tricks*
Men dreme al day of owles° or of apes,   *owls*
And of many a maze° therwithal.°   *delusion, with it all*
Men dreme of thyng° that nevere was ne shal.°   *[a] thing, nor shall [be]*
3095 But sith° I see that thou wolt heere abyde,°   *since, will wait here*
And thus forslewthen wilfully thy tyde,°   *willfully waste your time*
God woot,° it reweth me!° And have good day!'   *God knows, I regret it*
And thus he took his leve° and wente his way.   *leave*
But er° that he hadde° half his cours° yseyled,°   *before, had, course, sailed*
3100 Noot I nat° why ne° what myschaunce it eyled,°   *I do not know, nor, went wrong (ailed)*
But casuelly° the shippes botme° rente,°   *by chance, bottom, split*
And shipe and man under the water wente
In sighte of othere shippes it bisyde°   *beside it*
That with hem seyled° at the same tyde.°   *sailed with them, tide*
3105 And therfore, faire Pertelote, so deere,
By swiche ensamples° olde yet maistow leere°   *such examples, may you learn*
That no man sholde been to recchelees°   *should be too careless*
Of dremes. For I seye thee doutelees°   *say to you doubtless*
That many a dreem ful soore is for to drede!°   *to be feared*
3110 Lo in the *Lyf of Seint Kenelm*[1] I rede,
That was Kenulphus sone,° the noble kyng   *Cenwulf's son*
Of Mercenrike,° how Kenelm mette° a thyng°   *Mercia, MS Mertenrike, dreamed, something*
A lite er° he was mordred° on a day.   *little before, murdered*
His mordre in his avysioun° he say.°   *vision, saw*
3115 His norice° hym expowned every deel°   *nurse, explained every part to him*
His swevene and bad° hym for to kepe hym° weel   *commanded, protect himself*
For traisoun.° But he nas° but sevene° yeer oold,   *from treason, was only, MS vij*

---

1   This is a saint's life, or biography, of Kenelm (Cenhelm), a seven-year-old Anglo-Saxon king of Mercia, who was murdered at the command of his aunt. There is a Latin gloss in the margin: "Of the dream of Saint Kenelm."

And therfore litel tale hath he toold°   *paid little attention*
Of any dreem, so hooly° is his herte.   *holy*
3120 By God, I hadde levere than my sherte
That ye hadde rad his Legende as have I,[1]
Dame Pertelote! I sey yow trewely,
Macrobeus, that writ° the avisioun°   *who wrote, dream*
In Affrike° of the worthy Cipioun,°[2]   *Africa, Scipio*
3125 Affermeth° dremes and seith that they been   *affirms [the validity of]*
Warnynge of thynges that men after seen.°   *see afterwards*
AND forthermoore, I pray yow, looketh wel°[3]   *look well*
In the Olde Testament of Daniel,[4]
If he heeld dremes° any vanitee.°   *considered dreams, folly*
3130 REED eek of Joseph, and ther shul ye see
Wher dremes be somtyme—I sey nat alle°—   *not always*
Warnynge of thynges that shul after falle.°   *shall happen later*
LOOKE of Egipte° the kyng Daun Pharao,°   *Egypt, Lord Pharaoh*
His bakere° and his butiller° also,   *baker, butler*
3135 Wher° they ne felte noon° effect in dremes.   *whether, did not feel any*
Whoso wol seken° actes of sondry remes°   *whoever will seek, various realms*
May rede of dremes many a wonder thyng.
Lo Cresus,°[5] which that was of Lyde kyng,   *Croesus*
Mette he nat° that he sat upon a tree,   *did he not dream*
3140 Which signified he sholde anhanged bee?°   *should be hanged*
Lo heere Adromacha,° Ectores wyf,°   *Andromacha, Hector's wife*
That day that Ector sholde lese his lyf°   *lose his life*
She dremed on the same nyght biforn°   *the night before*
How that the lyf of Ector sholde be lorn°   *lost*
3145 If thilke° day he wente into bataille.   *that*

---

1 "I would rather (*levere*) that you had read this saint's life than that I had my shirt" or as we might
  say, "I'd give my shirt to have you read it."
2 The Roman writer Macrobius (c. 400 AD) wrote a *Commentary* on part of Cicero's *Republic*
  called *The Dream of Scipio*. This book tells how Scipio Africanus Minor, a Roman consul,
  dreamed of meeting his famous ancestor, Scipio Africanus Major (so called because he defeated
  Hannibal, the great general of Carthage, North Africa) and urged him to pursue virtue for the
  sake of reward in a future life. Chauntecleer misinterprets his name, assuming the dream hap-
  pened in Africa.
3 There is a Latin gloss in the margin: "Here for [more information on] dreams."
4 Both Daniel and Joseph, mentioned below, were famous for their ability to interpret dreams.
  Daniel interpreted the dream of King Nebuchadnezzar to predict that the king would be ban-
  ished for seven years. See Daniel 4. Joseph interpreted his own dream to predict that he would
  be lord over his brothers, interpreted the dreams of Pharaoh's butler and his baker to predict that
  the former would be restored to office but the latter hanged, and interpreted Pharaoh's dream
  to predict that Egypt would have seven years of good harvest followed by seven years of famine.
  See Genesis 37:5–11; 40:1–23; 41:1–32.
5 The Monk had mentioned the dream of Croesus, the fabulously rich king of Lydia who was
  conquered by King Cyrus of Persia, in the previous Tale.

She warned hym, but it myghte nat availle.°   *could not help*
He wente for to fighte natheles,°   *nevertheless*
But he was slayn anon of Achilles.[1]
But thilke is al to longe° for to telle,   *too long*
3150 And eek it is ny° day. I may nat dwelle.°   *near, not delay*
Shortly I seye as for conclusioun°   *conclusion*
That I shal han° of this avisioun°   *shall have, vision*
Adversitee.° And I seye forthermoor°   *adversity, furthermore*
That I ne telle of laxatyves no stoor!°   *do not rely on laxatives*
3155 For they been venymes!° I woot it weel!°   *venomous, know it well*
I hem diffye!° I love hem never a deel!°   *I reject them, not at all*
Now lat us speke of myrthe° and stynte al this.°   *mirth, be silent about*
Madame Pertelote, so have I blis,°   *happiness*
Of o thyng° God hath° sent me large grace.°   *one thing, has, great favor*
3160 For whan I se° the beautee of youre face—   *see*
Ye been° so scarlet reed° aboute youre eyen°—   *are, red, eyes*
It maketh° al my drede° for to dyen.°   *makes, fear, die*
For also siker° as *In principio*,[2]   *as certain*
Mulier est hominis confusio.[3]
3165 MADAME, the sentence° of this Latyn° is,   *meaning, Latin*
'Womman is mannes joye and al his blis.'°   *happiness*
For whan I feele anyght° youre softe syde—   *at night*
Albeit that I may nat on yow ryde,°   *although, ride on you*
For that° oure perche is maad° so narwe,° allas!—   *because, made, narrow*
3170 I am so ful of joye and of solas°   *comfort*
That I diffye° bothe swevene and dreem!"[4]   *defy*
And with that word he fly° doun fro the beem,°   *flew, beam*
For it was day, and eek hise hennes alle,°   *also [so did] all his hens*
And with a "chuk" he gan hem for to calle,°   *began to call for them*
3175 For he hadde founde a corn lay° in the yerd.   *kernel that lay*
Real° he was. He was namoore aferd,   *regal*
And fethered Pertelote twenty tyme
And trad as ofte er it was pryme.[5]

---

1   The narrative of the Trojan war recounted by Dares Phrygius, one of the standard versions of
    the story in the Middle Ages, includes the story of the dream of Hector's wife. Homer's *Iliad*,
    which was not well known in western Europe in the Middle Ages, does not include the episode.
2   The Latin words *In principio* begin both the book of Genesis and the gospel of John. Chauntecleer
    is saying, roughly, "As certain as is the Bible."
3   "Woman is the confusion of man."
4   Chauntecleer appears to distinguish between two kinds of dream here, but it is not clear what
    the difference is. Medieval dream theory distinguished between prophetic dreams and those
    that were merely the result of indigestion, but the terms "swevene" and "dreme" (and also
    "mete") cover both.
5   "He covered Pertelote with his feathers twenty times and copulated with her as often before it
    was the hour of prime" (prime is an hour for prayer in the early morning).

	He looketh as it were° a grym leoun,°	*as if he were, fierce lion*
3180	And on hise toos° he rometh° up and doun.	*his toes, roams*
	Hym deigned nat to sette his foot to grounde.¹	
	He chukketh° whan he hath a corn yfounde,	*clucks*
	And to hym rennen thanne° hise wyves alle.	*run then*
	Thus roial° as a prince is in an halle°	*regal, hall*
3185	Leve° I this Chauntecleer in his pasture,	*leave*
	And after wol I telle his aventure.°	*adventure*
	WHAN that the monthe in which the world bigan,	
	That highte° March, whan God first maked° man,²	*is named, made*
	Was compleet° and passed were also	*complete*
3190	Syn° March bigan thritty dayes and two,°³	*since, thirty-two days*
	Bifel° that Chauntecleer in al his pryde,°	*it happened, pride*
	Hise sevene wyves walkynge by his syde,	
	Caste up hise eyen° to the brighte sonne,	*looked up*
	That in the signe° of Taurus hadde yronne°	*[zodiac] sign, run*
3195	Twenty degrees and oon° and somwhat moore,	*twenty-one degrees*
	And knew by kynde° and by noon oother loore°	*nature, no other teaching*
	That it was pryme,° and crew° with blisful stevene.°	*9 a.m., crowed, voice*
	"The sonne," he seyde, "is clomben upon hevene	
	Fourty degrees and oon° and moore,° ywis.	*one, more*
3200	Madame Pertelote, my worldes blis,°	*worldly happiness*
	Herkneth thise blisful briddes,° how they synge,	*Listen to these happy birds*
	And se° the fresshe floures, how they sprynge.°	*see, bloom*
	Ful is myn herte of revel° and solas."°	*amusement, enjoyment*
	But sodeynly hym fil° a sorweful cas,°	*befell, event*
3205	For evere the latter ende° of joye is wo.°	*last end, woe*
	God woot° that worldly joye is soone ago!°	*God knows, soon gone*
	And if a rethor° koude faire endite,°	*rhetorician, write well*
	He in a cronycle° saufly° myghte it write	*chronicle, safely*
	As for a sovereyn notabilitee.°⁴	*very notable thing*
3210	Now every wys man, lat hym herkne me.°	*listen [to] me*
	This storie is also trewe,° I undertake,°	*as true, I swear*

---

1   "It did not seem fitting to him to set his foot on the ground."

2   According to various medieval authorities, including Saint Basil and the English monastic writer Bede, God created the world at the spring equinox.

3   The phrasing is ambiguous but the events seem to take place on 3 May, when all of March and a further thirty-two days had passed. This date is in keeping with the position of the sun in the sky and the other astrological information, which is accurate "almost to the minute," according to the calculations reported by Skeat. 3 May was considered an unlucky day and is also the day on which Palamon escapes from prison in the Knight's Tale (line 1462).

4   A Latin gloss in the margin notes, "Peter Comestor." The same gloss appears in Hengwrt and in some other manuscripts. The theologian Peter Comestor (c. 1100–78) was famous for his *Scholastic History* and other works of Biblical scholarship, but the reference has not been traced. Derek Pearsall, in the *Variorum* edition, suggests this is no better than "a hopeful shot by a literal-minded scribe" at which "cronycle" might contain the platitude of line 3205.

As is *The Book of Launcelot de Lake*,[1]
That wommen holde in ful greet reverence.°   *respect*
Now wol I come agayn to my sentence.°   *purpose*
3215 A COLFOX° ful of sly iniquitee,°   *fox with black feet, ears, and tail, malice*
That in the grove hadde woned yeeres three,°   *had lived three years*
By heigh ymaginacioun forncast,[2]
The same nyght thurghout° the hegges° brast°   *through, hedge, burst*
Into the yerd ther° Chauntecleer the faire   *where*
3220 Was wont° and eek° hise wyves to repaire,°   *accustomed, also, to retire*
And in a bed of wortes° stille° he lay,   *herbs, quietly*
Til it was passed undren° of the day,   *dawn*
Waitynge his tyme° on Chauntecleer to falle,   *watching for his opportunity*
As gladly doon° thise homycides alle°   *do, all these murderers*
3225 That in await liggen° to mordre men.   *lie in wait*
O false mordrour, lurkynge° in thy den!   *lurking*
O newe Scariot,° newe Genylon!°   *[Judas] Iscariot, Ganelon*
False dissymulour,° o Greek Synon,°[3]   *liar, Sinon*
That broghtest° Troye al outrely° to sorwe!   *brought, utterly*
3230 O Chauntecleer, acursed° be that morwe   *cursed*
That thou into that yerd flaugh fro the bemes!
Thou were ful wel ywarned° by thy dremes   *warned*
That thilke day° was perilous° to thee   *that same day, dangerous*
But what that God forwoot,° moot nedes bee,°   *foreknows, must necessarily be*
3235 After° the opinioun of certein clerkis.°   *according, scholars*
Witnesse on hym that any parfit clerk is,[4]
That in scole° is greet altercacioun°   *the universities, debate*
In this mateere° and greet disputisoun,°   *matter, dispute*
And hath been of an hundred thousand men.[5]

---

1   This is the title of any one of a number of Arthurian romances that recount the adventures of
    Sir Lancelot, including his love affair with Guinevere. The story was popular with the English
    gentry and aristocracy, but was regarded by many as immoral fiction. Dante describes two lovers
    on the outer edges of Hell, Paolo and Francesca, who are damned because of an affair they began
    while reading some version of this story (*Inferno*, canto 5).

2   The phrase can be roughly translated as "foreseen by exalted imagination," but the exact mean-
    ing is disputed. Many editors take it to refer to the mind or conception ("imaginacioun")
    of God, which foresees all events. Others take "imaginacioun" as a reference, expressed in
    deliberately and ridiculously grandiose language, to Chauntecleer's dream, or as a reference to
    the plotting of the fox. In each case, the word "forncast" introduces the theme of predestination
    discussed in lines 3234–51.

3   Judas Iscariot betrayed Christ in the gospels by identifying him to the Roman soldiers who came
    to arrest him; Ganelon betrayed Roland in *The Song of Roland*, with a plot that led to his death in
    the pass at Roncesvalles; and Sinon betrayed Troy in *The Iliad* by suggesting the Greeks conceal
    themselves in a wooden horse to gain access to the city.

4   "As any fully qualified scholar can testify."

5   The question of how God's foreknowledge could be reconciled with human free will was al-
    ways important in medieval theology, but the debate flared up in Chaucer's day. The radical
    theologian John Wycliffe (d. 1384), best known for initiating the translation of the Bible into

3240 But I ne kan nat bulte it to the bren[1]
     As kan the hooly doctour Augustyn°   *holy teacher Augustine*
     Or Boece or the Bisshope Bradwardyn[2]—
     Wheither° that Goddes worthy forwityng°   *whether, foreknowledge*
     Streyneth° me nedefully° to doon a thyng.   *constrains, necessarily*
3245 "Nedely" clepe° I symple necessitee°   *call, simple necessity*
     Or elles,° if free choys° be graunted me°   *else, choice, granted to me*
     To do that same thyng or do it noght,
     Though God forwoot° it er° that it was wroght,°   *foreknows, before, done*
     Or if his wityng° streyneth° never a deel°   *knowing, constrains, not at all*
3250 But by necessitee condicioneel.°[3]   *conditional necessity*
     I wol nat han to do of swich mateere.°   *not have to do with such matter*
     My tale is of a cok, as ye may heere,
     That took his conseil of his wyf with sorwe
     To walken in the yerd upon that morwe
3255 That he hadde met° that dreem that I of tolde.   *dreamed*
     Wommennes conseils been ful ofte colde.°   *bad*
     Wommannes conseil broghte us first to wo
     And made Adam out of Paradys to go,
     Theras° he was ful myrie° and wel at ese.°   *where, merry, well at ease*
3260 But for I noot° to whom it myghte displese,   *since I do not know*
     If I conseil of wommen wolde blame,
     Passe° over, for I seye° it in my game.°   *pass, say, in jest*
     Rede auctours° where they trete° of swich mateere,   *authors, treat*
     And what they seyn of wommen ye may heere.
3265 Thise been the cokkes wordes and nat myne!
     I kan noon harm of no womman divyne.[4]

English, argued that God's omniscience gave him absolute knowledge of who would be saved or damned. For Wycliffe, this meant that there was no justification for the institutions of the earthly church or for penitential practices such as confession or pilgrimage.

1   "But I cannot separate [the kernels] from the bran." That is, the Nun's Priest cannot sort out the issues in the debate about God's foreknowledge.

2   The great Church Father St. Augustine (354–430 AD), the late Roman scholar Boethius (d. 524 AD), and Thomas Bradwardine, chancellor of Oxford and very briefly archbishop of Canterbury (who died in the Black Death in 1349), all wrote about the concept of predestination. Although stressing God's omniscience, all three are thoroughly orthodox in their insistence that humans have free will.

3   Boethius distinguishes between simple necessity and conditional necessity in his *Consolation of Philosophy* Book 5, prose 6, and then draws on God's status outside time to resolve the theological dilemma. To use Boethius's example, that a man must die is a matter of simple necessity. But if you know someone is walking, while he must then necessarily be walking, the necessity is only conditional, i.e., it depends on the condition of the man having decided to take a walk. From your perspective, he could have chosen not to do so. "God sees those future events which happen of free will as present events; so that these things when considered with reference to God's sight of them do happen necessarily as a result of the condition of divine knowledge; but when considered in themselves they do not lose the absolute freedom of their nature" (trans. Victor Watts in the Penguin edition).

4   "I can imagine nothing wrong of women."

FAIRE in the soond° to bathe hire° myrily   *sand, herself*
Lith° Pertelote and alle hire sustres by°   *lies, nearby*
Agayn the sonne.° And Chauntecleer so free   *in the sunshine*
3270 Soong murier° than the mermayde° in the see.   *sang more merrily, mermaid*
For *Phisiologus*[1] seith sikerly°   *surely*
How that they syngen wel and myrily.
AND so bifel° that as he caste his eye   *it happened*
Among the wortes° on a boterflye,°   *herbs, butterfly*
3275 He was war° of this fox that lay ful lowe.°   *aware, very low*
Nothyng ne liste hym thanne for to crowe,[2]
But cride anon,° "Cok! Cok!" and up he sterte°   *cried immediately, jumped*
As man that was affrayed in his herte.
For natureelly a beest desireth flee°   *wants to escape*
3280 Fro his contrarie° if he may it see,   *enemy*
Though he never erst hadde seyn° it with his eye.   *never before had seen*
THIS Chauntecleer, whan he gan hym espye,°   *spotted him*
He wolde han fled but that the fox anon
Seyde, "Gentil sire,° allas, wher wol ye gon?°   *noble sir, where will you go*
3285 Be ye affrayed of me, that am youre freend?
Now certes, I were worse than a feend°   *fiend*
If I to yow wolde° harm or vileynye!°   *intended, villainy*
I am nat come youre conseil for t'espye.°   *to spy on your counsel*
But trewely, the cause of my comynge
3290 Was oonly for to herkne° how that ye synge.   *listen*
For trewely, ye have as myrie a stevene°   *voice*
As any aungel that is in Hevene.
Therwith° ye han° in musyk° moore feelynge°   *with it, have, music, feeling*
Than hadde Boece°[3] or any that kan synge.   *Boethius*
3295 My lord, youre fader, God his soule blese,
And eek youre mooder of hire gentillesse°   *her courtesy*
Han in myn hous ybeen° to my greet ese.°   *been, great ease*
And certes, sire, ful fayn wolde I yow plese.[4]
BUT for men speke of syngyng, I wol yow seye—
3300 So moote° I brouke wel° myne eyen tweye°[5]—   *might, use well, my two eyes*
Save yow,° herde I nevere man yet synge   *apart from yourself*

---

1   "Physiologus" was the supposed author of a bestiary, a book explaining the allegorical significances of various animals. According to this work, mermaids use their sweet singing to lure sailors to their deaths.

2   "He did by no means want then to crow."

3   Boethius not only wrote *The Consolation of Philosophy*, which Chaucer translated, but also wrote the basic university textbook used in the Middle Ages about music.

4   "And certainly, sir, very gladly would I please you."

5   "So may I enjoy the use of my eyes" is a common expression, meaning little more than "indeed," but it is ill suited for musical appreciation. The Ellesmere scribe, Adam Pinkhurst, has repeated this line and then crossed it out.

As dide youre fader in the morwenynge.
Certes, it was of herte al° that he song!°   *from the heart, sang*
And for to make his voys the moore strong,°   *stronger*
3305 He wolde so peyne hym° that with bothe hise eyen°   *take pains, his eyes*
He moste wynke°—so loude° he wolde cryen—   *had to wink, loudly*
And stonden on his tip-toonz° therwithal°   *tiptoes, in doing so*
And strecche forth his nekke long and smal.°   *slender*
And eek he was of swich discrecioun°   *such discernment*
3310 That ther nas no man in no regioun°   *was no one in any region*
That hym in song or wisedom myghte passe.°   *surpass*
I have wel rad° in *Daun Burnel the Asse*[1]   *read*
Among hise vers,° how that ther was a cok,   *verses*
For that° a preestes sone° yaf° hym a knok   *because, priest's son, gave*
3315 Upon his leg whil he was yong and nyce,°   *silly*
He made° hym for to lese° his benefice.   *caused, lose*
But certeyn, ther nys no comparisoun°   *is no comparison*
Bitwixe the wisedom and discrecioun
Of youre fader and of his subtiltee.°   *cleverness*
3320 Now syngeth, sire, for seinte charitee!°   *holy charity*
Lat se,° konne ye youre fader countrefete?"°   *Let us see, imitate*
THIS Chauntecleer hise wynges gan° to bete°   *began, beat*
As man that koude his traysoun° nat espie,°   *treason, not see*
So was he ravysshed° with his flaterie.°   *ravished, flattery*
3325 ALLAS, ye lordes, many a fals flatour°   *false flatterer*
Is in youre courtes° and many a losengeour°   *courts, flatterer*
That plesen° yow wel moore, by my feith,   *please*
Than he that soothfastnesse° unto yow seith.   *truth*
Redeth Ecclesiaste[2] of flaterye.°   *about flattery*
3330 Beth war,° ye lordes, of hir trecherye!°   *Beware, their treachery*
THIS Chauntecleer stood hye° upon his toos,°   *high, toes*
Strecchynge his nekke, and heeld° his eyen cloos°   *held, eyes closed*
And gan to crowe loude for the nones.°   *for the occasion*
And Daun Russell the fox stirte up atones°   *jumped up at once*
3335 And by the gargat° hente° Chauntecleer   *throat, grabbed*
And on his bak° toward the wode° hym beer,°   *back, woods, carried him*
For yet ne was ther no man that hym sewed.[3]

---

1 This is the title of a twelfth-century Latin satire by Nigel Wireker about a foolish donkey, Master Brunellus, who becomes a wandering scholar. The episode described below concerns a young man who was about to be ordained and to receive a benefice. The cock that he had hurt took its revenge by not crowing so that the man overslept.

2 Ecclesiasticus 12:16 warns against deceptive enemies but does not specifically mention flattery. The reference might be a mistake for Proverbs 29:5, another book of the Bible that was attributed to King Solomon, and so might be confused with Ecclesiasticus. Chaucer quotes Proverbs 29:5 in his *Tale of Melibee*.

3 "Because so far there was no one who pursued him."

O DESTINEE, that mayst nat been eschewed!°   *may not be avoided*
Allas, that Chauntecleer fleigh fro the bemes!°   *from the beams*
3340 Allas, his wyf ne roghte nat° of dremes!   *paid no attention*
And on a Friday fil° al this meschaunce!°   *happened, misfortune*
O VENUS, that art goddesse of plesaunce,°¹   *pleasure*
Syn° that thy servant was this Chauntecleer   *since*
And in thy servyce dide al his poweer°   *all he could*
3345 Moore for delit° than world to multiplye,°   *delight, increase the world (procreate)*
Why woldestow suffre hym° on thy day to dye?°²   *would you allow him, die*
O GAUFRED,°³ deere maister soverayn,°   *Geoffrey, sovereign teacher*
That whan thy worthy kyng Richard was slayn
With shot,° compleynedest° his deeth so soore,°   *arrow, lamented, sorely*
3350 Why ne hadde I now thy sentence° and thy loore°   *meaning, learning*
The Friday for to chide as diden ye?
For on a Friday soothly° slayn was he.   *truly*
Thanne wolde I shewe° yow how that I koude pleyne°   *show, could lament*
For Chauntecleres drede° and for his peyne!°   *fear, pain*
3355 CERTES swich cry ne lamentacioun
Was nevere of ladyes° maad° whan Ylioun°   *ladies, made, Troy*
Was wonne,° and Pirrus° with his streite swerd,°   *conquered, Pyrrhus, drawn sword*
Whan he hadde hent° Kyng Priam by the berd°   *seized, beard*
And slayn hym, as seith us *Eneydos*,°   *[Virgil's] Aeneid*
3360 As maden alle the hennes in the clos°   *yard*
Whan they had seyn° of Chauntecleer the sighte.   *seen*
But sodeynly Dame Pertelote shrighte°   *shrieked*
Ful louder° than dide Hasdrubales⁴ wyf   *much louder*
Whan that hir housbonde hadde lost his lyf
3365 And that the Romayns hadde brend Cartage.°   *burned Carthage*
She was so ful of torment and of rage
That wilfully° into the fyr° she sterte°   *voluntarily, fire, jumped*
And brende° hirselven with a stedefast herte.   *burned*
O WOFUL hennes, right so criden ye,°   *just so you cried*

---

1   In classical mythology, Venus was the goddess of love.

2   According to medieval astrology, each of the planets had special influence on a given day of the
    week. Venus, who gives her name to Friday (*Veneris dies*) in Romance languages, controlled that
    day, which is named after the Germanic goddess Freya in English.

3   This is Geoffrey of Vinsauf, whose treatise, *Poetria Nova*, a basic manual on how to write rhe-
    torically elaborate poetry, Chaucer alludes to in the following lines. King Richard is Richard I,
    the Lion-hearted, who in 1199 was wounded on a Friday while besieging a castle and later died
    of his wound.

4   Hasdrubales was the king of Carthage in the second century BC. He was defeated by Scipio
    Africanus, the grandfather of the man whose dream Cicero had related, mentioned by the Nun's
    Priest above, in line 3123–24. The fate of Hasdrubales' wife is also mentioned in the Franklin's
    Tale (lines 1399–1404), where it is taken from Jerome's *Against Jovinian*.

3370 As, whan that Nero¹ brende the citee
    Of Rome, cryden senatours wyves,
    For that hir housbondes losten alle hir lyves.
    Withouten gilt° this Nero hath hem slayn.   *although they were not guilty*
    Now turne I wole to my tale agayn.
3375 THIS sely wydwe° and eek hir doghtres two   *innocent widow*
    Herden° thise hennes crie° and maken wo,°   *heard, cry, woe*
    And out at dores stirten° they anon°   *jumped, immediately*
    And syen° the fox toward the grove gon°   *see, go*
    And bar upon his bak the cok away,
3380 And cryden, "Out! Harrow!" and "Weylaway!"²
    Ha! Ha! The fox!" And after hym they ran.
    And eek with staves° many another man   *clubs*
    Ran Colle oure dogge and Talbot and Gerland³
    And Malkyn with a dystaf° in hir° hand.   *spinning staff, her*
3385 Ran cow and calf and the verray hogges,°   *even the hogs*
    So fered° for berkyng° of the dogges   *afraid, barking*
    And shoutyng of the men and wommen eek.
    They° ronne so hem thoughte hir herte° breek.°   *MS The, their heart, break*
    They yolleden° as feendes° doon in Helle.   *yelled, fiends*
3390 The dokes° cryden° as men wolde hem quelle.°   *ducks, cried, kill them*
    The gees° for feere° flowen° over the trees.   *geese, fear, follow*
    Out of the hyve° cam° the swarm of bees.   *hive, came*
    So hydous° was the noyse, a, benedicitee,°   *hideous, ah bless you*
    Certes he Jakke Straw and his meynee°   *gang*
3395 Ne made nevere shoutes half so shrille,°⁴   *shrill*
    Whan that they wolden any Flemyng° kille,   *Fleming*
    As thilke day was maad° upon the fox.   *made*
    Of bras they broghten bemes and of box,
    Of horn, of boon, in whiche they blewe and powped,⁵
3400 And therwithal° they skriked° and they howped.°   *with this, shrieked, whooped*
    It semed as that Hevene sholde falle.
    Now, goode men, I prey yow, herkneth alle.
    Lo how Fortune turneth sodeynly°   *suddenly turns*
    The hope and pryde° of hir enemy.   *pride*

---

1   Nero is the emperor of Rome who had his city burned while he stood by, according to Suetonius,
    playing the bagpipes. The Monk, in the previous Tale, narrates his tragedy.
2   These words were used to call up help in an emergency.
3   These were typical names for dogs.
4   Ellesmere reads "shille." The emendation is from Hengwrt. Jack Straw was the name of one of
    the leaders of the Peasants' Revolt of 1381; about thirty or forty Flemish merchants and weavers
    were murdered in London during this period of violence and rioting. This is one of the few
    "current events" Chaucer mentions directly in his writings.
5   "They brought trumpets ['bemes'] made of brass and boxwood/And of horn and of bone."

3405 This cok that lay upon the foxes bak,
     In al his drede° unto the fox he spak   *fear*
     And seyde, "Sire, if that I were as ye,
     Yet wolde I seyn, as wys God helpe me,
     'Turneth agayn,° ye proude cherles° alle!   *turn again, peasants*
3410 A verray pestilence upon yow falle!°   *true plague fall upon you*
     Now I am come unto the wodes syde.°   *the border of the woods*
     Maugree youre heed, the cok shal heere abyde.¹
     I wol hym ete,° in feith, and that anon!'"   *will eat him*
     THE fox answerde, "In feith, it shal be don!"
3415 And as he spak that word al sodeynly,°   *suddenly*
     This cok brak° from his mouth delyverly°   *broke, quickly*
     And heighe upon a tree he fleigh anon.
     And whan the fox saugh that he was gon,
     "ALLAS!" quod he. "O Chauntecleer, allas!
3420 I have to yow," quod he, "ydoon trespas,°   *done a wrong*
     In as muche as I maked° yow aferd°   *made, afraid*
     Whan I yow hente° and broghte into this yerd.²   *seized*
     But sire, I dide it of no wikke entente.
     Com doun, and I shal telle yow what I mente.
3425 I shal seye sooth to yow,° God help me so!"   *tell you truth*
     "NAY, thanne," quod he, "I shrewe° us bothe two!   *curse*
     And first I shrewe myself, bothe blood and bones,
     If thou bigyle° me any ofter than ones!°   *trick, once*
     Thou shalt namoore thurgh thy flaterye
3430 Do° me to synge and wynke° with myn eye!   *cause me, wink*
     For he that wynketh whan he sholde see°   *should see*
     Al wilfully,°³ God lat hym nevere thee!"°   *voluntarily, let him never thrive*
     "NAY," quod the fox, "but God yeve hym meschaunce°   *give him misfortune*
     That is so undiscreet° of governaunce°   *indiscreet, behavior*
3435 That jangleth° whan he sholde holde his pees!"°   *chatters, peace*
     LO, swich° it is for to be recchelees°   *such, reckless*
     And necligent° and truste on flaterye!   *negligent*
     BUT ye that holden° this tale a folye°   *consider, folly*
     As of a fox or of a cok and hen,
3440 Taketh the moralite,° goode men.   *moral*

---

1 "Despite anything you can do, the rooster will remain here."
2 Both Hengwrt and Ellesmere have "into this yerd." This seems an obvious slip and many other
   manuscripts have the easier reading "out of" which has been adopted by most editors. Derek
   Pearsall, however, in the *Variorum* edition, defends "into" by suggesting that the fox is still try-
   ing to deceive Chauntecleer and so refers to the place they have come to as "this yerd," as if it
   were the kind of safe enclosure to which the rooster was accustomed.
3 "For he that winks willfully when he should see...."

For Seint Paul seith that al that writen is,
To oure doctrine° it is ywrite,° ywis.°[1]   *teaching, written, indeed*
Taketh the fruyt,° and lat the chaf be stille.°   *fruit, let the chaff alone*
Now, goode God, if that it be thy wille,
3445 As seith my lord,[2] so make us alle goode men,
And brynge us to his heighe blisse. Amen!

HEERE IS ENDED THE NONNES PREESTES TALE

[THE NUN'S PRIEST'S EPILOGUE][3]

"SIRE Nonnes Preest," oure Hoost seide anoon,
"Iblissed° be thy breche° and every ston!°   *blessed, buttocks, testicles*
This was a murie tale of Chauntecleer.
But by my trouthe, if thou were seculer°   *a lay man*
Thow woldest ben a tredefoul° aright.   *copulator with chickens*
For if thou have corage° as thou hast myght°   *spirit, power*
The were nede of hennes° as I wene,°   *You would need hens, think*
Ya,° moo° than sevene tymes seventene!   *Yes, more*
Se° which braunes° hath this gentil° preest   *see, muscle, fine*
So gret a nekke and swich a large breest.°   *chest*
He loketh as a sparhauke° with hise eyen   *sparrowhawk*
Him nedeth nat his colour° for to dyghen°   *complexion, dye*
With brasile ne with greyn of Portyngale[4]
Now sire, faire falle yow° for your tale."   *may good befall you*
And after that he with ful merie chere
Seide unto another as ye shuln heere.°[5]   *hear*

---

1 Romans 15:4. Chaucer cites the same lines in his Retraction and it is also paraphrased at the beginning of the medieval translation and allegorical interpretation of Ovid's *Metamorphoses*, the *Ovide Moralisé*.

2 A Latin gloss in the margin in both Ellesmere and Hengwrt notes, "Namely the lord Archbishop of Canterbury," but whether this is really the lord in question is uncertain. The Nun's Priest might also be referring to Christ or, since he is attached to the nunnery at Stratford-at-Bow near London, to his immediate ecclesiastical superior, the bishop of London.

3 This epilogue is found in nine manuscripts but not in either Ellesmere or Hengwrt. It seems most likely that the epilogue is part of an earlier draft, which Chaucer abandoned, incorporating some of the lines into the Host's words to the Monk. This version is based on that in Cambridge University Library, MS Dd. 4.24.

4 "Brasile" was a red dye made from wood, which in the Middles Ages was imported from Malaya. Similar wood was found in the Portuguese territories in South America in 1499, and the territory is named after the wood. "Greyn of Portingale" was another red dye and was imported from Portugal.

5 Skeat in his edition judged this appeal to another of the pilgrims "so absurdly indefinite that it can hardly be genuine." He believed that the last three lines were "either spurious, or were jotted down temporarily, to await the time of revision."

THE PARSON'S PROLOGUE

THE PARSON'S PROLOGUE

By that the Maunciple hadde° his tale al ended,	*had*
The sonne fro the south lyne° was descended	*meridian*
So lowe, that he nas nat° to my sighte	*was not*
Degrees nyne and twenty as in highte.	
5 Four of the clokke it was tho, as I gesse,¹	
For ellevene foot or litel moore or lesse	
My shadwe° was at thilke tyme° as there,	*shadow, that time*
Of swiche feet as my lengthe parted° were	*divided*
In sixe feet equal of proporcioun.°	*proportion*
10 Therwith the moones exaltacioun—	
I meene° Libra²—alwey° gan ascende,°	*mean, always, ascended*
As we were entryng° at a thropes° ende.	*entering, village's*
For which oure Hoost, as he was wont to gye,°	*used to guide*
As in this caas° oure joly compaignye,	*situation*
15 Seyde in this wise: "Lordynges everichoon,°	*everyone*
Now lakketh us no tales mo than oon.°	*we lack no more tales than one*
Fulfilled° is my sentence and my decree.°³	*completed, proposal*
I trowe° that we han herd of° ech degree.°	*believe, heard from, each rank*
Almoost fulfild° is al myn ordinaunce.°	*complete, my plan*
20 I pray to God so yeve hym right good chaunce°	*good luck*
That telleth this tale to us lustily.°	*pleasantly*
Sire Preest," quod he, "artow a vicary°	*are you a vicar*
Or art a persoun?°⁴ Sey sooth,° by thy fey.°	*parson, tell the truth, faith*
Be what thou be,° ne breke° thou nat oure pley.°	*whatever you are, break, play*

---

1 Both Ellesmere and Hengwrt read "ten of the clokke," as do most other manuscripts, but the long shadows described in the following line, which say that a six-foot man would cast an eleven-foot shadow, make it clear that it is late afternoon, and the Host confirms this at line 72. One possible explanation for the error is that both the Roman numeral IV and the medieval Arabic numeral for 4, as it was written in the Middle Ages, might be easily mistaken for the Roman numeral X. Another problem with the astrological account here is that according to Chaucer's source for the astrological information, Nicholas of Lynne's *Kalendarium* of 1386, Libra would have just begun to ascend over the horizon at four o'clock on 16 or 17 April. This conflicts with the astrological situation described in the introduction to the Man of Law's Tale, which could only occur on 18 April.

2 The moon's exaltation (the sign of the zodiac in which it is most powerful) is not Libra but Taurus. Libra, who holds the scales of justice, is symbolically appropriate.

3 Some early editors believed this indicated that the pilgrims had already visited Canterbury and were on the return journey, but it is simpler to imagine that the Host has abandoned his original plan for each pilgrim to tell four tales.

4 A parson holds a benefice (a church and the tithes it brings in), whereas a vicar performs the duties for a fixed stipend, which was usually considerably less.

25 For every man save° thou hath toold his tale.   *except*
   Unbokele° and shewe° us what is in thy male.°   *unbuckle, show, pouch*
   For trewely,° me thynketh° by thy cheere,°   *truly, I think, expression*
   Thou sholdest knytte up° wel a greet mateere.°   *complete, great matter*
   Telle us a fable anon,° for cokkes bones!"[1]   *immediately*
30 THIS Persoun answerde al atones,°   *at once*
   "Thou getest° fable noon ytoold° for me!   *get, told*
   For Paul, that writeth unto Thymothee,°[2]   *Timothy*
   Repreveth hem° that weyven soothfastnesse°   *reproaches them, depart from truth*
   And tellen fables and swich wrecchednesse.°   *such wretchedness*
35 Why sholde I sown draf° out of my fest°   *sow chaff, fist*
   Whan I may sowen whete,° if that me lest?°   *wheat, if I please*
   For which I seye, if that yow list to heere,°   *you wish to hear*
   Moralitee and° vertuous mateere°   *MS ad, virtuous matter*
   And thanne that ye wol yeve° me audience,   *give*
40 I wol fayn° at Cristes reverence°   *gladly, honor*
   Do yow plesaunce leefful,° as I kan.   *give you lawful pleasure*
   But trusteth wel,° I am a southren° man.   *trust well, southern*
   I kan nat° geeste° 'rum, ram, ruf,'[3] by lettre.°   *cannot, tell a story, letter*
   No, God woot,° rym° holde I but litel bettre.°   *God knows, rhyme, little better*
45 And therfore, if yow list, I wol nat glose.°   *will not flatter*
   I wol yow telle a myrie tale in prose
   To knytte° up al this feeste° and make an ende.   *knit, feast*
   And Jhesu for his grace wit me sende
   To shewe° yow the way in this viage°   *show, journey*
50 Of thilke° parfit,° glorious pilgrymage   *that, perfect*
   That highte° Jerusalem celestial.°[4]   *is named, heavenly*
   And if ye vouchesauf,° anon° I shal   *promise, immediately*
   Bigynne upon my tale, for which I preye°   *ask*
   Telle youre avys.° I kan° no bettre° seye.°   *advice, can, better, say*
55 BUT nathelees,° this meditacioun,°[5]   *nevertheless, meditation*

---

1   "Cock's bones" is a euphemism for the blasphemous oath "God's bones."

2   Paul criticizes fables in 1 Timothy 1:4 and 4:7 and 2 Timothy 4:4. A Latin gloss in the margin notes "Paul to Timothy."

3   These words indicate that the Parson is not willing to produce poetry that alliterates, as was common in the west Midlands and northern England.

4   The heavenly Jerusalem is described in Revelation 21:2.

5   Strictly speaking, the Parson's Tale is neither a tale nor a sermon but a penitential manual. Like a modern technical manual, it is comprehensive but schematic. It covers the seven deadly sins and all the ways of overcoming them through penance, but offers few of the vivid examples or the exemplary stories that might be found in a sermon. Penitential manuals were originally intended to help priests hear confessions; they proliferated in the wake of the Fourth Lateran Council of 1215, which obliged all Christians, both men and women, no matter what their social rank, to confess their sins once a year. The penitential manuals, especially when translated

I putte° it ay° under correccioun   *put, ever*
Of clerkes,° for I am nat° textueel.°   *scholars, not, learned*
I take but sentence,° trusteth weel.°   *substance, trust [it] well*
Therfore I make a protestacioun°   *declaration*

into the vernacular, were also used by lay people to prepare themselves for confession and to probe their own consciences.

The Parson's Tale is ultimately based on two penitential manuals, both compiled by Dominican friars. The first was the *Summa de poenitentia et matrimonio* (*Summa on Penance and Marriage*), composed between 1225 and 1227 by Raymond of Pennaforte, who was the confessor of Pope Gregory IX. This provided the outer framework of the Parson's Tale: the discussion of penance and contrition (lines 80–315), of confession and the distinction between mortal and venial sin (lines 316–86), and of satisfaction (lines 1029–80). The second source, the *Summa de vitiis* or *Summa vitiorum* (*Summa on sins*, c. 1236) of William Peraldus, covers the seven deadly sins. The summa, such as the famous *Summa Theologicae* (*Summa of Theology*) by Thomas Aquinas, was a particular form of academic treatise widely used in the thirteenth century. Like medieval or modern encyclopedias, summas ("summaries" or "summations") offered a comprehensive treatment of a subject, but unlike the earlier medieval encyclopedias, they presented their material in an elaborate scholastic fashion, dividing it up into categories and sub-categories and often posing and then resolving hypothetical questions. The penitential summas of Pennaforte and Peraldus were widely copied and were frequently reworked, abridged or expanded, or translated into the vernacular. Although the sections of the Parson's Tale that are derived from Pennaforte's summa differ from it significantly, offering a more straightforward list of moral conclusions and omitting much of the academic debate, no intermediate versions—that is, versions that are significantly closer to the Parson's Tale in organization or phrasing than the original—have yet been discovered. In the case of Peraldus, however, three intermediate versions have been discovered. These three, all of which were compiled in England, are often identified by their opening words: *Quoniam* ("*Since*, as the wise man says, the sinner is ensnared ..."), *Primo* ("*First* one must see what sin is ..."), and *Postquam* ("*After* describing the diseases of the soul, that is the sins, we must add their remedies, the virtues). *Quoniam* is a reworking of Peraldus's *Summa de vitiis*, which arranges the sins in the same order they occur in the Parson's Tale; *Primo* is a further reworking of *Quoniam*; and *Postquam* (whose proper title is the *Summa virtutum de remediis anime*) supplements Peraldus's *Summa de vitiis* by adding an account of the seven remedial virtues that combat the seven deadly sins. None of the works that has been discovered, however, is a perfect match for the Parson's Tale. Chaucer may have worked independently, combining several of these various sources himself, as Siegfried Wenzel, Lee Patterson, and A.E. Hartung have argued. Alternatively, as Jill Mann suggests in her edition of 2005, he may have simply translated someone else's lost compilation, which may yet be discovered, as was the case with the source of the Second Nun's Tale.

Like its sources, the Parson's Tale is in large part composed of quotations, which come chiefly from the Bible, the Church Fathers, especially Jerome, Augustine, and Gregory, and later theologians. Many of these quotations are identified by Wenzel in his notes to the *Riverside Chaucer* and other publications, now conveniently gathered and supplemented by Mann in her edition. *Postquam* has been edited and translated by Wenzel; Pennaforte's summa is available in a modern edition (but not a translation), edited by Xaverius Ochoa and Aloisius Diez (Rome, 1976); Peraldus's *Summa de vitiis* is available in early modern editions, one of which has been reproduced in facsimile; *Quoniam* and *Primo* are still only available in manuscript, but Wenzel cites sections in "Chaucer's Seven Deadly Sins." Sections from Pennaforte, Peraldus, and analogues such as the Anglo-Norman *Compileison de seinte penance* are available with translations in *Sources and Analogues of the Canterbury Tales*, now available in a second edition.

60 That I wol stonde° to correccioun."°   *will stand, correction*
     UPON this word we han assented soone.°   *have soon agreed*
     For as us semed,° it was for to doone°   *seemed to us, ought to be done*
     To enden in som vertuous sentence°   *some virtuous doctrine*
     And for to yeve° hym space and audience°   *give, time and attention*
65 And bede° our Hoost he sholde to hym seye   *asked*
     That alle we to telle his tale hym preye.
     OURE Hoost hadde the wordes for us alle.
     "Sire Preest," quod he, "now faire yow bifalle!°   *may you have good luck*
     Sey what yow list, and we wol gladly heere."
70 And with that word he seyde in this manere:[1]
     "Telleth," quod he, "youre meditacioun.
     But hasteth yow.° The sonne wole adoun.°   *make haste, sun will [go] down*
     Beth fructuous,° and that in litel space.°   *be fruitful, little space [of time]*
     And to do wel, God sende yow his grace."

EXPLICIT PROHEMIUM[2]

---

1   In most editions, lines 69 and 70 are moved to the end so that line 70 refers not to the Host but to the Parson. The Ellesmere order, however, which is supported by Hengwrt and most other manuscripts, can be defended as giving the Host's afterthought, which ends—perhaps significantly—with the Host blessing the Parson.

2   "Here ends the Prologue."

CHAUCER'S RETRACTION

Chaucer's *Retraction*. Ellesmere Manuscript EL 26 C9 f. 232v. Reprinted by permission of The Huntington Library

CHAUCER'S RETRACTION

Now preye° I to hem° alle that herkne° this
litel° tretys°[1] or rede,° that if ther be anythyng in
it that liketh hem,° that therof they thanken oure
Lord Jhesu Crist, of whom procedeth al wit and al
goodnesse. And if ther be anythyng that displese
hem, I preye hem also that they arrette° it to the
defaute° of myn unkonnynge° and nat to my wyl,°
that wolde ful fayn° have seyd bettre, if I hadde
had konnynge.° For oure book seith, "Al that is
writen is writen for oure doctrine."°[2] And that is
myn entente.°

Wherfore I biseke° yow mekely° for the mercy
of God that ye preye° for me, that Crist have mercy
on me and foryeve° me my giltes,° and namely°
of my translacions and enditynges° of worldly
vanitees,° the whiche I revoke in my retracciouns—
as is *The Book of Troilus, The Book* also *of Fame,
The Book of the Five and Twenty Ladies,*[3] *The Book
of the Duchesse, The Book of Seint Valentynes Day of
the Parlement of Briddes,*° *The Tales of Caunterbury*
(thilke° that sownen into synne°), *The Book of the
Leoun,*[4] and many another book (if they were in
my remembrance) and many a song and many a
leccherous° lay°—that Crist for his grete mercy
foryeve° me the synne.°

But of the translacioun of Boece,° *De
Consolacioun*[5] and othere bookes of legendes of
seintes° and omelies° and moralitee and devocioun,

ask, them, listen to
little, treatise, read
pleases them

ascribe
default, my lack of skill, will
very gladly
ability
instruction
my intent

ask, meekly
pray
forgive, sins, especially
writings
acts of folly

Parliament of Fowls
those, tend towards sin

lecherous, song
forgive, sin

Boethius

moral stories of saints, homilies

---

1 The reference to the "little treatise" has provoked much discussion. The Parson's Tale, while far
from little, could rightly be classified as a treatise (indeed, the Parson calls it so himself at line
957), but this would be an odd term for the *Canterbury Tales* as a whole.

2 2 Timothy 3:16.

3 This must be the *Legend of Good Women*, which Chaucer allegedly wrote to make amends for
insulting women by writing the story of Criseyde's betrayal of Troilus. The surviving copies of
the *Legend of Good Women*, however, preserve only ten stories, although there are some contem-
porary references which suggest the work might once have included several more.

4 This text, probably a translation of the *Dit de Leon* by the French poet and composer Guillaume
de Machaut (c. 1300–77), one of Chaucer's major early influences, does not survive.

5 This is the famous treatise of the late Roman scholar and statesman, Boethius, *The Consolation
of Philosophy*.

that thanke I oure Lord Jhesu Crist and his blisful
mooder° and alle the seintes of Hevene, bisekynge   *mother*
hem° that they from hennes forth° unto my lyves°   *asking them, henceforth, life's*
ende sende me grace to biwayle° my giltes° and to   *lament, sins*
studie° to the salvacioun of my soule and graunte   *take thought*
me grace of verray° penitence, confessioun, and   *true*
satisfaccioun to doon° in this present lyf thurgh   *do*
the benigne° grace of hym that is Kyng of kynges   *kind*
and preest° over alle preestes, that boghte us with   *priest*
the precious blood of his herte,° so that I may been   *heart*
oon° of hem° at the Day of Doome° that shulle° be   *one, them, Judgment Day, shall*
saved. *Qui cum patre, etc.*[1]

HEERE IS ENDED THE BOOK OF THE TALES OF CAUNTERBURY
COMPILED BY GEFFREY CHAUCER,
OF WHOS SOULE JHESU CRIST HAVE MERCY,
AMEN.

---

1   The full liturgical phrase that Chaucer begins here is *Qui cum patre et spiritu sancto vivit et regnat
deus per omnia secula. Amen,* translated, "Who with the Father and the Holy Spirit lives and
reigns, God forever and ever, Amen."

APPENDIX: BACKGROUND DOCUMENTS

1. SAINT JEROME, *AGAINST JOVINIAN* (400)

[Saint Jerome (c. 347–c. 420 AD) was one of the most influential of the early Christian theologians, famous for his work on the translation of the Bible into Latin, and also for his asceticism. The monk Jovinian, who had apparently claimed that "a virgin was no better than a wife in the eyes of God," is known only through Jerome's response, *Against Jovinian*, excerpted below. Jerome's work was widely copied in the Middle Ages and often circulated with attacks on marriage or on women in general.]

41. I have offered enough examples of Christian chastity and of angel-like virginity from Holy Scripture. But because I realize that my opponent has challenged us in his commentaries with the worldly-wise claim that this mode of life has never met with the approval of the world, and that our faith has dreamt up a novel teaching that is contrary to nature, I will quickly run through the histories of the Greeks, the Romans, and the other nations, and I will show that virginity has always held the first place among the virtues.

46. Let me move now to Roman women; and I put Lucretia first, who, not wishing to outlive her violated chastity, removed the spot from her body with her own blood. Duillius, who was the first to celebrate a triumph at Rome for a naval battle, married the virgin Bilia, a woman so chaste that she was held up as an example even in that age, to which unchastity was not just a vice, but a monstrosity. When he was old and his body shook, he heard himself taunted during an argument for his bad breath and went home sad. And when he complained to his wife that she had never warned him, so that he could have corrected this failing, she said, "I would have, had I not thought that was how all men's breath smelled." A chaste and noble woman, to be praised for both, whether she did not know her husband's fault or just endured it patiently, and because her husband learned of that unpleasantness of his body through his enemy's nasty comment and not through his wife's revulsion. Certainly, a woman who marries a second husband cannot say what she said.

47. I know that I have included far more in this catalogue of women than the conventions of examples allow, and that I may be justly blamed by a learned reader. But what else can I do, when women these days will push the authority of St. Paul at me, and recite the rules about multiple marriage by heart before their first husband is even buried? If they despise the fidelity that Christian chastity dictates, maybe they will at least learn chastity from the pagans.

48. Socrates had two wives, Xanthippe, and Myron the granddaughter of Aristides. They were always bickering with each other, and he was accustomed to laugh at them because they fought over him—the ugliest man, with

ape's nostrils, a bald forehead, hairy shoulders, and bowlegs. In the end they turned their energy on him and persecuted him for a long time, punishing him and putting him to flight. Once, when he had stood up to Xanthippe as she poured out endless abuse from an upper story, she poured dirty water on him, and he responded with nothing further than wiping his head and saying, "I knew it was coming, I knew it would rain after a thunder like that."

★ ★ ★

"It is better," Solomon says, "to dwell in a wilderness than with a quarrelsome and passionate wife." Any man who has been married knows how rare it is to find a wife without these vices. Hence Various Geminus, the sublime orator, said it beautifully: "The man who does not quarrel is a bachelor." "It is better to dwell in a corner of the roof than with a wrangling wife in a common house." If a house that belongs to both husband and wife raises the wife into pride and makes her treat her husband roughly, how much more if the wife is the richer one, and the man stays in her house? She begins to be not a wife, but a landlady; and if her husband offends her, he must leave. "Continuous drippings drive a man out of his house on a winter day; so will a wrangling woman drive him from his own house." In truth, she makes his house leak with her constant bickerings and her daily chatter and expels him from his home, that is, from the church. And so in an earlier passage the same Solomon commands, "Son, do not let these things leak away." And the apostle says in Hebrews, "Therefore ought we more diligently to observe the things which are spoken, lest perhaps we should let them leak away."

[Ed. and trans. Ralph Hanna III and Traugott Lawler, *Jankyn's Book of Wikked Wyves: Volume 1: The Primary Texts* (Athens: U of Georgia P, 1997), 160, 172, 174, 176, 188.]

2. BOETHIUS, *THE CONSOLATION OF PHILOSOPHY* (524)

[Anicius Boethius (c. 480–524 AD) came from a noble Roman family and became a senior administrator for Theodoric, king of the Ostrogoths, who ruled the western half of the Roman empire. As the political situation shifted, Theodoric came to distrust Boethius, and had him imprisoned and eventually executed. In prison Boethius wrote a long dialogue, alternating between prose and verse, in which he describes how he was visited by a beautiful but stern lady—Philosophy—who consoled him for his apparent misfortunes. Chaucer translated the entire *Consolation* into prose and translated passages into verse which he inserted into his *Troilus and Criseyde*.]

Book 2, Prose 8

"But I don't want you to think that I am rigidly opposed to Fortune, for there are times when she stops deceiving and helps man. I mean when she reveals herself, when she throws off her disguise and admits her game. Perhaps you still don't understand what I'm saying. What I want to say is a paradox, and so I am hardly able to put it into words. For bad fortune, I think, is more use to a man than good fortune. Good fortune always seems to bring happiness, but deceives you with her smiles, whereas bad fortune is always truthful because by change she shows her true fickleness. Good fortune deceives, but bad fortune enlightens. With her display of specious riches good fortune enslaves the minds of those who enjoy her, while bad fortune gives men release through the recognition of how fragile a thing happiness is. And so you can see Fortune in one way capricious, wayward and ever inconstant, and in another way sober, prepared and made wise by the experience of her own adversity. And lastly, by her flattery good fortune lures men away from the path of true good, but adverse fortune frequently draws men back to their true good like a shepherdess with her crook. Do you think it is of small account that this harsh and terrible misfortune revealed those friends whose hearts are loyal to you? She has shown you the friends whose smiles were true smiles, and those whose smiles were false; in deserting you Fortune has taken her friends with her and left those who are really yours. Had you remained untouched and, as you thought, blessed by Fortune, you would have been unable to get such knowledge at any price. So you are weeping over lost riches when you have really found the most precious of all riches—friends who are true friends.

Meter 8

"The world in constant change
Maintains a harmony
And elements keep peace
Whose nature is to war.
The sun in car of gold
Draws forth the rosy day,
And evening brings her night
When Luna holds her sway.
The tides in limits fixed
Confine the greedy sea;
No waves shall overflow
The rolling field and lea.
And all this chain of things
In earth and sea and sky

One ruler holds in hand:
If Love relaxed the reins
All things that now keep peace
Would wage continual war
And wreck the great machine
Which unity maintains
With motions beautiful.
Love, too, holds peoples joined
By sacred bond of treaty,
And weaves the holy knot
Of marriage's pure love.
Love promulgates the laws
For friendship's faithful bond.
O happy race of men
If Love who rules the sky
Could rule your hearts as well!"

Book 3, Prose and Meter 9

"... Now turn your mind's eye in the opposite direction and you will immediately see the true happiness that I promised."

"Even a blind man could see it," I said, "and you revealed it just now when you were trying to show the causes of false happiness. For unless I'm mistaken, true and perfect happiness is that which makes a man self-sufficient, strong, worthy of respect, glorious and joyful. And to show you that I have more than a superficial understanding, without a shadow of a doubt I can see that happiness to be true happiness which, since they are all the same thing, can truly bestow any one of them."

"You are blessed in this belief, my child, provided you add one thing."

"What is that?"

"Do you think there is anything among these mortal and degenerate things which could confer such a state?"

"No, I don't, and you have proved it as well as anyone could wish."

"Clearly, therefore, these things offer man only shadows of the true good, or imperfect blessings, and cannot confer true and perfect good."

"Yes."

"Since then you have realized the nature of true happiness and seen its false limitations, what remains now is that you should see where to find this true happiness."

"Which is the very thing I have long and eagerly been waiting for."

"But since in the *Timaeus* my servant Plato was pleased to ask for divine help even over small matter, what do you think we ought to do now in order to be worthy of discovering the source of that supreme good?"

"We ought to pray to the Father of all things. To omit to do so would not be laying a proper foundation."

"Right," she said, and immediately began the following hymn.

[The poem that follows summarizes much of the first book of Plato's *Timaeus*, the only Platonic dialogue widely known during the Middle Ages, but also draws on later Neoplatonic writings—especially for the suggestion in lines 6–7 that God carries the idea or model of all creation in his mind.]

"O Thou who dost by everlasting reason rule,
Creator of the planets and the sky, who time
From timelessness dost bring, unchanging Mover,
No cause drove Thee to mould unstable matter, but
The form benign of highest good within Thee set.
All things Thou bringest forth from Thy high archetype:
Thou, height of beauty, in Thy mind the beauteous world
Dost bear, and in that ideal likeness shaping it,
Dost order perfect parts a perfect whole to frame.
The elements by harmony Thou dost constrain,
That hot to cold and wet to dry are equal made,
That fire grow not too light, or earth too fraught with weight.
The bridge of threefold nature mad'st Thou soul, which spreads
Through nature's limbs harmonious and all things moves.
The soul once cut, in circles two its motion joins,
Goes round and to itself returns encircling mind,
And turns in patterns similar the firmament.
From causes like Thou bringst forth souls and lesser lives,
Which from above in chariots swift Thou dost disperse
Through sky and earth, and by Thy law benign they turn
And back to Thee they come through fire that brings them home.
Grant, Father, that our minds Thy August seat may scan,
Grant us the sight of true good's source, and grant us light
That we may fix on Thee our mind's unblinded eye.
Disperse the clouds of earthly matter's cloying weight;
Shine out in all Thy glory; for Thou art rest and peace
To those who worship Thee; to see Thee is our end,
Who art our source and maker, lord and path and goal."

Book 3, Meter 12

"Happy the man whose eyes once could
Perceive the shining fount of good;

Happy he whose unchecked mind
Could leave the chains of earth behind.
Once when Orpheus sad did mourn
For his wife beyond death's bourn,
His tearful melody begun
Made the moveless trees to run,
Made the rivers halt their flow,
Made the lion, hind's fell foe,
Side by side with her to go,
Made the hare accept the hound
Subdued now by the music's sound.
But his passions unrepressed
Burned more fiercely in his breast;
Though his song all things subdued,
It could not calm its master's mood.
Complaining of the gods above,
Down to hell he went for love.
There on sweetly sounding strings
Songs that soothe he plays and sings;
All the draughts once drawn of song
From the springs the Muses throng,
All the strength of helpless grief,
And of love which doubled grief,
Give their weight then to his weeping,
As he stands the lords beseeching
Of the underworld for grace.
The triform porter stands amazed,
By Orpheus' singing tamed and dazed;
The Furies who avenge men's sin,
Who at the guilty's terror grin,
Let tears of sorrow from them steal;
No longer does the turning wheel
Ixion's head send whirling round;
Old Tantalus upon the sound
Forgets the water and his thirst,
And while the music is rehearsed
The vulture ceases flesh to shred.
At last the monarch of the dead
In tearful voice, 'We yield,' he said:
'Let him take with him his wife,
By song redeemed and brought to life.
But let him, too, this law obey,
Look not on her by the way

Until from night she reaches day.'
But who to love can give a law?
Love unto love itself is law.
Alas, close to the bounds of night
Orpheus backwards turned his sight
And looking lost her twice to fate.
For you the legends I relate,
You who seek the upward way
To life your mind into the day;
For who gives in and turns his eye
Back to darkness from the sky,
Loses while he looks below
All that up with him may go."

[Trans. Victor Watts, *Boethius: The Consolation of Philosophy*, 2nd ed. (Harmondsworth: Penguin, 1969), 44–46, 65–67, 82–84.]

3. THE TWELVE CONCLUSIONS OF THE LOLLARDS (1395)

[According to one contemporary chronicler, the Twelve Conclusions were nailed to the doors of Westminster Hall—the part of Westminster Abbey that was used for large meetings—during the session of Parliament of 1395; another source maintains that they were also nailed to the doors of St. Paul's Cathedral. They were preserved in an account written by one of the opponents of the Lollards, the Dominican friar Roger Dymmock, who included them (in both Latin and English versions) in a refutation *Liber contra duodecim errores et hereses Lollardorum* ("A Book Against the Twelve Errors of the Lollards"), which he presented to Richard II in 1397. Dymmock preserves both Latin and English versions of the conclusions, but the ones nailed up at Westminster were probably in English.]

We poor men, treasurers of Christ and his apostles, denounce [i.e., present as a denunciation] to the lords and commons of the Parliament certain conclusions and truths for the reformation of the Holy Church of England, which has been blind and leprous for many years because of the support of the proud prelacy [i.e., bishops and the system of ecclesiastical government], raised up by the flattering of private religion [i.e., monks, nuns, and all those whose vows cut them off from the community], which has multiplied and become a great and heavy burden on the people of England.

    When the church of England began to involve itself foolishly in temporal matters following the example of her stepmother, the great church of Rome, and churches were killed because of the appropriation [of the incomes of benefices by religious houses, making it hard to find parish priests] in various places, faith, hope, and charity began to flee from our church ... This conclusion is generally acknowledged and proved by experience, custom, and habitual practice, as you shall see in this document.

The second conclusion is this. Our normal priesthood, which began in Rome and pretended to have a power higher than that of angels, is not the priesthood which Christ established for his apostles. This conclusion is proved because the priesthood of Rome is made with signs, rituals, and the blessings of bishops, and all that is of little value, and no examples can be found to support it in Holy Scripture, for the bishops' ordinals [books containing the services to ordain priests and consecrate bishops] are not recorded [in the Bible]. And we cannot see that the Holy Spirit gives any gifts because of any such signs, for he and his noble gifts may not co-exist with deadly sin in any kind of person. The corollary of this conclusion is that it is most inappropriate in the opinion of many who are wise to see bishops playing with the Holy Spirit in establishing orders [i.e., ordaining priests], for they give shaved crowns as symbols instead of giving badges of the white hart [as King Richard did][1] and that is the livery of Antichrist, which is introduced into the Holy Church to conceal idleness.

The third conclusion, which is sorrowful to hear, is that the law of continence, which is attached to the priesthood, which was first established concerning the private matters of women, causes sodomy in all the Holy Church; but we excuse ourselves by appealing to the Bible in opposition to the decretal [Papal Letter] that says we should not mention this sin, because we consider the letter suspect [i.e., possibly a forgery]. Reason and experience prove this conclusion, because the delicious food and drink of men in Holy Church needs to be purged, or worse. Experience, through the private investigation of such men, shows that they do not like women, and when you find such a man, mark him well, for he is one of those [i.e., homosexual]. The corollary of this conclusion is that the private religious orders [i.e., monks, nuns, etc.], which first started this sin, most deserve to be abolished. But may God, in his power, send open forgiveness of secret sin. The fourth conclusion, concerning that which most harms the people, is this: that the pretend miracle of the sacrament of bread [i.e., the Eucharist] induces all but a few men to idolatry, for they think that God's body, which will never leave heaven, is, by the power of the priest's words, enclosed in its essence in a little piece of bread which the priests show to the people. But, would to God, that they would believe what the Evangelical Doctor [i.e., Wycliffe] says in his *Trialogus* "*quod panis materialis est habitudinaliter corpus Christi*" [that the material bread is the body of Christ by a convention of speech]. For we believe that in this way every true man and woman under God's law may take the sacrament without any such miracle. The corollary of this conclusion is that if Christ's body is endowed with everlasting joy, the service of

---

1   Literally, "They give crowns in characters instead of white harts." King Richard's followers wore a badge with a white stag on it. Here the writers pun on crowns, which also means coins, which bore the king's image, and also on hart/heart.

Corpus Christi made by Friar Thomas [i.e., Thomas Aquinas] is untrue and painted full of false miracles.[1] And no wonder, for Friar Thomas, agreeing with the Pope on this matter, would have made a miracle of a hen's egg [i.e., the mysterious appearance of a chicken from an egg], and we know that every lie which is publicly preached is a disgrace to him [Christ] who was always faithful and without fault.

The fifth conclusion is this: that exorcisms and blessings made in church with wine, bread and wax, water, salt and oil and incense, the stone of the altar, upon vestments, mitres, crosses, and pilgrim staffs are truly the practice of black magic rather than of holy theology. This conclusion is proved thus: for by such exorcisms things are ordered to have a greater power than their own nature, and we see no change in any such object that has charms said over it except because of false belief, which is the principle of the devil's art. The corollary of this is that if the book that charms the holy water which is used in Holy Church were really true, we think that the holy water used in Holy Church should be the best medicine for all kinds of sickness; *cuius contrarium experimur* [and we experience the contrary].

The sixth conclusion, against a practice that supports great pride, is that a king and a bishop in the same person, a prelate acting as a judge in a temporal case, a religious official acting as an officer in worldly service disrupt good rule in every kingdom. This conclusion is clearly seen, because temporality [secular rule] and spirituality are two parts of Holy Church and therefore he who has assumed one should not interfere in the other, *"quia nemo potest duobus dominis servire"* [because nobody can serve two masters]. We think that hermaphrodite or ambidexterous were good names for this kind of man who has a double status. The corollary is that we, legal representatives of God in this case, plead to this Parliament that all types of religious officials, both high and low, be excused the temporal office and busy themselves with their religious duties and nothing else.

[The seventh conclusion rejects prayers for the souls of the dead.]

The eighth conclusion, which we need to tell to the people who have been tricked, is that the pilgrimages, prayers, and offerings made to blind crosses and deaf images of wood and stone are close relatives of idolatry and not proper acts of charity. And although this forbidden imagery is a book of error for the common people, yet the standard image of the Trinity is the most abominable. God openly shows this conclusion, commanding us to perform acts of charity for men who are needy for they are a closer image of God than the piece of wood or stone, for God did not say *"Faciamus lignum ad ymaginem et similitudinem nostram aut lapidem"* [Let us make wood or stone

---

1 At the request of Pope Urban IV, Thomas Aquinas wrote a liturgy to celebrate the feast of Corpus Christi, which was instituted in 1264 and became the occasion for cycles of religious plays in England.

in our image] but *"Faciamus hominem, etc."* [Let us make man, etc.]. For the high worship that the scholars call *latria* belongs to the godhead alone, and the lower worship which is called *dulia* belongs to man and the angels and the lower creatures. The corollary is that the service of the cross, performed twice every year in our church, is filled with idolatry, for if the cross, nails, and the spear and crown [of thorns] of God should be worshiped in such a holy manner, then the lips of Judas would be a most holy relic for whoever might get them. But we beg you, pilgrim, tell us when you make an offering to the bones of a saint that are enshrined somewhere, whether you believe the saint who is in bliss or the poor almshouse which is so well-endowed? For men are canonized as saints, God knows how and, to speak more plainly, true Christian men suppose that the positions of the noble whom men call Saint Thomas [Saint Thomas Becket] were no cause for martyrdom.[1]

The ninth conclusion, against a practice which suppresses the people, is that the articles of confession, which is said to be necessary for the salvation of man, and a pretended power of absolution increase the pride of priests and gives them opportunities for private visits beyond what we will discuss here. For lords and ladies are prevented by fear of their confessors so that they dare not tell a truth [about their confessors] and the time of confession is the best time for courting and the private performance of deadly sin. They say that they are representatives of God to judge every sin and to dirty or cleanse whomever they like. They say they have the keys of heaven and of hell, they may curse and bless, bind and unbind, at their own will, so for a bushel of wheat or twelve pence a year they will sell the bliss of heaven by a charter with a legal guarantee of satisfaction sealed with the common seal. This conclusion is so often seen in common use that it needs no other proof. *Correlarium* [the corollary]: the Pope of Rome who pretends to have the treasury of the Holy Church, having the valuable jewel of Christ's Passion, with all [the rewards] that the saints of heaven have deserved, on the strength of which he gives a feigned pardon *a pena et a culpa* (from the punishment and the guilt)—he is a treasurer who is completely lacking in charity, since he is able at will to deliver the prisoners who are in pain and make it so nobody will ever come there [to Hell].[2] Here every true Christian man can see that there is a great deal of secret falsehood hidden in our church.

The tenth conclusion is that manslaughter by battle or a pretense of legal right, whether for a temporal or a spiritual cause, unless one has had a special revelation, is expressly contrary to the New Testament, which is a law of grace and full of mercy. This conclusion is openly demonstrated by the example of Christ's preaching here on earth, which taught above all to love

---

1   Lollards objected to Becket's support for the church's powers and his defense of its endowments against royal power.

2   The Pope, when offering indulgences, drew on the accumulated merit of Christ, the Virgin Mary, and the saints, known as the "treasury of the church." Pardons only remitted the punishment in Purgatory, not the guilt, which could send one to Hell if one was not truly repentant, but many people, like Chaucer's Pardoner, attributed both powers to them.

and have mercy on your enemy and not to kill him. The reason for this is that for the most part when men fight after the first stroke charity is broken, and whoever dies out of charity goes the high way to Hell. And concerning this, we know that no scholar can find in scripture or by reason how there should be lawful punishment by death for one deadly sin and not for another. But the law of mercy is that the New Testament forbade all manslaughter: "*In evangelio dictum est antiquis, Non occides*" [In the Bible it is said in the Old Testament, do not kill]. The corollary is: it is a holy robbery from the poor people when lords purchase indulgences *a pena et a culpa* for those who join their armies and come together to kill Christian men in far lands to get worldly goods, as we have seen. And knights that run off to heathen lands to win a name for themselves by killing men cause much displeasure to the King of Peace [Christ], for our faith was multiplied by meekness and patient endurance and Jesus Christ hates fighters and man-slayers and said "*Qui gladio percutit, gladio peribit*" [Who uses the sword, will die by the sword].

The eleventh conclusion is shameful to speak about, that a vow of continence made in the church by women, who are fickle and imperfect by nature, causes the most horrible sin possible to mankind. For the slaying of children before they are christened, abortion, and the destroying of nature by medicine [i.e., abortion by taking a drug] are very sinful, yet masturbation or sex with an irrational animal or a dead creature deserves even more to be punished with the pains of Hell. The corollary is that we wish widows and those who have taken the mantle and the ring [i.e., the habit of a nun] who are richly fed, were married for we suspect them of secret sin.

The twelfth conclusion is that the multitude of unnecessary trades which are used in our church [i.e., the church in England] encourage much sin through waste, idle curiosity, and disguising [i.e., elaborate fashions]. Experience shows this and reason proves it for nature and a few trades are sufficient for the needs of man. The corollary is that, since St. Paul says, "We have our bodily food and clothing; we should be satisfied," we think that goldsmiths and armorers and all kinds of trades that are not necessary for people according to the Apostles should be abolished to increase virtue. For although these crafts we have mentioned were much more necessary under the old law, the New Testament has made them and many others unnecessary.

This is our diplomatic message, which Christ has commanded us to pursue at this time, which is a particularly suitable time for it for many reasons. And although these matters have been treated briefly here, they are set out fully in another book and in many other books in English, which we wish were communicated to all Christian men. We pray God of his endless goodness to reform our church which is all out of joint from the perfection it had when it just began. Amen.

[Trans. Andrew Taylor, from Anne Hudson, ed. *Selections from English Wycliffite Writings* (Cambridge: Cambridge UP, 1978), 24–29.]

4. JEAN DE MEUN, *THE ROMANCE OF THE ROSE* (c. 1275)

[*The Romance of the Rose* consists of two parts. The first 4058 lines were com-
posed by Guillaume de Lorris c. 1230–35, and describe a dream vision in
which a young man falls in love with a rose that he sees in the garden of the
God of Love. While he is in the garden, he meets a number of allegorical
figures—such as Fair Welcoming and Resistance—who either help or hinder
him in his efforts to win the rose. The second part, which adds over 17,000
lines, was composed by Jean de Meun, c. 1275. In his continuation, Jean
de Meun expands the basic allegory of a love affair by adding a lengthy
philosophical debate between Reason and Nature. He also adds a number
of speeches in which figures who represent different sections of society and
their usual sins reveal their tricks. Chaucer translated part of the work and
drew upon it for some of his characters, such as the Friar (who owes a good
deal to False Seeming), and the Wife of Bath (who owes a good deal to the
Old Woman).]

a. False Seeming

Then, without waiting any longer, False Seeming began his lecture and said
to all in hearing:

"Barons, hear my theme: he who wants to become acquainted with False
Seeming must seek him in the world or in the cloister. I dwell in no place
except these two, but more in one and less in the other. Briefly, I am lodged
where I think that I am better hidden. The safest hiding place is under the
most humble garment. The religious are very covert, the worldly more open.
I do not want to blame or defame the religious calling, in whatever habit one
may find it. I shall not, as I may, blame the humble and loyal religious life,
although I do not love it.

"I have in mind the false religious, the malicious criminals who want to
wear the habit but do not want to subdue their hearts. The religious are all
compassionate: you will never see a spiteful one. They do not care to fol-
low pride, and they all want to live humbly. I never dwell with such people,
and if I do, I pretend. I can indeed assume their habit, but I would rather let
myself be hanged than desert my main business, whatever face I put on it.

"I dwell with the proud, the crafty, the guileful, who covet worldly hon-
ors and who carry out large dealings, who go around tracking down large
handouts and cultivating the acquaintance of powerful men and becoming
their followers. They pretend to be poor, and they live on good, delicious
morsels of food and drink costly wines. They preach poverty to you while
they fish for riches with seines and trammel nets. By my head, evil will come
of them. They are neither religious nor worldly. To the world they pres-
ent an argument in which there is a shameful conclusion: this man has the
robe of religion; therefore he is a religious. This argument is specious, not

worth a knife of privet; the habit does not make the monk. Nevertheless no one knows how to reply to the argument, no matter how high he tonsures his head, even if he shave with the razor of the *Elenchis*, that cuts up fraud into thirteen branches. No man knows so well how to set up distinctions that he dare utter a single word about it. But whatever place I come to, no matter how I conduct myself, I pursue nothing except fraud. No more than Tibert the cat has his mind on anything but mice and rats do I think of anything except fraud. Certainly by my habit you would never know with what people I dwell, any more than you would from my words, no matter how simple and gentle they were. You should look at actions if your eyes have not been put out; for if people do something other than what they say, they are certainly tricking you, whatever robes they have or whatever estate they occupy, clerical or lay, man or woman, lord, sergeant, servant, or lady."

★ ★ ★

At this point False Seeming wanted to stay silent, but Love did not pretend that he was annoyed at what he heard; instead, to delight the company, he said to him:

"Tell us more especially in what way you serve disloyally. Don't be ashamed to speak of it, for, as you tell us of your habits, you seem to be a holy hermit."

"It is true, but I am a hypocrite."

"You go around preaching abstinence."

"True, indeed, but I fill my paunch with very good morsels and with wines such as are suitable for theologians."

"You go around preaching poverty."

"True, abundantly richly. But however much I pretend to be poor, I pay no attention to any poor person. I would a hundred thousand times prefer the acquaintance of the King of France to that of a poor man, by our lady, even though he had as good a soul. When I see those poor devils all naked, shivering with cold on those stinking dunghills, crying and howling with hunger, I don't meddle in their business. If they were carried to the Hôtel-Dieu, they wouldn't get any comfort from me, for they wouldn't feed my maw with a single gift, since they have nothing worth a cuttlefish. What will a man give who licks his knife? But a visit to a rich usurer who is sick is a good and pleasant thing. I go to comfort him, for I expect to bring away money from him. And if wicked death stifles him, I will carry him right up to his grave. And if anyone comes to reprove me for avoiding the poor, do you know how I escape from him? I give out behind my cloak that the rich man is more stained with sin than the poor, and has greater need of counsel, and that that is the reason that I see him and advise him."

★ ★ ★

"By my trickery I pile up and amass great treasure in heaps and mounds, treasure than cannot be destroyed by anything. For if I build a palace with it and achieve all my pleasures with company, the bed, with tables full of sweets—for I want no other life—my money and my gold increases. Before my treasure can be emptied, money comes to me again in abundance. Don't I make my bears tumble? My whole attention is on getting. My acquisitions are worth more than my revenues. Even if I were to be beaten or killed, I still want to penetrate everywhere. I would never try to stop confessing emperors, kings, dukes, barons, or counts. But with poor men it is shameful; I don't like such confession. If not for some other purpose, I have no interest in poor people, their estate is neither fair nor noble.

"The empresses, duchesses, queens, and countesses; their high-ranking palace ladies, these abbesses, beguines, and wives of bailiffs and knights; these coy, proud bourgeois wives, these nuns and young girls; provided that they are rich or beautiful, whether they are bare or well turned out, they do not go away without good advice.

"For the salvation of souls, I inquire of lords and ladies and their entire households about their characteristics and their way of life; and I put into their heads the belief that their parish priests are animals in comparison with me and my companions. I have many wicked dogs among them, to whom I am accustomed to reveal people's secrets, without hiding anything; and in the same way they reveal everything to me, so that they hide nothing in the world from me."

★ ★ ★

b. The Old Woman

"Know then, that if only, when I was your age, I had been as wise about the games of Love as I am now! For then I was a very great beauty, but now I must complain and moan when I look at my face, which has lost its charms; and I see the inevitable wrinkles whenever I remember how my beauty made the young men skip. I made them so struggle that it was nothing if not a marvel. I was very famous then; word of my highly renowned beauty ran everywhere. At my house there was a crowd so big that no man ever saw the like. At night they knocked on my door: I was really very hard on them when I failed to keep my promises to them, and that happened very often, for I had other company. They did many a crazy thing at which I got very angry. Often my door was broken down, and many of them got into such battles as a result of their hatred and envy that before they were separated they lost their members and their lives. If master Algus, the great calculator, had wanted to take the trouble and had come with his ten figures, by which he certifies and numbers everything, he could not, however well he knew how to calculate, have ascertained the number of these great quarrels. Those were the days when my body was strong and active! As I say, if I had been as wise then as I am now, I would possess the value of a thousand pounds of sterling silver more than I do now, but I acted too foolishly.

"I was young and beautiful, foolish and wild, and had never been to a school of love where they read in the theory, but I know everything by practice. Experiments, which I have followed my whole life, have made me wise in love. Now that I know everything about love, right up to the struggle, it would not be right if I were to fail to teach you the delights that I know and have often tested. He who gives advice to a young man does well. Without fail, it is no wonder that you know nothing, for your beak is too yellow. But, in the end, I have so much knowledge upon which I can lecture from a chair that I could never finish. One should not avoid or despise everything that is very old; there one finds both good sense and good custom. Men have proved many times that, however much they have acquired, there will remain to them, in the end, at least their sense and their customs. And since I had good sense and manners, not without great harm to me, I have deceived many a worthy man when he fell captive in my nets. But I was deceived by many before I noticed. Then it was too late, and I was miserably unhappy. I was already past my youth. My door, which formerly was often open, both night and day, stayed constantly near its sill.

"'No one is coming today, no one came yesterday,' I thought, 'unhappy wretch! I must live in sorrow.' My woeful heart should have left me. Then, when I saw my door, and even myself, at such repose, I wanted to leave the country, for I couldn't endure the shame. How could I stand it when those handsome young men came along, those who formerly had held me so dear that they could not tire themselves, and I saw them look at me sideways as they passed by, they who had once been my dear guests? They went by near me, bounding along without counting me worth an egg, even those who had loved me most; they called me a wrinkled old woman and worse before they had passed on by."

★ ★ ★

"Certainly, dear son, my tender young one, if my youth were present, as yours is now, the vengeance that I would take on them could not rightly be written. Everywhere I came I would work such wonders with those scoundrels, who valued me so lightly and who vilified me and despised me when they so basely passed by near me, that one would never have heard the like. They and others would pay for their pride and spite; I would have no pity on them. For with the intelligence that God has given me—just as I have preached to you—do you know what condition I would put them in? I would so pluck them and seize their possessions, even wrongly and perversely, that

I would make them dine on worms and lie naked on dunghills, especially and first of all those who loved me with more loyal heart and who more willingly took trouble to serve and honor me. If I could, I wouldn't leave them anything worth one bud of garlic until I had everything in my purse and had put them all into poverty; I would make them stamp their feet in living rage behind me. But to regret is worth nothing; what has gone cannot come. I would never be able to hold any man, for my face is so wrinkled that they don't even protect themselves against my threat. A long time ago the scoundrels who despised me told me so, and from that time on I took to weeping. O God! But it still pleases me when I think back on it. I rejoice in my thoughts and my limbs become lively again when I remember the good times and the gay life for which my heart so strongly yearns. Just to think of it and to remember it all makes my body young again. Remembering all that happened gives me all the blessings of the world, so that however they may have deceived me, at least I have had my fun. A young lady is not idle when she lives a gay life, especially she who thinks about acquiring enough to take care of her expenses."

★ ★ ★

"O fair, most sweet son," said the Old Woman, "O beautiful tender flesh, I want to teach you of the games of Love so that when you have learned them you will not be deceived. Shape yourself according to my art, for no one who is not well informed can pass through this course of games without selling his livestock to get enough money. Now give your attention to hearing and understanding, and to remembering everything that I say, for I know the whole story."

★ ★ ★

"A woman should be careful not to stay shut up too much, for while she remains in the house, she is less seen by everybody, her beauty is less well-known, less desired, and in demand less. She should go often to the principal church and go visiting, to weddings, on trips, at games, feasts, and round dances, for in such places the God and Goddess of Love keep their schools and sing mass to their disciples."

★ ★ ★

"But pay good attention to Nature, for in order that you may see more clearly what wondrous power she has I can give you many examples which will show this power in detail. When the bird from the green wood is captured and put in a cage, very attentively and delicately cared for there within, you think that he sings with a gay heart as long as he lives; but he longs for the branching woods that he loved naturally, and he would want to be on the tree, no matter how well one could feed him. He always plans and studies how to regain his free life. He tramples his food under his feet with the ardor that his heart fills him with, and he goes trailing around his cage, searching in great anguish for a way to find a window or hold through which he might fly away to the woods. In the same way, you know, all women of every condition, whether girls or ladies, have a natural inclination to seek out voluntarily the roads and paths by which they might come to freedom, for they always want to gain it."

★ ★ ★

"By my soul, if I had been wise, I would have been a very rich lady, for I was acquainted with very great people when I was already a coy darling, and I certainly was held in considerable value by them, but when I got something of value from one of them, then, by the faith that I owe God or Saint Thibaut, I would give it all to a rascal who brought me great shame but pleased me more. I called all the others lover, but it was he alone that I loved. Understand, he didn't value me at one pea, and in fact told me so. He was bad—I never saw anyone worse—and he never ceased despising me. This scoundrel, who didn't love me at all, would call me a common whore. A woman has very poor judgement, and I was truly a woman. I never loved a man who loved me, but, do you know, if that scoundrel had laid open my shoulder or broken my head, I would have thanked him for it. He wouldn't have known how to beat me so much that I would not have had him throw himself upon me, for he knew very well how to make his peace, however much he had done against me. He would never have treated me so badly, beaten me or dragged me or wounded my face or bruised it black, that he would not have begged my favor before he moved from the place. He would never have said so many shameful things to me that he would not have counseled peace to me and then made me happy in bed, so that we had peace and concord again. Thus he had me caught in his snare, for this false, treacherous thief was a very hard rider in bed. I couldn't live without him; I wanted to follow him always. If he had fled, I would certainly have gone as far as London in England to seek him, so much did he please me and make me happy. He put me to shame and I him, for he led a life of great gaiety with the lovely gifts that he received from me. He put none of them into saving, but played everything at dice in the taverns. He never learned any other trade, and there was no need then for him to do so, for I gave him a great deal to spend, and I certainly had it for the taking. Everybody was my source of income, while he spent it willingly and always on ribaldry; he burning everything with his lechery."

[Trans. Charles Dahlberg, *The Romance of the Rose by Guillaume de Lorris and Jean de Meun* (Princeton, NJ: Princeton UP, 1971), 194–95, 197–98, 202–03, 222–23, 223–24, 225, 233, 239, 247–48.]

5. WILLIAM LANGLAND, *PIERS PLOWMAN* (1360s–80s)

[William Langland, Chaucer's contemporary and a poet of great distinction, labored for years over his great poem, *Piers Plowman*, producing several versions of his long, rambling, allegorical satire of late fourteenth-century English society. Chaucer populates *The Canterbury Tales* with tradespeople— giving his great poem what we would today term a middle-class feel. By contrast, Langland's center of gravity is more towards the peasantry; this helps us partially to see his society through their eyes. The first of the following excerpts assembles people in a manner not too dissimilar to that of Chaucer's General Prologue; we see some carry-overs, notably the Pardoner. The second excerpt supports Chaucer's complaints about friars.]

a. The Fair Field of Folk

One summer season, when the sun was warm, I rigged myself out in shaggy woolen clothes, as if I were a shepherd; and in the garb of an easy-living hermit I set out to roam far and wide through the world, hoping to hear of marvels. But on a morning in May, among the Malvern Hills, a strange thing happened to me, as though by magic. For I was tired out by my wanderings, and as I lay down to rest under a broad bank by the side of a stream, and leaned over gazing into the water, it sounded so pleasant that I fell asleep.

And I dreamt a marvelous dream: I was in a wilderness, I could not tell where, and looking Eastwards I saw a tower high up against the sun, and splendidly built on top of a hill; and far beneath it was a great gulf, with a dungeon in it, surrounded by deep, dark pits, dreadful to see. But between the tower and the gulf I saw a smooth plain, thronged with all kinds of people, high and low together, moving busily about their worldly affairs.

Some laboured at ploughing and sowing, with no time for pleasure, sweating to produce food for the gluttons to waste. Others spent their lives in vanity, parading themselves in a show of fine clothes. But many, out of love for our Lord and in the hope of Heaven, led strict lives devoted to prayer and penance—for such are the hermits and anchorites who stay in their cells, and are not forever hankering to roam about, and pamper their bodies with sensual pleasures.

Others chose to live by trade, and were much better off—for in our worldly eyes such men seem to thrive. Then there were the professional entertainers, some of whom, I think, are harmless minstrels, making an honest living by their music; but others, babblers and vulgar jesters, are true Judas' children! They invent fantastic tales about themselves, and pose as half-wits, yet they show wits enough whenever it suits them, and could easily work for a living if they had to! I will not say all that St. Paul says about them; it is enough to quote, "He who talks filth is a servant of the Devil."

And there were tramps and beggars hastening on their rounds, with their bellies and their packs crammed full of bread. They lived by their wits, and fought over their ale—for God knows, they go to bed glutted with food and drink, these brigands, and get up with foul language and filthy talk; and all day long, Sleep and shabby Sloth are at their heels.

And I saw pilgrims and palmers banding together to visit the shrines at Rome and Compostella. They went on their way full of clever talk, and took leave to tell fibs about it for the rest of their lives. And some I heard spinning such yarns of the shrines they had visited, you could tell by the way they talked that their tongues were more tuned to lying than telling the truth, no matter what tale they told.

Troops of hermits with their hooked staves were on their way to Walsingham, with their wenches following after. These great, long lubbers, who hated work, were got up in clerical gowns to distinguish them from laymen, and paraded as hermits for the sake of an easy life.

I saw the Friars there too—all four Orders of them—preaching to the people for what they could get. In their greed for fine clothes, they interpreted the Scriptures to suit themselves and their patrons. Many of these Doctors of Divinity can dress as handsomely as they please, for as their trade advances, so their profits increase. And now that Charity has gone into business, and become confessor-in-chief to wealthy lords, many strange things have happened in the last few years; unless the Friars and Holy Church mend their quarrel, the worst evil in the world will soon be upon us.

There was also a Pardoner, preaching like a priest. He produced a document covered with Bishops' seals, and claimed to have power to absolve all the people from broken fasts and vows of every kind. The ignorant folk believed him and were delighted. They came up and knelt to kiss his documents, while he, blinding them with letters of indulgence thrust in their faces, raked in their rings and jewelry with his roll of parchment!—So the people give their gold to support these gluttons, and put their trust in dirty-minded scoundrels. If the Bishop were worthy of the name, if he kept his ears open to what went on around him, his seal would not be sent out like this to deceive the people. But it is not by the Bishop's leave that this rogue preaches; for the parish priest is in league with the Pardoner, and they divide the proceeds between them—money which, but for them, would go to the poor of the parish.

Then I heard parish priests complaining to the Bishop that since the Plague their parishes were too poor to live in; so they asked permission to

live in London, where they could traffic in Masses, and chime their voices
to the sweet jingling of silver. Bishops and novices, Doctors of Divinity and
other great divines—to whom Christ has given the charge of men's souls,
and whose heads are tonsured to show that they must absolve, teach, and
pray for their parishioners, and feed the poor—I saw them all living in Lon-
don, even in Lent. Some took posts at Court counting the king's money, or
in the Courts of Exchequer and Chancery, where they claimed his dues from
the wards of the City and his right to unclaimed property. Others went into
the service of lords and ladies, sitting like stewards and managing household
affairs—and gabbled their daily Mass and Office without devotion. Indeed,
I fear that there are many whom Christ, in His great Consistory Court, will
curse for ever.

Then I understood something of that power which was entrusted to
Peter, to "bind and unbind" as the Scripture puts it. Peter, by our Lord's
command, left it in the hands of Love, sharing it out among the four greatest
virtues, which are called Cardinal. For these are the hinges on which swing
the gates of Christ's kingdom, closing against some, and opening on the
bliss of Heaven to others. But as to those other Cardinals at Rome who have
assumed the same name, taking upon themselves the appointment of a Pope
to possess the power of St. Peter, I will not call them in question. The elec-
tion of a Pope requires both love and learning. There is much more I could
say about the Papal Court, but it is not for me to say it.

Then there came into the field a king, guided by the knights. The power
of the Commons gave him his throne, and Common Sense provided men of
learning to counsel him and to protect the people.

The king, with his nobles and counselors, decided that the common
people should provide them with resources; so the people devised different
trades, and engaged ploughmen to labour and till the soil for the good of
the whole community, as honest ploughmen should. Then the king and the
people, helped by Common Sense, established law and order, so that every
man might know his rights and duties.

b. The Friar

Yet I believe that those who preach this doctrine to ignorant people are liars.
For God, through Moses, gave men a law, "Thou shalt not covet that which
is thy neighbour's." And how little is this obeyed in the parishes of England!
For it is a parish priest's duty to hear his people's confessions; that is why he
is called a "curate" or keeper—because he must know all his parishioners and
heal them and exhort them to do penance and to feel ashamed of their sins
when they go to confession. Yet their very shame makes them abandon their
curates and run to the Friars, just as some swindlers flee to Westminster—
who borrow money, take it there with them, and then beseech their creditors

to let them off or extend the loan for a few more years. But while they are in Westminster, they go quickly to work, and make merry on other men's money. It is like that with many of those who confess to the Friars—jurymen and executors for example: they give the Friar a fee to pray for the dead man, and then have a good time with what is left of the money which he had laboured to earn. And so they leave the dead in debt till the Day of Judgement.

So Envy hated Conscience, and provided for the Friars to go to College and learn philosophy. Meanwhile Covetousness and Unkindness attacked Conscience, who held fast inside Unity. And Conscience appointed Peace as porter, commanding her to bar the gates to all tattlers and idle gossips. Then Hypocrisy made an assault on the castle, and struggled hard with Conscience at the gates. And he grievously wounded many a wise teacher who fought on the side of Conscience and the Cardinal Virtues.

So Conscience sent for a doctor skilled in hearing confessions. "Go and heal those that are sick or wounded with sin," he said. Then this Doctor Shrift concocted a lotion that smarted, and made men do penance for their misdeeds; and he saw to it that Piers' Pardon was properly paid for, with its condition "Pay back that which thou owest."

But some disliked this doctor, and sent out letters to ask if there were any surgeon in the town who could apply plasters more gently. For Sir Love-Living-in-Lechery lay there groaning, and whenever he had to fast on a Friday he acted as though he were dying. "There is a surgeon here," he said, "who knows how to handle you gently. He knows far more about Medicine than the parson does, and applies plasters much more pleasantly. They call him Doctor Friar Flatter, Physician and Surgeon."

"Let him come to Unity," said Contrition to Conscience, "for we have so many folk here wounded by Hypocrisy."

"We don't really need him," said Conscience; "I know of no better doctors than the parson, the penitentiary and the Bishop—except for Piers the Ploughman, who has power over them all, for he can grant an indulgence to any who are not in debt. But since you are so anxious, perhaps, after all, I will let Dr. Flatter come and treat your patients."

The Friar very soon heard of this, and hurried off to the Bishop to get a license to do parish work. He came before him as bold as brass, carrying his letters of recommendation, and very soon got written permission to hear confessions wherever he went. Then he came to the place where Conscience was, and knocked at the gate.

Peace, the porter of Unity, unfastened the gates, and said hurriedly, "What do you want?"

"I should like to speak with Contrition," answered the Friar. "It concerns the health and welfare of you all. That is why I have come."

"He is ill, and so are many others," said Peace. "Hypocrisy has wounded them so badly that they are not likely to get better."

"But I am a doctor," said the Friar, "and highly skilled in mixing medicines. Conscience knows me well, and has seen what I can do."

"Well, before you go any further, you had better tell me your name. And please don't try to conceal it."

Then the Friar's companion answered for him, saying, "Certainly. This is Father Creep-into-Houses."

"Oh! Then you can clear off!" said Peace. "I've heard of your medicine, by heaven! You will have to learn a better trade before you get in here! I knew a man like you, in a Friar's habit, eight years ago. He used to come to the house where I worked, to act as doctor to my master and mistress. And one day, when my master was out, he came and cured our women so well that some turned out to be with child!"

But Courtesy urged Peace to open the gate, saying, "Let the Friar and his friend in, and give them a good welcome. He may be very shrewd, and for all you know his teaching may persuade Life to leave Avarice and Pride, and begin to fear Death. We may yet see Life embrace Conscience and make his peace with him."

So, through Courtesy's intervention, the Friar came in, and going in to where Conscience was, he greeted him politely. "You are welcome," replied Conscience. "Can you heal the sick? My cousin Contrition here is wounded. Will you nurse him and look after his sores? The parson's plasters and powders are too strong for him; he is always unwilling to change them, and leaves them on too long. Why, he sometimes lets them go on chafing from one Lent to another."

"That is far too long," said the Friar, "but I think I know how to put things right."

So he went to examine Contrition, and gave him a fresh dressing called Private Subscription. "And I shall pray for you," he said, "and for all your loved ones, all my life." And to another patient he said, "I shall remember you, my lady, in my Masses and Matins, and you shall share all the spiritual gifts of our Order—for a small charge of course."

So he went about collecting money, and flattering those who came to him for confession. And Contrition had soon forgotten to weep for his sins, and no longer lay awake at night as he used to do. So, in return for the comfort of an easy confessor, he gave up repentance, the sovereign remedy for all sins.

Sloth and Pride saw this at once, and attacked Conscience more eagerly than ever. And Conscience begged Clergy to help him, and ordered Contrition to guard the gates.

"Contrition is on his back, asleep and dreaming," said Peace, "and most of the others are in the same state. The Friar has bewitched them with his cures; his plasters are so mild that they have lost all fear of sin."

"Then by Christ!" cried Conscience, "I will become a pilgrim, and walk to the ends of the earth in search of Piers the Ploughman. For he can destroy Pride, and find an honest livelihood for these Friars who live by flattery and set themselves against me. Now may Nature avenge me, and send me His help and healing, until I have found Piers the Ploughman!"

[Trans. J.F. Goodridge, *Piers the Ploughman* by William Langland (Harmondsworth: Penguin, 1959), 25–28; 253–56.]

6. GUILLAUME DE MACHAUT, *THE JUDGMENT OF THE KING OF NAVARRE* (1351)

[Machaut was a great composer as well as a great poet, and Chaucer, in his early career as a writer, was heavily influenced by him, echoing large amounts of Machaut's poetry in his *Book of the Duchess*. This excerpt is Machaut's take on the Black Plague of 1348–50, the catastrophic epidemic that carried off between a fourth and a half of the population of Europe. As a child, Chaucer lived through it, and, particularly in the Pardoner's Tale, it leaves its mark on his poetry.]

The Plague

When God from his house saw
The corruption in the world
Which was everywhere so great,
It's no wonder that he was eager
To revenge himself cruelly
For this great disorder;
And so at once, without waiting longer,
In order to exact justice and vengeance,
He made death come forth from his cage,
Full of rage and anger,
Without check, without bridle, without rein,
Without faith, without love, without measure,
So very proud and arrogant,
So gluttonous and so famished
That he could not be satisfied
By anything that he could consume.
And he raced across the world;
He killed and destroyed one and all,
Whomever he came across,
Nor could he be withstood.
And in short he killed so many,
Struck down and devoured such a multitude

That every day could be found
Great heaps of women, youths,
Boys, old people, those of all stations,
Lying dead throughout the churches;
And these were thrown all together
In great trenches, all of them dead from the buboes,
For one found the cemeteries
So full of bodies and biers
That it was necessary to make new ones.
These were strange new tidings.
And so there was many a fine town
Where no boy, no girl, no man or woman
Was seen to come and go,
Nor was anyone to be found there to talk to,
For they were all dead
From this devastating attack.
And they did not languish more than three days,
Sometimes less; it was a short time.
And there were certainly many who
Died of it suddenly;
For those same men who carried them
To the church did not return;
(One often witnessed this there)
Instead they were to die right on the spot,
And whoever wished himself to undertake
To learn or to put down in writing
The number of those who died,
Those who are still here and those who were,
And all those who are to come,
Never would they be able to arrive at a figure.
A great many they'd amount to;
For no one could number them,
Imagine, conceive, nor tell,
Compute, make known, or record them.
For to be sure many times
I've heard it said, and openly,
That in thirteen hundred and forty nine,
From one hundred only nine remained.
And so one saw because of a lack of people
That many a fine, noble estate
Lay unworked.
No one had his fields plowed,
His grain sowed, or the vines tended,

Who would have given triple wages,
No, surely, not for twenty to one,
So many had died; and so it happened
That the cattle roamed
Through the fields completely abandoned,
Grazing in the corn and among the grapes,
Anywhere at all that they wished,
Nor did they have a master, a cowherd,
Or any man to go among them;
Nor was there anyone to call them back,
None to claim them as his own.
There were many estates
Which remained without owners;
Nor did the living dare to remain
At all inside the houses
Where the dead had been,
Either in winter or in summer;
And if there was anyone who did this,
He put himself in peril of death.
And when I saw these events
So strange and so ominous,
I was not at all so brave
That I did not become very cowardly.
For all the bravest trembled
With the fear of death that came over them,
And so I confessed myself very thoroughly
Of all the sins I had committed,
And put myself into a state of grace
In order to accept death at that moment,
If it should please our Lord.
Therefore in doubt and fear
I closed myself up inside the house
And determined in my mind
Resolutely that I'd not leave it
Until that moment when I would know
What conclusion this might come to;
And I would leave it for God to decide.
And so for a long time, may God help me,
I remained there, knowing little
Of what was being done in the city,
And more than twenty thousand died,
Though I knew nothing of this,
And so I felt less melancholy;

For I did not wish to know anything
In order to have fewer worries,
Though many of my friends
Had died and had been put into the ground.

[Trans. R. Barton Palmer, *The Judgment of the King of Navarre* by Guillaume de Machaut (New York: Garland, 1988), 17–21.]

7. GIOVANNI BOCCACCIO, *THE DECAMERON* (1353)

[Boccaccio was arguably the author who most influenced Chaucer. Chaucer translated and adapted long works of Boccaccio for the Knight's Tale and his *Troilus and Criseyde*. *The Decameron*, like the later *The Canterbury Tales*, is a framework-story in which various characters tell tales to entertain each other. Several of the stories in *The Decameron* found their way into *The Canterbury Tales*, either directly or through the translations of others. The first excerpt is from the opening material of Boccaccio's work, which explains how ten young people escape the city of Florence during the Plague and spend the following ten days amusing themselves by telling stories. Boccaccio gives more details about the Plague than does Machaut, and it is clear that Boccaccio would not have agreed with Machaut's strategy for surviving the disease.]

a. The Black Death

In the year 1348 after the fruitful incarnation of the Son of God, that most beautiful of Italian cities, noble Florence, was attacked by deadly plague. It started in the East either through the influence of the heavenly bodies or because God's just anger with our wicked deeds sent it as a punishment to mortal men; and in a few years killed an innumerable quantity of people. Ceaselessly passing from place to place, it extended its miserable length over the West. Against this plague all human wisdom and foresight were vain. Orders had been given to cleanse the city of filth, the entry of any sick person was forbidden, much advice was given for keeping healthy; at the same time humble supplications were made to God by pious persons in processions and otherwise. And yet, in the beginning of the spring of the year mentioned, its horrible results began to appear, and in a miraculous manner. The symptoms were not the same as in the East, where a gush of blood from the nose was the plain sign of inevitable death; but it began both in men and women with certain swellings in the groin or under the armpit. They grew to the size of a small apple or an egg, more or less, and were vulgarly called tumours. In a short space of time these tumours spread from the two parts named all over the body. Soon after this the symptoms changed and black or purple spots appeared on the arms or thighs or any other part of the body, sometimes a few large ones, sometimes many little ones. These spots were a certain sign of death, just as the original tumour had been and still remained.

No doctor's advice, no medicine could overcome or alleviate this disease. An enormous number of ignorant men and women set up as doctors in addition to those who were trained. Either the disease was such that no treatment was possible or the doctors were so ignorant that they did not know what caused it, and consequently could not administer the proper remedy. In any case very few recovered; most people died within about three days of the appearance of the tumours described above, most of them without any fever or other symptoms.

The violence of this disease was such that the sick communicated it to the healthy who came near them, just as a fire catches anything dry or oily near it. And it even went further. To speak to or go near the sick brought infection and a common death to the living; and moreover, to touch the clothes or anything else the sick had touched or worn gave the disease to the person touching.

What I am about to tell now is a marvelous thing to hear; and if I and others had not seen it with our own eyes I would not dare to write it, however much I was willing to believe and whatever the good faith of the person from whom I heard it. So violent was the malignancy of this plague that it was communicated, not only from one man to another, but from the garments of a sick or dead man to animals of another species, which caught the disease in that way and very quickly died of it. One day among other occasions I saw with my own eyes (as I said just now) the rags left lying in the street of a poor man who had died of the plague; two pigs came along and, as their habit is, turned the clothes over with their snouts and then munched at them, with the result that they both fell dead almost at once on the rags, as if they had been poisoned.

From these and similar or greater occurrences, such fear and fanciful notions took possession of the living that almost all of them adopted the same cruel policy, which was entirely to avoid the sick and everything belonging to them. By so doing, each one thought he would secure his own safety.

Some thought that moderate living and the avoidance of all superfluity would preserve them from the epidemic. They formed small communities, living entirely separate from everybody else. They shut themselves up in houses where there were no sick, eating the finest food and drinking the best wine very temperately, avoiding all excess, allowing no news or discussion of death and sickness, and passing the time in music and suchlike pleasures. Others thought just the opposite. They thought the sure cure for the plague was to drink and be merry, to go about singing and amusing themselves, satisfying every appetite they could, laughing and jesting at what happened. They put their words into practice, spent day and night going from tavern to tavern, drinking immoderately, or went into other people's houses, doing only those things which pleased them. This they could easily do because everyone felt doomed and had abandoned his property, so that most houses became common property and any stranger who went in made use of them as if he had owned them. And with all this bestial behaviour, they avoided the sick as much as possible.

In this suffering and misery of our city, the authority of human and divine laws almost disappeared, for, like other men, the ministers and executors of the laws were all dead or sick or shut up with their families, so that no duties were carried out. Every man was therefore able to do as he pleased.

Many others adopted a course of life midway between the two just described. They did not restrict their victuals so much as the former, nor allow themselves to be drunken and dissolute like the latter, but satisfied their appetites moderately. They did not shut themselves up, but went about, carrying flowers or scented herbs or perfumes in their hands, in the belief that it was an excellent thing to comfort the brain with such odours; for the whole air was infected with the smell of dead bodies, of sick persons and medicines.

Others again held a still more cruel opinion, which they thought would keep them safe. They said that the only medicine against the plaguestricken was to go right away from them. Men and women, convinced of this and caring about nothing but themselves, abandoned their own city, their own houses, their dwellings, their relatives, their property, and went abroad or at least to the country round Florence, as if God's wrath in punishing men's wickedness with this plague would not follow them but strike only those who remained within the walls of the city, or as if they thought nobody in the city would remain alive and that its last hour had come.

Not everyone who adopted any of these various opinions died, nor did all escape. Some when they were still healthy had set the example of avoiding the sick, and, falling ill themselves, died untended.

One citizen avoided another, hardly any neighbour troubled about others, relatives never or hardly ever visited each other. Moreover, such terror was struck into the hearts of men and women by this calamity, that brother abandoned brother, and the uncle his nephew, and the sister her brother, and very often the wife her husband. What is even worse and nearly incredible is that fathers and mothers refused to see and tend their children, as if they had not been theirs.

Thus, a multitude of sick men and women were left without any care except from the charity of friends (but these were few), or the greed of servants, though not many of these could be had even for high wages. Moreover, most of them were coarse-minded men and women, who did little more than bring the sick what they asked for or watch over them when they were dying. And very often these servants lost their lives and their earnings. Since the sick were thus abandoned by neighbours, relatives and friends, while servants were scarce, a habit sprang up which had never been heard of before. Beautiful and noble women, when they fell sick, did not scruple to take a young or old manservant, whoever he might be, and with no sort of shame, expose every part of their bodies to these men as if they had been women, for they were compelled by the necessity of their sickness to do so. This, perhaps, was a cause of looser morals in those women who survived.

In this way many people died who might have been saved if they had been looked after. Owing to the lack of attendants for the sick and the violence of the plague, such a multitude of people in the city died day and night that it was stupefying to hear of, let alone to see.

★ ★ ★

The plight of the lower and most of the middle classes was even more pitiful to behold. Most of them remained in their houses, either through poverty or in hopes of safety and fell sick by thousands. Since they received no care and attention, almost all of them died. Many ended their lives in the streets both at night and during the day; and many others who died in their houses were only known to be dead because the neighbours smelled their decaying bodies. Dead bodies filled every corner. Most of them were treated in the same manner by the survivors, who were more concerned to get rid of their rotting bodies than moved by charity towards the dead. With the aid of porters, if they could get them, they carried the bodies out of the houses and laid them at the doors, where every morning quantities of the dead might be seen. They then were laid on biers, or, as these were often lacking, on tables.

★ ★ ★

Such was the multitude of corpses brought to the churches every day and almost every hour that there was not enough consecrated ground to give them burial, especially since they wanted to bury each person in the family grave, according to the old custom. Although the cemeteries were full, they were forced to dig huge trenches, where they buried the bodies by hundreds. Here they stowed them away like bales in the hold of a ship and covered them with a little earth, until the whole trench was full.

★ ★ ★

[S]uch was the cruelty of Heaven, and perhaps in part of men, that between March and July more than one hundred thousand persons died within the walls of Florence, what between the violence of the plague and the abandonment in which the sick were left by the cowardice of the healthy. And before the plague it was not thought that this whole city held so many people.

Oh, what great palaces, how many fair houses and noble dwellings, once filled with attendants and nobles and ladies, were emptied to the meanest servant! How many famous names and vast possessions and renowned estates were left without an heir! How many gallant men and fair ladies and hand-some youths, whom [the physicians] Galen, Hippocrates, and Æsculapius themselves would have said were in perfect health, at noon dined with their relatives and friends, and at night supped with their ancestors in the next world!

[Trans. Richard Aldington, *The Decameron of Giovanni Boccaccio* (New York: Dell Publishing, 1930), 30–36.]

b. Patient Griselda

[The next excerpt from *The Decameron* is the hundredth, or last story, of pa-tient Griselda. Francis Petrarch translated the story into Latin in 1373, and sent a revised version to Boccaccio the following year. Chaucer adapted Petrach's translation for his Clerk's Tale but may also have known Boccaccio's version.]

A very long time ago, there succeeded to the marquisate of Saluzzo a young man called Gualtieri, who, having neither wife nor children, spent the whole of his time hunting and hawking, and never even thought about marrying or raising a family, which says a great deal for his intelligence. His followers, however, disapproved of this, and repeatedly begged him to marry so that he should not be left without an heir nor they without a lord. Morever, they offered to find him a wife whose parentage would be such as to strengthen their expectations and who would make him exceedingly happy.

So Gualtieri answered them as follows:

"My friends, you are pressing me to do something that I had always set my mind firmly against, seeing how difficult it is to find a person who will easily adapt to one's own way of living, how many thousands there are who will do precisely the opposite, and what a miserable life is in store for the man who stumbles upon a woman ill-suited to his own temperament. Moreover it is foolish of you to believe that you can judge the character of daughters from the ways of their fathers and mothers, hence claiming to provide me with a wife who will please me. For I cannot see how you are to know the fathers, or to discover the secrets of the mothers; and even if this were pos-sible, daughters are very often different from either of their parents. Since, however, you are so determined to bind me in chains of this sort, I am ready to do as you ask; but so that I have only myself to blame if it should turn out badly, I must insist on marrying a wife of my own choosing. And I hereby declare that no matter who she may be, if you fail to honour her as your lady you will learn to your great cost how serious a matter it is for you to have urged me to marry against my will."

To this the gentlemen replied that if only he would bring himself to take a wife, they would be satisfied.

Now, for some little time, Gualtieri had been casting an appreciative eye on the manners of a poor girl from a neighbouring village, and thinking her very beautiful, he considered that a life with her would have much to commend it. So without looking further afield, he resolved to marry the girl; and having summoned her father, who was very poor indeed, he arranged with him that he should take her as his wife.

This done, Gualtieri brought together all his friends from the various parts of his domains, and said to them:

"My friends, since you still persist in wanting me to take a wife, I am prepared to do it, not because I have any desire to marry, but rather in order to gratify your wishes. You will recall the promise that you gave me, that no matter whom I should choose, you would rest content and honour her as your lady. The time has now come when I want you to keep that promise, and for me to honour the promise I gave to you. I have found a girl after my own heart, in this very district, and a few days hence I intend to marry her and convey her to my house. See to it, therefore, that the wedding-feast lacks nothing in splendour, and consider how you may honourably receive her, so that all of us may call ourselves contented—I with you for keeping your promise, and you with me for keeping mine."

As of one voice, the good folk joyously gave him their blessing, and said that whoever she happened to be, they would accept her as their lady and honour her as such in all respects.

[The wedding celebration is planned, a sumptuous feast prepared, and a number of beautiful dresses made for the mysterious bride-to-be.]

Early on the morning of the day he had fixed for the nuptials, Gualtieri, his preparations now complete, mounted his horse together with all the people who had come to do him honour, and said:

"Gentlemen, it is time for us to go and fetch the bride."

He then set forth with the whole of the company in train, and eventually they came to the village and made their way to the house of the girl's father, where they met her as she was returning with water from the fountain, making great haste so that she could go with other women to see Gaultieri's bride arriving. As soon as Gualtieri caught sight of her, he called to her by name, which was Griselda, and asked her where her father was, to which she blushingly replied:

"My lord he is at home."

So Gualtieri dismounted, and having ordered everyone to wait for him outside, he went alone into the humble dwelling, where he found the girl's father, whose name was Giannùcole, and said to him:

"I have come to marry Griselda, but first I want to ask her certain questions in your presence." He then asked her whether, if he were to marry her, she would always try to please him and never be upset by anything he said or did, whether she would obey him, and many other questions of this sort, to all of which she answered that she would.

Whereupon Gualtieri, having taken her by the hand, led her out of the house, and in the presence of his whole company and of all the other people there he caused her to be stripped naked. Then he called for the clothes and shoes which he had had specially made, and quickly got her to put them on, after which he caused a crown to be placed upon the dishevelled hair of her head.

[Having thus made public his bride-choice, Gualtieri marries Griselda "then and there before all the people present." Later there is much rejoicing at the wedding feast, as much "as if he had married the King of France's daughter." They live blissfully together until Griselda gives birth to a daughter, "to her husband's enormous joy."]

But shortly thereafter Gualtieri was seized by the strange desire to test Griselda's patience, by subjecting her to constant provocation and making her life unbearable.

At first he lashed her with his tongue, feigning to be angry and claiming that his subjects were thoroughly disgruntled with her on account of her lowly condition, especially now that they saw her bearing children; and he said they were greatly distressed about this infant daughter of theirs, of whom they did nothing but grumble.

The lady betrayed no sign of bitterness on hearing these words, and without changing her expression she said to him:

"My lord, deal with me as you think best for your own good name and peace of mind, for I shall rest content whatever you decide, knowing myself to be their inferior and that I was unworthy of the honour which you so generously bestowed upon me."

This reply was much to Gualtieri's liking, for it showed him that she had not been puffed with pride by any honour that he or others had paid her.

[Determined to test her further, however, Gualtieri sends one of his attendants to take away their infant daughter, with instructions to leave Griselda with the impression that the little girl is to be murdered at her father's behest. Her heart breaking, but determined to obey her husband, Griselda gives up her baby to the servant, saying:]

"There; do exactly as your lord, who is my lord too, has instructed you. But do not leave her to be devoured by the beasts and the birds, unless that is what he has ordered you to do."

The servant took away the little girl and reported Griselda's words to Gualtieri, who, marvelling at her constancy, sent him with the child to a kinswoman of his in Bologna, requesting her to rear and educate her carefully, but without ever making it known whose daughter she was.

[Time passes and Griselda gives birth to another child, a boy. Shortly thereafter, Gualtieri torments his wife as before, sending a servant to take away her baby, ostensibly to have him put to death but in fact to be fostered with his kinswoman in Bologna.]

To all of this his wife reacted no differently, either in her speech or in her looks, than she had on the previous occasion, much to the astonishment of Gualtieri, who told himself that no other woman could have remained so impassive. But for the fact that he had observed her doting upon the children for as long as he allowed her to do so, he would have assumed that she was glad to be rid of them, whereas he knew that she was too judicious to behave in any other way.

His subjects, thinking he had caused the children to be murdered, roundly condemned him and judged him a cruel tyrant, whilst his wife became the object of their deepest compassion. But to the women who offered her their sympathy in the loss of her children, all she ever said was that the decision of their father was good enough for her.

Many years after the birth of their daughter, Gualtieri decided that the time had come to put Griselda's patience to the final test. So he told a number of his men that in no circumstances could he put up with Griselda as his wife any longer, having now come to realize that his marriage was an aberration of his youth. [...] Shortly thereafter, Gualtieri arranged for some counterfeit letters of his to arrive from Rome, and led his subjects to believe that within these, the Pope had granted him permission to abandon Griselda and remarry.

He accordingly sent for Griselda, and before a large number of people he said to her:

"Woman, I have had a dispensation from the Pope, allowing me to leave you and take another wife. Since my ancestors were great noblemen and rulers of these lands, whereas yours have always been peasants, I intend that you shall no longer be my wife, but return to Giannùcole's house with the dowry you brought me, after which I shall bring another lady here. I have already chosen her and she is better suited to a man of my condition."

On hearing these words, the lady, with an effort beyond the power of any normal woman's nature, suppressed her tears and replied:

"My lord, I have always known that my lowly condition was totally at odds with your nobility, and that it is to God and yourself that I owe whatever standing I possess. Nor have I ever regarded this as a gift that I might keep and cherish as my own, but rather as something I have borrowed; and now that you want me to return it, I must give it back to you with good

grace. Here is the ring with which you married me: take it. As to your
ordering me to take away the dowry that I brought, you will require no
accountant, nor will I need a purse or a pack-horse, for this to be done. For
it has not escaped my memory that you took me as naked as on the day I was
born. If you think it proper that the body in which I have borne your chil-
dren should be seen by all the people, I shall go away naked. But in return
for my virginity, which I brought to you and cannot retrieve, I trust you will
at least allow me, in addition to my dowry, to take one shift away with me."

Gualtieri wanted above all else to burst into tears, but maintaining a stern
expression, he said:

"Very well, you may take a shift."

All the people present implored Gualtieri to let her have a dress, so that
she who had been his wife for thirteen years and more would not have to
suffer the indignity of leaving his house in a shift, like a pauper; but their
pleas were unavailing. And so Griselda, wearing a shift, barefoot, and with
nothing to cover her head, having bidden them farewell, set forth from
Gualtieri's house and returned to her father amid the weeping and the wail-
ing of all who set eyes upon her.

Giannùcole, who had never thought it possible that Gualtieri would keep
his daughter as his wife, and was daily expecting this to happen, had pre-
served the clothes she discarded on the morning Gualtieri had married her.
So he brought them to her, and Griselda, having put them on, applied her-
self as before to the menial chores in her father's house, bravely enduring the
hostile assault of cruel Fortune.

No sooner did Gualtieri drive Griselda away, than he gave his subjects
to understand that he was betrothed to a daughter of one of the Counts of
Panago. And having ordered that grandiose preparations were to be made
for the nuptials, he sent for Griselda and said to her:

"I am about to fetch home this new bride of mine, and from the moment
she sets foot inside the house, I intend to accord to her an honourable wel-
come. As you know, I have no women here who can set the rooms in order
for me, or attend to many of the things that a festive occasion of this sort
requires. No one knows better than you how to handle these household
affairs, so I want you to make all the necessary arrangements. Invite all the
ladies you need, and receive them as though you were mistress of the house.
And when the nuptials are over, you can go back home to your father."

Since Griselda was unable to lay aside her love for Gualtieri as readily as
she had dispensed with her good fortune, his words pierced her heart like so
many knives. But she replied, "My lord, I am ready to do as you ask."

And so, in her coarse, thick, woollen garments, Griselda returned to the
house she had quitted shortly before in her shift, and started to sweep and
tidy the various chambers. On her instructions, the beds were draped with
hangings, the benches in the halls were suitably adorned, the kitchen was

made ready; and she set her hand, as though she were a petty serving wench, to every conceivable household task, never stopping to draw breath until she had everything prepared and arranged as befitted the occasion.

Having done all this, she caused invitations to be sent, in Gualtieri's name, to all the ladies living in those parts, and began to await the event. And when at last the nuptial day arrived, heedless of her beggarly attire, she bade a cheerful welcome to each of the lady guests, displaying all the warmth and courtesy of a lady of the manor.

Gualtieri's children having meanwhile been carefully reared by his kinswoman in Bologna, who had married into the family of the Counts of Panago, the girl was now twelve years old, the loveliest creature ever seen, whilst the boy had reached the age of six. Gualtieri had sent word to his kinswoman's husband, asking him to do him the kindness of bringing this daughter of his to Saluzzo along with her little brother, to see that she was nobly and honourably escorted, and to tell everyone he met that he was taking her to marry Gualtieri, without revealing who she really was to a living soul.

In accordance with the Marquis's request, the gentleman set forth with the girl and her brother and a noble company, and a few days later, shortly before the hour of breakfast, he arrived at Saluzzo, where he found that all the folks thereabouts, and numerous others from neighbouring parts, were waiting for Gualtieri's latest bride.

After being welcomed by the ladies, she made her way to the hall where the tables were set, and Griselda, just as we have described her, went cordially up to meet her, saying:

"My lady, you are welcome."

The ladies, who in vain had implored Gualtieri to see that Griselda remained in another room, or to lend her one of the dresses that had once been hers, so that she would not cut such a sorry figure in front of his guests, took their seats at table and addressed themselves to the meal. All eyes were fixed upon the girl, and everyone said that Gaultieri had made a good exchange. But Griselda praised her as warmly as anyone present, speaking no less admiringly of her little brother.

Gualtieri felt that he had now seen all he wished to see of the patience of his lady, for he perceived that no event, however singular, produced the slightest change in her demeanour, and he was certain that this was not because of her obtuseness, as he knew her to be very intelligent. He therefore considered that the time had come for him to free her from the rancour that he judged her to be hiding beneath her tranquil outward expression. And having summoned her to his table before all the people present he smiled at her and said:

"What do you think of our new bride?"

"My lord," replied Griselda, "I think very well of her. And if, as I believe, her wisdom matches her beauty, I have no doubt whatever that your life with

her will bring you greater happiness than any gentleman on earth has ever
known. But with all my heart I beg you not to inflict those same wounds
upon her that you imposed upon her predecessor, for I doubt whether she
could withstand them, not only because she is younger, but also because she
has had a refined upbringing, whereas the other had to face continual hard-
ship from her infancy."

On observing that Griselda was firmly convinced that the young lady was
to be his wife, and that even so she allowed no hint of resentment to escape
her lips, Gualtieri got her to sit down beside him, and said:

"Griselda, the time has come for you to reap the reward of your unfail-
ing patience, and for those who considered me a cruel and bestial tyrant, to
know that whatever I have done was done of set purpose, for I wished to
show you how to be a wife, to teach these people how to choose and keep a
wife, and to guarantee my own peace and quiet for as long as we were living
beneath the same roof. When I came to take a wife, I was greatly afraid that
this peace would be denied me, and in order to prove otherwise I tormented
and provoked you in the ways you have seen. But as I have never known you
to oppose my wishes, I now intend, being persuaded that you can offer me
all the happiness I desired, to restore to you in a single instant that which
I took from you little by little and delectably to assuage the pains I have
inflicted upon you. Receive with gladsome heart, then, this girl whom you
believe to be my bride, and also her brother. These are our children, whom
you and many others have long supposed that I caused to be cruelly mur-
dered; and I am your husband, who loves you above all else, for I think I
can boast that there is no other man on earth whose contentment in his wife
exceeds my own."

Having spoken these words, he embraced and kissed Griselda, who by
now was weeping with joy; then they both got up from the table and made
their way to the place where their daughter sat listening in utter amazement
at these tidings. And after they had fondly embraced the girl and her brother,
the mystery was unravelled to her, as well as to many of the others who were
present.

The ladies rose from the table in transports of joy, and escorted Griselda
to a chamber, where, with greater assurance of her future happiness, they
divested her of her tattered garments and clothed her anew in one of her
stately robes. And as their lady and their mistress, a rôle which even in her
rags had seemed to be hers, they led her back to the hall, where she and
Gualtieri rejoiced with the children in a manner marvellous to behold.

Everyone being delighted with the turn that events had taken, the feast-
ing and the merrymaking were redoubled, and continued unabated for the
next few days. Gualtieri was acknowledged to be very wise, though the trials
to which he had subjected his lady were regarded as harsh and intolerable,
whilst Griselda was accounted the wisest of all.

The Count of Panago returned a few days later to Bologna, and Gualtieri, having removed Giannùcole from his drudgery, set him up in a style befitting his father-in-law, so that he lived in great comfort and honour for the rest of his days. As for Gualtieri himself, having married off his daughter to a gentleman of renown, he lived long and contentedly with Griselda, never failing to honour her to the best of his ability.

What more needs to be said, except that celestial spirits may sometimes descend even into the houses of the poor, whilst there are those in royal palaces who would be better employed as swineherds than as rulers of men? Who else but Griselda could have endured so cheerfully the cruel and unheard of trials that Gualtieri imposed upon her without shedding a tear? For perhaps it would have served him right if he had chanced upon a wife, who, being driven from the house in her shift, had found some other man to shake her skin-coat for her, earning herself a fine new dress in the process.

[Trans. G.H. McWilliam, *Giovanni Boccaccio, The Decameron* (Harmondsworth: Penguin, 1972), 813–24.]

8. RUDOLPH OF SCHLETTSTADT, *THE HOST AND LIBELS AGAINST THE JEWS* (1303)

[These stories, part of a collection of fifty-six compiled by their author, provide a glimpse into the widespread anti-semitism of the later Middle Ages, and thus a context for Chaucer's Prioress's Tale.]

In 1298 the lord Kraffto de Hohenloe had contracted large debts from the Jews which he was unable to pay without great loss of his property. The Jews who lived in his domain, fearing the lord Kraffto, went suppliantly to the bishop of Würzburg, asking him to compel their lord Kraffto to stand by the Christian oath he made to them that he would trouble no Jew in possession or body. The lord bishop assented to their request, went to the lord Kraffto, interceded humbly for the Jews, and what he asked he effectively got. By virtue of this success, the Jews grew bolder in making their contracts. Whatever it occurred to them to do they readily attempted. During this same time there were many Jews living at castle Wickersheim, which was in the domain of Lord Kraffto. By price or plea they persuaded a bellman or sacristan to open the church for them on Holy Thursday night before matins and let them go inside freely and do whatever they wanted to do. When the Jews went to the church on Holy Thursday night and found it open, with great glee they ran up to the altar, took the sacrament (that is, the hosts), tossed them on the altar, and stuck them with knives and heaped whatever abuse on them they were able. The hosts wounded by the blades shed the purest blood from their wounds and bled profusely so that the blood stained the Jews' hands and palms and spotted the pavement in many more places. With a loud cry the hosts shouted over and over the words of Christ as he hung on the cross: *Hely, hely lamma sabacthani?* that is, "My God, my God, why hast thou forsaken me?" They made such an uproar that nearly everyone in the neighborhood was terrified, and they all alike got up and went outside their houses where they all heard great shouting and horrifying voices inside the church. But those inside the church—the Jews—through Christ's permission could hear neither the shouting nor anything else. The people all together followed the crying and shouting to the church and found it open. Going inside they saw the Jews standing near the altar throwing hosts here and there and the blood flowing from the wounds. When the neighborhood poor saw this, they all seized the Jews and put them in custody. But the local priest seeing and hearing this, ran to the lord of Hohenloe and told him what they had done. The lord said to the priest, "At the behest of my lord the bishop, I promised that no harm would come to the Jews and I mean strictly to abide by this. But I will confer with the lord bishop and whatever he counsels me to do, I will do it." However after the lord went to the bishop and faithfully related all of the above, the bishop said: "It is written: Judge justly the sons of man. If a man kills a man, you know his punishment and you have often inflicted it. But what punishment is worthy for those who crucify our Lord Jesus Christ, son of the Virgin Mary, true God and man, our creator, redeemer, and judge in his sacramental form?—I cannot say. So this is my advice: judge your Jews in such a way that you will not eternally suffer the Almighty's punishment." After the lord of Hohenloe heard the lord bishop's response, he returned to his own place, seized all the Jews he could find, and, as best he could, he burned all of them to ashes.

2. Near the town of Möckmühl a river flowed that had formed a sort of island on which no one lived except paupers and prostitutes who concealed their excesses. On this island burning lights appeared several times to some men, which greatly frightened them. When this was reported to the governors of the town, some of them were told to visit the place and carefully investigate and inquire where the lights had been seen. For there was a great suspicion that the Jews, who had lived on the island shortly before, had perpetrated some crime that God wished to reveal. The next day the men deputized on the order of their superiors to discharge their wishes went to the island. They carefully probed around with a shovel and saw turned earth in many places and they found new dirt carelessly replaced. They re-opened these holes and in each hole they found hosts or pieces of the Lord's sacrament stolen by the Jews. They lifted these up with awe and reverently carried them back to the church.

8. Concerning the revelation of Christ's Body through boys

When the Jews suffered persecution by Rindfleisch through all Franconia, some of them deserted their houses and took themselves and their movable goods to safer places. Among them, one Jew from Iphofen abandoned his house and left for the time being. This Jew had a Christian neighbor who had two boys whom he dearly loved. These boys often played together, as boys are wont to do, in front of the deserted house of the absent Jew and passed their time there. Now and then they even peeked through the chinks into the house and one time they saw inside a lovely little boy scampering about. When they saw this, they quickly dashed to their father and shouted with a loud voice, saying, "Father, father! We saw a lovely little boy in the Jew's house!" The father did not believe that his boys had seen anything and said, "He's gone and we can't catch him." The boys went back and again saw the child in the Jew's house just as they had the first time. They returned to their father and told him that they had seen the boy again. Then the father said to them: "Let's go there and get him." Saying this, he went with the boys to the Jew's house, asking them exactly where they had seen the boy. But when he saw nothing there, he harshly scolded the boys and went back to tending his garden and the boys went back to their father's house. But several days later the boys again carefully looked around the Jew's house (since it was in their neighborhood). Then they saw through the chinks a woman dressed in the most beautiful attire with the handsomest boy walking around her. Again they swiftly ran with joy to their father, saying, "Father, father! We have seen our auntie in the Jew's house wearing the most beautiful clothes while a boy walks around her." The father was disturbed and amazed and said: "Let's go see this marvel." And when they got to the spot the boys showed him, just as the last time he saw absolutely none of the things that the boys had seen. Thinking that his boys were playing tricks on him, he said to his neighbors, "My boys have made a fool of me. They told me they saw a handsome boy resting in that house and their aunt wearing the loveliest clothes and taking care of the boy." His neighbors said: "There's not a doubt—the Lord's sacrament is hidden in that house. So let's call the priest and carefully look about; for God wants to reveal to us his power and marvels." When the priest arrived, all the neighbors gathered around him telling him what they heard from their rustic neighbor. Then the father began to recount everything above in the order it happened. The priest summoned both boys and questioned them, and they told him just what they told the father. Then the priest ordered the door of the Jew's house to be opened, and in the presence of everyone he asked them where and in what spot they had seen the boy resting. The boys said, "Here!" pointing their fingers at the spot. Then the priest dug into the ground with a stick and discovered three hosts of the Lord's sacrament. The priest called for his sacristan to bring large candles, clean corporal-cloths, and incense in a thurible, and to have the bells rung and the people called together. When the people had gathered, the priest had the above story recited and asked for advice as to what should be done about it. Everyone advised that the Lord's Body should be left lying there in order to prove the malice and envy of the Jews and Christ's suffering. After this the priest and people set up some people around the Body who would defend and guard it day and night so that no one would have free access to the Lord's Body. For a priest and two worthy lay men were always present there; and it was so arranged that whenever they wished to leave, two others would quickly take their place while they were gone. And they faithfully considered how to build a church on that spot.

[Trans. John Shinners, *Medieval Popular Religion: A Reader* (Peterborough, ON: Broadview Press, 1997), 105–08.]

9. *THE REMEDY AGAINST THE TROUBLES OF TEMPTATION* (LATE FOURTEENTH CENTURY)

[The following excerpt is taken from an anonymous devotional text of the late fourteenth century. Such treatises were enormously popular in Chaucer's day, and in his Retraction he laments not writing more in the way of this genre. The Friar's Tale and the Pardoner's Tale are exempla—"examples," or stories—employed by preachers in sermons and writers of devotional treatises to make moral points. The Friar's Tale is particularly close in content to the one offered below.]

An Exemplum about Despair

And even though you sometimes feel the stirrings of despair or of unnatural, evil thought, take comfort ever in the goodness of God and in the painful passion that his manhood suffered for you. For the fiend tempts many of God's servants to desperation and dread of salvation—worldly men as well as spiritual—putting in worldly men's minds the grievousness of their sins, and to the spiritual he puts dread and strict conscience in many more different ways than I can tell. And God has very graciously comforted them and brought them out of their errors.

And now am I stirred and moved to tell you about some one who was a squire by the name of John Holmes. This squire that I have named had been a great, sinful man, and so at the last, through the beholding of his great sins and by the temptation of the fiend he fell into despair so deeply and grievously that he almost lost his mind. And he was so troubled for forty days that he could neither sleep nor eat but wasted away and was almost at the point of destroying himself. But the blessed Lord, who is so full of mercy and pity, would not let him be lost. So once as he walked in a wood alone an angel came to him in the form of a man and saluted the squire very well and talked with him in a very courteous way, saying to him: "Man, you seem to have great sorrow and depression. Tell me, I pray you, the cause of your discomfort." "No," said the squire, "I cannot tell you." "Yes, hardly," said the angel, "you do not know how well I may help you and remove your discomfort. For a man in discomfort should always reveal his depression to some creature who might ease him. For through good counsel he might recover comfort and health or in some way have remedy."

The squire answered the angel again and said that he well knew that he neither could nor might help him and therefore would not tell it to him. This squire, still believing that this angel was an earthly man, dreaded that if he told it to him he should have said some word that would utterly have grieved him more. And when the angel saw that he would in no way tell it to him, he said this to the squire: "Now, since you will not tell me your grief, I will tell it to you. You are," said the angel, "in despair of your salvation, but trust me faithfully that you will be saved. For the mercy of God is so great that it surpasses all his works and surmounts all sins." "It is true," said the squire, "that I know well that God is merciful, but he is also righteous and his righteousness must needs punish sin, and therefore I dread his righteous judgments."

The angel spoke to him again and gave him many great examples of how gracious and merciful our Lord God is to sinners. But the squire of whom we are speaking was so deeply fallen into despair that he could take no comfort in anything that the angel could say. Then the angel spoke to him again in this way: "Oh," said he, "you are hard of belief! But do you wish to have a revelation about your salvation?" Then he said to the squire, "I have here three dice that I will throw and you shall throw them also. And the one who has the most of the dice shall surely be saved." "Ah," said the squire, "how can I be certain of my salvation in the throwing of dice?" And he considered it just a joke. But nevertheless the angel threw the dice, and he had on every die the number six. And then he bade the squire throw the dice. "O, then," said the squire, "certainly I dare not do that, for I know well that I cannot cast more than you have cast, and if I cast less, then I shall fall into further discomfort." But the angel desired it and spoke about it so much that at last the squire threw the dice. And in the cast by the gracious might and power of God every die divided in two and on each was the number six, and so he had double what the angel had.

And as he was marveling, the angel vanished out of his sight. Therefore he truly thought that it was an angel sent from God to bring him out of his sorrow, and then he took great comfort and joy in the mercy and goodness of God in such a way that all his dreads and sorrows completely departed and he became a virtuous man and the very servant of God and lived blessedly. And when he came to depart from this world, he devised that there should be a stone laid upon him with these words written on it: "Here lies John

Holmes who can speak about the generosity of God." I know a worshipful person who was in the same abbey here in England where he lies and who read these words written on his tomb.

Now since our merciful Lord God sent thus his gracious comfort to this man who was a worldly, sinful man and received him to grace and brought him out of despair, no one should be discomforted or despair in any temptation, for God will surely comfort him when he sees his time. And though he does not immediately send his comfort, it shall be for the greater reward. Therefore always think when you consider any bodily or spiritual temptations that you will stand with the blessing of all Holy Church. For holy scripture says: Blessed are those who suffer temptations, for when they are well proven they shall have the crown of life which Almighty God has promised to those who love him.

[Trans. Robert Boenig, "*The Profits of Tribulation* and *The Remedy against the Troubles of Temptation*: Translations from the Middle English," *Studia Mystica* 17 (1997): 260–62.]

10. *THE TALE OF BERYN* (1410–20)

[This description of the pilgrims' arrival at Canterbury comes from the prologue to the anonymous *The Tale of Beryn*, which survives in a single mid-fifteenth-century manuscript. *The Tale of Beryn* itself is given to the Merchant for the return journey and describes the adventures of a young nobleman who decides to become a merchant instead of a knight. The author is anonymous but may have been one of the monks who were responsible for taking care of the shrine of Saint Thomas Becket in Canterbury Cathedral. Whoever he was, he was certainly familiar with pilgrims' behavior, and misbehavior, during their visit. This excerpt draws in part on Edith Rickert's translation. As she notes, "the rhythm is as bad in the original as in the modernization."]

The Pilgrims Arrive at Canterbury and Visit the Shrine

When all this fellowship had come to Canterbury,
As you have already heard, with tales glad and merry,
Some of subtle *sentens*, of virtue and of lore,
And some of other kinds of mirth for them that do not care
For wisdom, nor for holiness, nor for chivalry,
Neither for virtuous matter, but only for folly,
Crude jokes, every kind of pleasure or disgrace,
Just like a company of goblins, hiding in every place,
Who go crazy in their minds when the leaves turn green
And spring up in better weather—they're the ones I mean.

But no more about them at this time
To preserve my *sentens*, my meaning, and my rhyme.
They took their inn and lodged themselves at mid-morning I trowe
At the Checker-of-the-Hoop, which many a man does know.
Their Host from Southwerk who with them went as you have heard before
Who was the ruler of them all, whether they were less or more,
Ordered their dinner wisely, before to church they went,
Such victuals as he found in town and for no others sent.
The Pardoner beheld the activity—how all the people were served
Withdrawing himself secretly and aside he swerved.
The innkeeper was so shouted for, from one place to another,
That the Pardoner took his staff to the barmaid. "A Welcome my own
        brother,"
Said she with a friendly look, all ready for a kiss.
And he, as a man well schooled in such kindness
Embraced her by the waist and made her merry cheer,
As if he had known her all the previous year.
She hauled him into the taproom, where her bed was made.
Lo, here I lie, said she, by myself all night naked
Without man's company, since my love died.

[The barmaid, Kit, proceeds to trick the Pardoner by promising
to meet him that night, only to have her real lover beat him as a thief.
While the Pardoner waits for evening to pursue his would-be love affair, he
and the other pilgrims visit the cathedral and then the city.]

The knight and all the fellowship in that company
When they were well lodged, according to reason,
Each one according to his rank, to church then was the season
To turn their way, and went to make their offerings,
Devoutly as each would, of silver brooches and rings.
Then at the church door the question of manners did arise,
Until the knight who of gentle ways knew right well the guise
Sent forth the clergymen, the Parson and his brother.
A monk then took the sprinkler with a manly air
And, as the custom is, wetted all their heads,
Each one after the other, according to their estates.
The friar acted winsomely and all in the hope
Of being allowed to sprinkle all the rest, because for his cope
He wouldn't have given up that job in that holy place
So longed his holy conscience to see the Nun's face.
The knight went with his companions towards the holy shrine
To do what they had come for, and after go to die.

The Pardoner and the Miller and the other ignorant sots
Went wandering about the church just like silly goats.
Peered at the stained glass up above them high
Pretending to be gentlemen, reading heraldry.
Pointing out the painters and the artist's plan
And getting everything as twisted up as the horn of an old ram.
"That man carries a short stick," said one, "just like a rake."
"You're wrong!" said the Miller, "You're making a mistake.
It's a spear, if you can see it, with a point well-honed.
To push down his enemy right through the shoulder bone."
"Peace!" said the Host of Southwark, "Let the windows be.
Go make your offering. You seem half dazed truly.
Since you are in the company of honest men and good
Behave as if you were one and don't be rude
For a time. I hold that for the best.
For he who behaves sensibly in public may better live in rest."
Then they moved on busily, goggling everywhere,
Kneeled down before the shrine and on their rosaries said their prayers.
Then they prayed to St. Thomas as they all wished
And then the holy relics each man with his mouth kissed
As a goodly monk taught them all the names,
And then to the other places of holiness they all came
And stayed in prayer until the service was done,
And then they went to lunch, as it was near noon.
Then, as the custom is, tokens there they brought
So that their neighbours should know whom they had sought.
Each man used his silver to buy enough
And in the meanwhile the Miller into his tunic stuffed
Tokens of Canterbury that were little brooches,
Which he and the Pardoner into their pouches,
Put afterwards, so that nobody knew a thing.
Except the Summoner who saw them and said, "Listen.
Give me half!" he said, whispering in their ear.
"Hush! Peace!" said the Miller, "Don't you see the Friar
How he glowers under his hood with greedy eye?
It would be a secret thing that he could not spy.
Of every trick he knows a bit, Our Lady give him sorrow!"
"Amen," then said the Summoner, "By eve and by the morrow!
So cursed a tale he told of me, may the devil take him hard
And me!—unless I pay him well and give him his reward.
If it happens that homeward bound each man tell his tale
As we did coming here, though I should avail
Myself of all the cunning I have, I will him nothing spare

Until I've dirtied his tunic and caused him sorrowful care."
They set their badges upon their heads, or upon their caps,
And then to the dinner they began to take their steps
Every man according to his rank washed and took his seat
As they were used to do at supper and at meat,
And they were silent for awhile, till their waist-bands did swell.
But then as nature demands, as wise men know well,
When our bodies are at last replete
Spirits are lively, and then foods that are sweet
Will often cause people amusements to seek.
And it was certainly then no time to be bleak.
Every man resolved not to be sad
And told his fellows of the good time they'd had
And of the funny things that happened along the way,
As is the pilgrim's custom, and has been for many a day.

[Trans. Andrew Taylor, from John M. Bowers, ed. *The Canterbury Tales: Fifteenth-Century Continuations and Additions* (Kalamazoo, MI: Medieval Institute Publications, 1992), 60–66, with some rhymes taken from Edith Rickert, *Chaucer's World* (London: Oxford UP, 1948), 261–64.]

A BASIC CHAUCER GLOSSARY

agayn, ayein	back, in return, against, toward
al, al be	although
alday	continually
alderbest	best of all
als	1. as
	2. also
anon, anoon	immediately
arn	are
artow	you are/are you (a contraction of *art thou*; cf. *hastow*, you have; *wiltow*, you will/wish, etc.)
as	1. as
	2. in phrases: *so as*, so; *ther as*, there/where; *wher as*, where
att	at the (contraction)
avysen	to look at, consider, reflect, understand
ay	always, all the time
ben	to be
bet	better
behove(n)	to be proper, right, necessary; an impersonal verb, with *me* as its indirect object: *me bihoveth*, I should (cf. *methinks*, it seems to me)
bihote(n)	to promise
blyve	quickly, soon, often in the phrase *as blyve*
bountee	goodness
brenne(n)	to burn
breyde(n)	to start (from sleep), to move suddenly, to snatch
buxom	obedient
cas	chance, accident
certes	certainly
clepe(n)	to call
conne(n)/konne(n)	1. to be able
also *cunne(n)/*	2. to know (how to)
kunne(n)	
corage	heart
coy	quiet
daungerous	distant, haughty (the appropriate attitude for a lady in the code of *amour courtois*)
descreyven	to describe
disese	distress, pain, discomfort
drenche(n)	to drown
dreynt	drowned
ech, ych	each
eek/eke	also

em	uncle
emforth	to the extent of
er, er that	before
ey	egg
eye/ye	eye (plural *eyen/yen*); *at eye*, plainly
fele/feele	many
fere/feere	companion
ferre(r)	farther
fonde(n)	1. to test
	2. to strive
forthy	therefore
forward	agreement, promise
free/fre	generous, noble
fro	from
gan	1. began
	2. past tense marker: *gan her kysse* could mean, depending on context, 'he began to kiss her' or simply 'he kissed her'
gentil	well-bred, courtly, genteel, kind
hem	them; Middle English often does not use the *th* marker for the 3rd person plural pronouns; Chaucer uses *they* but not *them*
henten	to seize, catch, attack
her/hir(e)	1. their
	2. her
hight	1. named, called
	2. promised
hit	it
ich	1. I
	2. each
ilke	same, very
in hye	quickly, soon
iwis, ywis	certainly
kepe(n)	to take care of, preserve; *take(n) kepe*, take heed
kouthe/couthe	known
kynde	nature
lette(n)	to hinder, prevent
lever	prefer; *him was lever*, he preferred
lewed	ignorant, uneducated, unsophisticated
list/lest	it pleases (impersonal verb: e.g., *hire listeth*, she likes)
lite	little
lust	pleasure
men	1. men
	2. one (cf. Fr. *on*, Ger. *Mann*)
me thinketh	it seems to me; I think. Impersonal verb, so also: *thee*

deyneth, you condescend; *hire seemeth*, she thinks; *us liketh*,
we like; *hem nedeth*, they need

met(e) food

mete fitting, suitable

mete(n) 1. to dream

2. to meet

mo more

moot/mot must, may

mowen may, be able to

n- negative prefix attached to common verbs, e.g., *nadde*,
hadn't;

nel/nil, won't; *nere*, weren't; *niste* (*ne* + *wiste*), didn't know;
nolde (*ne* + *wolde*), wouldn't; *not/noot*, doesn't know, etc.

neer 1. near

2. nearer

no fors no matter

nyce foolish

o/oo/oon one

or before

paraunter perhaps

parde by God!, assuredly (Fr. *par Dieu*)

quite(n) pay back, repay, requite, revenge

quod said

seistow you say

sely happy, innocent, pitiable

siker(ly) sure(ly)

sin, sithen since

sith/sith that since

skile/skille reason

somdeel somewhat

sooth truth

sowne(n) to conduce, to tend toward

spede(n) to succeed, to go quickly

stente(n)/stinte(n) stop, cease

steven(e) 1. voice

2. appointment

sweven dream

swich such

swynke(n) to labor

swythe quickly

syn/syn that since

thee 1. you (singular, thou)

2. to prosper (*so theech*, as I hope to prosper)

ther 1. there

2. (also *there as*) where

tho 1. then

2. those

trowe(n) to believe

vanite folly, worthless thing or pursuit of worthless things (more often than conceit)

verray true

war aware, cautious

wher 1. whether

2. (also *wher as*) where

wil/wol 1. to wish

2. future auxiliary (as in current useage)

wille desire

wisly certainly, surely

wite(n)/ wete(n) to know, to be familiar with

withoute(n) 1. outside

2. without, e.g., *withouten drede*, doubtless

wood mad, insane

worship honor or social prestige (often of a knight)

wrye(n) 1. to hide

2. to turn

y- past participle marker (e.g., *yhent*, taken; *yloren*, lost)

ye/yen eye/eyes

yerne eagerly

yeve(n) to give (past, *yaf*)

yfeere together

yif if

yliche alike, equally

ywis/iwis indeed, certainly

BIBLIOGRAPHY

Scholarly Editions of Chaucer's Works

Baugh, A.C., ed. *Chaucer.* New York: Appleton-Century-Crofts, 1968.

Benson, Larry, ed. *The Riverside Chaucer.* Boston: Houghton Mifflin, 1987.

Donaldson, E. Talbot. *Chaucer's Poetry.* 1958. New York: Wiley, 1975.

Fisher, John H., ed. *The Complete Poetry and Prose of Geoffrey Chaucer.* 2nd ed. New York: Holt, Rinehart and Winston, 1989.

Manly, John M., and Edith Rickert. *The Text of the Canterbury Tales.* 8 vols. Chicago: U of Chicago P, 1940.

Mann, Jill. *Geoffrey Chaucer: The Canterbury Tales.* Harmondsworth: Penguin, 2005.

Robinson, F.N., ed. *The Works of Geoffrey Chaucer.* 2nd ed. Boston: Houghton Mifflin, 1957.

Ruggiers, Paul G., ed. *Geoffrey Chaucer: The Canterbury Tales: A Facsimile and Transcription of the Hengwrt Manuscript, with Variants from the Ellesmere Manuscript.* Norman, OK: U of Oklahoma P, 1979.

Skeat, Walter W. *The Complete Works of Geoffrey Chaucer.* 7 vols. Oxford: Clarendon, 1894–97.

Tyrwhitt, Thomas. *The Canterbury Tales of Chaucer, with an Essay upon His Language and Versification, an Introductory Discourse, and Notes.* 4 vols. (London: T. Payne, 1775). Vol. 5, with glossary, 1778.

Woodward, Daniel, and Martin Stevens, eds. *Geoffrey Chaucer: The Canterbury Tales: The New Ellesmere Chaucer Monochromatic Facsimile.* San Marino, CA: Huntington Library, 1997.

Biographies of Chaucer

Brewer, Derek. *Chaucer and His World.* Cambridge: D.S. Brewer, 1978.

—. *The World of Chaucer.* Woodbridge, England: D.S. Brewer, 2000. [This is a revised edition of the item immediately above.]

Gardner, John. *The Life and Times of Chaucer.* New York: Knopf, 1977.

Howard, Donald R. *Chaucer: His Life, His Works, His World.* New York: Dutton, 1987.

Pearsall, Derek. *The Life of Geoffrey Chaucer.* Oxford: Blackwell, 1995.

Background Materials for Chaucer's Life and Works

Bryan, W.F., and Germaine Dempster, eds. *Sources and Analogues of Chaucer's Canterbury Tales.* Chicago: U of Chicago P, 1941.

Correale, Robert, with Mary Hamel, eds. *Sources and Analogues of Chaucer's Canterbury Tales.* 2 vols. Woodbridge, England: Boydell and Brewer, 2005.

Crow, Martin M., and Clair C. Olson. *Chaucer Life-Records*. Austin: U of
      Texas P, 1966.
Miller, Robert P. *Chaucer: Sources and Backgrounds*. New York: Oxford UP,
      1977.

Websites

The Chaucer Metapage is maintained by professional Chaucerians and con-
tains numerous links. It can be visited at:
http://www.unc.edu/depts/chaucer/aboutmp.htm.

For medieval culture in general, the Labyrinth, run by Georgetown
University, is very useful: http://labyrinth.georgetown.edu/.

Aids to Chaucer's Language

Davis, Norman, et al. *A Chaucer Glossary*. Oxford: Clarendon, 1979.
Kökeritz, Helge. *A Guide to Chaucer's Pronunciation*. 1961. Rpt. Toronto: U
      of Toronto P, 1978.
Kurath, Hans, ed., et. al. *The Middle English Dictionary*. 10 vols. with supple-
      ment. Ann Arbor: U of Michigan P, 1952–84.

Articles about *The Canterbury Tales*

There are very many scholarly articles about Chaucer and his works, too
many to include in this suggested reading list. The bibliographies in the edi-
tions of Fisher, Benson, and Mann above, are essential, and Cooper (below)
provides a useful survey of key articles. There are two scholarly journals
devoted almost entirely to Chaucer:

The Chaucer Review, published at the Pennsylvania State University.

Studies in the Age of Chaucer, published at Washington University, St. Louis
      for the New Chaucer Society.

Books about *The Canterbury Tales*

Aers, David. *Chaucer*. Brighton: Harvester, 1986.
Ames, Ruth M. *God's Plenty: Chaucer's Christian Humanism*. Chicago:
      Loyola UP, 1984.
Andrew, Malcolm. *Critical Essays on Chaucer's Canterbury Tales*. Toronto: U
      of Toronto P, 1991.
Astell, Ann W. *Chaucer and the Universe of Learning*. Ithaca: Cornell UP,
      1996.

Baldwin, Ralph. *The Unity of the Canterbury Tales*. Copenhagen: Rosenkilde and Beggen, 1955.

Beidler, Peter G., ed. *Geoffrey Chaucer: The Wife of Bath*. Boston: Bedford, 1996.

Benson, C. David. *Chaucer's Drama of Style*. Chapel Hill: U of North Carolina P, 1986.

Besserman, Lawrence L. *Chaucer's Biblical Poetics*. Norman: U of Oklahoma P, 1998.

Birney, Earle. *Essays on Chaucerian Irony*. Ed. Beryl Rowland. 1941–60. Toronto: U of Toronto P, 1985.

Bisson, Lillian M. *Chaucer and the Late Medieval World*. New York: St. Martin's, 2000.

Blamires, Alcuin. *The Canterbury Tales*. Atlantic Highlands, NJ: Humanities Press, 1987.

Boenig, Robert. *Chaucer and the Mystics*. Lewisburg: Bucknell UP, 1995.

Boitani, Piero, ed. *Chaucer and the Italian Trecento*. Cambridge: Cambridge UP, 1983.

Bowden, Betsy. *Chaucer Aloud: The Varieties of Textual Interpretation*. Philadelphia: U of Pennsylvania P, 1987.

Bowden, Muriel. *A Commentary on the General Prologue to the Canterbury Tales*. 2nd ed. New York: Macmillan, 1967.

Brewer, Derek. *Chaucer: The Critical Heritage*. 2 vols. London: Routledge and Kegan Paul, 1978.

—. *Chaucer: The Poet as Storyteller*. London: Macmillan, 1984.

Bronson, Bertrand. *In Search of Chaucer*. Toronto: U of Toronto P, 1960.

Burger, Glen. *Chaucer's Queer Nation*. Minneapolis: U of Minnesota P, 2003.

Burlin, Robert B. *Chaucerian Fiction*. Princeton: Princeton UP, 1977.

Carlson, David R. *Chaucer's Jobs*. New York: Palgrave, 2004.

Cawley, A.C., ed. *Chaucer's Mind and Art*. London: Oliver and Boyd, 1969.

Coghill, Nevil. *The Poet Chaucer*. London: Oxford UP, 1941.

Condren, Edward I. *Chaucer and the Energy of Creation: The Design and the Organization of the Canterbury Tales*. Gainesville: UP of Florida, 1999.

Cooke, Thomas D. *The Old French and Chaucerian Fabliaux: A Study of Their Comic Climax*. Columbia: U of Missouri P, 1978.

Cooper, Helen. *Oxford Guides to Chaucer, The Canterbury Tales*. 2nd ed. Oxford: Oxford UP, 1996.

—. *The Structure of the Canterbury Tales*. Athens, GA: U of Georgia P, 1984.

Cox, Catherine S. *Gender and Language in Chaucer*. Gainesville: UP of Florida, 1997.

Craik, T.W. *The Comic Tales of Chaucer*. London: Methuen, 1964.

Crane, Susan. *Gender and Romance in Chaucer's Canterbury Tales*. Princeton: Princeton UP, 1994.

Curry, Walter Clyde. *Chaucer and the Mediaeval Sciences*. 1942. Rpt. New York: Barnes and Noble, 1960.

David, Alfred. *The Strumpet Muse: Art and Morals in Chaucer's Poetry.* Bloomington, IN: Indiana UP, 1976.

Dinshaw, Carolyn. *Chaucer's Sexual Poetics.* Madison, WI: U of Wisconsin P, 1989.

Donaldson, E. Talbot. *Speaking of Chaucer.* New York: Norton, 1970.

Economou, George D., ed. *Geoffrey Chaucer: A Collection of Original Articles.* New York: McGraw-Hill, 1975.

Edwards, Robert R. *The Dream of Chaucer: Representation and Reflection in the Early Narratives.* Durham: Duke UP, 1989.

Ellis, Roger. *Patterns of Religious Narrative in the Canterbury Tales.* Totowa, NJ: Barnes & Noble, 1986.

Ferster, Judith. *Chaucer on Interpretation.* Cambridge: Cambridge UP, 1985.

Fisher, John H. *The Importance of Chaucer.* Carbondale and Edwardsville: Southern Illinois, 1992.

Fleming, John V. *Classical Imitation and Interpretation in Chaucer's Troilus.* Lincoln: U of Nebraska P, 1990.

Fradenburg, Aranye. *Sacrifice Your Love: Psychoanalysis, Historicism, Chaucer.* Minneapolis: U of Minnesota P, 2002.

Frese, Dolores Warwick: *An* Ars Legendi *for Chaucer's Canterbury Tales: Re-Constructive Reading.* Gainesville: U of Florida P, 1991.

Ganim, John M. *Chaucerian Theatricality.* Princeton: Princeton UP, 1990.

Gardner, John. *The Poetry of Chaucer.* Carbondale, IL: Southern Illinois UP, 1977.

Gellrich, Jesse M. *The Idea of the Book in the Middle Ages: Language Theory, Mythology, and Fiction.* Ithaca, NY: Cornell UP, 1985.

Grudin, Michaela Paasche. *Chaucer and the Politics of Discourse.* Columbia: U of South Carolina P, 1996.

Hadow, Grace. *Chaucer and His Times.* New York: Holt, 1914.

Hansen, Elaine Tuttle. *Chaucer and the Fictions of Gender.* Berkeley: U of California P, 1992.

Hill, John M. *Chaucerian Belief.* New Haven: Yale UP, 1991.

Holley, Linda Tarte. *Chaucer's Measuring Eye.* Houston: Rice UP, 1990.

Hornsby, Joseph Allen. *Chaucer and the Law.* Norman, OK: Pilgrim Books, 1988.

Howard, Donald. *The Idea of the Canterbury Tales.* Berkeley: U of California P, 1976.

Howes, Laura L. *Chaucer's Gardens and the Language of Convention.* Gainesville: UP of Florida, 1997.

Huppé, Bernard F. *A Reading of the Canterbury Tales.* Albany: State U of New York P, 1964.

— and D.W. Robertson, Jr. *Fruyt and Chaf: Studies in Chaucer's Allegories.* Princeton: Princeton UP, 1963.

Hussey, S.S. *Chaucer: An Introduction.* London: Methuen, 1971.

Jeffrey, David L. *Chaucer and Scriptural Tradition*. Ottawa: U of Ottawa P, 1984.

Jones, Terry. *Chaucer's Knight: The Portrait of a Medieval Mercenary*. New York: Methuen, 1980.

Jordan, Robert M. *Chaucer and the Shape of Creation: The Aesthetic Possibilities of Inorganic Structure*. Cambridge, MA: Harvard UP, 1967.

—. *Chaucer's Poetics and the Modern Reader*. Berkeley: U of California P, 1987.

Kean, P.M. *Chaucer and the Making of English Poetry*. 2nd ed. London: Routledge & Kegan Paul, 1972.

Kellogg, Alfred L. *Chaucer, Langland, Arthur: Essays in Middle English Literature*. New Brunswick, NJ: Rutgers UP, 1972.

Kendrick, Laura. *Chaucerian Play: Comedy and Control in the Canterbury Tales*. Berkeley: U of California P, 1988.

Kittredge, George Lyman. *Chaucer and His Poetry*. Cambridge, MA: Harvard UP, 1915.

Klassen, Norman. *Chaucer on Love, Knowledge and Sight*. Woodbridge: S.S. Brewer, 1995.

Knapp, Peggy. *Chaucer and the Social Contest*. London: Routledge, 1990.

Knight, Stephen. *Geoffrey Chaucer*. Oxford: Blackwell, 1986.

Koff, Leonard Michael. *Chaucer and the Art of Story-telling*. Berkeley: U of California P, 1988.

Kolve, V.A. *Chaucer and the Imagery of Narrative*. Volume I. Stanford: Stanford UP, 1984.

Lawler, Traugott. *The One and the Many in the Canterbury Tales*. Hamden, CN: Archon Books, 1980.

Lawlor, John. *Chaucer*. New York: Harper and Row, 1968.

Lawrence, W.W. *Chaucer and the Canterbury Tales*. New York: Columbia UP, 1950.

Leicester, H. Marshall, Jr. *The Disenchanted Self: Representing the Subject in the Canterbury Tales*. Berkeley: U of California P, 1990.

Lerer, Seth. *Chaucer and His Readers: Imagining the Author in Late-Medieval England*. Princeton: Princeton UP, 1993.

Lewis, C.S. *The Allegory of Love*. London: Oxford UP, 1936.

Lindahl, Carl. *Earnest Games: Folkloric Patterns in the Canterbury Tales*. Bloomington, IN: Indiana UP, 1987.

Lumiansky, R.M. *Of Sundry Folk: The Dramatic Principle in the Canterbury Tales*. 1955. Austin: U of Texas P, 1980.

Manly, John M. *Some New Light on Chaucer*. 1926. Rpt. Gloucester, MA: Peter Smith, 1959.

Mann, Jill. *Chaucer and the Medieval Estates Satire*. Cambridge: Cambridge UP, 1973.

—. *Feminist Readings: Geoffrey Chaucer*. Atlantic Highlands, NJ: Humanities, 1991.

Martin, Priscilla. *Chaucer's Women: Nuns, Wives, and Amazons.* Iowa City: U of Iowa P, 1990.

McCall, John P. *Chaucer Among the Gods: The Poetics of Classical Myth.* University Park, PA: Pennsylvania State UP, 1979.

McGerr, Rosemarie P. *Chaucer's Open Books: Resistance to Closure in Medieval Discourse.* Gainesville: UP of Florida, 1998.

Muscatine, Charles. *Chaucer and the French Tradition.* Berkeley: U of California P, 1957.

Neuse, Richard. *Chaucer's Dante: Allegory and Epic Theater in the Canterbury Tales.* Berkeley: U of California P, 1991.

North, J.D. *Chaucer's Universe.* London: Oxford UP, 1988.

Olson, Paul A. *The Canterbury Tales and the Good Society.* Princeton: Princeton UP, 1986.

Owen, Charles A., Jr. *Pilgrimage and Storytelling in the Canterbury Tales: the Dialectic of "Earnest" and "Game."* Norman, OK: U of Oklahoma P, 1977.

Patterson, Lee W. *Chaucer and the Subject of History.* Madison: U of Wisconsin P, 1991.

—. *Negotiating the Past: The Historical Understanding of Medieval Literature.* Madison: University of Wisconsin P, 1987.

Payne, Robert O. *The Key of Remembrance: A Study of Chaucer's Poetics.* New Haven, CN: Yale UP, 1963.

Pearsall, Derek. *The Canterbury Tales.* London: George Allen & Unwin, 1985.

Robertson, D.W., Jr. *A Preface to Chaucer.* Princeton: Princeton UP, 1962.

Roney, Lois. *Chaucer's Knight's Tale and Theories of Scholastic Psychology.* Tampa: U of South Florida P, 1990.

Rowland, Beryl, ed. *Companion to Chaucer Studies.* London: Oxford UP, 1968.

Ruggiers, Paul G. *The Art of the Canterbury Tales.* Madison: U of Wisconsin P, 1965.

Russell, J. Stephen. *Chaucer and the Trivium: The Mindsong of the Canterbury Tales.* Gainesville: UP of Florida, 1998.

Schoeck, Richard, and Jerome Taylor, eds. *Chaucer Criticism, Volume I: The Canterbury Tales.* Notre Dame, IN: U of Notre Dame P, 1960.

Sklute, Larry. *Virtue of Necessity: Inconclusiveness and Narrative Form in Chaucer's Poetry.* Columbus: Ohio State UP, 1984.

Spurgeon, Caroline F.E. *Five Hundred Years of Chaucer Criticism and Allusion.* 3 vols. Cambridge: Cambridge UP, 1925.

Strohm, Paul. *Social Chaucer.* Cambridge, MA: Harvard UP, 1989.

Wagenknecht, Edward, ed. *Chaucer: Modern Essays in Criticism.* New York: Oxford UP, 1959.

Wallace, David. *Chaucer and the Early Writings of Boccaccio.* Cambridge: D.S. Brewer, 1985.

—. *Chaucerian Polity: Absolutist Lineages and Associational Forms in England and Italy*. Stanford: Stanford UP, 1997.

Whittock, Trevor. *A Reading of the Canterbury Tales*. Cambridge: Cambridge UP, 1968.

Wilkins, Nigel. *Music in the Age of Chaucer*. Cambridge: D.S. Brewer, 1979.

Wimsatt, James I. *Chaucer and His French Contemporaries: Natural Music in the Fourteenth Century*. Toronto: U of Toronto P, 1991.

Wood, Chauncey. *Chaucer and the Country of the Stars*. Princeton: Princeton UP, 1970.

TEXTUAL SOURCE LIST

Ellesmere Manuscript. Translation based upon the Ellesmere Manuscript, permission courtesy of The Huntington Library.

ALDINGTON, Richard (Translator). "The Black Death" from *The Decameron of Giovanni Boccaccio*. New York: Dell Publishing, 1930. Copyright © The Estate of Richard Aldington. Reproduced by kind permission of the Estate of Richard Aldington c/o Rosica Colin Limited, London.

BOENIG, Robert. Excerpt from "The Profits of Tribulation and The Remedy Against the Troubles of Temptation: Translations from the Middle English." *Studia Mystica* 17 (1996): 260–62. Copyright © 1996, Robert Boenig. Reprinted by permission of Robert Boenig.

DAHLBERG, Charles (Translator). *The Romance of the Rose* by Guillaume de Lorris. Princeton: Princeton University Press, 1971. Copyright © 1971 Princeton University Press, 1999 renewed PUP. Reprinted by permission of Princeton University Press.

GOODRIDGE, J.F. (Translator, introduction). Excerpts from *William Langland: Piers the Ploughman*. Harmondsworth: Penguin Classics, 1959, revised 1966. Copyright © J.F. Goodridge, 1959, 1966. Reprinted by permission of Penguin Books Ltd.

HANNA III, Ralph and Traugott Lawler (Translators and Editors). Excerpts from *Jankyn's Book of Wikked Wyves*. Copyright © 1997 by the University of Georgia Press. Reprinted by permission of the University of Georgia Press.

McWILLIAM, G.H. (Translator, introduction). Excerpts from *The Decameron* by Giovanni Boccaccio. Harmondsworth: Penguin Classics, 1972, second edition 1995. Copyright © G.H. McWilliam, 1972, 1995. Reprinted by permission of Penguin Books Ltd.

PALMER, R. Barton (Translator). Excerpt from *Guillaume de Machaut: The Judgement of the King of Navarre*. New York: Garland Publishing, 1988. Reprinted by permission of Taylor & Francis Group LLC, via Copyright Clearance Center.

SHINNERS, John (Translator). "Benedict of Canterbury," "Rudolph of Schlettstadt," and other excerpts from *Medieval Popular Religion: A Reader*. Peterborough, ON: Broadview Press, 1997. Reprinted by permission of Broadview Press and John Shinners.

TAYLOR, Andrew (Translator). Translations based on excerpts in the original Middle English from *Selection from English Wycliffite Writings*, edited by Anne Hudson. Cambridge: Cambridge University Press, 1978. Reprinted by permission of Andrew Taylor. Translations based on excerpts in the original Middle English from *The Canterbury Tales: Fifteenth-Century Continuations and Additions* by John M. Bowers. Kalamazoo, Michigan: Medieval Institute Publications, 1992. Reprinted by permission of Andrew Taylor.

WATTS, Victor (Translator, introduction). Excerpts from *Boethius: The Consolation of Philosophy*, 2nd edition, by Boethius. Harmondsworth: Penguin, 1969. Copyright © V.E. Watts, 1969. Reprinted by permission of Penguin Books Ltd.

from the publisher

A name never says it all, but the word "broadview" expresses a good deal of the philosophy behind our company. We are open to a broad range of academic approaches and political viewpoints. We pay attention to the broad impact book publishing and book printing has in the wider world; we began using recycled stock more than a decade ago, and for some years now we have used 100% recycled paper for most titles. As a Canadian-based company we naturally publish a number of titles with a Canadian emphasis, but our publishing program overall is internationally oriented and broad-ranging. Our individual titles often appeal to a broad readership too; many are of interest as much to general readers as to academics and students.

Founded in 1985, Broadview remains a fully independent company owned by its shareholders—not an imprint or subsidiary of a larger multinational.

If you would like to find out more about Broadview and about the books we publish, please visit us at **www.broadviewpress.com**. And if you'd like to place an order through the site, we'd like to show our appreciation by extending a special discount to you: by entering the code below you will receive a 20% discount on purchases made through the Broadview website.

Discount code: **broadview20%**

Thank you for choosing Broadview.

Please note: this offer applies only to sales of bound books within the United States or Canada.

LIST
of products used:

2,054 lb(s) of Rolland Opaque50
50% post-consumer

RESULTS
Based on the Cascades products you selected compared to products in the industry made with 100% virgin fiber, your savings are:

 9 trees

 7,123 gal. US of water
77 days of water consumption

 1,804 lbs of waste
17 waste containers

 5,522 lbs CO2
10,470 miles driven

 27 MMBTU
132,429 60W light bulbs for one hour

 17 lbs NOx
emissions of one truck during 23 days